Alice in a World of Wonderlands

The English-Language Editions of the
Four *Alice* Books Published Worldwide

VOLUME TWO

Checklists and Appendices

SELF-PORTRAIT OF JOHN TENNIEL (1820–1914)

Tenniel created this pen-and-ink drawing in September or October 1889 as an experiment in technique and self-portraiture. He considered this picture to be "a very good likeness, but too serious," adding, "Well, taking one's own portrait is a serious business . . . ." From the National Portrait Gallery, image 2818

ALICE

In a World of Wonderlands

The English-Language Editions of the
Four Alice Books Published Worldwide

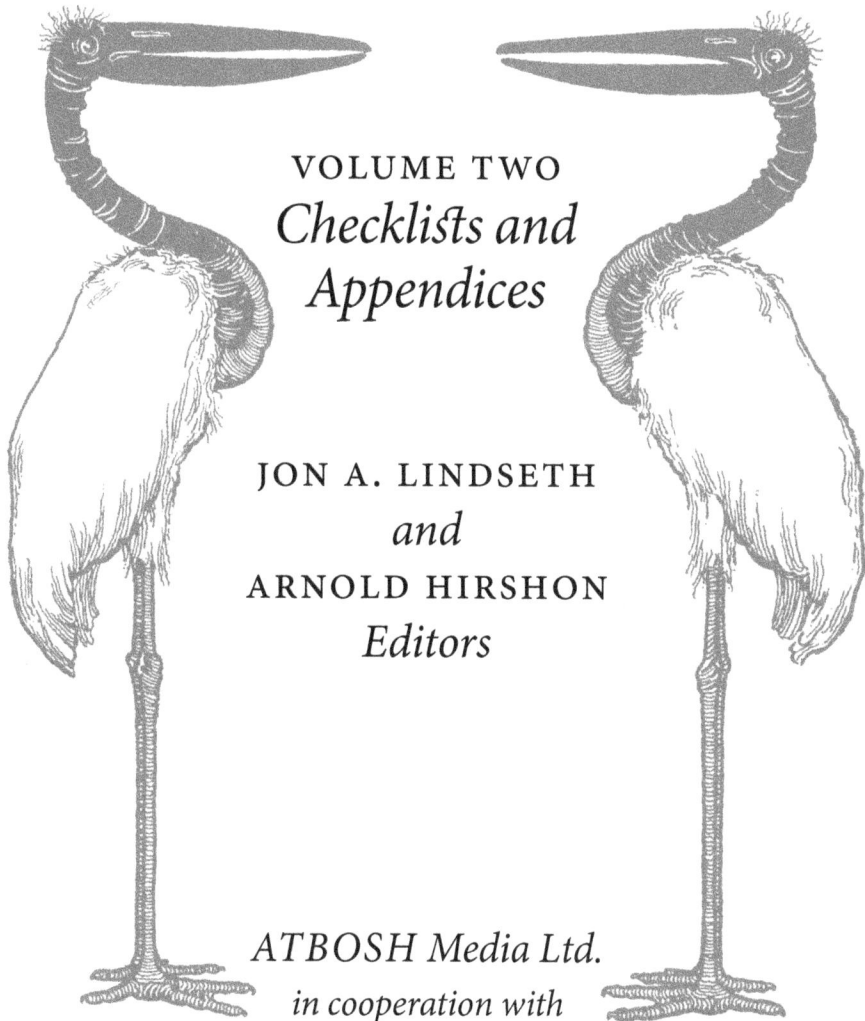

VOLUME TWO
Checklists and
Appendices

JON A. LINDSETH
and
ARNOLD HIRSHON
Editors

ATBOSH Media Ltd.
in cooperation with
The Lewis Carroll Society of North America · New York
2023

Alice in a World of Wonderlands:
The English Language of the Four Alice Books Published Worldwide
Volume 2 - Checklists and Appendices

Library of Congress Control Number
LCCN - 2023944842

ATBOSH Media Ltd.
Cleveland, Ohio 44120 USA

ISBN 9781626132580

Dedicated to the Memory of Morton N. Cohen

THE DEAN OF LEWIS CARROLL SCHOLARS

Life, what is it but a dream?

Through the Looking-Glass, CHAPTER XII

Contents

VOLUME TWO · CHECKLISTS AND APPENDICES

CHECKLISTS

APPENDICES

"When *I* use a word," Humpty Dumpty said in a rather scornful tone, "it means just what I chose it to mean — neither more nor less."

Through the Looking-Glass, CHAPTER VI

Introduction to the Checklists:
How They Were Compiled and Organized

Jon A. Lindseth and Arnold Hirshon

T HIS SECTION INCLUDES the checklists of the four *Alice* books: *Alice's Adventures in Wonderland*, *Through the Looking-Glass*, *Alice's Adventures under Ground*, and *The Nursery "Alice."* The checklists are not compiled in full bibliographic detail, but rather are meant to contain enough information to identify and distinguish among editions.

COVERAGE

The plan from the start was to include worldwide checklists of the English-language editions of the four *Alice* books no matter where they were published. It was apparent that, for this compilation task at least, the world divided into two parts: the English-speaking countries and the rest of the world.

The English-speaking countries as defined here are the United Kingdom, the United States, Australia, Canada, Ireland, and New Zealand. We located well-established bibliographers for all. Lenny de Rooy of the Netherlands, who conceived this project, worked with others to compile lists for the non-English-speaking countries. Assisting her were a number of contributors to our 2015 book, *Alice in a World of Wonderlands: The Translations of Lewis Carroll's Masterpiece*. So with these scholars from around the world, and Lenny's *Alice* skills, we had a good jump on the aspect of the project we refer to as "the rest of the world." A complete list of the checklist compilers appears in the Acknowledgments in Volume One.

In the introduction to his book on American *Alice* editions, Byron Sewell wrote: "As the title *Much of a Muchness* implies, this bibliography is incomplete. I wish that I could legitimately entitle it *All of a Muchness*. However, I have come around to the opinion that it is simply impossible to track down and describe every printing of the *Alice* books published in America." [1]

The same can be said of this book: it is necessarily incomplete. On February 21, 2022, when searching for *Alice in Wonderland* on Amazon's American and UK websites, both indicated matches with "over 10,000" entries. Both sites include many editions outside our scope of interest, such as coloring books and translations. Amazon descriptions tend to be vague, often including little usable information. Our checklists record some 4,358 unique entries for the four *Alice* books, and one would have to go to the Library of Congress, the British Library, and other notable repositories to find additional ones.

---

1. Byron W. Sewell in cooperation with Hilda Bohem, *Much of a Muchness: A Survey of the American Editions of the Alice Books Published from 1866 to 1960* (South Charleston, WV: Chicken Little's Press, 1992; reprinted in facsimile 2017).

ORDER OF THE CHECKLISTS

The checklists are presented in the following order:

First are the editions of *Alice's Adventures in Wonderland*, with separate sections for UK editions, American editions, other English-speaking country editions (Australia, Canada, Ireland, and New Zealand), and English-language editions published in the rest of the world. Each section also includes combined editions that contain both *Alice* and *Through the Looking-Glass* in a single volume.

Second are the editions of *Through the Looking-Glass*, including the same separate sections listed above for *Alice* but lacking combined editions.

Third are the editions of *Alice's Adventures under Ground*, with editions from all countries in a single list.

Fourth are the editions of *The Nursery "Alice,"* with all countries in a single list.

Fifth are the editions of *The Annotated Alice*, including all editions from all countries in a single list.

Sixth are the pop-up and movable editions that contain any or all portions of the four books, including editions from all countries in a single list.

Immediately following this introduction, you will find a summary table with the number of English-language editions of each of the four *Alice* books published worldwide. English-language editions of *Alice* have been published in twenty-nine non-English-speaking countries, including China with forty-two editions, Japan with thirty-one, Taiwan with twenty-eight, and even Singapore with one. *Looking-Glass* has appeared in English-language editions in twelve countries.

For the purposes of this book, an "edition" is a specific setting of type. Each hardcover, paperback, and e-book version usually has a unique International Standard Book Number (ISBN), thus making them different editions. Binding colors alone do not. We also include CDs, DVDs, and audio material only if they accompany a printed edition. See the "Editorial Note" in Volume One for more information about what we define as an "edition."

For the American editions, Byron Sewell's 2017 facsimile edition of *Much of a Muchness* was used as a starting point. The book is enormously detailed and informative, with numerous codes and abbreviations requiring significant study. A copy should be in every Carroll scholar's library.

The American *Through the Looking-Glass* checklist compiler is George Cassady, a retired medical school professor and now a professor of bibliography at the University of Southern California, which holds the extensive Cassady Collection of Carroll material. He has done a masterful job of explaining the vague publication dating system in use in America in the late nineteenth and early twentieth centuries. As a previously avocational and now vocational bibliographer, Cassady's original "Notes" in the checklist of American editions of *Looking-Glass* were extensive, enormously informative, and interesting. Since his entries far exceeded what any other checklist compiler provided for either this book or the prior *Translations* book, they were shortened for consistency. In the prospective online version of these checklists, perhaps his extensive notes may be added in full. For example, Cassady explains the Henry Altemus editions as follows:

> There are four formats of the Altemus *Looking-Glass* books: Format 1 (1895–1898), Format 2 (1898–1902), Format 3 (1902–1923), and Format 4 (1923–1933). The publication dates are principally determined by spine format and ads. American publishing practice did not often include dates printed on the title pages, so other means had to be used. Hence there are numerous date estimates in the date columns. The illustrations are by Tenniel although he is not credited. Even the titles and series numbers and names can be confusing. There are numerous Altemus book series, and *Looking-Glass* is found in series numbers 48, 57, 58, 59, 64, 82, 87, 115, 118, 130, 143, 180, 186, 200, and 202. The books are by publication date and not grouped by series number. There are 208 Altemus series and *Looking-Glass* is included in 15 of them.

Readers will note the omission in the checklists of any individual or institutional holding codes, which were included in the earlier *Translations* book. In an email of October 2, 2017, Cassady wrote: "I see no reason to include the 'Holdings' column. OCLC is almost useless in identifying who holds what. . . ."[2] A query of other checklist compilers produced unanimous agreement with Cassady. Although those codes indicated where an edition could be found, many were only in private collections, some were found only in other bibliographies, and for a number of editions no holder could be located. Since the information was spotty, eliminating holding codes greatly simplified the process while omitting little information of significant use to a reader.

In searching for the 1,952 copies of the 1866 Appleton edition of *Alice*, a similar problem arose. The sheets for the 1865 edition of *Alice* were rejected by Carroll due to poor illustration reproduction and sold to D. Appleton of New York. Assisted by Lila Harper and August Imholtz, we queried institutional libraries, finding only 114 copies. Of these, seventy-seven are in US libraries, two in Canada, one in the UK, one in Europe, and another in Japan. Only twenty were found in private collections and twelve in dealer catalogs. Each library listed by WorldCat was contacted. Several of them had no copy at all and no idea how they came to be included; others had the 1927 reprint, but it had been miscatalogued in WorldCat as the 1866 edition. Since there was a reprint, all 1,952 copies of the original 1866 edition must have been sold. But to whom we do not know, and neither does WorldCat.

CHECKLIST BIBLIOGRAPHICAL PRINCIPLES

This book is in American English. It is written for the Lewis Carroll scholar, the academic, and the general reader. The *Chicago Manual of Style* is silent about checklists. Ours are generally done to the standard used in our 2015 *Translations* book, but adapted for editions written in English. Unlike the earlier book, each separate edition, or "entry," has been given a unique identification number so that the various indexes (such as the illustrator index) can point directly to all the relevant entries.

Within each checklist, the editions are listed chronologically by publication date, usually the oldest first, with multiple sequences within a year (if applicable). When the year of publication is printed in the book, usually on the title page, that date is used and appears first. When derived from other sources, square brackets [year] are used if an exact date can be determined. Such dates appear second. Circa [ca. year] is used when the date is approximate, and appears third. When

---

2. OCLC (Online Computer Library Center) produces the WorldCat.org library catalog.

checklist compilers could only suggest a range of the date of publication, these appear as the last item within their chronological sequence. The last edition listed is not necessarily the last one published that year, but it is the last we found at the time the list was compiled. Finally, all undated books appear at the end of each checklist, labeled "n.d." [no date] in the date column.

The title of the book is taken from the title page rather than from the cover, as the two often differ. If a book had no title page, the cover title was used.

The city of publication is listed using American spelling. Diacritics are not always used. The country, state, or province may be included in the place of publication if the city is not widely known. If the city is unknown, N.P. [no place] is used.

The name of the publisher is listed using American spelling. If the name of the publisher is unknown, n.p. [no publisher] is used.

The International Standard Book Number (ISBN) or Standard Book Number (SBN) is included whenever one can be determined. Many editions were published before the ISBN system came into use. In recording the number, we include no spaces or hyphens. When a book has both a thirteen-digit and a ten-digit version, we generally use the thirteen-digit number and omit the ten-digit one. ISBN policy differs by country of publication and by publisher. As pointed out in the "Editorial Note" in Volume One, we caution that ISBNs, even ones found in the publication itself, can be incorrect or are shared among variant editions of the same title. Therefore, we include ISBNs for the reader's convenience, but we cannot ensure that the numbers are correct. If you wish to learn more about ISBNs, additional information is readily available online.

Print-on-demand editions posed a problem. Amazon acquired CreateSpace, a print-on-demand book publisher, in 2005. This is by far the most prolific print-on-demand publisher of both *Alice* and *Looking-Glass*. In August 2018, CreateSpace merged with Amazon's Kindle Direct Publishing (KDP) group. Between 2005 and 2018, CreateSpace printed literally hundreds of *Alice* and *Looking-Glass* editions, usually with different covers. Agonizingly, these usually, but not always, have different ISBNs. Most are available in paper wrappers or as e-books, many as audiobooks, and a few as hardcover printings. Often, the only information given on an internet site is a picture (often just a stock picture), an ISBN (not always correct), and a price.[3]

The name of the illustrator is listed if known. If the book is known to be illustrated but the name of the illustrator is unknown, the name is listed as "Anonymous." If the book was not seen and it is unknown if it is illustrated, the name is listed as "Unknown." In the "Illustrator Index," the variant forms of some of illustrators' names have been normalized.

The format and content of the Notes sections in the checklists are not always consistent and may contain a great variety of information that differs for different editions and by different checklist compilers. Many compilers contributed to each checklist, and they included what they found to be of interest or what was available. Some editions were not seen but were found in a published source and may have no notes. The number of pages appears in some notes.

In the notes, references to *Alice's Adventures in Wonderland* are often shortened to *Alice* (in

---

3. Our thanks to George Cassady for providing information on CreateSpace.

italics); references to Alice herself are not italicized. *Through the Looking-Glass and What Alice Found There* is usually shortened to *Through the Looking-Glass* or just *Looking-Glass*, and *Alice's Adventures under Ground* is shortened to *under Ground*. We also italicize *Alice* in the collective phrase "the four *Alice* books."

 Books are now published in more ways than the traditional codex or bound volume. We include other forms of publication, such as e-books and online books. We also include serial publications (including those in journals, newspapers, and magazines), abridged and retold books, graphic novels, comic books, and pop-up books. We do not include CDs, DVDs, or audiobooks (unless included with a bound edition), stage plays, films, sheet music, or radio broadcasts. Also omitted are fan fiction, parodies, coloring or paint books, and puzzle books. A complete list of all English-language audiobooks is left for a later project.

Finally, if you disagree with specific dates or other information listed in this book, please bring this matter, with your justification, to the attention of the Lewis Carroll Society of North America at LewisCarroll.org.

BIBLIOGRAPHICAL SOURCES. The following sources are referenced in the checklist, occasionally abbreviated as follows:

Davis: John Davis. "Introduction." In *The Illustrators of Alice in Wonderland and Through the Looking Glass*. Edited by Graham Ovenden. London: Academy Editions; NY: St. Martin's Press, 1972.

Harcourt Amory Collection: *The Harcourt Amory Collection of Lewis Carroll in the Harvard College Library*. Cambridge, MA: Harvard University Press, 1932.

Guiliano: Edward Guiliano. *Lewis Carroll: An Annotated International Bibliography, 1960–77.* Brighton, UK: Harvester Press, 1981.

Library Hub Discover: Contains the merged catalogs of UK national, university, and specialist libraries. This is now the official name, replacing the previous name of COPAC.

Lovett: Charles C. Lovett and Stephanie B. Lovett. *Lewis Carroll's Alice*. London: Meckler, 1990.

MoM: Byron W. Sewell. *Much of a Muchness: A Survey of the American Editions of the Alice Books Published from 1866 to 1960*. South Charleston, WV: Chicken Little's Press, 1992. Also the facsimile *Much of a Muchness: A Survey of the American editions of the Alice Books Published from 1866 to 1960*. N.P.: Word Type / CreateSpace, 2017.

Stern: Jeffrey Stern. *Lewis Carroll's Library: A Facsimile Edition of the Catalogue of the Auction Sale Following C. L. Dodgson's Death in 1898, with Facsimiles of Three Subsequent Booksellers' Catalogues Offering Books from Dodgson's Library*. Silver Spring, MD: The Lewis Carroll Society of North America, 1981.

Trove: Bibliographical database of the National Library of Australia.

OCLC: Publisher of the WorldCat database.

PTLA: *Publisher's Trade List Annual*.

WMGC: Sidney Herbert Williams and Falconer Madan, comps. *The Lewis Carroll Handbook: Being a New Version of a Handbook of the Literature of the Rev. C. L. Dodgson*. First published 1931. Revised and augmented by Roger Lancelyn Green, 1962. Further revised by Denis Crutch, 1979. Folkestone, Kent: Dawson, 1979.

Format of the Checklist Entries

Each checklist entry consists of the following elements in this order:

LINE 1:

>   Checklist entry reference number as provided in Appendix 2 (Publisher Index) and Appendix 3 (Illustrator Index)
>
>   Publication year
>
>   Title as found on the title page of the book

LINE 2:

>   Place of publication
>
>   Publisher
>
>   ISBN (if available)
>
>   Illustrator(s)

LINE 3, ETC.:

>   Edition, if identified
>
>   All other notes about the book

Note: It is possible for a single entry to be split across two pages. When an entry starts at the bottom of a page, readers are encouraged to go to the top of the next page to ensure that the full entry has been read.

ILLUSTRATION OF A TYPICAL ENTRY:

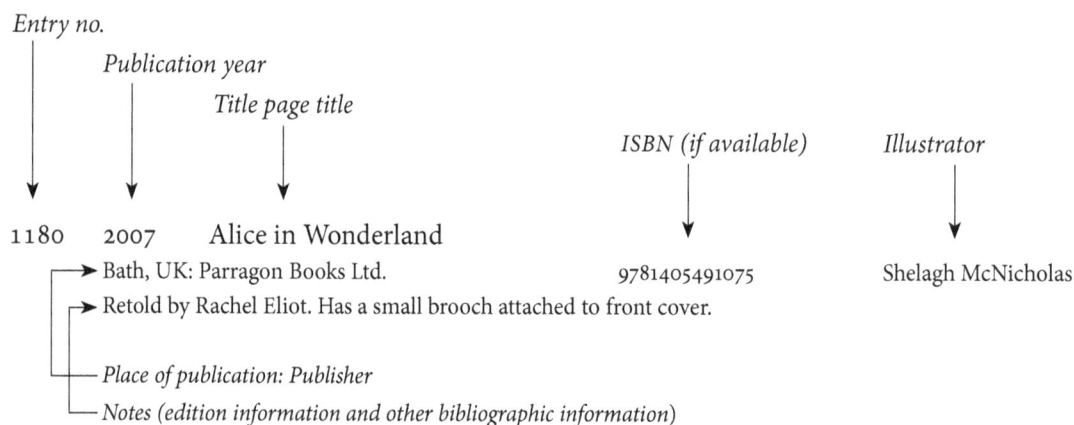

Entry no.

Publication year

Title page title

ISBN (if available)

Illustrator

1180   2007   Alice in Wonderland

Bath, UK: Parragon Books Ltd.   9781405491075   Shelagh McNicholas

Retold by Rachel Eliot. Has a small brooch attached to front cover.

Place of publication: Publisher

Notes (edition information and other bibliographic information)

Number of Checklist Entries
and Checklist Register for Each Book

Arnold Hirshon

1. UK *ALICE*, AND COMBINED *ALICE* AND *LOOKING-GLASS* EDITIONS

# OF ENTRIES	FIRST ENTRY	LAST ENTRY	SECTION NUMBER, BOOKS AND EDITIONS
101	1	101	1.1 Macmillan 6 shilling Red Cloth Edition
135	102	236	1.2 Macmillan *People's Edition*
19	237	255	1.3 Macmillan *Sixpenny Series*
13	256	268	1.4 Macmillan *Illustrated Pocket Classics for the Young* Edition
25	269	293	1.5 Macmillan *Miniature Edition*
16	294	309	1.6 Macmillan *Children's Edition*
14	310	323	1.7 Macmillan *Children's Books, New Children's Edition*
11	324	334	1.8 Macmillan *Children's Classics, Junior Series*
3	335	337	1.9 Macmillan Children's Books
7	338	344	1.10 Macmillan *Little Alice Edition*
29	345	373	1.11 Macmillan: Other Editions
33	374	406	1.12 Macmillan Combined *People's Edition* of *Alice* and *Looking-Glass*
21	407	427	1.13 Macmillan Combined *Sixpenny Series* of *Alice* and *Looking-Glass*
47	428	474	1.14 Macmillan Combined Other Editions of *Alice* and *Looking-Glass*
837	475	1311	1.15 Other Publishers of *Alice*
382	1312	1693	1.16 Other Publishers of Combined Editions of *Alice* and *Looking-Glass*

2. US *ALICE*, AND COMBINED *ALICE* AND *LOOKING-GLASS* EDITIONS

# OF ENTRIES	FIRST ENTRY	LAST ENTRY	SECTION NUMBER, BOOKS AND EDITION
77	1694	1770	2.1 Appleton and Macmillan *Alice* Editions
58	1771	1828	2.2 Macmillan: Combined Editions of *Alice* and *Looking-Glass*
557	1829	2385	2.3 Other Publishers of *Alice*
346	2386	2731	2.4 Other Publishers of Combined Editions of *Alice* and *Looking-Glass*

3. OTHER ENGLISH-SPEAKING COUNTRIES (AUSTRALIA, CANADA, IRELAND, AND NEW ZEALAND): *ALICE, LOOKING-GLASS,* AND COMBINED EDITIONS

# OF ENTRIES	FIRST ENTRY	LAST ENTRY	SECT. NO., BOOKS & EDITION	# OF ENTRIES	FIRST ENTRY	LAST ENTRY	SECT. NO., BOOKS & EDITION
69	2732	2800	3.1 Australia	12	2833	2844	3.3 Ireland
32	2801	2832	3.2 Canada	16	2845	2860	3.4 New Zealand

4. REST OF THE WORLD: *ALICE, LOOKING-GLASS,* AND COMBINED EDITIONS

# OF ENTRIES	FIRST ENTRY	LAST ENTRY	SECT. NO., BOOKS & EDITION	# OF ENTRIES	FIRST ENTRY	LAST ENTRY	SECT. NO., BOOKS & EDITION
2	2861	2862	4.1 Argentina	8	3119	3126	4.16 Netherlands
3	2863	2865	4.2 Austria	3	3127	3129	4.17 Peru
1	2866	2866	4.3 Belgium	6	3130	3135	4.18 Poland
3	2867	2869	4.4 Brazil	6	3136	3141	4.19 Romania
51	2870	2920	4.5 China	3	3142	3144	4.20 Russia
3	2921	2923	4.6 Colombia	2	3145	3146	4.21 Slovakia
3	2924	2926	4.7 Czech Republic	1	3147	3147	4.22 South Africa
1	2927	2927	4.8 Denmark	1	3148	3148	4.23 South Korea
24	2928	2951	4.9 France	35	3149	3183	4.24 Spain
45	2952	2996	4.10 Germany	8	3184	3191	4.25 Sweden
30	2997	3026	4.11 India	1	3192	3192	4.26 Switzerland
38	3027	3064	4.12 Italy	31	3193	3223	4.27 Taiwan
40	3065	3104	4.13 Japan[1]	1	3224	3224	4.28 Thailand
13	3105	3117	4.14 Malaysia	7	3225	3231	4.29 Turkey
1	3118	3118	4.15 Mexico				

1. See p. 18, note 2.

5. UK *THROUGH THE LOOKING-GLASS* EDITIONS

# OF ENTRIES	FIRST ENTRY	LAST ENTRY	SECTION NUMBER, BOOKS AND EDITION
57	3232	3288	5.1 Macmillan 6 shilling edition
92	3289	3380	5.2 Macmillan *People's Edition*
11	3381	3391	5.3 Macmillan *Sixpenny Series*
3	3392	3394	5.4 Macmillan *Little Folks' Edition*
14	3395	3408	5.5 Macmillan *Illustrated Pocket Classics for the Young* Edition

COUNTS BY BOOK AND COUNTRY OF PUBLICATION

	Alice	Looking-Glass	Under Ground	COMBINED EDITIONS[1]	POP-UPS & MOVABLES	TOTAL
UK	1,210	394	37	523	44	2,208
US	634	466	38	422	31	1,591
OTHER ENGLISH-SPEAKING COUNTRIES						
Australia	52	5	5	13	2	77
Canada	24	4	5	6	1	40
Ireland	9	2	2	3	0	16
New Zealand	8	8	0	0	0	16
REST OF THE WORLD						
Argentina	2	0	0	0	0	2
Austria	3	0	1	0	0	4
Belgium	1	0	0	0	0	1
Brazil	3	0	0	0	0	3
China	34	11	0	6	0	51
Colombia	3	0	0	0	0	3
Czechoslovakia / Czech Republic	2	0	0	1	1	4
Denmark	1	0	0	0	0	1
France	19	4	3	1	0	27
Germany	41	2	2	3	0	48
India	22	6	2	2	0	32
Italy	31	0	0	7	0	38
Japan[2]	32	8	7	15	1	63
Malaysia	13	0	0	0	0	13
Mexico	0	0	0	1	0	1
Netherlands	8	0	2	0	0	10
Peru	3	0	0	0	0	3
Poland	5	1	0	0	0	6
Romania	5	0	0	2	0	7
Russia	3	0	0	0	0	3
Slovakia	0	0	0	2	0	2
South Africa	1	0	1	0	0	2
South Korea	1	0	0	0	0	1
Spain	35	0	0	0	2	37
Sweden	2	1	0	5	0	8
Switzerland	1	0	0	0	0	1
Taiwan	27	1	0	3	0	31
Thailand	1	0	0	0	0	1
Turkey	7	0	0	0	0	7
TOTAL	2,243	913	105	1,015	82	4,358

1. This column includes combined editions of *Alice* and *Looking-Glass* as well as forty-eight instances where *The Nursery "Alice"* was published in a combined edition with *Looking-Glass*.

2. Japanese publishers in short runs and reprint frequently, sometimes in the same year. The reprint number is stated on the title page and the edition has the year of publication. In our 2015 book, *Alice in a World of Wonderlands: Translations*, we listed all reprints in the checklist. Here we are including in the Notes section the number of reprints when stated. For example, the second Japanese English-language edition was published in 1956 and the 29th printing was in 1981 according to its title page. In 1994 and 1996 the book was further reprinted but with a new ISBN, another peculiarity of Japanese publishing practice. Ordinarily we would consider a new ISBN to be a new edition, but this was not the case here.

CHECKLISTS

1. *Alice's Adventures in Wonderland* Editions Published in the UK, Including Combined Editions with *Through the Looking-Glass*

1.1 MACMILLAN 6 SHILLING RED CLOTH EDITION

1   1865   Alice's Adventures in Wonderland
London: Macmillan and Co.   John Tenniel
Macmillan 6 shilling red cloth. 1st edition. Suppressed by Carroll after Tenniel objected to the quality of the illustrations. Typical Macmillan red cloth. Only 22 copies known.

2   1866   Alice's Adventures in Wonderland
London: Macmillan and Co.   John Tenniel
Macmillan 6 shilling red cloth. 2nd edition. In typical Macmillan red cloth. 4,000 copies printed. Earlier copies have pale blue endpapers, later copies have black endpapers.

3   1866   Alice's Adventures in Wonderland
London: Macmillan and Co.   John Tenniel
Macmillan 6 shilling red cloth. 5th thousand. Also exists with an 1867 date.

4   1867   Alice's Adventures in Wonderland
London: Macmillan and Co.   John Tenniel
Macmillan 6 shilling red cloth. 5th thousand. Also exists with an 1866 date.

5   1867   Alice's Adventures in Wonderland
London: Macmillan and Co.   John Tenniel
Macmillan 6 shilling red cloth. 6th thousand.

6   1867   Alice's Adventures in Wonderland
London: Macmillan and Co.   John Tenniel
Macmillan 6 shilling red cloth. 7th thousand.

7   1867   Alice's Adventures in Wonderland
London: Macmillan and Co.   John Tenniel
Macmillan 6 shilling red cloth. 8th thousand.

8   1867   Alice's Adventures in Wonderland
London: Macmillan and Co.   John Tenniel
Macmillan 6 shilling red cloth. 9th thousand.

9   1867   Alice's Adventures in Wonderland
London: Macmillan and Co.   John Tenniel
Macmillan 6 shilling red cloth. 10th thousand. Also exists with an 1868 date.

10   1868   Alice's Adventures in Wonderland
London: Macmillan and Co.   John Tenniel
Macmillan 6 shilling red cloth. 10th thousand. Also exists with an 1867 date.

11   1868   Alice's Adventures in Wonderland
London: Macmillan and Co.   John Tenniel
Macmillan 6 shilling red cloth. 11th thousand. Also exists with an 1869 date.

12   1868   Alice's Adventures in Wonderland
London: Macmillan and Co.   John Tenniel
Macmillan 6 shilling red cloth. 12th thousand. Also exists with an 1869 date.

13   1868   Alice's Adventures in Wonderland
London: Macmillan and Co.   John Tenniel
Macmillan 6 shilling red cloth. 13th thousand. Also exists with an 1869 date.

14   1869   Alice's Adventures in Wonderland
London: Macmillan and Co.   John Tenniel
Macmillan 6 shilling red cloth. 11th thousand. Also exists with an 1868 date.

15   1869   Alice's Adventures in Wonderland
London: Macmillan and Co.   John Tenniel
Macmillan 6 shilling red cloth. 12th thousand. Also exists with an 1868 date.

16   1869   Alice's Adventures in Wonderland
London: Macmillan and Co.   John Tenniel
Macmillan 6 shilling red cloth. 13th thousand. Also exists with an 1868 date.

17   1869   Alice's Adventures in Wonderland
London: Macmillan and Co.   John Tenniel
Macmillan 6 shilling red cloth. 14th thousand. There are no known copies of the 15th thousand.

18   1869   Alice's Adventures in Wonderland
London: Macmillan and Co.   John Tenniel
Macmillan 6 shilling red cloth. 16th thousand. Some copies carry a fly leaf advertisement for *Phantasmagoria*.

19   1869   Alice's Adventures in Wonderland
London: Macmillan and Co.   John Tenniel
Macmillan 6 shilling red cloth. 17th thousand.

20   1869   Alice's Adventures in Wonderland
London: Macmillan and Co.   John Tenniel
Macmillan 6 shilling red cloth. 18th thousand. There are no known copies of the 19th thousand.

21   1870   Alice's Adventures in Wonderland
London: Macmillan and Co.   John Tenniel
Macmillan 6 shilling red cloth. 20th thousand. First advertisements for the French and German translations.

22   1870   Alice's Adventures in Wonderland
London: Macmillan and Co.   John Tenniel
Macmillan 6 shilling red cloth. 21st thousand.

23   1870   Alice's Adventures in Wonderland
London: Macmillan and Co.   John Tenniel
Macmillan 6 shilling red cloth. 22nd thousand. Advertisements for *Phantasmagoria*.

24   1870   Alice's Adventures in Wonderland

London: Macmillan and Co.   John Tenniel

Macmillan 6 shilling red cloth. 23rd thousand. Some copies have a "tri-star" device on the spine rather than the traditional Macmillan device found on other editions.

25	1870	Alice's Adventures in Wonderland	

London: Macmillan and Co.   John Tenniel

Macmillan 6 shilling red cloth. 24th thousand.

26	1870	Alice's Adventures in Wonderland	

London: Macmillan and Co.   John Tenniel

Macmillan 6 shilling red cloth. 25th thousand.

27	1871	Alice's Adventures in Wonderland	

London: Macmillan and Co.   John Tenniel

Macmillan 6 shilling red cloth. 26th thousand.

28	1871	Alice's Adventures in Wonderland	

London: Macmillan and Co.   John Tenniel

Macmillan 6 shilling red cloth. 27th thousand.

29	1871	Alice's Adventures in Wonderland	

London: Macmillan and Co.   John Tenniel

Macmillan 6 shilling red cloth. 28th thousand.

30	1872	Alice's Adventures in Wonderland	

London; New York: Macmillan and Co.   John Tenniel

Macmillan 6 shilling red cloth. 29th thousand. A copy is known with the January 15, 1898, obituary of Carroll from the *St. James Gazette* pasted in.

31	1872	Alice's Adventures in Wonderland	

London; New York: Macmillan and Co.   John Tenniel

Macmillan 6 shilling red cloth. 30th thousand.

32	1872	Alice's Adventures in Wonderland	

London; New York: Macmillan and Co.   John Tenniel

Macmillan 6 shilling red cloth. 31st thousand.

33	1872	Alice's Adventures in Wonderland	

London: Macmillan and Co.   John Tenniel

Macmillan 6 shilling red cloth. 32nd thousand.

34	1872	Alice's Adventures in Wonderland	

London: Macmillan and Co.   John Tenniel

Macmillan 6 shilling red cloth. 33rd thousand. Advertisements include the Italian translation.

35	1872	Alice's Adventures in Wonderland	

London: Macmillan and Co.   John Tenniel

Macmillan 6 shilling red cloth. 34th thousand.

36	1872	Alice's Adventures in Wonderland	

London: Macmillan and Co.   John Tenniel

Macmillan 6 shilling red cloth. 35th thousand. Also exists with a New York and London imprint.

| 37 | 1872 | Alice's Adventures in Wonderland | John Tenniel |

37   1872   Alice's Adventures in Wonderland
London: Macmillan and Co.   John Tenniel
Macmillan 6 shilling red cloth. 35th thousand.

38   1872   Alice's Adventures in Wonderland
London: Macmillan and Co.   John Tenniel
Macmillan 6 shilling red cloth. 36th thousand.

39   1872   Alice's Adventures in Wonderland
London: Macmillan and Co.   John Tenniel
Macmillan 6 shilling red cloth. 37th thousand.

40   1872   Alice's Adventures in Wonderland
London: Macmillan and Co.   John Tenniel
Macmillan 6 shilling red cloth. 38th thousand.

41   1872   Alice's Adventures in Wonderland
London: Macmillan and Co.   John Tenniel
Macmillan 6 shilling red cloth. 39th thousand.

42   1872   Alice's Adventures in Wonderland
London: Macmillan and Co.   John Tenniel
Macmillan 6 shilling red cloth. 40th thousand.

43   1872   Alice's Adventures in Wonderland
London: Macmillan and Co.   John Tenniel
Macmillan 6 shilling red cloth. 41st thousand. Also exists with an 1874 date.

44   1874   Alice's Adventures in Wonderland
London: Macmillan and Co.   John Tenniel
Macmillan 6 shilling red cloth. 41st thousand. Also exists with an 1872 date.

45   1874   Alice's Adventures in Wonderland
London: Macmillan and Co.   John Tenniel
Macmillan 6 shilling red cloth. 42nd thousand.

46   1874   Alice's Adventures in Wonderland
London: Macmillan and Co.   John Tenniel
Macmillan 6 shilling red cloth. 43rd thousand.

47   1874   Alice's Adventures in Wonderland
London: Macmillan and Co.   John Tenniel
Macmillan 6 shilling red cloth. 44th thousand.

48   1874   Alice's Adventures in Wonderland
London: Macmillan and Co.   John Tenniel
Macmillan 6 shilling red cloth. 45th thousand.

49   1874   Alice's Adventures in Wonderland
London: Macmillan and Co.   John Tenniel
Macmillan 6 shilling red cloth. 46th thousand.

50   1875   Alice's Adventures in Wonderland

Alice in a World of Wonderlands

London: Macmillan and Co.   John Tenniel

Macmillan 6 shilling red cloth. 47th thousand. There are no known copies of the 48th thousand.

51   1876   Alice's Adventures in Wonderland
London: Macmillan and Co.   John Tenniel

Macmillan 6 shilling red cloth. 49th thousand.

52   1876   Alice's Adventures in Wonderland
London: Macmillan and Co.   John Tenniel

Macmillan 6 shilling red cloth. 50th thousand. A copy exists signed by Edward Lear. This is the only known contact between the two great Victorian nonsense writers.

53   1876   Alice's Adventures in Wonderland
London: Macmillan and Co.   John Tenniel

Macmillan 6 shilling red cloth. 51st thousand.

54   1876   Alice's Adventures in Wonderland
London: Macmillan and Co.   John Tenniel

Macmillan 6 shilling red cloth. 52nd thousand.

55   1877   Alice's Adventures in Wonderland
London: Macmillan and Co.   John Tenniel

Macmillan 6 shilling red cloth. 53rd thousand.

56   1877   Alice's Adventures in Wonderland
London: Macmillan and Co.   John Tenniel

Macmillan 6 shilling red cloth. 54th thousand.

57   1877   Alice's Adventures in Wonderland
London: Macmillan and Co.   John Tenniel

Macmillan 6 shilling red cloth. 55th thousand.

58   1878   Alice's Adventures in Wonderland
London: Macmillan and Co.   John Tenniel

Macmillan 6 shilling red cloth. 56th thousand.

59   1878   Alice's Adventures in Wonderland
London: Macmillan and Co.   John Tenniel

Macmillan 6 shilling red cloth. 57th thousand.

60   1878   Alice's Adventures in Wonderland
London: Macmillan and Co.   John Tenniel

Macmillan 6 shilling red cloth. 58th thousand.

61   1879   Alice's Adventures in Wonderland
London: Macmillan and Co.   John Tenniel

Macmillan 6 shilling red cloth. 59th thousand.

62   1879   Alice's Adventures in Wonderland
London: Macmillan and Co.   John Tenniel

Macmillan 6 shilling red cloth. 60th thousand.

63   1879   Alice's Adventures in Wonderland

London: Macmillan and Co.
Macmillan 6 shilling red cloth. 61st thousand.

John Tenniel

64   1879   Alice's Adventures in Wonderland
London: Macmillan and Co.
Macmillan 6 shilling red cloth. 62nd thousand.

John Tenniel

65   1879   Alice's Adventures in Wonderland
London: Macmillan and Co.
Macmillan 6 shilling red cloth. 63rd thousand. Also exists with an 1881 date.

John Tenniel

66   1880   Alice's Adventures in Wonderland
London: Macmillan and Co.
Macmillan 6 shilling red cloth. 64th thousand. Also exists with an 1881 date.

John Tenniel

67   1881   Alice's Adventures in Wonderland
London: Macmillan and Co.
Macmillan 6 shilling red cloth. 63rd thousand. Also exists with an 1879 date.

John Tenniel

68   1881   Alice's Adventures in Wonderland
London: Macmillan and Co.
Macmillan 6 shilling red cloth. 64th thousand. Also exists with an 1880 date. There are no known copies of the 65th and 66th thousands.

John Tenniel

69   1881   Alice's Adventures in Wonderland
London: Macmillan and Co.
Macmillan 6 shilling red cloth. 67th thousand.

John Tenniel

70   1881   Alice's Adventures in Wonderland
London: Macmillan and Co.
Macmillan 6 shilling red cloth. 68th thousand.

John Tenniel

71   1882   Alice's Adventures in Wonderland
London: Macmillan and Co.
Macmillan 6 shilling red cloth. 69th thousand.

John Tenniel

72   1882   Alice's Adventures in Wonderland
London: Macmillan and Co.
Macmillan 6 shilling red cloth. 70th thousand.

John Tenniel

73   1883   Alice's Adventures in Wonderland
London: Macmillan and Co.
Macmillan 6 shilling red cloth. 71st thousand.

John Tenniel

74   1883   Alice's Adventures in Wonderland
London: Macmillan and Co.
Macmillan 6 shilling red cloth. 72nd thousand.

John Tenniel

75   1884   Alice's Adventures in Wonderland
London: Macmillan and Co.
Macmillan 6 shilling red cloth. 73rd thousand.

John Tenniel

76   1884   Alice's Adventures in Wonderland
London: Macmillan and Co.   John Tenniel
Macmillan 6 shilling red cloth. 74th thousand.

77   1885   Alice's Adventures in Wonderland
London: Macmillan and Co.   John Tenniel
Macmillan 6 shilling red cloth. 75th thousand. Known in typical red binding and one inscribed by Carroll in a white presentation binding. There are no known copies of the 76th thousand.

78   1886   Alice's Adventures in Wonderland
London: Macmillan and Co.   John Tenniel
Macmillan 6 shilling red cloth. 77th thousand. A copy is known signed on the title page by John Tenniel.

79   1886   Alice's Adventures in Wonderland
London: Macmillan and Co.   John Tenniel
Macmillan 6 shilling red cloth. 78th thousand.

80   1886   Alice's Adventures in Wonderland
London; New York: Macmillan and Co.   John Tenniel
Macmillan 6 shilling red cloth. 79th thousand. 2 pp. of advertisements.

81   1886   Alice's Adventures in Wonderland
London; New York: Macmillan and Co.   John Tenniel
Macmillan 6 shilling red cloth. 80th thousand.

82   1886   Alice's Adventures in Wonderland
London; New York: Macmillan and Co.   John Tenniel
Macmillan 6 shilling red cloth. 81st thousand.

83   1886   Alice's Adventures in Wonderland
London; New York: Macmillan and Co.   John Tenniel
Macmillan 6 shilling red cloth. 82nd thousand.

84   1886   Alice's Adventures in Wonderland
London; New York: Macmillan and Co.   John Tenniel
Macmillan 6 shilling red cloth. 83rd thousand. A copy exists with advertisements dated 1890.

85   1891   Alice's Adventures in Wonderland
London; New York: Macmillan and Co.   John Tenniel
Macmillan 6 shilling red cloth. 84th thousand. Mouse's tail on p. 37 is reset crudely. Alice on p. 91 is faceless. 3 pp. of advertisements start.

86   1892   Alice's Adventures in Wonderland
London; New York: Macmillan and Co.   John Tenniel
Macmillan 6 shilling red cloth. 85th thousand.

87   1897   Alice's Adventures in Wonderland
London: Macmillan and Co., Limited. New York: The Macmillan Company   John Tenniel
Macmillan 6 shilling red cloth. Also published in New York. 86th thousand. Newly set edition with text changes. Goodacre calls it the "Ninth Edition" although not stated in the book. In the preface, Carroll opens with: "Enquiries have been so often addressed to me, as to whether any answer to the Hatter's Riddle (see p. 97) can be imagined, that I may as well put on record here what seems to me to be a fairly appropriate answer, viz. 'Because it can produce a few notes, though they are very flat; and it is nevar [sic] put with the wrong end in front!'" Note that "nevar" is spelled thus in line six and changed to "never" in the 87th thousand. "Christmas-Greetings" is introduced on p. 195.

88   1898   Alice's Adventures in Wonderland
London: Macmillan and Co., Limited. New York: The Macmillan Company   John Tenniel
Macmillan 6 shilling red cloth. 87th thousand. The word "nevar" changes to "never."

89   1899   Alice's Adventures in Wonderland
London: Macmillan and Co., Limited. New York: The Macmillan Company   John Tenniel
Macmillan 6 shilling red cloth. 88th thousand.

90   1901   Alice's Adventures in Wonderland
London; New York: Macmillan and Co.   John Tenniel
Macmillan 6 shilling red cloth. 89th thousand.

91   1903   Alice's Adventures in Wonderland
London: Macmillan and Co., Limited. New York: The Macmillan Company   John Tenniel
Macmillan 6 shilling red cloth. 90th thousand.

92   1908   Alice's Adventures in Wonderland
London: Macmillan and Co., Limited / St. Martin's Street   John Tenniel
Macmillan 6 shilling red cloth. 91st thousand.

93   1911   Alice's Adventures in Wonderland
London: Macmillan and Co., Limited / St. Martin's Street   John Tenniel
Macmillan 6 shilling red cloth. 92nd thousand.

94   1915   Alice's Adventures in Wonderland
London: Macmillan and Co. Limited / St. Martin's Street   John Tenniel
Macmillan 6 shilling red cloth. 92nd thousand.

95   1915   Alice's Adventures in Wonderland
London: Macmillan and Co. Limited / St. Martin's Street   John Tenniel
Macmillan 6 shilling red cloth. 93rd thousand.

96   1919   Alice's Adventures in Wonderland
London: Macmillan and Co. Limited / St. Martin's Street   John Tenniel
Macmillan 6 shilling red cloth. 94th thousand. Last edition with advertisements.

97   1922   Alice's Adventures in Wonderland
London: Macmillan and Co. Limited / St. Martin's Street   John Tenniel
Macmillan 6 shilling red cloth. 95th thousand.

98   1927   Alice's Adventures in Wonderland
London: Macmillan and Co. Limited / St. Martin's Street   John Tenniel
Macmillan 6 shilling red cloth. 96th thousand. There is no known copy of the 97th thousand.

99   1932   Alice's Adventures in Wonderland
London: Macmillan and Co. Limited / St. Martin's Street   John Tenniel
Macmillan 6 shilling red cloth. 98th thousand.

100   1942   Alice's Adventures in Wonderland
London: Macmillan and Co. Limited / St. Martin's Street   John Tenniel
Macmillan 6 shilling red cloth. No thousand stated. In gray illustrated dust jacket. This issue would appear to be the last of the Macmillan 6 shilling red cloth editions.

101   1997   Alice's Adventures in Wonderland
London: Macmillan and Co.   0033337090   John Tenniel
Macmillan 6 shilling red cloth. Reprint in facsimile of the 1884 edition. Blue paper boards with dust jacket.
Also issued in paperback.

1.2 MACMILLAN *PEOPLE'S EDITIONS*

102   1887   Alice's Adventures in Wonderland
London; New York: Macmillan and Co.   John Tenniel
Macmillan People's Edition. 1st edition. 10,000 copies were printed. There are two variant bindings: one with
Wonderland on the spine in red, and one with Wonderland in black.

103   1888   Alice's Adventures in Wonderland
London; New York: Macmillan and Co.   John Tenniel
Macmillan People's Edition. 11th thousand.

104   1888   Alice's Adventures in Wonderland
London; New York: Macmillan and Co.   John Tenniel
Macmillan People's Edition. 12th thousand.

105   1888   Alice's Adventures in Wonderland
London; New York: Macmillan and Co.   John Tenniel
Macmillan People's Edition. 13th thousand.

106   1888   Alice's Adventures in Wonderland
London; New York: Macmillan and Co.   John Tenniel
Macmillan People's Edition. 14th thousand.

107   1888   Alice's Adventures in Wonderland
London; New York: Macmillan and Co.   John Tenniel
Macmillan People's Edition. 15th thousand. Also exists dated 1889.

108   1888   Alice's Adventures in Wonderland
London; New York: Macmillan and Co.   John Tenniel
Macmillan People's Edition. 16th thousand. Also exists dated 1889.

109   1888   Alice's Adventures in Wonderland
London; New York: Macmillan and Co.   John Tenniel
Macmillan People's Edition. 18th thousand.

110   1888   Alice's Adventures in Wonderland
London; New York: Macmillan and Co.   John Tenniel
Macmillan People's Edition. 20th thousand.

111   1889   Alice's Adventures in Wonderland
London; New York: Macmillan and Co.   John Tenniel
Macmillan People's Edition. 15th thousand. Also exists dated 1888.

112   1889   Alice's Adventures in Wonderland
London; New York: Macmillan and Co.   John Tenniel
Macmillan People's Edition. 16th thousand. Also exists dated 1888.

113	1889	Alice's Adventures in Wonderland	
		London; New York: Macmillan and Co.	John Tenniel
		Macmillan People's Edition. 17th thousand. 18th thousand known only in an 1888 edition.	

114	1889	Alice's Adventures in Wonderland	
		London; New York: Macmillan and Co.	John Tenniel
		Macmillan People's Edition. 19th thousand. 20th thousand known only in an 1888 edition.	

115	1890	Alice's Adventures in Wonderland	
		London; New York: Macmillan and Co.	John Tenniel
		Macmillan People's Edition. 21st thousand. Also exists dated 1891.	

116	1890	Alice's Adventures in Wonderland	
		London; New York: Macmillan and Co.	John Tenniel
		Macmillan People's Edition. 22nd thousand. Also exists dated 1891.	

117	1890	Alice's Adventures in Wonderland	
		London; New York: Macmillan and Co.	John Tenniel
		Macmillan People's Edition. 23rd thousand.	

118	1891	Alice's Adventures in Wonderland	
		London; New York: Macmillan and Co.	John Tenniel
		Macmillan People's Edition. 21st thousand. Alice lacks a face in the illustration on p. 82. Also exists dated 1890.	

119	1891	Alice's Adventures in Wonderland	
		London; New York: Macmillan and Co.	John Tenniel
		Macmillan People's Edition. 22nd thousand. A copy exists dated 1890. 23rd thousand exists only in an 1890 edition.	

120	1891	Alice's Adventures in Wonderland	
		London; New York: Macmillan and Co.	John Tenniel
		Macmillan People's Edition. 24th thousand.	

121	1891	Alice's Adventures in Wonderland	
		London; New York: Macmillan and Co.	John Tenniel
		Macmillan People's Edition. 25th thousand.	

122	1891	Alice's Adventures in Wonderland	
		London; New York: Macmillan and Co.	John Tenniel
		Macmillan People's Edition. 26th thousand.	

123	1891	Alice's Adventures in Wonderland	
		London; New York: Macmillan and Co.	John Tenniel
		Macmillan People's Edition. 27th thousand.	

124	1892	Alice's Adventures in Wonderland	
		London; New York: Macmillan and Co.	John Tenniel
		Macmillan People's Edition. 28th thousand.	

125	1892	Alice's Adventures in Wonderland	
		London; New York: Macmillan and Co.	John Tenniel
		Macmillan People's Edition. 29th thousand. In some copies Alice's face returns in the illustration on p. 82. Some copies still lack Alice's face, indicating the face was returned in the middle of the 29th thousand print run.	

| 126 | 1892 | Alice's Adventures in Wonderland | John Tenniel |

London; New York: Macmillan and Co.
Macmillan People's Edition. 30th thousand.

| 127 | 1893 | Alice's Adventures in Wonderland | John Tenniel |

London; New York: Macmillan and Co.
Macmillan People's Edition. 31st thousand.

| 128 | 1893 | Alice's Adventures in Wonderland | John Tenniel |

London; New York: Macmillan and Co.
Macmillan People's Edition. 32nd thousand. No copy of the 33rd thousand is known.

| 129 | 1893 | Alice's Adventures in Wonderland | John Tenniel |

London; New York: Macmillan and Co.
Macmillan People's Edition. 34th thousand.

| 130 | 1893 | Alice's Adventures in Wonderland | John Tenniel |

London; New York: Macmillan and Co.
Macmillan People's Edition. 35th thousand.

| 131 | 1893 | Alice's Adventures in Wonderland | John Tenniel |

London; New York: Macmillan and Co.
Macmillan People's Edition. 36th thousand. A copy exists dated 1894.

| 132 | 1894 | Alice's Adventures in Wonderland | John Tenniel |

London; New York: Macmillan and Co.
Macmillan People's Edition. 36th thousand. A copy exists dated 1893.

| 133 | 1894 | Alice's Adventures in Wonderland | John Tenniel |

London; New York: Macmillan and Co.
Macmillan People's Edition. 37th thousand.

| 134 | 1894 | Alice's Adventures in Wonderland | John Tenniel |

London; New York: Macmillan and Co.
Macmillan People's Edition. 38th thousand.

| 135 | 1894 | Alice's Adventures in Wonderland | John Tenniel |

London; New York: Macmillan and Co.
Macmillan People's Edition. 39th thousand.

| 136 | 1894 | Alice's Adventures in Wonderland | John Tenniel |

London; New York: Macmillan and Co.
Macmillan People's Edition. 40th thousand.

| 137 | 1894 | Alice's Adventures in Wonderland | John Tenniel |

London; New York: Macmillan and Co.
Macmillan People's Edition. 41st thousand.

| 138 | 1894 | Alice's Adventures in Wonderland | John Tenniel |

London; New York: Macmillan and Co.
Macmillan People's Edition. 42nd thousand.

| 139 | 1894 | Alice's Adventures in Wonderland |

London; New York: Macmillan and Co.   John Tenniel
Macmillan People's Edition. 43rd thousand.

140   1894   Alice's Adventures in Wonderland
London; New York: Macmillan and Co.   John Tenniel
Macmillan People's Edition. 44th thousand.

141   1894   Alice's Adventures in Wonderland
London; New York: Macmillan and Co.   John Tenniel
Macmillan People's Edition. 45th thousand. Also exists in an 1896 edition.

142   1896   Alice's Adventures in Wonderland
London; New York: Macmillan and Co.   John Tenniel
Macmillan People's Edition. 45th thousand. Also exists in an 1894 edition.

143   1896   Alice's Adventures in Wonderland
London; New York: Macmillan and Co.   John Tenniel
Macmillan People's Edition. 46th thousand.

144   1896   Alice's Adventures in Wonderland
London; New York: Macmillan and Co.   John Tenniel
Macmillan People's Edition. 47th thousand.

145   1896   Alice's Adventures in Wonderland
London; New York: Macmillan and Co.   John Tenniel
Macmillan People's Edition. 48th thousand.

146   1896   Alice's Adventures in Wonderland
London; New York: Macmillan and Co.   John Tenniel
Macmillan People's Edition. 49th thousand.

147   1896   Alice's Adventures in Wonderland
London; New York: Macmillan and Co.   John Tenniel
Macmillan People's Edition. 50th thousand. No copies of the 51st to the 62nd thousands are known.

148   1896   Alice's Adventures in Wonderland
London; New York: Macmillan and Co.   John Tenniel
Macmillan People's Edition. 63rd thousand.

149   1896   Alice's Adventures in Wonderland
London; New York: Macmillan and Co.   John Tenniel
Macmillan People's Edition. 64th thousand.

150   1896   Alice's Adventures in Wonderland
London; New York: Macmillan and Co.   John Tenniel
Macmillan People's Edition. 65th thousand. No copy of the 66th thousand is known.

151   1896   Alice's Adventures in Wonderland
London; New York: Macmillan and Co.   John Tenniel
Macmillan People's Edition. 67th thousand. This thousand includes the preface that also appears in the 1897 86th thousand of the 6 shilling red cloth edition. In the preface Carroll opens with: "Enquiries have been so often addressed to me, as to whether any answer to the Hatter's Riddle can be imagined, that I may as well put on record here what seems to me to be a fairly appropriate answer, viz. 'Because it can produce a few notes, though they are very flat; and it is nevar [sic] put with the wrong end in front!'"

152   1897   Alice's Adventures in Wonderland
London; New York: Macmillan and Co.   John Tenniel
Macmillan People's Edition. 68th thousand.

153   1897   Alice's Adventures in Wonderland
London; New York: Macmillan and Co.   John Tenniel
Macmillan People's Edition. 69th thousand.

154   1897   Alice's Adventures in Wonderland
London; New York: Macmillan and Co.   John Tenniel
Macmillan People's Edition. 70th thousand.

155   1897   Alice's Adventures in Wonderland
London; New York: Macmillan and Co.   John Tenniel
Macmillan People's Edition. 71st thousand.

156   1898   Alice's Adventures in Wonderland
London; New York: Macmillan and Co.   John Tenniel
Macmillan People's Edition. 72nd thousand. In the preface the word "never" is spelled as such. Starting in the 1886
67th thousand, it was spelled as "nevar."

157   1898   Alice's Adventures in Wonderland
London; New York: Macmillan and Co.   John Tenniel
Macmillan People's Edition. 73rd thousand.

158   1898   Alice's Adventures in Wonderland
London; New York: Macmillan and Co.   John Tenniel
Macmillan People's Edition. 74th thousand.

159   1898   Alice's Adventures in Wonderland
London; New York: Macmillan and Co.   John Tenniel
Macmillan People's Edition. 75th thousand.

160   1898   Alice's Adventures in Wonderland
London; New York: Macmillan and Co.   John Tenniel
Macmillan People's Edition. 76th thousand. No copies of the 77th, 78th, and 79th thousands are known.

161   1898   Alice's Adventures in Wonderland
London; New York: Macmillan and Co.   John Tenniel
Macmillan People's Edition. 80th thousand.

162   1898   Alice's Adventures in Wonderland
London; New York: Macmillan and Co.   John Tenniel
Macmillan People's Edition. 81st thousand.

163   1898   Alice's Adventures in Wonderland
London; New York: Macmillan and Co.   John Tenniel
Macmillan People's Edition. 82nd thousand.

164   1898   Alice's Adventures in Wonderland
London; New York: Macmillan and Co.   John Tenniel
Macmillan People's Edition. 83rd thousand. No copies of the 84th to the 87th thousands are known.

165	1898	Alice's Adventures in Wonderland	
		London; New York: Macmillan and Co.	John Tenniel
		Macmillan People's Edition. 88th thousand. Also exists in an 1899 edition.	

166	1899	Alice's Adventures in Wonderland	
		London; New York: Macmillan and Co.	John Tenniel
		Macmillan People's Edition. 88th thousand. Also exists in an 1898 edition. No copies of the 89th to the 93rd thousands are known.	

167	1899	Alice's Adventures in Wonderland	
		London; New York: Macmillan and Co.	John Tenniel
		Macmillan People's Edition. 94th thousand. No copy of the 95th thousand is known.	

168	1899	Alice's Adventures in Wonderland	
		London; New York: Macmillan and Co.	John Tenniel
		Macmillan People's Edition. 96th thousand.	

169	1899	Alice's Adventures in Wonderland	
		London; New York: Macmillan and Co.	John Tenniel
		Macmillan People's Edition. 97th thousand. Some copies are in a special binding for the Vaudeville Theatre's December 1900 production of *Alice*. No copy of the 98th thousand is known.	

170	1899	Alice's Adventures in Wonderland	
		London; New York: Macmillan and Co.	John Tenniel
		Macmillan People's Edition. 99th thousand. Some copies are in a special binding for the Vaudeville Theatre's December 1900 production of *Alice*.	

171	1899	Alice's Adventures in Wonderland	
		London; New York: Macmillan and Co.	John Tenniel
		Macmillan People's Edition. 100th thousand. Some copies are in a special binding for the Vaudeville Theatre's December 1900 production of *Alice*.	

172	1899	Alice's Adventures in Wonderland	
		London; New York: Macmillan and Co.	John Tenniel
		Macmillan People's Edition. 101st thousand.	

173	1899	Alice's Adventures in Wonderland	
		London; New York: Macmillan and Co.	John Tenniel
		Macmillan People's Edition. 102nd thousand.	

174	1899	Alice's Adventures in Wonderland	
		London; New York: Macmillan and Co.	John Tenniel
		Macmillan People's Edition. 103rd thousand. Copies are known dated 1901. No copy of the 104th thousand is known.	

175	1901	Alice's Adventures in Wonderland	
		London; New York: Macmillan and Co.	John Tenniel
		Macmillan People's Edition. 103rd thousand. Also exists with an 1899 date. No copy of the 104th thousand is known.	

176	1901	Alice's Adventures in Wonderland	
		London; New York: Macmillan and Co.	John Tenniel
		Macmillan People's Edition. 105th thousand.	

177	1901	Alice's Adventures in Wonderland	
		London; New York: Macmillan and Co.	John Tenniel
		Macmillan People's Edition. 106th thousand.	

| 178 | 1901 | Alice's Adventures in Wonderland | John Tenniel |

178 1901 Alice's Adventures in Wonderland
London; New York: Macmillan and Co.
Macmillan People's Edition. 107th thousand.
John Tenniel

179 1901 Alice's Adventures in Wonderland
London; New York: Macmillan and Co.
Macmillan People's Edition. 108th thousand.
John Tenniel

180 1901 Alice's Adventures in Wonderland
London; New York: Macmillan and Co.
Macmillan People's Edition. 109th thousand.
John Tenniel

181 1901 Alice's Adventures in Wonderland
London; New York: Macmillan and Co.
Macmillan People's Edition. 110th thousand. No copy of the 111th thousand is known.
John Tenniel

182 1901 Alice's Adventures in Wonderland
London; New York: Macmillan and Co.
Macmillan People's Edition. 112th thousand.
John Tenniel

183 1901 Alice's Adventures in Wonderland
London; New York: Macmillan and Co.
Macmillan People's Edition. 113th thousand.
John Tenniel

184 1902 Alice's Adventures in Wonderland
London; New York: Macmillan and Co.
Macmillan People's Edition. 114th thousand.
John Tenniel

185 1902 Alice's Adventures in Wonderland
London; New York: Macmillan and Co.
Macmillan People's Edition. 115th thousand.
John Tenniel

186 1902 Alice's Adventures in Wonderland
London; New York: Macmillan and Co.
Macmillan People's Edition. 116th thousand.
John Tenniel

187 1902 Alice's Adventures in Wonderland
London; New York: Macmillan and Co.
Macmillan People's Edition. 117th thousand.
John Tenniel

188 1902 Alice's Adventures in Wonderland
London; New York: Macmillan and Co.
Macmillan People's Edition. 118th thousand.
John Tenniel

189 1902 Alice's Adventures in Wonderland
London; New York: Macmillan and Co.
Macmillan People's Edition. 119th thousand.
John Tenniel

190 1902 Alice's Adventures in Wonderland
London; New York: Macmillan and Co.
Macmillan People's Edition. 120th thousand.
John Tenniel

191 1902 Alice's Adventures in Wonderland

London; New York: Macmillan and Co.   John Tenniel
Macmillan People's Edition. 121st thousand.

192   1904   Alice's Adventures in Wonderland
London; New York: Macmillan and Co.   John Tenniel
Macmillan People's Edition. 122nd thousand.

193   1904   Alice's Adventures in Wonderland
London; New York: Macmillan and Co.   John Tenniel
Macmillan People's Edition. 123rd thousand.

194   1904   Alice's Adventures in Wonderland
London; New York: Macmillan and Co.   John Tenniel
Macmillan People's Edition. 124th thousand.

195   1904   Alice's Adventures in Wonderland
London; New York: Macmillan and Co.   John Tenniel
Macmillan People's Edition. 125th thousand. No copies of the 126th and 127th thousands are known.

196   1904   Alice's Adventures in Wonderland
London; New York: Macmillan and Co.   John Tenniel
Macmillan People's Edition. 128th thousand. No copies of the 129th to the 134th thousands are known.

197   1905   Alice's Adventures in Wonderland
London; New York: Macmillan and Co.   John Tenniel
Macmillan People's Edition. 135th thousand. No copies of the 136th and 137th thousands are known.

198   1905   Alice's Adventures in Wonderland
London; New York: Macmillan and Co.   John Tenniel
Macmillan People's Edition. 138th thousand. No copy of the 139th thousands is known.

199   1905   Alice's Adventures in Wonderland
London; New York: Macmillan and Co.   John Tenniel
Macmillan People's Edition. 140th thousand. No copy of the 141st thousand is known.

200   1905   Alice's Adventures in Wonderland
London; New York: Macmillan and Co.   John Tenniel
Macmillan People's Edition. 142nd thousand.

201   1905   Alice's Adventures in Wonderland
London; New York: Macmillan and Co.   John Tenniel
Macmillan People's Edition. 143rd thousand. A copy exists dated 1907.

202   1907   Alice's Adventures in Wonderland
London; New York: Macmillan and Co.   John Tenniel
Macmillan People's Edition. 143rd thousand.

203   1907   Alice's Adventures in Wonderland
London; New York: Macmillan and Co.   John Tenniel
Macmillan People's Edition. 144th thousand.

204   1907   Alice's Adventures in Wonderland
London; New York: Macmillan and Co.   John Tenniel
Macmillan People's Edition. 145th thousand.

| 205 | 1907 | Alice's Adventures in Wonderland | | John Tenniel |
London; New York: Macmillan and Co.
Macmillan People's Edition. 146th thousand.

| 206 | 1907 | Alice's Adventures in Wonderland | | John Tenniel |
London; New York: Macmillan and Co.
Macmillan People's Edition. 147th thousand.

| 207 | 1907 | Alice's Adventures in Wonderland | | John Tenniel |
London; New York: Macmillan and Co.
Macmillan People's Edition. 148th thousand. No copies of the 149th to the 156th thousands are known.

| 208 | 1908 | Alice's Adventures in Wonderland | | John Tenniel |
London: Macmillan and Co.
Macmillan People's Edition. 157th thousand. The words "People's Edition" are omitted from the half title. The imprint is lacking on the title page. New York is removed from the imprint. No copies of the 158th to the 161st thousands are known.

| 209 | 1910 | Alice's Adventures in Wonderland | | John Tenniel |
London: Macmillan and Co.
Macmillan People's Edition. 162nd thousand. It is believed that from the 162nd thousand through to the 186th thousand, copies were printed in batches of 3,000, with all carrying the number of thousand of the first of the three.

| 210 | 1912 | Alice's Adventures in Wonderland | | John Tenniel |
London: Macmillan and Co.
Macmillan People's Edition. 165th thousand.

| 211 | 1914 | Alice's Adventures in Wonderland | | John Tenniel |
London: Macmillan and Co.
Macmillan People's Edition. 168th thousand.

| 212 | 1917 | Alice's Adventures in Wonderland | | John Tenniel |
London: Macmillan and Co.
Macmillan People's Edition. 171st thousand.

| 213 | 1920 | Alice's Adventures in Wonderland | | John Tenniel |
London: Macmillan and Co.
Macmillan People's Edition. 174th thousand. This is the first thousand to have "conversation" on p. 1, instead of the correct "conversations." It was never altered back.

| 214 | 1922 | Alice's Adventures in Wonderland | | John Tenniel |
London: Macmillan and Co.
Macmillan People's Edition. 177th thousand.

| 215 | 1925 | Alice's Adventures in Wonderland | | John Tenniel |
London: Macmillan and Co.
Macmillan People's Edition. 180th thousand.

| 216 | 1927 | Alice's Adventures in Wonderland | | John Tenniel |
London: Macmillan and Co.
Macmillan People's Edition. 183rd thousand.

217	1932	Alice's Adventures in Wonderland		
		London: Macmillan and Co.		John Tenniel
		Macmillan People's Edition. 186th thousand.		

218	1937	Alice's Adventures in Wonderland		
		London: Macmillan and Co.		John Tenniel
		Macmillan People's Edition. 189th thousand. This is the last edition to carry a thousand number.		

219	1943	Alice's Adventures in Wonderland		
		London: Macmillan and Co.		John Tenniel

Macmillan People's Edition. No thousand. This and all subsequent reprints are in a new-style shiny dust jacket. In addition, the title on the cloth spine now reads down rather than up. The preface is reduced to the one paragraph about the Hatter's riddle and is now titled "Author's Note." There are no advertisements at the end. A copy as above is known that contains the original preface to the 86th thousand (3 paragraphs), and 2 pp. of advertisements.

220	1948	Alice's Adventures in Wonderland		
		London: Macmillan and Co.		John Tenniel
		Macmillan People's Edition. No thousand. There was possibly a reprint in 1949, but no copy is known.		

221	1950	Alice's Adventures in Wonderland		
		London: Macmillan and Co.		John Tenniel
		Macmillan People's Edition. No thousand. There was possibly a reprint in 1951, but no copy is known.		

222	1952	Alice's Adventures in Wonderland		
		London: Macmillan and Co.		John Tenniel
		Macmillan People's Edition. No thousand.		

223	1953	Alice's Adventures in Wonderland		
		London: Macmillan and Co.		John Tenniel
		Macmillan People's Edition. No thousand.		

224	1959	Alice's Adventures in Wonderland		
		London: Macmillan & Co. Ltd.; New York: St. Martin's Press		John Tenniel
		Macmillan People's Edition. No thousand.		

225	1965	Alice's Adventures in Wonderland		
		London: Macmillan & Co. Ltd.; New York: St. Martin's Press		John Tenniel
		Macmillan People's Edition. No thousand.		

226	1968	Alice's Adventure		
		London; Melbourne, VIC; Toronto, ON: Macmillan. New York: St. Martin's Press		John Tenniel
		Macmillan People's Edition. No thousand.		

227	1972	Alice's Adventures in Wonderland		
		London; New York: Macmillan	0333066650	John Tenniel
		Macmillan People's Edition. No thousand.		

228	1973	Alice's Adventures in Wonderland		
		London; New York: Macmillan	0333066650	John Tenniel
		Macmillan People's Edition. No thousand.		

229	1975	Alice's Adventures in Wonderland		
		London; New York: Macmillan	0333066650	John Tenniel
		Macmillan People's Edition. No thousand.		

230	1978	Alice's Adventures in Wonderland		
		London; New York: Macmillan	0333066650	John Tenniel
		Macmillan People's Edition. 9th reprint. No thousand.		

231	1980	Alice's Adventures in Wonderland		
		London; New York: Macmillan	0333066650	John Tenniel
		Macmillan People's Edition. 10th reprint. No thousand.		

232	1981	Alice's Adventures in Wonderland		
		London; New York: Macmillan	0333066650	John Tenniel
		Macmillan People's Edition. 11th reprint. No thousand.		

233	1984	Alice's Adventures in Wonderland		
		London; New York: Macmillan	0333066650	John Tenniel
		Macmillan People's Edition. 12th reprint. No thousand.		

234	1985	Alice's Adventures in Wonderland		
		London: Macmillan Children's Books	0333066650	John Tenniel
		Macmillan People's Edition. 13th reprint. No thousand.		

235	1986	Alice's Adventures in Wonderland		
		London: Macmillan Children's Books	0333066650	John Tenniel
		Macmillan People's Edition. 14th reprint. No thousand. There was possibly a reprint in 1987, but no copy is known.		

236	1988	Alice's Adventures in Wonderland		
		London: Macmillan Children's Books	0333066650	John Tenniel
		Macmillan People's Edition. May be the 15th or the 16th reprint. No thousand. Believed to be the last People's Edition of *Alice*.		

1.3 MACMILLAN *SIXPENNY SERIES*

237	1898	Alice's Adventures in Wonderland		
		London; New York: Macmillan		John Tenniel
		Macmillan Sixpenny Series. 1st edition. Copies of the Sixpenny Series were issued in paper wrappers or blue cloth boards.		

238	1899	Alice's Adventures in Wonderland		
		London; New York: Macmillan		John Tenniel
		Macmillan Sixpenny Series. 1st reprint.		

239	1899	Alice's Adventures in Wonderland		
		London; New York: Macmillan		John Tenniel
		Macmillan Sixpenny Series. 2nd reprint.		

240	1900	Alice's Adventures in Wonderland		
		London; New York: Macmillan		John Tenniel
		Macmillan Sixpenny Series. Vaudeville Theatre Edition. No mention of reprint. Special binding in white cloth boards with photograph of Ellaline Terris as Alice on front cover. No advertisements.		

241	1900	Alice's Adventures in Wonderland		
		London; New York: Macmillan		John Tenniel
		Macmillan Sixpenny Series. 3rd reprint.		

| 242 | 1902 | Alice's Adventures in Wonderland | John Tenniel |

242   1902   Alice's Adventures in Wonderland
London; New York: Macmillan
Macmillan Sixpenny Series. 4th reprint.   John Tenniel

243   1903   Alice's Adventures in Wonderland
London; New York: Macmillan
Macmillan Sixpenny Series. 5th reprint.   John Tenniel

244   1905   Alice's Adventures in Wonderland
London; New York: Macmillan
Macmillan Sixpenny Series. 6th reprint.   John Tenniel

245   1906   Alice's Adventures in Wonderland
London; New York: Macmillan
Macmillan Sixpenny Series. 7th reprint.   John Tenniel

246   1907   Alice's Adventures in Wonderland
London; New York: Macmillan
Macmillan Sixpenny Series. 8th reprint.   John Tenniel

247   1908   Alice's Adventures in Wonderland
London: Macmillan
Macmillan Sixpenny Series. 9th reprint.   John Tenniel

248   1910   Alice's Adventures in Wonderland
London: Macmillan
Macmillan Sixpenny Series. 10th reprint.   John Tenniel

249   1913   Alice's Adventures in Wonderland
London: Macmillan
Macmillan Sixpenny Series. 11th reprint.   John Tenniel

250   1919   Alice's Adventures in Wonderland
London: Macmillan
Macmillan Sixpenny Series. 12th reprint.   John Tenniel

251   1921   Alice's Adventures in Wonderland
London: Macmillan
Macmillan Sixpenny Series. 13th reprint.   John Tenniel

252   1922   Alice's Adventures in Wonderland
London: Macmillan
Macmillan Sixpenny Series. 14th reprint.   John Tenniel

253   1923   Alice's Adventures in Wonderland
London: Macmillan
Macmillan Sixpenny Series. 15th reprint.   John Tenniel

254   1927   Alice's Adventures in Wonderland
London: Macmillan
Macmillan Sixpenny Series. 16th reprint.   John Tenniel

255   1938   Alice's Adventures in Wonderland
London: Macmillan   John Tenniel
Macmillan Sixpenny Series. 17th reprint.

1.4 MACMILLAN *ILLUSTRATED POCKET CLASSICS*
FOR THE YOUNG EDITION

256   1904   Alice's Adventures in Wonderland
London; New York: Macmillan   John Tenniel
Illustrated Pocket Classics for the Young edition. 1st edition. The series title Illustrated Pocket Classics for the Young is on the verso of the title page of this edition and in all reprints. Reprints up to and including the 5th issued in blue cloth boards, after this they were mostly issued in red cloth boards.

257   1905   Alice's Adventures in Wonderland
London; New York: Macmillan   John Tenniel
Illustrated Pocket Classics for the Young edition. 1st reprint.

258   1906   Alice's Adventures in Wonderland
London; New York: Macmillan   John Tenniel
Illustrated Pocket Classics for the Young edition. 2nd reprint but not stated as such on title page verso.

259   1907   Alice's Adventures in Wonderland
London: Macmillan   John Tenniel
Illustrated Pocket Classics for the Young edition. Reprint of the 1904 edition.

260   1908   Alice's Adventures in Wonderland
London; New York: Macmillan   John Tenniel
Illustrated Pocket Classics for the Young edition. 3rd reprint.

261   1910   Alice's Adventures in Wonderland
London: Macmillan   John Tenniel
Illustrated Pocket Classics for the Young edition. Reprint not stated on title page verso. One copy in blue leatherette.

262   1912   Alice's Adventures in Wonderland
London: Macmillan   John Tenniel
Illustrated Pocket Classics for the Young edition. 4th reprint but not stated as such on title page verso.

263   1917   Alice's Adventures in Wonderland
London: Macmillan   John Tenniel
Illustrated Pocket Classics for the Young edition. 5th reprint but not stated as such on title page verso. One copy in blue leatherette with dust jacket.

264   1919   Alice's Adventures in Wonderland
London: Macmillan   John Tenniel
Illustrated Pocket Classics for the Young edition. 6th reprint but not stated as such on title page verso. One copy known in red leatherette.

265   1925   Alice's Adventures in Wonderland
London: Macmillan   John Tenniel
Illustrated Pocket Classics for the Young edition. 7th reprint.

266   1925   Alice's Adventures in Wonderland
London: Macmillan   John Tenniel
Illustrated Pocket Classics for the Young edition. Stated as 4th reprint of "Illustrated Pocket Classics."

267   1928   Alice's Adventures in Wonderland
London: Macmillan   John Tenniel
Illustrated Pocket Classics for the Young edition. 8th reprint. Dust jacket.

268   1932   Alice's Adventures in Wonderland
London: Macmillan   John Tenniel
Illustrated Pocket Classics for the Young edition. 9th reprint.

1.5 MACMILLAN *MINIATURE EDITIONS*

269   1907   Alice's Adventures in Wonderland
London: Macmillan   John Tenniel
Macmillan Miniature Edition. 1st edition. Published in July 1907. On p. 172, the 2nd "fourteenth" should read
"fifteenth." Issued in red cloth boards. Later reprints have variant bindings. All reprints were issued in dust jackets,
but survivors are uncommon. A copy of the 1st edition in decorative dark bluish green leatherette is known.

270   1907   Alice's Adventures in Wonderland
London: Macmillan   John Tenniel
Macmillan Miniature Edition. 1st reprint. September 1907.

271   1907   Alice's Adventures in Wonderland
London: Macmillan   John Tenniel
Macmillan Miniature Edition. 2nd reprint. December 1907.

272   1908   Alice's Adventures in Wonderland
London: Macmillan   John Tenniel
Macmillan Miniature Edition. 3rd reprint.

273   1909   Alice's Adventures in Wonderland
London: Macmillan   John Tenniel
Macmillan Miniature Edition. 4th reprint.

274   1910   Alice's Adventures in Wonderland
London: Macmillan   John Tenniel
Macmillan Miniature Edition. 5th reprint.

275   1911   Alice's Adventures in Wonderland
London: Macmillan   John Tenniel
Macmillan Miniature Edition. 6th reprint.

276   1912   Alice's Adventures in Wonderland
London: Macmillan   John Tenniel
Macmillan Miniature Edition. 7th reprint.

277   1913   Alice's Adventures in Wonderland
London: Macmillan   John Tenniel
Macmillan Miniature Edition. 8th reprint.

278   1914   Alice's Adventures in Wonderland
London: Macmillan   John Tenniel
Macmillan Miniature Edition. 9th reprint.

279	1915	Alice's Adventures in Wonderland	John Tenniel

279   1915   Alice's Adventures in Wonderland   John Tenniel
London: Macmillan
Macmillan Miniature Edition. 10th reprint.

280   1916   Alice's Adventures in Wonderland   John Tenniel
London: Macmillan
Macmillan Miniature Edition. 11th reprint.

281   1918   Alice's Adventures in Wonderland   John Tenniel
London: Macmillan
Macmillan Miniature Edition. 12th reprint.

282   1919   Alice's Adventures in Wonderland   John Tenniel
London: Macmillan
Macmillan Miniature Edition. 13th reprint.

283   1920   Alice's Adventures in Wonderland   John Tenniel
London: Macmillan
Macmillan Miniature Edition. 14th reprint.

284   1920   Alice's Adventures in Wonderland   John Tenniel
London: Macmillan
Macmillan Miniature Edition. 15th reprint. On p 172 "fourteenth" is corrected to "fifteenth."

285   1922   Alice's Adventures in Wonderland   John Tenniel
London: Macmillan
Macmillan Miniature Edition. 16th reprint.

286   1925   Alice's Adventures in Wonderland   John Tenniel
London: Macmillan
Macmillan Miniature Edition. 17th reprint. Also issued in écrasé morocco, as were all later reprints.

287   1928   Alice's Adventures in Wonderland   John Tenniel
London: Macmillan
Macmillan Miniature Edition. 18th reprint.

288   1929   Alice's Adventures in Wonderland   John Tenniel
London: Macmillan
Macmillan Miniature Edition. 19th reprint. Also issued as later reprints in ledura binding with a special dust jacket.

289   1931   Alice's Adventures in Wonderland   John Tenniel
London: Macmillan
Macmillan Miniature Edition. 20th reprint.

290   1932   Alice's Adventures in Wonderland   John Tenniel
London: Macmillan
Macmillan Miniature Edition. Centenary edition. In green cloth boards.

291   1934   Alice's Adventures in Wonderland   John Tenniel
London: Macmillan
Macmillan Miniature Edition. 21st reprint.

292   1938   Alice's Adventures in Wonderland

London: Macmillan   John Tenniel

Macmillan Miniature Edition. 22nd reprint.

293   1941   Alice's Adventures in Wonderland

London: Macmillan   John Tenniel

Macmillan Miniature Edition. 23rd reprint.

1.6 MACMILLAN *CHILDREN'S EDITIONS*

294   1927   Alice's Adventures in Wonderland

London: Macmillan   John Tenniel; John Macfarlane

Macmillan Children's Edition. 1st edition. The series title Children's Edition is only on the verso of the title page of this edition and all reprints. Green and red pictorial cloth. 16 plates colored by John Macfarlane (unattributed).

295   1927   Alice's Adventures in Wonderland

London: Macmillan   John Tenniel; John Macfarlane

Macmillan Children's Edition. 1st reprint. The series title Children's Edition is only on the verso of the title page of this edition and all reprints. 16 plates colored by John Macfarlane (unattributed).

296   1932   Alice's Adventures in Wonderland

London: Macmillan   John Tenniel; John Macfarlane

Macmillan Children's Edition. 2nd reprint. The series title Children's Edition is only on the verso of the title page of this edition and all reprints. 16 plates colored by John Macfarlane (unattributed). A copy in écrasé morocco is known. How many reprints were also bound in this deluxe binding is not known.

297   1937   Alice's Adventures in Wonderland

London: Macmillan   John Tenniel; John Macfarlane

Macmillan Children's Edition. 3rd reprint. The series title Children's Edition is only on the verso of the title page of this edition and all reprints. 16 plates colored by John Macfarlane (unattributed). A copy in écrasé morocco is known.

298   1940   Alice's Adventures in Wonderland

London: Macmillan   John Tenniel; John Macfarlane

Macmillan Children's Edition. 4th reprint. The series title Children's Edition is only on the verso of the title page of this edition and all reprints. 16 plates colored by John Macfarlane (unattributed). A copy in écrasé morocco is known.

299   1942   Alice's Adventures in Wonderland

London: Macmillan   John Tenniel; John Macfarlane

Macmillan Children's Edition. 5th reprint. The series title Children's Edition is only on the verso of the title page of this edition and all reprints. 16 plates colored by John Macfarlane (unattributed).

300   1953   Alice's Adventures in Wonderland

London: Macmillan   John Tenniel; John Macfarlane

Macmillan Children's Edition. 6th reprint. The series title Children's Edition is only on the verso of the title page of this edition and all reprints. 16 plates colored by John Macfarlane (unattributed).

301   1954   Alice's Adventures in Wonderland

London: Macmillan   John Tenniel; John Macfarlane

Macmillan Children's Edition. 7th reprint. The series title Children's Edition is only on the verso of the title page of this edition and all reprints. 16 plates colored by John Macfarlane (unattributed).

302   1957   Alice's Adventures in Wonderland

London: Macmillan   John Tenniel; John Macfarlane

Macmillan Children's Edition. 8th reprint. The series title Children's Edition is only on the verso of the title page of this edition and all reprints. 18 plates colored by John Macfarlane (unattributed).

303   1962   Alice's Adventures in Wonderland

London: Macmillan   John Tenniel; John Macfarlane

Macmillan Children's Edition. 9th reprint. The series title Children's Edition is only on the verso of the title page of this edition and all reprints. 16 plates colored by John Macfarlane (unattributed).

304   1965   Alice's Adventures in Wonderland

London: Macmillan   0333029461   John Tenniel; John Macfarlane

Macmillan Children's Edition. 10th reprint. The series title Children's Edition is only on the verso of the title page of this edition and all reprints. 16 plates colored by John Macfarlane (unattributed).

305   1967   Alice's Adventures in Wonderland

London: Macmillan   0333029461   John Tenniel; John Macfarlane

Macmillan Children's Edition. 11th reprint. The series title Children's Edition is only on the verso of the title page of this edition and all reprints. 16 plates colored by John Macfarlane (unattributed).

306   1972   Alice's Adventures in Wonderland

London: Macmillan   0333029461   John Tenniel; John Macfarlane

Macmillan Children's Edition. 12th reprint. The series title Children's Edition is only on the verso of the title page of this edition and all reprints. 16 plates colored by John Macfarlane (unattributed).

307   1974   Alice's Adventures in Wonderland

London: Macmillan   0333029461   John Tenniel; John Macfarlane

Macmillan Children's Edition. 13th reprint. The series title Children's Edition is only on the verso of the title page of this edition and all reprints. 16 plates colored by John Macfarlane (unattributed).

308   1977   Alice's Adventures in Wonderland

London: Macmillan   0333029461   John Tenniel; John Macfarlane

Macmillan Children's Edition. 14th reprint. The series title Children's Edition is only on the verso of the title page of this edition and all reprints. 16 plates colored by John Macfarlane (unattributed).

309   1978   Alice's Adventures in Wonderland

London: Macmillan   0333029461   John Tenniel; John Macfarlane

Macmillan Children's Edition. 15th reprint. The series title Children's Edition is only on the verso of the title page of this edition and all reprints. 16 plates colored by John Macfarlane (unattributed). Some copies have "Books for Children" on the spine.

1.7 MACMILLAN *CHILDREN'S BOOKS, NEW CHILDREN'S EDITION*

310   1980   Alice's Adventures in Wonderland

London: Macmillan   0333290380   John Tenniel

Macmillan Children's Books, New Children's Edition. 1st edition. The series title Macmillan Children's Books, New Children's Edition is only on the verso of the title page in this edition and all reprints.

311   1980   Alice's Adventures in Wonderland

London: Macmillan   0333290380   John Tenniel

Macmillan Children's Books, New Children's Edition. 1st reprint. The series title Macmillan Children's Books, New Children's Edition is only on the verso of the title page in this edition and all reprints.

312   1980   Alice's Adventures in Wonderland

London: Macmillan   0333290380   John Tenniel

Macmillan Children's Books, New Children's Edition. 2nd reprint. The series title Macmillan Children's Books, New Children's Edition is only on the verso of the title page in this edition and all reprints.

313   1981   Alice's Adventures in Wonderland

London: Macmillan   0333290380   John Tenniel

Macmillan Children's Books, New Children's Edition. The so-called "2nd reprint," but is in fact the 3rd after the 1980 1st and 2nd reprints. The series title Macmillan Children's Books, New Children's Edition is only on the verso of the title page in this edition and all reprints.

314   1983   Alice's Adventures in Wonderland

London: Macmillan   0333290380   John Tenniel

Macmillan Children's Books, New Children's Edition. 4th reprint. The series title Macmillan Children's Books, New Children's Edition is only on the verso of the title page in this edition and all reprints.

315   1984   Alice's Adventures in Wonderland

London: Macmillan   0333290380   John Tenniel

Macmillan Children's Books, New Children's Edition. 5th reprint. The series title Macmillan Children's Books, New Children's Edition is only on the verso of the title page in this edition and all reprints.

316   1985   Alice's Adventures in Wonderland

London: Macmillan   0333290380   John Tenniel

Macmillan Children's Books, New Children's Edition. 6th reprint. The series title Macmillan Children's Books, New Children's Edition is only on the verso of the title page in this edition and all reprints.

317   1986   Alice's Adventures in Wonderland

London: Macmillan   0333290380   John Tenniel

Macmillan Children's Books, New Children's Edition. 7th reprint. The series title Macmillan Children's Books, New Children's Edition is only on the verso of the title page in this edition and all reprints.

318   1989   Alice's Adventures in Wonderland

London: Macmillan   0333290380   John Tenniel

Macmillan Children's Books, New Children's Edition. 8th reprint. The series title Macmillan Children's Books, New Children's Edition is only on the verso of the title page in this edition and all reprints.

319   1990   Alice's Adventures in Wonderland

London: Macmillan   0333290380   John Tenniel

Macmillan Children's Books, New Children's Edition. 9th reprint. The series title Macmillan Children's Books, New Children's Edition is only on the verso of the title page in this edition and all reprints.

320   1991   Alice's Adventures in Wonderland

London: Macmillan   0333290380   John Tenniel

Macmillan Children's Books, New Children's Edition. Reissue. The series title Macmillan Children's Books, New Children's Edition is only on the verso of the title page in this edition and all reprints.

321   1991   Alice's Adventures in Wonderland

London: Macmillan   0333290380   John Tenniel

Macmillan Children's Books, New Children's Edition. 1st reprint of 1991 reissue. The series title Macmillan Children's Books, New Children's Edition is only on the verso of the title page in this edition and all reprints.

322   1992   Alice's Adventures in Wonderland

London: Macmillan   0333290380   John Tenniel

Macmillan Children's Books, New Children's Edition. 2nd reprint of 1991 reissue. There were later reissues with changing number coding. The series title "Macmillan Children's Books, New Children's Edition is only on the verso of the title page in this edition and all reprints.

323   1997   Alice's Adventures in Wonderland
London: Macmillan   0333290380   John Tenniel
Macmillan Children's Books, New Children's Edition. Later reprint of the 1991 reissue. The series title Macmillan
Children's Books, New Children's Edition is only on the verso of the title page in this edition.

1.8 MACMILLAN *CHILDREN'S CLASSICS, JUNIOR SERIES*

324   1913   Alice's Adventures in Wonderland
London: Macmillan   John Tenniel
Macmillan Children's Classics, Junior Series. Adapted. Paperback. Greenish-blue wrappers.

325   1914   Alice's Adventures in Wonderland
London: Macmillan   John Tenniel
Macmillan Children's Classics, Junior Series. 1st reprint. Adapted. Paperback.

326   1917   Alice's Adventures in Wonderland
London: Macmillan   John Tenniel
Macmillan Children's Classics, Junior Series. 2nd reprint. Adapted. Paperback.

327   1919   Alice's Adventures in Wonderland
London: Macmillan   John Tenniel
Macmillan Children's Classics, Junior Series. 3rd reprint. Adapted. Paperback.

328   1919   Alice's Adventures in Wonderland
London: Macmillan   John Tenniel
Macmillan Children's Classics, Junior Series. 4th reprint. Adapted. Paperback.

329   1920   Alice's Adventures in Wonderland
London: Macmillan   John Tenniel
The Children's Classics, Junior Series. 5th reprint. Adapted. In the series The Children's Classics, Junior. Paperback.

330   1922   Alice's Adventures in Wonderland
London: Macmillan   John Tenniel
The Children's Classics, Junior Series. 6th reprint. Adapted. Paperback.

331   1922   Alice's Adventures in Wonderland
London: Macmillan   John Tenniel
Macmillan Children's Classics, Junior Series. No. 23. Ages 6 to 9. Bluish-gray pictorial wrappers. School textbook
adapted for children.

332   1924   Alice's Adventures in Wonderland
London: Macmillan   John Tenniel
Macmillan Children's Classics, Junior Series. No. 23. Ages 6 to 9. Light blue pictorial wrappers. School textbook
adapted for children.

333   1927   Alice's Adventures in Wonderland
London: Macmillan   John Tenniel
Macmillan Children's Classics, Junior Series. 7th reprint. Adapted. Paperback.

334   1927   Alice's Adventures in Wonderland
London: Macmillan   John Tenniel
Macmillan Children's Classics, Junior Series. 8th reprint. Adapted. Paperback.

1.9 MACMILLAN CHILDREN'S BOOKS

335   2015   Alice's Adventures in Wonderland
London: Macmillan Children's Books   9781447277781   John Tenniel
Macmillan Children's Books, Macmillan Little Folks' Edition. First published in 1907 by Macmillan. 32 brightly colored illustrations featuring Alice in a red dress for the first and only time.

336   2015   Alice's Adventures in Wonderland
London: Macmillan Children's Books   9781447286233   Eric Puybaret
Macmillan Children's Books. Adapted by Joe Rhatigan. 1 volume, 1 color map, and 1 CD read by Joanne Froggatt.

337   2016   Mable Lucie Attwell's Alice's Adventures in Wonderland
London: Macmillan Children's Books   9781509830336   Mable Lucie Attwell
Macmillan Children's Books. Mable Lucie Attwell (1879–1964) first illustrated *Alice* ca. 1910.

1.10 MACMILLAN *LITTLE ALICE* EDITION

338   1988   Alice's Adventures in Wonderland
London: Macmillan Children's Books   0333482247   John Tenniel; Harry Theaker
Macmillan Little Alice Edition. 1st edition. Issued in publisher's paper slipcase along with a copy of *Looking-Glass* as are all subsequent reprints. 8 Tenniel plates colored by Harry Theaker. All editions and reprints in dust jacket.

339   1990   Alice's Adventures in Wonderland
London: Macmillan Children's Books   0333482247   John Tenniel; Harry Theaker
Macmillan Little Alice Edition. 1st reprint. Issued in publisher's box along with a copy of *Looking-Glass*. 8 Tenniel plates colored by Harry Theaker. Dust jacket.

340   1991   Alice's Adventures in Wonderland
London: Macmillan Children's Books   0333482247   John Tenniel; Harry Theaker
Macmillan Little Alice Edition. 2nd reprint (called a "reissue"). Issued in publisher's box along with a copy of *Looking-Glass*. 8 Tenniel plates colored by Harry Theaker. Dust jacket.

341   1991   Alice's Adventures in Wonderland
London: Macmillan Children's Books   0333482247   John Tenniel; Harry Theaker
Macmillan Little Alice Edition. 3rd reprint. Issued in publisher's box along with a copy of *Looking-Glass*. 8 Tenniel plates colored by Harry Theaker. Dust jacket.

342   1992   Alice's Adventures in Wonderland
London: Macmillan Children's Books   0333482247   John Tenniel; Harry Theaker
Macmillan Little Alice Edition. 4th reprint. Issued in publisher's box along with a copy of *Looking-Glass*. 8 Tenniel plates colored by Harry Theaker. Dust jacket.

343   1992   Alice's Adventures in Wonderland
London: Macmillan Children's Books   0333482247   John Tenniel; Harry Theaker
Macmillan Little Alice Edition. 5th reprint. Issued in publisher's box along with a copy of *Looking-Glass*. 8 Tenniel plates colored by Harry Theaker. Dust jacket.

344   1995   Alice's Adventures in Wonderland
London: Macmillan Children's Books   0333482247   John Tenniel; Harry Theaker
Macmillan Little Alice Edition. 6th reprint. Issued in publisher's box along with a copy of *Looking-Glass*. 8 Tenniel plates colored by Harry Theaker. Dust jacket.

1.11 MACMILLAN: OTHER EDITIONS

345   1903   Alice's Adventures in Wonderland
London: Macmillan   John Tenniel
Macmillan Little Folks' Edition. 1st edition. Adapted version. Colored illustrations. Alice in blue dress. Red illustrated
cloth boards.

346   1907   Alice's Adventures in Wonderland
London: Macmillan   John Tenniel
Macmillan Little Folks' Edition. Reprint. The pictures are colored differently, with Alice now in a red dress.

347   1929   Alice's Adventures in Wonderland
London: Macmillan   John Tenniel
Not seen. Listed in *WMGC*. Reissued in October 1929.

348   1930   Alice's Adventures in Wonderland
New York; London: Macmillan and Co.   John Tenniel
Macmillan. New edition.

349   1932   Alice's Adventures in Wonderland
London: Macmillan and Co.   John Tenniel
Macmillan Centenary Edition with preface by Hugh Walpole.

350   1941   Alice's Adventures in Wonderland
London: Macmillan and Co.   John Tenniel
Macmillan's Cottage Library. Reprint of the 1932 edition.

351   1944   Alice's Adventures in Wonderland
London: Macmillan and Co.   John Tenniel

352   1948   Alice's Adventures in Wonderland
London: Macmillan and Co.   John Tenniel
Green cloth over boards. Title in black on spine. Upper cover with title in black and illustration in red and black.
Publisher's monogram on lower cover. Cream dust jacket.

353   1952   Alice's Adventures in Wonderland
London: Macmillan and Co.   John Tenniel

354   1954   Alice's Adventures in Wonderland
London: Macmillan and Co.; New York: St. Martin's Press   John Tenniel
Reprint of 1927 edition.

355   1958   Alice's Adventures in Wonderland
London: Macmillan   John Tenniel
St. Martin's Library edition.

356   1959   Alice's Adventures in Wonderland
London: Macmillan and Co.; New York: St. Martin's Press.   John Tenniel
Green cloth over boards.

357   1968   Alice's Adventures in Wonderland
London: Macmillan and Co.   John Tenniel
Green cloth over boards. Illustrated dust jacket.

358	1980	Alice's Adventures in Wonderland		
		London: Macmillan Children's Books	9780333290385	John Tenniel

359	1982	Alice's Adventures in Wonderland		
		London: Macmillan and Co.	0333315952	John Tenniel

1st edition. Retold by Deborah Tyler. A Ranger 3 Fiction book. Paperback. Abbreviated text with foot notes. Reprinted 1983 (twice), 1984, 1985, and 1986 (twice).

360	1983	Alice's Adventures in Wonderland		
		London: Macmillan and Co.	0333315952	John Tenniel

1st reprint of the 1982 edition. Retold by Deborah Tyler. A Ranger 3 Fiction book. Paperback. Abbreviated text with foot notes.

361	1983	Alice's Adventures in Wonderland		
		London: Macmillan and Co.	0333315952	John Tenniel

2nd reprint. Retold by Deborah Tyler. A Ranger 3 Fiction book. Paperback. Abbreviated text with foot notes.

362	1984	Alice's Adventures in Wonderland		
		London: Macmillan and Co.		John Tenniel

3rd reprint. Retold by Deborah Tyler. A Ranger 3 Fiction book. Paperback. Abbreviated text with foot notes.

363	1985	Alice's Adventures in Wonderland		
		London: Macmillan and Co.	0333315952	John Tenniel

4th reprint. Retold by Deborah Tyler. A Ranger 3 Fiction book. Paperback. Abbreviated text with foot notes.

364	1986	Alice's Adventures in Wonderland		
		London: Macmillan and Co.	0333315952	John Tenniel

5th reprint. Retold by Deborah Tyler. A Ranger 3 Fiction book. Paperback. Abbreviated text with foot notes.

365	1986	Alice's Adventures in Wonderland		
		London: Macmillan and Co.	0333315952	John Tenniel

6th reprint. Retold by Deborah Tyler. A Ranger 3 Fiction book. Paperback. Abbreviated text with foot notes.

366	1986	Alice's Adventures in Wonderland		
		London: Macmillan and Co.	0333433432	John Tenniel

Adapted by Margery Green. In the series Stories to Remember.

367	1986	Alice's Adventures in Wonderland		
		London: Macmillan and Co.	0333433432	John Tenniel

1st reprint of the 1986 Margery Green adaptation.

368	1986	Alice's Adventures in Wonderland		
		London: Macmillan and Co.	0333433432	John Tenniel

2nd reprint of the 1986 Margery Green adaptation.

369	1987	Alice's Adventures in Wonderland		
		London: Macmillan and Co.	0333433432	Unillustrated

Later reprint of the 1986 Margery Green adaptation. Photo on cover from the BBC TV production. No illustrations in the text.

370	1995	Alice's Adventures in Wonderland		
		London: Macmillan and Co.	9780333640494	John Tenniel; Harry Theaker; Diz Wallis

Coloring by Harry Theaker and Diz Wallis. Blue paper boards in pictorial dust jacket. A limited issue of 300 numbered copies leather bound in a plain white card slipcase. Also, an issue of 50 numbered copies leather bound with extra title page stating that the edition was specially printed for the Lewis Carroll Society.

371   2004   Alice's Adventures in Wonderland
London: Macmillan Collector's Library   9781904633327   John Tenniel
Afterword by Anna South. Dust jacket.

372   2015   Alice's Adventures in Wonderland
London: Macmillan and Co.   9781447279990   John Tenniel
1st edition in paperback. Blue printed wrappers. Logo on front cover reads "Macmillan Alice 150 years." Reprinted several times.

373   2015   Alice's Adventures in Wonderland
London: Macmillan and Co.   9780230469297   John Tenniel; Harry Theaker; Diz Wallis

Adapted by Gill Munton. In the series Macmillan English Explorers, with pictures colored by Harry Theaker and Diz Wallis. 1st edition. Reprinted several times all with same date.

1.12 MACMILLAN COMBINED *PEOPLE'S EDITION* OF *ALICE* AND *LOOKING-GLASS*

374   1887   Alice's Adventures in Wonderland and Through the Looking-Glass
London; New York: Macmillan   John Tenniel
Macmillan People's Edition. 1st combined edition. The front cover has the *Alice* title and the rear cover *Looking-Glass*. The spine shows both titles. The *Alice* and *Looking-Glass* editions have separate title pages both dated 1887. There is no thousand on any of the 3 title pages.

375   1888   Alice's Adventures in Wonderland and Through the Looking-Glass
London; New York: Macmillan   John Tenniel
Macmillan People's Edition. The main title page has no thousand. The *Alice* title page date is 1888 (lacks thousand). *Looking-Glass* title page date is 1888 (lacks thousand).

376   1888   Alice's Adventures in Wonderland and Through the Looking-Glass
London; New York: Macmillan   John Tenniel
Macmillan People's Edition. The main title page has no thousand. The *Alice* title page date is 1889, 20th thousand. The *Looking-Glass* title page date is 1889, 13th thousand. Another copy has no thousand on the *Alice* or *Looking-Glass* title pages.

377   1888   Alice's Adventures in Wonderland and Through the Looking-Glass
London; New York: Macmillan   John Tenniel
Macmillan People's Edition. No main title page. The *Alice* and the *Looking-Glass* title pages are both dated 1888 and lack a thousand. The book front cover has the *Alice* illustration and the rear cover the *Looking-Glass*.

378   1889   Alice's Adventures in Wonderland and Through the Looking-Glass
London; New York: Macmillan   John Tenniel
Macmillan People's Edition. The main title page has no thousand. The *Alice* title page date is 1889 with no thousand. The *Looking-Glass* title page date is 1889 with no thousand.

379   1890   Alice's Adventures in Wonderland and Through the Looking-Glass
London; New York: Macmillan   John Tenniel
Macmillan People's Edition. Not seen but believed to exist.

380   1891   Alice's Adventures in Wonderland and Through the Looking-Glass
London; New York: Macmillan   John Tenniel

Macmillan People's Edition. The main title page has no thousand. The title pages of *Alice* and *Looking-Glass* are missing.

381   1893   Alice's Adventures in Wonderland and Through the Looking-Glass
London; New York: Macmillan   John Tenniel

Macmillan People's Edition. Copies exist in several forms. One has the main title page with no thousand. *Alice* title page is 33rd thousand of 1893. *Looking-Glass* is 23rd thousand of 1893. Another has an 1893 title page with *Alice* the 32nd and *Looking-Glass* the 22nd thousand.

382   1894   Alice's Adventures in Wonderland and Through the Looking-Glass
London; New York: Macmillan   John Tenniel

Macmillan People's Edition. The main title page has no thousand. *Alice* has 32nd thousand of 1893. Another copy has the 38th of 1894. In *Looking-Glass* both have 24th thousand of 1894.

383   1894 and 1895   Alice's Adventures in Wonderland and Through the Looking-Glass
London; New York: Macmillan   John Tenniel

Macmillan People's Edition. The main title page has 11th thousand. *Alice* has the 46th thousand of 1894 and *Looking-Glass* has the 27th thousand of 1895. Another copy lacks the *Alice* and *Looking-Glass* title pages.

384   1896   Alice's Adventures in Wonderland and Through the Looking-Glass
London; New York: Macmillan   John Tenniel

Macmillan People's Edition. The main title page has 12th thousand. Lacks *Alice* and *Looking-Glass* title pages (possibly removed).

385   1897   Alice's Adventures in Wonderland and Through the Looking-Glass
London; New York: Macmillan   John Tenniel

Macmillan People's Edition. The main title page has no thousand. *Alice* has the 65th thousand of 1897 and *Looking-Glass* has 45th thousand of 1897. Another copy has no main title page.

386   1898   Alice's Adventures in Wonderland and Through the Looking-Glass
London; New York: Macmillan   John Tenniel

Macmillan People's Edition. The main title page has no thousand. *Alice* has the 73rd thousand of 1898 and *Looking-Glass* has 50th thousand of 1898. Another copy has *Alice* 93rd thousand and *Looking-Glass* 51st thousand of 1898.

387   1898   Alice's Adventures in Wonderland and Through the Looking-Glass
London; New York: Macmillan   John Tenniel

Macmillan People's Edition. The main title page has no thousand. *Alice* title page is 1889 83rd thousand and *Looking-Glass* is 1898 57th thousand.

388   1898   Alice's Adventures in Wonderland and Through the Looking-Glass
London; New York: Macmillan   John Tenniel

Macmillan People's Edition. The main title page has no thousand. In one copy *Alice* has 1898 76th thousand and *Looking-Glass* 1898 51st thousand. In another copy *Alice* has the 1898 83rd thousand and *Looking-Glass* the 1898 57th thousand.

389   1898   Alice's Adventures in Wonderland and Through the Looking-Glass
London; New York: Macmillan   John Tenniel

Macmillan People's Edition. The main title page has no thousand. *Alice* has the 117th thousand of 1902. *Looking-Glass* has the 73rd thousand of 1902.

390   1898   Alice's Adventures in Wonderland and Through the Looking-Glass
London; New York: Macmillan   John Tenniel

Macmillan People's Edition. The main title page has no thousand. *Alice* title page has the 133rd thousand of 1905. *Looking-Glass* title page has the 85th thousand of 1905.

391   1899   Alice's Adventures in Wonderland and Through the Looking-Glass
London; New York: Macmillan   John Tenniel

Macmillan People's Edition. The main title page has no thousand. *Alice* title page has the 93rd thousand of 1899. *Looking-Glass* has the 62nd thousand of 1899. In another copy *Looking-Glass* has the 63rd thousand of 1899.

392   1899   Alice's Adventures in Wonderland and Through the Looking-Glass
London; New York: Macmillan   John Tenniel

Macmillan People's Edition. The main title page is undated and has no thousand. Both the *Alice* title page and that of *Looking-Glass* are dated 1899.

393   1900 and 1899 Alice's Adventures in Wonderland and Through the Looking-Glass
London; New York: Macmillan   John Tenniel

Macmillan People's Edition. The main title page is dated 1900. The *Alice* title page is 1899. There is no *Looking-Glass* title page.

394   1901   Alice's Adventures in Wonderland and Through the Looking-Glass
London; New York: Macmillan   John Tenniel

Macmillan People's Edition. The main title page has no thousand. *Alice* has the 107th thousand of 1901 and *Looking-Glass* has 69th thousand of 1901.

395   1902   Alice's Adventures in Wonderland and Through the Looking-Glass
London; New York: Macmillan   John Tenniel

Macmillan People's Edition. The main title page has no thousand. *Alice* title page has the 113th thousand of 1902. *Looking-Glass* title page has 72nd thousand of 1902.

396   1902   Alice's Adventures in Wonderland and Through the Looking-Glass
London; New York: Macmillan   John Tenniel

Macmillan People's Edition. The main title page has no thousand. *Alice* has the 117th thousand of 1902. *Looking-Glass* has the 73rd thousand of 1902.

397   1904   Alice's Adventures in Wonderland and Through the Looking-Glass
London; New York: Macmillan   John Tenniel

Macmillan People's Edition. The main title page has no thousand. *Alice* title page has the 128th thousand of 1904. *Looking-Glass* title page has the 84th thousand of 1904.

398   1905   Alice's Adventures in Wonderland and Through the Looking-Glass
London; New York: Macmillan   John Tenniel

Macmillan People's Edition. The main title page has no thousand. *Alice* title page has the 133rd thousand of 1905. *Looking-Glass* title page has the 85th thousand of 1905.

399   1908   Alice's Adventures in Wonderland and Through the Looking-Glass
London; New York: Macmillan   John Tenniel

Macmillan People's Edition. There are several versions. Some have no main title page. *Alice* title page is dated 1908 with no thousand. There is no *Looking-Glass* title page and the book begins with Chapter 1 of *Alice*. Another copy has main title page dated 1908; *Alice* has no title page but is 86th thousand, and *Looking-Glass* has no title page.

400   1913   Alice's Adventures in Wonderland and Through the Looking-Glass
London; New York: Macmillan   John Tenniel

Macmillan People's Edition. The main title page has no thousand and no date. Lacks *Alice* title page. *Looking-Glass* title page has 1913 and 110th thousand (on verso).

401   1919   Alice's Adventures in Wonderland and Through the Looking-Glass
London; New York: Macmillan   John Tenniel

Macmillan People's Edition. A copy is known with 1919 on the main title page but lacking *Alice* and *Looking-Glass* title pages.

402   1925   Alice's Adventures in Wonderland and Through the Looking-Glass
London; New York: Macmillan   John Tenniel

Macmillan People's Edition. A copy is known with 1925 on the main title page. The *Alice* title page has 1925 and 180th thousand on the verso. The *Looking-Glass* has 1925 and 125th thousand. Another copy has 1925 on the main title page and 180th thousand on the verso. Lacks the *Alice* title page. *Looking-Glass* has 1925 and 121st thousand.

403   1928   Alice's Adventures in Wonderland and Through the Looking-Glass
London; New York: Macmillan   John Tenniel

Macmillan People's Edition. Some copies are in a white dust jacket with red lettering and illustration. The main title page is dated 1928 but has no thousand. *Alice* title page is dated 1928 with 183rd thousand on the verso. *Looking-Glass* title page is dated 1928 with 124th thousand on the verso. In another copy the dust jacket is beige and tan with black (may have originally been dark blue) printing. Only the Macmillan monogram is on the front and the base of the spine.

404   1932 and 1928 Alice's Adventures in Wonderland and Through the Looking-Glass
London; New York: Macmillan   John Tenniel

Macmillan People's Edition. No main title page. *Alice* title page is dated 1932 with 186th thousand. *Looking-Glass* title page is dated 1928 with 124th thousand on the verso.

405   1932 and 1933 Alice's Adventures in Wonderland and Through the Looking-Glass
London; New York: Macmillan   John Tenniel

Macmillan People's Edition. No main title page. *Alice* title page is dated 1932 and 186th thousand. *Looking-Glass* is dated 1933 and 127th thousand.

406   1937 and 1939 Alice's Adventures in Wonderland and Through the Looking-Glass
London; New York: Macmillan   John Tenniel

Macmillan People's Edition. No main title page. *Alice* title page is dated 1937 with 189th thousand. *Looking-Glass* title page is dated 1939 with 130th thousand on the verso. This is the last combined edition found.

1.13 MACMILLAN COMBINED *SIXPENNY SERIES* OF *ALICE* AND *LOOKING-GLASS*

407   1898 and 1898 Alice's Adventures in Wonderland and Through the Looking-Glass
London; New York: Macmillan   John Tenniel

Sixpenny Series. *Alice* and *Looking-Glass* are 1st issue. Both are 126 pp separately numbered, with *Looking-Glass* in a much smaller font. 6 pp. ads. Combined editions are usually found in boards – some in Macmillan boards, some not. It is likely that there are several other examples not listed here. One copy is bound with *Looking-Glass* first, in Macmillan's 6 shilling red cloth binding with roundels (Alice, Pig Baby, and Red Queen). Spine reads "ALICE AND LOOKING GLASS."

408   1898 and 1899 Alice's Adventures in Wonderland and Through the Looking-Glass
London; New York: Macmillan   John Tenniel

Sixpenny Series. *Alice* 1898 and *Looking-Glass* 1899.

409   1899 and 1898 Alice's Adventures in Wonderland and Through the Looking-Glass
London; New York: Macmillan   John Tenniel

Sixpenny Series. *Alice* 1899 (2nd or 3rd issue as there were two printings in 1899) and *Looking-Glass* 1898, 1st issue. Maroon cloth-covered boards. Spine titles lettered from foot to head in gilt. *Alice* 126 pp., *Looking-Glass* 122 in smaller font. Macmillan's Sixpenny Series recorded at the top of the *Alice* half title. No ads. One suggestion is that

Macmillan sold sheets of the Sixpenny Series to several publishers and binders. Myers & Company, London, may have been one of them. There was another issue of the same dates described below.

410   **1899 and 1898** Alice's Adventures in Wonderland and Through the Looking-Glass
London; New York: Macmillan   John Tenniel

Sixpenny Series. *Alice* 1899 (2nd or 3rd issue , as there were 2 printings in 1899), and *Looking-Glass* 1898. 1st issue. Dark gray-green cloth-covered boards. *Alice* 126 pp. *Looking-Glass* 122 in smaller font. 4 pages of ads. Macmillan's Sixpenny Series recorded at top of *Alice* half title.

411   **1899 and 1900** Alice's Adventures in Wonderland and Through the Looking-Glass
London; New York: Macmillan   John Tenniel

Sixpenny Series. *Alice* 1900, no reprint stated; *Looking-Glass* 1899, no reprint stated. One copy is in red cloth and has the lower part of the spine labeled "Samuels and Taylor." It seems likely that Macmillan sold sheets to be bound by other booksellers.

412   **1902 and 1902** Alice's Adventures in Wonderland and Through the Looking-Glass
London; New York: Macmillan   John Tenniel

Sixpenny Series. *Alice* 4th reprint of 1902 and *Looking-Glass* 2nd or 3rd reprint of 1902. Editions in pale red or covered boards. *Alice* 126 pp., *Looking-Glass* 122 in smaller font. Publisher identified on verso of each title page that also has an ad that lists 10 Carroll works. Verso of *Alice* title page: "First Edition Sixpenny Series published 1898. Reprinted 1899 (twice), 1900, 1902." Verso of *Looking-Glass* title page: "First Edition Sixpenny Series published 1898. Reprinted 1899, 1902."

413   **1902 and 1902** Alice's Adventures in Wonderland and Through the Looking-Glass
London; New York: Macmillan   John Tenniel

Sixpenny Series. *Alice* 4th reprint of 1902 and *Looking-Glass* 2nd or 3rd reprint of 1902. Tan cloth covered boards. Tenniel images on front cover and spine. *Alice* with 126 pp., *Looking-Glass* 122 in smaller font. No ads. Publisher identified on verso of each title page. Verso of *Alice* title page: "First Edition Sixpenny Series published 1898. Reprinted 1899 (twice), 1900, 1902." Verso of *Looking-Glass* title page: "First Edition Sixpenny Series published 1898. Reprinted 1899, 1902."

414   **1902 and 1902** Alice's Adventures in Wonderland and Through the Looking-Glass
London; New York: Macmillan   John Tenniel

Sixpenny Series. *Alice* 4th reprint of 1902 and *Looking-Glass* 2nd or 3rd reprint of 1902. Dark red flexible morocco covers. *Alice* with 126 pp., *Looking-Glass* 122 in smaller font. No ads. No publisher, copyright, or series statement on verso of either title page.

415   **1902 and 1902** Alice's Adventures in Wonderland and Through the Looking-Glass
London; New York: Macmillan   John Tenniel

Sixpenny Series. *Alice* 4th reprint of 1902 and *Looking-Glass* 2nd or 3rd reprint of 1902. Dark red flexible morocco covers. *Alice* with 126 pp., *Looking-Glass* 122 in smaller font. No ads. Separate frontispieces, title pages, paginations, and signatures. Publisher identified on verso of each title page. Verso of *Alice* title page: "First Edition Sixpenny Series published 1898. Reprinted 1899 (twice), 1900, 1902." Verso of *Looking-Glass* title page: "First Edition Sixpenny Series published 1898. Reprinted 1899, 1900, 1902." *Looking-Glass* reprint of 1900 appears here and in the next listing for the first time.

416   **1902 and 1902** Alice's Adventures in Wonderland and Through the Looking-Glass
London; New York: Macmillan   John Tenniel

Sixpenny Series. *Alice* 4th reprint of 1902 and *Looking-Glass* 2nd or 3rd reprint of 1902. Yellow-green cloth covers. *Alice* 126 pp., *Looking-Glass* 122 in smaller font. Publisher identified on verso of each title page, which also has an ad listing 10 Carroll works. Verso of *Alice* title page: "First Edition Sixpenny Series published 1898. Reprinted 1899 (twice), 1900, 1902." Verso of *Looking-Glass* title page: "First Edition Sixpenny Series published 1898. Reprinted 1899, 1900, 1902." *Looking-Glass* reprint of 1900 appears here and in the prior listing for the first time.

417   1902 and 1899 Alice's Adventures in Wonderland and Through the Looking-Glass
London; New York: Macmillan   John Tenniel
Sixpenny Series. *Alice* is dated 1902 and *Looking-Glass* is 1899.

418   1902 and 1902 Alice's Adventures in Wonderland and Through the Looking-Glass
London; New York: Macmillan   John Tenniel
Sixpenny Series. *Alice* 1902 no reprint stated and *Looking-Glass* 1902 no reprint stated.

419   1903 and 1902 Alice's Adventures in Wonderland and Through the Looking-Glass
London; New York: Macmillan   John Tenniel
Sixpenny Series. *Alice* 5th reprint of 1903 and *Looking-Glass* 2nd reprint of 1902.

420   1903 and 1902 Alice's Adventures in Wonderland and Through the Looking-Glass
London; New York: Macmillan   John Tenniel
Sixpenny Series. *Alice* 1903 no reprint stated and *Looking-Glass* 1902 no reprint stated.

421   1905 and 1904 Alice's Adventures in Wonderland and Through the Looking-Glass
London; New York: Macmillan   John Tenniel
Sixpenny Series. *Alice* 6th reprint of 1905 and *Looking-Glass* 3rd reprint of 1904.

422   1903 and 1902 Alice's Adventures in Wonderland and Through the Looking-Glass
London; New York: Macmillan   John Tenniel
Sixpenny Series. *Alice* 7th reprint of 1903 and *Looking-Glass* 3rd or 4th reprint of 1902. Red cloth, front and spine
with gold-gilt lettering and decorations; plain white endpapers; *Alice* 126 pp., *Looking-Glass* 122 in smaller font.
Separate frontispieces, title pages, paginations, and signatures. Neither publisher nor series printing dates identified
on verso of title pages. "Sixpenny Series" not recorded on *Alice* half title in this copy, but title pages, pagination, and
signatures identical to other Sixpenny Series issues.

423   1906 and 1904 Alice's Adventures in Wonderland and Through the Looking-Glass
London; New York: Macmillan   John Tenniel
Sixpenny Series. *Alice* 7th reprint of 1906 and *Looking-Glass* 3rd reprint of 1904. Dark-blue cloth. *Alice* 126 pp.,
Looking-Glass 122 in smaller font. 2 integral frontispieces. Verso of *Alice* title page has no ads but says, "Richard
Clay and Sons, Limited, Bread Street Bill, E. C., and Bungay, Suffolk. First Edition Sixpenny Series published 1898.
Reprinted, 1899 (twice), 1900, 1902, 1903, 1905, 1906." Verso of *Looking-Glass* title page ad lists 15 titles by Carroll.
Series statement says, "First Edition Sixpenny Series published 1989. Reprinted, 1899, 1902, 1904."

424   1907   Alice's Adventures in Wonderland and Through the Looking-Glass
London: Macmillan   John Tenniel
Sixpenny Series. *Alice* 8th reprint of 1907 and *Looking-Glass* 4th reprint of 1907.

425   1908 and 1907 Alice's Adventures in Wonderland and Through the Looking-Glass
London: Macmillan   John Tenniel
Sixpenny Series. *Alice* 9th reprint of 1908 and *Looking-Glass* 4th reprint of 1907.

426   1910 and 1907 Alice's Adventures in Wonderland and Through the Looking-Glass
London: Macmillan   John Tenniel
Sixpenny Series. *Alice* 10th reprint of 1910 and *Looking-Glass* 4th reprint of 1907.

427   1910 and 1911 Alice's Adventures in Wonderland and Through the Looking-Glass
London: Macmillan   John Tenniel
Sixpenny Series. *Alice* is dated 1910 and *Looking-Glass* is dated 1911. No reprint stated. This is the last combined
edition found.

428   1911   Alice's Adventures in Wonderland and Through the Looking-Glass
London: Macmillan   John Tenniel; Harry Theaker
Macmillan Combined Editions. 1st edition thus. 16 color plates by Harry Theaker (unattributed). Red cloth.

429   1916   Alice's Adventures in Wonderland and Through the Looking-Glass
London: Macmillan   John Tenniel; Harry Theaker
1st reprint of the 1911 edition. 16 color plates by Harry Theaker (unattributed).

430   1916   Alice's Adventures in Wonderland and Through the Looking-Glass
London: Macmillan Collector's Library   John Tenniel
Macmillan Collector's Library. 1st edition. Afterword by Anna Smith.

431   1916   Alice's Adventures in Wonderland and Through the Looking-Glass
London: Macmillan Collector's Library   John Tenniel
Macmillan Collector's Library. 1st edition. Afterword by Anna Smith.

432   1921   Alice's Adventures in Wonderland and Through the Looking-Glass
London: Macmillan   John Tenniel; John Macfarlane
2nd reprint of the 1911 edition. Only 8 of the original 16 color plates are included. Colored by John Macfarlane (unattributed).

433   1927   Alice's Adventures in Wonderland and Through the Looking-Glass
London: Macmillan   John Tenniel; John Macfarlane
3rd reprint of the 1911 edition. Only 8 of the original 16 color plates are included. Colored by John Macfarlane (unattributed). There may be a 1928 edition.

434   1928   Alice's Adventures in Wonderland and Through the Looking-Glass
London: Macmillan   John Tenniel
Two Shilling Library. 1st edition. Beige cloth boards with design in blind in pictorial dust jacket. Also issued in brown cloth boards, with vignettes of Tenniel characters and title all in gilt.

435   1928   Alice's Adventures in Wonderland and Through the Looking-Glass
London: Macmillan   John Tenniel
Two Shilling Library. 1st edition. Beige cloth boards with design in blind in pictorial dust jacket. Also issued in brown cloth boards, with vignettes of Tenniel characters and title all in gilt.

436   1932   Alice's Adventures in Wonderland and Through the Looking-Glass
London: Macmillan   John Tenniel
Cottage Library. 1st edition. Red paper boards in green dust jacket. Virtually identical to the Two Shilling Library edition of 1928.

437   1933   Alice's Adventures in Wonderland and Through the Looking-Glass
London: Macmillan   John Tenniel
1st reprint of the 1932 Cottage Library edition. Red paper boards. Also issued in decorative blue leatherette.

438   1934   Alice's Adventures in Wonderland and Through the Looking-Glass
New York; London: Macmillan Company   John Tenniel
Macmillan Children's Classics. Color frontispiece.

439 1934 Alice's Adventures in Wonderland and Through the Looking-Glass
London: Macmillan   John Tenniel; John Macfarlane
Later reprint of the 1911 edition. Only 8 of the original 16 color plates are included. Colored by John Macfarlane (unattributed).

440 1941 Alice's Adventures in Wonderland and Through the Looking-Glass
London: Macmillan   John Tenniel
2nd reprint of the 1932 Cottage Library edition. Orange cloth boards with "L.C.A." in blind on the front cover. Also issued in white paper boards with embossed wheat pattern.

441 1948 Alice's Adventures in Wonderland and Through the Looking-Glass
London: Macmillan   John Tenniel

442 1958 Alice's Adventures in Wonderland and Through the Looking-Glass
London: Macmillan   John Tenniel
St. Martin's Library Series. 1st edition. Variant paperback bindings.

443 1962 Alice's Adventures in Wonderland and Through the Looking-Glass
London: Collier Macmillan; New York: Collier   John Tenniel
With a new introduction by Louis Untermeyer.

444 1962 Alice's Adventures in Wonderland and Through the Looking-Glass
London: Collier-Macmillan Ltd.   John Tenniel
First Collier Books Edition. There was a 12th printing.

445 1963 Alice's Adventures in Wonderland and Through the Looking-Glass
London: Collier-Macmillan. New York: Macmillan   John Tenniel
Macmillan Classics. Afterword by Clifton Fadiman. First published in 1962.

446 1963 Alice's Adventures in Wonderland and Through the Looking-Glass
London: Collier-Macmillan. New York: Macmillan   John Tenniel
Afterword by Clifton Fadiman. First published in 1962. The 3rd printing is dated 1966.

447 1966 Alice's Adventures in Wonderland and Through the Looking-Glass
London: Collier-Macmillan Ltd.   0020423500   John Tenniel
Collier Books Edition. 3rd printing. Afterword by Clifton Fadiman. First published in 1962.

448 1966 Alice's Adventures in Wonderland and Through the Looking-Glass
London: Macmillan   John Tenniel
1st reprint of the 1958 St. Martin's Library edition but now styled Pocket Papermac. Paperback.

449 1966 Alice's Adventures in Wonderland and Through the Looking-Glass
London; Melbourne, VIC; Toronto, ON: Macmillan. New York: St. Martin's Press   John Tenniel
Pocket Papermac edition. Later printing of the 1958 Macmillan St. Martin's Library edition. Pictorial wrappers. Reprinted in 1968, 1971, 1973, and 1975. Paperback.

450 1968 Alice's Adventures in Wonderland and Through the Looking-Glass
London; Melbourne, VIC; Toronto, ON: Macmillan. New York: St. Martin's Press   John Tenniel
Pocket Papermac edition. Later printing of the 1958 Macmillan St. Martin's Library edition. Pictorial wrappers. Paperback.

451 1968 Alice's Adventures in Wonderland and Through the Looking-Glass
London: Macmillan   John Tenniel
Macmillan Pocket Papermac 2nd reprint of the 1958 edition. Paperback.

452	1968	Alice's Adventures in Wonderland and Through the Looking-Glass

London: Macmillan   John Tenniel

Macmillan Pocket Papermac. 3rd reprint of the 1958 edition. Paperback

453   1971   Alice's Adventures in Wonderland and Through the Looking-Glass

London: Macmillan   0333052609   John Tenniel

Macmillan Pocket Papermac. 4th reprint of the 1958 edition. Paperback

454   1971   Alice's Adventures in Wonderland and Through the Looking-Glass

London; Melbourne, VIC; Toronto, ON: 9780333052600   John Tenniel
Macmillan. New York: St. Martin's Press

Later printing of the Pocket Papermac edition of 1958. Macmillan St. Martin's Library edition. Pictorial wrappers.

455   1973   Alice's Adventures in Wonderland, and Through the Looking-Glass

London: Macmillan   0333052609   John Tenniel

Macmillan Pocket Papermac. 5th reprint of the 1958 edition. Paperback.

456   1973   Alice's Adventures in Wonderland and Through the Looking-Glass

London; Melbourne, VIC; Toronto, ON: 9780333052600   John Tenniel
Macmillan. New York: St. Martin's Press

Later printing of the Pocket Papermac edition of 1958. Macmillan St. Martin's Library edition. Pictorial wrappers.

457   1975   Alice's Adventures in Wonderland, and Through the Looking-Glass

London: Macmillan   0333052609   John Tenniel

Macmillan Pocket Papermac. 6th reprint of the 1958 edition. Paperback.

458   1975   Alice's Adventures in Wonderland and Through the Looking-Glass

London; Melbourne, VIC; Toronto, ON: 9780333052600   John Tenniel
Macmillan. New York: St. Martin's Press

Later printing of the Pocket Papermac edition of 1958. Macmillan St. Martin's Library edition. Pictorial wrappers.

459   1978   Alice's Adventures in Wonderland and Through the Looking-Glass

London; Melbourne, VIC; Toronto, ON: Macmillan. New York: St. Martin's Press   John Tenniel

Later printing of the Pocket Papermac edition of 1958. Macmillan St. Martin's Library edition. Pictorial wrappers.

460   1978   Alice's Adventures in Wonderland, and Through the Looking-Glass

London: Macmillan   0333052609   John Tenniel

Macmillan Pocket Papermac. 7th reprint of the 1958 edition. Paperback.

461   1980   Alice's Adventures in Wonderland, and Through the Looking-Glass

London: Macmillan   0333232704   John Tenniel

Macmillan Pocket Papermac. 8th reprint of the 1958 edition. Paperback.

462   1984   Alice's Adventures in Wonderland and Through the Looking-Glass

London: Macmillan Children's Books   John Tenniel

Macmillan Children's Books. Facsimile of the 1866 London *Alice* edition. Issued with or without publisher's slipcase along with a facsimile of the 1872 1st edition of *Looking-Glass*. Red cloth boards or maroon leather. Inserted is the Michael Hancher booklet "On the Writing, the Illustration and the Publication of Lewis Carroll's *Alice* Books."

463   1986   Alice's Adventures in Wonderland and Through the Looking-Glass

London: Macmillan Children's Books   John Tenniel

Macmillan New Children's Edition. 2-volume boxed set.

464 1991 Through the Looking-Glass
London: Macmillan   0333290378   John Tenniel
New Children's Edition reissue of the 1980 edition in a publisher's slipcase combined with *Alice*. Dust jacket.

465 1995 Alice's Adventures in Wonderland
London: Macmillan Children's Books   0333640497   John Tenniel; Harry Theaker;
                                                                             Diz Wallis

Macmillan Children's Books. Paperback edition with a new foreword by Philip Pullman. Coloring by Harry Theaker and Diz Wallis. Issued as a boxed set with *Looking-Glass*. A later edition in 2005. Dust jacket.

466 1998 Alice's Adventures in Wonderland, and Through the Looking-Glass
London: Macmillan Children's Books   9780333722725   John Tenniel
Combined edition.

467 1998 Alice's Adventures in Wonderland
London: Macmillan Children's Books   0333722728   John Tenniel
Macmillan Children's Books. Reprint of the 1995 edition of *Alice* in full-color and the 1996 *Looking-Glass* in full-color.

468 1998 Alice's Adventures in Wonderland and Through the Looking-Glass
London: Macmillan Children's Books   0333722728   John Tenniel; Harry Theaker;
                                                                             Diz Wallis

Macmillan Special Centenary Edition. Colored by Harry Theaker and Diz Wallis. Blue paper boards with illustrated dust jacket.

469 2004 Alice's Adventures in Wonderland and Through the Looking-Glass
London: Macmillan Collector's Library   9781904633327   John Tenniel
Afterword by Anna South.

470 2005 Alice's Adventures in Wonderland
London: Macmillan Children's Books   9781405053471   John Tenniel
Macmillan Children's Books. Paperback edition with a new foreword by Philip Pullman. Coloring by Harry Theaker and Diz Wallis. Issued as a boxed set with *Looking-Glass*. First published in 1995.

471 2007 The Complete Alice in Wonderland
London: Macmillan Children's Books   9780230015135   John Tenniel; Harry Theaker;
                                                                             Diz Wallis

In paperback. Boxed set of *Looking-Glass* and *Alice*. Foreword by Philip Pullman. Colored by Harry Theaker and Diz Wallis.

472 2014 Alice's Adventures in Wonderland
London: Macmillan Children's Books   9781509808762 set;   John Tenniel; John MacFarlane
                                               9781447273080 *Alice*; 9781447273097 *L-G*
Macmillan Children's Books. 2 volumes *Alice* and *Looking-Glass* issued in a slipcase. *Alice* foreword by Hilary McKay. *Looking-Glass* foreword by Philip Ardagh. 16 plates colored by John MacFarlane.

473 2015 The Complete Alice: Alice's Adventures in Wonderland and Through the
         Looking-Glass
London: Macmillan Children's Books   9781447275992;   John Tenniel; Harry Theaker;
                                               9781509811410 (e-book)   Diz Wallis

Foreword by Phillip Pullman. Die-cut cover with intricate embossed two-foil detail. Head and tail bands, red foiled edges, and a ribbon marker. Illustrations colored by Harry Theaker and Diz Wallis.

474 2016 Alice's Adventures in Wonderland and Through the Looking-Glass
London: Macmillan Collector's Library   9781909621589   John Tenniel
Afterword by Anna South.

UK Other *Alice* Publisher Editions

1.15 OTHER PUBLISHERS OF *ALICE*

475   ca. 1899   Alice's Adventures in Wonderland

London; Melbourne, VIC: Ward, Lock & Co., Ltd.   Blanche McManus

212 pp. 7 plates. Some of the illustrations are dated 1899.

476   1907   Alice's Adventures in Wonderland

London: Chatto and Windus   Millicent Sowerby

1st edition, 1st impression, published in October 2007. The St. Martin's Illustrated Library of Standard Authors. Dark blue illustrated cloth boards stamped in black and gilt with a circular full-color pictorial paste-on illustration of Alice and the creatures from Chapter III. Slightly reduced in size from the full-page illustration facing page 30. Back cover blank. Front and rear paste-downs and free endpapers are illustrated in gilt with Alice chasing the Rabbit. 12 full-color illustrations (including color frontispiece of the Mad Tea-Party) and chapters headed by black-and-white vignettes. Copies are known in olive green dust jacket with the front illustrated in black and the rear with ads as are both flaps. On the base of the jacket spine is the price of 5/=. Pp [8] + 166 + [7] ads.

477   1907   Alice's Adventures in Wonderland

London: Cassell and Company   Charles Robinson

1st edition. 1st impression, November 1907. Blue cloth, title and picture in gilt.

478   1907   Alice's Adventures in Wonderland

London: Grant Richards Children's Books   Norman Ault

Large octavo. Pictorial paper wrappers. Price one penny. Illustration in black-and-white.

479   1907   Alice's Adventures in Wonderland

London: The Bodley Head. New York: John Lane Company   W. H. Walker

1st edition. Decorated cloth boards in red, gold, white, or pale blue on green background. Other variant bindings are known in brown suede leather deluxe, paper boards, decorated in red, black, or white on green background. Later reprints give 1907 as the date of the 1st edition. 8 plates.

480   1907   Alice's Adventures in Wonderland

London: William Heinemann. New York: Doubleday, Page & Co.   Arthur Rackham

1st edition. Green cloth lettered in gilt and picture in dark green. In white dust jacket with frontispiece picture on the front. Proem by Austin Dobson. 21,000 copies printed.

481   1907   Alice's Adventures in Wonderland

London: William Heinemann. New York: Doubleday, Page & Co.   Arthur Rackham

Limited edition of 1,130 numbered copies, 30 of which were for presentation. White cloth lettered in gilt and dark green.

482   ca. 1907   Alice's Adventures in Wonderland

London: "Books for the Bairns" Office   Brinsley Le Fanu

1st edition. Red limp cloth. No. 142.

483   ca. 1907   Alice's Adventures in Wonderland

London: Aldine Co.   Anonymous

Not seen. In the series Tales for Little People. One penny for each part. Edited by Lady Kathleen. Many poor engravings. Details from *WMGC*.

484   ca. 1907   Alice's Adventures in Wonderland

London: Chatto and Windus   Millicent Sowerby

2nd impression of the 1907 1st edition. Blue illustrated cloth boards. Copies are known in dust jacket.

485   ca. 1907 *Alice's Adventures in Wonderland*
London: George Routledge & Sons, Ltd.   Thomas Maybank

1st edition. In cloth boards with elaborate design. Ruby Series. Maybank illustrated editions are not dated. *WMGC* gives November 1907 as the date of first publication. Color frontispiece with 28 black-and-white pictures.

486   ca. 1907 *Alice's Adventures in Wonderland*
London: George Routledge & Sons, Ltd.   Thomas Maybank

Broadway Series. Includes Routledge catalog that identifies this series. Copies are known in red cloth, blue cloth (with 1909 prize label), and green cloth (1908 inscription).

487   ca. 1907 *Alice's Adventures in Wonderland*
London: George Routledge & Sons, Ltd.   Thomas Maybank

Ruby Series. Front cover has picture of a lady with book in hand, below is the series name. Copies are known in orange cloth, pale blue cloth with 1909 prize label, dark blue cloth with a 1908 inscription, and red cloth with 1907 prize label.

488   ca. 1907 *Alice's Adventures in Wonderland*
London: George Routledge & Sons, Ltd.   Thomas Maybank

Red cloth. Alice and Pig Baby on cover. Lettering in gilt. Red and green decorations. Glassine cover.

489   ca. 1907 *Alice's Adventures in Wonderland*
London: George Routledge & Sons, Ltd.   Thomas Maybank;
                                                         H. L. Schindler

A One-Syllable Book. Quarto size. Cloth boards with picture on front cover. Copies in pictorial paper boards with cloth spine are known; some in red cloth with elaborate design and landscape shape picture; and in glazed paper boards with color picture on front cover signed H. L. Schindler.

490   ca. 1907 *Alice's Adventures in Wonderland*
Edinburgh, UK: W. P. Nemmo, Hay & Mitchell   Alice Ross

1st edition. Blue cloth with oval paste-on picture. Copies are known in red cloth and in orange cloth. There is an undated later edition in blue or beige cloth.

491   ca. 1907 *Alice's Adventures in Wonderland*
London; etc.: Ward Lock & Co. Ltd.   Blanche McManus

12 illustrations. 5 different binding styles are known, all undated. Priority impossible to identify. First style has title and author in gilt in oblong. frame on front cover. Advertisements suggest this is No. 81 in the Royal Series. Copies are known in blue cloth and in dark maroon cloth.

492   ca. 1907 *Alice's Adventures in Wonderland*
London; etc.: Ward Lock & Co. Ltd.   Blanche McManus

2nd-style binding has title and author in gilt in upright oblong frame on front cover with design of lilies below. Advertisements suggest this is No. 76 in The Lily Series. Copies are known in red cloth, cream cloth, dark green cloth, and blue cloth.

493   ca. 1907 *Alice's Adventures in Wonderland*
London; etc.: Ward Lock & Co. Ltd.   Blanche McManus

3rd-style binding has title and author in gilt in horizontal oblong frame on front cover with curtain-style design below. Copies are known in red cloth, blue cloth, and turquoise cloth.

494   ca. 1907 *Alice's Adventures in Wonderland*
London; etc.: Ward Lock & Co. Ltd.   Blanche McManus

Paperback. Story retold by Edith Robarts. Text in double columns with only 8 illustrations, one of which is from *Looking-Glass*. Front cover titled Stories For The Children and has the Tea-Party picture with design in red and black. There are variant copies with differing design on front cover but all with the same picture.

495   1908   Alice's Adventures in Wonderland
London: John Milne   Bessie Pease Gutmann
1st UK edition. Beige cloth, lettered in gilt, picture in red, black, white, and blue. Dust jacket.

496   1908   Alice's Adventures in Wonderland
London: S. W. Partridge & Co., Ltd.   K. M. R. (Roberts)
Everyone's Library. 1rst edition with dust wrapper,

497   1908   Alice's Adventures in Wonderland
London: S.W. Partridge & Co.   K. M. R. (Roberts)
1st edition. Red cloth.

498   1908   Alice's Adventures in Wonderland
London; etc.: Thomas Nelson and Sons   Harry Rountree
Small quarto edition. 8 color pictures with oval paste-on picture on front cover. Red cloth boards. It is likely that there were variant color boards.

499   ca. 1908 Alice's Adventures in Wonderland
London; Glasgow, UK: Collins Clear-Type Press   Charles Pears; T. H. Robinson
Collins Penny Library. Small format. Lewis Carroll signature in gilt on front cover. All editions with these two illustrators have color plates by Charles Pears and line drawings by T. H. Robinson in varying combinations.

500   ca. 1908 Alice's Adventures in Wonderland
London: George Routledge & Sons, Ltd.   Thomas Maybank
28 illustrations and colored frontispiece.

501   ca. 1908 Alice's Adventures in Wonderland
Dundee, UK; London: John Long & Co. Ltd.   Anonymous
Stapled paper wrappers with One Penny at top of front cover. Story in double columns. Date from inscription and comment that Alice has been known for "more than forty years."

502   ca. 1908 Alice's Adventures in Wonderland
London; Halifax, UK: Milner and Company   R. E. McEune
Olive green cloth boards. Date from *WMGC*.

503   ca. 1908 Alice's Adventures in Wonderland
London: S. W. Partridge & Co., Ltd.   K. M. R. (Roberts)
In all editions the illustrator is only given initials. Frontispiece in full-color. In dark maroon simulated leather boards. Date from *WMGC*.

504   ca. 1908 Alice's Adventures in Wonderland
London: S. W. Partridge & Co., Ltd.   K. M. R. (Roberts)
In all editions the illustrator is only given initials. Olive green, red, or blue cloth boards. Publisher's London address now includes Paternoster Row.

505   ca. 1908 Alice's Adventures in Wonderland
London: S. W. Partridge & Co., Ltd.   K. M. R. (Roberts)
In all editions the illustrator is only given initials. In various cloth board colors. Publisher's London address changes to Old Bailey.

506   ca. 1908 Alice in Wonderland
London: Sunday School Union   J. R. Sinclair
Red Sunday Series.

507   ca. 1908 Alice's Adventures in Wonderland
London; Felling-on-Tyne, UK: The Walter Scott Publishing Co., Ltd.   Walter Hawes

White cloth boards with gilt picture on front cover. Variant issues are known in red embossed cloth boards, in dark green cloth boards, and in brown cloth boards. All copies seen are undated.

508   ca. 1908 Alice's Adventures in Wonderland
London; etc.: Thomas Nelson and Sons   Harry Rountree

92 color illustrations. Cloth boards. Binding colors in blue, green, red, or gray are known, all lettered in gilt with on-laid picture. Few Rountree editions are dated, so precedence can be difficult to determine.

509   1909   Alice's Adventures in Wonderland
London; Glasgow, UK: Collins Clear-Type Press   Charles Pears

A miniature edition (10.2 x 7 cm). Soft suede purple stained leather. Frontispiece and title page also designed by Pears. Several variant bindings are known in different color suede, in pictorial boards, and in maroon leather boards with roundel of Carroll on the front.

510   1909   Alice's Adventures in Wonderland
London; etc.: Thomas Nelson and Sons   Harry Rountree

Small quarto edition. 8 color pictures with oval paste-on picture on front cover. Red cloth boards. Format exactly as the 1908 edition but with date change. Copies are known in gray cloth and green cloth.

511   ca. 1909 Alice's Adventures in Wonderland
London: British Books Ltd.   Charles Pears; T. H. Robinson

Undated reprint of one of the ca. 1908 editions.

512   ca. 1909 Alice's Adventures in Wonderland
London; Glasgow, UK: Collins Clear-Type Press   Charles Pears; T. H. Robinson

Red cloth boards with picture of a woman and children reading. One copy has a 1909 inscription.

513   ca. 1909 Alice's Adventures in Wonderland
London: The National Sunday School Union   J. R. Sinclair

Blue cloth boards, with picture on front of the Mouse.

514   1910   Alice's Adventures in Wonderland
London; New York; Toronto, ON; Melbourne, VIC: Cassell and Company, Ltd.   Charles Robinson

179 pp. 8 plates, some color illustrations.

515   1910   Alice's Adventures in Wonderland
London: The Bodley Head. New York: John Lane Company   W. H. Walker

1st reprint.

516   1910   Alice's Adventures in Wonderland
London; etc.: Thomas Nelson and Sons   Harry Rountree

Small quarto edition. 8 color pictures with oval paste-on picture on front cover. Red cloth boards. Format exactly as the 1909 edition but with date change. Copies are known in gray cloth, green cloth, and blue cloth.

517   1910   Alice's Adventures in Wonderland
London; Melbourne, VIC: Ward Lock & Co. Ltd.   Blanche McManus

Green cloth.

518   1910   Alice's Adventures in Wonderland
London; Melbourne, VIC: Ward Lock & Co. Ltd.   Blanche McManus

Pictorial wraps in red and black. Cover carries an ad for Steedman's Soothing Powders for Children Cutting Teeth.

519   ca. 1910 Alice's Adventures in Wonderland
London; Glasgow, UK: Collins Clear-Type Press   Charles Pears; T. H. Robinson
Blue cloth boards with non-Alice picture on front cover. In the series Collins Forward Library. One copy has a 1910
inscription. Copies are known in green and red cloth boards with different pictures on front cover. One with an
inscription dated 1915.

520   ca. 1910 Alice's Adventures in Wonderland
London; Glasgow, UK: Collins Clear-Type Press   Charles Pears; T. H. Robinson
Tales for the Children series.

521   ca. 1910 Alice's Adventures in Wonderland
London: E. Arnold   Olive Allen
Not seen. In the series Every Child's Stories. Priced at 4d. One plate only. Omits last 45 paragraphs. Details from
WMGC.

522   ca. 1910 Alice's Adventures in Wonderland
London: R. Tuck & Sons   Mabel Lucie Attwell
Deluxe binding. Title and picture in gilt on front cover. Green cloth boards. Also known in blue or red cloth boards
and in pictorial paper boards with cloth spine.

523   ca. 1910 Alice's Adventures in Wonderland
London: R. Tuck & Sons   Mabel Lucie Attwell
Raphael House Library. Pictorial paper boards with cloth spine. Otherwise as the 1st ca. 1910 edition.

524   ca. 1910s   Alice's Adventures in Wonderland
London; Melbourne, VIC: Ward, Lock & Co., Ltd.   Unillustrated
212 pp. Cover title: *Alice in Wonderland.* Undated.

525   1911   Alice's Adventures in Wonderland
London: Charles & Dible   Winifred A. Lee
Retold for little readers by Dora L. Shipley.

526   1911   Alice's Adventures in Wonderland
London: Headley Bros.   George Soper
Red cloth boards. Title on front cover in gilt.

527   1911   Alice's Adventures in Wonderland
London; etc: Thomas Nelson and Sons   Harry Rountree
Small quarto edition. 8 color pictures with oval paste-on picture on front cover. Red cloth boards. Format exactly as
the 1910 edition but with date change. Copies are known in blue cloth.

528   1911   Alice's Adventures in Wonderland
London: Ward Lock & Co. Ltd.   Blanche McManus
4th style binding. Front cover has design in blind. In The World Library series. Copies are known in olive green cloth.

529   1911   Alice's Adventures in Wonderland
London; Melbourne, VIC; Toronto, ON: Ward, Lock & Co., Ltd.   Blanche McManus
212 pp. 12 plates.

530   [1911]   Alice's Adventures in Wonderland
London: George Allen & Unwin   George Soper
Collins Forward Library 47.

531　ca. 1911　Alice's Adventures in Wonderland
London; Glasgow, UK: Collins Clear-Type Press　　　　　Charles Pears; T. H. Robinson
Tan paper-covered boards.

532　ca. 1911　Alice's Adventures in Wonderland told mostly in words of one syllable
London: George Routledge & Sons, Ltd.　　　　　Thomas Maybank
One-Syllable Books Series. Quarter-bound in red cloth. 29 illustrations.

533　1912　Alice's Adventures in Wonderland
London: William Heinemann. New York: Doubleday, Page & Co.　　　　　Arthur Rackham
1st reprint of the 1st Rackham 1907 edition.

534　ca. 1912　Alice's Adventures in Wonderland
London; Glasgow, UK: Blackie & Son, Ltd.　　　　　Frank Adams
Green cloth boards with paste-on picture on front cover. In the series Stories Old and New. Copies are known in pale green cloth boards, in dark green cloth boards, and in beige cloth boards. A cream paper boards issue probably came much later, ca. 1940s.

535　ca. 1912　Alice in Wonderland
London: Everett　　　　　Emily Overnell
Everett's Library. 2 leaves of plates.

536　ca. 1912　Alice's Adventures in Wonderland
London: John F. Shaw Ltd.　　　　　E. Stuart Hardy
The illustrator created 8 color plates, but only one issue has all 8. Most have 4 but the plates vary from issue to issue. There appear to be 5 different binding styles: Binding Style 1 in cloth boards with front cover having three filled circles, variously colored. Copies are known with "Lewis" spelled as "Louis."

537　ca. 1912　Alice's Adventures in Wonderland
London: John F. Shaw Ltd.　　　　　E. Stuart Hardy
Binding Style 2 has cloth boards with paste-on picture. Dated by inscription.

538　ca. 1912　Alice's Adventures in Wonderland
London: William Nicholson & Sons, Ltd.　　　　　K. M. R (Roberts)
Reprint.

539　1913　Alice's Adventures in Wonderland
London; New York; Toronto, ON; Melbourne, VIC: Cassell and Company, Ltd.　　　　　Charles Robinson
179 pp. 8 plates, some in color.

540　1913　Alice's Adventures in Wonderland
London: G. Bell & Sons Ltd.　　　　　Alice B. Woodward
Blue cloth with title and design in black. In the series Bell's Continuous Readers, deemed as Suitable for Standard III.

541　1913　Alice's Adventures in Wonderland
London: Henry Frowde; Hodder & Stoughton　　　　　Millicent Sowerby
1st edition thus; green cloth, with paste-on picture. New set of illustrations.

542　1913　Alice's Adventures in Wonderland
London: Longman　　　　　Unknown
Not seen. WMGC lists a 1913 edition priced at 8d.

543　1913　Alice's Adventures in Wonderland

London; etc.: Thomas Nelson and Sons   Harry Rountree
Small quarto edition. 8 color pictures with oval paste-on picture on front cover. In red, blue, or orange cloth boards. Format exactly as 1911 edition but with date change. There are very likely copies with variant color boards.

544   ca. 1913 Alice's Adventures in Wonderland
London: Collins Clear-Type Press   Charles Pears; T. H. Robinson
Large format. Front cover color picture by Pears of the Caucus Race. All line drawings by Robinson, including 16 with color highlights on glossy paper. 1913 inscription date.

545   1914   Alice's Adventures in Wonderland
London; New York; Toronto, ON; Melbourne, VIC: Cassell and Company, Ltd.   Charles Robinson
179 pp. 8 unnumbered plates, some in color.

546   1914   Alice's Adventures in Wonderland
London: G. Bell & Sons Ltd.   Alice B. Woodward
Bluish-gray cloth boards, title and picture in yellow. 8 color plates. In The Queen's Treasure Series.

547   1914   Alice's Adventures in Wonderland
London: Philip Lee Warner, Publisher to the Medici Society   John Tenniel
On handmade Riccardi paper. 1,000 numbered copies. 12 copies on vellum. Reprint of the 1865 edition.

548   1914   Alice's Adventures in Wonderland
London: Philip Lee Warner, Publisher to the Medici Society Ltd.   John Tenniel
Limp leather cover. Limited to 12 numbered copies on vellum and 1,000 copies on handmade Riccardi paper.

549   1914   Alice's Adventures in Wonderland
London; etc.: Thomas Nelson and Sons   Harry Rountree
Small quarto edition. 8 color pictures with oval paste-on picture on front cover. One copy is known in green cloth boards. Format exactly as 1913 edition but with date change. There are very likely copies with variant color boards.

550   1914   Alice's Adventures in Wonderland
London; etc.: Ward Lock & Co. Ltd.   Blanche McManus
4th-style binding as in the 1911 edition. Front cover has design in blind. In The World Library series.

551   1914   Alice's Adventures in Wonderland
London; Melbourne, VIC; Toronto, ON: Ward, Lock & Co., Ltd.   Blanche McManus
212 pp. 12 plates. Black-and-white plates are signed by Blanche McManus.

552   ca. 1914 Alice's Adventures in Wonderland
London; Glasgow, UK: Collins Clear-Type Press   Charles Pears; T. H. Robinson
Dated from an advertisement. Green cloth over boards.

553   ca. 1914 Alice's Adventures in Wonderland
London: John F. Shaw Ltd.   E. Stuart Hardy
Reprint of the ca. 1912 edition with Binding Style 1. Dated by inscription.

554   After 1914   Alice's Adventures in Wonderland
London; etc.: Ward Lock & Co. Ltd.   Blanche McManus
5th-style binding has front cover with title in gilt with design of black vertical lines. In red cloth.

555   [1915]   Alice's Adventures in Wonderland
London: Humphrey Milford   A. E. Jackson
Green cloth boards, lettered in gilt, picture in black. Large, opulent volume. Date from WMGC.

556   ca. 1915 Alice's Adventures in Wonderland
Leeds, UK; Glasgow, UK; Belfast, UK: E. J. Arnold & Son, Ltd.   E. Hatton Stanton
Edited by Alfonzo Gardiner. Bright Story Reader, No. 46. Cloth-lined bluish green cover.

557   ca. 1915 Alice's Adventures in Wonderland
London: John F. Shaw Ltd.   E. Stuart Hardy
Reprint of the ca. 1912 edition with Binding Style 1. Dated by inscription.

558   1916   Alice's Adventures in Wonderland
London: Charles H. Kelly   Gordon Robinson
6 color pictures and 19 black-and-white. Pale blue cloth boards.

559   1916   Alice's Adventures in Wonderland
London: Charles H. Kelly.   Gordon Robinson
A cheaper issue than the earlier 1916 edition with only 1 color plate. Pale blue cloth boards. Another copy is known in beige paper boards.

560   1916   Alice's Adventures in Wonderland
London; Melbourne, VIC; Toronto, ON: Ward Lock & Co.   Margaret W. Tarrant
Red diagonal rib grain cloth over boards. 48 color plates.

561   1916   Alice's Adventures in Wonderland
London; Melbourne, VIC: Ward, Lock & Co., Ltd.   Margaret W. Tarrant
332 pp. with color illustrations.

562   1916   Alice's Adventures in Wonderland
London: William Heinemann; New York: Doubleday, Page & Co.   Arthur Rackham
2nd reprint of the 1st Rackham 1907 edition.

563   ca. 1916 Alice's Adventures in Wonderland
London; Paris; New York: Raphael Tuck & Sons Ltd.   Mabel Lucie Attwell
The Raphael House Library of Gift Books. Blue cloth with gilt. 6 color plates.

564   ca. 1916 Alice's Adventures in Wonderland
London; Melbourne, VIC: Ward Lock & Co.   Margaret W. Tarrant
Tan cloth with pictorial cover. 48 color plates.

565   1917   Alice's Adventures in Wonderland
London: G. Bell & Sons Ltd.   Alice B. Woodward
Reprint of the 1913 edition. Soft cloth with title and design in black. In the series Bell's Continuous Readers, deemed as Suitable for Standard III.

566   1917   Alice's Adventures in Wonderland
London: William Heinemann. New York: Doubleday, Page & Co.   Arthur Rackham
3rd reprint of the 1st Rackham 1907 edition.

567   ca. 1917 Alice in Wonderland
London; Melbourne, VIC; Toronto, ON: Ward, Lock & Co., Ltd.   Anonymous
(after Blanche McManus)

Stories for the Children Series. Adaptation. Retold by Edith Robarts.

568   1918   Alice's Adventures in Wonderland
London: G. Bell & Sons Ltd.   Alice B. Woodward

Reprint of the 1913 edition. Soft cloth with title and design in black. In the series Bell's Continuous Readers, deemed as Suitable for Standard III.

569	1918	Alice's Adventures in Wonderland	
	London; Melbourne, VIC; Toronto, ON: Ward, Lock & Co., Ltd.		Margaret W. Tarrant
	4th edition. 332 pp. with 44 color plates.		

570   ca. 1918   Alice's Adventures in Wonderland
London; Paris; New York: Raphael Tuck & Sons Ltd.   Mabel Lucie Attwell
The Raphael House Library of Gift Books. Blue cloth with gilt. 12 color plates. Dated from inscription.

571   ca. 1919   Alice's Adventures in Wonderland
London; Paris; New York: Raphael Tuck & Sons Ltd.   Mabel Lucie Attwell
Modern Library for Boys and Girls. Brown paper over boards. 1 leaf of plates.

572   1919   Alice's Adventures in Wonderland
London: G. Bell & Sons Ltd.   Alice B. Woodward
Reprint of the 1913 edition. Soft cloth with title and design in black. In the series Bell's Continuous Readers, deemed as Suitable for Standard III.

573   1919   Alice's Adventures in Wonderland
London: Humphrey Milford   A. E. Jackson
May be the 1st reprint of the (1915) edition. Pale blue cloth boards, color plate on cover from p. 84.

574   1919   Alice's Adventures in Wonderland
London: Leopold B. Hill   G. Mawe
Miniature edition, brown paper boards. A similar copy dated ca. 1922 without illustrations exists.

575   1919   Alice's Adventures in Wonderland
London: T. Nelson   Unknown
8 color plates.

576   1919   Alice's Adventures in Wonderland
London: William Heinemann. New York: Doubleday, Page & Co.   Arthur Rackham
4th reprint of the 1st Rackham 1907 edition. Front cover picture now in dark green.

577   ca. 1919   Alice's Adventures in Wonderland
London: The Swarthmore Press   George Soper
Blue cloth boards with title on front cover in gilt.

578   ca. 1919   Alice's Adventures in Wonderland
London; Melbourne, VIC: Ward, Lock & Co., Ltd.   Margaret W. Tarrant
5th edition. 44 color plates. Olive green cloth, black lettering, with a colored, oval illustration of Alice and the rabbit mounted on the cover.

579   1920   Alice's Adventures in Wonderland
London: G. Bell & Sons Ltd.   Alice B. Woodward
Reprint of the 1914 edition. Bluish-gray cloth boards, title and picture in yellow. 8 color plates. In The Queen's Treasure Series. Reprinted in 1985 by Bell & Hyman.

580   1920   Alice's Adventures in Wonderland
London: George G. Harrap & Co., Ltd.   Bessie Pease Gutmann
Olive green cloth with paste-on picture on front cover. Dust jacket.

581   1920   Alice's Adventures in Wonderland

London: Humphrey Milford, Oxford University Press   A. E. Jackson

1st edition thus. In the series Herbert Strang's Library. Strang was the pseudonym of George Herbert Ely and James L'Estrange, two staff members of Oxford University Press, according to Lovett. Single color picture with black-and-white vignettes as chapter headings. Many variant bindings.

582   1920   Alice's Adventures in Wonderland

London; etc.: Thomas Nelson and Sons   Harry Rountree

Small quarto edition. 8 color pictures with oval paste-on picture on front cover. Format exactly as 1914 edition but with date change. There are copies with variant color boards.

583   ca. 1920 Alice's Adventures in Wonderland

London: John F. Shaw Ltd.   E. Stuart Hardy

Binding Style 4 has cloth boards with three rose designs. Dated by inscription. This binding style has only 1 plate, a frontispiece. Binding Styles 3 and 5 cannot be dated and are in the "n.d." portion of this checklist.

584   ca. 1920 Alice in Wonderland

London: L. B. Hill   Unknown

Langham Booklets for Children, No. 1. Illustrated.

585   ca. 1920 Alice's Adventures in Wonderland

London: Raphael Tuck & Sons Ltd.   Mabel Lucie Attwell

In the Treasure House Library. Illustrated paper boards, cloth spine. Dust jacket.

586   ca. 1920 Alice's Adventures in Wonderland

London: Sampson Low, Marston & Co., Ltd.   Anonymous; Alice Ross

Color frontispiece of Alice and Caterpillar. Red paper boards with picture in black of girl playing field hockey. Another copy has frontispiece of Robin Hood; another copy has frontispiece of Alice and Pool of Tears by Alice Ross but not attributed.

587   ca. 1920 Alice's Adventures in Wonderland

London: Thomas Nelson and Sons Ltd.   Agnes Richardson

Not seen. The Lewis Carroll Centenary Catalogue and *WMGC* list a copy illustrated by Richardson and published by Nelson dated 1920. No more is known about the copy.

588   ca. 1920 Alice's Adventures in Wonderland

London: Ward Lock & Co.   Margaret W. Tarrant

Prince Charming Colour Books for Children. 5th edition.

589   1921   Alice's Adventures in Wonderland

London: Leopold B. Hill   Unillustrated

Not seen. *WMGC* lists this reprint in the series Langham's Booklets for Children. Miniature edition in the series Langham Books for Children.

590   1921   Alice's Adventures in Wonderland

London: Raphael Tuck & Sons, Ltd.   Mabel Lucie Attwell

Attwell first illustrated *Alice* in a Raphael Tuck edition of ca. 1910.

591   1921   Alice's Adventures in Wonderland

London; etc.: Thomas Nelson and Sons   Harry Rountree

Small quarto edition. 8 color pictures with oval paste-on picture on front cover. Format exactly as 1920 edition but with date change. There are copies with variant color boards.

592   1921   Alice's Adventures in Wonderland

London: Ward Lock & Co.   Margaret W. Tarrant

Royal Series, No. 6. Margaret W. Tarrant illustration was frontispiece only.

593   1921   Alice's Adventures in Wonderland
London; Melbourne, VIC: Ward, Lock & Co. Ltd.   Unknown

Royal Series, No. 6. 212 pp, 1 leaf of plate.

594   ca. 1921 Alice's Adventures in Wonderland
London; Glasgow, UK: Collins Clear-Type Press   T. H. Robinson; Charles Pears

Decorated red boards. Frontispiece and title page in color by Pears, but uncredited. Many black-and-white illustrations by Robinson.

595   ca. 1921 Alice's Adventures in Wonderland
London: John F. Shaw Ltd.   E. Stuart Hardy

In the series Tell Me a Story. Abridged. Paper boards with paste-on picture. 8 pictures in full-color. A copy is known with a 1921 inscription. Other variants known.

596   ca. 1921 Alice's Adventures in Wonderland
London: Raphael Tuck & Sons, Ltd.   A. L. Bowley

In the series The Golden Treasury Library. 6 leaves of plates. Olive green or red cloth boards with paste-on picture on front cover of Alice and White Rabbit.

597   1922   Alice's Adventures in Wonderland
London: Hodder and Stoughton   Gwynedd Hudson

Cream cloth boards. Edition limited to 250 copies numbered and signed by Hudson. Large, opulent volume, with mounted color plates. Title page misspells author as "Lewis Caroll."

598   1922   Alice's Adventures in Wonderland
London: Hodder and Stoughton for Boots the Chemist   Gwynedd Hudson

Blue cloth boards. Title page has Boots the Chemist / Branches Everywhere. Title page verso has notes published by Hodder and Stoughton for Boots Pure Drug Co., Nottingham. In corn yellow illustrated dust jacket. Title page has the author's name still misspelled as "Lewis Caroll." Goodacre also has a copy with the correct spelling.

599   1922   Alice's Adventures in Wonderland
London: The Bodley Head. New York: John Lane Company   W. H. Walker

Later reprint.

600   1922   Alice's Adventures in Wonderland
London: The National Sunday School Union   J. R. Sinclair

Red Nursery Series. Illustrated paper boards, three interlocked color pictures.

601   1922   Alice's Adventures in Wonderland
London: Ward Lock & Co.   Margaret W. Tarrant

Green cloth. 48 color plates.

602   1922   Alice's Adventures in Wonderland
London: William Heinemann. New York: Doubleday, Page & Co. Arthur Rackham

5th reprint of the 1st Rackham 1907 edition.

603   ca. 1922 Alice's Adventures in Wonderland
London; New York: Geographica Ltd.   Agnes Richardson

Green paper boards with picture on front cover. 6 tipped-in color plates and other line drawings. Date from inscription.

604　ca. 1922 Alice's Adventures in Wonderland

London: Leopold B. Hill　　　　　　　　　　　　　　　　Unillustrated

Miniature edition, in the series Langham Booklets for Children. Date from inscription. It could be the 1919 or the 1921 edition.

605　ca. 1922 Alice's Adventures in Wonderland

London; Melbourne, VIC: Ward, Lock & Co. Ltd.　　　　　Margaret W. Tarrant

2nd edition. 340 pp. with 48 color plates. Published ca. 1922, according to library catalog but could have been earlier.

606　1923　Alice's Adventures in Wonderland

London: Humphrey Milford, Oxford University Press　　　A. E. Jackson

1st reprint. In the series Herbert Strang's Library. Single color picture with black-and-white vignettes as chapter headings. Many variant bindings.

607　1923　Alice's Adventures in Wonderland

London: The Bodley Head. New York: John Lane Company　W. H. Walker
Later reprint.

608　ca. 1923 Alice's Adventures in Wonderland

London: George Allen & Unwin, Ltd.　　　　　　　　　George Soper

Red cloth boards lettered in black. In illustrated dust jacket. Second Impression stated on jacket's front flap.

609　1924　Alice's Adventures in Wonderland

London: G. Bell & Sons Ltd.　　　　　　　　　　　　Alice B. Woodward

Reprint of the 1913 edition. Soft cloth with title and design in black. In the series Bell's Continuous Readers, deemed as Suitable for Standard III.

610　1924　Alice's Adventures in Wonderland

London: The New Era Publishing Company,　　　　　　Evelyn A. Friedenham
on behalf of The New Education Fellowship

In the series World Library for Children (English Edition). No. 17/18 edited by D. N. Northcroft.

611　1924　Alice's Adventures in Wonderland

London: William Heinemann. New York: Doubleday, Page & Co.　Arthur Rackham

6th reprint of the 1st Rackham 1907 edition.

612　ca. 1924 Alice's Adventures in Wonderland

London; Glasgow, UK: Collins Clear-Type Press　　　　Charles Pears; T. H. Robinson

Pale blue paper boards with paste-on picture on front cover. A copy with prize label dated 1924 is known.

613　ca. 1924 Alice's Adventures in Wonderland

London: Frederick Warne & Co.　　　　　　　　　　　K. M. Roberts;
　　　　　　　　　　　　　　　　　　　　　　　　　George Newsome

Red cloth. One color plate by George Newsome and 8 black-and-white plates by K. M. Roberts.

614　ca. 1924 Alice's Adventures in Wonderland

London: Raphael Tuck & Sons Ltd.　　　　　　　　　　Mabel Lucie Atwell

In the Treasure House Library. Illustrated paper boards with cloth spine. Dust jacket. Dated by inscription.

615　ca. 1924 Alice's Adventures in Wonderland

Vienna; London; New York: Sesame Publishing Company　Evelyn A. Friedenham

Not seen. The Columbia 1932 Centenary Catalogue lists a copy published by the Sesame Publishing Company (Vienna, London, and New York) similar to the 1924 New Era Publishing Company edition.

616   1925   Alice's Adventures in Wonderland
London: George G. Harrap & Co., Ltd.   Bessie Pease Gutmann
1st reprint. Olive green cloth with different paste-on picture than the 1920 edition on front cover.

617   1925   Alice's Adventures in Wonderland
London: Humphrey Milford, Oxford University Press   A. E. Jackson
2nd reprint. In the series Herbert Strang's Library. Single color picture with black-and-white vignettes as chapter headings. Many variant bindings.

618   1925   Alice's Adventures in Wonderland
London: J. Coker & Co., Ltd.   Bessie Pease Gutmann;
                                                                G. P. Micklewright

1st edition. Large octavo. Paper boards, red cloth spine. Front cover has paste-on picture by G. P. Micklewright, and all pages have elaborate border by Micklewright. 8 inserted plates by Pease.

619   1925   Alice's Adventures in Wonderland and Bruno's Revenge
London; etc.: Thomas Nelson and Sons   Harry Rountree;
                                                                E. Heber Thompson

Frontispiece line drawing of Lewis Carroll by E. Heber Thompson.

620   ca. 1925 Alice in Wonderland
London: Sampson Low   Walter Hawes
Not seen. Listed in *WMGC*.

621   1926   Alice's Adventures in Wonderland
London: Ernest Benn Ltd.   Brinsley Le Fanu
1st reissue of Ernest Benn's edition of 1926, although that edition has not been located.

622   1926   Alice's Adventures in Wonderland
London: Humphrey Milford, Oxford University Press   A. E. Jackson
3rd reprint. In the series Herbert Strang's Library. Single color picture with black-and-white vignettes as chapter headings. Many variant bindings. Another copy in matching dust jacket and slipcase.

623   1926   Alice's Adventures in Wonderland
London: Humphrey Milford, Oxford University Press   Millicent Sowerby; Anonymous
1st edition thus. Paper boards with paste-on picture by Anonymous. 2 Sowerby illustrations omitted.

624   1926   Alice's Adventures in Wonderland
London: Raphael Tuck & Sons Ltd.   A. L. Bowley
Reprint of the 1924 Treasure House Library edition.

625   1926   Alice's Adventures in Wonderland
London: The Readers Library Publishing Company   Hume Henderson
Maroon paper boards. In illustrated dust jacket with picture of Alice and White Rabbit.

626   ca. 1926 Alice's Adventures in Wonderland
London: Ward Lock & Co.   Margaret W. Tarrant
Green cloth. 30 color plates.

627   1927   Alice's Adventures in Wonderland
London: G. Bell & Sons Ltd.   Alice B. Woodward
Reprint of 1914 edition. Bluish-gray cloth boards, title and picture in yellow. 8 color plates. In The Queen's Treasure Series.

628	1927	Alice's Adventures in Wonderland	
		London: Hodder and Stoughton	Gwynedd Hudson
		Reprint of 1922 issue.	

628 1927 Alice's Adventures in Wonderland
London: Hodder and Stoughton   Gwynedd Hudson
Reprint of 1922 issue.

629 1927 Alice's Adventures in Wonderland
London: Humphrey Milford, Oxford University Press   A. E. Jackson
4th reprint. In the series Herbert Strang's Library. Single color picture, with black-and-white vignettes as chapter headings. Many variant bindings.

630 1927 Alice's Adventures in Wonderland
London: Humphrey Milford, Oxford University Press   A. E. Jackson
4th reprint. In the series Herbert Strang's Library. Single color picture, with black-and-white vignettes as chapter headings. Many variant bindings.

631 1927 Alice's Adventures in Wonderland
London: Raphael Tuck & Sons Ltd.   A. L. Bowley
Golden Treasury Library edition.

632 1927 Alice's Adventures in Wonderland and Bruno's Revenge
London; etc.: Thomas Nelson and Sons   Harry Rountree;
                                                                     E. Heber Thompson
1st reprint of 1925 edition. Frontispiece line drawing of Lewis Carroll by E Heber Thompson.

633 ca. 1927 Alice's Adventures in Wonderland
London: J. Brodie   Thomas Maybank
Listed in *WMGC*. Abridged.

634 1928 Alice's Adventures in Wonderland
London; etc.: Cassell and Company   Charles Robinson
New edition. Plain blue cloth boards lettered in dark blue.

635 1928 Alice's Adventures in Wonderland
London: James Brodie, Ltd.   Thomas Maybank
1st edition.

636 1928 Alice in Wonderland Reading Cards
London: Oxford University Press   A. E. Jackson
Abridged. 16 parts.

637 1928 Alice's Adventures in Wonderland
London: The Bodley Head. New York: John Lane Company   W. H. Walker
4th reprint. Dark blue cloth, decorated in pale blue, title in gilt. Goodacre has a copy in dust jacket with design exactly as the paper boards issue of the 1st edition with notes on a series of reprints of unknown dates.

638 [1928] Alice's Adventures in Wonderland
London: The Readers Library Publishing Company   Hume Henderson
Date from *WMGC*, p. 240.

639 1928 Alice's Adventures in Wonderland and Bruno's Revenge
London; etc.: Thomas Nelson and Sons   Harry Rountree;
                                                                     E. Heber Thompson
2nd reprint of 1925 edition. Frontispiece line drawing of Lewis Carroll by E. Heber Thompson.

640   1928   Alice's Adventures in Wonderland
London; Melbourne, VIC: Ward, Lock & Co., Ltd.   Margaret W. Tarrant
44 color plates. Light brown cloth, black lettering with a colored, oval illustration of Alice and the rabbit.

641   1928   Alice's Adventures in Wonderland
London: William Heinemann. New York: Doubleday, Page & Co.   Arthur Rackham
7th reprint of the 1st Rackham 1907 edition.

642   ca. 1928 Alice in Wonderland
London: Little Blue Book Co.   Unillustrated
Blue paper wrappers. Listed in *WMGC*. Little Blue Book Series, No. 67. 24mo.

643   ca. 1928 Alice's Adventures in Wonderland
London: The Readers Library Publishing Company   Dudley Jarrett
Red cloth decorated in gilt. This and other later copies omit the publisher's address in title page.

644   ca. 1928 Alice's Adventures in Wonderland
London; Melbourne, VIC: Ward, Lock & Co., Ltd.   Margaret W. Tarrant
48 color plates.

645   1929   Alice's Adventures in Wonderland
London: A. & C. Black Ltd.   Charles Folkard
1st edition. Blue cloth boards lettered in black. There were variant issues in red cloth boards, in olive green, and in blue cloth boards.

646   1929   Alice's Adventures in Wonderland
London: George G. Harrap & Co., Ltd.   Bessie Pease Gutmann
2nd reprint. Olive green cloth with different paste-on picture than the 1920 edition on front cover. Dust jacket with picture on the front titled The Pease Edition. Back of dust jacket has list of other titles in Harrap's Standard Children's Library. This is No. 15.

647   1929   Alice's Adventures in Wonderland
London: George G. Harrap & Co., Ltd.   Bessie Pease Gutmann
3rd reprint. Green cloth.

648   1929   Alice's Adventures in Wonderland
London: Humphrey Milford, Oxford University Press   A. E. Jackson
5th reprint. In the series Herbert Strang's Library. Single color picture, with black-and-white vignettes as chapter headings. Many variant bindings.

649   1929   Alice's Adventures in Wonderland
London: J. Coker & Co., Ltd.   Bessie Pease Gutmann;
                                                                  G. P. Micklewright
2nd printing, March 1929. Large octavo. Paper boards, red cloth spine. Front cover has paste-on picture by G. P. Micklewright, and all pages have elaborate border by Micklewright. 8 inserted plates by Pease.

650   1929   Alice's Adventures in Wonderland
London: J. Coker & Co., Ltd.   Bessie Pease Gutmann;
                                                                  G. P. Micklewright
3rd printing, September 1929. Large octavo. Paper boards. Copies have red cloth spine or blue cloth spine. Copies have the front cover paste-on picture by G. P. Micklewright. A copy is known by Bessie P. Guttmann. All pages have elaborate border by Micklewright, 8 inserted plates by Pease.

651	1929	Alice's Adventures in Wonderland	
		London: Longman Green and Co., Ltd.	Unillustrated
		Class-Books of English Literature.	

651   1929   **Alice's Adventures in Wonderland**
London: Longman Green and Co., Ltd.   Unillustrated
Class-Books of English Literature.

652   1929   **Alice's Adventures in Wonderland and Bruno's Revenge**
London; etc. Thomas Nelson and Sons   Harry Rountree;
                                             E. Heber Thompson
3rd reprint of 1925 edition. Frontispiece line drawing of Lewis Carroll by E. Heber Thompson.

653   1929   **Alice's Adventures in Wonderland**
London; Melbourne, VIC: Ward, Lock & Co., Ltd.   Margaret W. Tarrant
The Sunshine Series. 24 color plates, 175 pp.

654   1929   **Alice's Adventures in Wonderland**
London: William Heinemann. New York: Doubleday, Page & Co.   Arthur Rackham
8th reprint of the 1st Rackham 1907 edition.

655   ca. 1929 Alice's Adventures in Wonderland
London: George G. Harrap & Co., Ltd.   Bessie Pease Gutmann
Later issue of the 2nd reprint. Olive green cloth with different paste-on picture than the 1920 edition on front cover. Variant dust jacket from the 1929 2nd edition. With picture on the front of dust jacket titled The Pease Edition. Back of jacket has list of other titles in Harrap's Standard Children's Library. This is No. 15.

656   ca. 1920s   **Alice's Adventures in Wonderland**
London; Glasgow, UK: Charles and Son, Ltd.   Winifred A. Lee
Retold for Little Readers by Dora L Shipley. Illustrated paper wrappers.

657   ca. 1920s   **Alice's Adventures in Wonderland**
London: Raphael Tuck & Sons Ltd.   Mabel Lucie Attwell;
                                             A. L. Bowley
Color pictures by Atwell on spine, and front and back covers. Text pictures by Bowley.

658   ca. 1920s   **Alice's Adventures in Wonderland**
London: Simpkin, Marshall   Julia Greene; Helen Pettes,
                                           after John Tenniel
Pictorial boards. Green cloth.

659   ca. 1920s   **Adventures of Alice in Wonderland**
London: Simpkin, Marshall   Walter Hawes
The Beacon Library.

660   ca. 1920s   **Alice's Adventures in Wonderland**
London: The Epworth Press, J. Alfred Sharp   Gordon Robinson
The Rex Series for Boys, No. 37.

661   ca. 1920s   **Adventures of Alice in Wonderland**
Dundee, UK; London; Montreal, QC: Valentine & Sons Ltd.   Anonymous
A shaped book.

662   ca. 1920s   **Alice's Adventures in Wonderland**
London; Wakefield, UK: W. Nicholson & Sons, Ltd.   K. M. R (Roberts)
Copies in dark green, blue, and red cloth boards.

663   ca. 1920s   Alice's Adventures in Wonderland
London: William Nicholson & Sons, Ltd.   Blanche McManus
In the series Nicholson's Home Library.

664   1930   Alice in Wonderland
London; Glasgow, UK: Collins Clear-Type Press   Winifred M. Ackroyd
In the series Collins Boys & Girls Library. Yellow or orange paper boards with picture on front cover of a boy and girl reading.

665   1930   Alice's Adventures in Wonderland
London: G. Bell & Sons Ltd.   Alice B. Woodward
New Edition with Self-Study Exercises. In the series Bell's Continuous Readers, deemed as Suitable for Standard III.

666   1930   Alice's Adventures in Wonderland
London: Humphrey Milford   A. E. Jackson
Tan boards.

667   1930   Alice in Wonderland
London: J. M. Dent & Sons   John Tenniel; Henry Holiday
Kings Treasures of Literature Series. Includes *Snark* and several poems from *Sylvie and Bruno*. Blue cloth over boards.

668   1930   Alice's Adventures in Wonderland and Bruno's Revenge
London; etc.: Thomas Nelson and Sons   Harry Rountree;
          E Heber Thompson
4th reprint of 1925 edition. Frontispiece line drawing of Lewis Carroll by E. Heber Thompson.

669   1930   Alice's Adventures in Wonderland
London: William Heinemann. New York: Doubleday, Page & Co.   Arthur Rackham
9th reprint of the 1st Rackham 1907 edition. Green cloth.

670   ca. 1930 Alice's Adventures in Wonderland
London; Glasgow, UK: Collins Clear-Type Press   Charles Pears; T. H. Robinson
Pictorial boards, green cloth spine. 4 color plates by Pears and 15 black-and-white plates by Robinson.

671   ca. 1930 Alice's Adventures in Wonderland
London; Glasgow, UK: Collins Clear-Type Press   Charles Pears; T. H. Robinson
Illustrated Pocket Classics.

672   ca. 1930 Alice's Adventures in Wonderland
London; Glasgow, UK: Collins Clear-Type Press   Harry Rountree; Charles Pears
Popular Series.

673   ca. 1930 Alice's Adventures in Wonderland
London: Frederick Warne and Co. Ltd.   K. M. Roberts; Muriel Baines
The Magnet Library.

674   ca. 1930 Alice's Adventures in Wonderland
London: Hamlyn Classics   Unknown

675   ca. 1930 Alice's Adventures in Wonderland
London: Raphael Tuck & Sons Ltd.   Mabel Lucie Atwell
In the Treasure House Library. Illustrated paper boards with cloth spine. Dust jacket. Copy dated by inscription.

676   ca. 1930 Alice's Adventures in Wonderland
Leicester, UK: The Brockhampton Press   Gwynedd Hudson
The Nursery Books, sold by Boots.

677   ca. 1930 Alice's Adventures in Wonderland
London; Glasgow, UK: The Children's Press   Harry Rountree; D. Osborne;
                                                         Charles Pears

Green textured paper-covered boards, with front cover picture by D. Osborne. One copy has frontispiece by Charles
Pears. Binding variants known.

678   ca. 1930 Alice's Adventures in Wonderland
London: The Readers Library Publishing Company   Dudley Jarrett
Red cloth decorated in gilt. This and other later copies omit the publisher's address in title page.

679   ca. 1930 Alice's Adventures in Wonderland
London: Ward Lock & Co.   Margaret W. Tarrant
Tan cloth with pictorial cover. 16 color plates.

680   ca. 1930 Alice's Adventures in Wonderland
London: Ward Lock & Co.   Margaret W. Tarrant
Pictorial boards with green spine. 16 color plates. Dust jacket.

681   [1930–1933]   Children's Treasury of Great Stories
London: "Daily Express" Publications   Helen Monro; C. R. [Charles
                                                         Robinson]; Harry Rountree

Anthology of books by multiple authors. Contains the full text of Alice as the first book. Most illustrations by Monro,
with a color frontispiece by Rountree, and a half title page with an illustration by "C.R." [Charles Robinson].

682   1931   Alice's Adventures in Wonderland
London: J. Coker & Co., Ltd.   Bessie Pease Gutmann;
                                                         G. P. Micklewright

4th printing. Large octavo. Paper boards, red cloth spine. Front cover has paste-on picture by G. P. Micklewright, and
all pages have elaborate border by Micklewright. 8 inserted plates by Pease.

683   1931   Alice's Adventures in Wonderland
London: J. Coker & Co., Ltd.   Bessie Pease Gutmann;
                                                         G. P. Micklewright

5th printing. Large octavo. Paper boards, red cloth spine, front cover has paste-on picture by G. P. Micklewright, and
all pages have elaborate border by Micklewright, 8 inserted plates by Pease.

684   1932   Alice's Adventures in Wonderland
London: Hodder and Stoughton   Gwynedd Hudson
Red cloth boards, front cover includes the words Centenary Edition. In red illustrated dust jacket.

685   1932   Alice's Adventures in Wonderland
London: Humphrey Milford   A. E. Jackson
Reprint of 1920 issue.

686   1932   A Little Book of Alice in Wonderland
London: Humphrey Milford, Oxford University Press   A. E. Jackson; Anonymous
Little Big Book Series. Color frontispiece.

687   1932   Alice's Adventures in Wonderland
London: Raphael Tuck & Sons Ltd.   A.L. Bowley
Golden Treasury Library edition.

688   1932   Alice's Adventures in Wonderland
London: The Readers Library Publishing Company   Hume Henderson
Centenary Edition. Illustrated paper boards with picture of Alice by mushroom. Omits the publisher's address on title page.

689   1932   Alice's Adventures in Wonderland and Bruno's Revenge
London; etc.: Thomas Nelson and Sons   Harry Rountree;
                                              E. Heber Thompson
5th reprint of 1925 edition. Frontispiece line drawing of Lewis Carroll by E. Heber Thompson.

690   1932   Alice's Adventures in Wonderland
London; etc.: Thomas Nelson and Sons   Helen Monro
In the series Nelson's Famous Books. Includes *Bruno's Revenge*. Blue or red cloth boards. Advertisement at the end lists this as Ready September 1932. Other copies are known in darker blue or maroon cloth boards. A copy in black cloth boards is known in dust jacket with picture of Alice and White Rabbit. Later undated reprints are known in red or red pebble dash cloth boards.

691   ca. 1932 Alice's Adventures in Wonderland
London; Melbourne, VIC: Ward Lock & Co.   Margaret W. Tarrant
Royal Series, No. 6. Blue cloth over boards. Dust jacket.

692   ca. 1932 Alice's Adventures in Wonderland
London; Melbourne, VIC: Ward, Lock & Co., Ltd.   Unknown
Royal Series, No. 6. 212 pp. 14 color plates.

693   1933   Alice's Adventures in Wonderland
London: G. Bell & Sons Ltd.   Alice B. Woodward
New Edition with Self-Study Exercises. In the series Bell's Continuous Readers, deemed as Suitable for Standard III.

694   1933   Alice's Adventures in Wonderland
London: J. Coker & Co., Ltd.   Bessie Pease Gutmann;
                                      G. P. Micklewright
6th printing. Large octavo. Paper boards, red cloth spine. Front cover has paste-on picture by G. P. Micklewright, and all pages have elaborate border by Micklewright. 8 inserted plates by Pease.

695   1933   Alice's Adventures in Wonderland
London: Oxford University Press   A. E. Jackson
1st edition thus. Colored pictorial boards. 7 color plates.

696   1933   Alice in Wonderland
London: Raphael Tuck & Sons   A.L. Bowley
The Modern Library for Boys and Girls.

697   1933   Alice's Adventures in Wonderland
London: The Readers Library Publishing Company   Hume Henderson
Maroon paper boards. Dust jacket has a picture of Charlotte Henry from the Paramount film of 1933. Omits the publisher's address on title page.

698   1933   Alice's Adventures in Wonderland and Bruno's Revenge
London; etc.: Thomas Nelson and Sons   Harry Rountree;
                                              E. Heber Thompson
Later reprint of the 1925 edition. Frontispiece line drawing of Lewis Carroll by E. Heber Thompson.

699   1933   Alice's Adventures in Wonderland
London: William Heinemann   Arthur Rackham
10th reprint of the 1st Rackham 1907 edition styled Cheaper Edition. Lettered in black on pale blue cloth, slightly smaller size. Has 8 of the 13 color plates.

700   [1933]   Alice's Adventures in Wonderland
London; Beccles, UK: William Clowes and Sons Ltd.   J. Morton Sale
Yellow cloth boards printed in black.

701   ca. 1933 Alice's Adventures in Wonderland
London: Collins' Clear-Type Press   Harry Rountree
Large quarto edition. Dark green cloth boards, with front cover picture in blind. Title on spine in gilt. Copy dated by a 1933 inscription.

702   ca. 1933 Alice's Adventures in Wonderland
London: John F. Shaw & Co., Ltd.   D. R. Sexton
Large format. Pictorial paper boards, cloth spine. Front cover has color picture of Alice and Mouse. 8 color plates tipped in with 23 full-page pictures in black-and-white.

703   ca. 1933 Alice's Adventures in Wonderland
London: Juvenile Productions   D. R. Sexton; Anonymous
Large format. Pictorial paper boards with picture extending over both covers and spine of the Tea-Party by Anonymous. Two black-and-white pictures by Sexton omitted.

704   ca. 1933 Alice's Adventures in Wonderland
London; Melbourne, VIC: Ward, Lock, & Co   Margaret W. Tarrant
48 color plates.

705   1934   Alice's Adventures in Wonderland
London: A. & C. Black Ltd.   Charles Folkard
1st reprint. Blue cloth boards, lettered in red.

706   1934   Alice in Wonderland and Grimm's Fairy Tales
London: Foulsham & Co.   Gil Dyer
Foulsham's Two Books in One Library Series.

707   1934   Alice's Adventures in Wonderland
London: J. Coker & Co., Ltd.   Bessie Pease Gutmann;
                                                            G. P. Micklewright
7th printing. Large octavo. Paper boards, red cloth spine. Front cover has paste-on picture by G. P. Micklewright, and all pages have elaborate border by Micklewright. 8 inserted plates by Pease.

708   1934   Alice's Adventures in Wonderland and Bruno's Revenge
London; etc.: Thomas Nelson and Sons   Harry Rountree;
                                                            E. Heber Thompson
Later reprint of the 1925 edition. Frontispiece line drawing of Lewis Carroll by E. Heber Thompson.

709   ca. 1934 Alice's Adventures in Wonderland
London; Glasgow, UK: Collins   Irene Mountfort
Gray cloth boards. Photographs from Paramount Film.

710   ca. 1934 Alice's Adventures in Wonderland
London: Hutchinson & Co.   M. L. Clements
Date from WMGC. Full-color paper boards with picture of Alice holding Pig.

711	1935	Famous Animal Tales	
		London: G. G. Harrap	Ernest Aris

"The Mad Tea Party" appears on pp. 37–46. Color frontispiece and black-and-white illustrations by Ernest Aris. Also published in Philadelphia by David McKay.

712	1935	Alice's Adventures in Wonderland	
		London: Humphrey Milford, Oxford University Press	A. E. Jackson

6th reprint. Green cloth. Dust jacket with blurb. In the series Herbert Strang's Library. Single color picture, with black-and-white vignettes as chapter headings. Many variant bindings.

713	1935	Alice's Adventures in Wonderland	
		London: John Lane, The Bodley Head Ltd.	W. H. Walker

Red or blue cloth stamped in black. 8 color plates.

714	ca. 1935	Alice's Adventures in Wonderland	
		London; Dublin: Mellifont Press Ltd.	Anonymous

Mellifont Children's Books for Boys and Girls. Pictorial paper wrappers. Abridged. In wrappers with full-color picture on front cover and one anonymous illustration.

715	1936	The Children's Alice	
		London: George G. Harrap & Co., Ltd.	Honor C. A. Appleton; Richard Ogle

Adapted by F. H. Lee. Front cover picture by (Richard) Ogle. In corn yellow soft cloth wrapper.

716	1936	Alice's Adventures in Wonderland	
		London: Humphrey Milford	A. E. Jackson

Color plates laid in on glossy paper. Pink cloth boards. Roundel on front cover of girl dancing.

717	1936	Alice's Adventures in Wonderland	
		London: Humphrey Milford, Oxford University Press	Millicent Sowerby; Anonymous

Reprint. Brown cloth boards. In the series The Children's Bookcase.

718	1936	Alice's Adventures in Wonderland	
		London: Humphrey Milford, Oxford University Press	A. E. Jackson

7th reprint. In the series Herbert Strang's Library. Single color picture, with black-and-white vignettes as chapter headings. Many variant bindings.

719	1936	Alice's Adventures in Wonderland	
		London: Raphael Tuck & Sons, Ltd.	A. L. Bowley

Favourite Tales Library.

720	1936	Alice's Adventures in Wonderland	
		London; Edinburgh, UK: Thomas Nelson and Sons Ltd.	Helen Monro

Reprint of 1932 edition, in The Nelson Classics edition.

721	1936	Alice's Adventures in Wonderland	
		London: Ward, Lock & Co.	Margaret W. Tarrant

Royal Series, No. 6. Red cloth.

722	ca. 1936	Alice's Adventures in Wonderland	
		London: Collins' Clear-Type Press	Harry Rountree

Large quarto edition. Red cloth boards. Front cover paste-on picture. Dated by inscription.

723   1937   Alice's Adventures in Wonderland
London: G. Bell & Sons Ltd.   Alice B. Woodward
New Edition with Self-Study Exercises. In the series Bell's Continuous Readers, deemed as Suitable for Standard III.

724   1937   Alice's Adventures in Wonderland
London: J. Coker & Co., Ltd.   Bessie Pease Gutmann;
                                                               G. P. Micklewright

8th printing. Large octavo. Paper boards, red cloth spine. Front cover has paste-on picture by G. P. Micklewright, and all pages have elaborate border by Micklewright. 8 inserted plates by Pease. There are similar but undated reprints.

725   1937   Alice's Adventures in Wonderland
London: Juvenile Productions Ltd.   D. R. Sexton
In the Merlin Series. Color frontispiece of the Duchess. 18 black-and-white full-page pictures. Several variant copies are known with most including a list of books in the series. Alice's position varies. Copies are known in pale green, dark green, orange, red, beige, or brown cloth boards. Some are known with a dust jacket and with a picture of Alice and the Caterpillar.

726   1937   Alice's Adventures in Wonderland and Bruno's Revenge
London; etc.: Thomas Nelson and Sons   Harry Rountree;
                                                               E. Heber Thompson

Later reprint of the 1925 edition. Frontispiece line drawing of Lewis Carroll by E. Heber Thompson.

727   1938   Alice's Adventures in Wonderland
London: Collins   R. M. Tovey
Not seen. Listed in *WMGC*.

728   1938   Alice's Adventures in Wonderland
London: Hodder and Stoughton   Gwynedd Hudson
As the 1932 edition but title page verso has First Printing of this edition 1938.

729   1939   Alice's Adventures in Wonderland
London: A. & C. Black Ltd.   Charles Folkard
2nd reprint.

730   1939   Alice's Adventures in Wonderland
London: Juvenile Productions   D. R. Sexton
Not seen. *WMGC* lists this reprint dated 1939.

731   ca. 1930s   Story Lessons from Alice in Wonderland
London; Glasgow, UK: Charles and Son, Ltd.   Winifred A. Lee
Free adaptation by Dora L Shipley with school lessons added. Brown cloth boards. An edition is known in blue cloth boards.

732   ca. 1930s   Alice in Wonderland
London: Collins Clear-Type Press   Winifred M. Ackroyd
In the series Collins Bumper Reward Books.

733   ca. 1930s   The Adventures of Alice in Wonderland
London: The Children's Press   Edgar Norfield; Anonymous
Large volume (32.8 x 23 cm). With card covers stapled sideways. Unsigned full-color picture of the Tea-Party on front cover. Illustrations by Edgar Norfield.

734   ca. 1930s   The Adventures of Alice in Wonderland
London: The Children's Press   Edgar Norfield; Anonymous

Large volume (32.8 x 23 cm). With card covers stapled sideways. Unsigned full-color picture of the Tea-Party on front cover. Illustrations by Edgar Norfield.

735   ca. 1930s   Alice's Adventures in Wonderland
London; Melbourne, VIC: Ward Lock & Co.   Margaret W. Tarrant
Orange cloth over boards. 30 color plates. Illustrated endpapers. Illustrated dust jacket.

736   ca. 1930s   Alice's Adventures in Wonderland
London; Melbourne, VIC: Ward Lock & Co.   Margaret W. Tarrant
Light brown cloth over boards. 48 color plates.

737   ca. 1930s   Alice's Adventures in Wonderland
London; Melbourne, VIC; Cape Town, SA: Ward Lock & Co.   Anonymous
Red paper boards.

738   1940   Alice's Adventures in Wonderland and Bruno's Revenge
London; etc.: Thomas Nelson and Sons   Harry Rountree;
                                                                 E. Heber Thompson
Later reprint of the 1925 edition. Frontispiece line drawing of Lewis Carroll by E. Heber Thompson.

739   ca. 1940 Alice's in Wonderland
London: W. Foulsham & Co.   Gil Dyer
In the series Foulsham's Boy and Girl Fiction Library. Red cloth boards with perspective black lines on front cover. A war time edition, all issues are undated but have varying codes. Goodacre has 10 E, 11E, 13E, 15E 16E, 18E, 19E but the meaning is not known. 10E to 15E have frontispiece in black-and-white. 16E, 18E, and 19E have frontispiece and 4 other plates in color.

740   1941   The Children's Alice
London: George G. Harrap & Co., Ltd.   Honor C. A. Appleton;
                                                                 Richard Ogle
6th printing. Pictorial wraps. Front cover picture by (Richard) Ogle.

741   1941   Alice's Adventures in Wonderland
London: Humphrey Milford   A. E. Jackson
Reprint of 1920 issue.

742   1942   Alice's Adventures in Wonderland
London: A. & C. Black Ltd.   Charles Folkard
3rd reprint.

743   1942   Alice's Adventures in Wonderland
London: Fairylite Books   Unknown
Not seen. British Library catalog lists as 11 pp.

744   1942   Alice's Adventures in Wonderland and Bruno's Revenge
London; etc.: Thomas Nelson and Sons   Harry Rountree;
                                                                 E. Heber Thompson
Later reprint of the 1925 edition. Frontispiece line drawing of Lewis Carroll by E. Heber Thompson.

745   [1942] Some Adventures of Alice in Wonderland
Lower Chelston, UK: Gulliver Book Co.   Unknown
Gulliver Little Books. No. 2. Abridged.

746   1943   Alice in Wonderland
London: The Waverley Book Company Ltd.   Rene Cloke

Rene Cloke had previously supplied some pictures for a 1934 anthology with *Alice* extracts. The present issue has her 2nd set of illustrations. 8 color plates, 76 line drawings with single-color highlights. Dark blue cloth boards.

747   1943   Alice's Adventures in Wonderland and Bruno's Revenge
London; etc.: Thomas Nelson and Sons   Harry Rountree;
                                                               E. Heber Thompson
Later reprint of the 1925 edition. Frontispiece line drawing of Lewis Carroll by E. Heber Thompson.

748   1943   Alice's Adventures in Wonderland and Bruno's Revenge
London; etc.: Thomas Nelson and Sons   Harry Rountree;
                                                               E. Heber Thompson
Later reprint of the 1925 edition. Frontispiece line drawing of Lewis Carroll by E. Heber Thompson.

749   ca. 1943 Alice in Wonderland
London: Educational Book Company   Rene Cloke
Apart from change of publisher from The Waverley Book Company Ltd., same as another Cloke illustrated edition of 1943. Light blue cloth boards.

750   ca. 1943 Alice in Wonderland
London: P. R. Gawthorn, Ltd.   Rene Cloke
Apart from change of publisher, virtually as an earlier Rene Cloke issue. Red cloth boards. A copy is known in full-color dust jacket with Tea-Party picture. A variant issue is known with different prelims.

751   ca. 1943 Alice in Wonderland
London: P. R. Gawthorn, Ltd.   Rene Cloke
Variant issue of the ca. 1943 edition with different prelims.

752   1944   Alice's Adventures in Wonderland
London: Humphrey Milford   A. E. Jackson
Unspecified reprint. Corn yellow paper boards.

753   1944   Alice's Adventures in Wonderland
London; Leicester, UK: Newman Wolsey   A. Rado
Red cloth boards very similar to the other 1944 Rado illustrated edition.

754   1944   Alice's Adventures in Wonderland
London: W. H. Cornelius   A. Rado
1rst edition. Blue or red cloth boards. In illustrated dust jacket.

755   [1944]   Alice in Wonderland
London: The Waverley Book Company   Rene Cloke
Blue cloth over boards. 8 leaves of color plates.

756   ca. 1944 Alice in Wonderland
London: P. R. Gawthorn, Ltd.   Rene Cloke
2nd printing. Red cloth boards.

757   1945   Alice's Adventures in Wonderland
London: Arthur Barron, Ltd.   Harry Riley
In beige or green cloth boards or orange paper boards. One copy in a dust jacket with note from previous printing cites the 2nd impression as the 2nd edition.

758   1945   Alice's Adventures in Wonderland
London: Arthur Barron, Ltd.   Harry Riley
2nd impression.

759   1945   Alice in Wonderland
London: Collins Clear-Type Press   Anonymous
Retold. In The Silver Torch Series.

760   1945   Alice's Adventures in Wonderland
London: Martins Press   Unknown
Not seen.

761   1945   Alice in Wonderland
London: P. R. Gawthorn, Ltd.   Rene Cloke
3rd printing. Red cloth boards.

762   1945   Alice's Adventures in Wonderland and Bruno's Revenge
London; etc.: Thomas Nelson and Sons   Harry Rountree;
                                                                    E. Heber Thompson

Later reprint of the 1925 edition. Frontispiece line drawing of Lewis Carroll by E. Heber Thompson.

763   ca. 1945 Alice in Wonderland
London: Juvenile Productions Ltd.   D. R. Sexton
Merlin Series edition.

764   1946   Alice's Adventures in Wonderland
London: A. & C. Black Ltd.   Charles Folkard
4th reprint.

765   1946   Alice's Adventures in Wonderland
Piccadilly (London): Arandar Books, Ltd.   Richard Ogle
Retold by Monica Marsden. Pictorial boards. Color frontispiece and black-and-white illustrations.

766   1946   Alice's Adventures in Wonderland
London: Arthur Barron, Ltd.   Harry Riley
3rd edition. In red or orange cloth boards. Color plates.

767   1946   Alice in Wonderland
London: Birn Brothers Ltd.   Anonymous
Full-color glazed paper boards, green cloth spine, and matching dust jacket. Date from inscription. Variant copies
known with red or orange cloth spine, and one with the front picture continuing onto the spine. 4 full-page color
plates.

768   1946   Alice in Wonderland
London: George G. Harrap and Company Ltd.   Eileen Soper
1st edition thus. Blue cloth boards. Dust jacket with picture of Alice and White Rabbit.

769   1946   Alice in Wonderland
London: Juvenile Productions   Anonymous
Large format. Glazed pictorial boards with red cloth spine. Matching dust jacket. Variant copy known with blue cloth
spine.

770   1946   Alice's Adventures in Wonderland
London: Penguin Books   John Tenniel
A Puffin Book, 1st edition. Reprinted 1950, 1962, 1973, 1974, 1977, and 1997. Pictorial wrappers.

771   1946   Alice's Adventures in Wonderland

London; New York: Penguin Books   John Tenniel
Puffin Story Book. Yellow paper binding.

772   1946   Alice's Adventures in Wonderland
Harmondsworth, UK: Puffin   John Tenniel
Puffin Classics.

773   1946   Alice in Wonderland
South Croydon, UK: The Blue Book Company   Anonymous
In The Blue Book Library. Dust jacket.

774   ca. 1946 Alice in Wonderland
London: The Little Blue Book Company   Anonymous; T. D.
In The Little Blue Book Library. In illustrated dust jacket with picture of Alice signed with "TD" (some "DT") monogram.

775   1947   Alice in Wonderland
London; Toronto, ON: George G. Harrap   Eileen A. Soper
Some illustrations in color.

776   1947   Alice's Adventures in Wonderland and Bruno's Revenge
London; etc.: Thomas Nelson and Sons   Harry Rountree;
                                                                           E. Heber Thompson
Later reprint of the 1925 edition. Frontispiece line drawing of Lewis Carroll by E. Heber Thompson.

777   1947   Alice's Adventures in Wonderland
London: William Heinemann   Arthur Rackham
11th reprint of the 1st Rackham 1907 edition. Reverts to original size.

778   1948   Alice in Wonderland
London: Adprint Ltd., distributed by Max Parrish and Co., Ltd.   John Tenniel; Hugh Gee
Line drawings by Tenniel, 16 full-color pictures of scenes and figures created and photographed by Hugh Gee. In
matching dust jacket.

779   1948   Alice's Adventures in Wonderland
London: George Allen & Unwin, Ltd.   George Soper
2nd impression. Dust jacket.

780   1948   Alice in Wonderland
London: George G. Harrap and Company Ltd.   Eileen Soper
1st reprint. Silver decorations on blue cloth. 3 color plates and numerous black-and-white illustrations.

781   1948   Alice's Adventures in Wonderland
London: J. Coker & Co., Ltd.   Bessie Pease Gutmann;
                                                                           G. P. Micklewright
Not seen. WMGC lists this reprint of the 1937 edition.

782   1948   Alice in Wonderland
London: P. R. Gawthorn, Ltd.   Rene Cloke
4th printing. Red cloth boards.

783   1948   Alice's Adventures in Wonderland
London: William Heinemann   Arthur Rackham
12th reprint of the 1st Rackham 1907 edition.

784   [1948]   The Children's Omnibus

London: Peter Lunn   H. M. Brock

Brown cloth boards with color illustrated dust jacket that includes multiple characters, including Alice and the Queen of Hearts. Only 1 illustration in the text, a black-and-white frontispiece ("The Mad Tea Party") by Brock.

785   [ca. 1948]   Alice's Adventures in Wonderland with other stories and poems

London: Peter Lunn   H. M. Brock

Green cloth boards. Frontispiece only by Brock. The edition was originally part of The Children's Omnibus series, edited by John Keir Cross. Dust jacket. Contains *Alice*, but not *Looking-Glass*.

786   [1948]   Alice's Adventures in Wonderland, from the story by Lewis Carroll

London; Ewell, UK: The Studley Press   Arabella Blithe

In The Academy Series. Retold by Mary Farrer. Paperback.

787   1949   Alice's Adventures in Wonderland

London: A. & C. Black Ltd.   Charles Folkard

5th reprint.

788   1949   Alice in Wonderland

London: Adprint Ltd., distributed by Max Parrish and Co., Ltd.   John Tenniel; Hugh Gee

2nd impression. Line drawings by Tenniel, 16 full-color pictures of scenes and figures created and photographed by Hugh Gee. In matching dust jacket.

789   1949   Alice in Wonderland

London: George G. Harrap and Company Ltd.   Eileen Soper

7th reprint. The Children's Bookshelf.

790   1949   Alice's Adventures in Wonderland

London: J. Coker & Co., Ltd.   Bessie Pease Gutmann; Mary Smith

4 plates by Mary Smith, line drawings by Bessie Pease. Smith's name is on paste-on slip over Pease's name on the title page. In pictorial dust jacket with a 5th picture by Mary Smith on the front.

791   1949   Alice's Adventures in Wonderland

Harmondsworth, UK: Penguin Books   John Tenniel

Published first in Puffin Story Books in 1946.

792   1949   Alice's Adventures in Wonderland

London: Penguin Books   0140350381   John Tenniel, Elisa Trimby

Puffin Classics. Paperback. Elisa Trimby, color cover. Originally published in 1946, also reprinted 1952, 1955, 1985, and 1986 (twice).

793   1949   Alice's Adventures in Wonderland

London: Penguin Books Limited   John Tenniel

Reprint of 1946 issue.

794   1949   Alice's Adventures in Wonderland

Bungay, UK: Privately produced for Allen and Richard Lane   John Tenniel
by Richard Clay and Company

500 copies printed for Allen and Richard Lane by Richard Clay and Company. Blue cloth, blind stamped. Spine stamped in silver.

795   1949   Alice's Adventures in Wonderland and Bruno's Revenge
London; etc.: Thomas Nelson and Sons   Harry Rountree;
                                                                             E. Heber Thompson
Later reprint of the 1925 edition. Frontispiece line drawing of Lewis Carroll by E. Heber Thompson.

796   1949   Alice's Adventures in Wonderland
London: Ward, Lock & Co.   Margaret W. Tarrant
New Prize Library Edition, No. 2. There were later editions. Tarrant illustration is frontispiece only.

797   1949   Alice's Adventures in Wonderland
London: William Heinemann   Arthur Rackham
13th reprint of 1st Rackham 1907 edition.

798   ca. 1940s   Alice in Wonderland and Grimm's Fairy Tales
London: Foulsham & Co.   Gil Dyer
Paperback, with full-color front cover.

799   ca. 1940s   Some Adventures of Alice in Wonderland
Lower Chelston, UK: Gulliver Books, Ltd.   Anonymous
Card covers in Penguin Books style in blue and white, printed in black. Variant issues seen; some covers in blue and
silver; red and white; orange and white. All issues are small format.

800   ca. 1940s   Alice in Wonderland
Lower Chelston, UK: Gulliver Books, Ltd.   P. James
In The Magic Hour series. Blue paper boards lettered in white. In full-color dust jacket with picture on front by
P. James. Variant issues are known in red paper boards, lettered in white; a paperback issue with picture on front
cover of the Tea-Party. Title page says Gulliver's Everychild's Library of Best Stories. Back cover lists it as Gulliver's
Favourite Stories for Children.

801   ca. 1940s   Alice in Wonderland
London: H. F. & Co., Ltd.   Anonymous
14-page booklet. Card wrappers. Front cover has color picture of Tea-Party and back cover a picture of the Cheshire Cat.

802   ca. 1940s   Alice's Adventures in Wonderland
London: J. Coker & Co., Ltd.   Bessie Pease Gutmann;
                                                                             G. P. Micklewright
Large octavo in paper boards with blue cloth spine. Front cover with paste-on picture by Micklewright, and all pages
have elaborate border by Micklewright. 8 inserted plates by Pease. It is difficult to know which of these large issues
has precedence.

803   ca. 1940s   Alice in Wonderland
London: Juvenile Productions Ltd.   Anonymous
10-page booklet with abbreviated text. Card wrappers. Front and back covers have color picture of Alice and White
Rabbit.

804   ca. 1940s   Alice's Adventures in Wonderland
London: Martins Press   Helen Jacobs
In The Riverside Series. Large format. Retold and edited by Constance M. Martin. A war-time version with black-
and-white pictures. Front cover has orange additions.

805   ca. 1940s   Alice's Adventures in Wonderland
London: Philip & Tracey Ltd.   Helen Jacobs
A later version of another ca. 1940s. Jacobs illustrated edition published by Martins Press. With full-color wrappers
and text pictures with orange highlights. One copy lists the publisher as "Tacey" not Tracey.

806   ca. 1940s   Alice's Adventures in Wonderland

London; Glasgow, UK: The Children's Press   Harry Rountree

Undated. Ad for Nestle's milk on back cover.

807   ca. 1940s   Alice's Adventures in Wonderland

London; etc.: Thomas Nelson and Sons Ltd.   Helen Monro

In the series Nelson Classics. Introduction by Langford Reed. A dust jacket with picture of King and Queen is known. Varying copies are known with different lists of adverts; one is known in white dust jacket lettered in red, and another in blue dust jacket lettered in white. Later undated reprints are known in red cloth boards or dark blue paper boards.

808   ca. 1940s   Alice's Adventures in Wonderland

London: Thomas Nelson and Sons Ltd.   Helen Monro

Introduction by Langford Reed. Copies known in reddish orange cloth or blue leather with gilt lettering.

809   ca. 1940s   Alice's Adventures in Wonderland

London; Edinburgh, UK: Thomas Nelson and Sons Ltd.   Harry Rountree

Reprint.

810   ca. 1940s   Alice in Wonderland

London: W. Barton Ltd.   Unillustrated

In the series Mighty Midgets, No. 45. Miniature edition. A variant issue has an advert from Kiwi shoe polish on back cover.

811   ca. 1940s   Alice in Wonderland

London: W. H. CA   Jack Orr

Booklet with transfer pictures.

812   1950   Alice's Adventures in Wonderland

London: James Brodie, Ltd.   Thomas Maybank

In the series Brodie Books, No. 35. Paper wrappers.

813   1950   Alice's Adventures in Wonderland

London: Penguin Books Limited   John Tenniel

Reprint. A Puffin Book, 1st edition was 1946. Reprinted 1962, 1973, 1974, 1977, and 1997.

814   1950   Alice's Adventures in Wonderland and Bruno's Revenge

London; etc.: Thomas Nelson and Sons   Harry Rountree;
        E. Heber Thompson

Later reprint of the 1925 edition. Frontispiece line drawing of Lewis Carroll by E. Heber Thompson.

815   ca. 1950 Alice in Wonderland Story Book

London: Shaw's Children's Books   John Tenniel; Helen Haywood

Large format. Card wrappers. Front cover has color picture by Haywood and text pictures are colored versions of Tenniel.

816   ca. 1950s   Alice in Wonderland

London: Strato Publications   Alex A. Blum

Classics Illustrated (England) Series, No. 49. With a short biography of the author. Abridged.

817   ca. 1950 Alice's Adventures in Wonderland

London; Glasgow, UK: The Children's Press   Harry Rountree

Silver decorations on green cloth. 23 black-and-white illustrations.

818   ca. 1950 Alice in Wonderland
London: W. Foulsham & Co., Ltd.   Gil Dyer
Red cloth.

819   ca. 1950s   Alice's Adventures in Wonderland
London; Melbourne, VIC: Ward, Lock & Co.   Margaret W. Tarrant
Sunshine Series. 127 pp. with 16 leaves of color plates.

820   1951   Alice in Wonderland
London: Adprint Ltd., distributed by Max Parrish and Co., Ltd.   John Tenniel; Hugh Gee
3rd impression. Line drawings by Tenniel, 16 full-color pictures of scenes and figures created and photographed by
Hugh Gee. In matching dust jacket.

821   1951   Alice's Adventures in Wonderland
London; Glasgow, UK: Collins Clear-Type Press   G. W. Backhouse
Glazed pictorial paper boards. 8 color plates, in matching dust jacket. There is an undated reprint in pictorial boards
with 4 color plates.

822   1951   Walt Disney's Alice in Wonderland
London: Dean & Son Ltd.   Disney Studio
Copyright Walt Disney – Mickey Mouse Ltd. 1951. Glazed pictorial boards. Front cover has Tea-Party illustration and
back cover the Caterpillar.

823   ca. 1951 Walt Disney's Story of Alice in Wonderland and Cinderella
London; Glasgow, UK: Collins   Disney Studio
Glazed pictorial boards. Front cover has Tea-Party at the top and Cinderella at the bottom.

824   ca. 1951 Walt Disney's Alice in Wonderland
London; Glasgow, UK: Collins   Disney Studio
Adapted by Al Dempster. Pictorial paper wrappers. Front cover has Alice and Caterpillar with Hatter peeping around
a tree.

825   ca. 1951 Walt Disney's Alice in Wonderland
London; Glasgow, UK: Collins   Disney Studio
Adapted by Samuel Armstrong.

826   ca. 1951 Adventures from the Original Alice in Wonderland: Lewis Carroll's Story
Manchester, UK: World Distributors   Laszlo Matulay
Wonder Books 2 Series. Adapted and abridged for little children by Marcia Martin. In color.

827   1952   Alice's Adventures in Wonderland
London: A. & C. Black Ltd.   Charles Folkard
6th reprint. Light blue cloth. Pictorial dust jacket with blurb.

828   1952   Alice in Wonderland
London: Collins Clear-Type Press   Anonymous
5th impression. In The Silver Torch Series. Retold.

829   1952   Walt Disney's Alice in Wonderland
London; Glasgow, UK: Collins Clear-Type Press   Disney Studio
Collins Wonder Colour Book. Adapted by Samuel Armstrong. from the Disney motion picture.

830   1952   Alice in Wonderland
London: George G. Harrap & Company, Ltd.   Eileen Soper
2nd reprint of the 1946 edition.

831   1952   Alice's Adventures in Wonderland
London: Penguin Books   0140350381   John Tenniel, Elisa Trimby
Puffin Classics. Paperback. Elisa Trimby, color cover. Originally published in 1946, also reprinted 1949, 1955, 1985, and
1986 (twice).

832   1952   Alice's Adventures in Wonderland
London: Ward, Lock & Co.   Margaret W. Tarrant
New Royal Series. Tarrant illustration is the frontispiece only.

833   ca. 1952 Alice in Wonderland
London; Glasgow, UK: The Children's Press   Harry Rountree
Dated by inscription. Black-and-white illustrations. Green paper boards.

834   1953   Alice in Wonderland
London: Adprint Ltd., distributed by Max Parrish and Co., Ltd.   John Tenniel; Hugh Gee
4th impression. Line drawings by Tenniel, 16 full-color pictures of scenes and figures created and photographed by
Hugh Gee. In matching dust jacket.

835   1953   Alice's Adventures in Wonderland
London; Glasgow, UK: Collins Clear-Type Press   G. W. Backhouse
2nd reprint of the Backhouse edition. Glazed pictorial paper boards in matching dust jacket. 8 color plates.

836   1953   The Children's Alice
London: George G. Harrap & Company, Ltd.   Honor C. A. Appleton;
                                                                  Richard Ogle

8th reprint. Adapted by F. H. Lee. Paper wrappers. Front cover has picture by (Richard) Ogle. In corn yellow soft
cloth wrapper.

837   1953   Alice's Adventures in Wonderland
London; Edinburgh, UK: Thomas Nelson and Sons Ltd.   Helen Monro
Reprint of 1932 edition, in The Nelson Classics edition.

838   1954   Alice's Adventures in Wonderland
London; Glasgow, UK: Blackie & Son Ltd.   David Walsh
Red cloth stamped in silver.

839   1954   Alice's Adventures in Wonderland
London; Glasgow, UK: Collins Clear-Type Press   G. W. Backhouse
3rd reprint of the Backhouse edition. Pictorial boards with red cloth back strip. 8 color plates and numerous black-
and-white illustrations.

840   1954   The Children's Alice in Wonderland
London: George G. Harrap & Co., Ltd.   Honor C. A. Appleton;
                                                                 Richard Ogle

9th reprint in corn yellow soft cloth wrapper but with new title. Front cover picture by (Richard) Ogle.

841   1954   Alice in Wonderland
London: Juvenile Publications Ltd.   Willy Schermele
Glazed pictorial paper boards backed in bluish green cloth.

842   ca. 1954 Alice's Adventures in Wonderland
London: Hamlyn Classics   Pauline Baynes
Hamlyn Classics Series. Red paper boards.

843   ca. 1954 Alice in Wonderland
London: Purnell Books   Marjorie Torrey
Adapted and prepared under the supervision of Josette Frank. In the series Winner Books. The title page has
"Copyright 1946, 1949, 1950 and 1954 Random House, Inc." Presumably this is a UK edition of an original USA
Random House edition. There may be earlier UK editions but they have not been found. Lovett cites this as the first
British edition illustrated by Marjorie Torrey.

844   Not after 1954 Alice in Wonderland
London: Ward Lock & Co., Ltd.   Anonymous
Dated by inscription. 30 color plates.

845   1955   Alice in Wonderland
London: Adprint Ltd.; Random House Inc.; Purnell and Sons Ltd.   Marjorie Torrey
Reprint of 1946 copy.

846   1955   Alice's Adventures in Wonderland
London: Andrew Dakers Ltd.   Unknown
Hamlyn Classic.

847   1955   Alice's Adventures in Wonderland
London; Glasgow, UK: Collins Clear-Type Press   G. W. Backhouse
4th reprint of the Backhouse edition. Red paper boards. Now only 4 color plates and numerous black-and-white
illustrations.

848   1955   Alice's Adventures in Wonderland
London: Penguin Books   0140350381   John Tenniel; Elisa Trimby
Puffin Classics. Paperback. Elisa Trimby, color cover. Originally published in 1946, also reprinted 1949, 1952, 1985, and
1986 (twice).

849   ca. 1955 Alice in Wonderland
London: Publicity Products   Marjorie Torrey
Winner Books. Abridged by Josette Frank.

850   1956   Alice's Adventures in Wonderland
London; Glasgow, UK: Collins Clear-Type Press   G. W. Backhouse
5th reprint. Red paper boards. 4 color plates and numerous black-and-white illustrations. Copies known in dust
jacket.

851   1956   Alice in Wonderland
London: George G. Harrap and Company Ltd.   Eileen Soper
3rd reprint of the 1946 edition. Silver decorations on blue cloth. Pictorial dust jacket with blurb.

852   1956   Alice's Adventures in Wonderland
London: William Heinemann   Arthur Rackham
14th reprint of the 1st Rackham 1907 edition.

853   1956   Alice's Adventures in Wonderland
London: William Heinemann   Arthur Rackham
15th reprint of the 1st Rackham 1907 edition. A copy is known dated 1969.

854   1957   Alice's Adventures in Wonderland
London; Glasgow, UK: Collins Clear-Type Press   G. W. Backhouse
6th reprint. Red paper boards. 4 color plates and numerous black-and-white illustrations.

855   1957   Alice in Wonderland
[London]: Shaw's Children's Books   John Tenniel; Helen Haywood
Illustrated wrapper cover by Helen Haywood. Text pictures are colored versions by Tenniel. Abridged.

856   1957   Alice's Adventures in Wonderland
London: W. H. Allen & Co., Ltd.   Maraja
Pictorial paper-covered boards. Dust jacket replicates cover.

857   1958   Alice's Adventures in Wonderland
London; Glasgow, UK: Collins Clear-Type Press   G. W. Backhouse
7th reprint. Red paper boards. 4 color plates and numerous black-and-white illustrations.

858   1958   Alice in Wonderland
London: Collins Clear-Type Press   Anonymous
9th impression. In The Silver Torch Series. Retold.

859   1958   Alice's Adventures in Wonderland
London; Glasgow, UK: The Children's Press   Harry Rountree; Others
The New Challenge Library for Boys and Girls.

860   1958   Alice's Adventures in Wonderland
London: W. H. Allen & Co., Ltd.   Maraja
Pictorial paper-covered boards. In printed glassine dust jacket. Profusely illustrated in color.

861   1959   Alice's Adventures in Wonderland
London; Glasgow, UK: The Children's Press   Harry Rountree; Anonymous
Pictorial boards. In The New Challenge Series. 24 Rountree pictures and 5 pictures by an anonymous illustrator.

862   1959   Alice's Adventures in Wonderland
London; Glasgow, UK: Collins Clear-Type Press   G. W. Backhouse
8th reprint. Red paper boards. 4 color plates and numerous black-and-white illustrations.

863   1959   The Children's Alice in Wonderland
London: George G. Harrap & Co., Ltd.   Honor C. A. Appleton;
                                                       Richard Ogle
11th reprint. In corn yellow soft cloth wrapper but with new title. Front cover picture by (Richard) Ogle.

864   ca. 1950s   Alice's Adventures in Wonderland
London: Andrew Dakers   G. R. Ratcliff
Red paper boards. Dust jacket with picture signed GRR (Ratcliff), repeating frontispiece also by GRR.

865   ca. 1950s   Alice's Adventures in Wonderland
London; Glasgow, UK: Blackie & Sons, Ltd.   Pauline Baynes
In the series Blackie's Library of Famous Books. All Baynes editions have frontispiece and color picture by her on dust jacket, and a vignette of Alice on the title page. Several variant bindings are known: green paper boards; red paper boards; yellow paper boards; green cloth.

866   ca. 1950s   Alice's Adventures in Wonderland
London; Glasgow, UK: Blackie & Sons, Ltd.   Pauline Baynes
In the series Blackie Tower Classics. Red paper boards with no frontispiece.

867 ca. 1950s   Alice's Adventures in Wonderland
Leicester, UK: Brown Watson   Pauline Baynes; Hildegard Bone
Basically, the Blackie edition text. In the series Abbey Classics. The title page vignette is replaced by Abbey logo.
Laminated red boards with picture by Hildegard Bone on front cover.

868 ca. 1950s   Alice in Wonderland
London: Hampster Books   Anonymous
78-page adaptation with 26 illustrations. In the Early Reader Series 4. Illustrated paper boards, red cloth spine. Dust
jacket. A variant is known with blue cloth spine.

869 ca. 1950s   Alice's Adventures in Wonderland
London: Juvenile Productions   A. A. Nash
Pictorial boards with red cloth spine. Many full-color plates.

870 ca. 1950s   Alice in Wonderland
London: Mellifont Press   Unknown
Children's Classics T13 Series. Abridged 48 pp.

871 ca. 1950s   Alice in Wonderland
London: Murray's Sales & Service Co.   Anonymous
A miniature book. Treasure House logo on back cover. Author misspelled as "Lewis Carrol." One of a set of 12 books
called Classic Fairy Tales. Packaged in a box that looked like a bookshop with doors that swung open.

872 ca. 1950s   Alice's Adventures in Wonderland
London: Peal Press   Pauline Baynes; Anonymous
Basically, a reprint of the two Blackie editions of ca. 1950s illustrated by Baynes but no frontispiece. Dust jacket
picture by anonymous illustrator.

873 ca. 1950s   Alice in Wonderland
London: Rylee Ltd.   Reinhard Volker
Retold by Marie Joseph.

874 ca. 1950s   Alice in Wonderland
London: Sandle's   Anonymous
12 pp. card covers.

875 ca. 1950s   Alice's Adventures in Wonderland
London: The Sunshine Press   Harry Rountree; Anonymous
Large quarto. Laminated red paper boards. Front cover and some of the text pictures are by anonymous illustrator.

876 ca. 1950s   Alice's Adventures in Wonderland
London: Thomas Nelson and Sons Ltd.   Helen Monro
Introduction by Langford Reed. Red cloth. 9 full-page black-and-white illustrations.

877 ca. 1950s   Alice in Wonderland
Oadby, UK: Thorpe & Porter   Alex A. Blum
Classics Illustrated Series, No. 49.

878 ca. 1950s   Alice's Adventures in Wonderland
London: W. H. Allen & Co., Ltd.   Maraja
Glazed pictorial paper boards in large format. Color pictures on every page.

879 1960   Alice's Adventures in Wonderland

London: Hutchinson Educational Ltd.   Lewis Carroll; Douglas Hall
Junior Classics, edited by M. W. and G. Thomas.

880   1961   Alice's Adventures in Wonderland
London; Glasgow, UK: Collins Clear-Type Press   G. W. Backhouse
9th reprint. Red paper boards. Has only 1 color plate, the frontispiece.

881   1961   Alice in Wonderland
London: George G. Harrap and Company Ltd.   Eileen Soper
24th reprint of the 1946 edition.

882   1961   Alice in Wonderland
London: J. M. Dent & Sons. New York: E. P. Dutton   Lewis Carroll; Robin Jacques
First use of the term An Everyman Paperback. Preface by Roger Lancelyn Green, cover design by Robin Jacques. 37 black-and-white illustrations by Lewis Carroll. Preface first added in this edition. Reprinted in 1966, 1972, 1974, and 1976.

883   1961   Alice in Wonderland
London; Glasgow, UK: The Children's Press   Normy Robinson
1st edition thus. Red paper boards. Dust jacket. Reprinted 1963, 1965, 1971, and 1974.

884   1961   Alice's Adventures in Wonderland
London: The Folio Society   John Tenniel
1st edition. In publisher's slipcase. Reissued in 1990.

885   1961   Alice's Adventures in Wonderland and Bruno's Revenge
London; etc.: Thomas Nelson and Sons   Harry Rountree;
                                                                E. Heber Thompson

Later reprint of the 1925 edition. Frontispiece line drawing of Lewis Carroll by E. Heber Thompson.

886   ca. 1961 Alice in Wonderland
London: J. W. Dent   Lewis Carroll
Everyman's Library. Prefatory note by Roger Lancelyn Green. Paperback.

887   1962   Alice in Wonderland
London: Golden Pleasure Books   Leonard; Anonymous
Illustrated paper boards with picture signed Leonard. In the series Tales Told for Young Readers.

888   1962   Alice's Adventures in Wonderland
London: Penguin Books Limited   John Tenniel
Reprint. A Puffin Book, 1st edition was 1946. Reprinted 1950, 1973, 1974, 1977, and 1997.

889   1962   Alice's Adventures in Wonderland
London: The Folio Society   John Tenniel
Reissue of the 1961 edition. In publisher's slipcase.

890   ca. 1962 Alice in Wonderland
London: Hampster Books   Anonymous
Pictorial boards, red spine. Retold for Young Readers.

891   1963   Alice in Wonderland
London: Golden Pleasure Books   Leonard; Anonymous
2nd impression. In the series Tales Told for Young Readers.

892   1963   Alice in Wonderland
London: J. M. Dent   John Tenniel; Henry Holiday
Kings Treasures of Literature Series. Introduction by Guy Pocock. Includes *Snark* and several poems from *Sylvie and Bruno*. First published in 1930.

893   1963   Alice in Wonderland
London: Odhams Press Ltd.   Livraghi; Aquenza
In the series Odham's Golden Hour Story Books. Specially retold by Jane Carruth.

894   1963   Alice in Wonderland
London; Glasgow, UK: The Children's Press   Normy Robinson
Boys' and Girls' Library. Reprinted 1965, 1971, and 1974.

895   1964   The Children's Alice in Wonderland
London: George G. Harrap   Honor C.A. Appleton;
                                                                      Richard Ogle
Abridged by F. H. Lee. First published in January 1936. Front cover picture by (Richard) Ogle.

896   1964   Alice in Wonderland
London: Golden Pleasure Books   Leonard; Anonymous
3rd impression. Not seen. In the series Tales Told for Young Readers.

897   1964   Alice in Wonderland
London; Melbourne, VIC: Ward Lock & Co., Ltd.   Alice Huertas
A Rainbow Story Book 16. Glazed paper over boards. Illustrated endpapers. Color illustrations on both covers.

898   1964   Alice in Wonderland
London; Melbourne, VIC: Ward, Lock & Co.   Anonymous
Rainbow Story Book: 16. Adaptation. 93 pp. Illustrated.

899   ca. 1964 Alice in Wonderland
Paulton, UK; London: Purnell Books   Marjorie Torrey
Winner Books. Josette Frank, editor.

900   1965   Alice in Wonderland
London: Blackie   J. S. Goodall
In the series Stories Old and New.

901   1965   Alice in Wonderland
London; Glasgow, UK: The Children's Press   Normy Robinson
A later impression of the 1961 edition. Reprinted 1961, 1963, 1971, and 1974.

902   ca. 1965 Alice in Wonderland
Hackney, UK: L. Miller & Co. Ltd.   Rose Garcia; D. Hall
Card covers. Much abbreviated text. Appears to be a translation of a foreign edition by someone who does not know the original. D. Hall did cover only.

903   1966   Alice in Wonderland
London: Bancroft & Co.   Anonymous
1st reissue of the Bancroft 1st edition, also of 1966. In pictorial boards.

904   1966   Alice in Wonderland
London: Bancroft & Co.   Anonymous
1st edition. A Bancroft Classics. Red paper boards. Dust jacket.

905   1966   Alice in Wonderland
London: Dent. New York: E. P. Dutton   Lewis Carroll

Everyman Paperback. First appeared in the Everyman series in 1929. Preface first added in the 1961 edition.
Reprinted in 1972, 1974, and 1976.

906   1966   Alice in Wonderland
London: Golden Pleasure Books   Sergio Leone

907   1966   Alice in Wonderland
London: J. M. Dent & Sons. New York: E. P. Dutton   0460018361   Lewis Carroll; Robin Jacques

Later use of the term An Everyman Paperback. 1st edition was 1961. Preface by Roger Lancelyn Green, cover design
by Robin Jacques. 37 black-and-white illustrations by Lewis Carroll. Reprinted in 1972, 1974, and 1976.

908   1966   Alice in Wonderland
London: J. M. Dent & Sons. New York: E. P. Dutton   Lewis Carroll; Brian Robins

Later use of the term Everyman Paperback. 1st edition was 1961. Preface by Roger Lancelyn Green. 37 black-and-
white illustrations by Lewis Carroll. Cover design by Brian Robins. Dust jacket.

909   1966   Alice in Wonderland
London: Odhams Press, Ltd.   L'Alpino

An Odham's All-Color Book. Retold by Jane Carruth. A later undated issue is also known.

910   1966   Alice's Adventures in Wonderland
London: The Folio Society   John Tenniel

2nd reissue of the 1961 edition. Illustrations printed in red.

911   1966   Alice's Adventures in Wonderland
London; Melbourne, VIC: Ward Lock & Co., Ltd.   Alice Huertas

1st edition thus. In the Royal Series. Dust jacket with color picture similar to the frontispiece. Illustrations uncredited
but by Alice Huertas.

912   1966   Alice's Adventures in Wonderland
London; Melbourne, VIC: Ward, Lock & Co.   Alice Huertas; Anonymous

Royal Series, No. 8. Unsigned frontispiece plus four line drawings.

913   1966   Alice's Adventures in Wonderland
London: William Heinemann   Arthur Rackham

16th reprint of the 1st Rackham 1907 edition. Proem by Austin Dobson. Binding is now maroon cloth. One copy is in
a pictorial dust jacket. Another copy is dated 1972.

914   ca. 1966 Alice in Wonderland
Banbury, UK: Banbury Books   John Tenniel; Jonathan Miller

Introduction by Woodrow Wyatt. Contains 25 color plates from the Jonathan Miller BBC TV version.

915   ca. 1966 Alice's Adventures in Wonderland
London; Glasgow, UK: Blackie & Sons, Ltd.   Pauline Baynes

Reprint of ca. 1950s Blackie's Library of Famous Books. Green cloth in dust jacket.

916   ca. 1966 Alice in Wonderland: Specially Adapted for Young People
London: Ward Lock & Co., Ltd.   Anonymous

Rainbow Story Book.

917   1967   Alice in Wonderland

London: Denis Dobson   Ralph Steadman
Hard cover and paperback.

918   1967   Alice in Wonderland
Brighton, UK: Litor   M. Gorde
Abridged by D. M. (Dorothy May) Priestly. Silhouette Series.

919   1967   Alice in Wonderland
London; Glasgow, UK: The Children's Press   Normy Robinson; Anonymous
A later impression. In the series The Boys and Girls Library Classics. Laminated full-color pictorial boards with front
cover picture by anonymous illustrator of Alice approaching the Tea-Party. With a different anonymous illustrator of
the same scene on rear cover.

920   1967   Alice's Adventures in Wonderland
London: William Heinemann.   Arthur Rackham
17th reprint of the 1st Rackham 1907 edition. A copy dated 1974 is known.

921   1968   Alice in Wonderland
London: Bancroft & Co.   Anonymous
2nd reissue of the 1966 Bancroft edition.

922   1968   Alice in Wonderland
London: R. Watts   John Tenniel
Large Type Edition.

923   1968   Alice in Wonderland
London; Glasgow, UK: The Children's Press   Normy Robinson; Anonymous
A later impression. In the series The Boys and Girls Library Classics. Laminated full-color pictorial boards with front
cover picture by anonymous illustrator of Alice approaching the Tea-Party. With a different anonymous illustrator of
the same scene on rear cover.

924   1968   Alice's Adventures in Wonderland
London: W. H. Allen & Co., Ltd.   Maraja
Glazed pictorial paper boards in large format. Color pictures on every page.

925   1968   Alice in Wonderland
London: Ward Lock & Co., Ltd.   Alice Huertas
A Rainbow Story Book. Reprint of the 1964 edition.

926   1968   Alice in Wonderland
London; Melbourne, VIC: Ward, Lock & Co.   Anonymous
Rainbow Story Book. Abridged. 92 pp. Reprint of the 1964 edition.

927   1968   Alice in Wonderland
Manchester, UK: World Distributors, Ltd.   Janet Johnstone;
                                                                   Anne Grahame Johnstone
1st edition. Giant Fairy Story. Laminated pictorial boards. Full-color. Pictures on every page.

928   1969   Alice in Wonderland
London: Armada Paperbacks   0006925456   John Tenniel
1st Armada edition.

929   1969   Alice in Wonderland

Alice in a World of Wonderlands

London: Bancroft & Co.   0430000693   Anonymous
3rd reissue of the 1966 Bancroft edition.

930   1969   Alice in Wonderland
London: Dean & Sons, Ltd.   0603047572   Rene Cloke
Retold and illustrated by Rene Cloke. A Dean Gold Medal Book. Full-color pictures on every page. Glazed paper boards with extra picture on front. This edition has Rene Cloke's 3rd set of illustrations.

931   1969   Alice in Wonderland
London: May Fair   John Tenniel
Paperback.

932   1969   Alice in Wonderland
London: Mayflower   John Tenniel
A Mayflower paperback. A companion book to the *Looking-Glass* edition of 1969 by Mayflower.

933   1969   Alice's Adventures in Wonderland
Paulton, UK; London: Purnell & Sons   Rosemary Honeybourne
1st edition.

934   1969   Alice in Wonderland
London; Glasgow, UK: The Children's Press   Normy Robinson; Anonymous
A later impression. In the series The Boys and Girls Library Classics. Laminated full-color pictorial boards with front cover picture by anonymous illustrator of Alice approaching the Tea-Party.

935   1969   Alice in Wonderland
London; Glasgow, UK: William Collins Sons & Co.   John Tenniel
Armada Paperbacks for Boys and Girls.

936   1969   Alice's Adventures in Wonderland
London: William Heinemann   Arthur Rackham
18th reprint of the 1st Rackham 1907 edition.

937   ca. 1969 Alice in Wonderland
London: Brown Watson   Jose Luis Macias
Card covers and much abbreviated text. Author misspelled as "Lewis Carrol." The 1970s edition has it correctly spelled. Illustrated wrappers.

938   ca. 1969 Alice in Wonderland
Manchester, UK: World Distributors, Ltd.   0723538662   R. Canaider
A Giant Fairy Story.

939   ca. 1960s   Alice in Wonderland
Hackney, UK: L. Miller & Co.   D. Hall
Card covers. Front cover has triangular motif of A Jolly Miller Production.

940   ca. 1960s   Alice in Wonderland
London: Murray's Sales and Services Co.   Anonymous
One of 12 Classic Fairy Tales in a box designed as a bookshop with an opening as a wardrobe.

941   ca. 1960s   Alice in Wonderland
London: Rylee Ltd.   Hidalgo
Retold by Angela Bigton in A Storytime Book.

942	1970	Alice's Adventures in Wonderland		
		London: Abbey Classics, a division of Murray's Sales and Service	009701340	Pauline Baynes; Anonymous

Pictorial paper boards, with anonymous picture. Title page verso has Murray's Sales and Service Co. Title page Baynes vignette returns and Abbey logo added.

943	1970	Alice in Wonderland		
		London: Hamlyn	0601073584	Guy Doré

Small format. In the series Gold Star Library. An English version of a French original. Some color illustrations.

944	ca. 1970	Alice in Wonderland		
		London: Blackie	0216885744	A. A. Nash

Early Readers Series, No. 4. Blackie's Library of Famous Books 13.

945	1971	Alice's Adventures in Wonderland		
		London: Abbey Classics, a division of Murray's Sales and Service		Pauline Baynes; Anonymous

Reprint of the 1970 edition.

946	1971	Alice in Wonderland		
		London: Bancroft & Co.	0430000693	Anonymous

4th reissue of the 1966 Bancroft edition.

947	1971	Alice in Wonderland		
		London: Bancroft & Co.	0430000693	Anonymous

5th reissue of the 1966 Bancroft edition.

948	1971	Alice in Wonderland		
		London: Brown Watson		Marie-Jose Maury

16-page adaptation.

949	1971	Alice in Wonderland		
		London: J. M. Dent & Sons	0460018361	Lewis Carroll

Everyman's Library, No. 836, Reprint.

950	1971	Alice in Wonderland		
		London; Glasgow, UK: The Children's Press	0001660136	Normy Robinson

Boys' and Girls' Library. 1st printing 1963. Reprinted 1965 and 1974.

951	1972	Alice in Wonderland		
		London: Bancroft & Co.	0430000693	Anonymous

6th reissue of the 1966 Bancroft edition.

952	1972	Alice in Wonderland		
		London: Bancroft & Co.	0430000693	Anonymous

7th reissue and the 2nd of 1972. From the 1966 Bancroft edition.

953	1972	Alice in Wonderland		
		London: Bancroft & Co.	0430000693	Anonymous

8th reissue of the 1966 Bancroft edition.

954	1972	Alice in Wonderland		
		London: Bancroft & Co.	0430000693	Anonymous

9th reissue and the 2nd of 1972. From the 1966 Bancroft edition.

955   1972   Alice in Wonderland
London: Dent. New York: E. P. Dutton   9780460018364   Lewis Carroll
Everyman Paperback. First appeared in the Everyman series in 1929. Preface first added in the 1961 edition.
Reprinted in 1966, 1974, and 1976.

956   1972   Alice in Wonderland
London: J. M. Dent & Sons. New York: E. P. Dutton   0460018361   Lewis Carroll; Robin Jacques
Later use of the term An Everyman Paperback. 1st edition was 1961. Preface by Roger Lancelyn Green, cover design
by Robin Jacques. 37 black-and-white illustrations by Lewis Carroll. Reprinted in 1966, 1974, and 1976.

957   1972   Alice's Adventures in Wonderland
London: William Heinemann   0434958565   Arthur Rackham
19th reprint of the 1st Rackham 1907 edition.

958   1972   Alice in Wonderland
Manchester, UK: World Distributors   9780723505150   Janet Johnstone;
                                                                    Anne Grahame Johnstone

1st reprint of the 1968 edition. In pink laminated pictorial boards.

959   1973   Alice in Wonderland
London: Bancroft & Co.   0430000693   Anonymous
10th reissue of the 1966 Bancroft edition.

960   1973   Alice in Wonderland
London: Bancroft & Co.   0430000693   Anonymous
11th reissue of the 1966 Bancroft edition.

961   1973   Alice's Adventures in Wonderland
London: Pan Books Ltd.   0330236148   Peter Richardson
Paperback. 2nd printing. A Piccolo Book. Includes 22 color pictures from the Shaftel Film.

962   1973   Alice's Adventures in Wonderland
London: Penguin Books Ltd.   0140350381   John Tenniel
Reprint. A Puffin Book, 1st edition was 1946. Reprinted 1950, 1962, 1974, 1977, and 1997.

963   1973   Alice in Wonderland
London: Purnell Books   0361024630   Disney Studio
Adapted by Al Dempster. Laminated pictorial boards. Styled A Walt Disney Classic.

964   1973   Alice in Wonderland
Manchester, UK: World Distributors   0723505122   Janet Johnstone;
                                                                Anne Grahame Johnstone

2nd reprint. In pink laminated pictorial boards.

965   1974   Alice in Wonderland
London: Bancroft & Co.   0430000693   Anonymous
12th reissue of the 1966 Bancroft edition.

966   1974   Alice in Wonderland
Maidenhead, UK: Bancroft & Co.   0430000693   Anonymous
A Bancroft Classics. Pictorial boards. Black-and-white frontispiece and illustrations.

967   1974   Alice in Wonderland
London: Dean & Son Ltd.   0603057683   Georgina Hargreaves
Retold and illustrated by Georgina Hargreaves. Glazed pictorial boards.

968   1974   Alice in Wonderland
London: J. M. Dent & Sons. New York: E. P. Dutton   0460018361   Lewis Carroll; Robin Jacques
Later use of the term An Everyman Paperback. 1st edition was 1961. Preface by Roger Lancelyn Green, cover design
by Robin Jacques. 37 black-and-white illustrations by Lewis Carroll. Reprinted in 1966, 1972, and 1976.

969   1974   Alice in Wonderland
London: J. M. Dent & Sons. New York: E. P. Dutton   0460018361   Lewis Carroll; Brian Robins
Later use of the term An Everyman Paperback. 1st edition was 1961. Preface by Roger Lancelyn Green. 37 black-and-
white illustrations by Lewis Carroll. Cover design by Brian Robins.

970   1974   Alice in Wonderland
London: J. M. Dent. New York: E. P. Dutton   9780460018364   Lewis Carroll
Everyman Paperback. First appeared in the Everyman series in 1929. Preface first added in the 1961 edition.
Reprinted in 1966, 1972, and 1976.

971   1974   Alice's Adventures in Wonderland
London: Published by Penguin Books for Olivetti   Kuniyoshi Kaneko
Reprint of a Penguin edition stating, "This book is not for sale." Red cloth with pictorial plate on front cover.

972   1974   Alice's Adventures in Wonderland
London: Penguin Books Limited   0140350381   John Tenniel
Reprint. A Puffin Book, 1st edition was 1946. Reprinted 1950, 1962, 1973, 1977, and 1997.

973   1974   Walt Disney presents Alice in Wonderland
Paulton, UK; London: Purnell Books   Disney Studio
A Square Story Book.

974   1974   Alice in Wonderland
London: Purnell Books   9780361034500   Gordon King
Retold by Jane Carruth. Glazed pictorial boards. In the Purnell Color Classics Series.

975   1974   Alice in Wonderland
London; Glasgow, UK: The Children's Press   0001660136   Normy Robinson
Boys' and Girls' Library. 1st printing in 1963. Reprinted 1965 and 1971.

976   1974   Alice in Wonderland
London; Glasgow, UK: The Children's Press   0001660136   Normy Robinson
The Boys' and Girls' Library Classics reprint.

977   1974   Alice's Adventures in Wonderland
London; Glasgow, UK: The Children's Press   9780001660137   Normy Robinson
The Boys' and Girls' Library Classics.

978   1975   Alice's Adventures in Wonderland
London: Elsevier-Phaidon   0729000354   Moritz Kennel
1st English edition. A version of what is believed to be a French original. Bright yellow cloth. Numerous full-page
color plates. Pictorial dust jacket with blurb.

979   1975   Alice in Wonderland

Brighton, UK: Litor Publishers   Hutchings

Illustrated card covers. Abbreviated text. Front cover has Infant Series and another copy has Treasure Series. Back cover on both has at base Children's Books Ltd., Stafford.

980   1975   Alice in Wonderland
Manchester, UK: World Distributors   0723505152   Janet Johnstone;
                                                                Anne Grahame Johnstone

2nd impression of 1968 edition.

981   1975   Alice in Wonderland
Manchester, UK: World Distributors   0723546983   Hutchings

As in the 1975 Litor edition illustrated by Hutchings. Front cover lists Favourite Series.

982   1975   Alice in Wonderland
London: World International Publishing   R. Canaider

A Learn to Read Story Book. Pictorial wraps. Color illustrations on every page.

983   ca. 1975   Alice in Wonderland and Hansel and Gretel
London: Sandle Brothers Ltd.   0854130438   D'Agostini

Pictorial paper-covered boards. The illustrator was identified as D'Agostini from a 1985 New York edition with an illustration signed "D'Agostini 75."

984   1976   Walt Disney's Greatest Stories
[Maidenhead, UK]: [Purnell] for Marks and Spencer   0361939085   Disney Studio
Includes *Alice in Wonderland*, Snow White, and Cinderella.

985   1976   Alice's Adventures in Wonderland
London: Academy Editions. New York: St. Martin's Press   0856701890   John Tenniel
Glazed paper wrappers. Giant Illustrated Edition.

986   1976   Alice in Wonderland
London: Dent; New York: E. P. Dutton   9780460018364   Lewis Carroll

Everyman Paperback. First appeared in the Everyman series in 1929. Preface first added in the 1961 edition. Reprinted in 1966, 1972, and 1974.

987   1976   Alice in Wonderland
London: J. M. Dent & Sons. New York: E. P. Dutton   0460018361   Lewis Carroll; Robin Jacques

Later use of the term "An Everyman Paperback." 1st edition was 1961. Preface by Roger Lancelyn Green, cover design by Robin Jacques. 37 black-and-white illustrations by Lewis Carroll. Reprints in 1966, 1972, and 1974.

988   1976   Alice in Wonderland
London: J. M. Dent & Sons. New York: E. P. Dutton   0460018361   Lewis Carroll; Brian Robins

Reprint of the 1961 An Everyman Paperback. Preface by Roger Lancelyn Green. 37 black-and-white illustrations by Lewis Carroll. Cover design by Brian Robins.

989   1976   Alice in Wonderland
London: Longman   0582534143   Carol Tarrant

Simplified and brought within the vocabulary of the New Method Supplementary Readers, Stage 1. D. K. Swan, editor. Paperback.

990   1976   Alice's Adventures in Wonderland
Harlow, UK: Longman Group   0582534143   Carol Tarrant
2nd impression.

991   1976   Alice's Adventures in Wonderland
Harlow, UK: Longman Group   0582534143   Carol Tarrant
In wrappers. Simplified and brought within the vocabulary of the New Method Supplementary Readers, Stage 1, by
D. K Swan.

992   1976   Lewis Carroll's "Alice in Wonderland"
Maidenhead, UK: Purnell Books   0361034504   Gordon King
Retold by Jane Carruth.

993   1977   Alice in Wonderland
London: Bancroft & Co.   0430000693   Anonymous
Now styled "A Purnell Children's Classic."

994   1977   Alice in Wonderland
London: New English Library   0450032787   Disney Studio
1st New English Library paperback edition. Dated February 1977. A Read and Colour Book Series.

995   1977   Alice's Adventures in Wonderland
London: Penguin Books Limited   0140350381   John Tenniel
A Puffin Book, 1st edition was 1946. Reprinted 1950, 1962, 1973, 1974, and 1997.

996   1977   Alice's Adventures in Wonderland
London; Sydney, NSW: Piccolo Pan Books Ltd.   0330236148   Peter Richardson
Reissue of the 1973 edition. Color picture on cover by Peter Richardson. A Piccolo Book. Includes 22 color pictures
from the Shaftel Film.

997   1977   Alice in Wonderland
Maidenhead, UK: Purnell Books   036103556X   McB
A Purnell Classic. Illustration by McB is only of the cover.

998   1977   Alice's Adventures in Wonderland
London: William Heinemann   9780440000693   Arthur Rackham
21st reprint of the 1st Rackham 1907 edition.

999   1978   Alice in Wonderland
London: Bancroft & Co.   0430000693   Anonymous
1st reprint of the 1977 edition. Now styled A Purnell Children's Classic.

1000   1978   Alice in Wonderland
London; Sydney, NSW; Auckland, NZ; Toronto, ON: 0340233583   Art Studium
Hodder and Stoughton
English version of original Spanish edition of 1978.

1001   1978   Alice in Wonderland
London: Marvel Comics   094893607X   Frank Bolle
Comic book.

1002   1979   Alice in Wonderland
London: Armada Paperbacks   0006916198   John Tenniel
A reprint of the 1969 Armada edition with price change and with cover picture of Alice with Duchess. This edition
was originally published in London by Collins in 1955.

1003   1979   Alice in Wonderland

London: Hodder and Stoughton 0340233583 Art Studium

English version of original Spanish edition of 1978.

1004 1979 Alice's Adventures in Wonderland
London: Longman Group 9780582534148 Carol Tarrant
New impression. New Method Supplementary Readers, Stage 1.

1005 1979 Walt Disney Presents "Alice in Wonderland"
Maidenhead, UK: Purnell Books 0361043996 Disney Studio
A Square Story Book.

1006 1979 Alice's Adventures in Wonderland
Maidenhead, UK: Purnell Books 0361043961 Blasco
In the series Purnell Picture Classics. 32 pp.

1007 1979 Alice in Wonderland
London; Glasgow, UK: The Children's Press 0001800136 Normy Robinson; Anonymous
A later impression. Laminated full-color pictorial boards with front cover picture by anonymous illustrator of Alice approaching the Tea-Party.

1008 ca. 1970s Alice in Wonderland
London: Brown Watson 0709702175 Jose Luis Macias
Card covers with much-abbreviated text. In the 1969 edition the author is misspelled as "Lewis Carrol." This 1970s edition has it correctly spelled as "Carroll."

1009 ca. 1970s The Goose Girl / Alice in Wonderland
London: Brown Watson Jose Luis Macias
Glazed pictorial boards. Front cover has picture of Goose Girl, and Alice with Caterpillar. Later edition has picture of Goose Girl only.

1010 ca. 1970s The Goose Girl / Alice in Wonderland
London: Hemma Jose Luis Macias
Glazed pictorial boards. Front cover has picture of Goose Girl, and Alice with Caterpillar. Later edition has picture of Goose Girl only.

1011 ca. 1970s Alice in Wonderland
Maidenhead, UK: Sugar Puffs Library Unillustrated
Paperback. Front cover has photograph of girl with toy rabbit.

1012 1980 Alice's Adventures in Wonderland
London: Longman Group 9780582534148 Carol Tarrant
3rd impression.

1013 1980 Alice's Adventures in Wonderland
London: Octopus Books Ltd. 0706413121 John Tenniel
Treasury of Children's Classics. Red paper boards. Later edition in yellow paper boards.

1014 1981 Alice's Adventures in Wonderland
London: Book Club Associates 0333290380 John Tenniel
New Children's Edition but with this special imprint for the Book Club Associates.

1015 1981 Alice's Adventures in Wonderland
London: Octopus Books 0906320941 John Tenniel; Anne Isseyegh
Pictures colored by Anne Isseyegh. Blue paper boards, spine has St Michael. Front endpaper lists Marks and Spencer plc.

1016	1981	Alice's Adventures in Wonderland		
		London: Oxford University Press		John Tenniel
		The Oxford Library of the World's Great Books. Gray leather.		

1017	1981	Pinocchio / Alice in Wonderland		
		London: Ramboro Books	086288ooX	Iborro
		Card covers. Abbreviated text.		

1018	1981	Alice's Adventures in Wonderland		
		London: Victor Gollancz, Ltd.	0575032634	Justin Todd
		1st edition. Blue cloth. Dust jacket.		

1019	1981	Alice in Wonderland		
		Manchester, UK: World International Publishing Ltd.	0723538662	R. Canaider

1020	1982	Alice in Wonderland		
		London: Bancroft & Co.	0430000693	Anonymous
		2nd reprint. Now styled "A Purnell Children's Classic."		

1021	1982	Alice's Adventures in Wonderland		
		London: Hodder and Stoughton	0340283947	Gwynedd Hudson
		Reissue of the 1922 edition. Red leather. Limited to 500 numbered copies. Plates tipped in. A standard edition of this was issued in red cloth boards.		

1022	1982	Alice's Adventures in Wonderland		
		London: Hodder and Stoughton	0340283955	Gwynedd Hudson
		Navy blue bonded leather. An edition published for American Express that used overstocks of the earlier 1982 issue.		

1023	1982	Alice's Adventures in Wonderland		
		London: Octopus Books Ltd.	9780862730055	John Tenniel
		Reprint of 1981 Octopus edition.		

1024	1982	Alice's Adventures in Wonderland		
		Bristol, UK: Purnell Books	0361053355	Anonymous
		A "Purnell Children's Classic."		

1025	1983	Alice in Wonderland		
		London: J. M. Dent & Sons. New York: E. P. Dutton	0460118366	Lewis Carroll; Diana Stanley
		Reprint of the 1961 An Everyman Paperback. Preface by Roger Lancelyn Green. Cover design by Diana Stanley. 37 black-and-white illustrations by Lewis Carroll.		

1026	1984	Alice in Wonderland		
		London: Bancroft & Co.	0430000693	Anonymous
		3rd reprint. "A Purnell Children's Classic."		

1027	1984	Alice in Wonderland		
		London: Brown Watson	0709702620	Carlos Busquets
		In a box in the style of a house titled My House of Fairy Tales with 5 other books, all printed concertina style. UK version of a Spanish original.		

1028	1984	Alice's Adventures in Wonderland		
		Harmondsworth, UK: Penguin	0140350381	John Tenniel
		Reprint of the first 1984 edition.		

1029   1984   Alice's Adventures in Wonderland
London: Penguin Books   0140350381   John Tenniel, Elisa Trimby
Puffin Classics. Paperback. Elisa Trimby, color cover. Originally published in 1946, also reprinted 1949, 1952, 1955, 1985, and 1986 (twice).

1030   1984   Alice's Adventures in Wonderland
London: Puffin Books   John Tenniel
Later reprinted in the same year.

1031   1984   Alice in Wonderland and Other Stories
Paulton, UK: Purnell Books   9780361064286   Disney Studio
In the series Disney's Little Library.

1032   1984   Alice's Adventures in Wonderland
London: Victor Gollancz, Ltd.   0575032634   Justin Todd
A later reprint of the 1981 edition. Blue cloth with gilt title. 22 full-page color plates.

1033   1984   Alice in Wonderland
Manchester, UK: World International Publishing Ltd.   0723575975   Anonymous
In the series Best Loved Stories. Abridged edition. Front cover picture of Tea-Party.

1034   1985   Alice in Wonderland
London: Armada Paperbacks   0006925456   John Tenniel
A reprint of the 1969 Armada edition with cover picture from BBC TV production.

1035   1985   Alice's Adventures in Wonderland
London: Bell and Hyman   0713525428   Alice B Woodward; Sue Shields
St. Martin's Illustrated Library of Standard Authors. Full complement of Woodward pictures from the 1913 edition plus 8 colored plates by Shields. Reprint of the G. Bell 1920 edition.

1036   1985   Alice's Adventures in Wonderland
London: Bracken Books   0946495610   Gwynedd Hudson
Red paper boards. Text is a facsimile of the Hodder and Stoughton editions. Pictures in black-and-white, with orange highlights. In illustrated color dust jacket.

1037   1985   Alice's Adventures in Wonderland
London: Chancellor Press   0907486797   Arthur Rackham
Facsimile edition. Plain glazed cream paper boards, in illustrated dust jacket with picture. Poem by Austin Dobson. 13 color plates.

1038   1985   Alice in Wonderland, Lewis Carroll's Famous Story
Clifford, UK: Privately printed by Edward Wakeling   Harry Furniss
Card wrappers. Limited to 42 numbered copies. A facsimile of 3 fortnightly installments, numbers 28, 29, and 30, of The Children's Encyclopedia, edited by Arthur Mee. Published in 1908–1909.

1039   1985   The Adventures of Alice in Wonderland
London: Grandreams, Ltd.   0862273293   Ann McKie; Ken McKie
Retold and illustrated by Ann and Ken McKie.

1040   1985   Alice's Adventures in Wonderland
London: Methuen Children's Books   0416960006   Michael Hague
1st English edition of an American original.

1041   1985   Alice's Adventures in Wonderland

London: Penguin Books   0140350381   John Tenniel; Elisa Trimby

Puffin Classics. Paperback. Elisa Trimby, color cover. Originally published in 1946, also reprinted 1949, 1952, 1955, 1984, and 1986 (twice).

1042   1985   Walt Disney presents Alice in Wonderland

Paulton, UK: Purnell Books   0361024630   Disney Studio

Large format. Blue glazed boards with front cover picture of Alice under a tree.

1043   ca. 1985 Alice in Wonderland

London: Brown Watson   Anonymous

A shaped book.

1044   1986   Alice in Wonderland

London: Armada Paperbacks   0006925456   John Tenniel

A reprint of the 1969 Armada edition with cover picture of Alice and White Rabbit.

1045   1986   Alice's Adventures in Wonderland

London: Chancellor Press   0009074867   Arthur Rackham

1st reprint. Glazed cream paper boards. Front cover has the same picture as the dust jacket.

1046   1986   Walt Disney's Alice in Wonderland

London: Fleetway Books   0850376386   Disney Studio

Large format. Glazed pictorial paper boards. Front cover picture of Tea-Party.

1047   1986   Alice in Wonderland

London: Fleetway Books   0850378575   Disney Studio

Paperback. A smaller version of the earlier 1986 edition.

1048   1986   Alice in Wonderland

Loughborough, UK: Ladybird Books   0721409679   Debbie Boon-Jenkins

Ladybird Children's Classics. Glazed pictorial boards. Retold by Joan Collins. There were numerous undated reprints with prices rising from 75p to 99p.

1049   1986   Alice's Adventures in Wonderland

London: Methuen Children's Books   0416960006   David Hall

The pictures were designed by David Hall for a Walt Disney film but were never used. Afterword by Brian Sibley. Glazed pictorial paper boards. Dust jacket.

1050   1986   Alice's Adventures in Wonderland

London: Michael O'Mara Books Ltd.   0948397551   W. H. Walker

Facsimile edition, 1st impression. The 2nd impression was published in 1987 by Tiger Books.

1051   1986   Alice's Adventures in Wonderland

London: Penguin Books   0140350381   John Tenniel; Elisa Trimby

2nd 1986 reprint. Puffin Classics. Paperback. Elisa Trimby, color cover. Originally published in 1946, also reprinted 1949, 1952, 1955, 1984, 1985, and 1986 (twice).

1052   1986   Alice's Adventures in Wonderland

London: Penguin Books   0140350381   John Tenniel; Elisa Trimby

Puffin Classics. Paperback. Elisa Trimby, color cover. Originally published in 1946, also reprinted 1949, 1952, 1955, 1984, 1985, and 1986 (twice).

1053	1987	Alice in Wonderland		
	Esher, UK: Celebrity Group			Anonymous; Walt Disney Company

In *Tapes 'n' Tales Magazine*. 15 pp. and a tape of *Alice*, abridged and read by June Whitfield. 2 anonymous color illustrations and pictorial wrappers by Disney Studios.

1054	1987	Alice's Adventures in Wonderland		
	London: Chancellor Press	0907486797	Arthur Rackham

1055	1987	Alice in Wonderland		
	London: Fleetway Books	185277035X	Disney Studio

A reissue of the smaller 1986 paperback.

1056	1987	Alice in Wonderland		
	Loughborough, UK: Ladybird Books	0721410596	Disney Studio

Glazed pictorial paper boards, cover picture of Alice and White Rabbit. There were several reprints with differing prices, Ladybird logos, and wording on covers.

1057	1987	Alice in Wonderland		
	Harlow, UK: Longman	0582522781	John Tenniel

Longman Classics, Stage 2. Simplified by D. K. Swan. For English as a second language. Paperback.

1058	1987	Alice's Adventures in Wonderland		
	London: Penguin Books	0140350381	John Tenniel

A Story Book. Paperback.

1059	1987	Alice's Adventures in Wonderland		
	London: Tiger Books International Limited; Ward Lock Limited	1870461029	Margaret W. Tarrant

First thus.

1060	1987	Alice in Wonderland		
	London: World International Publishing Ltd.	0723588724	Kim Lane

In the series Little Owl Mini Classics. Abridged edition. Yellow glazed pictorial boards, picture on front cover of Alice and White Rabbit.

1061	1988	The Original Alice in Wonderland		
	Newmarket, UK: Brimar Books Ltd.	086112457X	Eric Kincaid

Glazed pictorial paper boards.

1062	1988	The Original Alice in Wonderland		
	Newmarket, UK: Brimar Books	086112457X	Eric Kincaid

2nd printing. Glazed pictorial paper boards.

1063	1988	Alice's Adventures in Wonderland		
	London: Lynx	0575043326	Justin Todd

1st paperback edition.

1064	1988	Alice's Adventures in Wonderland		
	Leicester, UK: Magna Books. Greenwich, CT: Twin Books		A. Van Gool; André M. Lefèvre; M. Loiseaux

1st UK edition.

1065   ca. 1988 Alice's Adventures in Wonderland
London: Julia Macrae Books   0862033241   Anthony Browne
2nd printing. Glazed pictorial paper boards. Dust jacket.

1066   1989   Alice's Adventures in Wonderland
London: Butler & Tanner   Peter Weevers
Limited edition. In full leather boards. Limited to 100 copies signed and numbered by the artist. May have been
published in 1995.

1067   1989   Alice in Wonderland
Hove, UK: Firefly Books Ltd.   0904724719   Francesc Rovira
Retold by Michael Rosen.

1068   1989   Alice's Adventures in Wonderland
London: Hamlyn Publishing Group   0600566854   John Tenniel; Paul Sullivan
In the Hamlyn Tribute series. Cover picture by Paul Sullivan.

1069   1989   Alice's Adventures in Wonderland
London: Hippo Books, Scholastic Publications Ltd.   059076148X   John Tenniel
Hippo Classics.

1070   1989   Alice's Adventures in Wonderland
London; Sydney, NSW; Auckland, NZ;   0091737648   Peter Weevers
Johannesburg, SA: Hutchinson Children's Books
1st edition. Glazed pictorial blue paper over boards. Yellow illustrated dust jacket. Later reprints.

1071   1989   Alice in Wonderland
Loughborough, UK: Ladybird Books   0721409679   Debbie Boon-Jenkins
Reprint of the 1986 edition with a Burger King logo on the front cover. Ladybird Children's Classics. Glazed pictorial
boards. Retold by Joan Collins.

1072   1989   Alice in Wonderland
Ipswich, UK: Studio Publications   0862156920   Stéphanie Birch
Retold by Pat Posner.

1073   1989   The Original Alice in Wonderland
Newmarket, UK: W. H. Smith Exclusive Books,   086112457X   Eric Kincaid
and Brimax Books, Ltd.
3rd printing. Glazed pictorial paper boards.

1074   1989   Alice's Adventures in Wonderland
London: William Heinemann   0434958565   Arthur Rackham
1st reissue of the 1907 1st edition.

1075   ca. 1980s   Alice in Wonderland
Brighton, UK: Litor Publishers, Ltd.   Monique Gorde
In the Topsy Series. Abbreviated text.

1076   ca. 1980s   Alice in Wonderland
Bridlington, UK: Peter Haddock Ltd.   0071050378   Anonymous
Published in the UK for the American market and priced at $5.95.

1077   ca. 1980s   Alice's Adventures in Wonderland
Bridlington, UK: Priory Books,   9780710501448   Pauline Baynes; Deno Caruana
A Peter Haddock Limited imprint

In the series Priory Classics. Laminated orange paper boards. Styled A Peter Haddock Limited Imprint Copyright
BW (Leicester Ltd.). Baynes vignette present. Cover by Deno Caruana. Other covers known.

1078   1990   Alice in Wonderland
London: Armada Paperbacks   0006925456   John Tenniel
1st edition thus.

1079   1990   Lewis Carroll's Alice in Wonderland
London: Award Publications   9780861633913   Rene Cloke

Classic Award Series. Adapted by Jane Carruth, illustrated by Rene Cloke. 92 pp. Full-color pictures on every page.
Glazed paper boards with extra pictures on front and back. In dust jacket which repeats cover design. This edition
has Rene Cloke's 4th set of illustrations. Republished in 2004 with a different ISBN.

1080   1990   Alice's Adventures in Wonderland
London: Carnival   0001949349   Kate Simpson
Adapted by Charles Moritz. 31 pp.

1081   1990   Alice in Wonderland
Bridlington, UK: Dean & Son, Priory Books   0710501447   Unillustrated; Deno Caruana

1st Priory Classic Series Edition, 1st issue, No. 1 in series. Glazed blue paper-covered boards, front with Alice
kneeling. No dust jacket. Unpaginated and unillustrated. Cover by Deno Caruana.

1082   1990   Alice in Wonderland
London: Harper Collins   0001004735   Anonymous

1st Harper Festival edition. Abridged by Charles Moritz. Paperback plus 1 . Cover illustrator is anonymous.

1083   1990   Alice's Adventures in Wonderland
Bridlington, UK: Peter Haddock Ltd.   071050523X   Gary Henderson
Glazed pictorial paper boards. In the Traditional Stories Simply Retold. In the series of Bonny Books.

1084   1990   Alice's Adventures in Wonderland
London: The Folio Society   John Tenniel
Reissue of the 1961 edition. In suede publisher's slipcase with matching copy of *Looking-Glass*.

1085   1990   Alice's Adventures in Wonderland
London: Tiger Books International   1855010496   W. H. Walker
2nd impression of the 1986 Michael P. O'Mara Books edition of the 1st impression.

1086   1990   The Original Alice in Wonderland
Newmarket, UK: W. H. Smith Exclusive Books,   086112457X   Eric Kincaid
and Brimax Books Ltd.

4th printing. Glazed pictorial paper boards. Later printings known.

1087   1990   Alice's Adventures in Wonderland
London: William Heinemann   0434958565   Arthur Rackham
1st reprint of the 1989 reissue.

1088   ca. 1990 Alice in Wonderland, Noah's Ark, the Magic Book, and Pinocchio
Bridlington, UK: Peter Haddock Ltd.   9780710507020   Anonymous
Glazed pictorial paper boards. In the series Favourite Fairy Stories.

1089   1991   Alice in Wonderland
London: Award Publications, Ltd.   0861633911   Rene Cloke

2nd impression. Adapted by Jane Carruth, illustrated by Rene Cloke. Full-color pictures on every page. Glazed paper boards with extra pictures on front and back. In dust jacket which repeats the cover design. This edition has Rene Cloke's 4th set of illustrations.

1090   1991   Alice in Wonderland
London: J. M. Dent & Sons. New York: E. P. Dutton.   9780460871075   Lewis Carroll; Arthur Rackham
Rutland, Vermont: Charles E. Tuttle Co., Inc.

Reprint of an earlier Everyman's edition. Cover illustration by Arthur Rackham.

1091   1991   Alice's Adventures in Wonderland
Limpsfield, UK: Dragon's World   185028105X   Malcolm Ashman

15 color plates. Glazed pictorial boards. Blue cloth. Dust jacket.

1092   1991   Alice in Wonderland
Loughborough, UK: Ladybird Books   0721440142   Disney Studio
Paperback.

1093   1991   Walt Disney's Alice and the Mad Hatter's Tea Party
London: Purnell Books   9780361013864   Anonymous
3 double-page scenes.

1094   1991   Alice in Wonderland
Manchester, UK: World International Publishing   0749802197   Kim Lane
Retold by Clive Hopwood. Little Owl Mini Classics.

1095   ca. 1991 Alice's Adventures in Wonderland
Bridlington, UK: Peter Haddock Ltd.   0710508131   Anonymous
Glazed pictorial paper boards. In the series Fantasy Land Fairy Tales. A UK version of an original foreign edition.

1096   1992   Alice in Wonderland
London: Award Publications, Ltd.   0861633911   Rene Cloke

3rd impression. Adapted by Jane Carruth, illustrated by Rene Cloke. Full-color pictures on every page. Glazed paper boards with extra pictures on front and back. In dust jacket which repeats the cover design. This edition has Rene Cloke's 4th set of illustrations.

1097   1992   Alice in Wonderland
London: Brown Watson   0709708556   Anonymous
Text by Maureen Spurgeon. In the series Bedtime Books. Later issues give the series as Fairy Tales.

1098   1992   The Alice in Wonderland Picture Book
London: Hodder & Stoughton   9780340567876   Mabel Lucie Attwell
Adapted by Jennifer Roberts. Attwell first illustrated *Alice* in a Raphael Tuck edition of ca. 1910.

1099   1992   Alice's Adventures in Wonderland
London: Red Fox   0099808609   Peter Weevers
Paperback edition. Covers repeat pictures from the Hutchinson Children's Books 1st edition of 1989. Dust jacket.

1100   1992   Alice's Adventures in Wonderland
London: Studio Editions   1851709355   Gwynedd Hudson
Glazed paper wrappers. Reprint of the 1985 Bracken Books edition. Covers use the same pictures as the dust jacket.

1101   1992   Alice's Adventures in Wonderland
London: The Folio Society   John Tenniel
5th printing. In publisher's slipcase with matching copy of *Looking-Glass*.

1102   1992   Alice in Wonderland
Northampton, UK: W. F. Graham   185128396X   Georgina Hargreaves
In the series Illustrated Classics for Everyone. Adapted and illustrated by Georgina Hargreaves.

1103   1992   Alice in Wonderland
London: William Clowes and Sons, Ltd.   1855873419   Anonymous
Front cover has anonymous picture of the Tea-Party.

1104   1992   Alice in Wonderland
Ware, UK: Wordsworth Editions   1853260029   John Tenniel; Henry Holiday
Introduction and notes by Michael Irwin. Also contains *Phantasmagoria* and *The Hunting of the Snark*.

1105   1993   Alice's Adventures in Wonderland
London: Andersen Press   1783442662   Tony Ross
Abridged and illustrated by Tony Ross. Laminated pictorial paper boards.

1106   1993   Alice in Wonderland
London: Armada Paperbacks   9780006940081   John Tenniel
Reprint of the 1990 Armada edition. Has Kids Classics on back cover.

1107   1993   Alice in Wonderland
London: Award Publications, Ltd.   0861633911   Rene Cloke
4th impression. Adapted by Jane Carruth, illustrated by Rene Cloke. Full-color pictures on every page. Glazed paper boards with extra pictures on front and back. In dust jacket which repeats the cover design. This edition has Rene Cloke's 4th set of illustrations.

1108   1993   Alice's Adventures in Wonderland
Bath, UK; Boston, MA: Barefoot Books   1898000158   John Tenniel
Little Barefoot Books.

1109   1993   Alice in Wonderland
Newmarket, UK: Brimax Books   086112457X   Eric Kincaid

1110   1993   Alice in Wonderland
London: Diamond Books   9780261660687   John Tenniel; Anonymous
Reprint of the 1990 Armada edition. Anonymous front cover picture of Tea-Party.

1111   1993   Alice in Wonderland
London: Grandreams, Ltd.   1858301769   Pamela Storey
Retold by Grace de la Touche. In the series Bow-Wow.

1112   1993   Alice in Wonderland
Loughborough, UK: Ladybird Books   0721442323   Disney Studio
Large format. Glazed pictorial paper boards with front cover picture of Alice with Dormouse in Teapot.

1113   1993   "Van Gool's" Alice in Wonderland
Wigston, UK: Magna Books   1854225316   A. Van Gool;
                                                            André M. Lefèvre; M. Loiseaux
In the series Magna Fairy Tale Classics. Produced by Twin Books. Glazed paper boards.

1114 1993 "Van Gool's" Alice in Wonderland
Wigston, UK: Magna Books   A. Van Gool;
                        André M. Lefèvre; M. Loiseaux

In the series Magna Little Fairy Tale. Abbreviated version of the earlier 1993 edition. Glazed paper wrappers.

1115 1993 Alice in Wonderland
London: Wordsworth Classics   1853260029   Lewis Carroll; Adelaide Claxton

2nd reprint of the 1st 1992 edition. Only *Alice* has Carroll pictures. Though not stated, this is a facsimile of the 1929 J. M. Dent Everyman edition but lacks introduction and *Tangled Tales* answers. Front cover has the Adelaide Claxton picture Wonderland.

1116 1994 Alice in Wonderland
London: Award Publications, Ltd. 0861633911   Rene Cloke

5th impression. Adapted by Jane Carruth, illustrated by Rene Cloke. Full-color pictures on every page. Glazed paper boards with extra pictures on front and back. In dust jacket which repeats the cover design. This edition has Rene Cloke's 4th set of illustrations.

1117 1994 Alice in Wonderland
Loughborough, UK: Ladybird Books 0721416543   David Frankland;
                        Jonathan Mercer

Retold by Joan Collins. Glazed pictorial paper boards. Price £1.50. Various reprints, some in a case with CD-ROM. Read by Prunella Scales. Includes woodcuts by Jonathan Mercer.

1118 1994 Alice in Wonderland
Leicester, UK: Magna Books   1854226096   Claudio Cernuschi;
                        Maria De Filippo

In the Magna Reed, Color and Play Series.

1119 1994 Alice's Adventures in Wonderland
Oxford: Oxford University Press 0195852745   K. Y. Chan
Oxford Progressive English Readers, Level 2. 2nd impression; the 1st was 1992.

1120 1994 Alice in Wonderland
Bristol, UK: Parragon Books   1858136350   Carole Gray
Mini Classics series. Retold by Stephanie Laslett. Miniature format. Dust jacket.

1121 1994 Alice's Adventures in Wonderland
London: Penguin Books   014036675X   John Tenniel; James Marsh
Penguin Books edition. Cover illustration by James Marsh.

1122 1994 Alice's Adventures in Wonderland
Harmondsworth, UK: Penguin   0140620869   John Tenniel
Penguin Popular Classics Series.

1123 1994 Alice's Adventures in Wonderland
London: Penguin Books   9780140620863 John Tenniel
Reissued as Penguin Popular Classics. In green wrappers lettered in white on 100% recycled paper.

1124 1994 Alice's Adventures in Wonderland
London: Puffin   014036675X   John Tenniel
Now styled Puffin Classics.

1125 1994 Alice's Adventures in Wonderland

Bath, UK: Robert Frederick Ltd.   1850812330   Gwynedd Hudson; Others

Color paper boards, imitating cloth. In the series Children's Classics. Text is a facsimile of the Hodder and Stoughton editions, including the misspelling "Caroll." In the middle of the book is a Picture Gallery of color plates, a collection of illustrations by well-loved artists: 4 by Hudson, others by Frank Adams, Harry Rountree, Arthur Rackham, Charles Robinson, and Bessie Pease.

| 1126 | 1995 | Alice's Adventures in Wonderland | | |

London: Bloomsbury Classics   978074752284   Jeff Fisher

Black cloth boards. Dust jacket. The pictures are all silhouettes.

| 1127 | 1995 | 3 Wonderland Tales | | |

London: Brown Watson   0709710240   Anonymous

Glazed pictorial paper boards with Fairy Tale Treasury at the top of the front cover. *Alice* is the first of 3 stories. It is a reprint of the 1992 Bedtime Books edition.

| 1128 | 1995 | Alice's Adventures in Wonderland | | |

London: The Templar Company   1898784353   Nick Hewetson

In the series Mini Classics. Retold by Stephanie Laslett. Miniature-format dust jacket.

| 1129 | 1995 | The Original Alice in Wonderland | | |

Newmarket, UK: W. H. Smith Exclusive Books,   086112457X   Eric Kincaid
and Brimax Books Ltd.

A later printing. Dust jacket. *Alice* is one of 4 Classic Stories.

| 1130 | 1995 | Alice in Wonderland | | |

Manchester, UK: World International Publishing Ltd.   R. Canaider; Anonymous

Cover now with anonymous illustrated picture of Alice and White Rabbit.

| 1131 | 1996 | 3 Wonderland Tales | | |

London: Brown Watson   0709710240   Anonymous

1st reprint of the 1995 edition with a different cover design. Glazed pictorial paper boards with Fairy Tale Treasury at the top of the front cover. *Alice* is the first of 3 stories and is a reprint of the 1992 Bedtime Books edition.

| 1132 | 1996 | Alice in Wonderland | | |

Loughborough, UK: Ladybird Books   978072143676   Disney Studio

Series D263, Easy Reader. Reprint of the 1993 Disney edition. Large-format glazed pictorial paper boards. Front cover has picture of Alice with Dormouse in Teapot.

| 1133 | 1996 | Alice in Wonderland | | |

Loughborough, UK: Ladybird Books   0721448224   Unillustrated

Classics Collection 4, with 2 sound cassettes.

| 1134 | 1996 | Alice's Adventures in Wonderland | | |

London: Leopard   0752903160   Peter Weevers

Essentially as earlier Weevers illustrated editions.

| 1135 | 1996 | Alice in Wonderland | | |

Bristol, UK: Parragon Book Service   978075251276   Carole Gray

In the series Sleepytime Tales. Retold by Dugald Steer.

| 1136 | 1996 | Tales from Alice in Wonderland | | |

London: Penguin   0146003209   Unknown

Penguin Children's Series 60s.

1137	1996	Alice's Adventures in Wonderland		
	London: Ted Smart		0091850770	Peter Weevers
	A Ted Smart Publication.			

1138	1996	Alice's Adventures in Wonderland		
	London: The Folio Society			John Tenniel
	Reissue of the 1961 edition.			

1139	1997	Alice's Adventures in Wonderland		
	Newmarket, UK: Brimar Books Ltd.		1858546028	Gill Guile
	Adapted by Lucy Kincaid. Designed for Children 8 and younger. In the series Brimar Classics. Dust jacket.			

1140	1997	3 Wonderland Tales		
	London: Brown Watson		0709710240	Anonymous
	2nd reprint of the 1995 edition with a different cover design. Glazed pictorial paper boards with Fairy Tale Treasury at the top of the front cover. *Alice* is the first of 3 stories and is a reprint of the 1992 Bedtime Books edition.			

1141	1997	Alice's Adventures in Wonderland		
	London: Penguin Books Limited		0140340381	John Tenniel
	A Puffin Book, 1st edition was 1946. Reprinted 1950, 1962, 1973, 1974, and 1977.			

1142	1997	Alice's Adventures in Wonderland		
	London: Penguin Books		014036675X	John Tenniel; James Marsh
	2nd printing of 1994 issue with cover by James Marsh.			

1143	1997	Alice's Adventures in Wonderland		
	Market Drayton, UK: The Tern Press			Nicholas Parry
	Privately printed. Limited edition of 90 copies signed by Mary Parry and Nicholas Parry.			

1144	1998	Alice's Adventures in Wonderland		
	Newmarket, UK: Brimar Books Ltd.		1858546028	Gill Guile
	1st reprint of the 1997 edition. Adapted by Lucy Kincaid. Designed for Children 8 and younger. In the series Brimar Classics. Dust jacket.			

1145	1998	Alice in Wonderland		
	Loughborough, UK: Ladybird Books		0721473792	David Frankland; Jonathan Mercer
	Reprint in larger paperback format. Retold by Joan Collins. Includes woodcuts by Jonathan Mercer.			

1146	1998	Alice's Adventures in Wonderland		
	Bath, UK: Robert Frederick Ltd.		9780907785729	Gwynedd Hudson
	Color paper boards in imitation quarter cloth. Also has the author's name misspelled as "Caroll." Dust jacket.			

1147	1999	Alice's Adventures in Wonderland		
	London: Micawber Fine Editions			Griff Jones
	Limited to 150 numbered copies signed by the artist and author of the afterword, with an extra suite of pictures signed by the artist. In publisher's box.			

1148	1999	Alice in Wonderland		
	London; New York: North-South Books		0735811660	Lisbeth Zwerger
	A Michael Neugebauer Book. Also issued in boxed set with *The Wizard of Oz.*			

1149	1999	Alice's Adventures in Wonderland		

London: Penguin Books   John Tenniel
Reissue.

1150   2000   Alice's Adventures in Wonderland
London: Dorling Kindersley   0751371106   Greg Backer
Adapted by Jane Fior. Dust jacket.

1151   2000   Alice's Adventures in Wonderland
London: HarperFestival   0694014540   John Tenniel
Paperback. 1st Harper Festival Edition. In the series Charming Classics. Has White Rabbit pendant attached to the
front cover.

1152   2000   Alice in Wonderland
Harlow, UK: Pearson Education   0582421233   Unknown
Penguin Readers, Level 2. Retold by Mary Tomlin.

1153   2000   Alice's Adventures in Wonderland
London: Ted Smart   0744561248   Helen Oxenbury
Dust jacket. This edition produced for The Book People.

1154   ca. 2001 Alice in Wonderland
Bridlington, UK: Peter Haddock Ltd.   0710510802   Carlos Busquets
The Busquets pictures originate in Spanish editions. The first English-language edition with his pictures appeared in 1984.

1155   2001   Alice's Adventures in Wonderland
London: Bloomsbury   9780747553687   Mervyn Peake

1156   2001   The Original Alice in Wonderland
London: Brimax, an imprint   086112457X   Eric Kincaid
of Octopus Publishing Group Ltd.
A later printing Alice is one of 4 Classic Stories series. Dust jacket.

1157   2001   Alice in Wonderland
Bath, UK: Parragon Books   0752549359   Jenny Press
In the series Little Tales. Retold by Stephanie Laslett. Issued in boxed set with 5 other children's stories.

1158   2002   Alice in Wonderland
Dorking, UK: Templar Publishing   1840114096   Cinzia Ratto
1st edition. Dust jacket. The 2007 reprint is also listed as "first edition."

1159   2003   Walt Disney's Classic Alice in Wonderland
London: Ladybird Books   9781904351832;   David Frankland
                                        9780721416540
Ladybird Classics. Retold by Joan Collins. Read by Prunella Scales. Woodcuts by Jonathan Mercer. 51 pp. plus 1 CD.

1160   2003   Alice in Wonderland
Loughborough, UK: Ladybird Books   1844220265   Disney Studio
With new picture on front cover of Alice with cup of tea.

1161   2003   Lewis Carroll's Alice in Wonderland
Bath, UK: Parragon Books   9781405416702   June Goulding
In the series Children's Classic Collection. Glazed paper boards. Dust jacket. A variant exists with different binding
and pictures.

1162 2003 Alice's Adventures in Wonderland
London: The Children's Golden Library 8497890566 Unillustrated
Includes note "Not to be sold separately from the Daily Mail." Dust jacket.

1163 2004 Lewis Carroll's Alice in Wonderland
London: Award Publications 1841353469 Rene Cloke
Adapted by Jane Carruth. Previously published in 1990. 92 pp.

1164 2004 Alice's Adventures in Wonderland
London: Chrysalis Children's Books 1843650568 Michael Foreman
Dust jacket.

1165 2004 Alice's Adventures in Wonderland
London: Chrysalis Children's Books 9781843651161 Michael Foreman
First paperback edition.

1166 2004 Alice's Adventures in Wonderland
London: Penguin Books 9780141317748 Walt Disney
A Puffin Book, Disney Classics adapted by Narinder Dhami.

1167 ca. 2004 Alice's Adventures in Wonderland
London; Philadelphia, PA: Courage Books 0762420081 Greg Hildebrandt
Adapted and abridged by Julia Suarez.

1168 ca. 2004 Alice's Adventures in Wonderland
Ringmer, UK: Leaf Enterprises Unillustrated
Issued in three volumes as a set of leather-bound copies. There was also an issue in decorated paper boards in illustrated dust jacket.

1169 2005 Alice's Adventures in Wonderland
London: Bounty Books, Octopus Publishing Group Ltd. 9780753712306 Margaret W. Tarrant
Reprint of 1990 issue.

1170 2005 Alice's Adventures in Wonderland
London: Ted Smart 0744561248 Helen Oxenbury
A later edition of the 2000 edition.

1171 2006 Alice in Wonderland
London: Berryland Books 9781845770945 Anonymous
Adapted by Bookmatrix Ltd. and edited by Claire Black. Anonymous line illustrations and color picture on front cover.

1172 2006 Alice's Adventures in Wonderland
Chichester, UK: Brimax Publishing Ltd., 0086112457 Eric Kincaid
Appledram Barns
Reprint.

1173 2006 Alice in Wonderland
Weston-Super-Mare, UK: Dateman Books Anonymous
Miniature edition (2.1 cm tall). Front cover color picture.

1174 2006 Walt Disney's Alice in Wonderland Read to Me Book
Bath, UK: Parragon Books 9781405469708 Disney Studio
CD included with a 24-page booklet.

1175   2006   Alice in Wonderland
Bath, UK: Parragon Publishing   1405468157   June Goulding
Paper-covered boards, front with Tea-Party. Dust jacket illustrated same as boards. 287 pp. Many color illustrations, of which 28 are integral full-page. Title on title page: "*Alice in Wonderland*." Verso title page: "This edition published in 2006. Copyright 2004, Parragon Books Ltd."

1176   2006   Alice's Adventures in Wonderland
London: Penguin Books   0141023554   John Tenniel
London Penguin Books reissued as Penguin Red Classic.

1177   2006   The Original Alice in Wonderland
London: The Five Mile Press Pty Ltd.   1742481485   Eric Kincaid
1st edition thus. As in the 1988 W. H. Smith edition but with CD attached to front cover.

1178   2006   Alice in Wonderland
London: Usborne Publishing, Ltd.   9780746076590   Mauro Evangelista
Glazed paper boards, small format.

1179   2007   Alice in Wonderland
Weston-Super-Mare, UK: Dateman Books   Anonymous
Miniature edition (2.9 cm tall). Front cover color picture same as 2006 edition.

1180   2007   Alice in Wonderland
Bath, UK: Parragon Books Ltd.   9781405491075   Shelagh McNicholas
Retold by Rachel Eliot. Has a small brooch attached to front cover.

1181   2007   Alice's Adventures in Wonderland
London: Penguin Books   9780141033440   John Tenniel

1182   2007   Alice in Wonderland
Dorking, UK: Templar Publishing   9781840114386   Cinzia Ratto
Reprint of the 2002 edition. A Waterstone's Classics Collection edition. On the front of the dust jacket is printed "first edition."

1183   2008   Alice in Wonderland
London: IBS Books   9781905863235   Unknown
Abridged English Classics Series.

1184   2008   Alice in Wonderland
Loughborough, UK: Ladybird Books   9781846469459   David Frankland; Jonathan
                                                                               Mercer; Fausto Bianchi
A new edition of the 1994 edition with woodcuts by Jonathan Mercer, but with a new front cover illustration by Fausto Bianchi.

1185   2008   Alice in Wonderland
Harlow, UK: Pearson Education   9781405855358 book;   Unknown
                                                 9781405878234 CD
Penguin Reader, Level 2. Retold by Mary Tomalin. 43-page book and 1 audio CD.

1186   2008   Alice's Adventures in Wonderland
London: Penguin Books   9780141321073   John Tenniel
Reissue of the 2006 London Penguin Books edition. Introduction by Chris Riddell.

1187	2008	Alice's Adventures in Wonderland		
		London; New York: Puffin Books	9780141321073; 0141321075 (paperback)	John Tenniel
		Puffin Classics. Introduction by Chris Riddell. Paperback.		

1188	2008	Lewis Carroll's Alice in Wonderland		
		Dorking, UK: Templar Publishing	978184011481	Robin Matthews
		Dust jacket. There was also a limited edition in slipcase.		

1189	2009	Alice in Wonderland		
		London: Arcturus Publishing, Ltd.	9781848373969	John Tenniel
		Dust jacket.		

1190	2009	Alice's Adventures in Wonderland		
		Church Hanborough, UK: Artists' Choice Editions		John Vernon Lord
		Introduction and bibliography by artist, textual corrections by Selwyn Goodacre. Limited edition of 280 standard numbered copies, 68 special numbered copies bound in quarter leather in printed box, and 5 copies specially bound by Chris Hicks.		

1191	2009	Alice in Wonderland		
		London: Harper Collins Children's Books	9780007316137 (hardcover); 9780007371310 (paperback with CD); 9780007351596 (paperback)	Emma Chichester Clark
		Text abridged by Alison Sage and retold by Emma Chichester Clark.		

1192	2009	Alice's Adventures in Wonderland		
		Dorking, UK: Templar Publishing	9781840119688	Robert Ingpen
		Dust jacket. Various later issues denoted by numbers 1–10, with one dropped incrementally, all with same date.		

1193	2009	Alice in Wonderland		
		London: Usborne Publishing, Ltd.	9780746099230	Mauro Evangelista
		Adapted by Lesley Sims, designed by Louise Flutter.		

1194	2009	Alice's Adventures in Wonderland		
		London; Sydney, NSW: Walker Books	9781921529023	Robert Ingpen

1195	2010	Alice in Wonderland		
		London: Alligator Books	1842392344	Anonymous
		One of 6 titles in boxed set entitled Classic Fairy Tales Mini Library.		

1196	2010	Lewis Carroll's Alice's Adventures in Wonderland		
		London: Carlton Books Ltd.	9781847324368	Zdenko Bašić
		With booklet attached to inside front cover, "The White Rabbit's Guide to Wonderland." 24 pp.		

1197	2010	Alice in Wonderland		
		London: Harper Collins Children's Books	9780007351596	Emma Chichester Clark
		3rd printing of the 2009 edition.		

1198	2010	Alice: An Adaptation		
		London: Oberon Books	9781849430678	Lindsey Turner
		Adapted by Laura Wade.		

1199	2010	Disney Alice in Wonderland		
		Bath, UK: Parragon Books	9781407586878	Disney Studio
		In the series Disney Classics. Front cover has a cut-out.		

1200   2010   Alice's Adventures in Wonderland
[Cookhill, UK]: Pook Press / Read Books   9781445505886 (paperback); Arthur Rackham
                                                 9781473327054 (hardback)

Various issues in 2010 and 2015 with the same ISBN.

1201   2010   Alice's Adventures in Wonderland
[Cookhill, UK]: Pook Press / Read Books   9781445506036 (paperback); Millicent Sowerby
                                                 9781445506067 (hardback)

Various issues in 2010, 2016, 2017, all with the same ISBN.

1202   2010   Alice in Wonderland
London: Puffin   9780141330464   Disney Studio

Adapted by T. T. Sutherland. Paperback.

1203   2010   Lewis Carroll's Alice in Wonderland
London: Raintree   9781406214147   Daniel Perez

Graphic Revolve Series. Retold by Martin Powell. Colored by Prontobunker Studio.

1204   2011   Lewis Carroll's Alice's Adventures in Wonderland
London: Carlton Books Ltd.   9781847327673   Zdenko Bašić

1st paperback edition. Retold by Harriet Castor. Various later issues with the same date but denoted by numbers 1–10, one being removed sequentially. Includes guide-book.

1205   2011   The Children's Alice
[Cookhill, UK]: Pook Press / Read Books   9781445508740   Honor C. Appleton

Various issues in 2011, 2015, and 2017, with the same ISBN.

1206   2011   Alice's Adventures in Wonderland
[Cookhill, UK]: Pook Press / Read Books   9781446533369 (paperback); Milo Winter
                                                 9781446533109 (hardback)

Various issues in 2011, 2015, and 2017, all with the same ISBN.

1207   2011   Alice's Adventures in Wonderland
London: QED Publishing   9781848355507   Robert Dunn

Adapted by Ronne Randall.

1208   2011   Alice in Wonderland
London: Tate, Sons   9781854379917   Various

Compiler Gavin Delahunty of Tate Liverpool, with contributions by Gillian Beer, Alberto Manguel, Carol Mavor, and Edward Wakeling.

1209   2012   Disney Alice in Wonderland
[London]: Hachette   9781906965228   Disney Studio

Disney Wonderful World of Reading Series.

1210   2012   Alice in Wonderland
London: Ladybird Books   9780723279624   Ester Garcia-Cortés;
                                                         Valeria Valenza

In the series Ladybird Classics. Glazed paper boards. Illustrated by Ester Garcia-Cortés, with chapter illustrations by Valeria Valenza.

1211   2012   Alice in Wonderland
Bath, UK: Parragon   9781445478517   Amanda Gulliver

A full-color picture book for children. 27 pp.

1212   2012   Alice in Wonderland
Bath, UK: Parragon   9781781860335   Disney
Magical Story Series. Edited by Gemma Louise Lowe. Designed by Jim Willmott. [26] pp.

1213   2012   Lewis Carroll's Alice's Adventures in Wonderland
London; New York: Penguin Classics   9780141197302   Yayoi Kusama
Penguin Classics. Kusama illustrations in full-color interspersed throughout the book, produced in collaboration
with Kusama Studio, Tokyo and Gagosian Gallery.

1214   2012   The Original Alice in Wonderland
London: The Five Mile Press Pty Ltd.   9781743003787   Eric Kincaid
A later issue of the 2006 edition, but omits "The Mock Turtle's Story" and "The Lobster Quadrille."

1215   2013   Alice in Wonderland
[London]: Cornerstones Education   9781909859043   Unknown
Love to Read Classics Vol. 1.

1216   2013   Alice's Adventures in Wonderland
London: Harper Collins Publishers   9780007350827   John Tenniel; Peter Newell
Paperback. In the series Collins Classics. Cover illustration is a detail from a Peter Newell picture.

1217   2013   Alice in Wonderland
London: Ladybird Books   9780723279624   Ester Garcia-Cortés
Ladybird Classics. Retold by Joan Collins.

1218   2013   Alice In Wonderland
[Cookhill, UK]: Pook Press / Read Books   9781473307049 (paperback);   Frank Adams
                                            9781473307353 (hardcover)
Various issues in 2013, 2015, and 2017, with the same ISBN.

1219   2013   Alice's Adventures in Wonderland
[Cookhill, UK]: Pook Press / Read Books   9781473307292 (hardback);   Ada L. Bowley
                                            9781473306981 (paperback)
Various issues in 2013 and 2017 with the same ISBN.

1220   2013   Alice's Adventures in Wonderland
[Cookhill, UK]: Pook Press / Read Books   9781473307001 (paperback);   Walter Hawes
                                            9781473307315 (hardback)
Various issues in 2014, 2015, and 2017 with the same ISBN.

1221   2013   Alice's Adventures in Wonderland
[Cookhill, UK]: Pook Press / Read Books   9781473307254 (hardback);   A. E. Jackson
                                            97781473306943 (paperback)

1222   2013   Alice's Adventures in Wonderland
[Cookhill, UK]: Pook Press / Read Books   9781473307513 (hardback);   Gertrude A. Kay
                                            97781473307209 (paperback)
Various issues in 2013 and 2015 with the same ISBN.

1223   2013   Alice's Adventures in Wonderland
[Cookhill, UK]: Pook Press / Read Books   9781473307285 (hardback);   M. L. Kirk; John Tenniel
                                            97781473306974 (paperback)
Includes 12 full-page color illustrations in color by M. L. Kirk and 42 illustrations by John Tenniel. Various issues in
2013 and 2017 with the same ISBN.

1224 2013 Alice's Adventures in Wonderland
[Cookhill, UK]: Pook Press / Read Books   9781473306998 (paperback); Willy Pogany
                                                  9781473307308 (hardback)

Various issues in 2013 and 2017 with the same ISBN.

1225 2013 Alice's Adventures in Wonderland
[Cookhill, UK]: Pook Press / Read Books   9781473307322 (hardback);   K. M. Roberts
                                                  97781473307018 (paperback)

Various issues in 2013 and 2017 with the same ISBN.

1226 2013 Songs from Alice in Wonderland and Through the Looking-Glass
[Cookhill, UK]: Pook Press / Read Books   9781473306967 (paperback); Charles Robinson
                                                  9781473307278 (hardback)

Various issues in 2013 and 2017 with the same ISBN.

1227 2013 Alice's Adventures in Wonderland
[Cookhill, UK]: Pook Press / Read Books   9781473307025 (paperback); T. H. Robinson; Charles Pears
                                                  9781473307339 (hardback)

Various issues in 2013, 2015, and 2017, all with the same ISBN.

1228 2013 Children's Treasure Book, Vol. II, Alice in Wonderland
[Cookhill, UK]: Pook Press / Read Books   9781447477402 (paperback); Harry Rountree; Charles Pears
                                                  9781447477730 (hardback)

Various issues in 2013 and 2017 with the same ISBN.

1229 2013 Alice's Adventures in Wonderland
[Cookhill, UK]: Pook Press / Read Books   9781473307346 (hardback);   George Soper
                                                  97781473307032 (paperback)

Various issues in 2013 and 2017 with the same ISBN.

1230 2013 Alice's Adventures in Wonderland
[Cookhill, UK]: Pook Press / Read Books   9781473307230 (hardback);   Margaret W. Tarrant
                                                  97781473306929 (paperback)

Various issues in 2013 and 2021 with the same ISBN.

1231 2013 Alice's Adventures in Wonderland
[Cookhill, UK]: Pook Press / Read Books   9781473307483   John Tenniel
Various issues in 2013 and 2020 with the same ISBN.

1232 2013 Alice's Adventures in Wonderland
London: Usborne Publishing Ltd.   9781409563822   Mauro Evangelista
Usborne Classics Stories. 5 volume set issued together in an illustrated gift box. *Alice in Wonderland* adapted by
Lesley Sims and illustrated by Mauro Evangelista. Other works in set adapted by other writers and illustrators: *The
Wind in the Willows*, *Around the World in Eighty Days*, *The Secret Garden*, and *The Railway Children*.

1233 2013 Alice's Adventures in Wonderland
London: Usborne Publishing Ltd.   9781409533016   Fran Parreño

1234 2014 Alice in Wonderland
Bath, UK: Parragon   9781472357236   Erin McGuire
Retold by Catherine Allison.

1235 2014 Alice in Wonderland
[Cookhill, UK]: Pook Press / Read Books   9781473312746 (paperback); Mabel Lucie Attwell
                                                  9781473312845 (hardback)

1236 2014   Songs from Alice in Wonderland and Through the Looking-Glass
[Cookhill, UK]: Pook Press / Read Books   9781473312814 (paperback)   Charles Folkard
Music by Lucy E. Broadwood. Various issues in 2017 with same ISBN.

1237 2014   Alice's Adventures in Wonderland
[Cookhill, UK]: Pook Press / Read Books   9781473312838   Gwynedd M. Hudson
Various issues in 2014 and 2017 with the same ISBN.

1238 2014   The Adventures of Alice in Wonderland
[Cookhill, UK]: Pook Press / Read Books   9781473312760   Thomas Maybank
Various issues in 2014, 2016, and 2017 with the same ISBN.

1239 2014   Alice's Adventures in Wonderland
[Cookhill, UK]: Pook Press / Read Books   9781473312777   Harry Rountree

1240 2014   Alice's Adventures in Wonderland
[Cookhill, UK]: Pook Press / Read Books   9781473312791 (paperback); W. H. Walker
                                                 9781473312890 (hardback)
Various issues in 2014, 2015, and 2017 with the same ISBN.

1241 2014   Alice in Wonderland
London: QED Publishing   9781781716021   Robert Dunn
Adapted by Ronne Randall. 46 pp. Color illustrations.

1242 2015   Alice in Wonderland
London: Bounty   9780753729687   John Tenniel
Classic Works Series.

1243 2015   Lewis Carroll's Alice's Adventures in Wonderland
London: Carlton Books Ltd.   9781783121588   Zdenko Bašić
Retold by Harriet Castor. With booklet attached to inside front cover: "The White Rabbit's Guide to Wonderland."
First published in 2010.

1244 2015   Alice's Adventures in Wonderland
London: Frances Lincoln's Children's Books   9781847806796   Yelena Bryksenkova
Later issues with the same date but denoted by numbers 1-10, one being moved sequentially.

1245 2015   Alice in Wonderland: Down the Rabbit Hole
Watertown, UK: Imagine Publishing   1623540496   Eric Puybaret
Retold by Joe Rhatigan and Charles Nurnberg. Published the same year by Macmillan Children's Books. Includes a
CD read by Joanne Froggatt.

1246 2015   Alice's Adventures in Wonderland
Oxford: Inky Parrot Press and Artists' Choice Editions 9780955834394;
                                                        0955834392   Kaori Ogawa; Mini Grey;

Clive Hicks-Jenkins; Jonny Hannah; Giovanni Robustelli; Ian Beck; Robi Dwi Antono; Ian Whadcock ; Vasilis
Papatsarouchas; Dagmar Sissolak; Kenneth Rougeau; Anne Vansweevelt; Janet Woolley; Lowri Mai Roberts;
Petra Brown; Schichinhoe Masaru; Katia Florentino; John Tenniel; Daria Palotti; Valery Kosachev; Annisa Krolik;
Yuri Laptev; Veronica Rowlands; Stanislawa Kodman; Victor Maristane (after Jan Švankmajer); Roland Topor
Sesquicentennial Edition. An Afterthought by Brian Sibley. Limited to 340 numbered copies plus 56 special copies
with a folder containing four signed prints, all in a solander box.

1247 2015   Alice in Wonderland, based on the classic tale by Lewis Carroll

London: Ladybird Books   9780723292180   Ailie Busby
In the series Ladybird First Favourite Tales. Glazed paper boards. Retold by Ronne Randall.

1248 2015 Alice's Adventures in Wonderland
Houghton-le-Spring, UK: My World   1909486132   Unillustrated
150th Anniversary Edition Celebrating Lewis Carroll's "North East Connections," meaning his childhood in Croft.

1249 2015 Alice in Wonderland
[Cookhill, UK]: Pook Press / Read Books 9781473306936   Dudley Jarrett
Various issues in 2013, 2015, and 2017, all with the same ISBN.

1250 2015 Alice's Adventures in Wonderland and Through the Looking-Glass
[Cookhill, UK]: Pook Press / Read Books 9781473322202 (paperback); Blanche McManus
                9781473335028 (hardback)
Includes 16 full-page illustrations by Blanche McManus.

1251 2015 Alice's Adventures in Wonderland
London: Puffin   9780141361345   Unknown

1252 2015 Alice in Wonderland
Woodbridge, UK: Top That Publishing 9781784452469   Alexandra Ball
Retold by Susie Linn. [25] pp. Paperback.

1253 2015 Usborne Classic Stories [Alice in Wonderland]
London: Usborne Publishing Ltd.   9781409563822   Mauro Evangelista
A later issue of the 2013 edition. Usborne Classics Stories. 5-volume set issued together in an illustrated gift box.
Alice in Wonderland adapted by Lesley Sims and illustrated by Mauro Evangelista. Other works in the set adapted by
other writers and illustrators: *The Wind in the Willows, Around the World in Eighty Days, The Secret Garden*, and *The
Railway Children*.

1254 2015 Alice
Cambridge, UK: Worth Press   9781849310284   John Tenniel
Color illustrations.

1255 ca. 2015 Alice in Wonderland
Ware, UK: Wordsworth Classics   9781840225990 (set); Various
                9781853261183 (*Alice*)
Alice is one of 8 classics in the set. The others are *Black Beauty, Peter Pan, The Jungle Book, The Little Prince, The
Secret Garden, The Wind In The Willows*, and *Treasure Island*.

1256 2016 The Alice in Wonderland Collection
London: Amazon   9781539022107   Unillustrated
Special Annotated Student and Teacher Edition. Edited by Vincent Verret.

1257 2016 Alice's Adventures in Wonderland
Worksop, UK: Award Publications   9781782701842   John Tenniel
Award Essential Classics Series.

1258 2016 Russian Alices: Illustrated Editions of Alice in Wonderland
        from the USSR and the Post-Soviet Era
Oxford; London: Artists' Choice Editions 9780995557000   Valerie Alfeyevsky; Eugene
Antonenkov; Alexander Antonyuk; Anastasia Arushanova; Diana Atoyan; Maria Babkina; Maria Bablova;
Anastasia Balantenysheva; Nikolay Batakov; Elena Bazanova; Dagmar Berkova; Yelena Bryksenkova;
Victor Chizhykov; Eugenia Christotinoy; Petr Chuklev; Vladimir Clavijo-Telepnev; Nataliya Derevyanko;
Elenka Deyn; Kosub Dmitry; Alexander Dodon; Vladislav Erko; Alessandra Fusi; Evgenia Gapchinska;

Andrei Gennadiev; E. S. Gorokhovski; Julia Gukova; Tatiana Ianovskaia; Nedezkda Illarionova; S. Ivancheva; Varya Kalesnikova; Gennady Kalinovski; Ivana Kazakova; Leila Kazbekova; Valerie Kazhin; Nicoli Kazlov; Maria Kolyshkina; Alexander Koshkin; Prezemyslaw Kossakowski; P. Kotov; Lucyny Telejko Kwiatowskiei; Eva Ladzinski; Diana Lapshina; Kosina Lavrova; Igor Lazarov; Oleg Lipchenko; M. Martynov; Andrei Martynov; Kasia Mickiewicz; Olga Minnibaeva; May Miturich; Maxim Mitrofanov; Vladimir Moldavsky; Ekaterina Mudrenko; Ekatrina Muratova; L. Mystratova; Julia Buhrle Nowikova; Vladimir Ovtcharov; Gergana Petkausa; Valeria Popova; Nina Povovska; Boris Pushkaroyov; Marja Rudska; Glenda Sburelin; I. Sergienko; Victor Shatunov; V. Shukayev; Lidia Shulgina; Anna Silivonchik; M. Svetlanov; Yuri Arstentyevich Vashchenko; Denis Vorobyev; Kataryzna Widmanska; Sergei Zalshupin; Natasha Zatulovskaya

The text is in English. Includes contributions by Tatiana Ianovskaia, Olia Harris, and Ella Parry-Davies. The checklist documents that the book contains illustrations by 54 illustrators who have completed a separate book, and 44 illustrators "who have done paintings or illustrations from *Alice in Wonderland* but, as far as we can establish, have not completed a book." There are 160 standard copies and 48 copies with a folder containing a signed aquatint.

1259	2016	Alice in Wonderland		
		London: Campbell	9781509812257	Colonel Moutarde
		First Stories Series.		

1260	2016	Alice in Wonderland		
		Newbury, UK: CCS Books	9781910619810	Unknown
		Classics Illustrated. 51 pp.		

1261	2016	Alice in Wonderland: The Complete Visual Guide		
		London: Dorling Kindersley	9780241256282	Disney Studios
		Written by Elizabeth Dowsett, Jo Casey, and Laura Gilbert. Copyright by Disney.		

1262	2016	Alice in Wonderland		
		Bath, UK: Parragon	9781474851435	Disney Studios
		Adapted by T. T. Sutherland. Based on the film by Tim Burton.		

1263	2016	The Illustrated Alice in Wonderland (The Golden Age of Illustration Series)		
		[Cookhill, UK]: Pook Press / Read Books	9781473335134; 9781473378100 (e-book)	Arthur Rackham Gwynedd M. Hudson; John Tenniel; Thomas Heath Robinson; Milo Winter

1264	2016	Alice's Adventures in Wonderland		
		London: The Folio Society		Charles van Sandwyk
		Limited to 1,000 numbered copies with original copper etching, signed and numbered by the artist. Illustrated cloth boards. In publisher's box.		

1265	2017	Foxton Readers: Alice in Wonderland		
		London: Foxton Books, CBL Distribution	9781911481119	Unknown
		Graded ESL / EAL / ELT Readers, Level 2 (600 headwords). Paperback.		

1266	2017	Alice in Wonderland		
		Sywell, UK: Igloo Books Ltd.	9781786705891	Eva Morales
		Retold by Jan Payne. Edited by Hannah Cather. Read by Blake Ritson and Katy Wix. Plus 1 CD.		

1267	2017	Alice's Adventures in Wonderland		
		London: Puffin	9780141385655	John Tenniel
		Puffin Classics.		

1268   2017   Alice in Wonderland
London: Scholastic Ltd.   9781407176161   Unknown
Read & Respond Series. Abridged by Sarah Ellen Burt and Debbie Ridgard. 47 pp.

1269   2017   Alice
Cambridge, UK: Worth Press   9781849311182   Anonymous
Colour My Classics Series.

1270   ca. 2017 Alice's Adventures in Wonderland
London: Carcas Publishing   9781975923631   John Tenniel
Front cover illustration is portion of Tenniel's White Rabbit as Herald. Book advertised in 2017 by Amazon.

1271   2018   Alice in Wonderland
Devon, UK: Centum Books   9781912396672   Disney Studios
A Treasure Cove Story 7. Adapted by Al Dempster.

1272   2018   Alice in Wonderland
Ware, UK: Wordsworth Editions   9781840227802   Unknown
Collector's Editions Series. Introductions and notes by Michael Irwin.

1273   2019   Alice's Adventures in Wonderland
Salisbury, UK: Books Illustrated, Ltd.   Christian Birmingham
The edition had 420 signed and numbered copies, 20 as "Artist's Prestige Editions in full vellum and with a presentation box, 100 as Deluxe Editions in Leather with a presentation box, 100 as Collectors Editions with a Slipcase, and 200 as standard editions.

1274   [2020] Alice's Adventures in Wonderland
Oxford: Inky Parrot Press   9780995557079   Willy Pogany
Limited edition of 126 copies. Paperbound. Illustration borders are in blue, red, green, or brown. Slightly enlarged from the original edition. Illustrations and typesetting by Charles Hall. Printed on Arcoprint paper by Palace Printers and bound by Ludlow Bookbinders.

1275   n.d.   Alice's Adventures in Wonderland
London: Bairns Books Ltd.   Anonymous
Three-way Tracing, Puzzle, and Story Book. Stiff pictorial boards. Abbreviated text.

1276   n.d.   Alice's Adventures in Wonderland
Leicester, UK: Brown Watson   9780709701347   Anonymous
Pictorial boards. Frontispiece illustration only, by anonymous illustrator. Rear cover has list of 12 Abbey Classics, of which this is No. 11.

1277   n.d.   Alice's Adventures in Wonderland
London, etc.: Cassell and Company   Anonymous
Story adapted. Illustrations unattributed. In the Playtime Series. Orange paper wrappers.

1278   n.d.   Alice's Adventures in Wonderland
London, etc.: Cassell and Company   Anonymous; Dorothy Rees
Story adapted. Illustrations unattributed. Title page vignette by Dorothy Rees. In the Storytime Series. Red limp cloth.

1279   n.d.   Alice's Adventures in Wonderland
London; Glasgow, UK: Collins Clear-Type Press   G.W. Backhouse
Undated reprint of the [1951] edition. In pictorial boards with 4 color plates.

1280   n.d.   Alice's Adventures in Wonderland
London; Glasgow, UK: Collins Clear-Type Press   G.W. Backhouse
Undated reprint of the Backhouse illustrated edition first published in [1951]. With 4 color plates and numerous
black-and-white illustrations. Red paper boards.

1281   n.d.   Alice's Adventures in Wonderland
London; Glasgow, UK: Collins Clear-Type Press   Charles Pears; T. H. Robinson
Beige or blue paper boards with paste on picture on front cover. Endpapers have scrolled reading Tales Told for the
Children.

1282   n.d.   Alice's Adventures in Wonderland
London; Glasgow, UK: Collins Clear-Type Press   Charles Pears; T. H. Robinson
Red or blue or beige paper boards with paste-on color picture. In the series Treasure Trove Picture Books.

1283   n.d.   Alice's Adventures in Wonderland
London; Glasgow, UK: Collins Clear-Type Press   Charles Pears; T. H. Robinson
Red paper boards with paste-on picture.

1284   n.d.   Alice's Adventures in Wonderland
London; Glasgow, UK: Collins Clear-Type Press   Harry Rountree
Paper boards and cloth spine. Oval paste-on picture on front cover. In the series Tales for the Children. Color
frontispiece and other line drawings.

1285   n.d.   Alice's Adventures in Wonderland
London; Glasgow, UK: Collins Clear-Type Press   Harry Rountree
Pictorial paper boards with pictures on spine and on front and back covers. Abbreviated text.

1286   n.d.   The Adventures of Alice in Wonderland
London: Collins Clear-Type Press   Harry Rountree; Edgar Norfield
Blue boards. Cover by Rountree and color drawings by Norfield.

1287   n.d.   Alice's Adventures in Wonderland
London: Collins' Clear-Type Press   Harry Rountree
Large quarto edition. Red cloth boards with title and roundel on front cover.

1288   n.d.   Alice's Adventures in Wonderland
London: Hodder and Stoughton   Gwynedd Hudson
Gray cloth boards, lettered in red. Color plates tipped in. In gray dust jacket, lettered in white.

1289   n.d.   Alice's Adventures in Wonderland
London: J. Coker & Co., Ltd.   Bessie Pease Gutmann;
                                                G. P. Micklewright
Internally similar to large octavo issues. Paper boards, red cloth spine, front cover has paste-on picture by Pease.

1290   n.d.   Alice's Adventures in Wonderland
London: J. M. Dent & Sons, Ltd.   0460008366   Anonymous
Green pictorial cloth. Introduction by Roger Lancelyn Green. Black-and-white illustrations. Everyman's Library.

1291   n.d.   Alice's Adventures in Wonderland
London: James Brodie, Ltd.   Thomas Maybank
Similar to No. 35 but styled The Owbridge Edition and Presented by the proprietors of Owbridge's Lung Tonic / The
Laboratory Hull.

1292   n.d.   **Alice's Adventures in Wonderland**
London: John F. Shaw Ltd.   E. Stuart Hardy
Binding Style 3. Cloth boards with candelabra-type design. Brown or blue cloth. Both have "Louis" instead of "Lewis."

1293   n.d.   **Alice's Adventures in Wonderland**
London: John F. Shaw Ltd.   E. Stuart Hardy
Binding Style 5. Green cloth boards with groups of flowers. This binding style only has 1 color plate, as the frontispiece.

1294   n.d.   **Alice in Pictures**
London: Oxford University Press   A. E. Jackson
Much abbreviated text. All but 2 pictures in full-color.

1295   n.d.   **Alice in Wonderland**
London: P. R. Gawthorn   Rene Cloke

1296   n.d.   **Walt Disney presents Alice in Wonderland**
Poulton, UK; Bristol, UK: Purnell and Sons   0361053681   Disney Studios
Closely parallels the American Little Golden Book D-19.

1297   n.d.   **Alice in Wonderland**
London: Simpkin Marshall, Ltd.   Walter Hawes; Anonymous
In the series Beacon Library. Frontispiece color illustration by another hand. Blue cloth boards.

1298   n.d.   **Alice's Adventures in Wonderland**
London: Stead's Publishing House   Brinsley Le Fanu
1st edition. In the series Stead's Prose Classics for Children.

1299   n.d.   **Alice's Adventures in Wonderland**
London; Glasgow, UK: The Children's Press   Harry Rountree
Front cover has picture by Rountree of Alice with Duchess.

1300   n.d.   **Alice's Adventures in Wonderland**
London; Glasgow, UK: The Children's Press   Harry Rountree
Large quarto edition, paper boards, red cloth spine. Front cover has picture of the Tea-Party.

1301   n.d.   **Alice's Adventures in Wonderland**
London; Glasgow, UK: The Children's Press   Harry Rountree
Large quarto edition, paper boards. Front cover has picture of Bill the Lizard, repeated on back cover.

1302   n.d.   **Alice's Adventures in Wonderland**
London; Glasgow, UK: The Children's Press   Harry Rountree; Peggy Earnshaw
Paper boards. Front cover has picture by Peggy Earnshaw. Dust jacket with same picture.

1303   n.d.   **Alice's Adventures in Wonderland**
London; Glasgow, UK: The Children's Press   Harry Rountree; Eulalie Banks
Paper boards. Front cover picture by Eulalie (Banks).

1304   n.d.   **Alice's Adventures in Wonderland**
London: The Epworth Press, J. Alfred Sharp   Gordon Robinson
Similar binding to first 1916 edition published by Charles Kelly and illustrated by Robinson. 1 color plate. A dust jacket with picture of Pool of Tears exists. Another copy has picture of Caterpillar on dust jacket. Several versions exist.

1305   n.d.   Alice's Adventures in Wonderland
London; etc.: Thomas Nelson and Sons   Harry Rountree
Quarto in purple paper boards, cloth spine, paste on picture on front cover. 8 illustrations mounted on gray paper.

1306   n.d.   Alice's Adventures in Wonderland
London; etc.: Thomas Nelson and Sons   Harry Rountree; Blampied
Small quarto edition. 8 color pictures, later issue. Green or blue cloth boards with silhouette of figures dancing. In
The Golden River Series. Another dust jacket with picture on front by Blampied.

1307   n.d.   Alice's Adventures in Wonderland and Bruno's Revenge
London; Edinburgh, UK: Thomas Nelson and Sons Ltd.   Helen Monro
Nelson's Famous Books edition.

1308   n.d.   Alice's Adventures in Wonderland
London: Thomas Nelson and Sons Ltd.   John Tenniel
Reprint of the 1932 Nelson Classics series. Introduction by Langford Reed.

1309   n.d.   Alice's Adventures in Wonderland
London; Melbourne, VIC: Ward Lock & Co   Anonymous (after
                                                            Margaret W. Tarrant)

16 color plates. Pictorial paper-covered boards.

1310   n.d.   Alice's Adventures in Wonderland
London: Ward Lock & Co   Anonymous
Sunshine Series.

1311   n.d.   Alice's Adventures in Wonderland
London: Young World Productions Ltd.   Anonymous
A Gold Token Book.

1.16 OTHER PUBLISHERS OF COMBINED EDITIONS OF *ALICE* AND *LOOKING-GLASS*

1312   ca. 1920s   Alice's Adventures in Wonderland and Through the Looking-Glass
London: Collins Clear-Type Press   Harry Rountree
Large format. Green cloth boards, vignette on front cover. Tipped-in plates. Also exists in a small format in dark blue
leatherette, lettered in gilt on spine, 1 color plate on the frontispiece.

1313   1920   Alice's Adventures in Wonderland and Through the Looking-Glass
London: George G. Harrap & Company   Bessie Pease Gutmann
8 color plates and 14 line drawings.

1314   1921   Alice's Adventures in Wonderland and Through the Looking-Glass
              (and The Rose of the Ring)
London: Odhams Press   Edgar B. Thurstan
Includes The Rose of the Ring by Thackeray. 22 illustrations.

1315   1925   Alice's Adventures in Wonderland and Through the Looking-Glass
London: George G. Harrap & Company   Bessie Pease Gutmann
Reprint of the 1920 edition. 8 color plates and 14 line drawings.

1316 [1928] Alice's Adventures in Wonderland and Through the Looking-Glass

London; Glasgow, UK: Collins Clear-Type Press   Harry Rountree

Undated but believed to be 1928. 1 color plate as frontispiece. 55 other illustrations. Tales for the Children edition. Illustrated front cover. Flexible blue cloth.

1317 [1928] Alice's Adventures in Wonderland and Through the Looking-Glass

London; Glasgow, UK: Collins Clear-Type Press   Harry Rountree

Undated but believed to be 1928. 8 tipped-in color plates with tissue guards. 125 other illustrations. Illustrated front cover. Green cloth. Also exists in a small format in dark blue leatherette, lettered in gilt on the spine. 1 color plate on the frontispiece.

1318 [1928] Alice's Adventures in Wonderland and Through the Looking-Glass

London; Glasgow, UK: Collins Clear-Type Press   Harry Rountree

Undated but believed to be 1928. 8 tipped-in color plates with tissue guards. 55 other illustrations. Illustrated Pocket Classics edition. Illustrated front cover. Green cloth.

1319 [1928] Alice's Adventures in Wonderland and Through the Looking-Glass

London; Glasgow, UK: Collins Clear-Type Press   Harry Rountree

Undated but believed to be 1928. Illustrated School Classics edition. Tipped in plates with tissue guards. Illustrated front cover.

1320 1929 Alice's Adventures in Wonderland and Through the Looking-Glass

London: George G. Harrap & Company   Bessie Pease Gutmann

Reprint of the 1920 edition in March 1929 and again in September 1929. 8 color plates and 14 line drawings.

1321 1929 Alice in Wonderland, Through the Looking Glass and Other Comic Pieces

London: J. M. Dent & Sons. New York: E. P. Dutton   Lewis Carroll

1st edition. Called the Dent Library Edition. Introduction by Ernest Rhys.

1322 1929 Alice in Wonderland and Through the Looking-Glass and Other Comic Pieces

London: J. M. Dent. New York: E. P. Dutton   Various

Everyman's Library for Young People, No. 836. Includes *Phantasmagoria*, *Snark*, and *A Tangled Tale*. Reprinted in 1992.

1323 1930 Alice in Wonderland, Through the Looking Glass and Other Comic Pieces

London: J. M. Dent & Sons. New York: E. P. Dutton   Lewis Carroll

1st reprint of the 1929 Library Edition. Dust jacket.

1324 1930 Alice in Wonderland, Through the Looking Glass and Other Comic Pieces

London: J. M. Dent & Sons. New York: E. P. Dutton   Lewis Carroll

1st reprint of the 1929 Library Edition. Dust jacket.

1325 ca. 1930 Alice's Adventures in Wonderland and Through the Looking-Glass

London; Glasgow, UK: Collins Clear-Type Press   Harry Rountree

Undated but believed to be ca. 1930. 4 tipped in color plates with tissue guards. 66 other illustrations. Illustrated front cover.

1326 ca. 1930 Alice's Adventures in Wonderland and Through the Looking-Glass

London; Glasgow, UK: Collins Clear-Type Press   Harry Rountree; Charles Pears

Undated but believed to be ca. 1930. The Children's Press edition. 5 tipped-in color plates; 1 of these by Charles Pears. 66 other illustrations. Illustrated front cover. Pictorial paper-covered boards backed in black cloth.

1327   ca. 1930 Alice's Adventures in Wonderland and Through the Looking-Glass
London; Glasgow, UK: Collins Clear-Type Press   Harry Rountree;
                                                       Charles Pears; D. Osborne
Undated but believed to be ca. 1930. The Children's Press edition. 8 tipped-in color plates; 4 of these by Charles Pears. 66 other illustrations. Illustrated front cover by D. Osborne.

1328   ca. 1930 Alice's Adventures in Wonderland and Through the Looking-Glass
London; Glasgow, UK: Collins Clear-Type Press   Harry Rountree; Charles Pears
Undated but believed to be ca. 1930. The Children's Press edition. 8 tipped-in color plates; 4 of these by Charles Pears. 66 other illustrations. Illustrated front cover.

1329   ca. 1930s Alice's Adventures in Wonderland, Through the Looking-Glass and
             The Rose and the Ring
London: Odhams Press   Edgar B. Thurstan
Undated. Dust jacket.

1330   ca. 1930s Alice's Adventures in Wonderland and Through the Looking-Glass
London; Beccles, UK: William Clowes and Sons Ltd.   J. Morton Sale
Yellow cloth boards printed in black.

1331   1931   Alice's Adventures in Wonderland and Through the Looking-Glass
London: J. Coker & Co., Ltd.   Bessie Pease Gutmann
Reprint of the 1920 Harrap edition. 8 color plates and 14 line drawings. There is an enlarged version with leaf measuring 248 x 195 mm vs 195 x 140. In the enlarged version the pictorial borders are signed P. Micklewright.

1332   1933   Alice's Adventures in Wonderland and Through the Looking-Glass
London: J. Coker & Co., Ltd.   Bessie Pease Gutmann
Reprint of the 1920 Harrap edition in the 248 x 195 mm format. 8 color plates and 14 line drawings. The pictorial borders are signed P. Micklewright.

1333   ca. 1933 Alice's Adventures in Wonderland and Through the Looking-Glass
London; Beccles, UK: William Clowes and Sons   J. Morton Sale
Yellow cloth boards printed in black. Color frontispiece. This edition dated from inscription.

1334   1934   Alice in Wonderland, Through the Looking Glass and Other Comic Pieces
London: J. M. Dent & Sons. New York: E. P. Dutton   Lewis Carroll
2nd reprint of the 1929 Library Edition. Dent logo in blind on the front cover. Dust jacket. In various bindings.

1335   ca. 1934 Alice's Adventures in Wonderland and Through the Looking-Glass
London: Hutchinson   M. L. Clements
In full-color paper boards. Spells "Carroll" incorrectly on title page as "Carrol."

1336   1938   Alice's Adventures in Wonderland and Through the Looking-Glass
London; Glasgow, UK: Collins Clear-Type Press   Harry Rountree
The Laurel and Gold Series, No. 106.

1337   1939   Alice's Adventures in Wonderland and Through the Looking-Glass
London; Glasgow, UK: Collins Clear-Type Press   A. H. Watson
1st edition June 1939. Dust jacket.

1338   1939   Alice in Wonderland, Through the Looking Glass and Other Comic Pieces
London: J. M. Dent & Sons. New York: E. P. Dutton   Lewis Carroll
3rd reprint of the 1929 Library Edition. Dust jacket.

1339   1939   The Complete Works of Lewis Carroll
London: Nonesuch Press   John Tenniel
1st edition, November 1939. Nonesuch Library. Introduction by Alexander Woollcott. Dust jacket.

1340   1940   The Complete Works of Lewis Carroll
London: Nonesuch Press   John Tenniel
2nd impression. Introduction by Alexander Woollcott

1341   1942   Alice in Wonderland, Through the Looking Glass and Other Comic Pieces
London: J. M. Dent & Sons. New York: E. P. Dutton   Lewis Carroll
Later reprint of the 1929 Library Edition. Dust jacket.

1342   1942   The Complete Works of Lewis Carroll
London: Nonesuch Press   John Tenniel
3rd impression.

1343   1943   Alice in Wonderland, Through the Looking Glass and Other Comic Pieces
London: J. M. Dent & Sons   Lewis Carroll
The Kings Treasuries of Literature, reprint.

1344   1943   The Complete Works of Lewis Carroll
London: Nonesuch Press   John Tenniel
4th impression.

1345   ca. 1943 The Complete Works of Lewis Carroll
London: Nonesuch Press   John Tenniel
5th impression.

1346   1944   Alice's Adventures in Wonderland and Through the Looking-Glass
London; Glasgow, UK: Collins Clear-Type Press   A. H. Watson
2nd reprint May 1944. Dust jacket.

1347   1946   Alice's Adventures in Wonderland and Through the Looking-Glass
London; Glasgow, UK: Collins Clear-Type Press   A. H. Watson
3rd reprint March 1946. Dust jacket. In orange cloth stamped in silver.

1348   1946   Alice in Wonderland, Through the Looking Glass and Other Comic Pieces
London: J. M. Dent & Sons. New York: E. P. Dutton   Lewis Carroll
The Kings Treasuries of Literature, reprint.

1349   1946   The Complete Works of Lewis Carroll
London: Nonesuch Press   John Tenniel
6th impression.

1350   1946   Alice's Adventures in Wonderland and Through the Looking-Glass
Stockholm; London: Zephyr Books and The Continental Book Company   Mervyn Peake
1st edition. Card covers and matching dust jacket.

1351   1947   The Complete Works of Lewis Carroll
London: Nonesuch Press   John Tenniel
7th impression.

1352   1947   Alice's Adventures in Wonderland and Through the Looking-Glass
London: Pan Books   John Tenniel
Great Pan Double Volume Series. Reprinted 1948 and 1952 with new publisher's note' Paperback.

1353   1948   Alice's Adventures in Wonderland and Through the Looking-Glass
London; Glasgow, UK: Collins Clear-Type Press   A. H. Watson
4th reprint January 1948.

1354   1948   Alice's Adventures in Wonderland and Through the Looking-Glass
London: Pan Books   John Tenniel
Great Pan Double Volume Series. 1st reprint of the 1947 edition with new publisher's note.

1355   1948   Alice's Adventures in Wonderland and Through the Looking-Glass
London; Ewell, UK: The Studley Press   Arabella Blithe; Anonymous
Children's Classics Series, 1st edition. 1 color plate as frontispiece signed "Blithe" and 4 color illustrations unsigned.
Dust jacket. In beige cloth stamped in gilt.

1356   ca. 1948 Alice's Adventures in Wonderland with other stories and poems
London: Peter Lunn   H. M. Brock
Green cloth boards. Frontispiece only by Brock. The edition was originally part of The Children's Omnibus series.
Dust jacket.

1357   1949   Alice's Adventures in Wonderland and Through the Looking-Glass
London: J. M. Dent & Sons   Lewis Carroll
Everyman's Library, No. 836. Reprint of 1929 issue.

1358   1949   The Complete Works of Lewis Carroll
London: Nonesuch Press   John Tenniel
8th impression.

1359   1949   Alice's Adventures in Wonderland and Through the Looking-Glass
London: The Heirloom Library   Philip Gough
1st edition. 8 color plates and 23 other illustrations. Dust jacket.

1360   1950   Alice's Adventures in Wonderland and Through the Looking-Glass
London: The Heirloom Library   Philip Gough
1st reprint of the 1949 edition. Paper boards with 8 color plates, some line drawings. Dust jacket.

1361   ca. 1950s   Alice's Adventures in Wonderland and Through the Looking-Glass
London: Andrew Dakers   G. R. Ratcliff
Red paper boards. Dust jacket with picture signed GRR (Ratcliff), repeating the frontispiece also by GRR. In various
bindings.

1362   ca. 1950s   Alice's Adventures in Wonderland and Through the Looking-Glass
London: Andrew Dakers, Ltd.   Anonymous; G. R. Ratcliff;
                                                     Sherborn?
Red paper boards. The Hamlyn Classics. Dust jacket with picture signed GRR (Ratcliff), repeating the frontispiece
also by GRR. With an illustration signed "Sherborn"?

1363   ca. 1950s   Alice in Wonderland and Through the Looking-Glass
London: Andrew Dakers Ltd.   M. Entwisle
The Hamlyn Classics. Yellow cloth. Color dust jacket and frontispiece by unattributed artist. One picture (p. 99)
signed M. Entwisle.

1364   ca. 1950 Alice's Adventures in Wonderland and Through the Looking-Glass
London; Glasgow, UK: Blackie & Son   Pauline Baynes
1 color frontispiece. Dust jacket cover also signed by Baynes. Blackie's Library of Famous Books. A copy is known
inscribed August 1953.

1365   ca. 1950s   Alice in Wonderland and Through the Looking-Glass
London: Blackie & Sons, Ltd.   Anonymous
Paper boards, dust jacket with anonymous picture of Alice and Caterpillar on front, Alice and Tweedles on back.
Famous Books series, No. 13.

1366   ca. 1950s   Alice's Adventures in Wonderland and Through the Looking-Glass
London: Dean & Son Ltd.   Anonymous
Red paper boards. Dust jacket has color picture of the Tea-Party. There are numerous variants, some with lists of titles in the series. Precedence is difficult to ascertain. The following have been seen: green and blue paper boards with the Tea-Party picture; red, and green paper boards with color picture of Duchess's kitchen on dust jacket; and yellow paper boards; laminated paper boards with a different Tea-Party picture on front cover; and laminated paper boards with picture of Alice with Gryphon on front cover. There are 14 issues in various bindings.

1367   ca. 1950s   Alice's Adventures in Wonderland and Through the Looking-Glass
London: Presentation Library, Beaverbrook Newspapers   Patricia Morriss
8 color plates and 12 other illustrations.

1368   ca. 1950s   Alice's Adventures in Wonderland and Through the Looking-Glass
London: Purnell Books   Anonymous
A later version of the Thames "Regent Classics." May have been issued in dust jacket.

1369   ca. 1950s   Alice's Adventures in Wonderland and Through the Looking-Glass
London: Reward Classics   Anonymous
The back cover lists *Alice* as number 3 in a list of 6 titles. This is a later version of one of the "Rylee Classics."

1370   ca. 1950s   Alice in Wonderland and Through the Looking-Glass
London: Rylee Classics   Anonymous
In the series Reward Classics. Laminated color paper boards, front cover has picture of Tea-Party. The back cover lists *Alice* as number 3 in a list of 6 titles.

1371   ca. 1950s   Alice in Wonderland and Through the Looking-Glass
London: Rylee Classics   Anonymous
Red decorated paper boards with frontispiece picture of Caucus Race. In full-color dust jacket with picture of Alice falling down rabbit-hole. Variant copy in blue paper boards; another variant in blue boards with frontispiece picture of Tea-Party; another in full-color paper boards with front picture of Alice falling down rabbit-hole.

1372   ca. 1950s   Alice's Adventures in Wonderland and Through the Looking-Glass
London; Birmingham, UK: Rylee Ltd.   Dorothy A. Doherty
Rylee Classics. 25 illustrations. A copy is known inscribed "September 1956." Various designs for covers and binding.

1373   ca. 1950s   Alice's Adventures in Wonderland and Through the Looking-Glass
London: The Thames Publishing Co.   Anonymous
The only illustration is on the dust jacket. May be a "Regent Classics."

1374   1951   Alice's Adventures in Wonderland and Through the Looking-Glass
London; Glasgow, UK: Collins Clear-Type Press   A. H. Watson
5th reprint. March 1949. Green cloth lettered in black.

1375   1951   Alice's Adventures in Wonderland and Through the Looking-Glass
London; Glasgow, UK: Collins Clear-Type Press   A. H. Watson
6th reprint. August 1951. Green cloth lettered in black.

1376   1951   Alice's Adventures in Wonderland and Through the Looking-Glass
London: The Heirloom Library   Philip Gough
2nd reprint of the 1949 edition. Paper boards with 8 color plates, some line drawings. Dust jacket.

1377   1952   Alice's Adventures in Wonderland and Through the Looking-Glass
London: J. M. Dent & Sons   Lewis Carroll
Everyman's Library, No. 836, reprint of 1929 issue.

1378   1952   The Complete Works of Lewis Carroll
London: Nonesuch Press   John Tenniel
9th impression.

1379   1952   Alice's Adventures in Wonderland and Through the Looking-Glass
London: Pan Books Ltd.   John Tenniel
Great Pan Double Volume Series. 2nd reprint of the 1947 edition with publisher's note as in the 1948 reprint.

1380   1953   Alice's Adventures in Wonderland and Through the Looking-Glass
London; Glasgow, UK: Collins Clear-Type Press   A. H. Watson
7th reprint.

1381   1953   Alice's Adventures in Wonderland and Through the Looking-Glass
London: The Heirloom Library   Philip Gough
3rd reprint of the 1949 edition. Paper boards with 8 color plates, some line drawings. Dust jacket.

1382   1954   Alice's Adventures in Wonderland and Through the Looking-Glass
London: Alan Wingate   Mervyn Peake
Foreword by Malcolm Muggeridge. Blue paper boards. Dust jacket.

1383   1954   Alice's Adventures in Wonderland, Through the Looking-Glass and other writings
London; Glasgow, UK: Collins Clear-Type Press   Dorothy Colles
                                                                (after John Tenniel)
1st edition. Illustrations after John Tenniel. Introduction by Robin Denniston. Many variant bindings. One listing "Collins Classics," including a "Collins School Classics" and "Olive Classics".

1384   1954   Alice's Adventures in Wonderland and Through the Looking-Glass
London; Glasgow, UK: Collins Clear-Type Press   A. H. Watson
8th reprint. Now called "Collins Standard Series." Dust jacket.

1385   1954   Alice's Adventures in Wonderland, Through the Looking-Glass and other writings
London; Glasgow, UK: Collins Clear-Type Press   After John Tenniel
The Olive Classics.

1386   1954   Alice's Adventures in Wonderland and Through the Looking-Glass
London: J. M. Dent & Sons Ltd. New York: E. P. Dutton & Co., Inc.   John Tenniel;
                                                                Diana Stanley
1st edition thus. After 8 Tenniel line drawings redrawn in color by Stanley. In the series The Children's Illustrated Classics. Dust jacket.

1387   1954   Alice's Adventures in Wonderland and Through the Looking-Glass
London: The Heirloom Library   Philip Gough
4th reprint of the 1949 edition. Paper boards with 8 color plates, some line drawings. Dust jacket.

1388   [1954]   Alice's Adventures in Wonderland and Through the Looking-Glass
London: Andrew Dakers Ltd.   G. R. Ratcliff; H. Entwhistle
The Hamlyn Classics.

1389   1955   Alice's Adventures in Wonderland and Through the Looking-Glass
London; Glasgow, UK: Collins Clear-Type Press   A. H. Watson
9th reprint. Dust jacket.

1390   1955   Alice's Adventures in Wonderland and Through the Looking-Glass
London: The Heirloom Library   Philip Gough
5th reprint of the 1949 edition. Paper boards with 8 color plates, some line drawings. Dust jacket.

1391   ca. 1955 Alice's Adventures in Wonderland and Through the Looking-Glass
London: The Thames Publishing Co.   Anonymous
In the series Regent Classics. There are at least 6 versions. Dust jacket has the only illustration.

1392   1956   Alice's Adventures in Wonderland and Through the Looking-Glass
London; Glasgow, UK: Collins Clear-Type Press   A. H. Watson
10th reprint. Labeled "This impression 1956." Dust jacket.

1393   1957   Alice's Adventures in Wonderland and Through the Looking-Glass
London; Glasgow, UK: Collins Clear-Type Press   A. H. Watson; Will Nickless
1st edition thus. Now called Collins Crusader Series. Dust jacket and frontispiece illustrated by Will Nickless.

1394   1957   Alice's Adventures in Wonderland and Through the Looking-Glass
London: Dean & Son Ltd.   Unillustrated; Anonymous
The book exists in 14 issues in various bindings. One is light green textured paper-covered boards. Pictorial dust
jacket with uncredited illustration. Variant edition in red paper-covered boards known. A later undated abridged
edition in dark green paper-covered boards is known. Only the dust jacket has a color picture by an anonymous
illustrator, which varies from issue to issue.

1395   1957   Alice in Wonderland, Through the Looking Glass and Other Comic Pieces
London: J. M. Dent & Sons   Lewis Carroll
The Kings Treasuries of Literature, reprint.

1396   1957   Alice's Adventures in Wonderland and Through the Looking-Glass
London: J. M. Dent & Sons Ltd. New York: E. P. Dutton & Co, Inc.   John Tenniel; Diana Stanley
Reprint of the 1954 edition of The Children's Illustrated Classics series. After 8 Tenniel line drawings redrawn in color
by Stanley. Dust jacket.

1397   1958   Alice's Adventures in Wonderland and Through the Looking-Glass
London; Glasgow, UK: Collins Clear-Type Press   A. H. Watson; Will Nickless
1st reprint. Dust jacket and frontispiece illustrated by Will Nickless.

1398   1958   Alice's Adventures in Wonderland and Through the Looking-Glass
London: The Heirloom Library   Philip Gough
6th reprint of the 1949 edition. Paper boards with 8 color plates, some line drawings. Dust jacket.

1399   1958   Alice's Adventures in Wonderland and Through the Looking-Glass
London: The Heirloom Library   Philip Gough
7th reprint of the 1949 edition. Paper boards with 8 color plates, some line drawings.

1400   [1958]   Alice's Adventures in Wonderland and Through the Looking-Glass

London; Glasgow, UK: Blackie & Son   Unillustrated

No. 13 in a series of 34 "Famous Books." In illustrated dust jacket. Undated, but British Library copy was received 18 December 18, 1958.

1401   1959   Alice's Adventures in Wonderland and Through the Looking-Glass

London; Glasgow, UK: Blackie & Son   Pauline Baynes

Blackie's Library of Famous Books.

1402   1959   Alice's Adventures in Wonderland and Through the Looking-Glass

London; Glasgow, UK: Blackie & Son   Pauline Baynes

The Tower Classics. Pauline Baynes illustrated only the cover.

1403   1960   Alice's Adventures in Wonderland and Through the Looking-Glass

London; Glasgow, UK: Collins Clear-Type Press   A. H. Watson; Will Nickless

Reprint of the 1958 edition. Dust jacket and frontispiece illustrated by Will Nickless.

1404   ca. 1960 Alice's Adventures in Wonderland, Through the Looking-Glass, and
                      The Rose and the Ring

London: Odhams Press Ltd.   Edgar B. Thurstan

1405   ca. 1960 Alice's Adventures in Wonderland and Through the Looking-Glass

London: Peal Press [Blackie and Son, Ltd.]   Pauline Baynes; Unknown

Peal Classic Library. Pauline Baynes listed on title page; unknown illustrator for the cover.

1406   ca. 1960s   Alice in Wonderland and Through the Looking-Glass

London: Rylee Classics   Anonymous

In the series Reward Classics. Laminated color paper boards. Front cover has picture of Tea-Party plus Caterpillar and Duchess. Frontispiece is Rabbit as Herald.

1407   ca. 1960s   Alice's Adventures in Wonderland and Through the Looking-Glass

London: Rylee Classics   D. A. Doherty

In the series Rylee Clear Print Classics. Glazed pictorial boards. Front cover picture of Tea-Party.

1408   ca. 1960s   Alice's Adventures in Wonderland and Through the Looking-Glass

London: Sandle Brothers Ltd.   D. A. Doherty

Similar to a 1960 edition published by Rylee Classics. Front cover has picture of Alice and Caterpillar.

1409   1960   Alice's Adventures in Wonderland and Through the Looking-Glass

London: The New English Library. New York: The New American Editions   John Tenniel

Foreword by Horace Gregory. Signet Classic with CD.

1410   ca. 1960s   Alice's Adventures and Through the Looking-Glass

London: The Thames Publishing Co.   Anonymous

In the series Regent Classics. Red paper boards. Anonymous picture on dust jacket. Several reprints all are undated but the list of other books in the series varies.

1411   1961   Alice's Adventures in Wonderland and Through the Looking-Glass

London: J. M. Dent & Sons Ltd. New York: E. P. Dutton & Co., Inc.   John Tenniel; Diana Stanley

Reprint of the 1954 edition of The Children's Illustrated Classics series. After 8 Tenniel line drawings redrawn in color by Stanley. Dust jacket. Reprinted 1966 and 1972.

1412   1962   Alice's Adventures in Wonderland and Through the Looking-Glass

London: Collier-Macmillan Ltd.   John Tenniel
First Collier Books Edition. There was a 12th printing.

1413   1962   Alice's Adventures in Wonderland and Through the Looking-Glass
London: Collier Macmillan. New York: Collier   John Tenniel
With a new introduction by Louis Untermeyer.

1414   1962   Alice's Adventures in Wonderland, Through the Looking-Glass and other writings
London; Glasgow, UK: Collins Clear-Type Press   Dorothy Colles
                                                                 (after John Tenniel)

Reprint of the 1954 edition. Illustrations after John Tenniel. Green cloth boards and in other covers. Dust jacket.
Collins Classics on spine.

1415   1962   Alice's Adventures in Wonderland and Through the Looking-Glass
Harmondsworth, UK: Penguin Books   0140301690   John Tenniel
1st Harmondsworth Penguin edition with both *Alice* and *Looking-Glass.*

1416   1962   Alice's Adventures in Wonderland and Through the Looking-Glass
London: Penguin Books Limited   John Tenniel
1st Puffin Book combined edition.

1417   1962   Alice's Adventures in Wonderland and Through the Looking-Glass
London: Ward, Lock & Co.   David Walsh; John Cooper
A Prince Charming Color Book. Pictorial paper boards Dust jacket.

1418   1963   Alice's Adventures in Wonderland and Through the Looking-Glass
London: Nonesuch Press   John Tenniel; Henry Holiday
1st edition. A Nonesuch Cygnet edition. With the illustrations of Tenniel and *The Hunting of the Snark*. In glazed or
glassine dust jacket.

1419   1963   Alice's Adventures in Wonderland, Through the Looking-Glass and The Hunting of
              the Snark
London: The Nonesuch Press   John Tenniel; Henry Holiday
1st edition. Yellow cloth stamped in gold and orange.

1420   1963   Alice's Adventures in Wonderland and Through the Looking-Glass
Harmondsworth, UK: Penguin Books   John Tenniel
1st Harmondsworth Penguin reprint.

1421   ca. 1964 Alice's Adventures in Wonderland and Through the Looking-Glass
London; Glasgow, UK: Blackie & Son   Unillustrated
Undated, but British Library copy received 9 October 9, 1964.

1422   1964   Alice's Adventures in Wonderland, Through the Looking-Glass and other writings
London; Glasgow, UK: Collins Clear-Type Press   Dorothy Colles
                                                                 (after John Tenniel)

Reprint of a 1954 edition. Illustrations after John Tenniel. Red paper boards. Collins School Classics on spine. Reprint
of 1954 edition.

1423   1964   Alice's Adventures in Wonderland and Through the Looking-Glass
London: J. M. Dent & Sons Ltd. New York: E. P. Dutton & Co, Inc.   John Tenniel;
                                                                   Diana Stanley

Reprint of the 1954 edition of The Children's Illustrated Classics series. After 8 Tenniel line drawings redrawn in color
by Stanley. Dust jacket.

1424   1965   Alice in Wonderland: Comprising both Alice's Adventures in Wonderland
        and Through the Looking-Glass
London; New York; Melbourne, VIC; Toronto, ON;   John Tenniel; Charles Mozley
Wellington, NZ: The Caxton Publishing Company
1st Caxton Edition. The Caxton Junior Classics Series. Yellow smooth cloth boards, Mad Hatter on front in black, gilt
lettering front and spine, 255 pp. 4 non-integral color plates including frontispiece + 92 black-and-white drawings.

1425   1965   Alice in Wonderland, Through the Looking Glass and Other Comic Pieces
London: J. M. Dent & Sons. New York: E. P. Dutton   Lewis Carroll
Reprint of the 1929 Library Edition. New introduction. Dust jacket.

1426   1965   The Works of Lewis Carroll
London: Paul Hamlyn, and Spring Books   John Tenniel
1st edition. Introduction by Roger Lancelyn Green. Dust jacket.

1427   1965   Alice's Adventures in Wonderland and Through the Looking-Glass
Harmondsworth, UK: Penguin Books   John Tenniel
2nd Harmondsworth Penguin reprint.

1428   1965   Alice's Adventures in Wonderland and Through the Looking-Glass
London; New York; Toronto, ON: The New English Library   John Tenniel
6th printing. Signets Classics Series.

1429   ca. 1965 Alice in Wonderland: Comprising both Alice's Adventures in Wonderland
        and Through the Looking-Glass
London: International Learning Systems Corporation   John Tenniel; Charles Mozley
1st International Learning Systems edition. The Caxton Junior Classics Series. Yellow cloth, gilt lettering front and
spine, 255 pp., 4 color plates, and 25 black-and-white Tenniel drawings (14 in *Alice*, 11 in *Looking-Glass*). This edition
first published 1965. Reprinted 1966, 1967, 1968, [1969?].

1430   ca. 1965 Alice's Adventures in Wonderland and Through the Looking-Glass
London: International Learning Systems Corporation   John Tenniel; Charles Mozley
5th printing. Caxton Junior Classics Series. 4 color plates plus 14 Tenniel illustrations in *Alice* and 11 in *Looking-Glass*.

1431   ca. 1965 Alice's Adventures in Wonderland and Through the Looking-Glass
London: International Learning Systems Corporation   John Tenniel; Charles Mozley
Caxton Junior Classics Series. 4 color plates and 14 Tenniel illustrations in *Alice* and 11 in *Looking-Glass*.

1432   1966   Alice' Adventures and Through the Looking-Glass
London: Caxton Publishing Company   John Tenniel; Charles Mozley
1st reprint. Caxton Junior Classics.

1433   1966   Alice's Adventures in Wonderland, Through the Looking-Glass and other writings
London; Glasgow, UK: Collins Clear-Type Press   Dorothy Colles
                                                                 (after John Tenniel)
Reprint of a 1954 edition. Illustrations after John Tenniel. Maroon soft leather.

1434   1966   Alice's Adventures in Wonderland and Through the Looking-Glass
London: J. M. Dent & Sons Ltd. New York: E. P. Dutton & Co., Inc.   John Tenniel;
                                                                     Diana Stanley
4th reprint of the 1954 edition of The Children's Illustrated Classics series. After 8 Tenniel line drawings redrawn in
color by Stanley. Dust jacket.

1435   1966   The Complete Works of Lewis Carroll
London: Nonesuch Press   John Tenniel
10th impression.

1436   1966   Alice's Adventures in Wonderland and Through the Looking-Glass
London: Nonesuch Press   John Tenniel; Henry Holiday
Reprint of the 1963 edition. With the illustrations of Tenniel and *The Hunting of the Snark*. Nonesuch Cygnet. In
glazed dust jacket.

1437   1966   Alice's Adventures in Wonderland and Through the Looking-Glass
Harmondsworth, UK: Penguin Books   John Tenniel
3rd Harmondsworth Penguin reprint.

1438   1966   Alice's Adventures in Wonderland and Through the Looking-Glass
Birmingham, UK: Rylee, Ltd.   Anonymous
Only illustrations are on the dust jacket and frontispiece. Later undated reissue styled Reward Classics.

1439   [1966] Alice's Adventures in Wonderland [and Through the Looking-Glass]
London: Rylee, Ltd.   D. A. Doherty
In the series Rylee Clear Print Classics. The publisher has a new address on Queen Victoria Street.

1440   [1966] Alice's Adventures in Wonderland and Through the Looking-Glass
London: Rylee, Ltd.   D. A. Doherty
Undated but the British Library copy was received July 22, 1966.

1441   ca. 1966 Alice's Adventures in Wonderland [and Through the Looking-Glass]
London: Sandle Brothers, Ltd.   D. A. Doherty
In the series Rylee Clear Print Classics. The back cover lists *Alice* as number 3 in a list of 6 titles. A later version of
Rylee Classics.

1442   1967   Alice's Adventures and Through the Looking-Glass
London: Caxton Publishing Company   John Tenniel; Charles Mozley
2nd reprint. Caxton Junior Classics.

1443   [1967] Alice's Adventures in Wonderland and Through the Looking-Glass
Maidenhead, UK: Quaker Oats Ltd. [McGraw-Hill Publishing Co., Ltd.]   Anonymous
Sugar Puffs Library. Cover by anonymous illustrator.

1444   1968   Alice's Adventures in Wonderland and Through the Looking-Glass
London: Caxton Publishing Company   John Tenniel; Charles Mozley
3rd reprint. Caxton Junior Classics.

1445   1968   Alice's Adventures in Wonderland and Through the Looking-Glass
London: Caxton Publishing Company   John Tenniel; Charles Mozley
4th reprint. Caxton Junior Classics.

1446   1968   Alice's Adventures in Wonderland and Through the Looking-Glass
London: Minster Classics   John Tenniel
Copyright Lancer Books, Inc.

1447   1968   Alice's Adventures in Wonderland and Through the Looking-Glass
                and The Hunting of the Snark
London: Minster Classics   John Tenniel; Henry Holiday
Paperback. Copyright date 1968 by Lancer Books Inc.

1448   1968   Alice's Adventures in Wonderland and Through the Looking-Glass
London: Penguin Books Limited   John Tenniel
4th Harmondsworth Penguin reprint.

1449   1968   The Works of Lewis Carroll
London: Spring Books   John Tenniel
2nd impression of the 1965 Hamlyn edition. Includes introduction by Roger Lancelyn Green.

1450   [Before 1970]   Alice's Adventures in Wonderland and Through the Looking-Glass
London: Heron Books, William Collins & Co. Ltd.   John Tenniel
Lacks the Diana Stanley plates from the 1954 J. M. Dent edition. A Young Person's Classic. Yellow or green paper boards.

1451   1970   Alice's Adventures in Wonderland and Through the Looking-Glass
London: Abbey Classics   Pauline Baynes; Unknown
Abbey Classics series. Pauline Baynes listed on title page; unknown illustrator for cover.

1452   1970   Alice's Adventures in Wonderland and Through the Looking-Glass
London: Cresta House   9780719600067   Anonymous
The only illustration is on the front cover.

1453   ca. 1970s   Alice's Adventures in Wonderland and Through the Looking-Glass
London: Dean & Son Ltd.   0603030092   John Tenniel; Unknown
1st Dean's Classics Series. Abridged Edition, No. 9. Paper-covered boards, front with Alice, Duchess & Cook. Rear cover with list of 50 numbered titles in the series, 184 pp., no illustrations. Cover artist uncredited.

1454   1970   Alice's Adventures in Wonderland and Through the Looking-Glass
London: J. M. Dent & Sons Ltd.   046005029X   John Tenniel; Diana Stanley
New York: E. P. Dutton & Co., Inc.
5th reprint. Children's Illustrated Classics Edition. Beige cloth. Pale-green dust jacket with Tea-Party on front. 61 unnumbered titles in the Children's Illustrated Classics Series (*Alice* and *Looking-Glass* listed 13th) and 28 titles in the Illustrated Classics for Older Readers Series on rear. 242 pp. + 4 ads. 8 non-integral color plates including frontispiece and black-and-white drawings. Verso half title page has no ads; verso of title page has short biography of Dodgson (33 lines) and colophon that states "First published in this edition 1954. Last reprinted 1970."

1455   1970   Alice's Adventures in Wonderland and Through the Looking-Glass
Harmondsworth, UK: Penguin Books   John Tenniel
5th Harmondsworth Penguin reprint.

1456   1970   Alice in Wonderland
London, Queen Street: Rylee Ltd.   0854082395   Unknown
The Clear Print Classics Series. Glazed paper-covered boards, front with Caterpillar and Alice, ads on rear cover, 256 pp. 3 non-integral full-page color plates including frontispiece.

1457   ca. 1970s   Alice's Adventures in Wonderland and Through the Looking-Glass
Paulton, UK; London: Purnell and Sons, Ltd.   Unillustrated
Regent Classics; advertising list ends at "*Oliver Twist.*" Not illustrated and unknown artist for cover.

1458   1971   Alice's Adventures in Wonderland and Through the Looking-Glass
London: Abbey Classics   0709701349   Pauline Baynes; Unknown
Abbey Classics reprint of 1970 edition. Pauline Baynes listed on title page; unknown illustrator for cover.

1459   1971   Alice's Adventures in Wonderland and Through the Looking-Glass
London: Book Club Associates   John Tenniel
In the series Oxford English Novels. Edited with introduction by Roger Lancelyn Green. Dust jacket.

1460   1971   Alice's Adventures in Wonderland and Through the Looking-Glass
London: Oxford University Press   0192553410   John Tenniel
1st edition. In the series Oxford English Novels. Edited with an introduction by Roger Lancelyn Green. Dust jacket. Issued in paperback in 1975 and reprinted in 1976.

1461   1971   Alice's Adventures in Wonderland and Through the Looking-Glass
London; New York: Oxford University Press   9780192553416   John Tenniel
Edited by Roger Lancelyn Green. Issued later in 1975 in paperback and reprinted in 1976.

1462   1971   Alice's Adventures in Wonderland and Through the Looking-Glass
Oxford: Oxford University Press   0192816209   John Tenniel
The World's Classics Series. Edited with an introduction by Roger Lancelyn Green.

1463   1971   Alice's Adventures in Wonderland and Through the Looking-Glass
Harmondsworth, UK: Penguin Books   John Tenniel
6th Harmondsworth Penguin reprint.

1464   1972   Alice's Adventures in Wonderland and Through the Looking-Glass
London: Collins Clear-Type Press   0460069209   John Tenniel; Diana Stanley
1st edition thus. A Jason Original. Red paper boards simulating leather in publisher's slipcase.

1465   1972   Alice's Adventures in Wonderland, Through the Looking-Glass and other writings
London; Glasgow, UK: Collins Clear-Type Press   Dorothy Colles
                                                                      (after John Tenniel)

Reprint of a 1954 edition. Illustrations after John Tenniel.

1466   1972   Alice's Adventures in Wonderland and Through the Looking-Glass
London: J. M. Dent & Sons Ltd.   0460069209   John Tenniel; Diana Stanley
Reprint of the 1954 edition of The Children's Illustrated Classics series. After 8 Tenniel line drawings redrawn in color by Stanley. Dust jacket. A Jason Original.

1467   ca. 1972 Alice's Adventures in Wonderland and Through the Looking-Glass
Maidenhead, UK: McGraw-Hill Publishing Co. for Quaker Oats Ltd.   Unknown
Sugar Puffs Library reprint. Cover by unknown artist.

1468   1972   Alice's Adventures in Wonderland and Through the Looking-Glass
Harmondsworth, UK: Penguin Books   John Tenniel
7th Harmondsworth Penguin reprint.

1469   1972   Alice's Adventures in Wonderland and Through the Looking-Glass
Bridlington, UK: Priory Books   0710501447   Deno Caruana
Priory Classics 12. Cover by Deno Caruana.

1470   1973   Alice's Adventures in Wonderland and Through the Looking-Glass
London: Book Club Associates   John Tenniel

A reprint of the 1971 Oxford University Press edition. Edited with an introduction by Roger Lancelyn Green. In dust jacket.

1471   1973   Alice's Adventures in Wonderland and Through the Looking-Glass
London: J. M. Dent & Sons Ltd.   0460069209   John Tenniel; Diana Stanley
Reprint of the 1972 edition. After 8 Tenniel line drawings redrawn in color by Stanley. "Jason" on front leatherette cover.

1472   1973   The Complete Works of Lewis Carroll
London: Nonesuch Press   9780370005072   John Tenniel
11th impression.

1473   1973   Alice's Adventures in Wonderland and Through the Looking-Glass
Harmondsworth, UK: Penguin Books   John Tenniel
8th Harmondsworth Penguin reprint.

1474   1973   Alice's Adventures in Wonderland and Through the Looking-Glass
Harmondsworth, UK: Penguin Books   John Tenniel
9th Harmondsworth Penguin reprint.

1475   1974   The Philosopher's Alice: Alice's Adventures in Wonderland and
                Through the Looking-Glass
London: Academy Editions   9856701262   John Tenniel
Introduction and notes by Peter Heath. Annotated from a philosophical perspective.

1476   1974   Alice's Adventures in Wonderland and Through the Looking-Glass
London; Sydney, NSW; Toronto, ON: Bodley Head   9370109279   John Tenniel; Henry Holiday
1st edition. Also contains *The Hunting of the Snark*. Dust jacket. Reissue of the Nonesuch Cygnet edition 1963. Green paper-covered boards.

1477   1974   Alice's Adventures in Wonderland and Through the Looking-Glass
London: Book Club Associates   John Tenniel
Reprint of the 1971 Oxford University Press edition. Edited with an introduction by Roger Lancelyn Green. Dust jacket.

1478   1974   Alice's Adventures in Wonderland and Through the Looking-Glass
Harmondsworth, UK: Penguin Books   John Tenniel
10th Harmondsworth Penguin reprint.

1479   1974   Alice's Adventures in Wonderland and Through the Looking-Glass and The Hunting of
                the Snark
London: The Bodley Head   0370109279   John Tenniel; Henry Holiday
1st edition. First published under the Bodley Head imprint 1974. Dust jacket.

1480   ca. 1974 Alice's Adventures in Wonderland and Through the Looking-Glass
London: Heron Books, William Collins & Co. Ltd.   Anonymous
A Young Person's Classic.

1481   1975   Alice's Adventures in Wonderland and Through the Looking-Glass
London: Bodley Head   0370109279   John Tenniel; Henry Holiday
1st reprint. Also contains *The Hunting of the Snark*. Dust jacket.

1482   1975   Alice's Adventures in Wonderland, Through the Looking-Glass and other writings
London; Glasgow, UK: Collins Clear-Type Press   Dorothy Colles
                                                                     (after John Tenniel)

Reprint of a 1954 edition. Illustrations after John Tenniel. Blue paper boards. Copies known in maroon soft leather.

1483   1975   Alice's Adventures in Wonderland and Through the Looking-Glass
London: J. M. Dent & Sons. New York: E. P. Dutton   0460027549   John Tenniel; Diana Stanley
Paperback reprint of the 1954 edition of The Children's Illustrated Classics series. After 8 Tenniel line drawings redrawn in color by Stanley. Title page lists 1975 but a copyright note gives 1977.

1484   1975   Alice's Adventures in Wonderland and Through the Looking-Glass
London: Oxford University Press   0001921186   John Tenniel
1st Oxford Paperbacks Edition. Edited with an introduction by Roger Lancelyn Green. In remainder sheets of the 1st edition of 1973.

1485   1975   Alice's Adventures in Wonderland and Through the Looking-Glass
London; New York: Oxford University Press   9780192811868;   John Tenniel
9780529050311 (hardcover); 9780529050328 (paperback)
Edited by Roger Lancelyn Green. Paperback issue of the 1971 edition. Reprinted in 1976.

1486   1975   Alice's Adventures in Wonderland and Through the Looking-Glass
London: Oxford University Press   0192553410   John Tenniel
In the series Oxford English Novels. Edited with an introduction by Roger Lancelyn Green. Dust jacket. Issued in paperback in 1975 and reprinted in 1976.

1487   1975   Alice's Adventures in Wonderland and Through the Looking-Glass
Harmondsworth, UK: Penguin Books   John Tenniel
11th Harmondsworth Penguin reprint.

1488   1975   Alice's Adventures in Wonderland and Through the Looking-Glass
Harmondsworth, UK: Penguin Books   John Tenniel
12th Harmondsworth Penguin reprint.

1489   1975   Alice's Adventures in Wonderland and Through the Looking-Glass
Maidenhead, UK: Purnell and Sons   0361028008   Jenny Thorne
A Purnell De Luxe Classic. Introduction by Jane Carruth.

1490   1975   Alice's Adventures in Wonderland and Through the Looking-Glass
Maidenhead, UK: Purnell Books   0361028008   Jenny Thorne
1st edition. A Purnell De Luxe Classic with 8 color plates.

1491   1975   Alice's Adventures in Wonderland and Through the Looking-Glass and The Hunting of the Snark
London: The Bodley Head   0370109279   John Tenniel; Henry Holiday
1st reprint. First published under the Bodley Head imprint in 1974. Dust jacket.

1492   ca. 1975 Alice's Adventures in Wonderland, Through the Looking-Glass and Other Writings
London: Heron Books, William Collins & Co. Ltd.   Dorothy Colles
(after John Tenniel)
A Young Person's Classic. Introduction by Robin Deniston.

1493   1976   Alice's Adventures in Wonderland and Through the Looking-Glass
London: Book Club Associates   John Tenniel
Reprint of the 1971 edition. Edited with introduction by Roger Lancelyn Green. Dust jacket.

1494   1976   Alice's Adventures in Wonderland and Through the Looking-Glass
London: Oxford University Press   0001921186   John Tenniel
Paperback reprint of the 1975 Oxford English Novels edition. Edited with an introduction by Roger Lancelyn Green.

1495   1976   Alice's Adventures in Wonderland and Through the Looking-Glass
London; New York: Oxford University Press   9780192553416   John Tenniel
Edited by Roger Lancelyn Green. First issued in 1971. Issued in 1975 in paperback. This is a reprint.

1496   1976   Alice's Adventures in Wonderland and Through the Looking-Glass
Harmondsworth, UK: Penguin Books   John Tenniel
13th Harmondsworth Penguin reprint.

1497   1977   Alice's Adventures in Wonderland and Through the Looking-Glass
London: Academy Editions.   9780856702167   John Tenniel
New York: St. Martin's Press
Giant Illustrated Edition.

1498   1977   Alice's Adventures in Wonderland and Through the Looking-Glass
London: J. M. Dent & Sons Ltd.   9780460027540   John Tenniel; Diana Stanley
Children's Illustrated Classics. Original engravings by John Tenniel of which 8 have been redrawn in color by Diana
Stanley.

1499   1977   Alice's Adventures in Wonderland and Through the Looking-Glass
London: J. M. Dent & Sons Ltd.   046005029X   John Tenniel; Diana Stanley
The Children's Illustrated Classics. Reprint.

1500   1977   The Complete Works of Lewis Carroll
London: Nonesuch Press   9780370005072   John Tenniel
Reset edition.

1501   1977   Alice's Adventures in Wonderland and Through the Looking-Glass
London: Pan Books Ltd.   Anonymous
Paperback.

1502   1977   Alice's Adventures in Wonderland and Through the Looking-Glass
Harmondsworth, UK: Penguin Books   John Tenniel
Listed as "13th" Harmondsworth Penguin reprint (possibly a numbering error).

1503   1977   Alice's Adventures in Wonderland and Through the Looking-Glass
Maidenhead, UK: Purnell Books   9361035527   Jenny Thorne
2nd impression of the 1975 edition. A Purnell De Luxe Classic with 8 color plates.

1504   1978   Alice's Adventures in Wonderland, Through the Looking-Glass, Phantasmagoria
                & Other Poems, The Hunting of the Snark and Others
London; etc.: J. M. Dent & Sons Ltd. New York: E. P. Dutton & Co.   Various
New Introduction by Roger Lancelyn Green. Blue paper-covered boards.

1505   1978   The Illustrated Lewis Carroll
London: Jupiter Books   0904041883   John Tenniel
1st edition. Introduction by Roy Gasson. Red paper over boards. Dust jacket. Includes *Alice* and *Looking-Glass* with
illustrations by Tenniel, and *Snark* (with illustrations by Henry Holiday (including the suppressed Boojum drawing).
Volume also includes "The Mad Gardener's Song" (unillustrated) and "Hiawatha's Photographing," with illustrations
by Arthur Burdett Frost from when the poem first was reprinted in *Phantasmagoria and Other Poems* in 1869. Black-
and-white plates also appear for *Alice* (with one each by W. H. Walker, Charles Robinson, Arthur Rackham, Thomas
Maybank, Millicent Sowerby, T. H. Robinson, Harry Furniss, and Mervyn Peake) and for *Looking-Glass* (with one
each by Blanche McManus, Peter Newell, E. B. Thurstan, J. Morton Sale, and Mervyn Peake).

1506   1978   The Illustrated Lewis Carroll
London: Jupiter Books   0904041883   John Tenniel; Others
Reprint edition. Introduction by Roy Gasson. Dust jacket. Includes *Alice* and *Looking-Glass* with illustrations by
Tenniel. See additional notes for 1st edition above.

1507	1978	Alice's Adventures in Wonderland and Through the Looking-Glass

London: Methuen Children's Books   0416552803   Mervyn Peake

With 66 illustrations. With a bibliographical note by Brian Sibley. Blue binding. Illustrated dust jacket.

1508	1978	Alice's Adventures in Wonderland and Through the Looking-Glass

London: Octopus Books   014035039X leather;   John Tenniel
0333370082 set

1st edition. Puffin Classics. Dust jacket.

1509	1978	Alice's Adventures in Wonderland and Through the Looking-Glass

Harmondsworth, UK: Penguin Books   John Tenniel

14th Harmondsworth Penguin reprint.

1510	1979	Alice's Adventures in Wonderland and Through the Looking-Glass

London: Book Club Associates   John Tenniel

A reissue of the 1971 Oxford University Press edition, edited and with introduction by Roger Lancelyn Green. Dust jacket.

1511	1979	Alice's Adventures in Wonderland and Through the Looking-Glass

Maidenhead, UK: Purnell Books   0361028008   Jenny Thorne

Reprint of the 1975 edition. A Purnell De Luxe Classic with 8 color plates.

1512	1980	Alice's Adventures in Wonderland and Through the Looking-Glass

London: Methuen   0001921186   Mervyn Peake

With 66 illustrations. Reprint.

1513	1980	Alice's Adventures in Wonderland and Through the Looking-Glass

London: Methuen Children's Books   0416552803   Mervyn Peake

Reprint of the 1978 edition. Dust jacket.

1514	1980	Alice's Adventures in Wonderland and Through the Looking-Glass

Harmondsworth, UK: Penguin Books   John Tenniel

16th Harmondsworth Penguin reprint.

1515	ca. 1980s	Alice's Adventures in Wonderland and Through the Looking-Glass

London: Dean & Son Ltd.   9780603030093   Unillustrated

Dean's Classics, No. 7. Not illustrated and unknown artist for cover.

1516	ca. 1980s	Alice's Adventures in Wonderland and Through the Looking-Glass

London: n.p.   Unillustrated

Pictorial paper-covered boards. Printed on light gray paper, including endpapers. Not illustrated and unknown artist for cover.

1517	1981	Alice's Adventures in Wonderland and Through the Looking-Glass

London, Toronto, ON: Bantam Books   0553213458   John Tenniel

Introduction by Morton N. Cohen.

1518	1981	Alice's Adventures in Wonderland and Through the Looking-Glass

London: Collins Clear-Type Press   John Tenniel; Diana Stanley

Later reprint. Dust jacket.

1519	1981	Alice in Wonderland and Through the Looking Glass

London; Toronto, ON;   046005029x   John Tenniel; Diana Stanley

Melbourne, VIC: J. M. Dent & Sons. New York: E. P. Dutton

Reprint of the 1954 edition of The Children's Illustrated Classics series. 8 after Tenniel line drawings redrawn in color by Stanley. Dust jacket.

1520   1981   Alice's Adventures in Wonderland and Through the Looking-Glass

Harmondsworth, UK: Penguin Books   John Tenniel

18th Harmondsworth Penguin reprint. Goodacre has a proof copy. There was possibly a 2nd printing dated 1981.

1521   1982   The Complete Illustrated Works of Lewis Carroll

London: Chancellor Press   0907486215   John Tenniel

1st edition. Red cloth. Dust jacket. Includes *Alice's Adventures in Wonderland* and *Looking-Glass*.

1522   1982   Journeys in Wonderland. Alice's Adventures in Wonderland and Through the Looking-Glass

Leicester, UK: Galley Press   9780861369348   John Tenniel

Foreword by Patricia Horan. Pictorial dust jacket designed by Mary Wheeler.

1523   1982   Alice's Adventures in Wonderland and Through the Looking-Glass

Oxford: Oxford University Press   0192816209   John Tenniel

1st reprint of the 1975 edition, now called the "World's Classics Paperback." Edited with an introduction by Roger Lancelyn Green.

1524   1982   Alice's Adventures in Wonderland and Through the Looking-Glass

London: Oxford University Press   0192816209   John Tenniel

2nd reprint of the 1975 edition, now called the "World's Classics Paperback." Edited with an introduction by Roger Lancelyn Green.

1525   1982   Alice's Adventures in Wonderland and Through the Looking-Glass

Harmondsworth, UK: Penguin Books   John Tenniel

19th Harmondsworth Penguin reprint.

1526   1982   The Complete Works of Lewis Carroll

Harmondsworth, UK: Penguin Books   0140090045   John Tenniel

1527   1982   The Complete Illustrated Works

London: Random House   Various

xxiii, 868 pp. Reprinted in 1995 by Leopard. Includes bibliographical references.

1528   1982   Alice's Adventures in Wonderland and Through the Looking-Glass and The Hunting of the Snark

London: The Bodley Head ·   9780370109275   John Tenniel; Henry Holiday

2nd reprint. First published under the Bodley Head imprint in 1974. Dust jacket.

1529   1983   The Complete Illustrated Works of Lewis Carroll

London: Chancellor Press   0907486215   John Tenniel

1st reprint. Dust jacket.

1530   1983   Alice's Adventures in Wonderland and Through the Looking-Glass

London: Methuen Children's   0416552803   Mervyn Peake

66 illustrations. Reprint.

1531   1983   Alice's Adventures in Wonderland and Through the Looking-Glass

Harmondsworth, UK: Penguin Books   John Tenniel

20th Harmondsworth Penguin reprint.

1532   1983   Alice's Adventures in Wonderland and Through the Looking-Glass
Maidenhead, UK: Purnell Books   0361028008   Jenny Thorne
Reprint of the 1975 edition. A Purnell De Luxe Classic with 8 color plates.

1533   1984   Alice's Adventures in Wonderland and Through the Looking-Glass
London: Bibliophile Books   0416552803   Mervyn Peake
Revised edition with introduction by Brian Sibley. Blue wrappers. Dust jacket.

1534   1984   Alice's Adventures in Wonderland and Through the Looking-Glass
London: Bibliophile Books   0416552803   Mervyn Peake
With 66 illustrations. May be a new edition of London: Methuen, 1978.

1535   1984   The Complete Illustrated Works of Lewis Carroll
London: Chancellor Press   0907486215   John Tenniel
2nd reprint. Orange-red cloth. Dust jacket.

1536   [1984]   Alice's Adventures in Wonderland and Through the Looking-Glass
London: Heron Books, William Collins & Co. Ltd.   9780004244501   John Tenniel
Undated. Reprint of the 1954 edition lacking the Stanley color plates. "A Young Person's Classic" edition. In various bindings. Date found on WorldCat.

1537   1984   Alice's Adventures in Wonderland and Through the Looking-Glass
Harmondsworth, UK: Penguin Books   John Tenniel
21st Harmondsworth Penguin reprint.

1538   1985   Alice's Adventures in Wonderland and Through the Looking-Glass
London: Bibliophile Books   0416552803   Mervyn Peake
Blue cloth, front with gilt Alice sleeping, spine with gold-gilt lettering, illustrated dust jacket, 221 pp. Illustrated title page. 66 black-and-white drawings.

1539   1985   The Complete Illustrated Works of Lewis Carroll
London: Chancellor Press   0907486215   John Tenniel
3rd reprint. Dust jacket.

1540   1985   Alice's Adventures in Wonderland and Through the Looking-Glass
London: Methuen Children's   10416596304   Mervyn Peake
66 illustrations. Reprint.

1541   1985   Alice's Adventures in Wonderland and Through the Looking-Glass
Oxford: Oxford University Press   0192816209   John Tenniel
3rd reprint of the 1975 edition as World's Classics Paperback. Edited with an introduction by Roger Lancelyn Green.

1542   ca. 1985   The Illustrated Lewis Carroll
Poole, UK: New Orchard Editions   9781850790006   John Tenniel
2nd impression. Introduction by Roy Gasson.

1543   1986   Alice's Adventures in Wonderland and Through the Looking-Glass
London: Cathay Books Limited;   9780861784103   Julia Christie
Octopus Books Limited
1st edition. Later published in 1987 by Chancellor Press. 16 pp. color plates.

1544   1986   Alice's Adventures in Wonderland and Through the Looking-Glass
London: Cathay Books   0861784103   Julia Christie
As in the earlier 1986 Cathay edition but with Marylebone Books at base of spine.

1545   1986   Alice's Adventures in Wonderland and Through the Looking-Glass
London: Cathay Books   0861784103   Julia Christie

1546   1986   The Complete Illustrated Works of Lewis Carroll
London: Chancellor Press   0907486215   John Tenniel
4th reprint. Dust jacket.

1547   1986   Alice in Wonderland [and Through the Looking-Glass]
London: Hamlyn   0600311627   Unknown
Classics S Series. Includes *Looking-Glass*.

1548   1986   Alice's Adventures in Wonderland and Through the Looking-Glass
Twickenham, UK: Hamlyn Publishing   0600311627   John Tenniel
1st edition in the Hamlyn Classics series. Blue paper boards.

1549   1986   The Complete Alice and The Hunting of the Snark
London: Jonathan Cape   0224028200   Ralph Steadman
1st edition. Dark-blue cloth, spine with silver-gilt lettering and decorations. Illustrated dust jacket. 336 pp. Many
black-and-white drawings. Includes "A Wasp in a Wig" as well as Steadman's introductions to his 1967 *Alice* and to
this *Looking-Glass*. 4 double pp. and 6 single pp. in color plus 21 other illustrations in *Snark*.

1550   1986   Alice's Adventures in Wonderland, Through the Looking-Glass, and Snark
London: Jonathan Cape Ltd.   0224028200   Ralph Steadman
Reprint. Includes "A Wasp in a Wig" and *Snark*.

1551   1986   Alice's Adventures in Wonderland and Through the Looking-Glass
Oxford: Oxford University Press   0192816209   John Tenniel
4th reprint of the 1975 edition as World's Classics Paperback. Edited with an introduction by Roger Lancelyn Green.

1552   1986   Alice's Adventures in Wonderland and Through the Looking-Glass
Harmondsworth, UK: Penguin Books   John Tenniel
23rd Harmondsworth Penguin reprint.

1553   1986   Alice's Adventures in Wonderland and Through the Looking-Glass
Paulton, UK; London: Purnell and Sons Ltd.   0361028008   Jenny Thorne
Reprint. A Purnell De Luxe Classic.

1554   1986   Alice's Adventures in Wonderland and Through the Looking-Glass
Maidenhead, UK: Purnell Books   0361028008   Jenny Thorne
Reprint of the 1975 edition. A Purnell De Luxe Classic. No color plates.

1555   1987   Alice's Adventures in Wonderland and Through the Looking-Glass
London: Bracken Books   9781851701094   John Tenniel; Ninon MacKnight
1st Bracken edition. Adapted for Little Folks from the Original Story. Illustrations in full-color from original designs
by John Tenniel with frontispiece by Ninon MacKnight. Orange paper-covered illustrated boards. 59 pp. 32 integral
color illustrations from original designs by John Tenniel; 2 color frontispieces by Ninon MacKnight.

1556   1987   Alice's Adventures in Wonderland and Through the Looking-Glass
London: Chancellor Press   1851520708   Julia Christie
1st Chancellor Edition. 16 color plates. Paper-covered illustrated boards, front with Tea-Party. 304 pp. 15 non-integral
full-page color plates on coated paper, all but frontispiece printed on both sides and many black-and-white drawings.
Edition first published 1986 by Octopus Books but illustrations and arrangement copyright 1985 by Octopus Books.

1557   1987   Alice's Adventures in Wonderland and Through the Looking-Glass
London: Chancellor Press   1851520708   Julia Christie
A later edition of the other Julia Christie illustrated Chancellor edition of this date, but with 12 color plates.

1558   1987   Alice's Adventures and Through the Looking-Glass
London: Chancellor Press   9781851520701   Julia Christie
Glazed pictorial paper boards with picture of Tea-Party on front cover.

1559   1987   The Complete Illustrated Works of Lewis Carroll
London: Chancellor Press   0907486215   John Tenniel
5th reprint. In laminated paper boards.

1560   1987   Alice's Adventures in Wonderland and Through the Looking-Glass and Other Works
London: Marshall Cavendish   0863076769   Lewis Carroll
The Great Writers Library. Illustrations by Lewis Carroll for *Alice*. Only the chess diagram is in *Looking-Glass* and the sea chart in *Snark*.

1561   1987   Alice's Adventures in Wonderland and Through the Looking-Glass and other works
London: Marshall Cavendish Ltd.   0863076769   Lewis Carroll
Great Writers Library. A facsimile reproduction of part of the 1961 J. M. Dent Everyman Paperback edition. 37 black-and-white illustrations by Lewis Carroll only for *Alice*.

1562   1987   Alice's Adventures in Wonderland and Through the Looking-Glass
Harmondsworth, UK: Penguin Books   John Tenniel
24th Harmondsworth Penguin reprint.

1563   1988   Journeys in Wonderland. Alice's Adventures in Wonderland and Through the Looking-Glass
Leicester, UK: Galley Press, W. H. Smith   0861366077   John Tenniel
1st Golden Heritage Series Edition. Blue cloth, spine with gilt lettering. White dust jacket, front with White Rabbit and diminutive Alice, rear lists 22 series titles. 224 pp. 92 black-and-white drawings including 2 frontispieces. First Galley Press issue was 1982.

1564   1988   Alice's Adventures in Wonderland and Through the Looking-Glass
London: Holland Enterprises Ltd.   9781850381563   Vicente
Glazed pictorial paper boards. Front cover illustration only by Vicente.

1565   1988   Alice's Adventures in Wonderland and Through the Looking-Glass
Harmondsworth, UK: Penguin Books   John Tenniel
25th Harmondsworth Penguin reprint.

1566   1988   The Complete Works of Lewis Carroll
Harmondsworth, UK: Penguin Books   0140105425   John Tenniel
2nd paperback edition.

1567   1989   Alice's Adventures in Wonderland and Through the Looking-Glass
London: Marks and Spencer,   0862730058   John Tenniel; Chris Hahner
by arrangement with the Octopus Publishing Group
1st edition thus. Cloth boards, with paste-on picture on front cover. Color plates by Hahner. Black-and-white pictures by Tenniel.

1568   1989   The Complete Works of Lewis Carroll
London: Reinhardt Books   0370005074   John Tenniel
Facsimile reprint of the Nonesuch edition of 1939. 1st edition thus. Includes *Looking-Glass*. Dust jacket.

1569   1989   Alice's Adventures in Wonderland and Through the Looking-Glass
Manchester, UK: World International Publishing   0723513635   Tony James Chance
1st World Classic Library Edition. In the series Classic Library. Pink laminated paper-covered boards, front with Alice and White Rabbit, rear lists 8 titles in series. 178 pp. 8 non-integral full-page color plates on coated paper.

1570   1990   The Complete Illustrated Works of Lewis Carroll
London: Chancellor Press   0907486215   John Tenniel
7th reprint. Includes *Looking-Glass*. In laminated paper boards.

1571   1990   Alice's Adventures in Wonderland; Through the Looking-Glass
London: The Folio Society   John Tenniel
Boxed set of *Alice* and *Looking-Glass*. Reissue of 1962 edition. Both volumes with pale-blue paper-covered boards illustrated front and rear with Tenniel drawings. No dust jackets. *Alice* with 113 pp. and *Looking-Glass* with 132. *Alice* with 42 drawings, *Looking-Glass* with 50, both printed in salmon from electrotypes made from the original Dalziel Bros. wood blocks.

1572   1991   Alice's Adventures in Wonderland and Through the Looking-Glass
Oxford: Oxford University Press   0192816209   John Tenniel
7th reprint of the 1975 edition as World's Classics Paperback. Edited with an introduction by Roger Lancelyn Green.

1573   1991   Alice's Adventures in Wonderland and Through the Looking-Glass
London: W. H. Smith Exclusive Books   0749805609   John Tenniel; Anonymous
In the series Children's Classics. Anonymous cover illustration. Paperback.

1574   1991   The Complete Works of Lewis Carroll
London: Wordsworth Editions   9781853269332   John Tenniel
Large print edition.

1575   1991   Alice's Adventures in Wonderland and Through the Looking-Glass
Manchester, UK: World International Publishing   9780723513636   Tony James Chance
1st reprint of the 1989 edition. In the series Classic Library.

1576   1992   Alice's Adventures in Wonderland and Through the Looking-Glass
London: David Campbell Publishers Ltd.   9781857159042   John Tenniel
Red cloth boards. Paste-on picture of Alice and Dodo from the Macmillan *Alice*. In the series Everyman's Library / Children's Classics.

1577   1992   Alice's Adventures in Wonderland and Through the Looking-Glass
London: Everyman's Library   1857159047   John Tenniel
First published by Dent as Everyman's Library for Young People in 1929.

1578   1992   Alice's Adventures in Wonderland and Through the Looking-Glass
Oxford: Oxford University Press   0192816209   John Tenniel
9th reprint of the 1975 edition published as a "World's Classics Paperback" edition. Edited with an introduction by Roger Lancelyn Green.

1579   1992   Alice's Adventures in Wonderland and Through the Looking-Glass
Maidenhead, UK: Purnell Books   0361028008   Jenny Thorne
6th reprint of the 1975 edition. A Purnell De Luxe Classic. No color plates.

1580   1992   Alice in Wonderland [and Through the Looking-Glass]
Horsham, UK: Ravette Books   1853044156   Anonymous
Paperback. Includes both *Alice* and *Looking-Glass*. Front cover has picture of Alice and Queen in procession.

1581   1992   Alice's Adventures in Wonderland and Through the Looking-Glass
London: Treasure Press   Dagmar Berková
1st edition.

1582   1992   Alice in Wonderland [and Through the Looking-Glass]
London: Wordsworth Classics   1853260029   Lewis Carroll; John Tenniel;
                                                          Adelaide Claxton

1st edition thus. Though not stated, the text is a facsimile of the 1929 Everyman's Library No. 836 edition. Published
by Dent and Dutton. It includes *Alice*, *Looking-Glass*, and other Carroll texts. The front cover illustration is by
Adelaide Claxton.

1583   1992   Alice's Adventures and Through the Looking-Glass
London: Wordsworth Classics   1853260029   Lewis Carroll; Adelaide Claxton
Paperback. Includes *Alice* and *Looking-Glass* and other Carroll texts. Only *Alice* has Carroll pictures. Though not
stated, this is a facsimile of the 1961 J. M. Dent Everyman Paperback edition but lacks introduction and *Tangled Tales*
answers. Front cover has the Adelaide Claxton picture titled Wonderland.

1584   1993   The Complete Illustrated Works of Lewis Carroll
London: Chancellor Press   1851525033   John Tenniel
1st edition thus. Includes *Looking-Glass*. In laminated boards and dust jacket, both of which have part of an Arthur
Rackham illustration.

1585   1993   Alice's Adventures and Through the Looking-Glass
London: J. M. Dent; Rutland, VT: Charles E. Tuttle   0460873598   Lewis Carroll; John Tenniel
Paperback in the Everyman series. Introduction by Penelope Lively. *Alice* has Lewis Carroll pictures and *Looking-
Glass* has Tenniel pictures.

1586   1993   The Works of Lewis Carroll
London: Magpie Books Ltd.   9781858133393   John Tenniel
Reprint of the 1965 Hamlyn edition. Omits the introduction by Roger Lancelyn Green.

1587   1993   Alice's Adventures in Wonderland and Through the Looking-Glass
Bristol, UK: Parragon Book Service Ltd.   1858135613   Anonymous
1st edition. In the series Children's Classics. Paperback. Verso of title page says it is A Parragon Classic. Anonymous
illustration on front cover. Undated reprints are known in various bindings.

1588   1993   Alice's Adventures in Wonderland and Through the Looking-Glass
Harmondsworth, UK: Penguin Books   John Tenniel
30th Harmondsworth Penguin reprint.

1589   1993   Alice's Adventures in Wonderland and Through the Looking-Glass
London: Tiger Books International   9781855014053   Lindsay Duff
1st edition thus. Dust jacket. In the Children's Treasury series.

1590   1993   Alice's Adventures in Wonderland and Through the Looking-Glass
Ware, UK: Wordsworth Classics   1853261181   John Tenniel
1st edition thus. Paperback.

1591   1993   Alice in Wonderland [and Through the Looking-Glass]
London: Wordsworth Classics   1853261181   Lewis Carroll; John Tenniel;
                                                          Adelaide Claxton

2nd reprint of the 1992 edition. Includes *Looking-Glass*.

1592   1993   Alice's Adventures in Wonderland and Through the Looking-Glass
Ware, UK: Wordsworth Classics   1853261181   John Tenniel
5th impression.

1593   1993   Alice's Adventures in Wonderland and Through the Looking-Glass
Ware, UK: Wordsworth Classics   1853261181   John Tenniel
6th impression.

1594   1993   Alice's Adventures in Wonderland and Through the Looking-Glass
Ware, UK: Wordsworth Classics   1853261183   John Tenniel; Lesley Fotherby
Paperback. Front cover has picture by Lesley Fotherby.

1595   1993   Alice's Adventures in Wonderland and Through the Looking-Glass
Ware, UK: Wordsworth Classics   1853261181   John Tenniel
Paperback. Larger format than the Wordsworth 1993 edition with Lobster Quadrille. Front cover here has Rackham picture of Duchess's kitchen.

1596   1993   Alice's Adventures in Wonderland and Through the Looking-Glass
Ware, UK: Wordsworth Classics   9781853260025   John Tenniel; Nathan Clair
Paperback. Michael Irwin notes included. Front cover has picture of Tea-Party by Nathan Clair.

1597   1993   Alice's Adventures in Wonderland and Through the Looking-Glass
Ware, UK: Wordsworth Classics   9781853261183   John Tenniel; Claire Ruddock
Paperback. No introduction or notes. Front cover has picture by Claire Ruddock.

1598   1993   Alice's Adventures in Wonderland and Through the Looking-Glass
Ware, UK: Wordsworth Classics   1853261181   John Tenniel
Paperback. Picture on front cover of Lobster Quadrille.

1599   1994   Alice's Adventures in Wonderland and Through the Looking-Glass
London: Bloomsbury Books   1854712373   Frank Adams; Anonymous
1st edition thus. Paperback. In the series Children's Classics. Cover illustrations by Frank Adams but not attributed.

1600   1994   The Complete Works of Lewis Carroll
London: Bracken Books   1858911419   John Tenniel
Reprint of the Nonesuch edition of 1939.

1601   1994   Alice's Adventures and Through the Looking-Glass
London: J. M. Dent; Rutland, VT: Charles E. Tuttle   0460873598   Lewis Carroll; John Tenniel
1st reprint of the 1993 edition. Paperback in the Everyman series. Introduction by Penelope Lively. *Alice* has Lewis Carroll pictures and *Looking-Glass* has Tenniel pictures.

1602   1994   Alice's Adventures in Wonderland and Through the Looking-Glass
Bristol, UK: Parragon Book Service Ltd.   1858135613   Anonymous
Dust jacket.

1603   1995   Alice's Adventures in Wonderland and Through the Looking-Glass
London: Anness Publishing Ltd.   John Tenniel
1st edition thus. Classic Library series. The English edition of the book originally published in America by Smithmark Publishers.

1604   1995   The Penguin Selected Works of Lewis Carroll
London: Claremont Books   John Tenniel
1st edition thus. Published under license from Penguin Books Ltd. Dust jacket.

1605   1995   Alice's Adventures and Through the Looking-Glass
London: J. M. Dent. Rutland, VT: Charles E. Tuttle   0460873598   Lewis Carroll; John Tenniel
2nd reprint of the 1993 edition. Paperback in the Everyman series. Introduction by Penelope Lively. *Alice* has Lewis Carroll pictures and *Looking-Glass* has Tenniel pictures.

1606   1995   The Complete Illustrated Works
London: Leopard   9780752900278   Various
xxiii, 868 pp. Includes *Looking-Glass*. Originally published by Random House in 1982. Includes bibliographical references.

1607   1996   The Complete Illustrated Works of Lewis Carroll
London: Chancellor Press   1851525033   John Tenniel
Reprint of a 1993 Chancellor Press edition. Dust jacket.

1608   1996   Alice's Adventures and Through the Looking-Glass
London: J. M. Dent; Rutland, VT: Charles E. Tuttle   0460873598   Lewis Carroll; John Tenniel
3rd reprint of the 1993 paperback in the Everyman series. Introduction by Penelope Lively. *Alice* has Lewis Carroll pictures and *Looking-Glass* has Tenniel pictures.

1609   1996   The Complete Illustrated Works of Lewis Carroll
London: Leopard Books, Random House   9780752900278   John Tenniel
Edited by Edward Guiliano. Dust jacket.

1610   1996   The Complete Illustrated Lewis Carroll
London: Wordsworth Editions   1853268976   John Tenniel
1st paperback edition thus.

1611   1997   Alice's Adventures in Wonderland and Through the Looking-Glass
London: Puffin Books   0140383514   John Tenniel; James Marsh
1st edition as Puffin Book. Prince Charming Color Books for Children Series. Cover illustration by James Marsh. Green paper wrappers, front with Mad Hatter, Alice, and White Rabbit. 311 pp. + 12 ads. 92 black-and-white drawings including single frontispiece. Includes Easter Greeting, Christmas Greetings, and Preface to the 61st thousand.

1612   1998   Alice's Adventures in Wonderland
London: Book People Ltd., Ted Smart   0333640497   John Tenniel
Coloring by Harry Theaker and Diz Wallis. A reissue of the Macmillan edition of 1995. Blue paper boards in pictorial dust jacket. Glazed pictorial paper boards. In boxed set with *Looking-Glass*.

1613   1998   Alice's Adventures in Wonderland and Through the Looking-Glass
Oxford: Oxford University Press   9780192833747   John Tenniel
Reissued as Oxford World's Classics Paperback. Edited with an introduction by Roger Lancelyn Green. There is a special edition overprinted on the front cover: "Alice's Day 2007 / Blackwell / The Knowledge Retailer."

1614   1998   Alice's Adventures in Wonderland and Through the Looking-Glass
London: Penguin Books   9780141439761   John Tenniel
Centenary Edition of the London Penguin Books. Edited with an introduction and notes by Hugh Haughton. Reprinted the same year. Includes "The Wasp in a Wig."

1615   1998   Alice's Adventures in Wonderland and Through the Looking-Glass
London: Penguin Books   9780140433173   Lewis Carroll; John Tenniel
Centenary edition. Edited with introduction and notes by Hugh Haughton. Includes *Alice's Adventures under Ground*.

1616   1998   Alice's Adventures in Wonderland and Through the Looking-Glass
London: Penguin Books   9780140433173   John Tenniel
Penguin Classics. Edited with an introduction and notes by Hugh Haughton. Reprint of the other 1998 edition.

1617   1998   The Complete Illustrated Works of Lewis Carroll
Ware, UK: Wordsworth Editions   1853268976   John Tenniel
Introduction by Alexander Woollcott. Reprint of 1996 edition.

1618   1999   Alice's Adventures in Wonderland and Through the Looking-Glass
Bristol, UK: Parragon Books Service   1858135613   Anonymous
Reprint of the 1993 1st edition. Paperback. In the series Children's Classics. Verso of title page has "A Parragon Classic." Anonymous illustration on front cover. Undated reprints are known.

1619   1999   The Complete Works of Lewis Carroll
Ware, UK: Wordsworth Classics   1853264962   John Tenniel
In 3 volumes, each with a different Rackham picture from *Alice*. In publisher's illustrated box, also with 3 Rackham illustrations.

1620   2001   Alice's Adventures in Wonderland and Through the Looking-Glass
London: Bloomsbury Books   0747556881 set;   Mervyn Peake
                                     0747553688 *Alice*; 0747553734 *L-G*
1st edition thus. Introduction by Will Self. In slipcase. Dust jacket. There was also a limited special edition of 60 numbered copies with portfolio of numbered set of prints in solander box. Also 120 numbered copies, 100 of which included a numbered set of the prints.

1621   2001   Alice's Adventures in Wonderland and Through the Looking-Glass
London: Bloomsbury Books   9781408805930   Mervyn Peake
1st edition. Introduction by Will Self and Zadie Smith. Later editions are 2003 and 2010.

1622   2001   Alice's Adventures in Wonderland and Through the Looking-Glass
London: Bloomsbury Books   0747564965   Mervyn Peake
Introduction by Will Self and Zadie Smith.

1623   2001   Alice's Adventures in Wonderland and Through the Looking-Glass
London: Egmont Books, Ltd.   Beverly Manson
1st edition. In boxed set with 9 other children's classics. Cover illustration by Manson.

1624   2001   Alice's Adventures in Wonderland and Through the Looking-Glass
London: Oberon   1840022566   Unillustrated
A new dramatization adapted by Adrian Mitchell.

1625   2001   Alice's Adventures in Wonderland and Through the Looking-Glass
Ware, UK: Wordsworth Classics   9781853260025   John Tenniel; Adelaide Claxton
New Edition. Introduction and notes by Michael Irwin.

1626   ca. 2001 Alice's Adventures in Wonderland and Through the Looking-Glass
Ware, UK: Wordsworth Classics   9781853260025   John Tenniel; Adelaide Claxton
Paperback. Notes by Michael Irwin included. Front cover has picture by Adelaide Claxton. The dating of Wordsworth editions is problematic. Some say this edition is from 1993 but in fact is later.

1627   2003   Alice's Adventures in Wonderland and Through the Looking-Glass
London: Bloomsbury Publishing   9781408805930   Mervyn Peake
Paperback edition of the 2001 edition. Introduction by Will Self and Zadie Smith. There is also a 2010 edition.

1628   2003   Alice's Adventures in Wonderland and Through the Looking-Glass
Bath, UK: Parragon Publishing   1405416742   June Goulding
1st Children's Classic Collection Series Edition. Paper-covered boards, front with Tea-Party. Illustrated dust jacket. 287 pp. Many color illustrations, 28 of which are integral full-page.

1629   2003   Alice's Adventures in Wonderland and Through the Looking-Glass
Bath, UK: Parragon Publishing   1405468157   June Goulding
Parragon Books series. Illustrated dust jacket.

1630   2003   Alice's Adventures in Wonderland and Through the Looking-Glass
London: Penguin   0141439769   John Tenniel
Penguin Classics. Centenary Edition. Introduction and notes by Hugh Haughton. First published in 1998. Paperback.

1631   2004   Alice's Adventures in Wonderland and Through the Looking-Glass
London: Collector's Library   9781904633327   John Tenniel
With an afterword by Anna South.

1632   2004   Alice's Adventures in Wonderland and Through the Looking-Glass
Lanark, Scotland, UK: Geddes & Grossett   9781842054116   John Tenniel

1633   2005   The Complete Works of Lewis Carroll
London: CRW Publishing   9781907360442; 1904633943 John Tenniel
1st edition. Collector's Library Editions. 479 pp.

1634   2005   The Complete Alice
London: Walker Books   9781406319699 (set);   Helen Oxenbury
                                9781406301965 (set); 9780744582673 (Alice);
                                9781406318265 (Looking-Glass)
Reprinted 2006 and 2009. In slipcase. Some copies list the set ISBN as 9781406301965. Includes both Alice and Looking-Glass.

1635   2005   Alice's Adventures in Wonderland and Through the Looking-Glass
Ware, UK: Wordsworth Classics   9781417027736   Anonymous
New issue, with DVD of the 1972 Fiona Fullerton Alice film. Covers have wrap-around picture from the film. Paperback.

1636   2006   Alice's Adventures in Wonderland and Through the Looking-Glass
Stroud, UK: Nonesuch Publishing Ltd.   9781845882341   John Tenniel; Robin Bennion
Nonesuch Classics series. Front cover picture is a watercolor by Robin Bennion of Alice and the Little Door based on a Tenniel picture.

1637   2006   Alice's Adventures in Wonderland and Through the Looking-Glass
London: Usborne Publishing   9780746076590   Mauro Evangelista
1st edition. Adapted by Lesley Sims. Published as The Usborne Illustrated Alice. Reprinted in 2009.

1638   2006   The Complete Alice
London: Walker Books   9781406301960 set   Helen Oxenbury
Reprint of Walker Books, 2005.

1639   2006   The Complete Alice
London: Walker Books   9781406319699 (set);   Helen Oxenbury
                                9780744582673 (Alice); 9781406318265 (Looking-Glass)
Reprint of Walker Books. First published in 2005. In slipcase. Some copies list the Set ISBN as 9781406301965.

1640   2006   The Complete Illustrated Lewis Carroll
London: Wordsworth Editions   9781853268977   Claire Ruddock
Cover illustration by Claire Ruddock.

1641   2007   Alice's Adventures in Wonderland and Through the Looking-Glass
London: Vintage Books   9781407087351;   John Tenniel
                                          9780099503859
1st edition thus. In the series Vintage Classics. Various later issues. Copies known with ISBN 9780099503859.
Reprinted in 2010 and other dates.

1642   2008   Alice's Adventures in Wonderland and Through the Looking-Glass
London: Arcturus Publishing, Ltd.;   0572034318   John Tenniel
Toronto, ON: Indigo Books
Dust jacket.

1643   2008   Alice's Adventures in Wonderland and Through the Looking-Glass
Lanark, Scotland, UK: Geddes & Grosset   1842054112   John Tenniel
Reprint of 2004 edition.

1644   2008   Sir John Gielgud reads Alice in Wonderland and Alice Through the Looking-Glass.
Hertfordshire, UK: Nimbus   Unillustrated
Online resource. Read by John Gielgud. 58 minutes.

1645   2008   Alice's Adventures in Wonderland and Through the Looking-Glass
Oxford: Oxford University Press   9780194791342   John Tenniel;
                                                                Frances Bloomfield
Oxford Bookworms Library. Classics Stage 3. Reissue of the 1998 edition with front cover picture by Frances Broomfield.

1646   2008   The Complete Illustrated Lewis Carroll
Ware, UK: Wordsworth Library Collection 9781840220742   John Tenniel

1647   2009   Alice's Adventures in Wonderland and Through the Looking-Glass
Oxford: Oxford University Press   9780199558292   John Tenniel;
                                                                Frances Bloomfield
Edited with an introduction and notes by Peter Hunt. In the series Oxford World Classics. Cover picture by Frances
Bloomfield. There are later issues. The 1st edition has code '1'. Later issues have a later number but the same date.

1648   2009   Alice's Adventures in Wonderland and Through the Looking-Glass
London: Penguin Books   9780141192468   Lewis Carroll; John Tenniel
Includes *Alice's Adventures under Ground*.

1649   2009   Alice's Adventures in Wonderland and Through the Looking-Glass
London: Usborne Publishing   9780746076590   Mauro Evangelista
2nd edition of a 2006 edition. Adapted by Lesley Sims. Published as *The Usborne Illustrated Alice*.

1650   2009   The Complete Alice
London: Walker Books   9781406301960 set   Helen Oxenbury
Reprint of Walker Books, 2005.

1651   2009   The Complete Alice
London: Walker Books   9781406319699 (set);   Helen Oxenbury
                                          9780744582673 (*Alice*); 9781406318265 (*Looking-Glass*)
Reprint of Walker Books. First published in 2005. In slipcase. Some copies list the Set ISBN as 9781406301965.

1652   2009   Alice's Adventures in Wonderland and Through the Looking-Glass
Cambridge, UK: Worth Literary Classics   9781849310048   John Tenniel; Peter Frith
1st edition. Introductions by Will Brooker, Morton N. Cohen, Hugues Lebailly, and Rose Lovell-Smith. With 1 map.
Colored by Peter Frith.

1653   2010   Alice's Adventures in Wonderland and Through the Looking-Glass
London: Bibliolis Books   9780956527752   Unknown
Bibliolis Classics edition.

1654   2010   Alice's Adventures in Wonderland and Through the Looking-Glass
London: Bloomsbury Publishing   9781408805930   Mervyn Peake
1st paperback edition. Introduction by Will Self and Zadie Smith. Later issues all have the same date. There is a 2003
edition. 1st edition 2001.

1655   2010   Lewis Carroll – Complete Illustrated Works
London: CRW Publishing   9781905716845   John Tenniel
1st edition thus. Collector's Library Omnibus Editions.

1656   2010   Alice's Adventures in Wonderland and Through the Looking-Glass
Oxford: Oxford University Press   9780192792631   Unillustrated
1st edition thus. In the series Oxford Children's Classics.

1657   2010   Alice's Adventures in Wonderland and Through the Looking-Glass
London: Vintage Classic   9781407087351   John Tenniel
"Curiouser and curiouser" Alice quote on cover. Reprint of a 2007 edition.

1658   2010   Alice's Adventures in Wonderland and Through the Looking-Glass
London: White's   9780956266828   Joe McLaren
White's Pocket Classic.

1659   2011   Alice's Adventures in Wonderland and Through the Looking-Glass
Oxford: Artist's Choice   John Vernon Lord
Textual corrections and foreword by Selwyn Goodacre and afterword by John Vernon Lord. Limited to 322 copies of
the "standard edition," and 98 copies of a Special Edition signed by the illustrator with a set of prints in slipcase.

1660   2011   Alice's Adventures in Wonderland and Through the Looking-Glass
London: Collector's Colour Library   9781907360367   John Tenniel
1st edition. Introduction by Anna Smith. Dust jacket, with wraparound band. There are later editions all with the
same date but denoted by numbers 1–10, one being removed sequentially.

1661   2011   The Complete Works of Lewis Carroll
London: CRW Publishing   9781907360442   John Tenniel
New edition or reissue of London: CRW / Collector's Library Edition, 2005.

1662   2011   Alice's Adventures in Wonderland [and Through the Looking-Glass]
Cambridge, UK: Proquest   9780141439761   Unillustrated
An online book. The Centenary Edition. Edited with an introduction and notes by Hugh Haughton.

1663   2012   Alice's Adventures in Wonderland and Through the Looking-Glass
London: Penguin Books   9780141199689   John Tenniel
Penguin English Library edition.

1664   2012   Alice's Adventures in Wonderland, Through the Looking-Glass
London: Penguin Classics   9780147509079   John Tenniel; Lewis Carroll
Includes *Alice's Adventures under Ground* illustrated by Carroll. Edited with an introduction and notes by Hugh Haughton.

1665   2012   Alice's Adventures in Wonderland and Through the Looking-Glass
London: Random House, Vintage Books   9781407087351   John Tenniel; Annelie Carlstrom
Cover illustration by Annelie Carlstrom.

1666   2012   Alice's Adventures in Wonderland and Through the Looking-Glass
London: Random House, Vintage Books   9780099572923   John Tenniel; Annelie Carlstrom
Vintage Classics Series Edition. Gray paper-wrappers. 348 pp. 92 black-and-white drawings including separate frontispieces.

1667   2012   The Complete Alice
London: Walker Books   9781406344400   Helen Oxenbury
22 volumes.

1668   2014   Alice in Wonderland – the Complete Collection
London: Classic Good Books   9780692228722   Unillustrated
Includes *Alice, Looking-Glass, Alice's Adventures under Ground,* and *The Hunting of the Snark.*

1669   2014   Alice in Wonderland: The Complete Collection
London: Classic Good Books   9780692228722   John Tenniel
Same as the 2014 edition but with illustrations by Tenniel. Includes *Alice, Looking-Glass, Alice's Adventures under Ground* (without the Carroll illustrations), and *The Hunting of the Snark.* Also has a study guide with quiz questions and numerous notes on adaptations, etc.

1670   2014   Alice's Adventures in Wonderland and Through the Looking-Glass
Oxford: Oxford University Press   9780192738295   Roland
An Oxford Children's Classics edition prepared by Steffan Nicholas, with summary, notes, and glossary. Cover illustration by Roland is the same as on title page.

1671   2015   Alice's Adventures in Wonderland and Through the Looking-Glass
Richmond, UK: Alma Classics   9781847494078   John Tenniel
Includes a facsimile of *Alice's Adventures under Ground.*

1672   2015   Alice's Adventures in Wonderland and Through the Looking-Glass
London: Bloomsbury Books   9781408868119   Mervyn Peake
The title page verso reads: This edition Geddes & Grosset Ltd., New Lanark.

1673   2015   Alice's Adventures in Wonderland and Through the Looking-Glass
London: Bounty   9780753729687   John Tenniel

1674   2015   The Complete Alice
London: Macmillan Children's Books   9781447275992   John Tenniel
Illustrations colored by Harry Theaker and Diz Wallis. Foreword by Philip Pullman.

1675   2015   Alice's Adventures in Wonderland and Through the Looking-Glass
Thaxted, Essex, UK; Miles Kelly Publishing   9781782098430   Martina Peluso
1st Mini-Classic Series Edition. Illustrated slipcase. Paper wrappers, front with White Rabbit, 320 pp. Many color illustrations. Single title page, no frontispieces. Issue identified on slipcase as Batch No. MC115, Jul-2015. Reprinted in 2017.

1676   2015   Alice's Adventures in Wonderland and Through the Looking-Glass
London: Penguin Classics   9780143107620   John Tenniel
Deluxe Edition. Introduction by Charlie Lovett.

1677   2015   Alice's Adventures in Wonderland and Through the Looking-Glass
London: Random House / Vintage Books   9781784870171   John Tenniel; Vivienne Westwood
Vintage Classics Series Edition. 150th Anniversary edition. Introduction and cover art by Vivienne Westwood. Cream cloth. Illustrated dust jacket. 348 pp. Black-and-white drawings. Various later issues.

1678   2015   Alice's Adventures in Wonderland and Through the Looking-Glass

London: Vintage Books   9781784870171   John Tenniel;
                                                                Vivienne Westwood

Vintage Classics Series Edition. 150th Anniversary edition. Introduction and cover art by Vivienne Westwood. Cream cloth. Illustrated dust jacket. 348 pp. Black-and-white drawings. Various later issues.

1679   ca. 2015 Alice's Adventures in Wonderland and Through the Looking-Glass
London: Simon & Schuster   9781471141614;   John Tenniel
                                      9781471134760 (e-book)

Also available as an e-book.

1680   2015   Alice's Adventures in Wonderland and Through the Looking-Glass
Cambridge, UK: Worth Press   9781849310046 cased;   John Tenniel; Peter Frith
                                      9781849310055 Skivertex edition

2nd edition of a 2009 edition. Introductions by Will Brooker, Morton N. Cohen, Hughes Lebailly, and Rose Lovell-Smith. With 1 map. Colored by Peter Frith.

1681   ca. 2015 Alice's Adventures in Wonderland and Through the Looking-Glass
Ware, UK: Wordsworth Editions   9781840225990   John Tenniel

Reprint of Ware, UK: Wordsworth, 1993. In a boxed set with 7 other classic children's books in paperback. "The Ultimate Children's Classic Collection."

1682   2016   Alice's Adventures in Wonderland and Through the Looking-Glass
Richmond, UK: Alma Classics   9781847494078   John Tenniel

Reprint of the 2015 edition lacking *Alice's Adventures under Ground*.

1683   2017   Alice's Adventures in Wonderland; Through the Looking-Glass
Oxford, London: Inky Parrot Press   9780995557031 (*Alice*);   Gennady Kalinovski
                                      9780995557031 (*Looking-Glass*); 9780995557048; 9780995557044 (Special)

English-language edition with illustrations taken from Kalinovsky's black-and-white edition of 1944 and from his colored version of 1988, both published by Detskaya Literatura, Moscow. Olia Harris provided "much help with the translations." There were 160 Standard copies and 48 Special copies. Issued as a boxed set.

1684   2017   Alice's Adventures in Wonderland and Through the Looking-Glass
Thaxted, Essex, UK; Miles Kelly Publishing   9781782098430   Martina Peluso

1st Mini-Classic Series Edition. Illustrated slipcase. Paper wrappers, front with White Rabbit, 320 pp. Many color illustrations. Single title page, no frontispieces. Reprint of 2015 edition.

1685   2017   Alice's Adventures in Wonderland and Through the Looking-Glass
London: Penguin Books   9780241331620   John Tenniel

Penguin Classics.

1686   2018   Alice's Adventures in Wonderland and Through the Looking-Glass
London: Arcturus Publishing   9781788883825 (hardback);   John Tenniel
                                      9781788882942 (pbk); 9781788883870 (slipcase)

In hardcover, paperback, and slipcase.

1687   2018   Alice's Adventures in Wonderland: poems, letters & bibliography
                [with Through the Looking-Glass]
London: Flame Tree Publishing   9781786647825   Various

Includes illustrations by A.B. Frost, Henry Holiday, John Tenniel, and Arthur Rackham.

1688   n.d.   Alice's Adventures in Wonderland and Through the Looking-Glass
Leicester, UK: Brown Watson   0709708556   Anonymous

Pictorial boards. Frontispiece illustration only by anonymous illustrator.

1689   n.d.   The Complete Novels of Lewis Carroll With All Original Illustrations.
N.P., UK: e-artnow Editions   9788026805106   Various
1 online resource. Maximum number of downloads 3. Includes: *The Life and Letters of Lewis Carroll*, *Alice's Adventures in Wonderland*, *Through the Looking-Glass*, *Sylvie and Bruno*, *Sylvie and Bruno Concluded*, and *Alice's Adventures under Ground*. 1,670 pp.

1690   n.d.   The Illustrated Lewis Carroll
London: Jupiter Books   0904041883   John Tenniel
Reprint of the 1978 Jupiter edition. Introduction by Roy Gasson. Dust jacket.

1691   n.d.   The Illustrated Lewis Carroll
Poole Dorset, UK: New Orchard Editions Ltd.   Various
Identical to the Jupiter Books Edition.

1692   n.d.   Alice's Adventures in Wonderland and Through the Looking-Glass
Bristol, UK: Parragon Books   1858135613   Anonymous
Undated reprint of the 1993 edition. Paperback. In the series Children's Classics. Verso of title page has A Parragon Classic. Anonymous illustration on front cover.

1693   n.d.   The Complete Works of Lewis Carroll
London: The Nonesuch Press;   9780370005072   John Tenniel
New York: Random House
Introduction by Alexander Woollcott. 1,165 pp.

2. *Alice's Adventures in Wonderland* Editions Published in the US, Including Combined Editions with *Through the Looking-Glass*

2.1 APPLETON AND MACMILLAN *ALICE* EDITION

1694   1866   Alice's Adventures in Wonderland

New York: D. Appleton   John Tenniel

1,952 sets of the rejected London 1865 *Alice* sheets were purchased by D. Appleton and published as the 2nd issue. August Imholtz, in his essay in Volume One of this book, provides evidence that the sheets were bound in England. The sheets exist in 2 variants, "A" and "a," as does the cancel Appleton title page in variants 1 and 2. Together these make a total of 4 variants of the D. Appleton edition with no priority. Red cloth with dark green endpapers. The 1865 sheets differ as described by Goodacre in *Yours Very Sincerely, C. L. Dodgson (alias Lewis Carroll)*, ed. Jon A. Lindseth (New York: Grolier Club, 1998), pp. 31–32, as Variant "A" and Variant "a." Easy identifiers are in the last stanza of the prefatory poem. Variant "A" begins "Alice! A childish—"; Variant "a" begins "Alice! a childish—." Also, in the Contents, Variant "A" shows an unhyphenated "rabbit hole," whereas Variant "a" shows "rabbit-hole" with a hyphen. The Appleton cancel title page was printed in duplicate and they differ slightly as described by Goodacre in the 1998 Lindseth Grolier Club catalog, pp. 113–115. In Appleton Variant 1, the "B" in "By" on the title page is directly over the "T" in "Tenniel," while in Variant 2 it is over and just to the right of the "T." This copy is Variant 1-A.

1695   1866   Alice's Adventures in Wonderland

New York: D. Appleton   John Tenniel

Appleton Variant 2-A. One of 4 variants of the 2nd issue of the 1865 1st edition. No priority. Red cloth with dark green endpapers.

1696   1866   Alice's Adventures in Wonderland

New York: D. Appleton   John Tenniel

Appleton Variant 1-a. One of 4 variants of the 2nd issue of the 1865 1st edition. No priority. Red cloth with dark green endpapers.

1697   1866   Alice's Adventures in Wonderland

New York: D. Appleton   John Tenniel

Appleton Variant 2-a. One of 4 variants of the 2nd issue of the 1865 1st edition. No priority. Red cloth with dark green endpapers.

1698   1877   Alice's Adventures in Wonderland

New York: Macmillan   John Tenniel

First American Macmillan edition. Title page reads "New edition." Printed and bound in England. Pictorial red cloth front cover stamped and lettered in gilt with Macmillan roundel. Back cover has no roundel. Spine in the standard Macmillan form. Macmillan emblem on the verso of the half title. There are 5 distinct variants of this edition: die used for front cover medallion, ad in terminals, shade of red cloth, color of endpapers, and printer identified as J. J. Little.

1699   1880   Alice's Adventures in Wonderland

New York: Macmillan   John Tenniel

Pictorial blue or green cloth. Triple-ruled circular device with Alice holding the pig, within triple-ruled outer border on the front cover. Stamped in gilt. Triple-ruled outer border in blind on the back cover. Spine has the same floral border at the top and the bottom in black and gilt, and a new decorative device in gilt above the lower border and above the Macmillan name.

1700   1881   Alice's Adventures in Wonderland

New York: Macmillan   John Tenniel

Red or green cloth. Covers as in the 1880 edition.

1701	1882	Alice's Adventures in Wonderland	
		New York: Macmillan	John Tenniel

Blue, red, or green cloth. Covers as in the 1880 edition.

1702	1884	Alice's Adventures in Wonderland	
		New York: Macmillan	John Tenniel

Red or green cloth. Covers as in the 1880 edition.

1703	1884	Alice's Adventures in Wonderland	
		New York: Macmillan & Co.	John Tenniel

Gold cloth, black and gold-gilt lettering and decorations front and spine, oval vignette of Gryphon and Tortoise in gold-gilt, spine with Cheshire Cat in gold-gilt within triangular device; endpapers with olive-green repetitive floral pattern; [15], 2-192, 1-12 (all ads) pp., all edges gilt. Verso title page says, "New York: J. J. Little & Co., Printers, 10 to 20 Astor Place." Also in a red binding.

1704	1885	Alice's Adventures in Wonderland	
		New York: Macmillan	John Tenniel

Blue or red cloth. Includes an ad for the "One Hundredth Thousand" printing of *Alice*. Covers as in the 1880 edition.

1705	1888	Alice's Adventures in Wonderland	
		New York: Macmillan	John Tenniel

Green or red cloth. Covers as in the 1880 edition.

1706	1889	Alice's Adventures in Wonderland	
		New York: Macmillan	John Tenniel

Red or blue cloth. Includes an ad for the "One Hundredth Thousand" printing of *Alice*. Covers as in the 1880 edition.

1707	1889	Alice's Adventures in Wonderland	
		New York: Macmillan	John Tenniel

Green floral cloth. Printed in New York by J. J. Little. Covers as in the 1880 edition.

1708	1893	Alice's Adventures in Wonderland	
		New York: Macmillan	John Tenniel

Red or green cloth. Covers as in the 1880 edition.

1709	1897	Alice's Adventures in Wonderland	
		New York: Macmillan	John Tenniel

Red cloth. Covers as in the 1880 edition.

1710	1898	Alice's Adventures in Wonderland	
		New York; London: Macmillan	John Tenniel

1st edition. Macmillan Children's Classic Series. Red floral cloth. Printed at the Norwood Press. This edition in blue non-floral cloth was printed by J. J. Little. Prior to 1898, the Macmillan editions in America were printed by J. J. Little. One copy on the verso of the title page states, "Printed March 1898," and lists 7 reprints, with the latest being August 1904.

1711	1900	Alice's Adventures in Wonderland	
		New York; London: Macmillan	John Tenniel

1st reprint of the Macmillan Children's Classic Series 1898 edition. Red or blue cloth.

1712	1901	Alice's Adventures in Wonderland	
		New York; London: Macmillan	John Tenniel

Reprint of the Macmillan Children's Classic Series 1898 edition. Red or blue cloth. March 1901.

1713   1901   Alice's Adventures in Wonderland
New York; London: Macmillan   John Tenniel
Reprint of the Macmillan Children's Classic Series 1898 edition. Red or blue cloth. July 1901.

1714   1902   Alice's Adventures in Wonderland
New York; London: Macmillan   John Tenniel
Reprint of the Macmillan Children's Classic Series 1898 edition. Red or blue cloth.

1715   ca. 1903 Alice's Adventures in Wonderland
New York; London: Macmillan   John Tenniel
Macmillan Little Folks' Edition. Red cloth. 90th thousand.

1716   1903   Alice's Adventures in Wonderland
New York; London: Macmillan   John Tenniel
Reprint of the Macmillan Children's Classic Series 1898 edition. Red or blue cloth.

1717   1904   Alice's Adventures in Wonderland
New York; London: Macmillan   John Tenniel
7th reprint of the Macmillan Children's Classic Series 1898 edition. Red or blue floral cloth. Printed at the Norwood
Press. Prior to 1898, the Macmillan editions in America were printed by J. J. Little. Verso of the title page lists 7
reprints, with the latest being August 1904.

1718   1905   Alice's Adventures in Wonderland
New York; London: Macmillan   John Tenniel
In the form of Pocket Classics, but not stated in the book. Red cloth.

1719   1906   Alice's Adventures in Wonderland
New York; London: Macmillan   John Tenniel
In the form of Pocket Classics, but not stated in the book. Red cloth.

1720   1906   Alice's Adventures in Wonderland
New York; London: Macmillan   John Tenniel
New edition of Macmillan Children's Classic Series. Red or blue cloth

1721   1908   Alice's Adventures in Wonderland
New York; London: Macmillan   John Tenniel
Reprint of the Macmillan Children's Classic Series 1906 edition. Red or blue cloth.

1722   1908   Alice's Adventures in Wonderland
New York: Macmillan   John Tenniel
Macmillan Pocket Classics Edition.

1723   1909   Alice's Adventures in Wonderland
New York; London: Macmillan   John Tenniel; Amy Richards
Reprint of the Macmillan Children's Classic Series 1906 edition. Red or blue cloth. Also exists in a rust and green
decorated cover designed by Amy Richards.

1724   1910   Alice's Adventures in Wonderland
New York; London: Macmillan   John Tenniel; Amy Richards
Reprint of the Macmillan Children's Classic Series 1906 edition. Rust and green decorated cover designed by Amy
Richards.

1725   1910   Alice's Adventures in Wonderland
New York: Macmillan   John Tenniel
Macmillan Pocket Classics Edition. In gray cloth.

1726   [1911]   Alice's Adventures in Wonderland
New York: Macmillan   John Tenniel
Red cloth.

1727   1912   Alice's Adventures in Wonderland
New York: Macmillan   John Tenniel
Macmillan Pocket Classics Edition.

1728   1913   Alice's Adventures in Wonderland
New York; London: Macmillan   John Tenniel
Reprint of the Macmillan Children's Classic Series 1906 edition. Red or blue cloth. March 1913.

1729   1913   Alice's Adventures in Wonderland
New York; London: Macmillan   John Tenniel
Reprint of the Macmillan Children's Classic Series 1906 edition. Red or blue cloth. July 1913.

1730   1914   Alice's Adventures in Wonderland
New York: Macmillan   John Tenniel
Macmillan Pocket Classics Edition.

1731   1914   Alice's Adventures in Wonderland
New York; London: Macmillan   John Tenniel; Amy Richards
Reprint of the 1906 edition Macmillan Children's Classic Series. Rust decorated cover designed by Amy Richards.
June 1914.

1732   1914   Alice's Adventures in Wonderland
New York; London: Macmillan   John Tenniel
Reprint of the 1906 edition Macmillan Children's Classic Series. Blue cloth. December 1914.

1733   1914   Alice's Adventures in Wonderland
New York; London: Macmillan   John Tenniel
Macmillan Miniature Edition.

1734   [1914]   Alice's Adventures in Wonderland
New York: Macmillan   John Tenniel
Macmillan Juvenile Library Edition.

1735   1915   Alice's Adventures in Wonderland
New York: Macmillan   John Tenniel
Reprint of the Macmillan Children's Classic Series 1906 edition. Blue cloth. July 1915.

1736   1915   Alice's Adventures in Wonderland
New York; London: Macmillan   John Tenniel
Reprint of the Macmillan Children's Classic Series 1906 edition. Blue cloth. December 1915.

1737   1916   Alice's Adventures in Wonderland
New York; London: Macmillan   John Tenniel
Reprint of the Macmillan Children's Classic Series 1906 edition. Blue cloth. June 1916.

1738   1916   Alice's Adventures in Wonderland
New York; London: Macmillan   John Tenniel
Reprint of the Macmillan Children's Classic Series 1906 edition. Blue cloth. July 1916.

1739   1916   Alice's Adventures in Wonderland
New York; London: Macmillan   John Tenniel
Reprint of the Macmillan Children's Classic Series 1906 edition. Blue cloth. September 1916.

1740   1916   Alice's Adventures in Wonderland
New York: Macmillan   John Tenniel
Macmillan Pocket Classics Edition.

1741   1917   Alice's Adventures in Wonderland
New York: Macmillan   John Tenniel
Macmillan Pocket Classics Edition.

1742   1917   Alice's Adventures in Wonderland
New York: Macmillan   John Tenniel
Reprint of the Macmillan Children's Classic Series 1906 edition. Blue cloth. April 1917.

1743   1917   Alice's Adventures in Wonderland
New York: Macmillan   John Tenniel
Reprint of the Macmillan Children's Classic Series 1906 edition. Blue cloth. July 1917.

1744   [1918] Alice's Adventures in Wonderland
New York: Macmillan   John Tenniel

1745   1919   Alice's Adventures in Wonderland
New York: Macmillan   John Tenniel
Reprint of the Macmillan Children's Classic Series 1906 edition. Red or blue cloth.

1746   1920   Alice's Adventures in Wonderland
New York: Macmillan   John Tenniel
Red cloth. Standard issue.

1747   1921   Alice's Adventures in Wonderland
New York: Macmillan   John Tenniel
Red cloth. Standard issue.

1748   1922   Alice's Adventures in Wonderland
New York: Macmillan   John Tenniel
Red or blue cloth. Standard issue.

1749   1923   Alice's Adventures in Wonderland
New York; London: Macmillan   John Tenniel
Red or blue cloth. Standard issue.

1750   1924   Alice's Adventures in Wonderland
New York; London: Macmillan   John Tenniel
Blue cloth. Standard issue.

1751   [1926] Alice's Adventures in Wonderland
New York: Macmillan   John Tenniel

1752   1927   Alice's Adventures in Wonderland
New York: D. Appleton   John Tenniel

The first Appleton reprint of their 1866 edition of the rejected London 1865 sheets. This of Variant 2-A. Typical Macmillan binding in red cloth with dark green endpapers. In the 61 years since the 1866 publication in 1,952 copies, all must have been sold to warrant a reprint. But a search locates very few of these 1866 copies. Here, the facsimile title page still reads 1866 but the verso says "Copyright, 1927, by D. Appleton and Company" and at the bottom of the page "Printed in the United States of America." The original 1866 edition was printed and bound in England. A 2nd reprint was done in 1943.

1753   1927   Alice's Adventures in Wonderland
New York: Macmillan   John Tenniel
Red cloth. Standard issue.

1754   1928   Alice's Adventures in Wonderland
New York: Macmillan   John Tenniel
Red cloth. Standard issue.

1755   1928   Alice's Adventures in Wonderland
New York: Macmillan   John Tenniel
Macmillan Pocket Classics Edition. Brown cloth.

1756   1929   Alice's Adventures in Wonderland
New York: Macmillan   John Tenniel
Reprint of the Macmillan Children's Classic Series 1906 edition. Red cloth. Dust jacket.

1757   1929   Alice's Adventures in Wonderland
New York: Macmillan   John Tenniel
Macmillan Little Library Edition.

1758   1929   Alice's Adventures in Wonderland
New York: Macmillan   John Tenniel
Red cloth. Standard issue.

1759   1930   Alice's Adventures in Wonderland
New York; London: Macmillan   John Tenniel
New edition. Macmillan Children's Classic Series. Red or blue cloth.

1760   1932   Alice's Adventures in Wonderland
New York; London: Macmillan   John Tenniel
Reprint of the 1930 New Edition. Macmillan Children's Classic Series. Red or blue cloth.

1761   1933   Alice's Adventures in Wonderland
New York: Macmillan   John Tenniel
Reprint of the 1930 New Edition. Macmillan Children's Classic Series. Red cloth.

1762   1935   Alice's Adventures in Wonderland
New York: Macmillan   John Tenniel
Red cloth. Standard issue.

1763   1937   Alice's Adventures in Wonderland
New York: Macmillan   John Tenniel
Red cloth. Standard issue.

1764   1943   Alice's Adventures in Wonderland
New York: D. Appleton   John Tenniel
2nd reprint of the Appleton Variant 2-A. Red cloth with dark green endpapers. The 1st reprint was 1927.

1765   ca. 1944 Alice's Adventures in Wonderland
New York; London: Macmillan   John Tenniel
Red cloth.

1766   1946   Alice's Adventures in Wonderland
New York; London: Macmillan   John Tenniel
Red or blue cloth. New edition. Reprint of the 1906 edition.

1767   1959   Alice's Adventures in Wonderland
New York: St. Martin's Press. London: Macmillan   John Tenniel

1768   1981   Classic Children's Literature
New York: Macmillan   9780023471902   Unknown
An anthology including *Alice's Adventures in Wonderland*. Softcover.

1769   1982   Classic Children's Literature
New York: Macmillan   9780023471902   Unknown
An anthology including *Alice's Adventures in Wonderland*. Likely a reprint of the 1981 edition.

1770   1987   Classic Children's Literature
New York: Macmillan   9780023473401   Unknown
2nd edition. An anthology including *Alice's Adventures in Wonderland*. Softcover.

2.2 MACMILLAN: COMBINED EDITIONS OF *ALICE* AND *LOOKING-GLASS*

1771   1881   Alice's Adventures in Wonderland and Through the Looking-Glass
New York: Macmillan and Co.   John Tenniel
First American 1-volume combined edition. Green cloth. The combined title page is undated and marked "New York: Macmillan and Co." Also marked "New Edition in One Volume." The *Alice* title page is dated 1881, marked "New Edition" and Macmillan & Co. The *Looking-Glass* imprint is London and New York: Macmillan, 1881. It is also marked "Fiftieth Thousand." Ads priced in US dollars.

1772   1883   Alice's Adventures in Wonderland and Through the Looking-Glass
London; New York: Macmillan and Co.   John Tenniel
2nd printing of the 1881 New York combined edition, but with dual imprint. Copies found in blue, red, or other colored cloth.

1773   1885   Alice's Adventures in Wonderland and Through the Looking-Glass
London; New York: Macmillan   John Tenniel
2nd American 1-volume combined edition. Green or red cloth. All title pages are dated 1885. Combined title page marked "New Edition in One Volume." The *Alice* title page is marked "New Edition" and Macmillan & Co. The *Looking-Glass* imprint is London and New York: Macmillan. It is also marked "Fiftieth Thousand." 12 pages of ads at the rear are priced in US dollars.

1774   1889   Alice's Adventures in Wonderland and Through the Looking-Glass
London; New York: Macmillan   John Tenniel
A later printing of the 1885 edition. Red cloth. All title pages dated 1889. Both the combined and *Alice* title pages are

marked "New Edition." *Looking-Glass* now the 52nd thousand. Title page is London and New York: Macmillan. 12 pages of ads at the rear are priced in US dollars.

1775   1892   Alice's Adventures in Wonderland and Through the Looking-Glass
New York: Macmillan   John Tenniel
1-volume combined edition. Red cloth. No combined title page. *Alice* title page dated 1892 and marked "New Edition." *Looking-Glass* imprint is London and New York: Macmillan & Co. 50th thousand. 1892. 12 pages of ads at the rear are priced in US dollars.

1776   1894   Alice's Adventures in Wonderland and Through the Looking-Glass
New York: Macmillan   John Tenniel
1-volume combined edition. Red cloth. All title pages dated 1894. Combined and *Alice* title pages both marked "New Edition." *Looking-Glass* imprint is London and New York: Macmillan & Co. 52nd Thousand.

1777   1899   Alice's Adventures in Wonderland and Through the Looking-Glass
New York: Macmillan   John Tenniel
A later printing of the 1885 2nd American 1-volume edition. Red cloth. All 3 title pages dated 1899. The combined and *Alice* title pages both marked "New Edition." *Looking-Glass* imprint is London and New York: Macmillan. 52nd thousand.

1778   1903   Alice's Adventures in Wonderland and Through the Looking-Glass
New York: Macmillan   John Tenniel
A later printing of the 1885 2nd American 1-volume edition. Red cloth. The combined and *Alice* title pages both marked "New Edition." *Looking-Glass* imprint is London and New York: Macmillan. 52nd thousand.

1779   1906   Alice's Adventures in Wonderland and Through the Looking-Glass
New York; London: Macmillan   John Tenniel
Red or green cloth.

1780   1906   Alice's Adventures in Wonderland and Through the Looking-Glass
New York: The Macmillan Company; London: Macmillan & Co., Ltd.   John Tenniel
Macmillan's Children's Classics Series. New Edition. Printed at the Norwood Press. Each with a separate title page. *Alice* includes "Preface of the 86th Thousand" [of *Alice*] and "Christmas Greeting." *Looking-Glass* includes "Preface to the 61st Thousand" [of *Looking-Glass*] and "Christmas Greeting." Reprints include 1910, twice in 1913, 3 times in 1914, twice in 1915, 1916, 1917, 1919, and 1921. According to Lovett, all copies of the combined edition published before 1930 are reprints of the 1906 combined edition. Red or blue cloth.

1781   1910   Alice's Adventures in Wonderland and Through the Looking-Glass
New York; London: Macmillan   John Tenniel
Macmillan Children's Classics Series. Red cloth. July 1910.

1782   1913   Alice's Adventures in Wonderland and Through the Looking-Glass
New York; London: Macmillan   John Tenniel
Macmillan Children's Classics Series. Dull green decorated cloth.

1783   1914   Alice's Adventures in Wonderland and Through the Looking-Glass
New York; London: Macmillan   John Tenniel
Macmillan Children's Classics Series.

1784   1915   Alice's Adventures in Wonderland and Through the Looking-Glass
New York; London: Macmillan   John Tenniel
Macmillan Children's Classics Series.

1785   1915   Alice's Adventures in Wonderland and Through the Looking-Glass

New York; London: Macmillan   John Tenniel
Macmillan Children's Classics Series. 2nd 1915 printing.

1786   1916   Alice's Adventures in Wonderland and Through the Looking-Glass
New York; London: Macmillan   John Tenniel
New edition of Macmillan Children's Classics Series in 1 volume. Green cloth. Both *Alice* and *Looking-Glass* with a separate title page dated 1916. Lovett 42 and 43 are separate printings of these editions.

1787   1917   Alice's Adventures in Wonderland and Through the Looking-Glass
New York; London: Macmillan   John Tenniel
Macmillan's Children's Classics Series.

1788   1919   Alice's Adventures in Wonderland and Through the Looking-Glass
New York; London: Macmillan   John Tenniel
Macmillan Children's Classics Series. Red cloth.

1789   ca. 1920s   Alice's Adventures in Wonderland and Through the Looking-Glass
New York: The Modern Library   John Tenniel
Introduction by Alexander Woollcott.

1790   1921   Alice's Adventures in Wonderland and Through the Looking-Glass
New York; London: Macmillan   John Tenniel
Macmillan Children's Classics Series. A later printing of the 1916 edition. Red cloth. Both *Alice* and *Looking-Glass* have a separate title page dated 1921.

1791   1922   Alice's Adventures in Wonderland and Through the Looking-Glass
New York; London: Macmillan   John Tenniel
Red cloth.

1792   1923   Alice's Adventures in Wonderland and Through the Looking-Glass
New York; London: Macmillan   John Tenniel
Blue cloth.

1793   1924   Alice's Adventures in Wonderland and Through the Looking-Glass
New York; London: Macmillan   John Tenniel
Blue cloth.

1794   1924   Alice's Adventures in Wonderland and Through the Looking-Glass
New York: Boni and Liveright   John Tenniel
Modern Library edition. Introduction by Alexander Woollcott. Dark green imitation leather.

1795   1925   Alice's Adventures in Wonderland and Through the Looking-Glass
New York; London: Macmillan   John Tenniel
Blue cloth.

1796   1926   Alice's Adventures in Wonderland and Through the Looking-Glass
New York; London: Macmillan   John Tenniel
Blue cloth.

1797   1927   Alice's Adventures in Wonderland and Through the Looking-Glass
New York; London: Macmillan Children's Classics   John Tenniel
Macmillan Children's Classics Series. Blue cloth.

1798   1928   Alice's Adventures in Wonderland and Through the Looking-Glass
New York; London: Macmillan   John Tenniel
Blue cloth.

1799   1929   Alice's Adventures in Wonderland and Through the Looking-Glass
New York; London: Macmillan   John Tenniel
Blue cloth.

1800   1930   Alice's Adventures in Wonderland and Through the Looking-Glass
New York: Macmillan Children's Classics   John Tenniel
New Edition. Macmillan Children's Classics Series. Includes the "Preface to the 86th Thousand" edition and "Christmas Greetings." Blue cloth. According to Lovett, all later editions are reprints of this 1930 edition.

1801   ca. 1930   Alice's Adventures in Wonderland and Through the Looking-Glass
New York: Boni and Liveright   John Tenniel
Modern Library edition. Introduction by Alexander Woollcott. Reddish brown cloth.

1802   1931   Alice's Adventures in Wonderland and Through the Looking-Glass
New York: Macmillan Children's Classics   John Tenniel
Later printing of the Macmillan Children's Classics Series 1930 edition. Blue cloth.

1803   1932   Alice's Adventures in Wonderland and Through the Looking-Glass
New York: Macmillan Children's Classics   John Tenniel
Later printing of the Macmillan Children's Classics Series 1930 edition. Blue cloth. Printed twice this year.

1804   1933   Alice's Adventures in Wonderland and Through the Looking-Glass
New York: Macmillan Children's Classics   John Tenniel
Later printing of the Macmillan Children's Classics Series 1930 edition. Blue cloth.

1805   1934   Alice's Adventures in Wonderland and Through the Looking-Glass
New York; London: Macmillan Company Children's Classics   John Tenniel
Macmillan Children's Classics Series. Blue cloth. According to Cassady, the University of Southern California copy on the verso of the half title lists 40 titles in the Macmillan Children's Classics Series. The verso of the title page says in part: Printed March 1898, Reprinted June 1899, August 1900, March 1901, [Ed. note: Omitting the July 1901 edition listed in the 1898 entry], January and September 1902, December 1903, August 1904, January 1906, New Edition September 1906, June 1908, June 1909, September 1910, September 1911, September 1912. Combined editions October 1906, July 1910, March and July 1813, January, June, and December 1914, July and December 1915, June, July, and September 1916, April and July 1917, New Edition October 1930, Reprinted February and May 1932, May 1933.

1806   1937   Alice's Adventures in Wonderland and Through the Looking-Glass
New York; London: Macmillan Children's Classics   John Tenniel
Later printing of the 1930 edition. Blue cloth.

1807   1940   Alice's Adventures in Wonderland and Through the Looking-Glass
New York: Macmillan Children's Classics   John Tenniel
Later printing of the 1930 edition. Blue cloth.

1808   1941   Alice's Adventures in Wonderland and Through the Looking-Glass
New York: Macmillan Children's Classics   John Tenniel
Later printing of the 1930 edition. Blue cloth.

1809   1943   Alice's Adventures in Wonderland and Through the Looking-Glass
New York: Macmillan Children's Classics   John Tenniel
Later printing of the 1930 edition. Blue cloth.

1810   1944   Alice's Adventures in Wonderland and Through the Looking-Glass
New York: Macmillan Children's Classics   John Tenniel
Later printing of the 1930 edition. Blue cloth.

1811   1946   Alice's Adventures in Wonderland and Through the Looking-Glass
New York: Macmillan Children's Classics   John Tenniel
Later printing of the 1930 edition. Blue cloth.

1812   ca. 1946 Alice's Adventures in Wonderland, Through the Looking-Glass and The Hunting of
                    the Snark
New York: The Modern Library   John Tenniel; Henry Holiday
Modern Library edition. Introduction by Alexander Woollcott. Medium blue cloth. Includes *Snark*.

1813   1950   Alice's Adventures in Wonderland and Through the Looking-Glass
New York: Macmillan Children's Classics   John Tenniel
Later printing of the 1930 edition. Blue cloth.

1814   1956   Alice's Adventures in Wonderland and Through the Looking-Glass
New York: Macmillan Children's Classics   John Tenniel
Later printing of the 1930 edition. Blue cloth.

1815   1958   Alice's Adventures in Wonderland and Through the Looking-Glass
London; Melbourne, VIC; Toronto, ON: Macmillan. New York: St. Martin's Press   John Tenniel
Pocket Papermac edition. 1st printing of this Macmillan St. Martin's Library edition. Pictorial wrappers. Reprinted in
1968, 1971, 1973, and 1975. Paperback.

1816   ca. 1960s   Alice's Adventures in Wonderland and Through the Looking-Glass
New York: The Modern Library   John Tenniel
Modern Library edition. Introduction by Alexander Woollcott. Dark blue cloth.

1817   1960   Alice's Adventures in Wonderland and Through the Looking-Glass
New York: Macmillan   John Tenniel
New Children's Classics Series.

1818   1962   Alice's Adventures in Wonderland and Through the Looking-Glass
New York: Collier. London: Collier-Macmillan   John Tenniel
1st edition. Introduction by Louis Untermeyer.

1819   1963   Alice's Adventures in Wonderland and Through the Looking-Glass
New York: Macmillan. London: Collier–Macmillan   John Tenniel
Afterword by Clifton Fadiman.

1820   1966   Alice's Adventures in Wonderland and Through the Looking-Glass
New York: Macmillan. London: Collier–Macmillan   John Tenniel
3rd printing. Afterword by Clifton Fadiman.

1821   1966   Alice's Adventures in Wonderland and Through the Looking-Glass
New York: Collier. London: Collier-Macmillan   John Tenniel
Reprint of the 1962 edition. Introduction by Louis Untermeyer.

1822   1967   Alice's Adventures in Wonderland and Through the Looking-Glass
New York: Collier. London: Collier-Macmillan   John Tenniel
Reprint of the 1962 edition. Introduction by Louis Untermeyer

1823   1968   Alice's Adventures in Wonderland and Through the Looking-Glass
London; Melbourne, VIC; Toronto, ON: Macmillan.   John Tenniel
New York: St. Martin's Press

Pocket Papermac edition. 1st printing of this Macmillan St. Martin's Library edition. Pictorial wrappers. Reprint of the 1958 edition. Paperback.

1824   1971   Alice's Adventures in Wonderland and Through the Looking-Glass
London; Melbourne, VIC; Toronto, ON: Macmillan.   John Tenniel
New York: St. Martin's Press

Pocket Papermac edition. 1st printing of this Macmillan St. Martin's Library edition. Pictorial wrappers. Reprint of the 1958 edition. Paperback.

1825   1973   Alice's Adventures in Wonderland and Through the Looking-Glass
London; Melbourne, VIC; Toronto, ON: Macmillan.   John Tenniel
New York: St. Martin's Press

Pocket Papermac edition. 1st printing of this Macmillan St. Martin's Library edition. Pictorial wrappers. Reprint of the 1958 edition. Paperback.

1826   1975   Alice's Adventures in Wonderland and Through the Looking-Glass
London; Melbourne, VIC; Toronto, ON: Macmillan.   John Tenniel
New York: St. Martin's Press

Pocket Papermac edition. 1st printing of this Macmillan St. Martin's Library edition. Pictorial wrappers. Reprint of the 1958 edition. Paperback.

1827   1975   Alice's Adventures in Wonderland and Through the Looking-Glass
New York: Collier. London: Collier-Macmillan   John Tenniel

Reprint of the 1962 edition. Introduction by Louis Untermeyer.

1828   2015   The Complete Alice
New York: Macmillan Children's Books, Henry Holt   9781627794350   John Tenniel; Harry Theaker;
                                                                       Diz Wallis

Includes *Alice* and *Looking-Glass*.

2.3 OTHER PUBLISHERS OF *ALICE*

1829   [1867]   Fun For All! A Collection of Mirthfull Morsels for Merry Moments.
                Served up by Mr. Merryman, who nose he nose how.
New York: American News Company   John Tenniel

The 1st Jesse Haney piracy of *Alice* in *Merryman's Monthly* for the January and February 1867 issues. Each issue with half of the *Alice* story. In an outer wrapper with the American News imprint and on the rear cover ads for "J.C. Haney & Co.'s Popular Publications. 109 Nassau Street." Title page lists the address as Nos. 119 and 121 Nassau Street. *Merryman's Monthly* is included in the ads. The illustration on the wrapper has no relationship to *Alice* or Tenniel. American News was General Agent for Haney. A copy exists of the January and February issues in original wrappers, unbound. One bound set of all 1867 *Merryman's Monthly* issues was sold at auction in 1992, present location unknown.

1830   [1868]   The Children's Library
New York: Jesse Haney   John Tenniel
The 2nd piracy of *Alice* by Jesse Haney. Known only in a copy at the New York Public Library.

1831   1869   Haney's Journal
New York: Jesse Haney   John Tenniel
The 3rd and last piracy of *Alice* by Jesse Haney. In 8 monthly parts. In Vol. II., Nos. 15-22., March–October 1869. Known in 8 copies, but only 1 is unbound and with some leaves unopened.

1832   1869   Alice's Adventures in Wonderland
Boston: Lee and Shepard   John Tenniel

First *Alice* book edition printed in America. Bindings in green, orange, or purple pebbled cloth. Macmillan roundels on front and back covers in gilt. Lee and Shepard device at foot of spine in gilt.

1833   1870   Alice's Adventures in Wonderland
Boston: Lee and Shepard   John Tenniel

In green, orange, or purple pebbled cloth. Macmillan roundels on front and back covers in gilt. Lee and Shepard device at foot of spine in gilt.

1834   1871   Alice's Adventures in Wonderland
Boston: Lee and Shepard. New York: Lee, Shepard and Dillingham   John Tenniel

In green or orange pebbled cloth and red smooth cloth. Macmillan roundels on front and back covers in gilt. Lee and Shepard device at foot of spine in gilt.

1835   1871   Alice's Adventures in Wonderland
New York: Lee, Shepard and Dillingham   John Tenniel

In orange pebbled cloth. Macmillan roundels on front and back covers in gilt. Lee and Shepard device at foot of spine in gilt.

1836   1872   Alice's Adventures in Wonderland
Boston: Lee and Shepard. New York: Lee, Shepard and Dillingham   John Tenniel

In green, blue, orangish-brown, yellow, or purple pebbled cloth, and in smooth red cloth with gilt Cat. Macmillan roundel on front cover in gilt and back cover in blind. Lee and Shepard device at foot of spine in gilt.

1837   1874   Alice's Adventures in Wonderland
Boston: Lee and Shepard   John Tenniel

In blue or green pebbled cloth. Macmillan roundel on front cover in gilt and back cover in blind. Lee and Shepard device at foot of spine in gilt.

1838   1875   Alice's Adventures in Wonderland
Boston: Lee and Shepard. New York: Lee, Shepard and Dillingham   John Tenniel

In green or rough red cloth.

1839   1876   Alice's Adventures in Wonderland
Boston: Lee and Shepard   John Tenniel

Green ribbed cloth. In *Jabberwocky* (Autumn 1981): 95–97, Byron Sewell reported that Lee and Shepard advertised *Alice* through 1878 and then from 1880 to 1886.

1840   ca. 1884 Alice's Adventures in Wonderland
New York: George Munro   John Tenniel

Seaside Library edition. Green cloth.

1841   1885   Alice's Adventures in Wonderland
New York: George Munro   John Tenniel

Seaside Library. Pocket edition. Wraps.

1842   1885   Alice's Adventures in Wonderland
New York: John W. Lovell   John Tenniel

Lovell's Library series. Wraps.

1843   1886   Alice's Adventures in Wonderland
New York: National Book Company   John Tenniel

Rugby Edition of Books for Boys and Girls.

1844   ca. 1890 Alice's Adventures in Wonderland
        Chicago: Belford, Clarke & Co.   John Tenniel

1845   ca. 1890 Alice's Adventures in Wonderland
        New York: John W. Lovell   John Tenniel
        Lovell's Standard set. In a boxed set with *Looking-Glass*.

1846   ca. 1890 Alice's Adventures in Wonderland
        New York: United States Book Company   John Tenniel
        Rugby Edition.

1847   ca. 1890 Alice's Adventures in Wonderland
        New York: United States Book Company   John Tenniel
        Seaside Library.

1848   ca. 1890 Alice's Adventures in Wonderland
        New York: Worthington Co.   John Tenniel
        Franklin Edition of Popular 12 mos.

1849   ca. 1890s Alice's Adventures in Wonderland
        New York: Hurst   John Tenniel
        Tan cloth.

1850   ca. 1890–1900 Alice's Adventures in Wonderland
        New York: New York Publishing Co.   John Tenniel
        Empire Edition.

1851   ca. 1890–1900 Alice's Adventures in Wonderland
        New York: R. F. Fenno   John Tenniel

1852   ca. 1892 Alice's Adventures in Wonderland
        New York: Hovenden   John Tenniel
        Juvenile Books in Sets. Boxed with *Looking-Glass* and *Rhyme? and Reason?*

1853   ca. 1892 Alice's Adventures in Wonderland
        Chicago: Morrill, Higgins & Co.   John Tenniel; Anonymous
        Illustrated Quarto Juveniles. With anonymous cover illustration.

1854   ca. 1892 Alice's Adventures in Wonderland
        New York: National Book Company   John Tenniel
        Rugby Household Library.

1855   ca. 1892 Alice's Adventures in Wonderland
        New York: Worthington Co.   John Tenniel
        Children's Hours.

1856   1893   Alice's Adventures in Wonderland
        New York; Boston: Thomas Y. Crowell   L. J. (Lewis Jesse) Bridgman;
                                                            Anonymous (after Tenniel); Charles Copeland
        Children's Favorite Classics. Color frontispiece signed "Copeland." 4 black-and-white plates, 3 after Tenniel and 1
        with L. J. Bridgman's monogram; cover by (Charles) Copeland.

1857   1893   Alice's Adventures in Wonderland
        New York: Maynard, Merrill   John Tenniel

1858   ca. 1893 Alice's Adventures in Wonderland
New York: Tait, Sons and Co.   John Tenniel
Rugby Edition.

1859   ca. 1894 Alice's Adventures in Wonderland
Chicago: Donohue, Henneberry & Co.   John Tenniel
Pictorial boards in brown cloth.

1860   ca. 1894 Alice's Adventures in Wonderland
Boston; New York; Chicago; San Francisco: Educational Publishing Co. John Tenniel

1861   ca. 1894 Alice's Adventures in Wonderland
New York: International Book Company   Unknown
Comic Tales for Girls. Boxed with *Looking-Glass* and *Rhyme? and Reason?* Not seen.

1862   ca. 1894 Alice's Adventures in Wonderland
New York: International Book Company   Unknown
Adventure Series. Not seen.

1863   1895   Alice's Adventures in Wonderland
Chicago: Donohue, Henneberry & Co.   John Tenniel
Watered Silk Series.

1864   ca. 1895 Alice's Adventures in Wonderland
Chicago: Donohue, Henneberry & Co.   John Tenniel
Full Morocco Leather Series.

1865   ca. 1895 Alice's Adventures in Wonderland
Chicago: E. A. Weeks & Co.   John Tenniel
Handy Volume Series. Green cloth. A copy is known in red cloth lettered in silver.

1866   ca. 1895 Alice's Adventures in Wonderland
Philadelphia: Henry Altemus   John Tenniel
Altemus' Young People's Library. Light green or buff cloth. According to Lovett, the series was published until ca.
1920.

1867   ca. 1895 Alice's Adventures in Wonderland
New York; Boston: Thomas Y. Crowell   L. J. (Lewis Jesse) Bridgman;
                                                Anonymous (after Tenniel); Charles Copeland
Children's Favorite Classics. Color frontispiece signed "Copeland." Reduced format. 4 black-and-white plates, 3 after
Tenniel and 1 with L. J. Bridgman's monogram; cover by (Charles) Copeland.

1868   ca. 1895–1900 Alice's Adventures in Wonderland
New York: John W. Lovell   John Tenniel
"The Prudential Library of Popular and Standard Works." "Published by JOHN W. LOVELL" in banner at top of
cover. 2-color illustration of the Mad Tea-Party in center of cover. At bottom is another banner: "Compliments of The
Prudential Insurance Co. of America, Newark, N.J."

1869   [1896] Alice's Adventures in Wonderland
New York: Hurst   Anonymous (after Tenniel)
Cinderella Series.

1870   ca. 1896 Alice's Adventures in Wonderland

New York: A. L. Burt — John Tenniel
Little Woman Series. Includes the first 10 chapters from *Sylvie and Bruno*. Dated by *PTLA*.

1871 ca. 1896 Alice's Adventures in Wonderland
New York: A. L. Burt — John Tenniel
The Fireside Series for Girls. Copies in 2 private collections.

1872 ca. 1896 Alice's Adventures in Wonderland
New York: American Publishers Corporation — John Tenniel
St. Nicholas Series for Boys and Girls.

1873 ca. 1896 Alice's Adventures in Wonderland
New York; Boston: H. M. Caldwell — John Tenniel
The De Novo Library.

1874 ca. 1896 Alice's Adventures in Wonderland
New York; Boston: H. M. Caldwell — John Tenniel
Calumet Series. Issued with *Looking-Glass* in a boxed set.

1875 ca. 1896 Alice's Adventures in Wonderland
New York; Boston: H. M. Caldwell — John Tenniel
Chef D'Ouvre Series.

1876 ca. 1896 Alice's Adventures in Wonderland
New York; Boston: H. M. Caldwell — John Tenniel
Superb Series.

1877 ca. 1896 Alice's Adventures in Wonderland
Philadelphia: Henry Altemus — John Tenniel
Altemus' Young People's Library. Bluish gray cloth.

1878 ca. 1896 Alice's Adventures in Wonderland
New York: Hurst — John Tenniel
Cambridge Classics.

1879 ca. 1896 Alice's Adventures in Wonderland
New York: Hurst — John Tenniel
Argyle Series.

1880 ca. 1896 Alice's Adventures in Wonderland
New York: Hurst — John Tenniel
Universal Library Series.

1881 ca. 1896 Alice's Adventures in Wonderland
New York: Merrill and Baker — John Tenniel
Celluloid Edition. Cover hand decorated in gilt.

1882 ca. 1896 Alice's Adventures in Wonderland
Philadelphia: Rodgers — John Tenniel
Popular Classics Series of 16 Mos. Excelsior Edition. A copy is known inscribed December 29, 1896.

1883 ca. 1896 Alice's Adventures in Wonderland
New York; Chicago: Siegel-Cooper Co. — John Tenniel
Dated by inscription of "Dec. 1896."

1884   1897   Alice's Adventures in Wonderland
        Philadelphia: Henry Altemus   John Tenniel;
                                                                             E. Gertrude Thomson
        Altemus' Young People's Library. Copyright 1897. In cream or beige cloth. Frontispiece by E. Gertrude Thomson.

1885   [1897]   Alice's Adventures in Wonderland
        New York: Henry Altemus   John Tenniel
        Pictorial tan cloth.

1886   [1897]   Alice's Adventures in Wonderland
        New York: Hurst   John Tenniel
        Arlington Edition Series.

1887   [1897]   Alice's Adventures in Wonderland
        Chicago: W. B. Conkey   John Tenniel
        Wonderland Series.

1888   1898   Alice's Adventures in Wonderland
        Chicago: Donohue, Henneberry & Co.   John Tenniel
        Red cloth.

1889   1898   Alice's Adventures in Wonderland
        Boston: Lothrop, Lee and Shepard   John Tenniel; Anonymous
        World Famous Quarto Series. 4 color plates by an uncredited illustrator. Greenish-gray cloth.

1890   1898   Alice's Adventures in Wonderland
        New York: McLoughlin Brothers   After John Tenniel
        Color frontispiece after Tenniel, and 40 black-and-white illustrations drawn after Tenniel. Several later printings.

1891   [1898]   Alice's Adventures in Wonderland
        Boston: D. Lothrop & Company   Anonymous (after Tenniel)
        In cloth and glazed boards.

1892   [1898]   Alice's Adventures in Wonderland
        Chicago: Rand McNally   Unknown
        Twentieth Century Series.

1893   [1898]   Alice's Adventures in Wonderland
        Chicago: Rand McNally   Unknown
        The Rand-McNally Alpha Library.

1894   ca. 1898 Alice's Adventures in Wonderland
        New York: A. L. Burt   John Tenniel
        The Cornell Series of 12 mos. Dated by *PTLA*.

1895   ca. 1898 Alice's Adventures in Wonderland
        Boston: DeWolfe, Fiske & Co.   John Tenniel
        The Favorite Library. Title page reads "Alberta's Little Friends." Beige cloth.

1896   ca. 1898 Alice's Adventures in Wonderland
        New York: F. M. Lupton Publishing Co.   John Tenniel
        In cloth and glazed boards.

1897	ca. 1898 Alice's Adventures in Wonderland New York; Boston: H. M. Caldwell Florentine Series.	John Tenniel
1898	ca. 1898 Alice's Adventures in Wonderland New York; Boston: H. M. Caldwell Commonwealth Series.	John Tenniel
1899	ca. 1898 Alice's Adventures in Wonderland New York; Boston: H. M. Caldwell The Young Folks Library.	John Tenniel
1900	ca. 1898 Alice's Adventures in Wonderland New York: McLoughlin Brothers Includes *Sylvie and Bruno* poems.	Harry Furniss
1901	ca. 1898 Alice's Adventures in Wonderland New York: McLoughlin Brothers Tan or brown cloth with pictorial cover.	Anonymous (after Tenniel)
1902	1899 Alice's Adventures in Wonderland New York: Gilbert H. McKibbin Manhattan Young People's Library. Tenniel illustrations have been colored. Anonymous colored frontispiece. Buff cloth.	John Tenniel; Anonymous
1903	1899 Alice's Adventures in Wonderland New York: Mansfield and Wessels 12 color plates. Tan or gray pictorial cloth.	Blanche McManus
1904	1899 Alice's Adventures in Wonderland New York: Hurst Hurst's Gilt Top Library Editions.	John Tenniel
1905	[1899] Alice's Adventures in Wonderland New York: Hurst Laurelhurst Series. Boxed together with *Looking-Glass*.	John Tenniel
1906	[1899] Alice's Adventures in Wonderland New York: Gilbert H. McKibbin Manhattan Young People's Library. Color illustrations throughout.	John Tenniel
1907	ca. 1899 Alice's Adventures in Wonderland New York: Gilbert H. McKibbin Red cloth. Illustrations in color.	Anonymous (after Tenniel)
1908	ca. 1899 Alice's Adventures in Wonderland New York: A. L. Burt Burt's Young Folks Library. Ivory cloth. Dated by *PTLA*.	John Tenniel
1909	ca. 1899 Alice's Adventures in Wonderland New York: A. L. Burt Little Woman Series. Includes the first 10 chapters of *Sylvie and Bruno*. Dated by *PTLA*.	John Tenniel

Alice in a World of Wonderlands

1910   ca. 1899 Alice's Adventures in Wonderland
        New York: A. L. Burt   John Tenniel
        The Wellesley Series for Girls. Red or ivory cloth. Includes the first 10 chapters of *Sylvie and Bruno*. Dated by *PTLA*.
        Could be earlier based on ads.

1911   ca. 1899 Alice's Adventures in Wonderland
        New York: Bay View Publishing   John Tenniel
        Excelsior Edition.

1912   ca. 1899 Alice's Adventures in Wonderland
        Boston: D. Lothrop & Company   John Tenniel; Anonymous
        Chromolithographed frontispiece by Anonymous.

1913   ca. 1899 Alice's Adventures in Wonderland
        Chicago: George M. Hill   John Tenniel
        Handy Volume Series.

1914   ca. 1899 Alice's Adventures in Wonderland
        Philadelphia: Henry Altemus   John Tenniel
        Altemus' Young People's Library. Bluish gray or cream cloth.

1915   ca. 1899 Alice's Adventures in Wonderland
        Philadelphia: Henry Altemus   John Tenniel
        Altemus' Illustrated Marqueterie Series.

1916   ca. 1899 Alice's Adventures in Wonderland
        Philadelphia: Henry Altemus   John Tenniel
        Altemus' Illustrated Petit Trianon Series.

1917   ca. 1899 Alice's Adventures in Wonderland
        Philadelphia: Henry Altemus   John Tenniel
        Altemus' Illustrated Sanspareil Series.

1918   ca. 1899 Alice's Adventures in Wonderland
        Philadelphia: Henry Altemus   John Tenniel
        Altemus' Illustrated Vademecum Series.

1919   ca. 1899 Alice's Adventures in Wonderland
        New York: Mershon   John Tenniel
        Standard Series.

1920   ca. 1899 Alice's Adventures in Wonderland
        New York: Mershon   John Tenniel

1921   ca. 1899 Alice's Adventures in Wonderland
        New York: Mershon   John Tenniel
        Sterling Series.

1922   ca. 1899 Alice's Adventures in Wonderland
        New York: Mershon   John Tenniel
        Golden Gem Series.

1923   ca. 1899 Alice's Adventures in Wonderland

New York: Thomas Y. Crowell

L. J. (Lewis Jesse) Bridgman;
Anonymous (after Tenniel); Charles Copeland

The Wonderland Series. 4 black-and-white plates, 3 after Tenniel and 1 with L. J. Bridgman's monogram; cover by (Charles) Copeland.

1924   ca. 1899 Alice's Adventures in Wonderland
New York: Thomas Y. Crowell

L. J. (Lewis Jesse) Bridgman;
Anonymous (after Tenniel); Charles Copeland

The Waldorf Library. 4 black-and-white plates, 3 after Tenniel and 1 with L. J. Bridgman's monogram; cover by (Charles) Copeland.

1925   1900   Alice's Adventures in Wonderland
New York: A. Wessels   Blanche McManus
12 color plates.

1926   1900   Alice's Adventures in Wonderland
Chicago; New York: Donohue Brothers   John Tenniel
The Donohue Brothers only published in 1900 under this name. Prior to this, they were "Donohue, Henneberry & Co." From 1901 onward, they were "M. A. Donohue and Company."

1927   [1900]   Alice's Adventures in Wonderland
New York: Hurst   John Tenniel
Emerson Series of Popular 16mos.

1928   [1900]   Alice's Adventures in Wonderland
Chicago: W. B. Conkey   John Tenniel
Amaranth Series. Includes *Flower Fables* by Louisa May Alcott. Red cloth.

1929   ca. 1900 Alice's Adventures in Wonderland
Buffalo, NY: Berger Publishing   John Tenniel
Adapted for Very Little Folks.

1930   ca. 1900 Alice's Adventures in Wonderland
Philadelphia: Henry Altemus   John Tenniel
Altemus' New Illustrated Beauxarts Series.

1931   ca. 1900 Alice's Adventures in Wonderland
Philadelphia: Henry Altemus   John Tenniel
Altemus' Illustrated Boys' and Girls' Classics.

1932   ca. 1900 Alice's Adventures in Wonderland
New York: Prudential Book Company   Anonymous
Wakefield Series item number 159.

1933   ca. 1900 Alice's Adventures in Wonderland
Chicago: W. B. Conkey   John Tenniel
Rosalind Series. Includes a truncated version of *Flower Fables* by Louisa May Alcott.

1934   ca. 1900 Alice's Adventures in Wonderland
Chicago: W. B. Conkey   John Tenniel
Young People's Cloth Library. Includes a truncated version of *Flower Fables* by Louisa May Alcott.

1935   ca. 1900 Alice's Adventures in Wonderland
Chicago: W. B. Conkey   John Tenniel; Others

Alice is followed by *The Secret of True Happiness*. Pictorial paper-covered boards backed in red cloth.

1936   ca. 1900–1905   Alice's Adventures in Wonderland
Chicago: W. B. Conkey   John Tenniel; Anonymous
Young People's Cloth Library. Anonymous color frontispiece.

1937   ca. 1900–1910   Alice's Adventures in Wonderland
Boston: Small, Maynard & Co.   George Soper

1938   ca. 1900–1915   Alice's Adventures in Wonderland
Chicago: Homewood Publishing   John Tenniel; Anonymous
Also contains *Flower Fables* by Louisa May Alcott.

1939   1901   Alice's Adventures in Wonderland
New York; London: Harper and Brothers   Peter Newell;
                                                                        Robert Murray Wright

Introduction by E. S. Martin. White paper-covered boards with gilt title and image of Alice holding a twig in lower
left corner. Border decorations by Robert Murray Wright. Contains a misprint on p. x ("Mary" corrected in later
printings to "Murray").

1940   1901   Alice's Adventures in Wonderland
Chicago: M. A. Donohue and Company   After John Tenniel

1941   1901   Alice's Adventures in Wonderland
Chicago: M. A. Donohue and Company   John Tenniel
Includes Andersen's fairy tales.

1942   [1901] Alice's Adventures in Wonderland
New York: Hurst   John Tenniel
Hurst's Home Series for Girls.

1943   ca. 1901   Alice's Adventures in Wonderland
Chicago: George M. Hill   John Tenniel
Popular Series.

1944   ca. 1901   Alice's Adventures in Wonderland
New York; Boston: H. M. Caldwell   John Tenniel
Kalon Series.

1945   ca. 1901   Alice's Adventures in Wonderland
New York; Boston: H. M. Caldwell   John Tenniel

1946   ca. 1901   Alice's Adventures in Wonderland
New York; Boston: H. M. Caldwell   John Tenniel
Famous Books for Girls.

1947   ca. 1901   Alice's Adventures in Wonderland
Chicago; New York: Henneberry   John Tenniel
Henneberry's Illustrated Boys' and Girls' Library.

1948   ca. 1901   Alice's Adventures in Wonderland
Chicago; New York: Henneberry   John Tenniel
Henneberry's Illustrated New Century Library of Standard Books by Popular Authors.

1949   ca. 1901 Alice's Adventures in Wonderland
        Philadelphia: Henry Altemus   John Tenniel
        Altemus' Illustrated La Belle Fleur Series.

1950   ca. 1901 Alice's Adventures in Wonderland
        Philadelphia: Henry Altemus   John Tenniel
        Altemus' Illustrated L'Art Nouveau Series.

1951   ca. 1901 Alice's Adventures in Wonderland
        Philadelphia: Henry Altemus   John Tenniel
        Altemus' Illustrated Favorite Series.

1952   ca. 1901 Alice's Adventures in Wonderland
        Philadelphia: Henry Altemus   Anonymous (after Tenniel)
        White cloth. No series listed.

1953   ca. 1901 Alice's Adventures in Wonderland
        Chicago; New York: M. A. Donohue   John Tenniel
        Little Folks' Edition. Contains other stories.

1954   ca. 1901 Alice's Adventures in Wonderland
        Chicago; New York: M. A. Donohue   John Tenniel

1955   [1901–1906]   Alice's Adventures in Wonderland
        Chicago: M. A. Donohue and Company   John Tenniel
        Date based on the address in the imprint.

1956   [1901–1909]   Alice's Adventures in Wonderland
        Chicago: M. A. Donohue and Company   Anonymous (after Tenniel)
        Young Folks Classics. Abridged. Contains other stories.

1957   [1901–1909]   Alice's Adventures in Wonderland
        Chicago: M. A. Donohue and Company   John Tenniel
        The Fairy Book Library. With other stories.

1958   [1901–1910]   Alice's Adventures in Wonderland
        Chicago: M. A. Donohue and Company   Anonymous (after Tenniel)

1959   [1901–1920]   Alice's Adventures in Wonderland
        Chicago; New York: M. A. Donohue and Company   John Tenniel
        Young Folks Classics. Contains other stories.

1960   1902   Alice's Adventures in Wonderland
        New York; London: Harper and Brothers   Peter Newell
        White paper-covered boards. Later red cloth bindings known.

1961   1902   Alice's Adventures in Wonderland
        New York: A. L. Burt   John Tenniel
        Decorated green cloth.

1962   [1902]   Alice's Adventures in Wonderland
        New York: Hurst   John Tenniel
        Aunt Virginia Series.

1963   [1902]   Alice's Adventures in Wonderland
        New York: Hurst   John Tenniel
        Cosmos Series.

1964   ca. 1902 Alice's Adventures in Wonderland
        New York: A. L. Burt   John Tenniel
        Little Woman Series. Dated by *PTLA*.

1965   ca. 1902 Alice's Adventures in Wonderland
        New York: A. L. Burt   John Tenniel
        The Wellesley Series for Girls. Dated by *PTLA*. Could be earlier based on ads.

1966   ca. 1902 Alice's Adventures in Wonderland
        New York: Globe School Book Co.   Anonymous

1967   ca. 1902 Alice's Adventures in Wonderland
        New York: Hurst   John Tenniel
        Arlington Series. Green cloth printed in black.

1968   ca. 1902 Alice's Adventures in Wonderland
        Chicago; New York; London: Rand McNally   F. Y. Cory
        Canterbury Classics. Edited by Florence Milner. Brown cloth.

1969   ca. 1902 Alice's Adventures in Wonderland
        New York; London: Street and Smith   John Tenniel
        Girl's Popular Library.

1970   1903   Alice's Adventures in Wonderland
        New York; Boston: H. M. Caldwell   John Tenniel
        Editha Series.

1971   1903   Alice's Adventures in Wonderland
        Chicago: Madison Book Co.   Anonymous
        Alice and other stories. Some later stories are copyright 1901. Greenish-yellow pictorial cloth printed in many colors.

1972   1903   Alice's Adventures in Wonderland
        New York: P. F. Collier & Son   Beatrice Stevens;
                                                                           Anonymous (after Tenniel)
        Library for Young People. Dark blue cloth over boards, blind stamped.

1973   1903   Alice's Adventures in Wonderland
        New York: McLoughlin Brothers   Anonymous (after Tenniel)

1974   1903   Alice's Adventures in Wonderland
        New York: McLoughlin Brothers   Harry Furniss
        Includes *Sylvie and Bruno* poems.

1975   [1903]   Alice's Adventures in Wonderland
        Chicago: Rand McNally   Unknown
        The Atlantic Library.

1976   [1903]   Alice's Adventures in Wonderland
        Chicago: Rand McNally   Unknown
        The Independent Library.

1977   ca. 1903 Alice's Adventures in Wonderland
New York: A. L. Burt   John Tenniel
The Wellesley Series for Girls. Dated by *PTLA*. Could be earlier based on ads. Uniform with a ca. 1903 *Looking-Glass* dated by *PTLA*.

1978   ca. 1903 Alice's Adventures in Wonderland
New York: Mansfield   Blanche McManus
12 color plates, including frontispiece.

1979   ca. 1903 Alice's Adventures in Wonderland
Chicago: Otto Hattrem   Anonymous
Includes 2 other stories not by Carroll.

1980   ca. 1903 Alice's Adventures in Wonderland
New York: Thomas Y. Crowell   L. J. (Lewis Jesse) Bridgman;
                                          Anonymous (after Tenniel); Charles Copeland
Pocket Edition. 4 black-and-white plates, 3 after Tenniel and 1 with L. J. Bridgman's monogram; cover by (Charles) Copeland.

1981   1904   Alice's Adventures in Wonderland
Chicago: M. A. Donohue and Company   John Tenniel
Title page lists only Chicago, but cover lists Chicago and New York, No. 191. Includes other stories and music.

1982   [1904]   Alice's Adventures in Wonderland
New York: Frederick A. Stokes   John Tenniel; M. L. Kirk
12 color plates by M. L. Kirk. Gray cloth. There is an undated later printing. Red cloth.

1983   [1904]   Alice's Adventures in Wonderland
Chicago: Rand McNally   Unknown
The Advance Library.

1984   ca. 1904 Alice's Adventures in Wonderland
New York; Boston: H. M. Caldwell   John Tenniel
Alcazar Classics.

1985   ca. 1904 Alice's Adventures in Wonderland
New York; Boston: H. M. Caldwell   John Tenniel
Miniature edition.

1986   ca. 1904–1913 Alice's Adventures in Wonderland
New York: Thomas Y. Crowell   L. J. (Lewis Jesse) Bridgman;
                                          Anonymous (after Tenniel); Charles Copeland
The Astor Prose Series. 4 black-and-white plates, 3 after Tenniel and 1 with L. J. Bridgman's monogram; cover by (Charles) Copeland.

1987   after 1904   Alice's Adventures in Wonderland
Boston: Lothrop, Lee and Shepard   John Tenniel; Anonymous
World Famous Quarto Series. 4 color plates by Anonymous.

1988   1905   Alice's Adventures in Wonderland Edited for School Use
New York: Charles A. McMurry. London: Macmillan   John Tenniel
First published February 1905.

Alice in a World of Wonderlands

1989   ca. 1905 Alice's Adventures in Wonderland
        New York: A. L. Burt   John Tenniel
        The Cornell Series of 12 mos. Includes the first 10 chapters of *Sylvie and Bruno*. Dated by *PTLA*.

1990   ca. 1905 Alice's Adventures in Wonderland
        New York: A. L. Burt   John Tenniel; J. Watson Davis
        8 color plates by J. Watson Davis. Blue cloth. Date based on collectors.

1991   ca. 1905 Alice's Adventures in Wonderland
        New York: A. L. Burt   John Tenniel; J. Watson Davis
        Retold in Words of One Syllable. By Mrs. J. C. Gorham. Color frontispiece by J. Watson Davis. Tan cloth. 2 other editions of
        ca. 1905 exist, identical except for format size and bindings. No credit in the book is given to Lewis Carroll or John Tenniel.

1992   ca. 1905 Alice's Adventures in Wonderland
        Chicago: M. A. Donohue and Company   John Tenniel
        Snug Corner Series.

1993   ca. 1905 Alice's Adventures in Wonderland
        Chicago; New York; London: Rand McNally   F. Y. Cory
        Canterbury Classics. Edited by Florence Milner. Gray cloth.

1994   1906   Alice's Adventures in Wonderland Edited for School Use
        New York: Charles A. McMurry. London: Macmillan   John Tenniel
        Reprint of the 1905 edition.

1995   [1906]   Alice's Adventures in Wonderland
        New York: Hurst   John Tenniel; Anonymous
                                                                      (after Tenniel)
        Fleur de Lis Classics. Boxed together with *Looking-Glass*.

1996   [1906]   Alice's Adventures in Wonderland
        New York: Hurst   John Tenniel; Anonymous
                                                                      (after Tenniel)
        Boy's Own Library.

1997   [1906]   Alice's Adventures in Wonderland
        New York: Hurst   John Tenniel; Anonymous
                                                                      (after Tenniel)
        Ideal Series of Standard Classics.

1998   [1906]   Alice's Adventures in Wonderland
        New York: McLoughlin Brothers   Unknown
        Young Folks Standard Library.

1999   [1906]   Alice's Adventures in Wonderland
        Chicago: Rand McNally   Unknown
        The Greek Lamp Library.

2000   ca. 1906 Alice's Adventures in Wonderland
        New York: A. L. Burt   John Tenniel
        Little Woman Series. Dated by *PTLA*.

2001   ca. 1906 Alice's Adventures in Wonderland
        New York; Boston: H. M. Caldwell   John Tenniel
        Editha Series. Tan, blue, or green cloth.

2002   ca. 1906 Alice's Adventures in Wonderland
New York; Boston: H. M. Caldwell   John Tenniel
Green cloth with pictorial cover.

2003   ca. 1906 Alice's Adventures in Wonderland
New York; London: Harper and Brothers   Peter Newell
Harper's Young People Series.

2004   ca. 1906 Alice's Adventures in Wonderland
Chicago: Monarch Book Co.   John Tenniel
Boys' and Girls' Series.

2005   ca. 1906 Alice's Adventures in Wonderland
Chicago: Monarch Book Co.   John Tenniel
Holiday Series. An anthology.

2006   ca. 1906 Alice's Adventures in Wonderland
New York: Thomas Y. Crowell   L. J. (Lewis Jesse) Bridgman;
                                              Anonymous (after Tenniel); Charles Copeland
Children's Handy Library. Copies include different numbers of titles. One has 37; another, 49.

2007   1907   Alice's Adventures in Wonderland
New York: Dodge Publishing Company   Bessie Pease Gutmann
11 color plates. Blue cloth.

2008   [1907] Alice's Adventures in Wonderland
New York: Cassell   Charles Robinson

2009   [1907] Alice's Adventures in Wonderland
New York: Doubleday, Doran & Co. London: William Heinemann   Arthur Rackham
1st American edition. Illustrated Holiday Edition. Red cloth.

2010   [1907] Alice's Adventures in Wonderland
New York: E. P. Dutton. London: George Routledge and Sons   Thomas Maybank
Pictorial cloth on green boards.

2011   [1907] Alice's Adventures in Wonderland
New York: John Lane Company. London: John Lane, The Bodley Head   W. H. Walker
1st American edition. 8 color plates and 42 line drawings. Limp green suede.

2012   [1907] Alice's Adventures in Wonderland
Chicago: M. A. Donohue and Company   John Tenniel

2013   [1907] Alice's Adventures in Wonderland
London: William Heinemann. New York: Doubleday Page & Co.   Arthur Rackham
1st edition. With "Proem" by Austin Dobson.

2014   [1907] Alice's Adventures in Wonderland
London: William Heinemann. New York: Doubleday Page & Co.   Arthur Rackham
1st American trade edition. With "Proem" by Austin Dobson. Some differences from the 1st edition.

2015   ca. 1907 Alice's Adventures in Wonderland
Boston; New York; Chicago; San Francisco: Educational Publishing Co. John Tenniel
Green or brownish-orange cloth.

2016	1908	Alice's Adventures in Wonderland	
		New York: Charles A. McMurry. London: Macmillan	John Tenniel
		First published in 1905.	

2017	1908	Alice's Adventures in Wonderland	
		New York: Duffield & Co. London: Chatto and Windus	Millicent Sowerby
		1st American edition. 12 color plates. Pinkish brown cloth.	

2018	1908	Alice's Adventures in Wonderland	
		Chicago; Akron, OH; New York: Saalfield	Anonymous (after Tenniel)
		In Words of One Syllable series. 10 chapters. "Pig and Pepper" and "Lobster Quadrille" are omitted. Blue cloth or tan boards.	

2019	[1908]	Alice's Adventures in Wonderland	
		Chicago: Brewer, Barse & Co.	Hugo von Hofsten
		6 color plates.	

2020	[1908]	Alice's Adventures in Wonderland	
		New York: Cassell	Charles Robinson
		Popular Edition.	

2021	[1908]	Alice's Adventures in Wonderland	
		New York: Cassell	Charles Robinson
		Cheap Edition. May have been published in 1910.	

2022	[1908]	Alice's Adventures in Wonderland	
		New York: Sully and Kleinteich	Harry Rountree

2023	[1909]	Alice's Adventures in Wonderland	
		New York: Hurst	John Tenniel; Anonymous (after Tenniel)
		Ansonia Classics.	

2024	[1909]	Alice's Adventures in Wonderland	
		New York: Hurst	John Tenniel; Anonymous (after Tenniel)
		Knickerbocker Classics.	

2025	[1909]	Alice's Adventures in Wonderland	
		New York: Hurst	John Tenniel; Anonymous (after Tenniel)
		Girl's Own Library.	

2026	[1909]	Alice's Adventures in Wonderland	
		New York: Hurst	John Tenniel; Anonymous (after Tenniel)
		Hurst's Alligator Classics.	

2027	ca. 1909	Alice's Adventures in Wonderland	
		Chicago: A. Flanagan	Anonymous

2028	ca. 1909	Alice's Adventures in Wonderland	
		New York: A. L. Burt	John Tenniel
		Oxford Series. Decorated cloth blocked in red. Dated by *PTLA*.	

2029	ca. 1909	Alice's Adventures in Wonderland	
		New York: A. L. Burt	John Tenniel
		The Wellesley Series for Girls. Dated by *PTLA*. Uniform with a ca. 1909 *Looking-Glass* dated by *PTLA*.	

2030	ca. 1909 Alice's Adventures in Wonderland	
	Philadelphia: Henry Altemus	John Tenniel
	Altemus' Illustrated Boys' and Girls' Own Library Series.	

2031	ca. 1909–1912 Alice's Adventures in Wonderland	
	New York: Chatterton-Peck	Anonymous (after Tenniel)

2032	1910 Alice's Adventures in Wonderland Edited for School Use	
	New York: Charles A. McMurry. London: Macmillan	John Tenniel
	First published in 1905.	

2033	1910 Alice's Adventures in Wonderland	
	New York; Boston: H. M. Caldwell	John Tenniel
	Tan cloth with picture of winter sunset on front cover.	

2034	[1910] Alice's Adventures in Wonderland	
	New York: E. P. Dutton	Thomas Maybank
	In Words of One Syllable series.	

2035	ca. 1910 Alice's Adventures in Wonderland	
	Philadelphia: Henry Altemus	John Tenniel
	Altemus' Illustrated Boys' and Girls' Classics Holiday Edition Series.	

2036	ca. 1910 Alice's Adventures in Wonderland	
	Chicago: M. A. Donohue and Company	John Tenniel
	The Fairy Book Library.	

2037	ca. 1910 Alice's Adventures in Wonderland	
	Chicago: M. A. Donohue and Company	John Tenniel
	Reddish-brown cloth.	

2038	ca. 1910 Alice's Adventures in Wonderland	
	New York: McCarthy	John Tenniel
	Identical to the Donohue edition of the same date. Pictorial paper-covered boards. Cover illustration is uncredited and after Tenniel.	

2039	ca. 1910 Alice's Adventures in Wonderland	
	New York: Platt and Peck	John Tenniel; E. C.
	The frontispiece is by the anonymous "E. C." Pictorial paper-covered boards. Copies found in a box with the same color illustration on the cover, and state "A to Z Juvenile Library."	

2040	ca. 1910 Alice's Adventures in Wonderland	
	New York; London; Paris: Raphael Tuck and Sons	John Tenniel; A. L. Bowley
	Golden Treasury Library series. Red cloth-covered boards with onlay by Bowley.	

2041	1911 Alice's Adventures in Wonderland	
	New York: Baker Taylor	George Soper
	2nd American edition. Red cloth.	

2042	1911 Alice's Adventures in Wonderland	
	New York: Charles E. Merrill	John Tenniel
	Merrill's Story Books.	

2043   1911   Alice's Adventures in Wonderland
New York: G. P. Putnam   John Tenniel

2044   1911   Alice's Adventures in Wonderland
New York: Thomas Y. Crowell   L. J. (Lewis Jesse) Bridgman;
                                            Anonymous (after Tenniel); Charles Copeland
16 mo. Green cloth. 4 black-and-white plates, 3 after Tenniel and 1 with L. J. Bridgman's monogram; cover by
(Charles) Copeland.

2045   [1911]   Alice's Adventures in Wonderland
New York: Platt and Peck   Margaret Winifred Tarrant

2046   ca. 1911 Alice's Adventures in Wonderland
New York: Barse and Hopkins   Hugo von Hofsten
Pleasant Hour Series. Red cloth.

2047   ca. 1911 Alice's Adventures in Wonderland
New York; Newark, NJ: Barse and Hopkins   Hugo von Hofsten
Pleasant Hour Series. Yellowish-tan cloth with color onlay. Color frontispiece by Hugo von Hofsten.

2048   ca. 1911 Alice's Adventures in Wonderland
Philadelphia: David McKay   Anonymous
                                                    (after Tenniel); Ada L. Bowley

McKay's Young People's Classics. Green cloth.

2049   ca. 1911 Alice's Adventures in Wonderland
New York: Manhattan Press   Anonymous; Anonymous
                                                        (after Tenniel)

Pictorial green cloth. Color frontispiece.

2050   ca. 1911 Alice's Adventures in Wonderland
New York: New York Book Co.   Anonymous (after Tenniel)
Our Young Folks Illustrated Books.

2051   1912   Alice's Adventures in Wonderland
New York: Grolier Society. London: Educational Book Co.   Harry Furniss
The Book of Knowledge, vol. 10.

2052   1912   Alice's Adventures in Wonderland
Chicago; New York: M. A. Donohue and Company   John Tenniel
The Fairy Book Library.

2053   ca. 1912 Alice's Adventures in Wonderland
Philadelphia: Henry Altemus   John Tenniel
Altemus' Young Folks Quarto Series.

2054   ca. 1912 Alice's Adventures in Wonderland
New York: McLoughlin Brothers   Anonymous
Frontispiece after Tenniel. 25 anonymous illustrations. Excludes final 5 paragraphs of text. Pictorial boards backed
with blue cloth.

2055   ca. 1912 Alice's Adventures in Wonderland
New York: P. F. Collier   Beatrice Stevens; Anonymous
                                                        (after Tenniel)
The Junior Classics. Part of an anthology. There were 46 printings of this edition.

2056   ca. 1912 Alice's Adventures in Wonderland
Nashville, TN: S. WN. Co.   Unknown

2057   ca. 1912–1919 Alice's Adventures in Wonderland
Dansville, NY: F. A. Owen   John Tenniel
Instructor Literature Series. For 1st volume (No. 201 in series), WorldCat lists a copy with imprint of [1912]; one other
copy has a 1919 inscription. In linen covers, with cover image of the White Rabbit; brown border. Continued by *Alice's
Further Adventures in Wonderland* (No. 202 in series), beginning with "Pig and Pepper" (shown as chapter I) and
continuing through "The Lobster-Quadrille," (shown as chapter IV). In linen covers, with cover image of the Lobster-
Quadrille; green border. Variant editions include imprint of Dansville, NY: F. A. Owen; Chicago: Hall & McCreary.
Lovett No. 69 describes a later edition with parts 1 and 2 in a single volume.

2058   1913   Alice's Adventures in Wonderland
New York: Longmans   John Tenniel

2059   ca. 1913 Alice's Adventures in Wonderland
New York: A. L. Burt   John Tenniel
Oxford Series. Dated by *PTLA*.

2060   ca. 1913 Alice's Adventures in Wonderland
New York: A. L. Burt   John Tenniel
The Cornell Series of 12 mos. Dated by *PTLA*.

2061   ca. 1913 Alice's Adventures in Wonderland
New York: A. L. Burt   John Tenniel
Young People's Classics. Holiday Edition. 8 color plates. Dated by *PTLA*.

2062   ca. 1913 Alice's Adventures in Wonderland
New York: Frederick A. Stokes   John Tenniel; Maria L. Kirk
Stokes Library for Young People.

2063   ca. 1913 Alice's Adventures in Wonderland
Philadelphia: Henry Altemus   John Tenniel
Altemus' Illustrated Children's Gift Series.

2064   ca. 1913 Alice's Adventures in Wonderland
Philadelphia: John C. Winston Co.   John Huehnergarth
General Classics.

2065   ca. 1913 Alice's Adventures in Wonderland
New York: McLoughlin Brothers   After John Tenniel
Dated by inscription.

2066   ca. 1913 Alice's Adventures in Wonderland
New York: Sully and Kleinteich   Harry Rountree
Children's Colored Classics.

2067   ca. 1913 Alice's Adventures in Wonderland
New York: Thomas Y. Crowell
                                                      L. J. (Lewis Jesse) Bridgman;
                                          Anonymous (after Tenniel); Charles Copeland
Children's Home Library. 4 black-and-white plates, 3 after Tenniel and 1 with L. J. Bridgman's monogram; cover by
(Charles) Copeland. An undated later printing exists.

2068   after 1913 Alice's Adventures in Wonderland
New York: A. L. Burt   [John Tenniel]; J. Watson Davis
Retold in Words of One Syllable. By Mrs. J. C. Gorham. Date based on ad addresses. Color frontispiece by J. Watson
Davis.

2069   1914   Alice's Adventures in Wonderland
New York: Funk and Wagnalls   Charles Robinson

2070   1914   Alice's Adventures in Wonderland
New York: George H. Doran   A. E. Jackson
Yellow brown cloth. 16 color plates. There have been 5 reprints.

2071   1914   Alice's Adventures in Wonderland
New York: Hodder and Stoughton   A. E. Jackson
1st edition. 16 color plates. Blue cloth. Printed by Clay in England.

2072   ca. 1914 Alice's Adventures in Wonderland
Garden City, NY: Garden City Publishing   A. E. Jackson
8 color plates. Orange cloth. There have been 5 reprints. Reprint of a 1914 Doran edition.

2073   1915   Alice's Adventures in Wonderland
New York: Little Leather Library   Unillustrated
Leaf size 2 x 3 inches. Purple cloth or tan leather. An undated edition in flexible green leather is known.

2074   ca. 1915 Alice's Adventures in Wonderland
Philadelphia: Henry Altemus   John Tenniel
Altemus' Illustrated Stories Children's Love Series.

2075   1916   Alice's Adventures in Wonderland
New York: Platt and Peck   Margaret W. Tarrant
48 color plates by Tarrant.

2076   1916   Alice's Adventures in Wonderland
New York: Platt and Peck   Blanche McManus
4 color plates by McManus. Abridged edition.

2077   1916   Alice's Adventures in Wonderland
New York: Sam'l Gabriel Sons & Co.   Gordon Robinson; H. K.
4 color plates. One signed by Robinson, and 22 line drawings, most signed "H. K." Red cloth. 1 copy lacks place of
publication, and publisher reads "Pictured by Linenette." Abridged.

2078   [1916] Alice's Adventures in Wonderland
New York: Doubleday, Doran & Co. London: William Heinemann   Arthur Rackham
1st reprint of the 1st American edition of 1907.

2079   [1916] Alice's Adventures in Wonderland
New York: E. P. Dutton   Thomas Maybank
Color frontispiece and 28 black-and-white illustrations.

2080   ca. 1916 Alice's Adventures in Wonderland
New York: Barse and Hopkins   Hugo von Hofsten
Tan cloth.

2081   ca. 1916 Alice's Adventures in Wonderland
        Philadelphia: Henry Altemus   John Tenniel
        Altemus' Illustrated Ever New Books for Young People Series.

2082   1917   Alice's Adventures in Wonderland
        Boston; New York; etc.: Ginn & Co.   Oliver Herford
        Blue cloth.

2083   [1917] Alice's Adventures in Wonderland
        New York: Charles E. Graham   John Tenniel
        Color pictorial boards backed with blue cloth.

2084   [1917] Alice's Adventures in Wonderland
        New York: Cupples and Leon   Julia Greene; Helen Pettes
        1st edition. Pictorial paper-covered boards. Cut-out pictures illustrated by Helen Pettes and frontispiece illustrated by
        Julia Greene (after Tenniel). 3 different versions exist, each having a different frontispiece.

2085   [1917] Alice's Adventures in Wonderland
        New York: Cupples and Leon   Julia Greene; Helen Pettes
        Leather bound. Cut-out pictures illustrated by Helen Pettes and frontispiece illustrated by Julia Greene (after
        Tenniel). Has all 3 different versions of the frontispiece.

2086   [1917] Alice's Adventures in Wonderland
        New York: Doubleday, Doran & Co. London: William Heinemann   Arthur Rackham
        2nd reprint of the 1st American edition of 1907.

2087   [1917] Alice's Adventures in Wonderland
        New York: Graham and Matlack   John Tenniel; Anonymous
        A reprint of the 1898 Lothrup, Lee and Shepard edition. Blue cloth. An undated later edition exists.

2088   ca. 1917 Alice's Adventures in Wonderland
        Philadelphia: Henry Altemus   John Tenniel
        Altemus' Illustrated New Books and New Editions Series.

2089   1918   Alice's Adventures in Wonderland
        New York: P. F. Collier   Beatrice Stevens; Anonymous
                                                                       (after Tenniel)
        Young Folks Shelf of Books. At least 18 reprints.

2090   ca. 1918 Alice's Adventures in Wonderland
        New York: American Book Company   John Tenniel
        Orange cloth. Edited by Clifton Johnson.

2091   ca. 1919 Alice's Adventures in Wonderland
        Boston: Charles E. Brown   John Tenniel

2092   [1919] Alice's Adventures in Wonderland
        New York: Doubleday, Doran & Co.   Arthur Rackham
        3rd reprint of the 1st American edition of 1907.

2093   1920   Alice's Adventures in Wonderland
        New York: A. L. Burt   John Tenniel
        Listed in 2 libraries with no other information.

2094   ca. 1920s Alice's Adventures in Wonderland
New York: Cupples and Leon   Julia Greene; Helen Pettes
Later printing of the 1917 edition. Pictorial paper-covered boards. Cut-out pictures illustrated by Helen Pettes and
frontispiece illustrated by Julia Greene (after Tenniel). 3 different versions exist, each having a different frontispiece.

2095   ca. 1920s Alice's Adventures in Wonderland
Garden City, NY: Garden City Publishing   A. E. Jackson
Orange cloth.

2096   ca. 1920 Alice's Adventures in Wonderland
New York; London: Harper and Brothers   Peter Newell
Introduction by E. S. Martin. Black or light blue cloth.

2097   ca. 1920s Alice's Adventures in Wonderland
Boston: Jordan, Marsh & Co.   John Tenniel
Editha Series.

2098   ca. 1920 Alice's Adventures in Wonderland
Chicago; New York: M. A. Donohue and Company   John Tenniel; Anonymous
Anonymous frontispiece.

2099   ca. 1920s Alice's Adventures in Wonderland
Chicago; Toronto, ON: Shrewsbury Publishing Co.   John Tenniel
Flexible red fabric printed in black.

2100   [1920–1929] Alice's Adventures in Wonderland
Chicago; New York: M. A. Donohue and Company   John Tenniel
Dated based on inscription. Cover lists "M. A. Donohue No. 191."

2101   1921   Alice's Adventures in Wonderland
Philadelphia: David McKay   Anonymous (after Tenniel);
                                                                    Ada L. Bowley
Newberry Classics. Blue cloth. Other versions known.

2102   [1921]   Alice's Adventures in Wonderland Edited for School Use
New York: Charles A. McMurry. London: Macmillan   John Tenniel
Later printing of the 1905 edition.

2103   ca. 1921 Alice's Adventures in Wonderland
Philadelphia: Henry Altemus   John Tenniel
Pictorial cloth with children playing in a garden. All pages bordered with pictorial scene in light green.

2104   ca. 1921–1928 Alice's Adventures in Wonderland
New York: E. P. Dutton. London; Melbourne, VIC; Toronto, ON: J. M. Dent   Thomas Maybank
Color frontispiece and 28 black-and-white illustrations. Seen in red or blue cloth.

2105   1922   Alice's Adventures in Wonderland
New York: Dodd, Mead & Co.   Gwynedd M. Hudson
12 color plates. Green cloth.

2106   [1922]   Alice's Adventures in Wonderland
New York: Doubleday, Doran & Co. London: William Heinemann   Arthur Rackham
4th reprint of the 1st American edition of 1907.

2107	[1922] Alice's Adventures in Wonderland	L. J. Bridgman; Anonymous
	Garden City, NY: Doubleday, Page & Co.	(after Tenniel)
	Likely a reprint of a Crowell edition. Red leather.	

2108	ca. 1922 Alice's Adventures in Wonderland	
	New York; London: Harper and Brothers	Peter Newell
	Harper's Selected Juveniles.	

| 2109 | ca. 1922 Alice's Adventures in Wonderland | |
| | Chicago; New York: M. A. Donohue and Company | John Tenniel |

2110	1923 Alice's Adventures in Wonderland	
	Philadelphia; London: J. B. Lippincott	John Tenniel; Gertrude A. Kay
	1st edition. The Stories All Children Love. 8 color plates. Red cloth. Later printings exist.	

2111	[1923] Alice's Adventures in Wonderland	
	Garden City, NY: Garden City Publishing	Arthur Rackham
	Lambskin Library. ca. 1893 by Thomas Y. Crowell.	

2112	ca. 1923 Alice's Adventures in Wonderland	
	New York; London: Harper and Brothers	Peter Newell
	Imaginative Stories for Children.	

2113	ca. 1923 Alice's Adventures in Wonderland	
	Chicago; New York: M. A. Donohue and Company	John Tenniel
	Green cloth. *Alice* plus a number of other stories. Several later undated printings according to Lovett.	

2114	[1924] Alice's Adventures in Wonderland	
	New York: Doubleday, Doran & Co. London: William Heinemann	Arthur Rackham
	5th reprint of the 1st American edition of 1907.	

2115	ca. 1924 Alice's Adventures in Wonderland	
	New York; London: Harper and Brothers	Peter Newell
	Twilight Series.	

2116	ca. 1924 Alice's Adventures in Wonderland	
	New York; London: Harper and Brothers	Peter Newell
	Wonderland Series.	

2117	1925 Alice's Adventures in Wonderland	
	New York: A. L. Burt	John Tenniel; E. Clark
	In Words of One Syllable series. 4 color plates by Clark. In green or tan cloth with pictorial onlay.	

2118	ca. 1925 Alice's Adventures in Wonderland	
	Philadelphia: Henry Altemus	John Tenniel
	Wee Folks Edition.	

2119	ca. 1925 Alice's Adventures in Wonderland	
	Chicago; New York: M. A. Donohue and Company	John Tenniel; D. E. Saunders
	Brown cloth. Color frontispiece by Saunders.	

2120	ca. 1926 Alice's Adventures in Wonderland	
	New York: Cupples and Leon	Julia Greene; Helen Pettes
	Cut-out pictures illustrated by Helen Pettes and frontispiece illustrated by Julia Greene (after Tenniel).	

2121   ca. 1926 Alice's Adventures in Wonderland
New York: Little Leather Library Corporation   Unknown
Brown leather.

2122   1928   Alice's Adventures in Wonderland
New York: Doubleday, Doran & Co. London: William Heinemann   Arthur Rackham
6th reprint of the 1st American edition of 1907.

2123   1928   Alice's Adventures in Wonderland
Chicago; New York: M. A. Donohue and Company   John Tenniel
Blue cloth.

2124   ca. 1928 Alice's Adventures in Wonderland
New York: Doubleday, Doran & Co.   A. E. Jackson

2125   ca. 1928 Alice's Adventures in Wonderland
Chicago: Whitman Publishing   John Tenniel
Albert Whitman Illustrated $1.00 Classics.

2126   1929   Alice's Adventures in Wonderland
New York: E. P. Dutton   Willy Pogany
Limited to 200 copies. Decorated paper-covered boards backed in pink cloth. Large paper edition.

2127   1929   Alice's Adventures in Wonderland
New York: E. P. Dutton   Willy Pogany
1st trade edition. Purple cloth.

2128   1929   Alice's Adventures in Wonderland
Chicago: M. A. Donohue and Company   John Tenniel
1 volume. Unpaginated. Includes other stories.

2129   [1929]   Alice in Wonderland
Chicago; New York: M. A. Donohue and Company   Anonymous
Pictorial covered boards backed in olive-green cloth.

2130   ca. 1929 Alice's Adventures in Wonderland
New York: A. L. Burt   John Tenniel; E. Clark
In Words of One Syllable series. Dated by *PTLA*.

2131   ca. 1929 Alice's Adventures in Wonderland
New York: A. L. Burt   John Tenniel
Best Young Folks Library. Dated by *PTLA*.

2132   ca. 1929 Alice's Adventures in Wonderland
New York: A. L. Burt   John Tenniel
Young People's Classics. Holiday Edition. 8 color plates. Dated by *PTLA*.

2133   ca. 1929 Alice's Adventures in Wonderland
Philadelphia: Henry Altemus   John Tenniel
Gray pictorial boards.

2134   ca. 1929 Alice's Adventures in Wonderland
Philadelphia: Henry Altemus   John Tenniel
Adapted for very little folks. Purple pictorial boards backed in red cloth.

2135   ca. 1929 Alice in Wonderland
Chicago; New York: M. A. Donohue and Company   John Tenniel
Blue cloth stamped in black.

2136   ca. 1929–1930 Alice's Adventures in Wonderland
Chicago; New York: M. A. Donohue and Company   John Tenniel
Select Reading Series.

2137   1930   Alice's Adventures in Wonderland
New York: Doubleday, Doran & Co. London: William Heinemann   Arthur Rackham
9th reprint of the 1st American edition of 1907.

2138   1930   Alice's Adventures in Wonderland
New York: Garden City Publishing   A. E. Jackson
8 color plates. Orange cloth. There have been 5 reprints. Reprint of a 1914 Doran edition.

2139   ca. 1930 Alice's Adventures in Wonderland
Boston: Cornhill Co.   John Tenniel

2140   ca. 1930 Alice's Adventures in Wonderland
New York: Garden City Publishing   A. E. Jackson; C. A. Federer
1 color plate signed by Federer. Orange cloth.

2141   ca. 1930 Alice's Adventures in Wonderland
New York: Little Leather Library Corporation   Anonymous
Red or green imitation leather.

2142   ca. 1930 Alice's Adventures in Wonderland
New York: Sam'l Gabriel Sons & Co.   Gordon Robinson
Color illustrations. Abridged.

2143   ca. 1930–1936 Alice's Adventures in Wonderland
Garden City, NY: Doubleday, Doran & Co.   A. E. Jackson; C. A. Federer
Garden City Children's Books.

2144   ca. 1930s Alice's Adventures in Wonderland
Chicago: M. A. Donohue   John Tenniel
With other stories.

2145   ca. 1930s Alice in Wonderland
Cleveland, OH: Goldsmith Publishing Co.   Anonymous; Buttiers
Includes *Alice* and *Children of the World: Verses* by M. A. Goldsmith. Cover illustrated by Buttiers. Pictorial paper-
covered boards backed by dark red cloth.

2146   1931   The Lewis Carroll Book
New York: Dial Press   Anonymous (after Tenniel)
1st printing, October 1931. 2nd printing, December 1931. Reprinted 5 more times. An anthology including both *Alice*
and *Lookimg-Glass*.

2147   [1931] Alice's Adventures in Wonderland
Garden City, NY: Junior Deluxe Editions   A. E. Jackson
The Junior Star Editions.

2148   ca. 1931 Alice's Adventures in Wonderland
Philadelphia: David McKay   Anonymous (after Tenniel);
                                                                    Ada L. Bowley
Raphael House.

2149   ca. 1931 Alice's Adventures in Wonderland
New York; London: G. P. Putnam's Sons   John Tenniel
Ariel Books.

2150   ca. 1931 Alice's Adventures in Wonderland
Chicago; New York: M. A. Donohue   John Tenniel
Golden Days Series. Unpaginated.

2151   1932   Alice's Adventures in Wonderland
New York: Limited Editions Club   John Tenniel
Limited to 1,500 copies. Some copies signed by the binder Frederic Warde and Alice Hargreaves. Red leatherette.
Glassine cover in blue slipcase. Signed editions of *Looking-Glass* are also known.

2152   1934   Alice in Wonderland
Racine, WI: Whitman Publishing Company   Paramount Pictures
Big Little Book series. Pictorial paper-covered boards. Illustrated with stills from the Paramount Pictures film of 1933.

2153   ca. 1934 Alice's Adventures in Wonderland
Boston: International Pocket Library   John Tenniel
1st printing 5,000 copies; 2nd printing 5,000 copies; 3rd printing 10,000 copies. Pictorial wrappers.

2154   1935   Alice's Adventures in Wonderland
New York: Dial Press   Gwynedd M. Hudson
New Edition. 12 color plates.

2155   ca. 1935 Famous Animal Tales
Philadelphia: David McKay   Ernest Aris
"The Mad Tea Party" appears on pp. 37–46. Color frontispiece and black-and-white illustrations by Ernest Aris. Also
published in London by G. G. Harrap.

2156   1938   Alice's Adventures in Wonderland
[Jamaica, NY]: Minia Press   John Tenniel
Miniature edition. Red cloth.

2157   1940   Alice's Adventures in Wonderland
Springfield, MA: McLoughlin Brothers   John Tenniel
Little Color Classics Series. Pictorial boards.

2158   ca. 1940 Alice in Wonderland
Girard, KS: Haldeman-Julius   Unillustrated
Ten Cent Pocket Series, No. 158. Light bluish-gray wrappers. Undated later printings exist.

2159   ca. 1940 Alice in Wonderland
Girard, KS: Haldeman-Julius   Unillustrated
Little Blue Book, No. 158. Blue wrappers.

2160   ca. 1940 Alice in Wonderland
Girard, KS: Haldeman-Julius   Unillustrated
Gray or tan wrappers.

2161   ca. 1940 Alice's Adventures in Wonderland
        Mount Vernon, NY: Peter Pauper   John Tenniel
        Floral paper over ivory cloth.

2162   ca. 1940s Alice's Adventures in Wonderland
        Chicago; New York: M. A. Donohue   John Tenniel

2163   ca. 1940s Alice's Adventures in Wonderland
        Jamaica, NY: Minia Press   John Tenniel
        Miniature edition; 2 1/4 x 1 5/8 inches. Red cloth.

2164   1941   Alice's Adventures in Wonderland
        New York: Book League of America   John Tenniel
        Facsimile of the 1865 1st edition. Published for members of the Book League. Introduction by Kathleen Norris. Dust
        jacket. Red cloth.

2165   1942   Alice's Adventures in Wonderland
        New York: Doubleday, Doran & Co.   John Tenniel
        Facsimile of the 1865 1st edition. Introduction by Kathleen Norris. Dust jacket. Red cloth.

2166   1943   Alice in Wonderland
        Springfield, MA: McLoughlin Brothers   Emma C. McKean
        Magic Fairy Tales, No. 2943. 1st edition. Printed on fold-over cardboard. Spiral bound in pictorial paper-covered
        boards. Lewis Carroll is not attributed as the author.

2167   ca. 1943 Alice's Adventures in Wonderland
        New York: Heritage Press   John Tenniel
        The Heritage Reprints. Issued separately and in a slipcase with *Looking-Glass*.

2168   1946   Alice's Adventures in Wonderland
        Girard, KS: Haldeman-Julius   Anonymous
        Little Blue Book, No. 36. Pink cloth. Pictorial dust jacket.

2169   1946   Alice's Adventures in Wonderland
        London; New York: Penguin Books   John Tenniel
        Introduction by series editor Eleanor Graham. Pictorial wrappers. This edition was reset in 1949 and remained in
        print until the 1990s.

2170   1946   Alice's Adventures in Wonderland
        New York: Random House   John Tenniel; Fritz Kredel
        Illustrated Modern Library Series. Tenniel illustrations colored by Fritz Kredel. Issued in a slipcase with a volume of
        Looking-Glass. Decorated paper-covered boards backed in blue.

2171   1946   Alice's Adventures in Wonderland
        New York: Random House   Marjorie Torrey
        Pictorial covered boards. Also issued in green cloth.

2172   1947   Alice's Adventures in Wonderland
        New York: International Readers League   John Tenniel
        The Child's Classics.

2173   1947   Alice in Wonderland
        New York: Maxton Publishers   Marjorie Collison
        22 illustrations. Pictorial paper-covered boards backed in black. Version for young readers by Roselle Ross.

2174   ca. 1947 Alice's Adventures in Wonderland
Mount Vernon, NY: Peter Pauper Press   John Tenniel
Paper-covered boards decorated with playing card pattern. In red slipcase.

2175   1948   Alice in Wonderland
New York: Gilbertson Company, Inc.   Alex A. Blum
Classics Illustrated No. 49. Comic book. 10 cents in July 1948; later increased to 15 cents in June 1966 and to 25 cents
in Fall 1968.

2176   ca. 1948 Alice's Adventures in Wonderland
New York: Chanticleer Press   John Tenniel; Hugh Gee
16 color plates.

2177   1949   Walt Disney's Alice in Wonderland
New York: Simon and Schuster   Al Dempster
A Big Golden Book.

2178   1950   Alice's Adventures in Wonderland
Jamaica, NY: Minia Press   John Tenniel
2 vol. miniature edition, 3 1/8 x 2 1/8 inches. Red leather in slipcase.

2179   1950   Alice's Adventures in Wonderland
Chicago: Rand McNally   Suzanne Bruce
Blue boards. Abridged.

2180   ca. 1950 Alice's Adventures in Wonderland
Baltimore, MD: Ottenheimer   Anonymous
Black-and-white anonymous illustrations.

2181   ca. 1950s   Alice's Adventures in Wonderland
Garden City, NY: Junior Deluxe Editions   John Tenniel
194 pp. Gray decorated boards on blue cloth.

2182   1951   Alice in Wonderland
New York: Dell Publishing Company   Walt Disney
Illustrated after the Walt Disney 1951 film.

2183   1951   Alice in Wonderland
New York: Walt Disney Productions   Walt Disney
Big Golden Book. Number 10426. Adapted by Al Dempster from the motion picture. Pictorial paper-covered boards.

2184   1951   Alice in Wonderland
New York: Golden Press   Walt Disney
Big Golden Book. Adapted by Al Dempster from the motion picture. Pictorial paper-covered boards. Number
omitted.

2185   1951   Alice's Adventures in Wonderland
New York: Greystone Press   John Tenniel
Castle Books. Marbleized boards.

2186   1951   Alice's Adventures in Wonderland
Chicago: Rand McNally   Suzanne Bruce
Pictorial paper-covered boards. Abridged.

2187 1951   Alice in Wonderland Meets the White Rabbit
New York: Simon and Schuster   Walt Disney
Little Golden Book. Number D-19. Excerpts adapted by Al Dempster from the motion picture. Pictorial paper-covered boards.

2188 1951   Alice in Wonderland Finds the Garden of Live Flowers
New York: Simon and Schuster   Walt Disney
Little Golden Book. Number D-20. Excerpts adapted by Campbell Grant from the motion picture. Pictorial paper-covered boards.

2189 1951   Mad Hatter's Tea Party: Alice in Wonderland
New York: Simon and Schuster   Walt Disney
Little Golden Book. Number D-23. Excerpts adapted by Richmond Kelsey and Don Griffith from the motion picture. Pictorial paper-covered boards. A variant edition is known.

2190 1951   Alice in Wonderland
Racine, WI: Whitman Publishing Company   Walt Disney
Cozy Corner Series. Adapted by Samuel Armstrong. Pictorial paper-covered boards.

2191 1951   Alice in Wonderland
New York: Wonder Books   Laszlo Matulay (after Tenniel)
Published by "A Division of Grosset & Dunlap." Adapted and abridged for Little Children by Marcia Martin. Pictorial paper-covered boards.

2192 1951   Alice in Wonderland
New York: Wonder Books   Laszlo Matulay (after Tenniel)
Adapted and abridged for Little Children by Marcia Martin. Pictorial paper-covered boards. With code number 574.

2193 ca. 1951 Alice in Wonderland
New York: Wonder Books, a Division of Grosset & Dunlap, Inc.   Laszlo Matulay
                                                                (after Tenniel)
Revised edition with "New Long-life binding." Adapted and abridged for Little Children by Marcia Martin. Pictorial paper-covered boards. Text further edited. 35 cents. There is a later issue at 39 cents.

2194 ca. 1951 Alice's Adventures in Wonderland
Chicago: Rand McNally   Janice Holland
Abridged by Marion E. Gridley. An Elf Book. Orange boards.

2195 [1952]   Alice's Adventures in Wonderland
Philadelphia: John C. Winston Co.   John Huehnergarth
1st edition. Winston Pixie Books. Decorated boards. There are 2 copies that state 1st edition but are of different heights.

2196 [1954]   Alice's Adventures in Wonderland
Chicago: Rand McNally   Unknown
A textbook edition.

2197 1955   Alice in Wonderland
New York: K.K. Publications, in cooperation with Golden Press   Walt Disney

2198 1955   Alice's Adventures in Wonderland
New York: Random House   Marjorie Torrey
Pictorial covered boards. Red cloth. Also in green.

2199   1955   Alice's Adventures in Wonderland and Peter Pan
New York: Random House   Marjorie Torrey
Pictorial covered boards.

2200   1955   Alice's Adventures in Wonderland
New York: Random House   Marjorie Torrey
Pictorial covered boards. Abridged by Josette Frank.

2201   1955   Alice's Adventures in Wonderland
New York: Random House   Marjorie Torrey
Green cloth with onlay. Abridged by Josette Frank.

2202   ca. 1955 Alice's Adventures in Wonderland
New York: Mansfield, Gulliver Books   Unillustrated
Magic Hour Series. Blue cloth.

2203   ca. 1955 Alice's Adventures in Wonderland
Philadelphia: John C. Winston Co.   John Huehnergarth
5th edition. Winston Pixie Books. Purple cloth.

2204   [1956] Alice's Adventures in Wonderland
Garden City, NY: Doubleday   A. E. Jackson
Doubleday Junior Classics.

2205   1957   Alice's Adventures in Wonderland
New York: Riverside Records   John Tenniel
Red cloth. Accompanied by a recording of Cyril Ritchard reading *Alice*.

2206   ca. 1950s–1960s Alice's Adventures in Wonderland
Boston: International Pocket Library   John Tenniel

2207   ca. 1960s Alice's Adventures in Wonderland
New York: Award Books, Inc.   John Tenniel
Family Classics series. Bright red textured paper wrappers.

2208   ca. 1960s Alice's Adventures in Wonderland
Garden City, NY: Nelson Doubleday   John Tenniel
Identical to the ca. 1950s Junior Deluxe Edition.

2209   ca. 1960s Alice's Adventures in Wonderland and Through the Looking-Glass
New York: The Modern Library   John Tenniel
Introduction by Alexander Woollcott. Dark blue cloth.

2210   ca. 1960 Alice's Adventures in Wonderland
New York; Washington, DC: Books, Inc.   John Tenniel
A Sunbeam Classic.

2211   [1961] The Big Book of Animal Stories
N.P.: Mulberry Books   0531020517   Janusz Grabiański
Anthology containing "The Mad Tea-Party" chapter with 9 illustrations (5 in full-color, 4 in sepia).

2212   1963   Alice in Wonderland
New York: Duell, Sloan and Pearce   Maraja
Color illustrations. Reprint of a 1957 Grosset & Dunlap edition.

2213   1963   Alice's Adventures in Wonderland
Chicago: Great Books Foundation   Unillustrated
Great Books series, volume 4 of 5.

2214   1963   Alice in Wonderland
New York: Wonder Books   Sergio Leone
Adapted and abridged by Oscar Weigle. A variant exists on larger paper.

2215   1965   Alice's Adventures in Wonderland
New York: Random House   John Tenniel
Centennial Edition. Sold in slipcase with *Looking-Glass*.

2216   1965   Alice's Adventures in Wonderland
New York: Random House   John Tenniel
A Centennial Edition. Reprint of a 1946 edition. Boxed in a slipcase with *Looking-Glass*.

2217   1965   Walt Disney's Story of Alice in Wonderland
New York: Walt Disney Productions   Walt Disney
Issued with a sound recording and a 24-page book. There are variant editions.

2218   [1965]   Alice's Adventures in Wonderland
New York: Airmont   John Tenniel
Airmont Classics.

2219   1966   Alice's Adventures in Wonderland
New York: Franklin Watts   Arthur Rackham
Later edition of the Doubleday first American trade edition of [1907]. "Proem" by Austin Dobson.

2220   1966   Alice in Wonderland
New York: Gilbertson Company, Inc.   Alex A. Blum
Classics Illustrated No. 49. Comic book. 10 cents in July 1948, later increased to 15 cents in June 1966 and to 25 cents in Fall 1968.

2221   1966   Alice in Wonderland
New York: Scholastic Book Services   John Tenniel
Paperback. Reprinted in 1972 and 1974.

2222   1966   Alice's Adventures in Wonderland
Ann Arbor, MI: University Microfilms   John Tenniel
A Legacy Library facsimile. From the 1897 edition.

2223   1966   Alice in Wonderland
Cleveland, OH: World Publishing Co.   R. Garcia
A Holly Book. Retold by Adele Wright.

2224   ca. 1966 Alice in Wonderland
Mount Vernon, NY: Peter Pauper Press   John Tenniel
Illustrations in red.

2225   1967   Alice's Adventures in Wonderland
New York: Crown Publishers   Ralph Steadman

2226   1967   Alice's Adventures in Wonderland and Through the Looking-Glass
New York: Collier. London: Collier-Macmillan   John Tenniel
4th edition. Introduction by Louis Untermeyer. Reprint of the 1962 edition.

2227   1968   Alice's Adventures in Wonderland
San Rafael, CA: Classic Press   Brigitte Bryan; Don Irwin

2228   1968   Alice in Wonderland
New York: Gilbertson Company, Inc.   Alex A. Blum
Classics Illustrated, No. 49. Comic book. 10 cents in July 1948.

2229   1969   Alice's Adventures in Wonderland
Avon, CT: Heritage Press   John Tenniel

2230   1969   Alice's Adventures in Wonderland
New York: Random House / Maecenas Press   Salvador Dalí
Issued in a limited edition of 2,700 copies. 2,500 on Mandeure paper; 200 numbered I to CC on Rives paper with an etching signed in pencil and including a double suite of 12 illustrations on Japan Nacre.

2231   1969   Alice's Adventures in Wonderland: A Critical Handbook
Belmont, CA: Wadsworth   Various
Edited by Donald Rackin. For details on this edition, see Guiliano p. 51.

2232   ca. 1970s   Alice in Wonderland
Baltimore, MD: Ottenheimer   Normy Robinson

2233   ca. 1970s   Alice's Adventures in Wonderland
New York: Tempo Books   0448170485   John Tenniel; Walt Disney
                                                                 Company

Color illustration on the dust jacket.

2234   1972   Alice in Wonderland
New York: Scholastic Book Services   9780590085038   John Tenniel
Paperback. First printed in 1966. Reprinted 1974.

2235   1972   Alice's Adventures in Wonderland
Deposit, NY: Valley Offset   John Tenniel
Limited to 1,000 copies.

2236   1973   Alice in Wonderland
New York: Clarkson N. Potter   9780517501351   Ralph Steadman
In hardcover and paperback. Reprinted 1974.

2237   [1973]   Alice's Adventures in Wonderland
New York: Avenel Books   John Tenniel

2238   1974   Alice in Wonderland
New York: Clarkson N. Potter   9780517501351   Ralph Steadman
In hardcover and paperback. Reprint of a 1973 edition.

2239   1974   Alice in Wonderland
New York: Scholastic Book Services   9780590085038   John Tenniel
Paperback. First printed in 1966. Reprinted 1972.

2240   ca. 1974   Alice in Wonderland
New York: Grosset & Dunlap   John Tenniel
Paperback.

2241   1975   Alice's Adventures in Wonderland
New York: Thomas Y. Crowell   9780690009842   Moritz Kennel
Color illustrations.

2242   1975   Alice's Adventures in Wonderland
New York: Viking Press   9780670112777   Arthur Rackham
Includes "Proem" by Austin Dobson. Illustrations first appeared in 1907, and some are in color.

2243   ca. 1975   Alice's Adventures in Wonderland
Franklin Center, PA: Franklin Mint   John Tenniel
Leather-bound edition. The 100 Greatest Books of All Time series.

2244   1976   Alice in Wonderland
New York: St. Martin's. London: Academy   9780856701894   John Tenniel
Giant Illustrated Edition. Greatly enlarged Tenniel illustrations.

2245   1976   Alice in Wonderland
New York: Wonder Books, a Division of Grosset & Dunlap, Inc.   Laszlo Matulay (after Tenniel)
Revised edition with "New Long-life binding." Adapted and abridged for Little Children by Marcia Martin. Pictorial
paper-covered boards. Text further edited. 49 cents. A later 1976 edition with 49 cents cancelled and 59 cents printed
below.

2246   [1976]   Lewis Carroll's Alice in Wonderland
New York: Golden Press. Racine, WI: Western Pub. Co. 9780307147554   Gordon King
Retold by Jane Carruth.

2247   [1976]   Alice in Wonderland
Chicago: Science Research Associates   9780574442406   John Tenniel
SRA Pilot Library.

2248   1977   Alice's Adventures in Wonderland
New York: Delacorte Press / Seymour Lawrence   9780440000693   Tove Jansson
A Merloyd Lawrence Book. Brown cloth stamped in gold.

2249   1977   Alice's Adventures in Wonderland
Norwalk, CT: Easton Press   John Tenniel; James Lewicki
Collector's Edition. Introduction by John T. Winterich. Frontispiece by James Lewicki.

2250   1977   Alice's Adventures in Wonderland
New York: St. Martin's Press   9780312018214   John Tenniel

2251   1977   Alice in Wonderland
New York: Wonder Books, a Division of Grosset & Dunlap, Inc.   Laszlo Matulay (after Tenniel)
Revised edition with "New Long-life binding." Adapted and abridged for Little Children by Marcia Martin. Pictorial
paper-covered boards. Text further edited. 59 cents.

2252   1978   Alice's Adventures in Wonderland
Austin, TX: Amistad Press   Yolanda Carter
A miniature book adapted by Yolanda Carter.

2253   1978   Walt Disney's Story of Alice in Wonderland
New York: Golden Book   9780307660862   Walt Disney

2254	1978	Alice in Wonderland		

2254   1978   Alice in Wonderland
Racine, WI: Western Publishing Company   Walt Disney
10th printing of D19. price 59 cents. An undated later printing as a New York Golden Book is priced at 89 cents.

2255   1978   Walt Disney's Story of Alice in Wonderland
New York: Wonder Books   9780448161051   Walt Disney
Adapted by Ann Spano.

2256   [1978]   Alice's Adventures in Wonderland
New York: Weathervane Books   9780517255162   Arthur Rackham
Otherwise, identical to the 1966 edition published by Franklin Watts. Blue cloth.

2257   1979   Walt Disney's Alice in Wonderland
Racine, WI: Western Publishing Co.   9780307104267   Walt Disney Studio
Adapted by Al Dempster.

2258   1980   Alice's Adventures in Wonderland
Franklin Center, PA: Franklin Library   9780333285701   John Tenniel

2259   1980   Alice's Adventures in Wonderland
Mahwah, NJ: Troll Associates   9780816718627   Kathryn A. Couri
Adapted by Earle Hitchner.

2260   [1980]   Alice's Adventures in Wonderland
Boston: G. K. Hall   9780816130702   Anthony Browne

2261   1982   Alice's Adventures in Wonderland
North Hatfield, MA: Pennyroyal Press   9780527100272   Barry Moser
Pennyroyal Edition. Limited to 350 copies.

2262   1983   Alice's Adventures in Wonderland
Mount Vernon, NY: Press of A. Colish   John Tenniel
Limited edition.

2263   1983   Alice's Adventures in Wonderland
New York: Bantam Books   9780553053852   Various
Classic Illustrated Edition. Edited by Cooper Edens.

2264   1983   Alice's Adventures in Wonderland
Franklin Center, PA: Franklin Library   9780906320945   Susan Palamara
Deluxe edition.

2265   1983   Alice's Adventures in Wonderland
New York: Knopf   9780394532271   S. Michelle Wiggins

2266   1983   Alice in Wonderland
Baltimore, MD: Ottenheimer Publishers Inc.   R. Canaider
1st edition thus.

2267   1983   Alice's Adventures in Wonderland
Berkeley, CA: University of California Press   9780520048201   Barry Moser
Also, a deluxe trade edition in a slipcase with an etching of the Hatter.

2268   ca. 1983 Alice's Adventures in Wonderland
Jackson, MS: University Press of Mississippi   0878051880   Walter Anderson
Book cover titled *Anderson's Alice*.

2269   1984   Alice's Adventures in Wonderland
New York: Alfred A. Knopf   039486915X; 0394869362   John Tenniel
Facsimile of the Macmillan London 1866 edition. Red cloth stamped in gold. Included in a slipcase with *Looking-Glass* facsimile of the London 1872 first edition. With a pamphlet by Michael Hancher "On the Writing, Illustration and Publication of Lewis Carroll's *Alice* Books."

2270   1984   Alice by Anselm: New Illustrations for Lewis Carroll's
                  Alice's Adventures in Wonderland
Decatur, GA: Oudepote Press   Anselm Atkins
Abridged edition with quotes and contour drawings. Staple bound with original dust jacket. Limited edition of 300 copies, numbered and signed by the illustrator.

2271   ca. 1984 Alice's Adventures in Wonderland
New York: Capricorn Press   9780870300226   John Tenniel

2272   ca. 1984 Alice's Adventures in Wonderland
New York: Crown Publishers   Justin Todd

2273   1985   Alice's Adventures in Wonderland
New York: Chancellor Press   Arthur Rackham
Otherwise, identical to the [1966] edition published by Franklin Watts. Ivory paper-covered boards.

2274   1985   Alice's Adventures in Wonderland
Norwalk, CT: Easton Press   Michael Hague
Collector's Edition, including a signed sketch.

2275   1985   Alice's Adventures in Wonderland
New York: Holt, Rinehart and Winston   9780030020377   Michael Hague

2276   1986   Alice's Adventures in Wonderland
New York: Simon and Schuster   0671635654   David Hall

2277   1988   Alice in Wonderland
New York: Abrams   9780810918726   Unknown
Magic Lantern slide illustrations. In the "Introduction," Brian Sibley states that the 24 slides in this book were "produced by Primus, the London photographic company of William Butcher. . . . The original colorist is unknown but was probably an employee of Butcher's. The illiustrations are after Tenniel, with some that "closely follow the originals. Others, however, contain small but fascinating differences." Alice has been added to some pictures.

2278   1988   Alice's Adventures in Wonderland
New York: Knopf   394805925; 039490592X   Anthony Browne
                        (library binding)

2279   [1988]   Alice in Wonderland
[Elgin, IL]: Child's World   9780895654670   Francesc Rovira
Adaptation by Eduard José; retold by Janet Riehecky.

2280   [1988]   Alice's Adventures in Wonderland
Oregon City, OR: Dilithium   9780517659618   Bessie Pease Gutmann;
                                                          John Tenniel

2281 1989 Alice in Wonderland
Baltimore, MD: Ottenheimer Publishers Inc.   R. Canaider
1st reprint. A Bancroft edition.

2282 1989 Alice's Adventures in Wonderland
New York: Philomel Books /   0399222413   Peter Weevers
Putnam and Grosset Group
There also was a special leather-bound edition in 1992.

2283 [1989] Alice's Adventures in Wonderland
New York: Bantam Books   9780553053852   Various
Classic Illustrated Edition. Edited by Cooper Edens.

2284 ca. 1990 Alice's Adventures in Wonderland
Morris Plains, NJ: Unicorn Publishing House   9780881011098   Greg Hildebrandt
Adapted and abridged by Julia Suarez. Hardcover.

2285 1990 Alice in Wonderland
Baltimore, MD: Ottenheimer Publishers Inc.   R. Canaider
2nd reprint. A Bancroft edition.

2286 1991 Walt Disney's Alice in Wonderland
Racine, WI: Western Publishing Company   Franc Mateu
A Little Golden Book. Abridged. Adapted by Terry Slater. Miniature book (6.7 cm).

2287 1992 Alice's Adventures in Wonderland
New York: Alfred A. Knopf   0679417958   John Tenniel

2288 1992 Alice's Adventures in Wonderland
New York: Alfred A. Knopf   0394805925   Anthony Browne

2289 1992 Alice's Adventures in Wonderland: a young reader's edition of the classic story
Philadelphia: Courage Books   9781561381005   John Bradley
Retold by David Blair. Illustrated by John Bradley. Edited by Gregory C. Aaron. Design and art direction by Alastair
Campbell. Courage Books is an imprint of Running Press Book Publishers.

2290 1992 Little Treasury of Alice in Wonderland
New York: Derrydale   9780517067208   Rene Cloke
Retold by Jane Carruth. Miniature 6-volume boxed set.

2291 1992 Alice's Adventures in Wonderland
New York: Philomel Books /   0399222413   Peter Weevers
Putnam and Grosset Group
A special leather-bound edition of the 1989 edition.

2292 1992 Alice's Adventures in Wonderland
New York: TOR   0812504186   Unknown

2293 [1992] Alice's Adventures in Wonderland
New York: William Morrow   9780688110871   John Tenniel
Books of Wonder series.

2294 1993 Alice's Adventures in Wonderland

Boston; Bath, UK: Bristol Books   9781569579008   John Tenniel

Little Barefoot Books. 1st edition. Miniature edition (12 cm). Unabridged. Series designed by Dede Cummings. Distributed in the United States by Random House. Colophon states UK edition ISBN as 1898000158.

2295   1993   Alice in Wonderland
Nashville, TN: Nelson Regency   9780840749260   John Tenniel
Little Classics. Miniature book. Abridged. Some illustrations in color.

2296   1993   Alice's Adventures in Wonderland
Philadelphia: Running Press   9781561382460   Graham Evernden
Retold by David Blair. Issued with dust jacket. Color illustrations. Miniature book (8.4 cm).

2297   [1993]   Alice's Adventures in Wonderland
Saratoga, NY: Book Club of America   Robin DeWitt; Patricia DeWitt
Adapted by Carolyn Magner.

2298   1994   Alice's Adventures in Wonderland
New York: Barnes and Noble   9781566194778   John Tenniel

2299   1995   Alice in Wonderland
New York: Barnes and Noble   9781566197441   Gwynedd Hudson;
Frank Adams; Harry Rountree; Charles Robinson; Bessie Pease Gutmann; Arthur Rackham

2300   1995   Walt Disney's Alice in Wonderland
New York: Disney Press   9780786830343;   Franc Mateu; Holly Hannen
                                9780786850174
Adapted from the 1951 film by Teddy Slater. Illustrated by Franc Mateu and Holly Hannen.

2301   1995   Alice's Adventures in Wonderland
New York: Gramercy Books / Random House   0517124203   Arthur Rackham

2302   1995   Classic Children's Literature
New York: Prentice Hall   9780133479645   Unknown
4th edition. An anthology including *Alice's Adventures in Wonderland*. Softcover.

2303   [1995]   Alice in Wonderland
New York: Modern Publishing   9781561442942   Shōgō Hirata
Honey Bear Books. Adapted and abridged.

2304   [1996]   Alice's Adventures in Wonderland
New York: Artisan   188518347X   Angel Dominguez

2305   1997   Alice in Wonderland
New York: Smithmark   9780765191885   Monique Gorde
Abridged.

2306   [1997]   Alice's Adventures in Wonderland
New York: Baronet Books   9780866118736   Lea Kaster
Adapted by Eliza Gatewood Warren. Great Illustrated Classics.

2307   [1997]   Alice's Adventures in Wonderland
New York: GT Publishing   9781577190806   Carolyn Ewing
Adapted by Wofford Williams.

2308	1998	Alice's Adventures in Wonderland		
		Mineola, NY: Dover Publications	9780486403458	Marty Noble
		Dover Children's Thrift Classics. Adapted by Bob Blaisdell.		

2309	1998	Alice's Adventures in Wonderland		
		New York: Dutton Children's Books	9780525460947	Abelardo Morell; John Tenniel
		Introduction by Leonard S. Marcus. Photographic collages with Tenniel illustrations.		

2310	1998	Alice in Wonderland		
		New York: Smithmark	9780831766948	Monique Gorde
		Abridged.		

2311	1999	Alice's Adventures in Wonderland		
		Cambridge, MA: Candlewick Press	0763608041	Helen Oxenbury

2312	1999	Alice's Adventures in Wonderland		
		Denver, CO: Micawber Fine Editions		Griff Jones

2313	1999	Alice's Adventures in Wonderland		
		New York: North–South Books	0735811660	Lisbeth Zwerger

2314	1999	Classic Children's Literature		
		New York: Prentice Hall	9780130837899	Unknown
		5th edition. An anthology including *Alice's Adventures in Wonderland*. Softcover.		

2315	2000	Alice's Adventures in Wonderland		
		San Francisco: Chronicle Books	9780811822749	Various
		Classic Illustrated Edition. Edited by Cooper Edens.		

2316	2000	Alice's Adventures in Wonderland		
		New York: Dorling Kindersley	9780789459022	Greg Becker
		Adapted by Jane Fior.		

2317	2000	Alice's Adventures in Wonderland		
		New York: HarperCollins	9780694014545	John Tenniel
		Charming Classics.		

2318	2000	Alice's Adventures in Wonderland		
		New York, etc.: Simon and Schuster	068983375X	John Tenniel

2319	ca. 2000	Alice's Adventures in Wonderland		
		McLean, VA: IndyPublish.com	9781588274939	Unknown
		Millennium fulcrum edition 3.0.		

2320	2001	Alice's Adventures in Wonderland		
		Franklin, TN: Dalmatian Press	9781577595502	Jason Alexander
		Adapted by Debbie Guthery.		

2321	2001	Alice's Adventures in Wonderland		
		Mineola, NY: Dover Publications	0486416585	John Tenniel
		New Dover edition.		

2322	2001	Alice's Adventures in Wonderland		
		New York: HarperCollins	978006029150	DeLoss McGraw

2323	ca. 2001 Alice's Adventures in Wonderland			
	New York: Bloomsbury	9781582341743	Mervyn Peake	

2324 ca. 2002 Alice's Adventures in Wonderland
San Anselmo, CA: Blushing Rose Publishing   1884807194   John Tenniel;
                                                                                Wendy Cogan Toyoda

2325 2003   Alice's Adventures in Wonderland
Buffalo, NY: Firefly Books   0789459027   Ralph Steadman
Paper wrappers.

2326 2004   Alice's Adventures in Wonderland
New York: CRW Publishing   0760750769   John Tenniel

2327 2004   Classic Children's Literature
New York: Longman Publishing Group   9780131891838   Unknown
6th edition. An anthology including *Alice's Adventures in Wonderland*. Softcover.

2328 2004   Alice's Adventures in Wonderland
New York: Sterling Publishing   9781402716522   Michael Foreman

2329 ca. 2004 Alice's Adventures in Wonderland
Philadelphia: Courage Books   9780762420087   Greg Hildebrandt
Adapted and abridged by Julia Suarez.

2330 ca. 2004 Alice's Adventures in Wonderland
New York: Modern Publishing   9780766607729   Rex Schneider
Adapted by Susan Linney.

2331 2005   Alice's Adventures in Wonderland
Boston: Paperview   9782874272172   Thomas de Coster
Boston Globe Family Classics series.

2332 2005   Alice's Adventures in Wonderland
New York: Sterling Publishing   9781402725029   Scott McKowen

2333 ca. 2005 Alice's Adventures in Wonderland
New York: Penguin Group   0803729405   Alison Jay

2334 2006   Alice's Adventures in Wonderland
Ann Arbor, MI: Borders Classics   9781587264146   Unknown

2335 2007   Alice's Adventures in Wonderland
Scituate, MA: DSI [Digital Scanning Incorporated]   9781582187914;   John Tenniel
                                                     9781582187907; 9781582187914
Print-on-demand book. Hardcover and softcover. Digital facsimile of an undated McLoughlin Brothers edition.

2336 2008   Walt Disney's Alice in Wonderland
New York: Disney Press   9781423107286   Mary Blair
The story retold by Jon Scieszka, with the original illustrations for the 1951 Disney film by Mary Blair.

2337   2008   Alice's Adventures in Wonderland
        Palo Alto, CA: Modernbook Editions   9780980104417;   Maggie Taylor
                                                     9780980104400 (limited edition)

2338   2008   Alice's Adventures in Wonderland
        New York; London: Puffin Books   9780141321073; 141321075   John Tenniel
        Puffin Classics. Introduction by Chris Riddell.

2339   2009   Alice's Adventures in Wonderland
        Somerville, MA: Candlewick Press   Rodney Matthews
        Illustrations in a fantasy style.

2340   2009   Alice's Adventures in Wonderland
        North Charleston, SC : CreateSpace   9781441400857   Glenn Diddit
        Graphic novel in color. "A Literature Through Art Novel." Adapted and illustrated by Glenn Diddit. The author noted,
        "It is very cool how Alice's dress begins yellow and ends blue, an effect you can only experience in color." A later
        edition appeared in black-and-white in 2015 as "the official 150th anniversary edition unabridged graphic novel."

2341   2009   Alice's Adventures in Wonderland
        Canandaigua, NY: Wiley O'Brien Workspace   9780615294926   Nancy Wiley

2342   ca. 2009 Alice's Adventures in Wonderland
        New York; London: Sterling Publishing   9781402768354   Robert Ingpen

2343   2010   Alice's Adventures in Wonderland
        [Clearfield, UT]: Capitalized Living   9780980247985   A.in.Z; Madalina Andronic;
        Raphael Armando; Allison Ball; Aaron Bartlett; Dan Bergevin (editing and publication); Marina Busteros;
        Jhonatan Medina Caguana; Justas Cekauskas; Kelly Chehardy; Yucci Chen; Antigoni Chryssanthopoulou
        (paperback cover artwork); Pedro Corrêa; Peter Danielsen (hardback cover text); Reuben Van Dijk; Mille Dørge;
        Guillermo Fajardo; Raquel Figueira; Victor van Gaasbeek; Federico Reyes Galván; Daisy Gam; Lina Gavėnaitė;
        Clémence Gerardin; Ramon E Gerena (paperback cover text); Marius Gherasim; Giovanni Girardi; Carmen
        Virginia Grisolfa; Francesco Gulina; Samir Hamiche; Pablo Lara Henriquez; Ali J; William Jamison; Andrew
        Johnson; Haley Jones; Loukia Kyriakidou; Andre Leonard; Tena Letica; Maria do Carmo Louceiro; Elizabeth
        Matlack; Ryan McDougal; Jodie McGuinness; Deni Medina; Ruchi Mhasane; Lorenzo Milito; Mel Muraca;
        Kristiaan der Nederlanden; Marc K Park; Josh Payne; Charlotte Peter; Elric Petit; Christian Poschmann
        (chapter titles); Ali Pye; Natalie Shau; Ana Šimon; Luke Stephen Smith; Ileana Surducan; Maria Surducan; Selena
        Tabakovic; Nicole Tan; Kim Triebsee (hardcover art); Ralf Wandschneider

        Collaboratively illustrated edition published as the "Alice Project" with works by 58 different illustrators. Edited by
        Dan Bergevin, owner of Capitalized Living.

2344   2010   Alice's Adventures in Wonderland
        Milwaukie, OR: Dark Horse.   1595822666   POP (a group of illustrators)
        London: Diamond [distributor]
        Translated from the Japanese. Michiyo Hayano is the Japanese editor.

2345   2010   Alice's Adventures in Wonderland
        New York: HarperCollins / Collins Design   9780061886577   Camille Rose Garcia

2346   2010   Alice in Wonderland
        New York: Penguin Young Readers   9780448452692   Kathryn Rathke
        Level 4 reader (fluent level). Text abridged and adapted by Deborah Hautzig.

2347   2011   Alice's Adventures in Wonderland
        Edina, MN: Magic Wagon   9781602707412   Ute Simon
        Calico Illustrated Classics. Adapted by Lisa Mullarkey.

2348	2012	Alice's Adventures in Wonderland		Andrew Sawyer
		Oakland, CA: Andrew Sawyer		
		Limited to 10 copies. A Unique Book Art Design.		

2349	2012	Alice's Adventures in Wonderland		
		North Charleston, SC: CreateSpace	9781448657919	Unknown
		Paperback. Print-on-demand book.		

| 2350 | 2012 | Alice's Adventures in Wonderland | | |
| | | East Bridgewater, MA: World Publishing Group | 9781464301520 | Eric Kincaid |

2351	2013	Alice's Adventures in Wonderland		
		North Charleston, SC: CreateSpace	9781494308629; 9781493771264	Unknown
		Paperback. Large print edition. Print-on-demand book.		

| 2352 | 2013 | Alice's Adventures in Wonderland | | |
| | | Tulsa, OK: EDC Publishing | 9780794547011 | Fran Parreño |

2353	2014	Alice's Adventures in Wonderland		
		North Charleston, SC: CreateSpace	9781505488340	M. C. Iglesias
		Paperback.		

2354	2014	Alice's Adventures in Wonderland		
		New York: Puffin Books	9780147510983	John Tenniel
		Puffin Chalk Series. Published by an imprint of Penguin Group (USA). First published in 1946.		

| 2355 | 2014 | Alice's Adventures in Wonderland | | |
| | | New York: Random House / Puffin Books | 9780147515872 | Anna Bond |

2356	2015	Alice's Adventures in Wonderland		
		Frostburg, MD: Box Books	9781517274405	Jamison Odone
		Retold by Jamison Odone.		

2357	2015	Alice's Adventures in Wonderland: "Official 150th Anniversary Edition Unabridged Graphic Novel"		
		North Charleston, SC : CreateSpace	9781511733007	Glenn Diddit
		Graphic novel. "A Literature Through Art Novel." Adapted and illustrated by Glenn Diddit. The author noted, "It is very cool how Alice's dress begins yellow and ends blue, an effect you can only experience in color." Original copyright 1988. An earlier 2009 edition appeared with color illustrations black-and-white."		

| 2358 | 2015 | Alice's Adventures in Wonderland | | |
| | | Princeton, NJ: Princeton University Press | 9780691170022 | Salvador Dalí |

2359	2015	Alice's Adventures in Wonderland		
		New York: Puffin Books	9780147515872	Anna Bond
		Published by an imprint of Penguin Group (USA). New deluxe hardcover oversized edition. A 150th Anniversary Edition. Illustrated in color. Some reviews give this edition and particularly the illustrator, Anna Bond, high marks.		

| 2360 | 2015 | Alice's Adventures in Wonderland | | |
| | | Beverly, MA: Quarto Publishing Group | 9781631590757 | Andrea D'Aquino |

| 2361 | 2015 | Alice's Adventures in Wonderland Decoded | | |
| | | New York: Random House | 9780385682268 | Various |

Annotations and essays by David Day. Hardcover won an Alcuin Society Book Design Award. Also available in e-book Kindle format with no ISBN, and Kobo format 9780385682275.

2362   2015   Alice in Manhattan: a photographic trip down New York City's rabbit holes
New York: Six State Press   9780996796101   Dan Hirshon

1st hardback edition. As a street photographer's view of Manhattan, the book juxtaposes Alice quotes in chapter order with over 60 black-and-white photographs of real-life characters, architecture, gardens, and underground tunnels. The front cover shows the 1959 Central Park José de Creeft sculpture. Back cover is from the 1994 New York Subway system (50th and Broadway station) Tenniel-based mosaic by New York-based Argentinian artist Liliana Porter.

2363   2015   Alice in Manhattan: a photographic trip down New York City's rabbit holes
New York: Six State Press   9781523837564   Dan Hirshon

1st paperback edition. As a street photographer's view of Manhattan, the book juxtaposes Alice quotes in chapter order with over 60 black-and-white photographs of real-life characters, architecture, gardens, and underground tunnels. The photographs vary from the hardback edition, as does the front cover of Alice profile from the 1994 New York Subway system (50th and Broadway station) Tenniel-based mosaic by New York-based Argentinian artist Liliana Porter, pulling back a curtain on the New York skyline at night. The back cover is the same as the hardback edition.

2364   2016   Alice in Wonderland
Los Angeles: Disney Press   9781484776421   Disney
Retold by T. T. Sutherland.

2365   2016   Alice's Adventures in Wonderland: 150th Anniversary edition
                with ninety-six illustrations by David Delamare
Portland, OR: Wendy Ice   9780996720649 (Standard);   David Delamare
        9780996720601 (Gold edition); 9780996720618 (Silver edition); 9780996720625 (Bronze edition)

Published in multiple editions. Gold edition had 25 numbered copies, signed in gold ink and issued with one 8 x 10 pencil drawing of Alice and five 9 x 12 posters, all signed by the publisher. Silver edition had 75 numbered copies, signed in silver ink and issued with three 8 x 10 giclées and five 9 x 12 posters, all signed by the publisher. The Bronze edition had 400 numbered copies, signed in copper ink and issued with one 8 x 10 giclée and five 9 x 12 posters, all signed by the publisher. The Standard edition had approximately 2,000 unnumbered copies.

2366   2017   Alice's Adventures in Wonderland: the classic edition
Kennebunkport, ME: Applesauce,   9781604337112   Charles Santore
an imprint of Cider Mill Press
Contains 3 foldout pages.

2367   2017   European Classics: The Lighter Side
Solon, OH: Findaway World, LLC   9781509456352   Various
Electronic text of numerous novels, including *Alice*.

2368   2020   Alice's Adventures in Wonderland
[Los Angeles]: Linda and George Cassady   Alp Ozberker

Limited unbound folio edition. 1st issue in 2020 with 20 copies, with separate edition of the portfolio of 22 folio prints in archival box issued in limited edition of 10 copies. 2nd issue in 2021 with 20 copies, some issued with separate print portfolio. Hand-colored illustrations commissioned by Linda and George Cassady in 2004–5 were etched on copper plates, with prints hand-colored by the artist. The original hand-colored art, black-and-white prints, and copper plates reside in the Cassady Collection at the Doheny Memorial Library of the University of Southern California.

2369   n.d.   Alice's Adventures in Wonderland
New York: A. L. Burt   John Tenniel

Series title unknown. Sewell believes this could be part of the Wellesley Series. Includes the first 10 chapters of *Sylvie and Bruno*. For details see *MoM*, p. 113.

2370   n.d.   Alice's Adventures in Wonderland
New York: A. L. Burt Company   John Tenniel
Series title unknown. Includes the first 10 chapters of *Sylvie and Bruno*. For details see *MoM*, p. 113.

2371   n.d.   Alice's Adventures in Wonderland
New York: Award Books, Inc.   John Tenniel
Family Classics.

2372   n.d.   Alice's Adventures in Wonderland
New York: Award Books, Inc.   John Tenniel
Best Seller Classics.

2373   n.d.   Alice's Adventures in Wonderland
New York: Best-Loved Classics   John Tenniel
Best-Loved Classics. A division of HarperCollins.

2374   n.d.   Alice's Adventures in Wonderland
Chicago: Book Supply Company   John Tenniel
Peerless Library. Also contains 10 chapters of *Sylvie and Bruno*.

2375   n.d.   Alice's Adventures in Wonderland
Garden City, NY: Children's Classics   John Tenniel
Peerless Library. Also contains 10 chapters of *Sylvie and Bruno*.

2376   n.d.   Alice's Adventures in Wonderland
Garden City, NY: Doubleday Classics   John Tenniel
Large paper edition. Gray pictorial boards.

2377   n.d.   Alice's Adventures in Wonderland and Peter Pan
New York: Hartsdale House   John Tenniel
Old English Style headings at the top of each page. A reprint of the 1936 Three Sirens Press edition.

2378   n.d.   Alice's Adventures in Wonderland
New York: Hodder and Stoughton   A. E. Jackson
Undated later printing, same as the 1914 edition. 16 color plates. Blue cloth.

2379   n.d.   Alice's Adventures in Wonderland
Chicago: J. G. Ferguson & Associates   John Tenniel
Art-Type Edition.

2380   n.d.   Alice's Adventures in Wonderland
New York: Little Leather Library   Unillustrated
Leaf size 2 x 3 inches. Flexible green leather.

2381   n.d.   Alice's Adventures in Wonderland
New York: New York Post   Unknown
A New York Post Families Classic Library, number 4.

2382   n.d.   Alice's Adventures in Wonderland
Green Bay, WI: Northern Paper Mills   Milo Winter
Blue paper-covered boards with color illustration on front cover.

2383   n.d.   Alice's Adventures in Wonderland
New York: Random House   Marjorie Torrey
Dandelion Library series. *Peter Pan* upside down to *Alice*.

2384   n.d.   Alice's Adventures in Wonderland
New York: Sam'l Gabriel & Sons   R. A. Burley
Linnette trademark on cover. Abridged.

2385   n.d.   Alice's Adventures in Wonderland
New York: Thomas Y. Crowell   L. J. (Lewis Jesse) Bridgman;
                                            Anonymous (after Tenniel); Charles Copeland
The Astor Prose Series. 4 black-and-white plates, 3 after Tenniel and 1 with L. J. Bridgman's monogram: cover by
(Charles) Copeland. Later printing identical to the ca. 1904–1913 edition.

2.4 OTHER PUBLISHERS OF COMBINED EDITIONS OF *ALICE* AND *LOOKING-GLASS*

2386   ca. 1892 Alice's Adventures in Wonderland and Through the Looking-Glass
New York: Lovell, Coryell & Co.   John Tenniel
Century series.

2387   ca. 1892 Alice's Adventures in Wonderland and Through the Looking-Glass
New York: National Book Company   John Tenniel
Library Editions of 12 mos.

2388   ca. 1893 Alice's Adventures in Wonderland and Through the Looking-Glass
New York: A. L. Burt   L. J. (Lewis Jesse) Bridgman;
                                            Anonymous (after Tenniel); Charles Copeland
The Fireside Series for Girls. Blue cloth. Dated by *PTLA*.

2389   ca. 1893 Alice's Adventures in Wonderland and Through the Looking-Glass
New York: Tait, Sons and Co.   John Tenniel
Library Edition.

2390   ca. 1894 Alice's Adventures in Wonderland and Through the Looking-Glass
New York: A. L. Burt   John Tenniel
A World of Girls. This series is advertised in Fireside ca. 1894, so must be around that date.

2391   ca. 1894 Alice's Adventures in Wonderland and Through the Looking-Glass
New York: A. L. Burt   John Tenniel; L. J. (Lewis Jesse)
                                                      Bridgman; Charles Copeland
The Fireside Series for Girls. Date based on terminal ads.

2392   ca. 1894 Alice's Adventures in Wonderland and Through the Looking-Glass
Boston: Estes & Lauriat   John Tenniel
Roxburgh Classics.

2393   ca. 1895 Alice's Adventures in Wonderland and Through the Looking-Glass
Philadelphia: Henry Altemus   John Tenniel
Altemus' Illustrated Famous Series. Brown cloth.

2394   [1896]   Alice's Adventures in Wonderland and Through the Looking-Glass
New York; Boston: H. M. Caldwell   John Tenniel
The Illustrated Library of Famous Books by Famous Authors. Gray cloth stamped in gilt figure. A dark red ribbed
cloth binding exists.

2395   ca. 1896 Alice's Adventures in Wonderland and Through the Looking-Glass
New York: A. L. Burt   John Tenniel; L. J. (Lewis Jesse)
                                                                       Bridgman; Charles Copeland
The Fireside Series for Girls. Date based on cover description.

2396   ca. 1896 Alice's Adventures in Wonderland and Through the Looking-Glass
New York: American Publishers Corporation   John Tenniel
New Century Series.

2397   ca. 1897 Alice's Adventures in Wonderland and Through the Looking-Glass
New York: A. L. Burt   John Tenniel
A World of Girls. No copy seen. Sewell believes this might be a ghost edition.

2398   ca. 1897 Alice's Adventures in Wonderland and Through the Looking-Glass
New York: A. L. Burt   John Tenniel
Burt's Home Library. Maroon cloth. Dated by *PTLA*.

2399   ca. 1897 Alice's Adventures in Wonderland and Through the Looking-Glass
New York: A. L. Burt   John Tenniel; L. J. (Lewis Jesse)
                                                                       Bridgman; Charles Copeland
The Fireside Series for Girls. Date based on ads. There is a 2nd ca. 1897 edition. For more information see *MoM,* p. 115.

2400   ca. 1897 Alice's Adventures in Wonderland and Through the Looking-Glass
New York: American Publishers Corporation   John Tenniel
New Oxford Series.

2401   ca. 1897 Alice's Adventures in Wonderland and Through the Looking-Glass
Philadelphia: Henry Altemus   John Tenniel
Altemus' Illustrated Library of Standard Authors.

2402   ca. 1897 Alice's Adventures in Wonderland and Through the Looking-Glass
Philadelphia: Henry T. Coates & Co.   John Tenniel
The Laurel Library. Green cloth. Text from a Macmillan edition.

2403   1898   Alice's Adventures in Wonderland
Boston: Lothrop, Lee and Shepard   Anonymous (after Tenniel)
New Edition, in One Vol. Pictorial greenish-gray cloth printed in dark green and orange. 4 color plates, including
frontispiece. 41 Tenniel illustrations for *Alice* and 42 for *Looking-Glass*. Title of the book is *Alice*, but it includes
Looking-Glass, each with its own half title. Verso of title page says, "Copyright 1898 by Lothrop Publishing
Company." Appears to be identical to a Newark, NJ: Charles E. Graham edition of 1917 that has on verso of the title
page "Copyright 1898 by Lothrop Publishing Company."

2404   ca. 1898 Alice's Adventures in Wonderland and Through the Looking-Glass
Boston: Lothrop Publishing Company   Anonymous (after Tenniel)
Pictorial brown-green cloth. States "New Ed, in One Vol." 4 color plates.

2405   1899   Alice's Adventures in Wonderland and Through the Looking-Glass
Chicago: Donohue, Henneberry & Co.   John Tenniel

2406   [1899] Alice's Adventures in Wonderland and Through the Looking-Glass
New York; Boston: H. M. Caldwell   John Tenniel
Berkeley Library.

2407   1900   Alice's Adventures in Wonderland and Through the Looking-Glass
New York: A. Wessels   Blanche McManus
16 color plates.

2408   1900   Alice's Adventures in Wonderland and Through the Looking-Glass
        Chicago; New York: Donohue Brothers   John Tenniel
        2 vols in 1 The Donohue Brothers only published under this name only in 1900. Prior to this, they were "Donohue, Henneberry & Co." From 1901 onward, they were "M. A. Donohue and Company."

2409   1900   Alice's Adventures in Wonderland and Through the Looking-Glass
        New York: Platt and Nourse   Blanche McManus
        Reprint of the Platt & Peck edition.

2410   1900   Alice's Adventures in Wonderland and Through the Looking-Glass
        New York: Platt and Peck   Blanche McManus
        Identical to the Wessels edition. Dark beige cloth.

2411   ca. 1900 Alice's Adventures in Wonderland and Through the Looking-Glass
        New York: Wm. L. Allison   John Tenniel
        Vassar Series. Blue cloth.

2412   [1901] Alice's Adventures in Wonderland and Through the Looking-Glass
        New York; Boston: H. M. Caldwell   John Tenniel
        Lotus Series. A 2-volume set boxed together.

2413   [1901] Alice's Adventures in Wonderland and Through the Looking-Glass
        Chicago: M. A. Donohue and Company   Anonymous (after Tenniel)

2414   ca. 1901 Alice's Adventures in Wonderland and Through the Looking-Glass
        New York: A. L. Burt   John Tenniel
        The Irving 12 mos. Dated by *PTLA*.

2415   ca. 1901 Alice's Adventures in Wonderland and Through the Looking-Glass
        New York: A. L. Burt   John Tenniel; L. J. (Lewis Jesse)
                                                                     Bridgman; Charles Copeland
        The Fireside Series for Girls. Date based on inscription.

2416   ca. 1901 Alice's Adventures in Wonderland and Through the Looking-Glass
        New York: A. L. Burt   John Tenniel
        Burt's Home Library. Date based on ads.

2417   ca. 1901 Alice's Adventures in Wonderland and Through the Looking-Glass
        Chicago; New York: Henneberry   John Tenniel
        Title on spine is *Through the Looking-Glass*, which is bound in before *Alice*.

2418   ca. 1901 Alice's Adventures in Wonderland and Through the Looking-Glass
        Philadelphia: Henry Altemus   John Tenniel
        Altemus' Illustrated Library of Standard Authors.

2419   ca. 1901 Alice's Adventures in Wonderland and Through the Looking-Glass
        Philadelphia: Henry Altemus   John Tenniel
        Altemus' Illustrated Riviere Series of 12 mos.

2420   ca. 1901 Alice's Adventures in Wonderland and Through the Looking-Glass
        Philadelphia: Henry T. Coates & Co.   John Tenniel
        The Favorite Library.

2421   ca. 1901 Alice's Adventures in Wonderland and Through the Looking-Glass

Philadelphia: Henry T. Coates & Co.   John Tenniel
The New Alpha Library.

2422   ca. 1901–1910   Alice's Adventures in Wonderland and Through the Looking-Glass
Chicago: Union School Furnishing Co. Publishers   John Tenniel
Union School Library. *Looking-Glass* bound before *Alice.*

2423   [1902]   Alice's Adventures in Wonderland and Through the Looking-Glass
New York: McLoughlin Brothers   Anonymous (after Tenniel)

2424   ca. 1902 Alice's Adventures in Wonderland and Through the Looking-Glass
New York: A. L. Burt   John Tenniel
Burt's Home Library. Date based on ads.

2425   ca. 1902 Alice's Adventures in Wonderland and Through the Looking-Glass
Philadelphia: Henry Altemus   John Tenniel
Altemus' Illustrated Popular Library.

2426   ca. 1903 Alice's Adventures in Wonderland and Through the Looking-Glass
New York: Hurst   John Tenniel; Anonymous
                                                                     (after Tenniel)
Fairy Tale Series.

2427   ca. 1903–1904   Alice's Adventures in Wonderland and Through the Looking-Glass
New York: Hurst   John Tenniel; Anonymous
                                                                     (after Tenniel)
Hurst's Presentation Series.

2428   ca. 1904 Alice's Adventures in Wonderland and Through the Looking-Glass
New York: A. Wessels   Blanche McManus
16 color plates.

2429   ca. 1904 Alice's Adventures in Wonderland and Through the Looking-Glass
New York: Hurst   John Tenniel; Anonymous
                                                                     (after Tenniel)
Red cloth. 6 uncredited color plates. In various bindings.

2430   ca. 1906 Alice's Adventures in Wonderland and Through the Looking-Glass
New York: A. L. Burt   John Tenniel; L. J. (Lewis Jesse)
                                                     Bridgman; Charles Copeland
The Fireside Series for Girls. Dated by *PTLA.*

2431   ca. 1906 Alice's Adventures in Wonderland and Through the Looking-Glass
New York: A. L. Burt   John Tenniel
Burt's Juvenile Classics for Young People. Dated by *PTLA.*

2432   ca. 1906 Alice's Adventures in Wonderland and Through the Looking-Glass
New York: A. L. Burt   John Tenniel
Series title unknown. Dated by *PTLA.*

2433   ca. 1907 Alice's Adventures in Wonderland and Through the Looking-Glass
Philadelphia: Henry Altemus   John Tenniel
Altemus' Illustrated Little Men and Women Series.

2434   1908   Alice's Adventures in Wonderland and Humpty Dumpty
Chicago: Reilly & Lee Co.   John R. Neill
Children's Red Book Series. 1st use of John R. Neill illustrations.

2435 [1908] Alice's Adventures in Wonderland and Through the Looking-Glass
New York; Boston: H. M. Caldwell   John Tenniel
Six to Sixteen Series.

2436 ca. 1908 Alice's Adventures in Wonderland and Through the Looking-Glass
Philadelphia: Henry Altemus   John Tenniel
Beige cloth.

2437 ca. 1908 Alice's Adventures in Wonderland and Through the Looking-Glass – Humpty Dumpty
Chicago: Reilly and Britton   John R. Neill
Children's Stories That Never Grow Old, adapted by Mary Stone. An omnibus edition containing 19 stories.

2438 [1909] Alice's Adventures in Wonderland and Through the Looking-Glass
New York: Hurst   John Tenniel; Anonymous
Every Girl's Library.   (after Tenniel)

2439 ca. 1909 Alice's Adventures in Wonderland and Through the Looking-Glass
New York: A. L. Burt   John Tenniel
The Meade Series for Girls. Dated by *PTLA*. Sewell speculates that the sheets may be from unsold earlier editions of
other series.

2440 ca. 1910 Alice's Adventures in Wonderland and Through the Looking-Glass
New York: A. L. Burt   John Tenniel; J. Watson Davis
Burt's Juvenile Classics for Young People.

2441 ca. 1910 Alice's Adventures in Wonderland and Through the Looking-Glass
Akron, OH; New York: Saalfield   John Tenniel;
                                                     Frances B. (Brundage)
The front cover is signed with the last name obscured, so known only by the first name and middle initial (Frances B.
[Brundage]). Pictorial paper-covered boards backed in beige cloth.

2442 1911 Alice's Adventures in Wonderland and Through the Looking-Glass
Boston: D. Lothrop, Lee & Shepard Co.   John Tenniel; Anonymous
World Famous Quarto Series.

2443 1911 Alice's Adventures in Wonderland and Through the Looking-Glass
New York: G. P. Putnam   John Tenniel

2444 [1912] Alice's Adventures in Wonderland and Through the Looking-Glass
Philadelphia: George W. Jacobs & Co.   John Tenniel; Elenore Abbott
Washington Square Classics. Yellowish-tan cloth. 7 color plates by Abbott.

2445 ca. 1912 Alice's Adventures in Wonderland and Through the Looking-Glass
Philadelphia: David McKay   Anonymous
                                                     (after Tenniel); Ada L. Bowley
McKay's Colored Classics. 10 full-color plates by Ada L. Bowley. Yellow cloth.

2446 ca. 1912 Alice's Adventures in Wonderland and Through the Looking-Glass
New York: McLoughlin Brothers   Anonymous (after Tenniel)
Date based on *WMGC*. Beige cloth.

2447 ca. 1912–1914 Alice's Adventures in Wonderland and Through the Looking-Glass
Philadelphia: George W. Jacobs   John Tenniel; Elenore Abbott
Washington Square Classics. Gift edition.

2448   ca. 1912–1925 Alice's Adventures in Wonderland and Through the Looking-Glass
Philadelphia: George W. Jacobs   John Tenniel; Elenore Abbott
Washington Square Classics. Regular edition.

2449   [1913]   Alice's Adventures in Wonderland and Through the Looking-Glass
New York: Doubleday, Doran & Co.   George Soper

2450   [1913]   Alice's Adventures in Wonderland and Through the Looking-Glass
New York: Hurst   John Tenniel; Anonymous
Best Value Books.   (after Tenniel)

2451   ca. 1913 Alice's Adventures in Wonderland and Through the Looking-Glass
New York: A. L. Burt   John Tenniel
Our Girl's Series. Dated by *PTLA*.

2452   ca. 1913 Alice's Adventures in Wonderland and Through the Looking-Glass
New York: D. Lothrop, Lee & Shepard Co.   John Tenniel; Anonymous

2453   [1916]   Alice's Adventures in Wonderland and Through the Looking-Glass
New York: Grosset & Dunlap   Nonpareil Film
Illustrated with scenes from the 1915 Nonpareil Feature Film. Color frontispiece and 32 black-and-white plates. Beige cloth. There is a later issue with 7 plates. Date from a copy inscribed "April 20th 1916."

2454   ca. 1916 Alice's Adventures in Wonderland and Through the Looking-Glass
Philadelphia: Henry Altemus   John Tenniel
Altemus' New Books and New Editions Series.

2455   ca. 1916 Alice's Adventures in Wonderland and Through the Looking-Glass
Chicago; New York: Rand McNally   Milo Winter
Windermere Series. 12 color plates and 6 black-and-white. Blue cloth.

2456   1917   Alice's Adventures in Wonderland and Through the Looking-Glass
Newark, NJ: Charles E. Graham   John Tenniel; Anonymous
                                                     (after Tenniel)

New edition in 1 volume. Greenish-gray cloth printed in dark green and orange. 4 color plates including frontispiece. 41 Tenniel illustrations for *Alice* and 42 for *Looking-Glass*. The illustration of *Alice* and chess pieces also appears in Lovett 208. Title of the book is *Alice*, but it includes *Looking-Glass*, each with its own half title. Verso of title page says, "Copyright 1898 by Lothrop Publishing Company."

2457   1917   Alice's Adventures in Wonderland and Through the Looking-Glass
New York: Grosset & Dunlap   John Tenniel
Pictorial dust jacket. Brown cloth.

2458   [1917]   Alice's Adventures in Wonderland and Through the Looking-Glass
Newark, NJ; New York: Charles E. Graham   John Tenniel
Brownish-orange cloth.

2459   ca. 1919 Alice's Adventures in Wonderland and Through the Looking-Glass
New York: McLoughlin Brothers   Anonymous (after Tenniel)
Beige cloth. Lovett believes this edition could be as early as 1912, but an inscription date of 1919 was found in a variant edition.

2460   ca. 1920 Alice's Adventures in Wonderland and Through the Looking-Glass
Newark, NJ; New York: Charles E. Graham   John Tenniel; Anonymous
Junior Classic Series. Black cloth.

2461 ca. 1920s   Alice's Adventures in Wonderland and Through the Looking-Glass
Chicago: M. A. Donohue and Company   John Tenniel

2462 ca. 1920s   Alice's Adventures in Wonderland and Through the Looking-Glass
New York: Modern Library   John Tenniel
A later printing of the ca. 1925–1929 Modern Library edition. Title reads Number 79 in the Modern Library.

2463 ca. 1920s   Alice's Adventures in Wonderland, Through the Looking-Glass and
               The Hunting of the Snark
New York: The Modern Library   John Tenniel
Introduction by Alexander Woollcott.

2464 [1921]   Alice's Adventures in Wonderland and Through the Looking-Glass
Chicago: M. A. Donohue and Company   John Tenniel

2465 1923   Alice's Adventures in Wonderland and Through the Looking-Glass
New York: A. L. Burt   John Tenniel
2 volumes in 1, each with a separate title page.

2466 1923   Alice in Wonderland: Comprising the two books / Alice's Adventures in Wonderland
               and Through the Looking-Glass
New York: Holt, Rinehart and Winston   John Tenniel; Donald E. Cooke
10 color plates by Donald E. Cooke. Later reprints.

2467 1923   Alice's Adventures in Wonderland and Through the Looking-Glass
Chicago; Philadelphia; Toronto, ON: John C. Winston Co.   John Tenniel; Edwin J. Prittie
4 color plates by Prittie. Blue cloth with onlay.

2468 ca. 1923 Alice's Adventures in Wonderland and Through the Looking-Glass
New York: J. H. Sears & Co.   Unillustrated
Red cloth.

2469 1924   Alice's Adventures in Wonderland and Through the Looking-Glass
New York: Boni and Liveright   John Tenniel
Introduction by Alexander Woollcott. Modern Library edition. Includes *The Hunting of the Snark*. Limited edition of
300 copies. Dark green imitation leather.

2470 1924   Alice's Adventures in Wonderland, Through the Looking-Glass and The Hunting of
               the Snark
Philadelphia: George W. Jacobs   John Tenniel; Elenore Abbott
Washington Square Classics. Yellowish tan cloth. Color pictorial plate; 92 Tenniel illustrations.

2471 ca. 1924 Alice's Adventures in Wonderland and Through the Looking-Glass
Chicago; Philadelphia; Toronto, ON: John C. Winston Co.   John Tenniel; Edwin J. Prittie
Winston Clear-Type Popular Classics. 4 color plates by Prittie. Pictorial blue cloth.

2472 ca. 1924–1940 Alice's Adventures in Wonderland, Through the Looking-Glass and The
               Hunting of the Snark
Garden City, NY: Blue Ribbon Books   John Tenniel
Blue Ribbon Specials. An imprint of Doubleday.

2473   [After 1924]   Alice's Adventures in Wonderland, Through the Looking-Glass and Snark
New York: Blue Ribbon Books   John Tenniel
A Burt Book. Famous Books for Young Americans Series. The text for this edition is from a 1924 Modern Library edition.

2474   [After 1924]   Alice's Adventures in Wonderland and Through the Looking-Glass
New York: Walter J. Black   John Tenniel
Dark red cloth.

2475   1925   Alice's Adventures in Wonderland and Through the Looking-Glass
New York: Boni and Liveright   John Tenniel
Introduction by Alexander Woollcott. Modern Library edition. Includes *The Hunting of the Snark*. Dark green imitation leather.

2476   1925   Alice's Adventures in Wonderland and Through the Looking-Glass
Chicago; Philadelphia; Toronto, ON: John C. Winston Co.   John Tenniel; Edwin J. Prittie
As in the 1923 edition. Blue cloth.

2477   ca. 1925 Alice's Adventures in Wonderland and Through the Looking-Glass
Philadelphia: Macrae Smith Publishing Company   Elenore Abbott; John Tenniel
Franklin Classics. 1 color plate by Abbott.

2478   ca. 1926 Alice's Adventures in Wonderland and Through the Looking-Glass
New York: J. H. Sears & Co.   Gertrude Welling
Sears Illustrated Juveniles series. Purple cloth.

2479   1929   Alice's Adventures in Wonderland, Through the Looking-Glass
        and Other Comic Pieces
New York: E. P. Dutton. London; Toronto, ON: J. M. Dent   Lewis Carroll
Everyman's Library for Young People, No. 836. Includes *Phantasmagoria*, *Snark*, and *A Tangled Tale*. Verso of the title page states: "First published in this edition in 1929." Introduction by Ernest Rhys. Orange and black dust jacket. Blue cloth.

2480   ca. 1929 Alice's Adventures in Wonderland and Through the Looking-Glass
Philadelphia: Henry Altemus   After John Tenniel
Wee Folks Edition. 31 color illustrations after Tenniel.

2481   ca. 1929 Alice's Adventures in Wonderland and Through the Looking-Glass
New York: J. H. Sears & Co.   Anonymous
Cream cloth illustrated in red and black.

2482   ca. 1929 Alice's Adventures in Wonderland and Through the Looking-Glass
Philadelphia: Macrae Smith Publishing Company   John Tenniel
Washington Square Classics.

2483   1930   Alice's Adventures in Wonderland and Through the Looking-Glass
Chicago: Albert Whitman   After John Tenniel
Albert Whitman's Illustrated $1.00 Classics Series. At least 2 issues. Dust jacket. Very dark green cloth; front with cream paste-on of Alice and Humpty in orange, lettering in dark blue and orange. Black-and-white illustrations.

2484   1930   Alice's Adventures in Wonderland and Through the Looking-Glass
New York: E. P. Dutton. London; Toronto, ON: J. M. Dent   Lewis Carroll
Everyman's Library. Blue cloth.

2485 ca. 1930 Alice's Adventures in Wonderland and Through the Looking-Glass
New York: Arden Book Co. John Tenniel
Arden Library.

2486 ca. 1930 Alice's Adventures in Wonderland and Through the Looking-Glass
Philadelphia: Henry Altemus John Tenniel

2487 ca. 1930 Alice's Adventures in Wonderland and Through the Looking-Glass
New York: Modern Library John Tenniel
A later printing of the ca. 1925–1929 Modern Library edition. Reddish-brown cloth.

2488 ca. 1930 Alice's Adventures in Wonderland, Through the Looking-Glass and The Hunting of
the Snark
New York: Boni and Liveright John Tenniel
Modern Library edition. Introduction by Alexander Woollcott. Reddish brown cloth.

2489 ca. 1930s A Lewis Carroll Omnibus
New York: Carlton House John Tenniel; Others
A Carlton House Book. Includes *The Hunting of the Snark*.

2490 ca. 1930s Alice's Adventures in Wonderland and Through the Looking-Glass
New York: Deluxe Editions John Tenniel; Anonymous
(after Tenniel)
No series title. *Alice* illustrations by Anonymous and *Looking-Glass* illustrated by Tenniel.

2491 ca. 1930s Alice's Adventures in Wonderland and Through the Looking-Glass
New York: Deluxe Editions John Tenniel; Anonymous
Old Ivory Library of Beloved Books. *Alice* illustrations by Anonymous and *Looking-Glass* illustrated by Tenniel.

2492 ca. 1930s Alice's Adventures in Wonderland and Through the Looking-Glass
New York: Tarry at the Taft Unillustrated; Anonymous
Orange cloth. Illustration of the Hotel Taft and "Compliments of Hotel Taft New York" on the front cover. Cover
illustration by Anonymous.

2493 [After 1930] Alice's Adventures in Wonderland and Through the Looking-Glass
Chicago: Albert Whitman After John Tenniel
Albert Whitman's Illustrated $1.00 Classics Series. Dust jacket with Alice and Humpty Dumpty printed in red and
green. Red cloth.

2494 [After 1930] Alice's Adventures in Wonderland and Through the Looking-Glass
New York: Deluxe Editions John Tenniel; Anonymous
Alice illustrations by Anonymous and *Looking-Glass* illustrated by Tenniel.

2495 1931 The Lewis Carroll Book
New York: Dial Press Anonymous (after Tenniel)
1st printing, October 1931. 2nd printing, December 1931. Reprinted 5 more times. An anthology including both *Alice*
and *Looking-Glass*.

2496 [1931] Alice's Adventures in Wonderland and Through the Looking-Glass
New York: Illustrated Editions Company John Tenniel
Old English Style headings at the top of each page. Reprinted numerous times and by different publishers.

2497   ca. 1931 Alice's Adventures in Wonderland and Through the Looking-Glass
New York: Deluxe Editions   John Tenniel; Anonymous
                                                                             (after Tenniel)

Palace Edition. *Alice* illustrations by Anonymous and *Looking-Glass* illustrated by Tenniel.

2498   ca. 1931 Alice's Adventures in Wonderland and Through the Looking-Glass
New York: G. P. Putnam   Charles Kirtland Stevens
Favorite Stories for Boys and Girls.

2499   1932   Alice's Adventures in Wonderland and Through the Looking-Glass
Chicago; New York: Rand McNally   Milo Winter
As in the 1916 edition, but with 8 color plates.

2500   ca. 1932 Alice's Adventures in Wonderland and Through the Looking-Glass
Washington, D.C.: National Home Library Foundation   John Tenniel
Jacket Library. Introduction by Mrs. Franklin D. Roosevelt.

2501   ca. 1932 Alice's Adventures in Wonderland and Through the Looking-Glass
New York: P. W. Wolson / Liveright Publishers   John Tenniel
The Black and Gold Library.

2502   ca. 1933 Alice's Adventures in Wonderland and Through the Looking-Glass
New York: Grosset & Dunlap   Paramount Pictures
Blue cloth. 16 plates. Illustrated with pictures from the Paramount film of 1933.

2503   1934   The Lewis Carroll Book
New York: Dial Press   Anonymous (after Tenniel)
4th printing. An anthology including both *Alice* and *Looking-Glass*.

2504   1934   Alice's Adventures in Wonderland and Through the Looking-Glass
New York: E. P. Dutton. London; Toronto, ON: J. M. Dent   Lewis Carroll
3rd printing. Everyman's Library, No. 836. Introduction by Ernest Rhys. Orange and black dust jacket. Blue cloth.

2505   [1934]   Alice's Adventures in Wonderland, Through the Looking-Glass and Snark
New York: Blue Ribbon Books   John Tenniel
Later published by Carlton House, ca. 1940s–1950s.

2506   ca. 1934 Alice's Adventures in Wonderland and Through the Looking-Glass
New York: A. L. Burt   John Tenniel; J. Watson Davis
Famous Books for Young Americans. Dated by *PTLA*. Could be ca. 1932.

2507   ca. 1934 Alice's Adventures in Wonderland and Through the Looking-Glass
New York: Blue Ribbon Books   John Tenniel
The text of a Modern Library edition. Blue cloth.

2508   ca. 1934 Logical Nonsense
New York: G. P. Putnam's Sons   Unillustrated
Contains *Alice*, *Looking-Glass*, and other Carroll books. Dark green cloth.

2509   ca. 1934 Alice's Adventures in Wonderland and Through the Looking-Glass
New York: Grosset & Dunlap   Paramount Photoplay
Blue cloth. Illustrations from Paramount Photoplay.

2510   ca. 1934 Alice's Adventures in Wonderland and Through the Looking-Glass
Cleveland, OH; New York: World Syndicate Publishing Co.   Anonymous (after Tenniel)
Children's Classics.

2511   ca. 1935 Alice's Adventures in Wonderland and Through the Looking-Glass
Cleveland, OH: Goldsmith Publishing Co.   Unillustrated
Olive cloth stamped in black.

2512   ca. 1935 Alice's Adventures in Wonderland and Through the Looking-Glass
Cleveland, OH; New York: World Syndicate Publishing Co.   Anonymous
Olive cloth.

2513   1936   The Lewis Carroll Book
New York: Dial Press   Anonymous (after Tenniel)
6th printing. An anthology including both *Alice* and *Looking-Glass*.

2514   1936   The Complete Works of Lewis Carroll
New York: Modern Library   John Tenniel
Number G28 in the Modern Library Giant series. Introduction by Alexander Woollcott. Dark red cloth. Two undated
later printings are known.

2515   1936   Alice's Adventures in Wonderland and Through the Looking-Glass
Chicago; New York: Rand McNally   Milo Winter
Identical to the 1932 edition. Darker blue cover.

2516   [1936]   Alice's Adventures in Wonderland and Through the Looking-Glass
New York: Three Sirens Press   John Tenniel
Plaza Edition. Old English Style headings at the top of each page. A reprint of the 1931 Illustrated Editions Company edition.

2517   ca. 1936 Alice's Adventures in Wonderland and Through the Looking-Glass
New York: Deluxe Editions   John Tenniel; Anonymous
                                                                                       (after Tenniel)

Plaza Edition. *Alice* illustrations by Anonymous and *Looking-Glass* illustrated by Tenniel.

2518   1937   Alice's Adventures in Wonderland and Through the Looking-Glass
New York: Platt and Munk   Anonymous (after Tenniel);
                                                                                       Ninon MacKnight

62 color illustrations after John Tenniel. 2 color plates (each used as a frontispiece) by Ninon MacKnight. Green
paper or cloth-covered boards.

2519   1937   The Complete Works of Lewis Carroll
New York: Random House   John Tenniel
Number G28 in the Modern Library Giant series. Introduction by Alexander Woollcott. Blue cloth. Undated later
printings known.

2520   ca. 1937 Alice's Adventures in Wonderland and Through the Looking-Glass
Chicago; New York: M. A. Donohue and Company   John Tenniel; Anonymous
Golden Days Series. 1 copy has an inscription dated 1937. Dust jacket has unattributed illustration by C. Burd. Color
frontispiece by Anonymous. In light green or red cloth.

2521   1939   The Complete Works of Lewis Carroll
New York: Random House   John Tenniel
1st edition published November 1939. Later published in 1939 in a smaller type size and with 1,165 pp. as in this copy.
A copy inscribed by Warren Weaver and containing a review by Evelyn Waugh from *The Spectator* of October 13,
1939, is known.

2522 ca. late 1930s Alice's Adventures in Wonderland and Through the Looking-Glass
New York: Grosset & Dunlap   John Tenniel
Reprint of the 1917 edition. Pictorial dust jacket. Blue cloth. Sewell believes this was in the Famous Stories for Young People Series.

2523 ca. 1940 Alice's Adventures in Wonderland
New York: Books, Inc.   John Tenniel
The title page only lists *Alice*, but it is a combined edition with *Looking-Glass*. Blue paper-covered boards. Undated variant editions exist.

2524 ca. 1940 Alice's Adventures in Wonderland and Through the Looking-Glass
New York: Illustrated Editions Company   John Tenniel
Old English Style headings at the top of each page. A reprint of the 1936 Illustrated Editions Company edition. Blue cloth.

2525 ca. 1940 Alice's Adventures in Wonderland and Through the Looking-Glass
Philadelphia: J. B. Lippincott   John Tenniel; Gertrude A. Kay
Lippincott Juniors. 8 color plates. Red cloth.

2526 ca. 1940 Alice's Adventures in Wonderland and Through the Looking-Glass
Philadelphia: John C. Winston Co.   John Tenniel; Edwin J. Prittie
Winston Clear-Type Popular Classics.

2527 ca. 1940 Alice's Adventures in Wonderland and Through the Looking-Glass
Racine, WI: Whitman Publishing Company   Unknown
Whitman Home Library.

2528 ca. 1940s   Alice's Adventures in Wonderland, Through the Looking-Glass and Snark
New York: Carlton House   John Tenniel
World's Great Literature. Reprint of the 1934 Blue Ribbon Books edition.

2529 ca. 1940s   Alice's Adventures in Wonderland, Through the Looking-Glass and
                        The Hunting of the Snark
New York: Carlton House   John Tenniel
First published in 1934 by Blue Ribbon Books. A variant edition exists.

2530 ca. 1940s   Alice's Adventures in Wonderland and Through the Looking-Glass
Chicago: Goldsmith Publishing Co.   After John Tenniel
Brown or purple cloth. An undated variant from the Boys and Girls Books series exists.

2531 ca. 1940s   Alice's Adventures in Wonderland and Through the Looking-Glass
New York: Windsor Press   John Tenniel

2532 1941   Alice's Adventures in Wonderland and Through the Looking-Glass
New York: Heritage Press   John Tenniel
Heritage Illustrated Bookshelf series. Yellow cloth in blue slipcase. An undated later edition in glossy yellow cloth is known.

2533 1943   Alice's Adventures in Wonderland and Through the Looking-Glass
New York; London: G. P. Putnam's Sons   John Tenniel
Facsimile of the 1865 first *Alice* edition. Red cloth.

2534 ca. 1943 Alice's Adventures in Wonderland and Through the Looking-Glass
Cleveland, OH; New York: World Publishing Co.   Anonymous (after Tenniel);
                                                                               Corydon
World Juvenile Library series. Color frontispiece signed "Corydon." Light blue cloth.

2535 1944 Alice's Adventures in Wonderland and Through the Looking-Glass
New York: International Readers League   John Tenniel; A. L. Bowley
Color frontispiece by Bowley.

2536 1944 The Lewis Carroll Book
New York: Tudor Publishing   Anonymous (after Tenniel)
An anthology including both *Alice* and *Looking-Glass*. A version of the Dial Press edition of 1934.

2537 1945 Alice's Adventures in Wonderland and Through the Looking-Glass
Racine, WI: Whitman Publishing Company   Linda Card
Classic Series. Tan paper-covered boards. With additional binding variants in green and one in brown. Many dust jacket variants.

2538 [1945] Alice's Adventures in Wonderland and Through the Looking-Glass
New York; London: Whittlesey House; McGraw-Hill   John Tenniel
The Heritage Illustrated Bookshelf series. Beige cloth or gray boards. A copy of the 2nd printing is known.

2539 ca. 1945 Alice's Adventures in Wonderland and Through the Looking-Glass
New York: Heritage Press   John Tenniel
The Heritage Illustrated Bookshelf series.

2540 ca. 1945 Alice's Adventures in Wonderland and Through the Looking-Glass
New York: Heritage Press   John Tenniel
The Heritage Reprints.

2541 1946 Alice's Adventures in Wonderland and Through the Looking-Glass
New York: E. P. Dutton. London; Toronto, ON: J. M. Dent   Lewis Carroll
Later printing. Everyman's Library, No. 836. Includes *Alice*, *Looking-Glass*, *Phantasmagoria*, *Snark*, and *A Tangled Tale*. Verso of the title page states "Last reprinted in 1946," but there are later reprintings. Introduction by Ernest Rhys. Orange and black dust jacket. Blue cloth.

2542 1946 Alice's Adventures in Wonderland and Through the Looking-Glass
New York: Grosset & Dunlap   John Tenniel
Illustrated Junior Library edition. Deluxe Edition. Beige cloth.

2543 1946 Alice's Adventures in Wonderland and Through the Looking-Glass
New York: Grosset & Dunlap   John Tenniel
Illustrated Junior Library edition. Popular Edition. Light tan cloth.

2544 [1946] Alice's Adventures in Wonderland and Through the Looking-Glass
Cleveland, OH; New York: World Publishing Co.   Anonymous (after Tenniel)
Rainbow Classics series. Introduction by May Lamberton Becker. Pictorial cloth.

2545 ca. 1946 Alice's Adventures in Wonderland, Through the Looking-Glass
          and The Hunting of the Snark
New York: The Modern Library   John Tenniel
Introduction by Alexander Woollcott. Medium blue cloth. Later printings known in dark blue cloth and dust jacket.

2546 ca. 1946 Alice's Adventures in Wonderland and Through the Looking-Glass
New York: Modern Library   John Tenniel
A later printing of the 1924 Boni and Liveright edition. Medium-blue cloth. Several later printings.

2547 1949 Alice's Adventures in Wonderland and Through the Looking-Glass

New York; London: Harper and Brothers   Leonard Weisgard
Paper-covered boards backed in light green cloth.

2548   1949   The Complete Works of Lewis Carroll
New York: Nonesuch Press   John Tenniel
The 1st edition was published in November 1939.

2549   ca. late 1940s to early 1950s Alice's Adventures in Wonderland, Through the Looking-Glass
                and The Hunting of the Snark
New York: Crown Press   John Tenniel

A later printing of the 1924 Boni and Liveright edition. Greenish-tan cloth. This edition was reprinted many times
with the Avenel Books imprint.

2550   1950   Alice's Adventures in Wonderland and Through the Looking-Glass
New York: Arcadia House   Anonymous
1 black-and-white illustration, only on the title page. Blue paper-covered boards backed by blue cloth.

2551   [1950]   Alice's Adventures in Wonderland and Through the Looking-Glass
Garden City, NY: Blue Ribbon Books   John Tenniel
Halcyon House Illustrated Library.

2552   ca. 1950 Alice's Adventures in Wonderland and Through the Looking-Glass
New York: Beaverbrook Newspapers   Patricia Morriss
Presentation Library. 8 color plates. Green cloth.

2553   ca. 1950s Alice's Adventures in Wonderland and Through the Looking-Glass
New York: Books, Inc.   John Tenniel; Jim Jones
Giant Junior Classics. Cover illustration by Jim Jones. A later printing is known.

2554   ca. 1950s Alice's Adventures in Wonderland and Through the Looking-Glass
New York: Grosset & Dunlap   John Tenniel
Companion Library Series. Later printing of the 1917 edition. Pictorial dust jacket. Blue paper-covered boards.

2555   ca. 1950s–1960s Alice's Adventures in Wonderland and Through the Looking-Glass
New York: Carlton House   John Tenniel
A later printing of the 1924 Boni and Liveright edition. Black cloth.

2556   1951   Alice in Wonderland and Other Favorites
New York: Pocket Books   John Tenniel; Others
Pocket Book edition published in July 1951. 2nd printing, August 1951. Pictorial wrappers.

2557   1951   Alice's Adventures in Wonderland and Through the Looking-Glass
New York: Pocket Books   John Tenniel
Pocket Book, No. 835.

2558   1951   Alice in Wonderland and Other Favorites
New York: Simon and Schuster   John Tenniel
Classic Pocket Book. Contains other Carroll works, as well as *Alice* and *Looking-Glass*.

2559   1951   Alice in Wonderland and Other Favorites
New York: Washington Square Press   John Tenniel; Henry Holiday
An edited version of the Pocket Book edition published in August 1951. Pictorial wrappers. Includes *Looking-Glass*
and *Snark*. Later reprints.

2560   ca. 1951   Alice's Adventures in Wonderland and Through the Looking-Glass
New York: D. Lothrop, Lee & Shepard Co.   Unknown

2561   1952   Alice's Adventures in Wonderland and Through the Looking-Glass
New York: E. P. Dutton. London; Toronto, ON: J. M. Dent   Lewis Carroll
Everyman's Library. Dust jacket. Verso of title page reads "Last reprinted in 1952," but there were later reprintings.

2562   1952   Alice's Adventures in Wonderland and Through the Looking-Glass
Philadelphia; Toronto, ON: John C. Winston Co.   John Tenniel

2563   1954   Alice's Adventures in Wonderland and Through the Looking-Glass
New York: E. P. Dutton; London: J. M. Dent   John Tenniel; Diana Stanley
Children's Illustrated Classics Series. 8 color plates after John Tenniel by Diana Stanley.

2564   1954   Alice's Adventures in Wonderland and Through the Looking-Glass
New York; Chicago; San Francisco: Rand McNally   Milo Winter
Paperback.

2565   1955   Alice's Adventures in Wonderland and Through the Looking-Glass
Racine, WI: Whitman Publishing Company   Roberta Paflin
Whitman Famous Classics. Pictorial paper-covered boards. A number of later variants exist.

2566   ca. 1956   Alice's Adventures in Wonderland and Through the Looking-Glass
New York: Chanticleer Press   Philip Gough
The Heirloom Library. 8 color plates.

2567   ca. 1956   Alice's Adventures in Wonderland and Through the Looking-Glass
New York: William Collins Sons   Dorothy Colles (after Tenniel)
In Masterpiece Binding or Leather Classics.

2568   1957   Alice's Adventures in Wonderland and Through the Looking-Glass
New York: Grosset & Dunlap   John Tenniel
Companion Library edition. Pictorial cloth. *Looking-Glass* also has an undated later printing.

2569   1957   Alice in Wonderland: Comprising the two books /
                    Alice's Adventures in Wonderland and Through the Looking-Glass
New York: Holt, Rinehart and Winston   John Tenniel; Donald E. Cooke
4 color plates by Donald E. Cooke. Reprint of the 1923 edition.

2570   1957   Alice's Adventures in Wonderland and Through the Looking-Glass
Philadelphia; Toronto, ON: John C. Winston Co.   John Tenniel
Dark red paper-covered boards.

2571   1960   Alice's Adventures in Wonderland and Through the Looking-Glass
New York: New American Library of World Literature   John Tenniel
A Signet Classic edition. 1st printing May 1960. Foreword by Horace Gregory. Later reprints.

2572   1960   Alice's Adventures in Wonderland and Through the Looking-Glass
New York: New American Library of World Literature   John Tenniel
A Signet Classic edition. 2nd printing of the May 1960 edition.

2573   1960   Lewis Carroll's Alice in Wonderland and Other Favorites
New York: Washington Square Press   John Tenniel
Reprint of the 1951 edition. Includes *Looking-Glass* and *Snark*.

2574   ca. 1960 Alice's Adventures in Wonderland and Through the Looking-Glass
New York: Hartsdale House   John Tenniel
Puffin Story Books. In 1975, Puffin Books editions were priced in UK and US currency so must have been published in America as well. Later reprints.

2575   ca. 1960s   Alice's Adventures in Wonderland and Through the Looking-Glass
New York: Black's Readers Service Company   John Tenniel
A later printing of the 1924 Boni and Liveright edition. Red or dark blue cloth.

2576   ca. 1960s   Alice's Adventures in Wonderland and Through the Looking-Glass
New York: Modern Library   John Tenniel
A later printing of the 1924 Boni and Liveright edition. Dark blue cloth.

2577   1961   The Complete Works of Lewis Carroll
Chester Springs, PA: Dufour   John Tenniel
Reissue of a 1939 edition. Introduction by Alexander Woollcott.

2578   1961   Alice's Adventures in Wonderland and Through the Looking-Glass
New York: E. P. Dutton. London: J. M. Dent   John Tenniel; Diana Stanley
1st reprint. Children's Illustrated Classics Series. First published in 1954. 8 color plates after John Tenniel by Diana Stanley. Later reprints.

2579   1961   Alice in Wonderland: Comprising the two books Alice's Adventures in Wonderland
       and Through the Looking-Glass
New York: Holt, Rinehart and Winston   John Tenniel; Donald E. Cooke
10 color plates by Donald E. Cooke. Reprint of a 1923 edition.

2580   ca. 1961 Alice's Adventures in Wonderland and Through the Looking-Glass
New York: Holt, Rinehart and Winston   John Tenniel; Donald E. Cooke
Great Books for Children Edition. Blue cloth.

2581   1962   Alice's Adventures in Wonderland and Through the Looking-Glass
New York: Collier. London: Collier-Macmillan   John Tenniel
Introduction by Louis Untermeyer. Later reprints.

2582   1962   Alice's Adventures in Wonderland and Through the Looking-Glass
New York: New American Library of World Literature   John Tenniel
A Signet Classic Edition.

2583   1962   Alice's Adventures in Wonderland and Through the Looking-Glass
New York: New American Library of World Literature   John Tenniel
Reprint of the 1960 edition. A Signet Classic edition. 3rd edition. Foreword by Horace Gregory.

2584   1962   Alice's Adventures in Wonderland and Through the Looking-Glass
Baltimore, MD: Penguin   John Tenniel

2585   [1962] Alice's Adventures in Wonderland and Through the Looking-Glass
New York: Collier   John Tenniel

2586   1963   Lewis Carroll's Alice in Wonderland and Other Favorites
New York: Washington Square Press   John Tenniel; Henry Holiday
Reprint of the 1951 edition. Includes *Looking-Glass* and *Snark*.

2587   ca. 1963 Alice's Adventures in Wonderland and Through the Looking-Glass
New York: Grosset & Dunlap   John Tenniel
Bound back-to-back with *Five Little Peppers*.

2588   1964   Alice's Adventures in Wonderland and Through the Looking-Glass
New York: Frederick Watts   John Tenniel
Reprinted in 1966.

2589   1964   Alice's Adventures in Wonderland and Through the Looking-Glass
New York: New American Library of World Literature   John Tenniel
Reprint of the 1960 edition. A Signet Classic edition. Foreword by Horace Gregory.

2590   1964   Alice's Adventures in Wonderland and Through the Looking-Glass
New York: Parents' Magazine Press   John Tenniel

2591   [1964] Alice's Adventures in Wonderland and Through the Looking-Glass
New York: Parents' Magazine Press   John Tenniel

2592   1965   Alice's Adventures in Wonderland and Through the Looking-Glass
New York: Airmont   John Tenniel
Airmont Classics Series, C179. Introduction by C. L. Bennet.

2593   1965   Alice in Wonderland and Other Favorites
New York: Washington Square Press   John Tenniel; Henry Holiday
An edited version of the Pocket Book edition published in August 1951. Pictorial wrappers. Includes *Looking-Glass* and *Snark*. Later reprints.

2594   1965   Lewis Carroll's Alice in Wonderland and Other Favorites
New York: Washington Square Press   John Tenniel; Henry Holiday
Reprint of the 1951 edition. Includes *Looking-Glass* and *Snark*.

2595   1966   Alice's Adventures in Wonderland and Through the Looking-Glass
New York: Collier. London: Collier-Macmillan   John Tenniel
Reprint of the 1962 edition. Introduction by Louis Untermeyer.

2596   1966   Alice's Adventures in Wonderland and Through the Looking-Glass
New York: E. P. Dutton. London: J. M. Dent   John Tenniel; Diana Stanley
Reprint of 1961 edition. Children's Illustrated Classics Series. 8 color plates after John Tenniel by Diana Stanley.

2597   1966   Alice's Adventures in Wonderland and Through the Looking-Glass
New York: Frederick Watts   John Tenniel

2598   1966   Alice's Adventures in Wonderland and Through the Looking-Glass
Ann Arbor, MI: University Microfilms   John Tenniel
Legacy Library. Facsimile of the 1886 Macmillan edition.

2599   1968   Alice's Adventures in Wonderland and Through the Looking-Glass
Rutland, VT: Charles E. Tuttle Company   Peter Newell;
                                                              Robert Murray Wright
1st Tuttle edition. Pictorial dust jacket and slipcase. Green cloth. Combined volume of editions originally published by Harper & Brothers in New York in 1901 and 1902, respectively. Text pages have decorated borders by Wright. 80 full-page black-and-white plates by Newell. Only one copy located.

2600   1968   Alice's Adventures in Wonderland and Through the Looking-Glass
New York: Lancer Books   John Tenniel
1st Lancer edition. Magnum Easy Eye Books. Later reprints.

2601   1968   Alice's Adventures in Wonderland and Through the Looking-Glass
New York: Magnum Books   John Tenniel
Magnum Easy Eye Books. Same as the Lancer edition of this date.

2602   1968   Alice's Adventures in Wonderland and Through the Looking-Glass
Rutland, VT; Hemel Hempstead, UK: Tuttle Prentice Hall   0804800057; 9780804800051   Peter Newell
529 pp. Only 2 copies located.

2603   [1969]   Alice's Adventures in Wonderland and Through the Looking-Glass
Chicago: Childrens Press   Brigitte Bryan

2604   ca. 1969   Alice's Adventures in Wonderland and Through the Looking-Glass
San Rafael, CA: Classic Publishing   Brigitte Bryan; Don Irwin

2605   1970   Alice's Adventures in Wonderland and Through the Looking-Glass
San Rafael, CA: Classic Publishing   Brigitte Bryan; Don Irwin

2606   1970   Alice's Adventures in Wonderland and Through the Looking-Glass
Racine, WI: Whitman Publishing Company   9780307216168   Ted Schroeder
Whitman Classics. Green-and-white illustrations. Variant editions exist.

2607   1971   Alice in Wonderland: Authoritative Texts of Alice's Adventures in Wonderland,
Through the Looking-Glass, The Hunting of the Snark. Backgrounds / Essays in Criticism
New York: Norton   9780393043433; 9780393099775   Various
1st Norton Critical Edition. Donald Grey, editor. 434 pp. For extensive details on this book, see Guiliano, pp. 57–58.
Hardcover and paperback.

2608   1971   Lewis Carroll's Alice in Wonderland and Other Favorites
New York: Washington Square Press   9780671466268   John Tenniel; Henry Holiday
Reprint of the 1951 edition. Includes *Looking-Glass* and *Snark*.

2609   1972   Alice's Adventures in Wonderland and Through the Looking-Glass
New York: E. P. Dutton. London: J. M. Dent   John Tenniel; Diana Stanley
Reprint of 1961 edition. Children's Illustrated Classics Series. 8 color plates after John Tenniel by Diana Stanley.

2610   1972   Alice's Adventures in Wonderland and Through the Looking-Glass
New York: Lancer Books   John Tenniel
Reprint of the 1968 edition. Magnum Easy Eye Books.

2611   1974   The Philosopher's Alice: Alice's Adventures in Wonderland
               & Through the Looking-Glass
New York: St. Martin's. London: Academy   0856701262; 9780312605186   John Tenniel
Introduction and annotations by Peter Heath from a philosophical perspective. Dust jacket.

2612   [1974]   Alice's Adventures in Wonderland and Through the Looking-Glass
Cleveland, OH; New York: World Publishing Co.   Anonymous (after Tenniel)
Later printing of the [1946] Rainbow Classics edition. Introduction by May Lamberton Becker. Pictorial cloth.

2613   1975   Alice's Adventures in Wonderland and Through the Looking-Glass
New York: Collier; London: Collier-Macmillan   9780020423508   John Tenniel
Reprint of the 1962 edition. Introduction by Louis Untermeyer.

2614   1975   Alice's Adventures in Wonderland and Through the Looking-Glass
Cleveland, OH: Collins World   9780529050311 (hardcover);   John Tenniel
                                        9780529050328 (paperback)
Later printing of the [1946] Rainbow Classics edition. Introduction by May Lamberton Becker.

2615   1975   Alice's Adventures in Wonderland and Through the Looking-Glass
New York: E. P. Dutton. London: J. M. Dent   John Tenniel; Diana Stanley
Reprint of Children's Illustrated Classics Series 1961 edition. 8 color plates after John Tenniel by Diana Stanley.

2616   1975   Alice's Adventures in Wonderland and Through the Looking-Glass
New York: Lancer Books   John Tenniel
Reprint of Magnum Easy Eye Books 1968 edition.

2617   ca. 1975 Alice's Adventures in Wonderland and Through the Looking-Glass
New York: Grosset & Dunlap   9780448060040   John Tenniel
Illustrated Junior Library edition. Deluxe Edition. New Edition. Textured paper illustrated.

2618   1976   Alice's Adventures in Wonderland and Through the Looking-Glass
New York: Hartsdale House   John Tenniel
Reprint of a Puffin Story Books ca. 1960. Puffin Books editions were priced in UK and US currency so must have
been published in America as well. Editions were published twice in 1976.

2619   1976   Alice's Adventures in Wonderland and Through the Looking-Glass
New York: Lancer Books   John Tenniel
Reprint of Magnum Easy Eye Books 1968 edition.

2620   1976   The Complete Works of Lewis Carroll
New York: Vintage   9780394716619   John Tenniel
Reissue of a 1939 edition. Introduction by Alexander Woollcott.

2621   1977   Alice's Adventures in Wonderland and Through the Looking-Glass
New York: E. P. Dutton. London: J. M. Dent   John Tenniel; Diana Stanley
Reprint of a Children's Illustrated Classics Series 1961 edition. 8 color plates after John Tenniel by Diana Stanley.

2622   1977   Alice's Adventures in Wonderland and Through the Looking-Glass
New York: Hartsdale House   John Tenniel
Reprint of a Puffin Story Books ca. 1960. Puffin Books editions were priced in UK and US currency so must have
been published in America as well.

2623   1978   Lewis Carroll, Alice in Wonderland
New York: E. P. Dutton. London; Melbourne, VIC;   9780460008365   Lewis Carroll; Others
Toronto, ON: J. M. Dent
Everyman's Library, No. 836. Later printing. Includes *Alice*, *Looking-Glass*, *Phantasmagoria*, *Snark*, and *A Tangled Tale*. Pictorial dust jacket. Blue paper-covered boards. New introduction by Roger Lancelyn Green.

2624   1978   Alice's Adventures in Wonderland and Through the Looking-Glass
New York: Hartsdale House   John Tenniel
Reprint of a Puffin Story Books ca. 1960. Puffin Books editions were priced in UK and US currency so must have
been published in America as well.

2625   1978   Alice's Adventures in Wonderland and Through the Looking-Glass
New York: Schocken Books   9780805205947   John Tenniel
Also includes *The Hunting of the Snark*.

2626　[1978]　Alice's Adventures in Wonderland, Through the Looking-Glass, Phantasmagoria
　　　　　　& Other Poems, The Hunting of the Snark, and A Tangled Tale
New York: E. P. Dutton. London; Melbourne, VIC;　9780460008365　Lewis Carroll; Others
Toronto, ON: J. M. Dent
Everyman's Library. Dust jacket. Blue paper-covered boards. Introduction by Roger Lancelyn Green.

2627　ca. 1978　The Illustrated Lewis Carroll
New York: Jupiter Books, distributed by Bookthrift　　　　　John Tenniel
Reprint edition with original imprint of London: Jupiter Books on title page, and a notation below: "This is a reprint edition distributed by Bookthrift, New York." Introduction by Roy Gasson. Green paper boards. Dust jacket. Includes *Alice* and *Looking-Glass* with illustrations by Tenniel, and *Snark* with illustrations by Henry Holiday (including the suppressed Boojum drawing). This edition also includes "The Mad Gardener's Song" (unillustrated) and "Hiawatha's Photographing," with illustrations by Arthur Burdett Frost from when the poem first was reprinted in *Phantasmagoria and Other Poems* in 1869. Black-and-white plates also appear for *Alice* (with one each by W. H. Walker, Charles Robinson, Arthur Rackham, Thomas Maybank, Millicent Sowerby, T. H. Robinson, Harry Furniss, and Mervyn Peake) and for *Looking-Glass* (with one each by Blanche McManus, Peter Newell, E. B. Thurstan, J. Morton Sale, and Mervyn Peake).

2628　1979　Alice's Adventures in Wonderland and Through the Looking-Glass
Woodbury, NY: Bobley Publishing　　　　　　　　John Tenniel
Title on cover is *Alice's Adventures in Wonderland*.

2629　1979　Journeys in Wonderland
New York: Derrydale　　　　　　　9780517301326　　　　John Tenniel
Contains *Alice's Adventures in Wonderland* and *Through the Looking-Glass*.

2630　[1979]　Alice's Adventures in Wonderland and Through the Looking-Glass
New York: Illustrated Editions　　　　9780517301326　　　　John Tenniel

2631　ca. 1979　Alice's Adventures in Wonderland and Through the Looking-Glass
New York: Modern Promotions　　　　　　　　　　Brigitte Bryan

2632　1980　Alice's Adventures in Wonderland and Through the Looking-Glass
Boston: Hall　　　　　　　　0893759937　　　　Unillustrated
Classics in Large Print.

2633　1981　Alice's Adventures in Wonderland and Through the Looking-Glass
New York: Bantam Books　　　　　0553210521　　　　John Tenniel
A Bantam Classic. Introduction by Morton N. Cohen.

2634　1981　Alice's Adventures in Wonderland and Through the Looking-Glass
New York: E. P. Dutton. London: J. M. Dent　9780460050296　　John Tenniel; Diana Stanley
Reprint of a Children's Illustrated Classics Series 1954 edition. 8 color plates after John Tenniel by Diana Stanley.

2635　1981　Alice's Adventures in Wonderland and Through the Looking-Glass
New York: Hartsdale House　　　　　　　　　　John Tenniel
Reprint of a Puffin Story Books ca. 1960. Puffin Books editions were priced in UK and US currency so must have been published in America as well. Published twice this year.

2636　1981　Alice's Adventures in Wonderland and Through the Looking-Glass
Closter, NJ: Sharon　　　　　　　9780895310590　　John Tenniel; Richard Moss

2637　1982　Alice's Adventures in Wonderland and Through the Looking-Glass
New York: Hartsdale House　　　　　　　　　　John Tenniel
Reprint of a Puffin Story Books ca. 1960. Puffin Books editions were priced in UK and US currency so must have been published in America as well.

2638   1982   The Works of Lewis Carroll: Complete and Unabridged
[New York]: Longmeadow Press   0681400358; 9780681400351 John Tenniel; Others
Edited by Edward Guiliano. Includes *Alice* and *Looking-Glass*. Copyright by Crown Publishers, Inc. This edition
published exclusively for Longmeadow Press by Avenel Books, Inc. Designed by Brian Mallow. Bound in green
leather with gold lettering on spine and cover, and decorative border on cover.

2639   1982   Alice's Adventures in Wonderland and Through the Looking-Glass
New York: Modern Promotions   John Cooper

2640   ca. 1982 Lewis Carroll: The Complete, Fully Illustrated Works
Avenel, NJ: Gramercy Books   9780307290373   John Tenniel
Alice's Adventures in Wonderland, *Through the Looking-Glass*, and other Carroll works.

2641   ca. 1982 Alice's Adventures in Wonderland and Through the Looking-Glass
New York: Julian Messner / Simon and Schuster   0671456490   John Speirs

2642   1983   The Philosopher's Alice: Alice's Adventures in Wonderland
                & Through the Looking-Glass
New York: St. Martin's   0312605188; 9780312605186 John Tenniel
Introduction and annotations by Peter Heath. Annotated from a philosophical perspective. Paperback edition.

2643   1983   Alice's Adventures in Wonderland and Through the Looking-Glass
Mahwah, NJ: Watermill Press   0893759937   John Tenniel; Anonymous

2644   [1983] Alice's Adventures in Wonderland and Through the Looking-Glass
New York: Grosset & Dunlap   9780448060040   John Tenniel
Later printing of the ca. 1975 Illustrated Junior Library edition.

2645   [1983] Alice's Adventures in Wonderland and Through the Looking-Glass
New York: Grosset & Dunlap   9780448110042   John Tenniel
Paperback issue of the 1946 Illustrated Junior Library edition. Pictorial wrappers.

2646   1984   Alice's Adventures in Wonderland and Through the Looking-Glass
New York: Alfred A. Knopf   0394869362 (set);   John Tenniel
                                    039486915X (*Alice*); 0394869168 (*Looking-Glass*)
Macmillan Children's Books. Facsimile of the 1866 London *Alice* edition. Issued with or without publisher's slipcase
along with a facsimile of the 1872 1st edition of *Looking-Glass*. Red cloth boards or maroon leather. Inserted is a
Michael Hancher booklet "On the Writing, the Illustration and the Publication of Lewis Carroll's *Alice* Books." First
published in the United States by Knopf, and first published in the United Kingdom by Macmillan Children's Books.

2647   1984   Alice's Adventures in Wonderland and Through the Looking-Glass
New York: Bantam Books   9780553213454   John Tenniel
Bantam Classics. Paperback.

2648   1985   Alice's Adventures in Wonderland and Through the Looking-Glass
Stamford, CT: Longmeadow Press   0681311975   John Tenniel; Julia Christie

2649   1986   Alice's Adventures in Wonderland and Through the Looking-Glass
New York: Hartsdale House   John Tenniel
Reprint of a Puffin Story Books ca. 1960. Puffin Books editions were priced in UK and US currency so must have
been published in America as well.

2650   1988   Alice's Adventures in Wonderland
New York: Dial Books   0803705891   John Tenniel
Packaged in a slipcase along with *Through the Looking-Glass*.

2651   1988   Alice's Adventures in Wonderland and Through the Looking-Glass
New York: Dial Press   9780803705890   Unknown

2652   1988   Alice's Adventures in Wonderland and Through the Looking-Glass
Chicago: Contemporary Books, Inc.   0809244888   T. Lewis
A Calico Book

2653   ca. 1988 Alice's Adventures in Wonderland and Through the Looking-Glass
Chicago: World Book, Inc.   0716631989   Marlene Ekman

2654   1989   Alice's Adventures in Wonderland and Through the Looking-Glass
New York: Choice Publishing   0945260210   John Tenniel
Reader's Digest Best Loved Books for Young Readers. Condensed edition.

2655   1989   Alice's Adventures in Wonderland and Through the Looking-Glass
Chicago: Wellington Press   0922984018N   Markéta Prachatická

2656   1990   Alice's Adventures in Wonderland and Through the Looking-Glass
New York: Bantam Doubleday, Dell Publishing Group   9780553213454   John Tenniel
Paperback.

2657   ca. 1991 Alice's Adventures in Wonderland and Through the Looking-Glass
Boston: Twayne Publishers   9780805794304;   Unknown
                                                9780805785531
Masterwork Studies Series, No 81. Hardcover and softcover.

2658   1993   Alice's Adventures in Wonderland & Through the Looking-Glass
[Mahwah, NJ]: Watermill Press   9780816728756   John Tenniel; Anonymous
This special and unabridged Watermill Classics edition has been completely reset in a size and style designed for easy
reading. Copyright 1992. Cover by anonymous illustrator.

2659   1994   Alice's Adventures in Wonderland and Through the Looking-Glass
New York: Book-of-the-Month Club   John Tenniel; Monica Elias
Monica Elias illustrated the dust jacket.

2660   1995   Lewis Carroll: The Complete, Fully Illustrated Works
New York: Gramercy Books   9780517147818   John Tenniel
Alice's Adventures in Wonderland, *Through the Looking-Glass*, and other Carroll works.

2661   1995   Alice's Adventures in Wonderland and Through the Looking-Glass
New York: Smithmark   9780831766948   John Tenniel

2662   1996   Alice's Adventures in Wonderland and Through the Looking-Glass
San Anselmo, CA: Blushing Rose Publishing   1884807194   John Tenniel;
                                                                        Wendy Cogan Toyoda
Title on cover is *Alice in Wonderland*. Illustrations colored by Wendy Cogan Toyoda.

2663   1996   Alice's Adventures in Wonderland and Through the Looking-Glass
Warwick, RI: North Books   9780939495078   Unknown
Large print.

2664   1998   Alice's Adventures in Wonderland [and Through the Looking-Glass]
Warwick, RI: North Books   9781582870120   John Tenniel
Includes *Through the Looking-Glass*.

2665　1999　Alice's Adventures in Wonderland and Through the Looking-Glass
New York: Barnes and Noble　　　　　　　9780760716199　　　　John Tenniel

2666　1999　Alice's Adventures in Wonderland and Through the Looking-Glass
Los Angeles: Hallmark Entertainment Books　9780787119782　　Hallmark Entertainment
Includes photos from the Hallmark Entertainment television movie.

2667　1999　Alice's Adventures in Wonderland and Through the Looking-Glass
Old Saybrook, CT: Konecky and Konecky　　1568523815　　　　John Tenniel

2668　ca. 1999　Alice's Adventures in Wonderland and Through the Looking-Glass
Los Angeles: Hallmark Entertainment Books　0787119784　　Oliver Upton; Rick Penn-Kraus
Title on cover: *Alice in Wonderland*.

2669　2000　Alice's Adventures in Wonderland and Through the Looking-Glass
New York: Signet Classic　　　　　　　　9780451527745　　　　John Tenniel

2670　2001　Alice's Adventures in Wonderland; Through the Looking-Glass
Detroit, MI: Elibron Classics　　　　　　9781402199936 (paperback);
　　　　　　　　　　　　　　　　　　　9781402147364 (hardcover)　John Tenniel
"This book was produced on August 11, 2001 for the participants of the IFLA Library Consortium Preconference
using print-on-demand technology developed by Adamant Media Corporation" (later Adegi Media Corporation).
Illustrations colorized (no artist listed for colorization). Later editions have ISBN of 9781402199936 (paperback).

2671　2002　Alice's Adventures in Wonderland and Through the Looking-Glass
New York: Gramercy　　　　　　　　　　9780517220771　　　　Unknown
Cover title is *The Complete Stories and Poems of Lewis Carroll*.

2672　2003　Alice's Adventures in Wonderland and Through the Looking-Glass
Asbury Park, NJ: Wordsworth Editions　　068983375X　　　　　John Tenniel

2673　2004　Alice's Adventures in Wonderland and Through the Looking-Glass
New York: Barnes and Noble　　　　　　　9781593080150　　　　John Tenniel

2674　2004　Alice's Adventures in Wonderland and Through the Looking-Glass
Franklin, TN: Dalmatian Press　　　　　　9781403737038　　　Jason Alexander
Adapted by Debbie Guthery.

2675　2005　Alice's Adventures in Wonderland and Through the Looking-Glass
New York: CFM Gallery　　　　　　　　　0976907100; 0976907143;　Anne Bachelier
　　　　　　　　　　　　　　　　　　　0972862090; 0972862080
Comes in standard edition; deluxe cloth-bound edition limited to 598; deluxe leatherette-bound limited to 250; and
deluxe leather-bound limited to 100.

2676　2006　Alice's Adventures in Wonderland and Through the Looking-Glass
New York: Bantam Books　　　　　　　　9780553213454　　　　John Tenniel
Bantam Classics. Paperback.

2677　2006　Alice's Adventures in Wonderland and Through the Looking-Glass
New York: Chelsea　　　　　　　　　　　780791085868　　　　John Tenniel

2678　2007　Lewis Carroll: The Complete, Fully Illustrated Works
New York: Gramercy Books　　　　　　　9780307290373　　　　John Tenniel
Alice's Adventures in Wonderland, *Through the Looking-Glass*, and other Carroll works. New edition.

2679   2009   Alice's Adventures in Wonderland and Through the Looking-Glass
New York: Penguin Classics   9780141924656   John Tenniel
Introduction and notes by Hugh Haughton.

2680   2010   The Complete Alice in Wonderland
Runnemede, NJ: Dynamite Entertainment   9781606900857   Erica Awano; Ale Starling;
                                                                    Jezreel Rojales
Includes issues 1–4 of the Dynamite Entertainment Series. *Alice* and *Looking-Glass* with "The Wasp in a Wig."
Adapted by Leah Moore and John Reppion. Colored by P. C. Siqueira, Ale Starling, and Jezreel Rojales.

2681   2010   Alice's Adventures in Wonderland and Through the Looking-Glass
Whitefish, MT: Kessinger Publishing   9781163987537   John Tenniel
Print-on-demand book. Paperback.

2682   2010   Alice's Adventures in Wonderland and Through the Looking-Glass
New York: Penguin Books   9780143117735   John Tenniel
Introduction and notes by Hugh Haughton.

2683   2010   Alice's Adventures in Wonderland and Through the Looking-Glass
Vancleave, MS: Ramble House   9781605435862   Gavin L. O'Keefe
Print-on-demand book. Issued in hardcover and softcover.

2684   2012   Alice's Adventures in Wonderland and Through the Looking-Glass
New York: Barnes and Noble   9781435142886   John Tenniel

2685   2012   Alice's Adventures in Wonderland, Through the Looking-Glass, and Alice's Adventures
               under Ground
New York: Penguin Classics   9780147509079   John Tenniel; Lewis Carroll
Introduction and notes by Hugh Haughton.

2686   2013   Alice in Wonderland: Authoritative Texts of Alice's Adventures in Wonderland,
           Through the Looking-Glass, The Hunting of the Snark. Backgrounds / Essays in Criticism
New York: Norton   9780393932348   Various
3rd edition. A Norton Critical Edition. Donald Grey, editor. 434 pp. For extensive details on this book, see Guiliano,
pp. 57–58. Hardcover and paperback. First published in 1971.

2687   2014   Alice's Adventures in Wonderland and Through the Looking-Glass
New York: Barnes and Noble   9781435160736   John Tenniel

2688   2014   Alice's Adventures in Wonderland and Through the Looking-Glass
North Charleston, SC: CreateSpace   9781495243530   Unknown
Paperback.

2689   2014   Alice's Adventures in Wonderland and Through the Looking-Glass
New York: Fall River Press   9781435153011   John Tenniel
Title on the cover is *Alice's Adventures in Wonderland*.

2690   2014   Alice's Adventures in Wonderland and Through the Looking-Glass
Los Angeles: Seven Seas Entertainment   9781626920613   Kriss Sison
Illustrations in black-and-white and in color.

2691   2014   The Wonderland Collection
Birmingham, AL: Sweet Water Press   9781492473848   Unknown
A Literary Classics Series. Includes *Alice*, *Looking-Glass*, and *A Tangled Tale*.

2692   2015   Alice's Adventures in Wonderland and Through the Looking-Glass
New York: Barnes and Noble   9781435159549   John Tenniel

2693   2015   Alice's Adventures in Wonderland and Through the Looking-Glass
New York: Penguin Books   9780143107620   John Tenniel
150th Anniversary Edition. Introduction by Charlie Lovett.

2694   [2015] Alice's Adventures in Wonderland and Through the Looking-Glass
Wilmington DE: Chartwell Books   9780785834199   John Tenniel
Knickerbocker series. Includes other Carroll works.

2695   2016   Alice in Wonderland [Deluxe Complete Collection]
[Lexington, KY]: [Christian Books Today]   9781499336924   Anonymous
Includes *Alice*, *Looking-Glass*, *under Ground*, and *The Hunting of the Snark*.

2696   2016   Alice in Wonderland [Deluxe Complete Collection]
[Lexington, KY]: [Christian Books Today]   9781499336925   Anonymous
Includes *Alice*, *Looking-Glass*, *under Ground*, and *The Hunting of the Snark*.

2697   2016   Alice's Adventures in Wonderland and Through the Looking-Glass
San Diego, CA: Canterbury Classics   9781626866072   John Tenniel
Word Cloud Classics.

2698   2016   Alice's Adventures in Wonderland and Through the Looking-Glass
San Diego, CA: Canterbury Classics   9781626866072   John Tenniel
Word Cloud Classics. Paperback.

2699   2016   Alice in Wonderland Collection
Los Angeles: Enhanced Media   9781530917563   Unknown
Includes *Alice*, *Looking-Glass*, *under Ground*, and *The Hunting of the Snark*.

2700   2016   Alice's Adventures in Wonderland and Through the Looking-Glass
New York: Race Point Publishing   9781631061707   John Tenniel

2701   2016   Alice's Adventures in Wonderland and Through the Looking-Glass
Birmingham, AL: Sweet Water Press   9781492473848   Anonymous

2702   [2016] The Complete Alice in Wonderland
Mt. Laurel, NJ: Dynamite   9781606909737   Erica Awano; Ale Starling;
                                                                           Jezreel Rojales
Includes *Alice* and *Looking-Glass* with "The Wasp in a Wig." Adapted by Leah Moore and John Reppion. Colored by
Erica Awano, Ale Starling, and Jezreel Rojales.

2703   2017   Alice's Adventures in Wonderland and Through the Looking-Glass
San Diego, CA: Canterbury Classics   9781684120369   John Tenniel

2704   2017   Alice's Adventures in Wonderland and Through the Looking-Glass
New York: Puffin Books   9780425289280   John Tenniel
Puffin + Pantone Collection. In color.

2705   2018   Alice's Adventures in Wonderland and Through the Looking-Glass
New York: Fantastica   9781787248373   Anonymous
New edition.

2706   2018   Alice's Adventures in Wonderland and Through the Looking-Glass
New York: Racehorse for Young Readers   9781631582752;   John Tenniel
                                                9781631582790 (e-book)

Illustrations in black-and-white and in color.

2707   2019   Alice's Adventures in Wonderland and Through the Looking-Glass
New York: Harper Design   9780062936615;   Minalima Design
                                   9780062936639

2708   n.d.   Alice's Adventures in Wonderland and Through the Looking-Glass
New York: Best-Loved Classics   John Tenniel
Best-Loved Classics. A division of HarperCollins.

2709   n.d.   Alice's Adventures in Wonderland and Through the Looking-Glass
                & The Hunting of the Snark
New York: Blue Ribbon Books   John Tenniel
Red cloth. According to Lovett, the text for this edition taken from a Boni and Liveright Modern Library edition of 1924.

2710   n.d.   Alice's Adventures in Wonderland and Through the Looking-Glass
Chicago: Book Supply Company   John Tenniel
Peerless Library. Also contains 10 chapters of *Sylvie and Bruno*.

2711   n.d.   Alice's Adventures in Wonderland and Through the Looking-Glass
New York: De Luxe Editions   John Tenniel
Old English Style headings at the top of each page. A reprint of the 1936 Three Sirens Press edition.

2712   n.d.   Alice's Adventures Underground & Alice's Adventures in Wonderland
Garden City, NY: Dolphin Books / Doubleday & Company   Lewis Carroll; John Tenniel;
                                                             Sydney Butchkes

In the series A Doubleday Dolphin Master. The cover includes a Tenniel illustration adapted by Sydney Butchkes.
Pictorial wrappers. 95 cents.

2713   n.d.   Alice's Adventures in Wonderland and Through the Looking-Glass
New York: Halcyon House   John Tenniel
Old English Style headings at the top of each page. A reprint of the 1936 Three Sirens Press edition.

2714   n.d.   Alice's Adventures in Wonderland and Through the Looking-Glass
New York: Hartsdale House   John Tenniel
Old English Style headings at the top of each page. A reprint of the 1936 Three Sirens Press edition.

2715   n.d.   The Complete Works of Lewis Carroll
New York: Hodder and Stoughton   A. E. Jackson
Undated later printing, same as the 1914 edition. 16 color plates. Blue cloth.

2716   n.d.   Alice's Adventures in Wonderland and Through the Looking-Glass
Chicago: J. G. Ferguson & Associates   John Tenniel
Art-Type Edition.

2717   n.d.   Alice's Adventures in Wonderland and Through the Looking-Glass
Philadelphia; Toronto, ON: John C. Winston Co.   John Tenniel; Edwin J. Prittie
The Winston Bookshelf edition. 4 color plates by Prittie. Orange cloth.

2718   n.d.   Alice's Adventures in Wonderland and Through the Looking-Glass
Philadelphia; Toronto, ON: John C. Winston Co.   John Tenniel; Edwin J. Prittie
Children's Classics edition. 4 color plates by Prittie. Reddish-brown cloth.

2719   n.d.   Alice's Adventures in Wonderland and Through the Looking-Glass
New York: Little Leather Library   Unillustrated
Leaf size 2 x 3 inches. Flexible green leather.

2720   n.d.   Alice's Adventures in Wonderland and Through the Looking-Glass
New York: Peebles Press International   Dorothy Colles
                                                                  (after John Tenniel)
Peebles Classic Library. Distributed by Walden Books, Resale Division.

2721   n.d.   Alice's Adventures in Wonderland and Through the Looking-Glass
New York: Peebles Press International   Unknown
Peebles Classic Library. Sandy Lesberg, editor. Includes *Alice*, *Looking-Glass*, and *Snark*. Blue paper-covered boards.

2722   n.d.   Alice's Adventures in Wonderland and Through the Looking-Glass
New York: Playmore, Inc.   John Tenniel; Jim Jones
Giant Junior Classics. Cover illustration by Jim Jones. Printed on thin paper.

2723   n.d.   Alice's Adventures in Wonderland and Through the Looking-Glass
New York: R. H. Macy   John Tenniel
A special printing of the Three Sirens Press edition.

2724   n.d.   Alice's Adventures in Wonderland and Through the Looking-Glass
New York: Random House   John Tenniel
Number G28 in the Modern Library Giant series. Introduction by Alexander Woollcott.

2725   n.d.   The Complete Works of Lewis Carroll
New York: Random House   John Tenniel
Number G28 in the Modern Library Giant series. Introduction by Alexander Woollcott.

2726   n.d.   Alice's Adventures in Wonderland and Through the Looking-Glass
Racine, WI: Western Printing and Lithographing Company   Roberta Paflin
Whitman Famous Classics.

2727   n.d.   Alice's Adventures in Wonderland and Through the Looking-Glass
Racine, WI: Whitman Publishing Division / Western Publishing Company   Roberta Paflin
Whitman Famous Classics.

2728   n.d.   Alice's Adventures in Wonderland and Through the Looking-Glass
New York: Windsor Press   John Tenniel
Old English Style headings at the top of each page. A reprint of the 1936 Three Sirens Press edition.

2729   n.d.   Alice's Adventures in Wonderland, Through the Looking-Glass
                and The Hunting of the Snark
New York: World Library Guild   Anonymous (after Tenniel)
Juvenile Library.

2730   n.d.   Alice's Adventures in Wonderland and Through the Looking-Glass
New York: World Library Guild   Anonymous (after Tenniel)
Juvenile Library.

2731   n.d.   Alice's Adventures in Wonderland and Through the Looking-Glass
Cleveland, OH; New York: World Publishing Co.   Anonymous (after Tenniel)
Jumbo Books. Includes *Heidi*.

3. *Alice's Adventures in Wonderland, Through the Looking-Glass,* and Combined Editions Published in Other English-Language Countries

3.1 AUSTRALIA

2732   1870   Alice's Adventures in Wonderland

Adelaide, SA: Adelaide Observer   Unknown

Chapter 1 only. Appeared in "The Children's Column." Exclusively for the *Adelaide Observer* newspaper, Christmas issue. *Evening Journal*, April 26, 1870: "In the Christmas number of the *Observer* we gave the first chapter of this very interesting work, containing an account of the wonderful things that happened after Alice descended the rabbit-hole. A great many things followed...."

2733   ca. 1899 Alice's Adventures in Wonderland

Melbourne, VIC: E. W. Cole, Book Arcade   Blanche McManus

Adaptation. 94 pp. Spine title: *Alice in Wonderland*. Printed in England for E. W. Cole, Book Arcade, Melbourne; 333 George Street, Sydney; 67 Rundle Street, Adelaide. Publication year is not stated, but "Illustrations by Blanche McManus, 1899" is visible.

2734   1936   Through the Looking-Glass

London; Melbourne, VIC: Ward, Lock & Co.   Unknown

191 pp.

2735   ca. 1937 Children's Treasury of Great Stories

Melbourne, VIC: United Press   Anonymous

2736   1938   Alice Through the Looking-Glass

Sydney, NSW: Publicity Press   Anonymous

John Mystery Pocket Books. Abridged.

2737   1938   Alice in Wonderland

Sydney, NSW: Publicity Press   Unknown

1st edition. 140 pp. Edited and compiled by local song and children's book writer John Mystery (a.k.a. Lester Sinclair). Later editions.

2738   1941   The Children's Alice

Sydney, NSW: Australasian Publishing   Honor C. Appleton

Adapted by F. H. Lee.

2739   ca. 1942 Alice's Adventures in Wonderland and Through the Looking-Glass

Melbourne, VIC: Colourgravure Publications   Donald Glue

117 pp. Beige paper-covered boards. Colourgravure was the publication arm of the *Herald and Weekly Times Ltd.*

2740   1943   Alice's Adventures in Wonderland and Through the Looking-Glass

Sydney, NSW: Consolidated Press   Kate O'Brien

205 pp. Reprinted in 1944, 1946, and 1947. Contains 11 full-page black-and-white images along with several small vignettes of Alice and animals such as an owl. O'Brien was an Australian comic book artist and book illustrator.

2741   1944   Alice's Adventures in Wonderland and Through the Looking-Glass

Sydney, NSW: Consolidated Press   Kate O'Brien

Name of illustrator not listed but signature on illustration belongs to O'Brien. O'Brien was an Australian comic book artist and book illustrator.

2742   1945   Alice's Adventures in Wonderland
Melbourne, VIC: Oxford University Press   Anonymous
1st Australian edition. Introduction by Herbert Strang. 173 pp.

2743   1946   Alice's Adventures in Wonderland and Through the Looking-Glass
Sydney, NSW: Consolidated Press   Kate O'Brien
Name of illustrator not listed but signature on illustration is O'Brien. O'Brien was an Australian comic book artist and book illustrator.

2744   ca. 1946 Alice in Wonderland
Melbourne, VIC: Oxford University Press   A. E. Jackson
1st edition. Reprinted in 1947 and 1949. Not listed in Trove or WorldCat.

2745   1947   Alice's Adventures in Wonderland and Through the Looking-Glass
Sydney, NSW: Consolidated Press   Kate O'Brien
O'Brien was an Australian comic book artist and book illustrator. Gray cardboard wrappers.

2746   1947   Alice's Adventures in Wonderland
Melbourne, VIC: Oxford University Press   A. E. Jackson
Reprint of the 1st Australian edition of 1946.

2747   1949   Alice in Wonderland and Through the Looking Glass
Melbourne, VIC: Colorgravure Press   Donald Glue
Herald Classic for Children Series.

2748   1949   Alice's Adventures in Wonderland
Melbourne, VIC: Oxford University Press   Unknown
Reprint of 1945 edition. Reprinted in 1989.

2749   1949   Alice in Wonderland
Sydney, NSW: Sydney Sunday Herald   Nan Fullarton
Comic strip. Adapted and illustrated by Nan Fullarton.

2750   1950   Through the Looking-Glass
Sydney, NSW: Sydney Sunday Herald   Nan Fullarton
Comic strip. Adapted and illustrated by Nan Fullarton.

2751   ca. 1950s   Walt Disney's Alice in Wonderland Finds the Garden of Live Flowers
Sydney, NSW: The Golden Press   Campbell Grant
Golden Library Series. Retold by Jane Werner. Abridged.

2752   ca. 1950s   Alice's Adventures
Sydney, NSW: The Golden Press   Maraja
In clear plastic dust wrapper printed in gold.

2753   1982   Alice's Adventures in Wonderland
Frenchs Forest, NSW: Reed   9780589503505   Charles Blackman
Edited by Nadine Amadio.

2754   1982   Alice's Adventures in Wonderland
Frenchs Forest, NSW: Reed   0589503502   Charles Blackman
Edited by Nadine Amadio. 128 pp. Dust jacket contains an incorrect ISBN.

| 2755 | 1982 | Alice's Adventures in Wonderland & Through the Looking-Glass and What Alice Found There | | |

Melbourne, VIC: Macmillan   0333338715   John Tenniel
for the Library of Imperial History

The 150th Anniversary edition to commemorate of the birth of Lewis Carroll. The Library of Imperial History commissioned Macmillan to release worldwide a leather-bound edition limited to 2,000 copies with owner's certificate and 5,000 copies of a deluxe cloth-bound edition.

| 2756 | 1983 | Alice's Adventures in Wonderland | | |

Sydney, NSW: Collins   0001843133   S. Michelle Wiggins
Simultaneously published in New York by Alfred Knopf.

| 2757 | 1985 | Alice's Adventures in Wonderland | | |

Caulfield East, VIC: Edward Arnold Australia   0713182261   Alice B. Woodward; Sue Shields

Simultaneously published in London by Bell & Hyman. First published in London by G. Bell & Sons in 1920.

| 2758 | 1987 | Walt Disney's Alice in Wonderland | | |

Melbourne, VIC: Budget Books   0868019526   Walt Disney Company
Adapted. WorldCat records shows it is also published by "Happy Time Books" under the same ISBN.

| 2759 | 1988 | Alice in Wonderland: A Full-Color Storybook | | |

Melbourne, VIC: Budget Books   073230279X   Unknown
16 pp.

| 2760 | 1989 | Alice's Adventures in Wonderland | | |

Melbourne, VIC: Carroll Foundation   1875244018; 9781875244010   Unillustrated
1 floppy disc.

| 2761 | 1989 | Alice's Adventures in Wonderland | | |

Flemington, VIC: Carroll Foundation   1875244042   Gavin O'Keefe

| 2762 | 1989 | Alice's Adventures in Wonderland | | |

Melbourne, VIC: Oxford University Press   0600566854   Unknown
Reprint of a 1985 edition.

| 2763 | 1990 | Alice's Adventures in Wonderland | | |

Flemington, VIC: Carroll Foundation   1875244034   Pixie O'Harris
Also titled *Pixie Alice.*

| 2764 | 1990 | Alice's Adventures in Wonderland | | |

Flemington, VIC: Carroll Foundation   1875244042   Gavin O'Keefe

| 2765 | 1993 | The Complete Stories of Lewis Carroll | | |

Sydney, NSW: The Book Co.   1854873784   Various

This edition first published by Magpie Books Ltd. in 1993. Includes *Alice's Adventures in Wonderland, Through the Looking-Glass, A Wonderland Miscellany, Bruno's Revenge* and other stories, *Sylvie and Bruno, Sylvie and Bruno Concluded, The Hunting of the Snark,* and *Original Games and Puzzles.*

| 2766 | 1993 | Alice's Adventures in Wonderland & Through the Looking Glass | | |

Baxter, VIC: Modern Publishing Group   9781875481309   Unknown
Seen for sale on AbeBooks. Copies with the same ISBN by McPherson's Printing are also available.

2767	1995	Disney's Alice in Wonderland		
		Port Melbourne, VIC: Reed for Kids	0732324068	Unknown
		Adapted. 25 pp.		

2768	1996	Great Works: Lewis Carroll		
		Sydney, NSW: The Book Company		Various
		470 pp. Includes *Alice's Adventures in Wonderland*, *Through the Looking-Glass*, *A Wonderland Miscellany*, *Bruno's Revenge*, *The Hunting of the Snark*, and *Original Games and Puzzles*.		

2769	1997	Alice in Wonderland		
		Geelong, VIC: Sands Print Group		Anonymous
		Adapted. 24 pp.		

2770	1998	Alice's Adventures in Wonderland		
		Heatherton, VIC: Hinkler Books	9781865150048	Unknown
		307 pp. Combined with *Through the Looking-Glass*.		

2771	1998	Disney's Alice in Wonderland		
		Camberwell: Penguin	9780721487328	Atelier Philippe Harchy
		Based on the movie *Alice in Wonderland*.		

2772	1999	Alice's Adventures in Wonderland		
		[Ringwood, VIC]: Claremont Classics	0734301529	Anonymous

2773	2003	Walt Disney's Alice in Wonderland		
		Camberwell, VIC: Puffin Books		Al Dempster
		Adapted and illustrated by Al Dempster.		

2774	2003	Alice's Adventures in Wonderland		
		Adelaide, SA: The University of Adelaide Library		Unknown
		The University of Adelaide Library e-books.		

2775	2003	Through the Looking-Glass		
		Adelaide, SA: The University of Adelaide Press		Unknown
		Electronic text.		

2776	2004	Alice's Adventures in Wonderland		
		Dingley, VIC: Hinkler Books	9781741210187	Unknown
		A new version of the classic tale by Archie Oliver.		

2777	2006	Alice in Wonderland		
		Rowville, VIC: Five Mile Press	9781741781373	Eric Kincaid
		Abridged. First published in Rowville by Brimax Books in 1988. With a CD.		

2778	2006	Alice in Wonderland		
		Rowville, VIC: Funtastic	9781741503371	Atelier Philippe Harchy
		95 pp. Adapted by Catherine McCafferty.		

2779	2007	Walt Disney's Alice in Wonderland		
		Collingwood, VIC: Funtastic	9781741921687	Walt Disney Company
		Pictures adapted by Al Dempster.		

2780	2007	Bedtime Collection Alice in Wonderland		
		Heatherton, VIC: Hinkler Books	9781741811599	Unknown

2781   2008   Alice in Wonderland
        Heatherton, VIC: Hinkler Books   9781741828528   Rodney Matthews
        95 pp. Some color illustrations.

2782   2009   Alice's Adventures in Wonderland: Through the Looking-Glass
                and What Alice Found There
        Wingfield, SA: Cameron House   9781741730456   John Tenniel

2783   2010   Michael Foreman's Alice's Adventures in Wonderland
        Scoresby, VIC: Five Mile Press   9781742481487   Michael Foreman
        Includes *Alice's Adventures under Ground.*

2784   2010   Alice in Wonderland and The Hunting of the Snark
        Scoresby, VIC: Five Mile Press   9781742119700   Cinzia Ratto
        153 pp.

2785   2010   Alice's Adventures in Wonderland
        Camberwell, VIC: Penguin   9780141194752   John Tenniel
        Paperback.

2786   2011   Alice's Adventures in Wonderland & Through the Looking-Glass
        Millers Point, NSW: Murdoch Books Australia   9781742665245   Miriam Steenhauer;
                                                                       Tania Comes

        Target Kids Classics. Retold by Harriet Castor. Paperback. Cover illustration by Tania Comes.

2787   2012   Alice's Adventures in Wonderland: The Original Classic Edition
        Dayboro, QLD: Emereo Publisher   9781486143733   Unknown
        Emereo Classics edition. Paperback.

2788   2012   Through the Looking-Glass: the Original Classic Edition
        Brisbane, QLD: Emereo Publishing   9781486410644   Unknown
        52 pp.

2789   2012   Alice's Adventures in Wonderland
        Scoresby, VIC: The Five Mile Press   9781743003787   Eric Kincaid

2790   2012   Alice in Wonderland
        Sydney, NSW: Scholastic   9781742832975   Unknown
        Scholastic Junior Classics.

2791   2013   The Classic Library
        Scoresby, VIC: The Five Mile Press   Eric Kincaid
        3 volumes. *Peter Pan* by J. M. Barrie; *Alice's Adventures in Wonderland* by Lewis Carroll; and *Oliver Twist* by Charles
        Dickens.

2792   2014   Alice in Wonderland
        Richmond, VIC: Chirpy Bird,   9781742978215   Kristy Lund-White
        an imprint of Hardie Grant Egmont
        Disney Vintage Collection for Primary School Age Readers. 30 pp. Color illustrations. Design by Kristy Lund-White.

2793   2015   Alice's Adventures in Wonderland: Alice Series
        Sydney, NSW: Harlequin Books   9781489205568   Unknown
        Brand Harlequin Teen. Online resource.

2794   2015   Alice in Wonderland: Down the Rabbit Hole
Gosford, NSW: Scholastic Australia   9781742761411   Eric Puybaret
For primary school age readers. Retold by Joe Rhatigan and Charles Nurnberg.

2795   2016   Alice's Adventures in Wonderland
Strawberry Hills, NSW: 9781458789556   Unknown
Read How You Want Classics Library
Dyslexic Books Edition. 132 pp. Paperback.

2796   2017   Alice's Adventures in Wonderland
Freshwater, NSW: Michelle's Miniatures   Michelle Burns
Miniature book by Michelle Burns. 29 pp.

2797   2017   Alice's Adventures in Wonderland
Newtown, NSW: The Shepherd Moon   9780648118435   Unknown
Includes *Through the Looking Glass*. Edited and annotated by Bogdan Meunier.

2798   2018   Alice's Adventures in Wonderland
Newtown, NSW: Walker Books Australia   9781760650780   Robert Ingpen
Abridged edition.

2799   n.d.   Alice in Wonderland
Wahroonga, NSW: St. Lucy's School for Blind and Visually Handicapped   Unillustrated
3 volumes of interpoint Braille

2800   n.d.   Alice in Wonderland
Kew, VIC: St. Paul's School for the Blind and Visually Handicapped   Unillustrated
1 volume of interline Braille

3.2 CANADA

2801   1907   Alice's Adventures in Wonderland
Toronto, ON: Musson Book Co.   Bessie Pease Gutmann
Copyright 1907 by Dodge Publishing. Also available as print-on-demand from India's ReInk Books (2015).

2802   1910   Alice's Adventures in Wonderland
Toronto, ON: The Macmillan Company of Canada, Ltd.   E. Hatton Stanton
A. L. Bright Story Readers, No.46. School edition, grade 4. With 4 illustrations signed by the illustrator.

2803   1948   Alice in Wonderland
Toronto, ON: Gilbertson Co.   Unknown
Classics Illustrated, No. 49. The series retells classics as comics for children.

2804   1951   Alice in Wonderland and Other Favorites
Montreal, QC: Pocket Books of Canada   Unknown
Pocket Book series , No. 835. Includes *Alice, Looking-Glass, The Hunting of the Snark, Puzzles from Wonderland,* and *Phantasmagoria*.

2805   1969   Alice in Wonderland
Toronto, ON: McClelland and Stewart   0361010982   Unknown

2806   1985   Alice's Wonderland Adventure

Toronto, ON; New York: Bantam   9780553054057;   Walt Disney Company

9780553172270

Part of Walt Disney Choose Your Own Adventure series.

2807   1985   Alice in Wonderland

Toronto, ON: Omniprose   9780921111443   Unknown

2808   1988   Alice's Adventures in Wonderland

Toronto, ON: The Cheshire Cat Press   George A. Walker

Limited edition of 177 copies.

2809   1991   Alice's Adventures in Toronto

Toronto, ON: The Cheshire Cat Press   George A. Walker

Limited edition of 177 copies. A companion to the Cheshire Cat Press's 1988 *Alice* edition. Includes the published *Alice* engravings, as well as the unpublished engravings and sketches for the published engravings.

2810   1998   Through the Looking-Glass

Toronto, ON: The Cheshire Cat Press   George A. Walker

Limited edition of 177 copies. Some copies were combined by the publisher in a 2-volume portfolio with the Cheshire Cat Press's edition of *Alice* (1988).

2811   2000   Alice's Adventures in Wonderland

Peterborough, ON: Broadview Press   9781551112237; 155111223X   John Tenniel

Includes *Alice, Alice's Adventures under Ground*, and *The Nursery "Alice,"* as well as selected reviews, parodies, remembrances of Carroll, and extracts from Carroll's diaries and letters.

2812   2003   Alice's Adventures in Wonderland

Toronto, ON; Buffalo, NY: Firefly   9781552977545   Ralph Steadman

Reprint of London: Dobson, 1967 edition. Illustrated with woodcuts by Ralph Steadman and designed by George Walker of the Cheshire Cat Press.

2813   2003   Alice's Adventures in Wonderland

Vancouver, BC: Simply Read Books   9781894965002   Iassen Ghiuselev

A surrealist interpretation of *Alice*. Designed by Judith Steedman.

2814   2005   Alice in Wonderland

Toronto, ON: Tania Press   0973735309   Tatiana Ianovskaia

2815   2007   Alice's Adventures in Wonderland

Toronto, ON: Studio Treasure   9780978361303   Oleg Lipchenko

Limited edition published by small press founded by illustrator Oleg Lipchenko.

2816   2008   Alice in Wonderland

Toronto, ON: Tania Press   9780973735321   Tatiana Ianovskaia

2817   2009   Alice's Adventures in Wonderland

Toronto, ON; Plattsburgh, NY: Tundra Books   9780887769320   Oleg Lipchenko

Trade edition of Studio Treasure (2007) limited edition. Winner of IBBY Canada Elizabeth Mrazik-Cleaver Picture Book Award.

2818   2009   Alice in Wonderland

Montreal, QC: Phidal   9782764317426   Walt Disney Company

| 2819 | 2010 | Alice's Adventures in Wonderland | | |
| | | Vancouver, BC: AD Classics / Engage Books | 9781926606286 | John Tenniel |

| 2820 | 2010 | Alice's Adventures in Wonderland | | |
| | | Calgary, AB: Qualitas | 9781897093535 | John Tenniel |

| 2821 | 2010 | Alice's Adventures in Wonderland and Through the Looking-Glass | | |
| | | Vancouver, BC: Engage Books | 9781926606316 | John Tenniel |

Facsimile of the Macmillan 1866 *Alice* and the 1872 *Looking-Glass*.

| 2822 | 2010 | Through the Looking-Glass | | |
| | | Calgary, AB: Qualitas | 9781897093658 | John Tenniel |

Part of the Library of the Classics series. This volume includes Carroll's text and Tenniel's illustrations only. No introduction, annotations, etc.

| 2823 | 2010 | Through the Looking-Glass and What Alice Found There | | |
| | | Toronto, ON: Tania Press | 9780973735345 | Tatiana Ianovskaia |

Limited edition of 50 copies.

| 2824 | 2011 | Alice's Adventures in Wonderland | | |
| | | Erin, ON: The Porcupine's Quill | 9780889843394; 9781122977128 (e-book) | George A. Walker |

Reuses George Walker's engravings and preserves much of the page layout from the Cheshire Cat Press edition of 1988. Also available as an e-book.

| 2825 | 2011 | Alice's Adventures in Wonderland | | |
| | | Vancouver, BC: Simply Read Books | 9781897476420 | Iassen Ghiuselev |

2nd edition.

| 2826 | 2011 | Alice's Adventures in Wonderland | | |
| | | Peterborough, ON: Broadview Press | 9781554810390 | John Tenniel |

2nd edition.

| 2827 | 2013 | Alice's Adventures in Wonderland and Through the Looking-Glass | | |
| | | Toronto, ON: HarperPerennial Classics | 9781443428118 | Unknown |

E-book.

| 2828 | 2014 | Alice's Adventures in Wonderland and Through the Looking-Glass | | |
| | | Toronto, ON: Indigo Library | 9780670068883 | John Tenniel |

Prepared by Penguin Random House for Indigo Library, imprint of Canada's largest book retailer chain, Indigo Books & Music.

| 2829 | 2015 | Alice's Adventures in Wonderland | | |
| | | Vancouver, BC: Engage Books | 9781772261714 | John Tenniel |

Limited edition of 1,000 copies. Cover illustrated by Arthur Rackham.

| 2830 | 2015 | Alice's Adventures in Wonderland | | |
| | | Toronto, ON: The Cheshire Cat Press | 9780385682268 | Harry Furniss |

Limited edition of 66 copies. Introduced, signed, and numbered by Edward Wakeling.

| 2831 | 2015 | Alice's Adventures in Wonderland Decoded: The Full Text of Lewis Carroll's Novel with Its Many Hidden Meanings Revealed | | |
| | | Toronto, ON: Doubleday | 9780385682268 | Various |

Annotations and essays by David Day. Hardcover won an Alcuin Society Book Design Award. Also available in e-book Kindle format with no ISBN, and Kobo format 9780385682275.

2832   2020   Through the Looking-Glass & What Alice Found There
Toronto, ON: Studio Treasure   9780978361358   Oleg Lipchenko
Limited edition of 100 copies. Bound in brown leather with title on in gold leaf on front cover, and gilt on all edges. Signed by Oleg Lipchenko.

3.3 IRELAND

2833   2008   Alice's Adventures in Wonderland
Westport, Ireland: Evertype   9781904808169   John Tenniel; Valerie Seery
1st edition. Cover designed by Valerie Seery, who also designed the 2003 Irish-language edition (Coiscéim and Evertype). The Rabbit's tabard has red hearts on alternating gold and white panels; the banner and trumpet are also gold, as is the shoulder piece; his shirtsleeve is white; his collar is pink; shadowing behind him is blue. The back cover has Alice and the Cheshire Cat in gray scale. Foreword by Michael Everson. Out of print September 9, 2015.

2834   2009   Through the Looking-Glass and What Alice Found There
Westport, Ireland: Evertype   9781904808381   John Tenniel
1st edition. Foreword by Michael Everson, and a note on Victorian pricing following Carroll's 1897 preface. Contains "The Wasp in a Wig," with an introduction and Ken Leeder's illustration. Green cover, colored by Valerie Seery; Alice has a blue dress, the White Knight's armor is bluish.

2835   2010   Through the Looking-Glass and What Alice Found There
Westport, Ireland: Evertype   9781904808381   John Tenniel; Ken Leeder;
                                                                  Michael Everson
1st reissue of the 2009 edition with a new cover. Foreword by Michael Everson, and a note on Victorian pricing following Carroll's 1897 preface. Contains "The Wasp in a Wig," with an introduction and with Ken Leeder's illustration. Green cover, colored by Michael Everson; Alice has a yellow dress, the White Knight's armor is white, and his sword is wooden.

2836   2010   Alice's Adventures in Wonderland: Retold in words of one syllable
Westport, Ireland: Evertype   9781904808442   John Tenniel
1st edition. Abridged and retold in words of one syllable by Mrs. J. C. Gorham. The cover is typical of the Evertype Alices, but has a gray background indicative of "altered English" Alices in different formats or alphabets. The number of spades on one of the gardeners in the 1st of Tenniel's illustrations to Chapter VIII is 6 rather than 7 due to the name change to a single syllable. An illustration of the front cover of the 1905 edition appears at the end of Michael Everson's foreword.

2837   2013   Alice's Adventures in Wonderland
Westport, Ireland: Evertype   9781782010371   June Lornie
1st edition. In color. Foreword by June Lornie.

2838   2014   The Complete Novels of Lewis Carroll with All the Original Illustrations
[Cork, Ireland]: E-artnow Editions   9788026805106   Lewis Carroll; John Tenniel
E-book. Includes: *Alice's Adventures under Ground*; *Alice's Adventures in Wonderland*; *Through the Looking-Glass*; *Sylvie and Bruno*; *Sylvie and Bruno Concluded*; *The Life and Letters of Lewis Carroll*. Page counts may vary depending on e-reader. Amazon Kindle copy has 1,382 pp.; others may have as many as 1,670 pp. *Under Ground* contains Carroll's illustrations, and *Looking-Glass* contains Tenniel illustrations. Other illustrated books contain the original illustrations.

2839   2015   Alice's Adventures in Wonderland
Portlaoise, Ireland: Evertype   9781782011255   John Tenniel; Michael Everson
2nd edition. Cover recolored by Michael Everson. The Rabbit's tabard has red hearts on white panels; the banner and shoulder piece are also white; the trumpet is gold; his shirtsleeve is green; his collar is off-white; shadowing

behind him is black. The back cover has Alice and the Cheshire Cat in color; Alice wears a yellow dress. Foreword by Michael Everson. Text establishes the Evertype definitive edition.

2840   2015   Alice's Adventures in Wonderland: An edition printed in Dyslexic-Friendly Fonts
Portlaoise, Ireland: Evertype   9781782011262   John Tenniel
1st edition. Printed in dyslexic-friendly fonts. The cover is typical of the Evertype *Alices*, but has a gray background indicative of "altered English" *Alices* in different formats or alphabets. Text follows the Evertype definitive edition.

2841   2015   Elucidating Alice: A Textual Commentary on Alice's Adventures in Wonderland
Portlaoise, Ireland: Evertype   9781782011057   John Tenniel
1st edition. Preface, introduction, and 635 annotations by Selwyn Goodacre. Full text of the book, which establishes the Goodacre definitive edition.

2842   2015   Alice's Adventures in Wonderland
Portlaoise, Ireland: Evertype   9781782011286   Mathew Staunton
1st edition. Foreword by Michael Everson. Illustrator's foreword by Mathew Staunton. Illustrations inspired by Staunton's family and friends; Staunton himself can be seen in illustrations for "You are old, Father William." A drawing and photograph vignette of Aoife Staunton at the end of the book echoes Carroll's paste-down over the Alice photo in *Alice's Adventures under Ground*. Text follows the Evertype definitive edition.

2843   2016   Alice's Adventures in Wonderland
Portlaoise, Ireland: Evertype   9781782011354   Harry Furniss
1st edition. With an introduction by Selwyn Goodacre and Edward Wakeling. Typical cover color is purple; on the back Alice is with the Cheshire Cat and wears a yellow dress. Furniss did not illustrate the Herald-Rabbit, so the front cover has Alice and the Caterpillar (as does the Evertype edition of *Alice's Adventures under Ground*). Text follows the Evertype definitive edition.

2844   2017   Alice's Adventures in Wonderland
Portlaoise, Ireland: Evertype   9781782012108   J. Michael Rolen
1st edition. Front and back cover have Rolen's illustrations of the Herald-Rabbit and Alice with the Cheshire Cat, as is typical in Evertype *Alices*, and coloration follows suit, with a blue cover. Foreword by Brian R. Basore. Text follows the Evertype definitive edition.

3.4 NEW ZEALAND

2845   1912   Through the Looking-Glass and What Alice Found There
Christchurch, NZ: Whitcombe & Tombs   Gwyneth Richardson
WorldCat has an entry for a 1912 edition but no holding library information. May be a ghost edition.

2846   1924   Alice's Adventures in Wonderland
Auckland, NZ: Whitcombe & Tombs   Christian Yandell
68-page primary school reader edited by E. A. Stewart for the Australian education market. First known illustration of *Alice in Wonderland* by an Australian artist. No extant copy of the original 1924 edition is known though the print run numbered 10,000. Not in New Zealand National Library's online catalog but mentioned in Michael Organ's article about *Alice* in Australia and New Zealand. Organ notes that "nine editions appeared to 1960, with the majority printed in Christchurch. Some 74,700 had been issued." The illustrator married in 1930 and became Christian Waller.

2847   1924   Through the Looking-Glass and What Alice Found There
Christchurch, NZ: Whitcombe & Tombs   Gwyneth Richardson
Whitcombe's Story Books Series, No. 443. First published in 1924, but no extant copy is known, according to Michael Organ. Adaptation. The research librarian at the Alexander Turnbull Library, NZ, confirmed the existence of editions for 1924, 1934, 1936, 1946, and 1949. A scan was reviewed of the relevant page from Whitcombe's Story Books: a trans-Tasman survey by Ian F. McLaren with the note "[£4.4.0, 22.4.1924]." The publishing dates generally do not appear in these books, and dating is done through the "G" numbers in the colophon.

2848   ca. 1934 Through the Looking-Glass and What Alice Found There
Christchurch, NZ: Whitcombe & Tombs Ltd.   Gwyneth Richardson
Whitcombe's Story Books, No. 443. 74 pp. Ian F. McLaren in Whitcombe's Story Books: a trans-Tasman survey notes
that "[p]ossibly issued from English sheets." "If adapted [from the] 1924 [edition] it could have been issued at that time
without numbering. As other numbers in series were published in 1934, it is possible that it was also released that year."

2849   1936   Through the Looking-Glass and What Alice Found There
Christchurch, NZ: Whitcombe & Tombs Ltd.   Various
Whitcombe & Tombs job no. G890. Adapted by E. A. Stewart. Whitcombe's Story Books. Dark blue and orange on
buff. Bottom right corner of cover printed "6d." Online catalog states publication year as 1934, but the worksheet
inside the book states "31.6.1936."

2850   1940   Alice in Wonderland
Christchurch, NZ: Whitcombe & Tombs   Christian Yandell (Waller)
                                                                            and the Carlton Studio

Adaptation. 68 pp. With original cover design by the Carlton Studio. Whitcombe & Tombs job no. G2028. Christian
Yandell is listed as an author. The illustrator married in 1930 and became Christian Waller.

2851   1945   Alice in Wonderland
Christchurch, NZ: Whitcombe & Tombs   Christian Yandell;
                                                                            Carlton Studio

Adaptation. 64 pp. With original cover design by the Carlton Studio.

2852   1946   Through the Looking-Glass and What Alice Found There
Christchurch, NZ: Whitcombe & Tombs Ltd.   Gwyneth Richardson
Whitcombe & Tombs job no. G3250. Published February 9, 1946. Blue and orange on buff. Adapted by E.A. Stewart.
74 pp. Whitcombe's Story Books, No. 443c. Bottom right corner of cover printed "8d." Released in Christchurch,
Auckland, Wellington, Dunedin, and Invercargill NZ, as well as London, Melbourne, Sydney, and Perth.
"Explanations for young readers" provided at the back of the book.

2853   1948   Alice in Wonderland
Christchurch, NZ: Whitcombe & Tombs   Christian Yandell
Adapted by E. A. Stewart. 64 pp. Whitcombe's Story Books: No. 415.

2854   1949   Through the Looking-Glass and What Alice Found There
Christchurch, NZ: Whitcombe & Tombs   Gwyneth Richardson
SG3726. Published December 10, 1949. Blue and orange on buff. 74 pp. Reprint of 1924 edition. Whitcombe's Story
Books, No. 443.

2855   1960   Alice in Wonderland
Christchurch, NZ: Whitcombe & Tombs   Christian Yandell

2856   1982   Alice's Adventures in Wonderland
Wellington, NZ: Reed   Charles Blackman
Edited by Nadine Amadio. 128 pp.

2857   2008   Alice in Wonderland
Auckland, NZ: Floating Press   9781877527814   Unillustrated
E-book.

2858   2008   Through the Looking-Glass
Auckland, NZ: Floating Press   9781877527586 (EPUB format);   Unillustrated
                                        9781775565604 (PDF)

Electronic document (PDF).

2859   2009   Alice in Wonderland
         Auckland, NZ: Floating Press   9781877527814   Unillustrated
         E-book.

2860   2009   Through the Looking-Glass
         Waiheke Island, NZ: Floating Press   1877527580   Unknown
         Online resource.

4. *Alice's Adventures in Wonderland, Through the Looking-Glass,* and Combined Editions Published in the Rest of the World

4.1 ARGENTINA

2861   2006   Alice in Wonderland. Other Titles: Alice's Adventures in Wonderland
Buenos Aires: Ediciones Dos Amigos   Alicia Scavino; Facundo Alí
Press Collection (Library of Congress). 1st edition. 176 pp. Edition of 25, of which 20 for sale. 21 unbound quires in a clamshell box covered in red cloth with cork on the upper cover. Inside the upper and lower covers are 10 double-page watercolor illustrations. Due to the artist's death, the final 2 chapters lack illustration. Facundo Alí provided the cover illustrations and hand-coloring of the images.

2862   2011   Alice's Adventures in Wonderland
Buenos Aires: Vi-Da Global   9789873407048   Unknown
E-book. 1st edition.

4.2 AUSTRIA

2863   2016   Alice's Adventures in Wonderland
Ramsau im Zillertal: Wartelsteiner   9783861843962   Unknown
Minibook.

2864   2018   Alice's Adventures in Wonderland
Innsbruck: Helbling   9783990458624 (with CD);   Anonymous
9783990458631 (without CD)
Helbling Readers Classics/Red Series, Level 2 (A1/A2). Revised edition. With audio CD, 96 pp. Color illustrations. Also available without CD, 88 pp.

2865   2019   Alice's Adventures in Wonderland
Innsbruck: Helbling   9783990458624 (with CD);   Anonymous
9783990458631 (without CD)
Helbling Readers Classics/Red Series, Level 2 (A1/A2). Revised edition. With audio CD, 96 pp. Color illustrations. Also available without CD, 88 pp.

4.3 BELGIUM

2866   ca. 2000 to 2010   Alice's Adventures in Wonderland
Brussels: Paperview; New York: New York Post   Unknown
New York Post Family Classics Library, No. 4. Unabridged. 128 pp. Not dated but believed to be ca. 2000 to 2010.

4.4 BRAZIL

2867   1999   Alice's Adventures in Wonderland
São Paulo: Editora Scipione   John Tenniel; Enzo Marciante
Black Cat, Reading & Training series: Level elementary 1. First edition. Text adaptation and exercises by Gaia Lerace.

2868   2003   Alice's Adventures in Wonderland
São Paulo: Editora Scipione   8526235915   John Tenniel; Enzo Marciante
Black Cat, Reading & Training series: Level elementary 1. 1st edition, 4th impression. Text adaptation and exercises by Gaia Lerace.

2869   2011   Alice in Wonderland
        São Paulo: HUB Editorial   9788563623867   Margherita Micheli
        Retold by Richard B. A. Brown. 32 pp.

4.5 CHINA

2870   1916   Alice's Adventures in Wonderland
        Shanghai: The Commercial Press   Unknown
        Student's Library Series.

2871   1921   Alice's Adventures in Wonderland
        Shanghai: The Commercial Press   Unknown
        Student's Library Series. 74 pp.

2872   1925   Alice's Adventures in Wonderland
        Shanghai: The Commercial Press   Unknown
        Student's Library Series. 7th edition. 74 pp.

2873   1927   Alice's Adventures in Wonderland
        Shanghai: The Commercial Press   Unknown
        Student's Library Series.

2874   1930   Alice's Adventures in Wonderland
        Shanghai: World Book Co.   Anonymous
        Elementary Readings in English series. 1st edition. With Chinese notes and vocabulary. Annotated by Lin Handa.

2875   1933   Alice's Adventures in Wonderland
        Shanghai: World Books   Unknown
        Elementary Readings in English series. 2nd edition. Annotated in Chinese by Lin Handa. 97 pp.

2876   1934   Alice's Adventures in Wonderland
        Shanghai: The Commercial Press   Unknown
        Student's Library Series.

2877   1958   Alice in Wonderland after Lewis Carroll
        Beijing: Foreign Language Press   Unknown
        134 pp.

2878   1961   Alice in Wonderland
        Hong Kong: Tsin Hsiu Press   Unknown
        Edited by Wang P'ei. Abridged version with notes in Chinese and a vocabulary. 93 pp.

2879   1962   Alice in Wonderland
        Beijing: The Commercial Press   Unknown
        Edited by G. K. Maghidson-Stepanova. Abridged version with notes in Chinese and a vocabulary. 74 pp.

2880   1962   Alice's Adventures in Wonderland
        Beijing: The Commercial Press   Unknown
        Simplified by G. K. Maghidson-Stepanova. With Chinese footnotes and a glossary given by the Department of
        English of Beijing Foreign Languages Institute.

2881 1974 Alice's Adventures in Wonderland
Hong Kong: Oxford University Press   9780195807134   Carol Owen
Oxford Progressive English Readers series, Grade 1. Retold by Richard Croft. 70 pp. 16 illustrations in pink and black.
Simplified according to the language grading scheme especially compiled by D. H. Howe. Text edited and annotated
to explain words not in this language grade. Intended for students studying English as a second or foreign language.

2882 1980 Alice's Adventures in Wonderland
Hong Kong: Oxford University Press   9780195807134   Carol Owen
Oxford Progressive English Readers series, Grade 1. Retold by Richard Croft. 70 pp. Color illustrations. Part of a
series of both classic and modern fiction rewritten for "learners of English." Includes questions for students.

2883 1981 Alice's Adventures in Wonderland and Through the Looking-Glass
Beijing: Foreign Language Press   Unknown
218 pp.

2884 1982 Alice's Adventures in Wonderland
Hong Kong: Oxford University Press   9780195807134   Carol Owen
Oxford Progressive English Readers series, Grade 1. 1st edition, 7th impression (of the 1974 edition). 70 pp.

2885 1983 Alice's Adventures in Wonderland
Hong Kong: Mandarin   9780906320945   John Tenniel
Reprint. 144 pp. Some color illustrations. Originally published in 1981 by Octopus Books (UK).

2886 1984 Alice's Adventures in Wonderland
Hong Kong and others: Oxford University Press   9780195807134   Carol Owen
Oxford Progressive English Readers series, Grade 1. Retold by Richard Croft. 70 pp.

2887 1987 Alice's Adventures in Wonderland
Hong Kong: Oxford University Press   9780195807134   Carol Owen
Oxford Progressive English Readers series, Grade 1. 10th impression. 70 pp.

2888 1988 Alice's Adventures in Wonderland and Through the Looking-Glass
Shanghai: Shanghai Foreign Language Education Press   Anonymous

2889 1988 Alice's Adventures in Wonderland and Through the Looking Glass
          and What Alice Found There
Beijing: The Commercial Press   0710000438   John Tenniel
Combined edition, unabridged; bilingual English-Chinese (*Looking-Glass* translated by Y. R. Chao in 1969), page to
page, from pp. 175–381; illustrations on the pages of Chinese translation.

2890 1989 Alice's Adventures in Wonderland
Hong Kong: Oxford University Press   9780195807134   Carol Owen
Oxford Progressive English Readers series, Grade 1. 12th impression. Retold by Richard Croft. 70 pp.

2891 1992 Through the Looking-Glass
Hong Kong: Oxford University Press   0195852680   Anonymous
Oxford Progressive English Readers series, Grade 2. Revised edition of abridged edition. 73 pp.

2892 1993 Through the Looking-Glass
Hong Kong: Oxford University Press   9780195852684   K. Y. Chan
Oxford Progressive English Readers series, Grade 2. Revised edition of abridged edition. Edited by D. H. Howe. With
teaching appendix. 78 pp.

2893 1994 Through the Looking-Glass
Hong Kong: Oxford University Press　　　　　9780195852684　　　　K. Y. Chan
Oxford Progressive English Readers series, Grade 2. 2nd edition.

2894 1994 Through the Looking Glass and What Alice Found There
Beijing: China Translation & Publishing House　　7500102437　　　　John Tenniel
Bilingual English-Chinese (translated by Xu Jihong), page to page, illustrations on the pages of English (photoprint).

2895 1998 Alice's Adventures in Wonderland
Shanghai: Shanghai Foreign Language Education Press. 9787810463911　　Unknown
Oxford University Press
Oxford Progressive English Readers series. Annotated by Wu Qiyao. Part of a set of stories including *Jane Eyre*, *Tales from the Arabian Nights*, *Treasure Island*, and *The Call of the Wild*. 486 pp.

2896 2003 Alice's Adventures in Wonderland
Shanghai: Shanghai Foreign Language Education Press　　　　　Unknown
Easy English for Classics series. Simplified by Margery Green. Annotated by Wang Jue. 95 pp.

2897 2003 Alice's Adventures in Wonderland
Hefei: Anhui Science & Technology Publishing House　　　　　Unknown
Illustrated World Masterpieces in English series. 232 pp. Authorized by Playmore and Waldman Publishing Co.

2898 2004 Alice's Adventures in Wonderland
Shanghai: East China Normal University Press　　9787561735824　　　Unknown
Black Cat, Reading & Training series: Level 3. Simplified by Gaia Lerace. 144 pp. Authorized by The Commercial Press (HK).

2899 2006 Alice's Adventures in Wonderland
Shanghai: Shanghai Foreign Language Education Press. 9787810463911　　Unknown
Oxford University Press
Oxford Progressive English Readers series. Annotated by Wu Qiyao. Reprint of the 1998 edition. Part of a set of stories including *Jane Eyre*, *Tales from the Arabian Nights*, *Treasure Island*, and *The Call of the Wild*. 486 pp.

2900 2006 Alice in Wonderland
Beijing: World Publishing Company　　　　　Unknown
Penguin English Readings series. Simplified by Mary Tomalin. 40 pp.

2901 2008 A Collection of English Language Children's Literature
Shanghai: World Publishing Corporation　　　　　Unknown
Alice and *Looking-Glass*. Together with *Happy Prince and Other Tales* by Oscar Wilde, *Peter Pan* by J. M. Barrie, and *Water-Babies* by Charles Kingsley.

2902 2009 Through the Looking Glass and What Alice Found There
Beijing: China Translation & Publishing House　　9787500122470　　　Unknown
269 pp. Bilingual English-Chinese (translated by Xu Jihong), page to page.

2903 2012 Through the Looking-Glass and What Alice Found There
Beijing: China Translation & Publishing House　　9787500134602　　　Unknown
269 pp. Bilingual English-Chinese (translated by Xu Jihong), page to page.

2904 2012 Through The Looking-Glass and What Alice Found There
Shanghai: Shanghai Translation Publishing House　　9787532756193　　Pete Newell
333 pp. Bilingual English-Chinese (translated by Wu Juntao).

2905   2012   Alice in Wonderland
Nanjing: Yilin Press   Unknown
Reading Classics, Level 2. Simplified by Ken Methold and Sheila Lyne. 64 pp.

2906   2013   Alice's Adventures in Wonderland
Nanjing: Yilin Press   Unknown
Readings in English series. 185 pp.

2907   2013   Alice in Wonderland
Nanjing: Yilin Press   Unknown
Reading Classics, Level 2. Simplified by Ken Methold and Sheila Lyne. 92 pp.

2908   2014   Alice's Adventures in Wonderland and Through the Looking-Glass
Beijing: Central Compilation and Translation Press   Unknown
Reader in Classics of World Literature. 222 p.

2909   2014   Alice's Adventures in Wonderland
Nanjing: Yilin Press   Unknown
1st English-language edition. Combined with *Looking-Glass*. 185 pp.

2910   2014   Through the Looking-Glass and What Alice Found There
Shanghai: Shanghai Scientific and   9787543957855   Unknown
Technological Literature Press
287 pp. Bilingual English-Chinese. Translated by Wang Renfang.

2911   2015   Alice in Wonderland
Hong Kong: Minedition   9789888341016   Lisbeth Zwerger
Mini-books Minedition series. Michael Neugebauer edition. 125 pp.

2912   2015   Alice's Adventures in Wonderland
Beijing: Zhongyi chubanshe   Unknown
Helbling English Reader for Junior High Schools, No. 2. Adapted by Lu Minmin. 91 pp. Authorized by Helbling
Languages.

2913   2015   Alice's Adventures in Wonderland
[Beijing]: Pickatale   Tim Budden (cover);
Beñiat Olaberria Egiguren; João Faissal; Sara Sánchez Núñez; Ekaterina Mudrenko; Bojan Petricevic;
Wendi M. Keels; Daria Makiela; Guan Wei; Allyson Kelley; Daniel Ramos; Elena Budenna; Marina Bello;
Ruxandra Socaciu; Georgia Stylou; Kizel Cotiw-an; Brenda Figueroa; Alexandra Dzhiganskaya; Robert William
Askew; Luke Parker; Tatyana Popovichenko; Angela Takagui; Vladan Zhervanov-Vamsi; Cecilia Daude;
Kseniya Eliseeva; Snezana Pupovic; Landis Blair; Daniel Vincent; Santiago Lozano; Jessica Cooper; Björn Dahlgren;
Regina Hammarlund; Andrea Maiorana; Dagmara Gąska; Xingwen Shi; Nikolas Hagialas; Nune Hovhannisyan;
Benjamin Mitchley; Irene Katsouri; Petra van Berkum; Dora Mitchell; Thiago Trapo; Isaiah Bolima; Eric Ashby;
Aitch; Svetlana Paluhina; Jun Hun Yap; Ilaria Bozzini; Rosen Marinov-Oummaia; Eric Bird; Juliana Fiorese;
Amgalan Sukhbaatar; Nela Krzewniak; Inga Shalvashvili; Lilla Kuizs; Rin Kurohana; John Frederik Federis;
Alexandra Stefanel Bejenaru; Miranda Mundt; Tony Ganem; Jack Herbert; Sergey Loginov; Anja Gram; Leandro
Luna; Krzysztof Krygier; Vinca Kumala; Anna Gorban; Irina Anatolieva Pamyatnih; Bill 5onic Fricke; Theo Chronis;
Mominur Rahman; Rebecca Weaver; Niharika Singh; Alexander Vidal; Milena Radeva; Davide Raimondi; Ekaterina
Muratova; Alizia Vence; Daria Atoyan; Pilar Criado; Clare Rosean; Luminita Cosareanu; John Monteiro; Vladimir
Nospherate; Rob Peters; Bruno Sousa; Erin T. Whalen; Katie Nolan; Ricardo De los Angeles; Lianna Tai; Peter
Máhr; Rebecca Crockett; Karolina Urbańczyk; Francesco Paolo Ardizzone; Gilly Ceder; Maryna Rudko; Gergana
Petanska; Jeremy Jones; Kasia Mickiewicz; Diana Stanciulescu; Anna Grinchuka; Igor Tadeu Paiva Guimarães;
Elvira Makienko; Mike Paschal; Paula Pakk; Vivian Mirelly de Freitas Vieira; Julia Steffy Berman; Ralitsa Yaneva;
Patricia Fidalgo; Matias Sariego; Anda Dragomir; Sarah Waterfield; Justin Moore; Estefanía de Castro; Ablena
Georgieva; Mollie d'Onofrio; Adriana Danaila; Iskra Gadularova; Gustavo Wenzel; Giuseppe Lira; Alexandra

Gheorghiu; Eduardo Alejandro Ramírez Hernández; Rowan Abbott; Johan Louw; Maria Kristina Windayani; Zhanna Dryha; Nina Popovska; Olga Dabrowska; Milos Tutus; John Daily; Amanda Lanzone; Vinicius Meira; David John Dunthorne; Ricardo Jaime; Juan Hernández Sánchez; Oscar Dominguez Pazo; Kaja Szechowsko; Maisa Chaves; Irina Zenuk; Madmanstan Johnson; Jehanne Silva-Freimane; Tetsuya Toshima; Tanya Francis-Day; Joanna Rzepińska; Vladimir Matic-Kuriljov; Maria Fernanda Fierro Fimbres; Vojislav Sarcevic; Jenay M. Elder; Olga Kovalyova; Varya Kolesnikova; Kristina Muñoz; Shiko

"150Alice Project: The World's Most Collaborative Artbook." 150 pp. of text and 150 pp. of color illustrations (all from different illustrators). 300 pp. Created by the 150Alice Project, celebrating 150 years of *Alice in Wonderland*. The original text was restyled into 150 segments, and each piece was sent to an artist to imagine that piece in their own way. Sold on Indiegogo.com as part of a crowd-funding campaign. The proceeds were used to fund the building of a school in Mongolia. Measures 28 x 28 cm.

2914	2016	Alice's Adventures in Wonderland			
		Beijing: Zhongyi chubanshe		Unknown	
		Zhongyi Classics Library – Masterpieces in World Literature (6).			

2915 2016 Alice's Adventures in Wonderland
Shanghai: Shanghai Foreign Language Education Press   Unknown
Annotated by Wu Qiyao and Tao Yi. 99 pp.

2916 2016 Alice Through the Looking-Glass
Beijing: Knowledge Press   9787501593194   Incco
Rewritten by Martin Mellish.

2917 2017 Disney Alice Through the Looking-Glass
Shanghai: East China University of   9787562851455
Science and Technology Press
236 pp. Rewritten by Disney.

2918 2017 Through the Looking-Glass
Beijing: Tsinghua University Press   9787302423638   Unillustrated
194 pp. Translated by Wang Tianxiang. Comes in 2 separate books: 1 English, 1 Chinese.

2919 2017 Alice's Adventures in Wonderland & Through the Looking-Glass
Tianjin: Tianjin People's Publishing House   9787201112282   Unknown
Holybird New Classics. 234 pp.

2920 2019 Alice's Adventures in Wonderland
Beijing: Foreign Language Teaching and Research Press   Unknown
Oxford Bookworms Library, Level 2.

4.6 COLOMBIA

2921 2001 Alice's Adventures in Wonderland
Bogotá: Panamericana Editorial   9789583007675   Rocío Parra
The English Bookmarks series. 1st edition. Unabridged. 159 pp.

2922 2003 Alice's Adventures in Wonderland
Bogotá: Panamericana Editorial   9789583007675   Rocío Parra
The English Bookmarks series. Unabridged. Reprint of the 2001 edition. 159 pp.

2923 2010 Alice's Adventures in Wonderland
Bogotá: Panamericana Editorial   9789583007675   Rocío Parra
The English Bookmarks series. Unabridged. Reprint of the 2001 edition. 159 pp.

4.7 CZECH REPUBLIC

2924   2007   Alice's Adventures in Wonderland
Brno: Tribun EU   9788087139820   Unillustrated
1st edition. 72 pp. Not illustrated (except cover).

2925   2009   Alice's Adventures in Wonderland
Brno: Tribun EU   9788073997021   Klára Mikulcová
Revised edition based on the 2007 edition. 72 pp.

2926   2017   Alice's Adventures in Wonderland and Through the Looking-Glass
Prague: Athanor   9788027022328   Jan Švankmajer
1st edition published with text in English. Previously available only in a Japanese edition.

4.8 DENMARK

2927   1996   Alice in Wonderland
Copenhagen: Aschehoug. Stockholm,   9788711090503 (Aschehoug);   Peter Bay Alexandersen
Sweden: Almqvist & Wiksell   9789121149843 (Almqvist & Wiksell)
Easy Classics, Level 3. Retold by Britt-Katrin Keson. 92 pp.

4.9 FRANCE

2928   1930   Alice in Wonderland
Paris: Black Sun Press   Marie Laurencin
114 pp. 6 color lithographs. Limited edition of 420 numbered copies for the US, 370 numbered copies for Europe of which 300 on Rives Paper, 50 on Japanese Vellum, and 20 on Hollande Van Gelder, each of these containing a supplementary suite of the 6 illustrations in sanguine, and 1 copy on Vieux Japon containing a suite in sanguine to be sold with the 6 lithographs colored and signed by Marie Laurencin. Printed under the direction of Caresse Crosby.

2929   1930   Alice's Adventures in Wonderland
Paris: Henri Didier (Villeneuve-Saint-Georges: Impr. Union typographique)   G. W. Irwin
Tales from England series, 1st degree, No. 1. 1st edition. Abridged and simplified by Ronald Windross. 72 pp. With engravings.

2930   1933   Alice's Adventures in Wonderland
Paris: Henri Didier   G. W. Irwin
Tales from England series, 1st degree, No. 1. 2nd edition. Abridged and simplified by Ronald Windross. 72 pp.

2931   1934   Alice's Adventures in Wonderland
[Paris]: Henri Didier   G.W. Irwin
Tales from England series, 1st degree, No. 1. 3rd edition. Abridged and simplified by Ronald Windross. 72 pp.

2932   1936   Alice's Adventures in Wonderland
Paris: Henri Didier   G.W. Irwin
Tales from England series, 1st degree, No. 1. 4th edition. Abridged and simplified by Ronald Windross. 72 pp.

2933   1939   Alice's Adventures in Wonderland
Paris: Henri Didier   G.W. Irwin
Tales from England series, 1st degree, No. 1. 5th edition. Abridged and simplified by Ronald Windross. 72 pp.

2934	1942	Alice's Adventures in Wonderland	
		Paris: Henri Didier	G.W. Irwin

Tales from England series, 1st degree, No. 1. 6th edition. Abridged and simplified by Ronald Windross. 72 pp.

2935	1946	Alice's Adventures in Wonderland	
		Paris: Henri Didier	G.W. Irwin

Tales from England series, 1st degree, No. 1. 7th edition. Abridged and simplified by Ronald Windross. 72 pp.

2936	1950	Alice's Adventures in Wonderland	
		Paris: Edmund S. Wood	John Tenniel

Miniature books. (2 volumes. In a tan slipcase. *Looking-Glass* is in that checklist.) *Alice* 174 pp. Bound in half red leather over marbled paper-covered boards. Spines stamped in gold with title, author, and rules. The Minia Press and Edmund S. Wood imprints are used on miniature books published in Jamaica, New York. However, this edition appears under the Edmund S. Wood imprint with Paris listed as the place of publication.

2937	1950	Alice's Adventures in Wonderland	
		Paris: Minia Press	John Tenniel

Miniature books. (2 volumes. In a tan slipcase. *Looking-Glass* is in that checklist.) *Alice* 174 pp. Bound in half red leather over marbled paper-covered boards. Spines stamped in gold with title, author, and rules. The Minia Press and Edmund S. Wood imprints are used on miniature books published in Jamaica, New York. However, this edition appears under the Minia Press imprint with Paris listed as the place of publication.

2938	1950	Through the Looking-Glass	
		Paris: Edmund S. Wood	John Tenniel

Miniature books. (2 volumes. In a tan slipcase. *Alice* is in that checklist.) *Looking-Glass* 204 pp. Bound in half red leather over marbled paper-covered boards. Spines stamped in gold with title, author, and rules. The Minia Press and Edmund S. Wood imprints are used on miniature books published in Jamaica, New York. However, this edition appears under the Edmund S. Wood imprint with Paris listed as the place of publication.

2939	1950	Through the Looking-Glass	
		Paris: Minia Press	John Tenniel

Miniature books. (2 volumes. In a tan slipcase. *Alice* is in that checklist.) *Looking-Glass* 204 pp. Bound in half red leather over marbled paper-covered boards. Spines stamped in gold with title, author, and rules. The Minia Press and Edmund S. Wood imprints are used on miniature books published in Jamaica, New York. However, this edition appears under the Minia Press imprint with Paris listed as the place of publication.

2940	1951	Through the Looking-Glass	
		Paris: Didier	Marjorie Whittington

Tales from England series, 1st degree, No. 16. Abridged and simplified by Ronald Windross. Includes a list of useful words with their translation. 60 pp.

2941	1951	Alice's Adventures in Wonderland	
		Paris: Henri Didier (Mesnil: impr. de Firmin-Didot)	G. W. Irwin

Tales from England series, 1st degree, No. 1. 10th edition. Abridged and simplified by Ronald Windross. 72 pp.

2942	1975	Alice's Adventures in Wonderland	
		Paris: Librairie Hachette	Paul Woolfenden

Facts and Fiction in Easy English series, 1st grade. General editor: Gilbert Quénelle. Adapted by Lynette Vaughan. Booklet with a listening tape. Black-and-white illustrations. 64 pp. Some vocabulary footnotes with a definition in English of the words. 1st illustrations have vocabulary included in it with arrows pointing at objects.

2943	2004	Through the Looking-Glass	
		Paris: Didier Mutel	John Tenniel, Didier Mutel

224 pp. With 50 engravings by Didier Mutel and 50 illustrations by Tenniel. Limited edition of 51 copies. With slipcase. The text is printed backwards, except for the introductory poem by Carroll and the colophon.

2944   1975   Alice's Adventures in Wonderland and Through the Looking-Glass
Paris: Librairie Hachette   9782010003608   Anonymous
Facts and Fiction in Easy English series. Adapted by Lynette Vaughan. 64 pp.

2945   1997   Alice in Wonderland
Paris: Fleurus Editions.   9780765191885   Monique Gorde
New York: Smithmark Publishers
57 pp.

2946   1998   Alice in Wonderland
Paris: Fleurus Editions.   9782215061922   Monique Gorde
New York: Smithmark Publishers
57 pp.

2947   2002   Alice's Adventures in Wonderland
Paris: D. Mutel   Didier Mutel
192 pp. With 42 original copper engravings by Didier Mutel and 42 illustrations after John Tenniel. In slipcase.
Limited edition of 50 copies.

2948   2007   L'anglais c'est facile avec Alice au pays des merveilles
Paris: Univers poche   9782266168366   Carole Gourrat
Adaptation by Céline Meur and Katia Tanant. With audio CD. 47 pp. Color illustrations. Very simple text for
teaching English to primary school children, with exercises at the end.

2949   2016   Alice in Wonderland
Paris: Larousse   9782818704523   Julien Akita
Harrap's School Yes, you can! series. 32 pp. Color illustrations. Adaptation to teach English to 11- and 12-year-old
pupils. Includes a list of words with their phonetic transcription and their translation into French at the end.

2950   2017   Alice in Wonderland
Paris: L'Orée des fees   9782322137213   Unknown
Original text with commentary and glossary of terms used both in Lewis Carroll's books and in Tim Burton's 2010
movie. 62 pp. Does not include "All in the golden afternoon." Reprint of a US edition of 1916 by Sam L. Gabriel Sons
and Company, New York. Printed by: Books on Demand GmbH, Norderstedt, Germany.

2951   2017   The Tale of Alice in Wonderland
Paris: Larousse   9782035919564   Julien Akita
Extremely simplified and adapted text. "To learn English by immersing yourself in the right accent." 12 pp. With
electronic device inserted in the book so you can hear the text by pressing on a dot on each page. Cover from
Shutterstock.

4.10 GERMANY

2952   ca. 1920s   Alice in Wonderland
Paderborn: F. Schöningh   Unknown
Schöninghs Englische Schulausgaben, nr. 38. Adaptation, with notes and dictionary. Edited by Dr. Franz Ewald. 94
pp.

2953   1926   Alice's Adventures in Wonderland
Frankfurt am Main: Diesterweg   Unknown
Diesterwegs Neusprachliche Schulausgaben/Englische Reihe, 2. Edited by Marie Mundt and G. Kirchner. 75 pp.

2954	1930	Alice in Wonderland		
		Paderborn: F. Schöningh		Unknown
		Schöninghs Englische Schulausgaben, nr. 38. Edited by Dr. Franz Ewald. 94 pp.		

2955	1930	Alice's Adventures in Wonderland		
		Munich: M. Kellerer		John Tenniel
		Kellerers Englische Ausgaben, Bd. 4/5. Adaptation with comments by Alfred Bernhard and Wilfrid H. Wells. 68 pp. Front wrapper has date 1928.		

2956	1935	Alice's Adventures in Wonderland		
		Bielefeld, Leipzig: Velhagen & Klasing		Anonymous
		No. 226. Edited by Adolf Püttmann. 74 pp.		

2957	1936	Alice's Adventures in Wonderland		
		Bielefeld, Leipzig: Velhagen & Klasing		Anonymous
		With 7 illustrations.		

2958	1946	Alice in Wonderland		
		Paderborn/Bremen/Mainz: F. Schöningh		Unknown
		Schöninghs Englische Schulausgaben, nr. 38. Edited by Dr. Franz Ewald. 94 pp.		

2959	1953	Alice's Adventures in Wonderland		
		Munich: Max Hueber Verlag		John Tenniel

2960	1953	Alice's Adventures in Wonderland		
		Leipzig: Paul List Verlag		Unknown
		Panther Books edition.		

2961	1968	Alice in Wonderland		
		Munich: Max Hueber Verlag		John Tenniel
		Edited by Alfred Bernhard. With notes in German. Copyright 1953.		

2962	1969	Alice's Adventures in Wonderland		
		Munich: Kunstverlag E. Praeger		Salvador Dalí
		With original wood engravings and 1 original etching by Salvador Dalí. One-time world publication of 2,500 numbered items, with 150 reserved for the German market. 150 pp.		

2963	1980	Alice's Adventures in Wonderland: language and communication		
		Frankfurt am Main: Hirschgraben-Verlag	9783454665100; 9783454665209	Anonymous
		Language & Communication series. Literarische Texte für den Englischunterricht auf der Sekundarstufe II. 1st edition. Edited by Dieter Wolff. 79 pp. Text in English, glossary etc. in German, textbook (study section) in German. Teacher book ('Lehrerheft') has ISBN 9783454665209.		

2964	1991	Alice's Adventures in Wonderland: language and communication		
		Frankfurt am Main: Cornelsen Hirschgraben	9783454665100	Anonymous
		Language & Communication series. 2nd edition. Edited by Dieter Wolff. 80 pp.		

2965	1994	Alice's Adventures in Wonderland		
		Berlin: Cornelsen	9783454665100	Anonymous
		Language & Communication series. 3rd edition. Edited by Dieter Wolff. 80 pp.		

2966	1997	Alice's Adventures in Wonderland		

Berlin: Cornelsen   9783454665100   Anonymous
Language & Communication series. 4th edition. Edited by Dieter Wolff. 80 pp.

2967   1998   Alice's Adventures in Wonderland
        Frankfurt am Main: Diesterweg   9783425030920   Unknown
        Black Cat, Reading & Training series: Step 2, level B1.1. Text adaption and activities by Gaia Lcrace. 124 pp.

2968   2005   Alice's Adventures in Wonderland
        Garching bei München: Miniaturbuchverlag Leipzig   9783861840572; 9783861840589   John Tenniel
        No. 11. 1st edition. 508 pp. In slipcase with gold stamping.

2969   2005   Alice's Adventures in Wonderland
        Simbach am Inn: Miniaturbuchverlag Leipzig (owned by Wartelsteiner GmbH)   John Tenniel;
                                                                                         Susanne Smajic
        Miniature book. Unabridged. 512 pp. With slipcase. Limited edition of 250. Hand-painted and inlaid bindings by
        Roland Meuter; stamp-signed on lower rear turn-ins. Fore-edge painted by Susanne Smajic. Later available as a set
        with miniature book *Through the Looking-Glass* published in 2013.

2970   2007   Alice's Adventures in Wonderland
        Munich: Langenscheidt ELT   9783526521334   Lucia Mattioli
        Black Cat, Reading & Training series: Step 2, level B1.1. For English language teaching. Text adaptation and activities
        by Kenneth Brodey. Other authors and contributors: Emma Berridge. 1 Audio/CD-ROM. 112 pp. Rights bought from
        Cideb, Italy (ISBN 9788877542991, 1997).

2971   2008   Alice's Adventures in Wonderland
        Munich: Black Cat Publishing, at Langenscheidt ELT   9783526520146   Anonymous
        Black Cat, Green Apple series: Starter (A1). With audio CD. 64 pp.

2972   2008   Alice's Adventures in Wonderland
        Leipzig: Miniaturbuchverlag   9783861841487   John Tenniel
        G. Edward Cassady Collection. 221 pp. In blue illustrated cardboard slipcase as issued.

2973   2010   Alice in Wonderland
        Stuttgart: Klett Ernst/Schulbuch   9783125148123   Margherita Micheli
        Young ELI Readers series, stage 4. Retold by Richard Brown. With audio CD. 32 pp.

2974   2012   Alice's Adventures in Wonderland: illustrated & annotated edition
        Frankfurt am Main: Jazzybee Verlag   9783849621698   Arthur Rackham
        E-book. Extended and annotated edition with extensive biographical information about the author and his life, all
        the original illustrations, and 2 essays about Alice and her place in Carroll's life.

2975   ca. 2012 Alice's Adventures in Wonderland
        Simbach am Inn: Miniaturbuchverlag Leipzig (owned by Wartelsteiner GmbH)   John Tenniel
        Miniature book. Unabridged. 1st edition. With slipcase.

2976   2013   Alice's Adventures in Wonderland
        Simbach am Inn: Miniaturbuchverlag Leipzig (owned by Wartelsteiner GmbH)   John Tenniel;
                                                                                         Susanne Smajic
        Miniature book set in a slipcase with a 2013 *Looking-Glass*. Unabridged. The *Alice* edition first published in a
        miniature book in 2005. Limited edition of 250. Hand-painted and inlaid bindings by Roland Meuter; stamp-signed
        on lower rear turn-ins. Fore-edge painted by Susanne Smajic.

2977   2013   Through the Looking-Glass
        Simbach am Inn, Germany: Miniaturbuchverlag Leipzig   John Tenniel; Susanne Smajic
        (owned by Wartelsteiner GmbH)

Miniature book set in a slipcase with a 2013 *Alice*. Unabridged. Limited edition of 250. Hand-painted and inlaid bindings by Roland Meuter; stamp-signed on lower rear turn-ins. Fore-edge painted by Susanne Smajic.

| 2978 | 2014 | Alice's Adventures in Wonderland | | |

Munich: Langenscheidt Verlag   9783526521549   Unknown

Black Cat, Reading & Training series: Step 2, level B1.1. With audio CD. Rights bought from Cideb, Italy (ISBN 9788877542991, 1997).

| 2979 | 2014 | Alice's Adventures in Wonderland – Reclams Universal-Bibliothek: Fremdsprachentexte: English | | |

Leipzig: Reclam Verlag   9783159604848   John Tenniel

E-book. Unabridged. Translated by Dietrich Klose. 118 pp. Includes translations of difficult words, epilogue, and literary references. With page numbering of the print version.

| 2980 | 2015 | Alice's Adventures in Wonderland | | |

Cologne: MSK GmbH   Tanika

Limited edition of 50. Published through crowdfunding.

| 2981 | 2015 | Alice's Adventures in Wonderland | | |

Munich: Langenscheidt   9783526521549   Giovanni Manna

Black Cat, Reading & Training series: Step 2, level B1.1. Adaptation and activities by Gina D. B. Clemen. With CD. 111 pp. Rights bought from Cideb, Italy (ISBN 9788877542991, 1997).

| 2982 | 2016 | Alice's Adventures in Wonderland – Englishe Lektüre für das 1, 2, und 3, Lernjahr | | |

Stuttgart: Ernst Klett Verlag GmbH   9783125000162   Unknown

Black Cat, Green Apple series: Starter (A1). Adapted by Gina D. B. Clemen, activities by Mary Johnson. With audio CD-ROM. 64 pp.

| 2983 | 2016 | Alice's Adventures in Wonderland – Englishe Lektüre für das 3, 4, und 5, Lernjahr | | |

Stuttgart: Ernst Klett Verlag GmbH   9783125000926   Unknown

Black Cat, Reading & Training series: Step 2, level B1.1. Edited by Gina D. B. Clemen. With audio CD. 112 pp.

| 2984 | 2016 | Alice's Adventures in Wonderland | | |

Norderstedt: Norderstedt Books on Demand   9783741221989   John Tenniel

E-book. 1st Page Publishing Classics Collection, Book 4. Unabridged.

| 2985 | 2016 | Alice's Adventures in Wonderland | | |

Norderstedt: Norderstedt Books on Demand   9783741205606 (e-book); 1011116100177 (print)   John Tenniel

E-book and print book. 1st Page Publishing Classics Collection, Book 5. 192 pp.

| 2986 | 2016 | Alice's Adventures in Wonderland | | |

Norderstedt: Norderstedt Books on Demand   9783741205101; 9783741205484 (e-book); 1011101601965 (print)   John Tenniel

E-book and print book. 1st Page Publishing Classics Collection, Book 6. Unabridged. 192 pp.

| 2987 | 2016 | Alice's Adventures in Wonderland | | |

Norderstedt: Norderstedt Books on Demand   9783741221972   Unknown

E-book. 91 pp.

| 2988 | 2016 | Alice's Adventures in Wonderland | | |

Dinslaken: Andre Hoffmann   9783736408500   Unknown

E-book. 96 pp.

2989   2016   **Alice's Adventures in Wonderland**
Simbach am Inn: Miniaturbuchverlag Leipzig   9783861840572   John Tenniel
(owned by Wartelsteiner GmbH)
Miniature book. Unabridged. 2nd edition. With slipcase.

2990   2017   **Alice's Adventures in Wonderland**
Norderstedt: Norderstedt Books on Demand   9783741281624   John Tenniel
1st Page Publishing Classics Collection, Book 1. 140 pp.

2991   2017   **Alice's Adventures in Wonderland**
Norderstedt: Norderstedt Books on Demand   9783743195042   Unknown
E-book. All-time Favorites Collection, No. 6. 84 pp.

2992   2017   **The complete novels of Lewis Carroll (Illustrated Edition)**
Frankfurt am Main: Musaicum Books   9788027218509   Lewis Carroll; John Tenniel;
    Others

E-book. 1,670 pp. Includes: *Alice's Adventures under Ground, Alice's Adventures in Wonderland, Through the Looking-Glass, Sylvie and Bruno, Sylvie and Bruno Concluded,* and *The Life and Letters of Lewis Carroll.*

2993   2017   **Alice in Wonderland: The Complete Collection**
Frankfurt am Main: Oregan Publishing   9782377939190;   Lewis Carroll; John Tenniel;
    9791097338756   Others

E-book. The Greatest Fictional Characters of All Time Book Center series. 483 pp. Includes *Alice's Adventures under Ground, Alice's Adventures in Wonderland, Through the Looking Glass, The Hunting of the Snark, The Nursery 'Alice,'* and the lost chapter, "The Wasp in a Wig," from *Through the Looking-Glass.*

2994   2017   **Alice's Adventures in Wonderland**
Frankfurt am Main: Prometheus Classics   9782378075316   Unknown
E-book. 200 pp.

2995   2019   **Alice in Wonderland**
Weimar: Aionas Verlag   9783965450066   John Tenniel
1st edition. Unabridged. 120 pp.

2996   2019   **Through the Looking-Glass**
Weimar: Aionas   9783965450073   John Tenniel
1st edition. Unabridged. 144 pp.

4.11 INDIA

2997   2004   **Alice in Wonderland**
Delhi: Printline Books   8175739398   Unknown
Printline Classic. Reprint. 104 pp.

2998   2005   **Great selected short stories**
Delhi: Printline Books   8130403153   John Tenniel; Others
Cover title: World's Great Selected Short Stories.

2999   2007   **Alice's Adventures in Wonderland**
New Delhi: Mahaveer Publishers   9788183520539   John Tenniel

3000   2010   **Alice's Adventures in Wonderland**
New Delhi: Mahaveer Publishers   9788183520539   John Tenniel
127 pp. Distributed by Vaibhav Book Service.

3001	2010	Alice's Adventures in Wonderland		
		Uttar Pradesh: Harper Collins India	9780007350827	Unknown

3002	2010	Alice in Wonderland		
		Mumbai: Alka Publications	9788180066467	Unknown
		32 pp.		

3003	2010	Alice in Wonderland		
		New Delhi: Kalyani Navyug Media	9789380028231	Rajesh Nagulakonda
		Graphic novel. "A Campfire Classic." Adapted by Lewis Helfand and illustrated by Rajesh Nagulakonda.		

3004	2011	Alice's Adventures in Wonderland		
		New Delhi: Maple Press	9789380816715	Unknown
		Maple Classics series. 256 pp.		

3005	2011	Alice in Wonderland		
		New Delhi: Dreamland Publications	9781730119668	Anonymous
		Uncle Moon's Fairy Tales series. Abridged. 16 pp.		

3006	2011	Through the Looking-Glass		
		New Delhi: Worldview	9788186423516	Unknown
		Edited by Brinda Bose.		

3007	2013	Alice in Wonderland		
		New Delhi: Ramesh Publishing House	9789381438466	Unknown
		Immortal Illustrated Classics series. Edited by LS Editorial Team.		

3008	2014	Alice in Wonderland and Through the Looking-Glass complete and unabridged		
		New Delhi: Sparrow Books	9789382382652	Unknown
		1st edition. Reprint. 196 pp.		

3009	2015	Alice in Wonderland		
		Uttar Pradesh: Om Books International	9789383202720	Manish Singh; Manoj Kumar Prasad
		Om Illustrated Classics/Om Kidz series. Adapted by Subhojit Sanyal. 240 pp.		

3010	2015	Alice in Wonderland		
		New Delhi: Dreamland Publications	9781730119668	Anonymous
		Uncle Moon's Fairy Tales series. 16 pp. Abridged.		

3011	2015	Through the Looking-Glass		
		Uttar Pradesh: Vishv Books Private Ltd.	9789350653388	Unknown
		Graded Readers series. 1st edition. Abridged by Shradha Anand. 80 pp.		

3012	2015	Through the Looking-Glass		
		New Delhi: Om Books International	9789384225490	Anonymous
		Om Illustrated Classics series. 240 pp.		

3013	2016	Alice in Wonderland		
		New Delhi: Dreamland Publications	9781730119668	Anonymous
		Uncle Moon's Fairy Tales series. 16 pp. Abridged. Reprint.		

3014	2016	Alice's Adventures in Wonderland and Through the Looking-Glass		
		New Delhi: Pan Macmillan Press	9781509849024	Unknown
		Macmillans Popular Classics series.		

3015 2016 Alice in Wonderland
Uttar Pradesh: Vishv Books Private Ltd. 9789350653326 Unknown
Graded Readers series. 96 pp. Abridged.

3016 2016 Alice in Wonderland
New Delhi: Ramesh Publishing House 9789381438466 Anonymous
Immortal Illustrated Classics series. 192 pp.

3017 2016 Alice's Adventures in Wonderland
Delhi: VIJ Books PVT Ltd. 9789386834669 Unknown
E-book. World Classics series. Unabridged. 88 pp.

3018 2016 Through the Looking-Glass
Uttar Pradesh: Vishv Books Private Ltd. 9789350653388 Unknown
Graded Readers series. 1st reprint. Abridged by Shradha Anand. 80 pp.

3019 2017 Alice's Adventures in Wonderland
Delhi: VIJ Books PVT Ltd./Alpha editions 9789386019462 Unknown
World Classics series. Unabridged. 90 pp.

3020 2017 Alice in Wonderland
Uttar Pradesh: Om Books International 9789386410047 Unknown
Illustrated Classics/Om Kidz series. 16 pp.

3021 2018 Alice's Adventures in Wonderland
New Delhi: Gyan Publishing House 9788121214513 Unknown
238 pp.

3022 2018 Alice's Adventures in Wonderland
New Delhi: Vayu Education of India (VEI) 9789386000538 Anonymous
126 pp. Black-and-white illustrations.

3023 2018 Through the Looking-Glass
New Delhi: Om Books International 9789384225490 Anonymous
Om Illustrated Classics series. 240 pp.

3024 2018 Through the Looking-Glass
New Delhi: Rupa Publications 9789350653388 Unknown

3025 2019 Alice's Adventures in Wonderland
New Delhi: Vayu Education of India (VEI) 9789386000538 Anonymous
126 pp. Black-and-white illustrations.

3026 2019 Alice in Wonderland
New Delhi: Ramesh Publishing House 9789386063274 Anonymous
Everlasting Illustrated Classics series.

4.12 ITALY

3027   1945   Alice's Adventures in Wonderland
Rome: Societal editorale G. Volterra   Anonymous
"By Lewis Carrol" [*sic*]. Preface by Edoardo Bizzarri. 202 pp.

3028   1969   Alice in Wonderland
Bologna: G. Malipiero   R. Canaider
Happiness Story Book series. 1st edition. Adaptation (text severely edited). 16 pp. 14 color illustrations, including
one partially repeated. Pictorial wrappers with among others "A story by Carrol" [*sic*]. Color pictorial scene. Later
printing in 1977.

3029   1974   Alice's Adventures in Wonderland
Milan: Olivetti   Kuniyoshi Kaneko
1st edition. Unabridged. 121 pp. With 13 large black-and-white illustrations and 1 colored on the cover. There is a
large 2-page illustration on the inside front cover and repeated on the inside back cover. Republication of the work
published by Penguin Books Ltd., London. Copyright 1974 by Olivetti for the illustrations by Kuniyoshi Kaneko.
Privately printed book (known as "Libri Strenna"); given as Christmas gifts to Olivetti clients and suppliers. Not for
sale to the public.

3030   1977   Alice in Wonderland
Bologna: G. Malipiero, under arrangement with Ottenheimer Publishers Inc.   R. Canaider
A learn to read story book. 16 pp. 1st printing in 1969.

3031   1995   Alice in Wonderland
Legnano: Gruppo EdiCart   9781552804902   Claudio Cernuschi;
                                                                                Maria De Filippo
Enchanted Fairy Tales series. Text adaptation by Giulia Baiocchi. Unpaginated. Large size.

3032   1996   Alice's Adventures in Wonderland
Colognola ai Colli: Giunti Demetra   9788844005160   Unknown
Scuola di Inglese series. 144 pp.

3033   1997   Alice's Adventures in Wonderland
Colognola ai Colli: Demetra; Florence: Giunti   8844005162;   Constantina Fiorini
                                                 9788844005160
Palestra di Inglese series. Edited by Lia Cavalli. 144 pp. Cover design by Constantina Fiorini.

3034   1997   Alice's Adventures in Wonderland
Genoa; Canterbury, UK: Cideb/Black Cat Publishing   9788877542991;   Unknown
                                                 9788877547064; 9783526521211
Black Cat, Reading & Training series: Step 2, level B1.1 – Beginner. 1st edition. Unabridged. Text adaptation and
activities by Gaia Lerace. Edited by Elvira Poggi Repetto and Rebecca Raynes. With audiocassette. 125 pp.

3035   1998   Alice's Adventures in Wonderland
Colognola ai Colli: Demetra   9788844005160   Constantina Fiorini
Palestra di Inglese series. Edited by Lia Cavalli. 144 pp. Cover design by Constantina Fiorini.

3036   1998   Alice's Adventures in Wonderland
Genoa: Cideb Editrice   9788877542991;   Unknown
                                     9788877547064; 9783526521211
Black Cat, Reading & Training series: Step 2, level B1.1 – Beginner. Unabridged. Text adaptation and activities by Gaia
Lerace. With audiocassette.

3037   2002   **Alice's Adventures in Wonderland and Through the Looking-Glass**
Florence/Milan: Giunti   9788809025714   Unknown
Giunti Classics. 1st edition. Edited with an introduction by Luciana Pirè. 254 pp.

3038   2005   **Alice's Adventures in Wonderland**
Genoa: Cideb/Black Cat Publishing   9788431665371;   Lucia Mattioli
Barcelona, Spain: Vicens Vives   9788853003225; 9788853006349
Black Cat, Reading & Training series: Step 2, level B1.1 – Beginner. Text adaptation and activities by Kenneth Brodey. 2nd edition. With audio CD. 112 pp.

3039   2005   **Alice's Adventures in Wonderland and Through the Looking-Glass**
Florence/Milan: Giunti   Unknown
Giunti Classics. 2nd edition. Edited with an introduction by Luciana Pirè. 254 pp.

3040   2006   **Alice's Adventures in Wonderland**
Genoa: Cideb/Black Cat Publishing   9788853006356;   Lucia Mattioli
Berlin, Muenchen, Germany: Langenscheidt   9788853006349; 9783526521358
Black Cat, Reading & Training series: Step 2, level B1.1. Text adaptation and activities by Kenneth Brodey. 1 audio CD-ROM. 112 pp. Rights bought from Cideb, Italy (ISBN 9788877542991, 1997).

3041   2006   **Alice's Adventures in Wonderland and Through the Looking-Glass**
Florence, Milan: Giunti   9788809025714   Unknown
Giunti Classics. 3rd edition. Edited with an introduction by Luciana Pirè. 254 pp.

3042   2007   **Alice's Adventures in Wonderland and Through the Looking-Glass**
Florence, Milan: Giunti   Unknown
Giunti Classics. 4th edition. Edited with an introduction by Luciana Pirè. 254 pp.

3043   2007   **Alice's Adventures in Wonderland**
Genoa: Black Cat. Barcelona, Spain: Vicens Vives   9788431665371   Lucia Mattioli
Black Cat, Reading & Training series: Step 2, level B1.1 – Beginner. 2nd edition, 1st reprint. Adaptation and activities by Kenneth Brodey. With CD. 112 pp.

3044   2008   **Alice's Adventures in Wonderland**
Genoa: Black Cat Cideb   9788853007681;   Alida Massari
        9788853007698
Black Cat, Green Apple series: Starter (A1). Adapted by Gina D. B. Clemen, activities by Mary Johnson. With audio disc (ISBN 9783526520146). 66 pp.

3045   2008   **Alice's Adventures in Wonderland and Through the Looking-Glass**
Florence, Milan: Giunti   Unknown
Giunti Classics. 5th edition. Edited with an introduction by Luciana Pirè. 254 pp.

3046   2008   **Alice's Adventures in Wonderland**
Florence, etc.: Giunti Demetra   9788844035129   Unknown
Scuola di Inglese – Testi. 1st edition of this version based on the 1997 edition. With annotations. 123 pp.

3047   2009   **Alice in Wonderland**
Recanati: Young ELI Readers   9788853604309   Margherita Micheli
Young ELI Readers Series: stage 4. Retold by Richard B. A. Brown. With audio CD. 32 pp.

3048   2010   **Alice's Adventures in Wonderland**
Florence; Milan: Giunti Demetra   9788844035129   Unknown
2nd edition. Scuola di Inglese – Testi. With learning activities. 123 pp.

3049   2011   Alice's Adventures in Wonderland
Milan: Hoepli   9788820347123   Anonymous
Simplified Classics, Level A2. Adaptation and teaching material by Lidia Parodi and Marina Vallacco. With learning activities. With CD. 80 pp.

3050   2011   Alice in Wonderland
Recanati: ELI   9788563623867   Margherita Micheli
Young ELI Readers, Stage 4. Retold by Richard B. A. Brown. 32 pp.

3051   2012   Alice's Adventures in Wonderland
Florence, etc.: Giunti Demetra   9788844035129   Unknown
3rd edition. Scuola di Inglese – Testi. With annotations. 123 pp.

3052   2013   Alice's Adventures in Wonderland
Florence, etc.: Giunti Demetra   9788844035129   Unknown
4th edition. Scuola di Inglese – Testi. With annotations. 123 pp.

3053   2013   Alice's Adventures in Wonderland
Genoa: Cideb   9788853013279   Giovanni Manna
Black Cat, Reading & Training series: Step 2, level B1.1 – Beginner. Web adaptation and activities by Gina D. B. Clemen. Free web activities. With audio CD. 64 pp.

3054   2013   Alice's Adventures in Wonderland
Novara: White Star Publishers   Manuela Adreani
80 pp.

3055   2014   Alice's Adventures in Wonderland
Florence, etc.: Giunti Demetra   9788844035129   Unknown
5th edition. Scuola di Inglese – Testi. With annotations. 123 pp.

3056   2014   Alice in Wonderland
Novara: White Star Publishers   9788854408203   Manuela Adreani
Adaptation of the text by Giada Francia. "Inspired by the masterpiece by Lewis Carroll." Translation from an Italian book into English. 80 pp.

3057   2015   Alice's Adventures in Wonderland
Florence, etc.: Giunti Demetra   9788844035129   Unknown
6th edition. Scuola di Inglese – Testi. With annotations. 123 pp.

3058   2015   Alice's Adventures in Wonderland
Milan: Streetlib Lt.   9788892522374   Unknown
E-book. Alice Series, Book 1. Self-published by Anthony Cyprien/Tyché, distributed through Publishdrive.

3059   2016   Alice's Adventures in Wonderland
Milan: Streetlib Lt.   9788892589902   Unknown
E-book.

3060   2016   Alice's Adventures in Wonderland and Through the Looking-Glass
Florence: Giunti   9788809817654   Unknown
Giunti Classics. Edited with an introduction by Luciana Pirè. 256 pp.

3061   2016   The Illustrated Alice in Wonderland Collection (+ 12 Other Works by Lewis Carroll)
Milan: Shdn Books   9786050463170   Various

E-book. Contains *Alice's Adventures in Wonderland, Through the Looking-Glass, Sylvie and Bruno, Sylvie and Bruno Concluded, A Tangled Tale, Bruno's Revenge and Other Stories, What the Tortoise Said to Achilles, Early Verse, Puzzles from Wonderland, Prologues to Plays, Rhyme? and Reason? A Wonderland Miscellany, College Rhymes and Notes by an Oxford Chiel,* Acrostics, *Inscriptions and Other Verses, Three Sunsets and Other Poems.*

3062   2017   Alice's Adventures in Wonderland
Florence: Demetra   9788844049980   Unknown
Scuola di Inglese – Testi. 128 pp. Based on the 1997 and 2008 editions.

3063   2018   Alice in Wonderland
Vercelli: White Star Publishers   9788854412552   Manuela Adreani
Reissue in a new, smaller format. Adaptation of the text by Giada Francia. Translation from Italian by Angela Arnone. 80 pp.

3064   2018   Alice in Wonderland: from a story by Lewis Carroll
Milan: White Star   9788854413153   Francesca Cosanti
White Star Kids series. Adaptation. Translated from Italian. 40 pp.

4.13 JAPAN

3065   1909   Alice in Wonderland
Tokyo: Kaiseikwan   John Tenniel
Included in The Language Readers Book Four. Annotated by Sioya Sakae. Lesson XI: *Alice in Wonderland*. pp. 51–58. Lesson XII: *Alice in Wonderland*. pp. 58-65. Revised edition first published in 1910.

3066   1956   Alice's Adventures in Wonderland
Tokyo: Kaibunsha   Unillustrated
Annotated by Hideko Inoue. The 29th printing of this book was in 1981 (ISBN of 9784875711100).

3067   1957   Alice's Adventures in Wonderland
Tokyo: Schinozaki Shorin   Unknown
New Diamond Reading series. Annotated by the editorial staff of Shinozaki Shorin. The 2nd printing of this book was on March 30, 1957.

3068   [1958]   Alice's Adventures in Wonderland
Tokyo: Gakusei-sha   4311001169   Unillustrated
Edited and annotated by Tadashi Ohsato. English edition with extensive Japanese notes. 99 pp. Colophon does not mention publishing year. Reprinted in 1963. Later editions have ISBN 4311001169.

3069   1967   Alice's Adventures in Wonderland
Tokyo: Kasama Shoin   Unillustrated
Annotated by Ryuzo Okuma and Chuken Okada.

3070   1975   Alice's Adventures in Wonderland
Tokyo: Hokuseido Press   4590004399   John Tenniel
Edited with notes by Shigeru Watanabe. With 2 audiocassettes. 166 pp. Reprinted in 1978 and 1993.

3071   1976   Through the Looking-Glass
Tokyo: Hokuseido Press   4590004798   John Tenniel
Edited with notes by Shigeru Watanabe. Reprinted in 1993 and 1999.

3072   1977   Alice in Wonderland (title of later editions: Alice's Adventures in Wonderland)
Tokyo: Yohan Publications   9784896845624   John Tenniel
Yohan Pearl Library series, YP10. 130 pp. 1st edition has the introduction "About the story and its author." Later

editions have the introduction "The man we call Lewis Carroll" by Anne Clark Amor. The 18th printing of this book was in 1997 (special edition, with 2 audiocassettes and a booklet in box: "Twelve Carroll Scholars read Alice with Jabberwocky in Six Tongues").

3073   1980   Through the Looking-Glass
Tokyo: Yohan Publications   John Tenniel
Pearl Library Edition.

3074   1984   Alice's Adventures in Wonderland
Tokyo: Hokuseido Press   4590007177   Unknown
Edited with notes by Masakazu Matsushima. Retold by Vivienne Kenrick. Reprinted in 1993 with the title changed to *Alice in Wonderland*.

3075   1984   Alice in Wonderland
Tokyo: Nihon Eigo Kyoiku Kyokai   4817713925   Atsushi Ogata;
                                                                       Yukimasa Matsuda

Includes *Looking-Glass*. Rewritten by John S. Lander. Reprinted in 1986. Cover design by Yukimasa Matsuda.

3076   1984   Alice in Wonderland
Tokyo: Obunsha   4010913924   Atsushi Ogata
Includes *Looking-Glass*. Rewritten by S. Lander. Issued with a pamphlet in Japanese by Teruko Nagai on the translation of *Alice in Wonderland* and *Through the Looking-Glass*. Reprinted in 1986 and 1993.

3077   1986   Alice in Wonderland
Tokyo: Nichieisha   John Tenniel
Choice Reading series, No. 134. With preface and annotations in Japanese by Tetsuo Aramaki. 68 pp. Issued with a pamphlet.

3078   1986   Alice in Wonderland
Tokyo: Nihon Eigo Kyoiku Kyokai   4817713925   Atsushi Ogata;
                                                                       Yukimasa Matsuda

Includes *Looking-Glass*. Rewritten by John S. Lander. Reprint of the 1984 edition. Cover design by Yukimasa Matsuda.

3079   1986   Alice in Wonderland
Tokyo: Obunsha   4010913924   Atsushi Ogata
Includes *Looking-Glass*. Rewritten by S. Lander. Issued with a pamphlet in Japanese by Teruko Nagai on the translation of *Alice in Wonderland* and *Through the Looking-Glass*. Reprint of 1984 edition.

3080   1986   Alice in Wonderland
Tokyo: Linguaphone   Unillustrated
Linguaphone Listening Theater Series, 18. Read by William Rushton. With cassette tapes.

3081   1987   Alice in Wonderland
Tokyo: Eichosha   Carol Tarrant
Annotated by Sachiko Watanabe, simplified by D. K. Swan. The 10th printing of this book was in 1999. Joint publication by Longman and Eichosha, distributed exclusively in Japan. Similar to the 1976 edition published by Longman (UK) (New Method Supplementary Readers, stage 1; ISBN 0582534143), but with a preface, notes instead of questions, and a different cover.

3082   1988   Alice's Adventures in Wonderland
Tokyo: Kodansha   4061860402   John Tenniel
Kodansha English Library 40. Annotated by Takeo Seto. 188 pp. The 11th printing of this book was in 1995. The 36th printing was in 2019. Later editions have ISBN 4770022239.

3083   1989   **Alice in Wonderland**
Tokyo: Yohan Publications   4896843274   John Tenniel; Mayumi Abe
A Ladder edition at the 1,000-word level. Adapted by Anna Udagawa. The 4th printing of this book was in 1997. Cover design by Mayumi Abe.

3084   1989   **Mad Tea Party**
Tokyo: Kawade Shobo Shinsha   4309731058   Unillustrated
Kawade Sound Bunko 5. With cassette tapes.

3085   1993   **Through the Looking-Glass**
Tokyo: Hokuseido Press   4590004798   John Tenniel
Edited with notes by Shigeru Watanabe. Reprint of 1976 edition.

3086   1993   **Alice in Wonderland**
Tokyo: Obunsha   4010913924   Atsushi Ogata
Includes *Looking-Glass*. Rewritten by S. Lander. Issued with a pamphlet in Japanese by Teruko Nagai on the translation of *Alice in Wonderland* and *Through the Looking-Glass*. Reprint of 1984 edition.

3087   1993   **Through the Looking-Glass**
Tokyo: Hokuseido Press   4590004798   John Tenniel
Edited with notes by Shigeru Watanabe. Reprint of 1976 edition.

3088   1995   **Through the Looking-Glass**
Tokyo: Charles E. Tuttle Company   080482066X   Peter Newell
Introduction by Charles V. S. Borst

3089   1999   **Alice's Adventures in Wonderland**
Tokyo: Kodansha International / Ruby Books   9784770025494   John Tenniel
The 6th printing of this book was in 2005.

3090   1999   **Alice in Wonderland**
Tokyo: Atelier Escarpolette   Masami Iida
Abridged miniature edition. Designed and bound by Chinatsu Nakata. Produced by Atsuko Kudoh. The 2nd printing of this book was in 2007.

3091   1999   **Through the Looking-Glass**
Tokyo: Hokuseido Press   4590004798   John Tenniel
Edited with notes by Shigeru Watanabe. Reprint of 1976 edition.

3092   1999   **Alice in a Miniature Book: Alice's Adventures in Wonderland**
Toride: Ichibyo Shobo   Youichi Nakajima;
                                                 Naoko Okamoto
Abridged miniature edition. Includes both *Alice* and *Looking-Glass*, drastically abridged. 56 pp. Hand coloring by Naoko Okamoto. Copyright: Annie's Coloring Studio.

3093   2005   **Alice's Adventures in Wonderland**
Tokyo: IBC Publishing   4896840372   John Tenniel
(distributed by Nihon Yosho Hanbai, Tokyo)
Yohan Ladder, Level 2 (1300-word). Adapted by Anna Udagawa. The 19th printing of this book was in 2018.

3094   2007   **Alice's Adventures in Wonderland**
Tokyo: IBC Publishing   9784896844757   John Tenniel
(distributed by Nihon Yosho Hanbai, Tokyo)
The 7th printing of this book was in 2015.

3095	2008	A Selection from Alice's Adventures in Wonderland		
		Kyoto: Marnavi Kyozai; Kaihatsu	9784903719061	John Tenniel
		(Multimedium Learning System)		
		Studying English through *Alice's Adventures in Wonderland* with Multimedia. Annotated by Shohei Koike. With CD-ROM.		

3096	2009	Alice's Adventures in Wonderland		
		Tokyo: IBC Publishing		John Tenniel
		Adapted by Anna Udagawa. With CD.		

3097	2009	Alice's Adventures in Wonderland		
		Tokyo: Toshimi Yoshida		Toshimi Yoshida
		Abridged edition.		

3098	2010	Alice's Adventures in Wonderland		
		Tokyo: Eiko-sha	9784870971295	John Tenniel
		Notes by Yoshio Maruhashi and Kayoko Ito. The 4th printing of this book was in 2013.		

3099	2011	An outline of Alice in Wonderland		
		Tokyo: Kujakudo Zakkaten		John Tenniel
		Miniature edition. Edited by Kana Kujakudo.		

3100	2012	Alice's Adventures in Wonderland		
		Mitaka: Hannalice		H. Hanna
		Limited edition of 1,000 copies.		

3101	2012	An outline of Through the Looking-Glass		
		Tokyo: Kujakudo Zakkaten		John Tenniel
		Miniature edition. Edited by Kana Kujakudo.		

3102	2013	Alice's Adventures in Wonderland		
		Ichikawa: Kototsubo		John Tenniel
		Miniature edition. Book designed and bound by Miyako Akai. The 2nd printing of this book was in 2014.		

3103	2014	Alice's Adventures in Wonderland		
		Tokyo: Kadokawa	9784046001870	Arina Utashiro; Azusa Yabe
		Let's read *Alice in Wonderland* in easy English. Annotated by Sally Kanbayashi. Supervised by Christopher Belton. Cover design by Azusa Yabe. With MP3 CD-ROM.		

3104	2017	Through the Looking-Glass, and What Alice Found There		
		Tokyo: Goma-books	9784814914104	Unillustrated

4.14 MALAYSIA

3105	1992	Alice in Wonderland		
		Kuala Lumpur: Agents Digest	9789837100558; 9789837100589	Anonymous
		Happy Fairy Tales Kingdom series. Color illustrations. 15 pp.		

3106	1997	Alice in Wonderland		
		Bangi: Penerbitan Pelangi	9789838787338	Anonymous
		Pelangi Little Book series. Color illustrations. 16 pp.		

3107　2002　Alice in Wonderland
Kuala Lumpur: Kohwai & Young Pub.　　　　9789831489994;　　　Anonymous
9789831911525
Favorite Fairy Tales series. Edited by Bob Williams. Color illustrations. 16 pp.

3108　2003　Aladdin and the Magic Lamp; Alice in Wonderland
Kuala Lumpur: Kohwai & Young Publications　9789831912287　　Anonymous
Selected Fairy Tales for Children series. Color illustrations. 35 pp. Also published in Malay language.

3109　2004　Alice in Wonderland
Kuala Lumpur: Kohwai & Young Pub.　　　　9789831489994　　　Anonymous
Favorite Fairy Tales series. Edited by Bob Williams. Color illustrations. 16 pp.

3110　2006　Alice in Wonderland
Kuala Lumpur: Kohwai & Young Publications　　　　　　　　Anonymous
Favorite Fairy Tales series. Revised edition. Edited by Bob William. Color illustrations. 16 pp.

3111　2006　Alice in Wonderland
Seri Kembangan, Selangor: Pernerbitan Daya　9789833481903　　Anonymous
I Can Read All by Myself Fairy Tales, Level 4. Adapted by Bob Williams. Color illustrations. 45 pp.

3112　2006　Alice in Wonderland
Kuala Lumpur: Kohwai & Young Publications　9789833664924　　Anonymous
I Can Read All by Myself Fairy Tales, Level 4, Book 2. Adapted by Bob Williams. Color illustrations. 45 pp.

3113　2009　Alice in Wonderland
Kuala Lumpur: Kohwai & Young Publications　9789831912683　　Anonymous
Favorite Fairy Tales series. Edited by Bob Williams. 16 pp.

3114　ca. 2010s　Alice in Wonderland
Batu Caves, Selangor: Little Sun　　　　　9789673241576;　　Anonymous
9789673241613
Best to Read Favorite Fairy Tales series. Color illustrations. 15 pp.

3115　2010　Alice's Adventures in Wonderland
Shah Alam: Gerak Ilmu　　　　　　　　9789675909085　　　Anonymous
Fun Classic for Young Learners series. Color illustrations. 56 pp.

3116　2010　Alice in Wonderland
Kuala Lumpur: Kohwai & Young Publications　9789833664924　　Anonymous
I Can Read All by Myself Fairy Tales, Level 4, Book 2. Adapted by Bob Williams. Color illustrations. 45 pp.

3117　2018　Alice in Wonderland
Sungai Buloh: Mind to Mind　　　　　　9789674474270　　　Anonymous
All Time Favorite Fairy Tales series.

4.15 MEXICO

3118　1961　Alice in Wonderland: comprising the two books, Alice's Adventures in Wonderland
and Through the Looking-Glass
Mexico: C. I. John W. Clute　　　　　　　　　　　John Tenniel; Donald E. Cooke
The Children's Classics, No. 3. 1st edition. 276 pp. Combined edition of *Alice* and *Looking-Glass*. Published by
arrangement with Holt, Rinehart and Winston, Inc. Color illustrations by Donald E. Cooke.

3119   1914 or 1919   Alice's Adventures in Wonderland
Amsterdam: Meulenhoff & Co   J. Wiegman
My First Collection series, 4. 1st edition. Abridged text with explanatory Dutch notes. Adapted by W. H. Sonius. 72 pp. For use in secondary schools.

3120   ca. 1925   Alice's Adventures in Wonderland
Amsterdam: Meulenhoff & Co   J. Wiegman
My First Collection series, 4. 2nd edition. Abridged text with explanatory Dutch notes. Adapted by W. H. Sonius. 72 pp. For use in secondary schools.

3121   1946   Alice in Wonderland
Amsterdam: Meulenhoff & Co   John Tenniel
My First Collection series, 4. 3rd edition. Abridged text with explanatory Dutch notes. Adapted by C. J. Knop. 76 pp. For use in secondary schools. 2 versions, in blue and white bindings.

3122   1949   Alice in Wonderland
Amsterdam: Meulenhoff   John Tenniel
My First Collection series, 4. 4th edition. Abridged text with explanatory Dutch notes. Adapted by C. J. Knop. 76 pp. For use in secondary schools.

3123   ca. 1960s   Alice in Wonderland – book and record
Amsterdam: Mulder & Zoon. Newark, NJ: Peter Pan Records   Walton
No. 1943. Severely abridged text. With 45 RPM audio record. 24 pp. Other book covers known. A later printing exists. Book published by Mulder & Zoon, the record by Peter Pan Records.

3124   1976   Alice's Adventures in Wonderland
Utrecht: Knippenberg's Uitgeverij   John Tenniel
Bulkboek No. 4. Preface by Lenny Bouman. With a selection of annotations from Martin Gardner's *Annotated Alice*. 28 pp. In newspaper format used in Dutch schools.

3125   1999   Alice's Adventures in Wonderland
Groningen: Gopher Publishers   9789076249155   Unknown
Gopher Classics series, 2. 67 pp.

3126   2002   Alice's Adventures in Wonderland
Amsterdam: Intertaal Dist. Genoa,   9789054511250;   Unknown
Italy: Cideb Editrice   9788877547064
Black Cat, Reading & Training series: Beginner. Text adaptation and activities by Gaia Lerace. With audio CD. 125 pp. Rights bought from Cideb, Italy (ISBN 9788877542991, 1997).

4.17 PERU

3127   2005   Alice in Wonderland
Lima: Santillana   9789972009105   Dario Zorzato
Richmond Readers, Level 1. Reprint. Adaptation, exercises and notes by Barbara Chatwin. With audiocassette. 31 pp.

3128   2006   Alice in Wonderland
Lima, London: Santillana-Richmond   9789972009105   Dario Zorzato
Richmond Readers, Level 1. Reprint. Adaptation, exercises and notes by Barbara Chatwin. With audiocassette. 31 pp.

3129   2014   Alice in Wonderland
Lima: Los Libros más Pequeños del Mundo E.I.R.L.   9786123031558   Mark Torres Escuadra
Miniature book. 1st edition. 442 pp.

4.18 POLAND

3130   2004   Alice's Adventures in Wonderland
Warsaw: KOG   9788389702159   Unillustrated
"English Classics Library" series. Edited by Marek Skierkowski. Author's name misspelled on cover, title page, and author biography as "Lewis Caroll." Cover illustration is a detail from Ilya Repin, *Portrait of the Daughter*, 1884.

3131   2004   Through the Looking-Glass
Warsaw: KOG   9788389702647   Unillustrated
English Classics Library series. Edited by Marek Skierkowski. Author's name misspelled on cover as "Lewis Carol," on title page and author biography as "Lewis Caroll." Cover illustration is a detail from Auguste Renoir *Dziewczeta przy pianinie*.

3132   2013   Alice's Adventures in Wonderland – Alicja w krainie czarów
Kraków: Global Metro   9788363035624   Małgorzata Flis
Czytamy w Oryginale series. Adapted by Scotia Victoria Gilroy. In English and Polish. 100 pp. Reprinted in 2018.

3133   2014   Alice's Adventures in Wonderland
Warsaw: Stefania Frączkowska   9788393769599   Unknown
E-book. Studio Aviva Art.

3134   2017   Alice in Wonderland
Warsaw: Wydawnictwo Zielona Sowa   9788380735064   Marianna Schoett
Już czytam po angielsku (I already read English). By Daniel Pycz. 48 pp.

3135   2018   Alice's Adventures in Wonderland – Alicja w krainie czarów
Kraków: Global Metro   9788363035624   Małgorzata Flis
Czytamy w Oryginale series. Adapted by Scotia Victoria Gilroy. In English and Polish. 100 pp. Reprint of 2013 edition.

4.19 ROMANIA

3136   1971   Alice's Adventures in Wonderland
Bucharest: Editura Didactică Și Pedagogică   John Tenniel
Notes, vocabulary, preface, and chronological table by Herminia Jocobsohn and Stefan Stoenescu. 193 pp.

3137   1999   Alice's Adventures in Wonderland
Bucharest: Editura All Educational   9789736840043   Unknown
Exercises on English literature, English Readers, Lower Secondary, Intermediate. With notes and follow-up activities by Alexandra Costin. 109 pp.

3138   2001   Alice's Adventures in Wonderland
Bucharest: Editura All Educational   9789736844744   Unknown
2nd edition of the 1999 edition. 92 pp.

3139   2002   Alice's Adventures in Wonderland and Through the Looking-Glass
Bucharest: Editura Prietenii Cărții   9789735730369   Anonymous
288 pp.

3140   [2006]   Alice's Adventures in Wonderland
       Brașov: Academic   9789738642492   Anonymous
       Read in English series. 93 pp.

3141   2009   Alice in Wonderland
       Iași: Gama   9789731491202   Nicolae Tonița
       Learn to Read in English, Level 1. Edited by Diana Mocanu. 16 pp.

4.20 RUSSIA

3142   1960   Alice in Wonderland
       Leningrad: Publishing House of the Ministry of Education of the RSFSR   A. Krutcev
       Adaptation for the 6th form of English students, with vocabulary. By G. K. Maghidson-Stephanova. 78 pp.

3143   1967   Alice's Adventures in Wonderland
       Moscow: Progress Publishers   Evgenij Aleksandrovič Šukaev
       Introduction in Russian by Dmitrij Mihajlovič Ûrnov and commentary in Russian by Lidiâ Semenovna Golovčinska.
       44 illustrations in both black-and-white and reddish-brown. 234 pp. Includes Russian versions of "Jabberwocky"
       and "The Walrus and the Carpenter." Beige cloth stamped in reddish-brown and black with author and title within
       decorative illustration on front cover and checker pattern on spine. Pictorial endpapers printed in brown and orange.
       Edition intended for learning English.

3144   1979   Alice's Adventures in Wonderland
       Moscow: Progress Publishers   Evgenij Aleksandrovič Šukaev
       Introduction in Russian by Dmitrij Mihajlovič Urnov and commentary in Russian by Lidiâ Semenovna Golovčinska
       and Nina M. Demurova. Illustrations on lining papers not related to *Alice in Wonderland*. Illustrations in both color
       and black-and-white. 234 pp.

4.21 SLOVAKIA

3145   2004   Alice's Adventures in Wonderland and Through the Looking-Glass
       Bratislava: Slovart   8071459690   Dušan Kállay
       Combined edition. 191 pp. Dust jacket. In the same format as the Slovak-language edition.

3146   2018   Alice's Adventures in Wonderland and Through the Looking-Glass
       Bratislava: Slovart   9788071459699   Dušan Kállay
       Reprint of the 2004 edition with note on the dust jacket cover that the Slovak-language edition won the "Outstanding
       Book Award" at the New York "Alice in a World of Wonderlands" exhibit in 2015. Combined edition. 191 pp. In the
       same format as the Slovak-language edition.

4.22 SOUTH AFRICA

3147   ca. 2000s   For the Love of Reading, Volume 1: 50 Classic Titles for the Ultimate
                    Reading Experience
       Johannesburg: Modern Publisher   9780620268769   Unknown
       CD-ROM, containing among others *Alice in Wonderland*.

4.23 SOUTH KOREA

3148   2009   Alice in Wonderland
Seoul: Compass Publishing   9781599662022   John Tenniel

Print textbook with accompanying audiobook with CD in MP3 format. Compass Classic Readers, Level 2. Retold by Ken Methold. Color illustrations. 68 pp. With questions and vocabulary.

4.24 SPAIN

3149   1976   Alice in Wonderland
Bilbao: Vasco Americana   9788431912147   Gutmaga
                                                                       [Manuel Gutiérrez Garulo]
1st edition. 12 pp.

3150   1997   Alice's Adventures in Wonderland
Barcelona: Vicens Vives   8431641312   Anonymous
Black Cat, Reading & Training series: Beginner. 1st edition. 16 pp.

3151   1997   Alice's Adventures in Wonderland
Barcelona: Vicens Vives   9788431640804   John Tenniel; Enzo Marciante
Black Cat, Reading & Training series: Beginner. 1st edition. Edited by Elvira Poggi Repetto and Rebecca Raynes. Text adaptation and activities by Gaia Lerace. With audiocassette. 125 pp.

3152   1998   Alice's Adventures in Wonderland
Barcelona: Vicens Vives   9788431640804   John Tenniel; Enzo Marciante
Black Cat, Reading & Training series: Beginner. 1st edition, 1st reprint. Text adaptation and activities by Gaia Lerace. With cassette. 125 pp.

3153   2000   Alice's Adventures in Wonderland
Barcelona: Vicens Vives   9788431640804   John Tenniel; Enzo Marciante
Black Cat, Reading & Training series: Beginner. 1st edition, 2nd reprint. Text adaptation and activities by Gaia Lerace. With cassette. 125 pp.

3154   2001   Alice in Wonderland
León: Everest   9788424185763   Belén Eizaguirre Alvear;
                                                                       María Isabel Nadal Romero; Juan Pablo Navas Rosco
Cometa Roja. 1st edition. Translated from Spanish to English by Esther Sarfatti. 16 pp.

3155   2002   Alice's Adventures in Wonderland
Barcelona: Vicens Vives   9788431640804   John Tenniel; Enzo Marciante
Black Cat, Reading & Training series: Beginner. 1st edition, 3rd reprint. Text adaptation and activities by Gaia Lerace. With CD. 125 pp. Also published in Italy.

3156   2003   Alice's Adventures in Wonderland
Madrid: Del Prado   9788483728321   Unillustrated
Miniature Classics Library. 383 pp. Author's name written as "Lewiss Carroll" on title page.

3157   2003   Alice's Adventures in Wonderland
Madrid: MDS Books / Mediasat   9788497890564   Unillustrated
The Children's Golden Library, No. 2. 128 pp. Special edition for the British newspaper *Daily Mail*. Page opposite title page reads: "Not to be sold separately from the *Daily Mail*." Cover illustration by anonymous illustrator.

3158 2003 Alice's Adventures in Wonderland
Madrid: MDS Books / Mediasat 9788497890137 Unillustrated
The Children's Golden Library, No. 22. 128 pp. Special edition for the UK. Cover illustration by anonymous illustrator.

3159 2004 Alice's Adventures in Wonderland
Madrid: MDS Books. Mediasat Group 9788497897013 Unillustrated;
Esteban Quintana de la Fuente
Vancouver Sun Classic Children's Book Collection, No. 7. 1st edition. 128 pp. Special edition for the Canadian newspaper *The Vancouver Sun*. Page opposite title page reads: "Not to be sold separately from *The Vancouver Sun*." Cover illustration by Esteban Quintana de la Fuente.

3160 2004 Alice in Wonderland
Madrid: Richmond (Grupo Santillana) 9788466804691 Dario Zorzato
Richmond Readers, Level 1. Adaptation. Exercises and notes by Barbara Chatwin. 1st edition. 32 pp.

3161 2005 Alice in Wonderland
León: Everest / Evergráficas 9788424185763 Belén Eizaguirre Alvear;
María Isabel Nadal Romero; Juan Pablo Navas Rosco
Cometa Roja. 1st edition, 2nd reprint. Translated from Spanish by Esther Sarfatti. 16 pp.

3162 2005 Alice's Adventures in Wonderland
Barcelona: Vicens-Vives. Genoa, Italy: Black Cat 9788431665371 Lucia Mattioli
Black Cat, Reading & Training series: Beginner. 2nd edition. Text adaptation and activities by Kenneth Brodey. With CD. 112 pp.

3163 2007 Alice's Adventures in Wonderland
Barcelona: Vicens Vives. Genoa, Italy: Black Cat 9788431665371 Lucia Mattioli
Black Cat, Reading & Training series: Beginner. 2nd edition, 1st reprint. Adaptation and activities by Kenneth Brodey. With CD. 112 pp.

3164 2007 Alice in Wonderland
León: Everest 9788444100371 Belén Eizaguirre Alvear;
María Isabel Nadal Romero; Juan Pablo Navas Rosco
Cometa Roja Grande. Translated from Spanish by Esther Sarfatti. 16 pp.

3165 2008 Alice in Wonderland
León: Everest 9788444100371 Belén Eizaguirre Alvear;
María Isabel Nadal Romero; Juan Pablo Navas Rosco
Cometa Roja. Translated from Spanish by Esther Sarfatti.

3166 2008 Alice in Wonderland
Madrid: Richmond (Grupo Santillana) 9788466804691 Dario Zorzato
Richmond Readers, Level 1. Reprint. Adaptation. Exercises and notes by Barbara Chatwin. 31 pp.

3167 2009 Alice's Adventures in Wonderland
Barcelona: Vicens Vives. Genoa, Italy: Black Cat 9788431665371 Lucia Mattioli
Black Cat, Reading & Training series: Step 2, level B1.1. 2nd edition, revised, 2nd reprint. Text adaption and activities by Kenneth Brodey. With CD. 112 pp.

3168 2009 Alice's Adventures in Wonderland
Barcelona: Vicens Vives 9788431692834 Alida Massari
Black Cat, Green Apple series: Starter (A1). 1st edition. Adapted by Gina D. B. Clemen, activities by Mary Johnson. With CD-ROM. 64 pp.

3169   2009   Alice's Adventures in Wonderland
Barcelona: Vicens Vives. Genoa, Italy: Black Cat   9788431665371   Lucia Mattioli
Black Cat, Reading & Training series: Step 2, level B1.1 – Beginner. 2nd edition. 2nd reprint. Text adaption and activities by Kenneth Brodey. With CD. 112 pp.

3170   2010   Alice's Adventures in Wonderland
Barcelona: Vicens Vives. Genoa, Italy: Black Cat   9788431665371   Lucia Mattioli
Black Cat, Reading & Training series: Step 2, level B1.1. 2nd edition, revised, 3rd reprint. Text adaption and activities by Kenneth Brodey. With CD. 112 pp.

3171   2010   Alice's Adventures in Wonderland
Barcelona: Vicens Vives   9788431692834   Alida Massari
Black Cat, Green Apple series: Starter (A1). 1st edition, 2nd reprint. Adapted by Gina D. B. Clemen, activities by Mary Johnson. With CD-ROM. 64 pp.

3172   2011   Alice in Wonderland
León: Everest   9788424185763   Huella ilustración
Cometa Roja. 1st edition, 3rd reprint. Translated from Spanish by Esther Sarfatti. 16 pp.

3173   2012   Alice's Adventures in Wonderland
Barcelona: Nórdica   9788492683741   Marta Gómez-Pintado Valero
E-book. 1st edition. 120 pp.

3174   2012   Alice's Adventures in Wonderland
Barcelona: Vicens Vives   9788431692834   Alida Massari
Black Cat, Green Apple series: Starter (A1). 1st edition, 3rd reprint. Adapted by Gina D. B. Clemen, activities by Mary Johnson. With CD-ROM. 64 pp.

3175   2013   Alice in Wonderland
León: Everest   9788444100371   Belén Eizaguirre Alvear;
                                            María Isabel Nadal Romero; Juan Pablo Navas Rosco
Cometa Roja. 2nd edition. Translated from Spanish by Esther Sarfatti. 16 pp.

3176   2013   Alice in Wonderland
Arganda del Rey: Madrid Estudio Didáctico D.L.   9788497865913   André M. Lefèvre; Various
I Can Read series, Level 3, 10. Adaptation by André M. Lefevre et al. 24 pp.

3177   2014   Alice in Wonderland
Oiartzun: Ediciones Saldaña   9788499395272;   Carlos Busquets
                                   9788499395265
Leo en inglés, nivel 3, 1. 1st edition. 32 pp.

3178   2014   Alice in Wonderland
Barcelona: Plutón   9788494543753   John Tenniel
English Classic Books series. With exercises. 152 pp.

3179   2015   Alice in Wonderland
Oiartzun: Faro Editores   9788499395272   Unknown
Leo en inglés, nivel 3, 1. 2nd edition of the 2014 edition.

3180   2015   Alice's Adventures in Wonderland
Valladolid: Maxtor   9788490019061   John Tenniel; Maria L. Kirk
Maxtor Classics, No. 6. 1st edition. 130 pp. Cover by Maria L. Kirk.

3181	2016	Alice in Wonderland		
		Barcelona: Plutón	9788494543753	John Tenniel
		1st edition. English Classic Books series. With exercises. 152 pp.		

3182	2017	Alice in Wonderland		
		Barcelona: Plutón	9788494543753	John Tenniel
		2nd edition. English Classic Books series. With exercises. 160 pp.		

3183	2019	Alice in Wonderland		
		Barcelona: Plutón	9788494543753	John Tenniel
		3rd edition. English Classic Books series. With exercises. 160 pp.		

4.25 SWEDEN

3184	1923	Alice's Adventures in Wonderland	
		Lund: C.W.K. Gleerup	After Tenniel
		With annotations by G. Björkelund and S.B.T. Danielsson. 119 pp. Accompanied by "a dictionary to *Alice's Adventures in Wonderland*" (44 pp.). Compiled by Björkelund and Danielsson.	

3185	1945	Alice in Wonderland and Through the Looking-Glass	
		Stockholm: Jan Förlag	Robert Högfeldt
		1st edition. 10 color plates plus 31 other illustrations. 221 pp. Red paper-covered boards backed in beige cloth. With Dust jacket.	

3186	1945	Alice in Wonderland and Through the Looking-Glass	
		Stockholm: Jan Förlag	Lewis Carroll
		268 pp. Printer: Victor Pettersons Bokindustriaktiebolag.	

3187	1946	Alice in Wonderland and Through the Looking-Glass	
		Stockholm: The Continental Book Company AB	Mervyn Peake
		Zephyr Books, volume 67. 352 pp. This was the 1st edition with Mervyn Peake's illustrations; it was published 2 years prior to the UK edition. Zephyr Books ("The Continental Book Company") was a subsidiary of the publishing company Bonnier.	

3188	1946	Alice in Wonderland and Through the Looking-Glass	
		Stockholm: Jan Förlag	Anonymous
		268 pp. "With illustrations by the author."	

3189	1949	Alice in Wonderland and Through the Looking-Glass	
		Stockholm: Jan Förlag	Robert Högfeldt
		2nd edition of the 1945 book. 221 pp.	

3190	1951	Alice's Adventures in Wonderland	
		Lund: Gleerup	Anonymous
		School edition with annotations by G. Björkelund and S.B.T. Danielsson. 119 pp.	

3191	2015	Through the Looking-Glass		
		Stockholm: Svenska Ljud Classica	9789176393628	Unknown
		Print book and computer file. Author: Lewis Carrol [*sic*].		

4.26 SWITZERLAND

3192   1942   Alice's Adventures in Wonderland
Bern: A. Francke   Unknown
Collection of English texts for use in schools, volume 40. Selected by Rudolf Stamm. 47 pp.

4.27 TAIWAN

3193   1978   Alice in Wonderland
Taipei: Ma Ling Publishing Co.   John Tenniel
434 pp. Reprint of the Norton Critical Edition published in the UK in 1971. (Original ISBN 0393043436 and
0393099776.)

3194   1981   Alice's Adventures in Wonderland
Taipei: Hua Hsing   Peter Newell
Oxford Progressive English Readers, Grade 1. 1st edition. Adapted. Edited by D. H. Howe. 70 pp.

3195   1981   Alice's Adventures in Wonderland
Taipei: Bookman Books   Anonymous
Oxford Progressive English Readers, Grade 1. 1st edition. Adapted. Edited by D. H. Howe. 70 pp.

3196   1985   Alice in Wonderland
Taipei: Wen Shin   Unknown
Shin Graded English Reading, No. 132. 2nd edition. Abridged to 9 chapters. Edited by Wen Shin Editing and
Screening Committee with Chinese footnotes on Vocabularies. 68 pp.

3197   1989   Alice's Adventures in Wonderland
Taipei: Bookman Books   9780333433430   Unknown
Macmillan "Stories to Remember." Adapted by Margery Green. 90 pp. Omnibus edition of two stories. Reprint of the
London Macmillan 1986 edition.

3198   1991   Alice's Adventures in Wonderland
Taipei: Bookman Books   Unknown
Simplified Editions in Memory of Masterpieces series. 90 pp.

3199   1996   Alice's Adventures in Wonderland and Through the Looking-Glass
Taipei: Bookman Books   9789575866532   John Tenniel; Diana Stanley
Illustrated Junior Library series. 352 pp. With 92 illustrations by John Tenniel, of which 8 have been redrawn in color
by Diana Stanley. Probably based on the 1954 edition from Dent, London.

3200   2004   Alice's Adventures in Wonderland
Taipei: Classic Communications Co. 9789574763719   Unknown
144 pp.

3201   2005   Alice's Adventures in Wonderland
Taipei: Bookman Books   9574450864   Anonymous
Macmillan Classic Readers Series, Level A, No. 1. With notes and annotations. 94 pp. Contains 15 stories with *Alice's
Adventures in Wonderland* as No. 8. Reprint. Originally published by Macmillan in London. The book is in 3 levels.
Level A is 1,500–2,000 words; Level B is 2,000–2,500 words; and Level C is 2,500–3,500 words. Levels A and C have
5 states and Level B has 4. Each has a different ISBN so is a different edition.

3202   2005   Alice's Adventures in Wonderland
Taipei: Bookman Books   9574450988   Anonymous

Macmillan Classic Readers Series, Level A, No. 2. With notes and annotations. 94 pp. Contains 15 stories with *Alice's Adventures in Wonderland* as No. 8. Reprint. Originally published by Macmillan in London. The book is in 3 levels. Level A is 1,500–2,000 words.

3203   2005   Alice's Adventures in Wonderland
Taipei: Bookman Books   9574450996   Anonymous
Macmillan Classic Readers Series, Level A, No. 3. With notes and annotations. 94 pp. Contains 15 stories with *Alice's Adventures in Wonderland* as No. 8. Reprint. Originally published by Macmillan in London. The book is in 3 levels. Level A is 1,500–2,000 words.

3204   2005   Alice's Adventures in Wonderland
Taipei: Bookman Books   9574451135   Anonymous
Macmillan Classic Readers Series, Level A, No. 4. With notes and annotations. 94 pp. Contains 15 stories with *Alice's Adventures in Wonderland* as No. 8. Reprint. Originally published by Macmillan in London. The book is in 3 levels. Level A is 1,500–2,000 words.

3205   2005   Alice's Adventures in Wonderland
Taipei: Bookman Books   957445116X   Anonymous
Macmillan Classic Readers Series. Level A, No. 5. With notes and annotations. 94 pp. Contains 15 stories with *Alice's Adventures in Wonderland* as No. 8. Reprint. Originally published by Macmillan in London. The book is in 3 levels. Level A is 1,500–2,000 words.

3206   2005   Alice's Adventures in Wonderland
Taipei: Bookman Books   9574450856   Anonymous
Macmillan Classic Readers Series. Level B, No. 1. With Notes and annotations. 94 pp. Contains 15 stories with *Alice's Adventures in Wonderland* as No. 8. Reprint. Originally published by Macmillan in London. The book is in 3 levels. Level B is 2,000–2,500 words.

3207   2005   Alice's Adventures in Wonderland
Taipei: Bookman Books   9574450872   Anonymous
Macmillan Classic Readers Series, Level B, No. 2. With Notes and annotations. 94 pp. Contains 15 stories with *Alice's Adventures in Wonderland* as No. 8. Reprint. Originally published by Macmillan in London. The book is in 3 levels. Level B is 2,000–2,500 words.

3208   2005   Alice's Adventures in Wonderland
Taipei: Bookman Books   9574451003   Anonymous
Macmillan Classic Readers Series, Level B, No. 3. With notes and annotations. 94 pp. Contains 15 stories with *Alice's Adventures in Wonderland* as No. 8. Reprint. Originally published by Macmillan in London. The book is in 3 levels. Level B is 2,000–2,500 words.

3209   2005   Alice's Adventures in Wonderland
Taipei: Bookman Books   9574451143   Anonymous
Macmillan Classic Readers Series. Level B, No. 4. With notes and annotations. 94 pp. Contains 15 stories with *Alice's Adventures in Wonderland* as No. 8. Reprint. Originally published by Macmillan in London. The book is in 3 levels. Level B is 2,000–2,500 words.

3210   2005   Alice's Adventures in Wonderland
Taipei: Bookman Books   9574450880   Anonymous
Macmillan Classic Readers Series. Level C, No. 1. With notes and annotations. 94 pp. Contains 15 stories with *Alice's Adventures in Wonderland* as No. 8. Reprint. Originally published by Macmillan in London. The book is in 3 levels. Level C is 2,500–3,500 words.

3211   2005   Alice's Adventures in Wonderland
Taipei: Bookman Books   957445097X   Anonymous

Macmillan Classic Readers Series, Level C, No. 2. With notes and annotations. 94 pp. Contains 15 stories with *Alice's Adventures in Wonderland* as No. 8. Reprint. Originally published by Macmillan in London. The book is in 3 levels. Level C is 2,500–3,500 words.

3212   2005   Alice's Adventures in Wonderland
Taipei: Bookman Books   9574451011   Anonymous
Macmillan Classic Readers Series. Level C, No. 3. With notes and annotations. 94 pp. Contains 15 stories with *Alice's Adventures in Wonderland* as No. 8. Reprint. Originally published by Macmillan in London. The book is in 3 levels. Level C is 2,500–3,500 words.

3213   2005   Alice's Adventures in Wonderland
Taipei: Bookman Books   9574451151   Anonymous
Macmillan Classic Readers Series. Level C, No. 4. With notes and annotations. 94 pp. Contains 15 stories with *Alice's Adventures in Wonderland* as No. 8. Reprint. Originally published by Macmillan in London. The book is in 3 levels. Level C is 2,500–3,500 words.

3214   2005   Alice's Adventures in Wonderland
Taipei: Bookman Books   9574451184   Anonymous
Macmillan Classic Readers, Series. Level C, no. 5. With Notes and annotations. 94 pp. Contains 15 stories with *Alice's Adventures in Wonderland* #8. Reprint. Originally published by Macmillan in London. The book is in three levels. Level C is 2,500–3,500 words.

3215   2005   Alice's Adventures in Wonderland
Taipei: Caves Books   9576065518   Unknown
Caves Classic Readers, Level 2. 155 pp.

3216   2008   Alice's Adventures in Wonderland
Taipei: Cosmos Culture   9789861843247   Anonymous
Reading Room, No. 38, Grade 7. Adapted by Norman Fung. With 2 CD-ROMs. 137 pp. With black-and-white and some color illustrations.

3217   2010   Alice's Adventures in Wonderland
Taipei: Bookman Books   9789574453955   Unknown
With vocabulary and test. 144 pp.

3218   2011   Alice's Adventures in Wonderland
Taipei: Cosmos Culture   9789861848839   Anonymous
Cosmos Classics 3 series. 1st edition. Edited by Rebecca Lu. 221 pp. Color illustrations.

3219   2011   Alice's Adventures in Wonderland
Taipei: Cosmos Culture   9789861848839   Anonymous
Cosmos Classics 3 series. 2nd edition. Edited by Rebecca Lu. 221 pp. Color illustrations.

3220   2011   Alice's Adventures in Wonderland
Taipei: Cosmos Culture   9789861848839   Anonymous
Cosmos Classics 3 series. 3rd edition. Edited by Rebecca Lu. 221 pp. Color illustrations.

3221   2016   Through the Looking-Glass
Taipei: Morning Star   9789864431151   John Tenniel
384 pp. Translated by Liao Xiuyu. Bilingual English and Chinese.

3222   2016   Alice's Adventures in Wonderland and Through the Looking Glass
Taipei: Deeten Publishing   9789577106698   John Tenniel
Combined edition. 656 pp. Translated by Sheng Shi Jiao Yu. Bilingual English and Chinese.

3223   2019   Alice's Adventures in Wonderland Through the Looking-Glass
Taipei: Deeten Publishing   9789577107749   John Tenniel
Bilingual English and Chinese. Translated by Sheng Shi Jiao Yu. 656 pp.

4.28 THAILAND

3224   2019   Alice in Wonderland
Bangkok: SE-Education, Plc.   9786160833412   Anonymous
In English with sidebar annotations in Thai language. Abridged by Chloe Black. In Se-Ed World Readers series.
Famous Stories: Stage 3 Intermediate. Illustrated. 80 pp. Paperback.

4.29 TURKEY

3225   2000   Alice in Wonderland
Istanbul: Beşir Kitabevi   9789758406821   Anonymous
Worldwide Readers, Level 1. Retold by Sema Babacan. Edited by Ebru Yener Gökşenli. 54 pp. 3 illustrations. Without
audio CD.

3226   2007   Alice in Wonderland
Istanbul: Beşir Kitabevi   9789758406821   Anonymous
A later edition. First published in 2000. Worldwide Readers, Level 1. Retold by Sema Babacan. Edited by Ebru Yener
Gökşenli. 54 pp. 3 illustrations. Without audio CD.

3227   2009   Alice in Wonderland
Istanbul: Beşir Kitabevi   9789758406821   Anonymous
A later edition. First published in 2000. Worldwide Readers, Level 1. Retold by Sema Babacan. Edited by Ebru Yener
Gökşenli. 54 pp. 3 illustrations. Without audio CD.

3228   2011   Alice in Wonderland
Istanbul: Beşir Kitabevi   9789758406821   Anonymous
A later edition. First published in 2000. Worldwide Readers, Level 1. Retold by Sema Babacan. Edited by Ebru Yener
Gökşenli. 54 pp. 3 illustrations. Without audio CD.

3229   2012   Alice in Wonderland
Istanbul: Beşir Kitabevi   9789758406821   Anonymous
A later edition. First published in 2000. Worldwide Readers, Level 1. Retold by Sema Babacan. Edited by Ebru Yener
Gökşenli. 54 pp. 3 illustrations. Without audio CD.

3230   2015   Alice in Wonderland
Istanbul: Beşir Kitabevi   9789758406821   Anonymous
A later edition. First published in 2000. Worldwide Readers, Level 1. Retold by Sema Babacan. Edited by Ebru Yener
Gökşenli. 54 pp. 3 illustrations. Without audio CD.

3231   2015   Alice in Wonderland
Ankara: Engin Publishing   9789753205221; 1000320001267   Unknown
Engin Gold Star Classics, Stage 1. With contributions by Merve Dikiciler and Zeynep Yağmur Mert. Translated by
Suzy Usanmaz. 48 pp.

5. *Through the Looking-Glass* Editions Published in the UK

5.1 MACMILLAN 6 SHILLING RED CLOTH EDITION

3232   1872   Through the Looking-Glass
London: Macmillan   John Tenniel

Macmillan 6 shilling red cloth edition. 1st edition, 1st issue. Published December 14, 1871, according to Hilda Bohem in *Jabberwocky* (Autumn, 1984). The title page reads 1872, a dating policy typical of the period. Page 21 has a typo of "wade," not the correct "wabe." Several minor corrections were made over the years, until publication of the 2nd edition in 1897. See *Jabberwocky* (Spring 1978) for details of the changes, and *The Carrollian*, (Autumn, 2008) for the 1897 changes. A 3rd edition was published in 1901. See Edward Wakeling's essay, "Inscribed Presentation Copies" in Volume One for the list of inscribed copies dated "Xmas 1871." Dark green endpapers. 1 page of ads continues to 40th thousand. Many copies have a Burn binder's ticket.

3233   1872   Through the Looking-Glass
London: Macmillan   John Tenniel

Macmillan 6 shilling red cloth edition. 10th thousand. With "wade" corrected to "wabe" on p. 21. 1 page of ads.

3234   1872   Through the Looking-Glass
London: Macmillan   John Tenniel

Macmillan 6 shilling red cloth edition. 11th thousand. 1 page of ads.

3235   1872   Through the Looking-Glass
London: Macmillan   John Tenniel

Macmillan 6 shilling red cloth edition. 12th thousand. 1 page of ads.

3236   1872   Through the Looking-Glass
London: Macmillan   John Tenniel

Macmillan 6 shilling red cloth edition. 13th thousand. 1 page of ads.

3237   1872   Through the Looking-Glass
London: Macmillan   John Tenniel

Macmillan 6 shilling red cloth edition. 14th thousand. 1 page of ads.

3238   1872   Through the Looking-Glass
London: Macmillan   John Tenniel

Macmillan 6 shilling red cloth edition. 15th thousand. No copies of the 16th to 20th thousand, published in the UK, are known to exist as they were believed sent to America. But no copy shows up in any American library or private collection.

3239   1872   Through the Looking-Glass
London: Macmillan   John Tenniel

Macmillan 6 shilling red cloth edition. 21st thousand. 1 page of ads.

3240   1872   Through the Looking-Glass
London: Macmillan   John Tenniel

Macmillan 6 shilling red cloth edition. 22nd thousand. 1 page of ads.

3241   1872   Through the Looking-Glass
London: Macmillan   John Tenniel

Macmillan 6 shilling red cloth edition. 23rd thousand. 1 page of ads.

3242   1872   Through the Looking-Glass
London: Macmillan   John Tenniel
Macmillan 6 shilling red cloth edition. 24th thousand. 1 page of ads.

3243   1872   Through the Looking-Glass
London: Macmillan   John Tenniel
Macmillan 6 shilling red cloth edition. 25th thousand. The 1st edition with the Kings missing from the chess board.
1 page of ads.

3244   1872   Through the Looking-Glass
London: Macmillan   John Tenniel
Macmillan 6 shilling red cloth edition. 26th thousand. 1 page of ads.

3245   1872   Through the Looking-Glass
London: Macmillan   John Tenniel
Macmillan 6 shilling red cloth edition. 27th thousand. 1 page of ads.

3246   1872   Through the Looking-Glass
London: Macmillan   John Tenniel
Macmillan 6 shilling red cloth edition. 28th thousand. 1 page of ads.

3247   1872   Through the Looking-Glass
London: Macmillan   John Tenniel
Macmillan 6 shilling red cloth edition. 29th thousand. 1 page of ads.

3248   1872   Through the Looking-Glass
London: Macmillan   John Tenniel
Macmillan 6 shilling red cloth edition. 30th thousand. 1 page of ads.

3249   1872   Through the Looking-Glass
London: Macmillan   John Tenniel
Macmillan 6 shilling red cloth edition. 31st thousand. Some copies have no ads and some 1 page.

3250   1872   Through the Looking-Glass
London: Macmillan   John Tenniel
Macmillan 6 shilling red cloth edition. 32nd thousand. 1 page of ads.

3251   1872   Through the Looking-Glass
London: Macmillan   John Tenniel
Macmillan 6 shilling red cloth edition. 33rd thousand. 1 page of ads.

3252   1873   Through the Looking-Glass
London: Macmillan   John Tenniel
Macmillan 6 shilling red cloth edition. 34th thousand. 1 page of ads.

3253   1873   Through the Looking-Glass
London: Macmillan   John Tenniel
Macmillan 6 shilling red cloth edition. 35th thousand. 1 page of ads.

3254   1873   Through the Looking-Glass
London: Macmillan   John Tenniel
Macmillan 6 shilling red cloth edition. 36th thousand. 1 page of ads.

3255   1873   Through the Looking-Glass
London: Macmillan   John Tenniel
Macmillan 6 shilling red cloth edition. 37th thousand. 1 page of ads.

3256   1873   Through the Looking-Glass
London: Macmillan   John Tenniel
Macmillan 6 shilling red cloth edition. 38th thousand. 1 page of ads. The 39th thousand is known only with a New York: Macmillan imprint. Macmillan records indicate it was published only for that market. Copies dated 1875 do show up in American libraries and private collections.

3257   1877   Through the Looking-Glass
London: Macmillan   John Tenniel
Macmillan 6 shilling red cloth edition. 40th thousand. 1 page of ads. A copy is known in a white presentation binding.

3258   1877   Through the Looking-Glass
London: Macmillan   John Tenniel
Macmillan 6 shilling red cloth edition. 41st thousand. 1 page of ads.

3259   1877   Through the Looking-Glass
London; New York: Macmillan   John Tenniel
Macmillan 6 shilling red cloth edition. 42nd thousand. 1 page of ads. Variant copies are known dated 1878 and 1880.

3260   1877   Through the Looking-Glass
London; New York: Macmillan   John Tenniel
Macmillan 6 shilling red cloth edition. 43rd thousand. 1 page of ads.

3261   1877   Through the Looking-Glass
London; New York: Macmillan   John Tenniel
Macmillan 6 shilling red cloth edition. 44th thousand. 1 page of ads. A copy is known with "Presented for the Use of Sick Children" stamped on the cover.

3262   1878   Through the Looking-Glass
London: Macmillan   John Tenniel
Macmillan 6 shilling red cloth edition. 45th thousand. Missing Kings (since 1872, 25th thousand) replaced on the chess board. The Kings symbols differ from the 24th thousand and earlier editions. 1 page of ads.

3263   1878   Through the Looking-Glass
London: Macmillan   John Tenniel
Macmillan 6 shilling red cloth edition. 46th thousand. 1 page of ads.

3264   1880   Through the Looking-Glass
London: Macmillan   John Tenniel
Macmillan 6 shilling red cloth edition. 47th thousand. 1 page of ads.

3265   1880   Through the Looking-Glass
London: Macmillan   John Tenniel
Macmillan 6 shilling red cloth edition. 48th thousand. 1 page of ads.

3266   1880   Through the Looking-Glass
London: Macmillan   John Tenniel
Macmillan 6 shilling red cloth edition. 49th thousand. 1 page of ads. There are copies of this thousand dated 1881.

3267 1881   Through the Looking-Glass
London: Macmillan   John Tenniel
Macmillan 6 shilling red cloth edition. 50th thousand. 1 page of ads.

3268 1882   Through the Looking-Glass
London: Macmillan   John Tenniel
Macmillan 6 shilling red cloth edition. 50th thousand. 1 page of ads.

3269 1882   Through the Looking-Glass
London: Macmillan   John Tenniel
Macmillan 6 shilling red cloth edition. 51st thousand. 1 page of ads.

3270 1882   Through the Looking-Glass
London: Macmillan   John Tenniel
Macmillan 6 shilling red cloth edition. 52nd thousand. 1 page of ads.

3271 1883   Through the Looking-Glass
London: Macmillan   John Tenniel
Macmillan 6 shilling red cloth edition. 53rd thousand. 1 page of ads. There may be copies of this thousand dated 1882.

3272 1883   Through the Looking-Glass
London: Macmillan   John Tenniel
Macmillan 6 shilling red cloth edition. 54th thousand. 1 page of ads.

3273 1885   Through the Looking-Glass
London: Macmillan   John Tenniel
Macmillan 6 shilling red cloth edition. 55th thousand. 1 page of ads.

3274 1885   Through the Looking-Glass
London: Macmillan   John Tenniel
Macmillan 6 shilling red cloth edition. 56th thousand. 1 page of ads.

3275 1887   Through the Looking-Glass
London; New York: Macmillan   John Tenniel
Macmillan 6 shilling red cloth edition. 57th thousand. 2 pages of ads.

3276 1887   Through the Looking-Glass
London; New York: Macmillan   John Tenniel
Macmillan 6 shilling red cloth edition. 58th thousand. 2 pages of ads.

3277 1887   Through the Looking-Glass
London; New York: Macmillan   John Tenniel
Macmillan 6 shilling red cloth edition. 59th thousand. 2 pages of ads.

3278 1893   Through the Looking-Glass
London; New York: Macmillan   John Tenniel
Macmillan 6 shilling red cloth edition. 60th thousand. According to Goodacre, there are 5 variants of this thousand and 17 known copies. See his analysis in Volume One titled "The Rejected 60th Thousand of *Through the Looking-Glass*: A Census of Known Copies." The edition was suppressed by Carroll because of poor illustrations. Only 60 copies were sold, and Carroll advertised for copies to be returned. None were as of September 20, 1894 according to Morton Cohen in his book *Lewis Carroll and the House of Macmillan*, p. 309, n. 1. 4 pages of ads including a page titled "[Specimen Page] *Alice's Adventures under Ground*." With a Carroll illustration of Alice. Two copies of the Mechanics Institute version of the 60th thousand are known. Both are in rough pebbled red cloth with roundels front and back,

not gilded. Embossed on the front cover in blind "Presented for the use of Mechanics' Institutes · Reading Rooms, Etc." Of the two copies, one has 2 pages of ads and the other has none. See Goodacre's essay referred to above for more information.

3279   1897   Through the Looking-Glass
London; New York: Macmillan   John Tenniel
Macmillan 6 shilling red cloth edition. 2nd edition. 61st thousand. 3 pages of ads including one for the 86th thousand of *Alice*, the last revised version during Carroll's lifetime.

3280   1898   Through the Looking-Glass
London; New York: Macmillan   John Tenniel
Macmillan 6 shilling red cloth edition. 62nd thousand. 3 pages of ads.

3281   1901   Through the Looking-Glass
London; New York: Macmillan   John Tenniel
Macmillan 6 shilling red cloth edition. 3rd edition. 63rd thousand. 3 pages of ads.

3282   1908   Through the Looking-Glass
London: Macmillan   John Tenniel
Macmillan 6 shilling red cloth edition. 64th thousand. 3 pages of ads.

3283   1913   Through the Looking-Glass
London: Macmillan   John Tenniel
Macmillan 6 shilling red cloth edition. 65th thousand. 3 pages of ads.

3284   1919   Through the Looking-Glass
London: Macmillan   John Tenniel
Macmillan 6 shilling red cloth edition. 66th thousand. 3 pages of ads.

3285   1922   Through the Looking-Glass
London: Macmillan   John Tenniel
Macmillan 6 shilling red cloth edition. 67th thousand. 3 pages of ads.

3286   1927   Through the Looking-Glass
London: Macmillan   John Tenniel
Macmillan 6 shilling red cloth edition. 68th thousand. No copy is known of the 69th thousand.

3287   1932   Through the Looking-Glass
London: Macmillan   John Tenniel
Macmillan 6 shilling red cloth edition. 70th thousand. 2 pages of ads. Copies in gray illustrated dust jacket are known. Most copies in standard red bindings. Remainder bindings exist.

3288   1942   Through the Looking-Glass
London: Macmillan   John Tenniel
Macmillan 6 shilling red cloth edition. No thousand on the title page. Dust jacket. Other than the 1872 facsimile editions of 1984 and 1997, both published as Macmillan Children's Books, this edition is believed to be the last of the Macmillan 6 shilling editions.

5.2 MACMILLAN *PEOPLE'S EDITION*

3289   1887   Through the Looking-Glass
London; New York: Macmillan   John Tenniel
Macmillan People's Edition. 1st edition. 10,000 copies were printed. In olive-green cloth.

3290   1889   Through the Looking-Glass
London; New York: Macmillan   John Tenniel
Macmillan People's Edition. 11th thousand. In olive-green cloth.

3291   1889   Through the Looking-Glass
London; New York: Macmillan   John Tenniel
Macmillan People's Edition. 12th thousand. In olive-green cloth.

3292   1889   Through the Looking-Glass
London; New York: Macmillan   John Tenniel
Macmillan People's Edition. 13th thousand. In olive-green cloth.

3293   1889   Through the Looking-Glass
London; New York: Macmillan   John Tenniel
Macmillan People's Edition. 14th thousand. In olive-green cloth.

3294   1889   Through the Looking-Glass
London; New York: Macmillan   John Tenniel
Macmillan People's Edition. 15th thousand. Copies dated 1891 are known. In olive-green cloth.

3295   1890   Through the Looking-Glass
London; New York: Macmillan   John Tenniel
Macmillan People's Edition. 16th thousand. A copy dated 1891 is known. Copies of the 18th thousand dated 1890 are known. In olive-green cloth.

3296   1891   Through the Looking-Glass
London; New York: Macmillan   John Tenniel
Macmillan People's Edition. Copies dated 1891 with 15th thousand and another with 16th thousand are known. In olive-green cloth.

3297   1892   Through the Looking-Glass
London; New York: Macmillan   John Tenniel
Macmillan People's Edition. 17th thousand. In olive-green cloth.

3298   1892   Through the Looking-Glass
London; New York: Macmillan   John Tenniel
Macmillan People's Edition. 18th thousand. Copies dated 1890 are known. In olive-green cloth.

3299   1892   Through the Looking-Glass
London; New York: Macmillan   John Tenniel
Macmillan People's Edition. 20th thousand. In olive-green cloth.

3300   1892   Through the Looking-Glass
London; New York: Macmillan   John Tenniel
Macmillan People's Edition. 21st thousand. In olive-green cloth.

3301   1893   Through the Looking-Glass
London; New York: Macmillan   John Tenniel
Macmillan People's Edition. 22nd thousand. A copy of the 24th thousand dated 1893 is known. In olive-green cloth.

3302   1894   Through the Looking-Glass
London; New York: Macmillan   John Tenniel
Macmillan People's Edition. 23rd thousand. In olive-green cloth.

3303   1894   Through the Looking-Glass
London; New York: Macmillan   John Tenniel
Macmillan People's Edition. 24th thousand. A copy dated 1893 is known. In olive-green cloth.

3304   1894   Through the Looking-Glass
London; New York: Macmillan   John Tenniel
Macmillan People's Edition. 25th thousand. In olive-green cloth.

3305   1895   Through the Looking-Glass
London; New York: Macmillan   John Tenniel
Macmillan People's Edition. 26th thousand. In olive-green cloth.

3306   1895   Through the Looking-Glass
London; New York: Macmillan   John Tenniel
Macmillan People's Edition. 27th thousand. In olive-green cloth.

3307   1896   Through the Looking-Glass
London; New York: Macmillan   John Tenniel
Macmillan People's Edition. 27th thousand. In olive-green cloth.

3308   1896   Through the Looking-Glass
London; New York: Macmillan   John Tenniel
Macmillan People's Edition. 28th thousand. In olive-green cloth. No copy of the 29th thousand is known.

3309   1896   Through the Looking-Glass
London; New York: Macmillan   John Tenniel
Macmillan People's Edition. 30th thousand. In olive-green cloth. No copies of the 31st to the 42nd thousand are known.

3310   1896   Through the Looking-Glass
London; New York: Macmillan   John Tenniel
Macmillan People's Edition. 43rd thousand. In olive-green cloth.

3311   1896   Through the Looking-Glass
London; New York: Macmillan   John Tenniel
Macmillan People's Edition. 44th thousand. In olive-green cloth.

3312   1897   Through the Looking-Glass
London; New York: Macmillan   John Tenniel
Macmillan People's Edition. 45th thousand. In olive-green cloth.

3313   1897   Through the Looking-Glass
London; New York: Macmillan   John Tenniel
Macmillan People's Edition. 46th thousand. In olive-green cloth.

3314   1897   Through the Looking-Glass
London; New York: Macmillan   John Tenniel
Macmillan People's Edition. 47th thousand. In olive-green cloth.

3315   1898   Through the Looking-Glass
London; New York: Macmillan   John Tenniel
Macmillan People's Edition. 48th thousand. In olive-green cloth.

3316	1898	Through the Looking-Glass	
		London; New York: Macmillan	John Tenniel
		Macmillan People's Edition. 49th thousand. In olive-green cloth.	

3317	1898	Through the Looking-Glass	
		London; New York: Macmillan	John Tenniel
		Macmillan People's Edition. 50th thousand. In olive-green cloth.	

3318	1898	Through the Looking-Glass	
		London; New York: Macmillan	John Tenniel
		Macmillan People's Edition. 51st thousand. In olive-green cloth.	

3319	1898	Through the Looking-Glass	
		London; New York: Macmillan	John Tenniel
		Macmillan People's Edition. 52nd thousand. In olive-green cloth.	

3320	1898	Through the Looking-Glass	
		London; New York: Macmillan	John Tenniel
		Macmillan People's Edition. 53rd thousand. In olive-green cloth.	

3321	1898	Through the Looking-Glass	
		London; New York: Macmillan	John Tenniel
		Macmillan People's Edition. 54th thousand. In olive-green cloth.	

3322	1898	Through the Looking-Glass	
		London; New York: Macmillan	John Tenniel
		Macmillan People's Edition. 55th thousand. In olive-green cloth.	

3323	1898	Through the Looking-Glass	
		London; New York: Macmillan	John Tenniel
		Macmillan People's Edition. 56th thousand. In olive-green cloth.	

3324	1898	Through the Looking-Glass	
		London; New York: Macmillan	John Tenniel
		Macmillan People's Edition. 57th thousand. In olive-green cloth.	

3325	1898	Through the Looking-Glass	
		London; New York: Macmillan	John Tenniel
		Macmillan People's Edition. 58th thousand. In olive-green cloth.	

3326	1898	Through the Looking-Glass	
		London; New York: Macmillan	John Tenniel
		Macmillan People's Edition. 59th thousand. In olive-green cloth.	

3327	1898	Through the Looking-Glass	
		London; New York: Macmillan	John Tenniel
		Macmillan People's Edition. 60th thousand. In olive-green cloth.	

3328	1899	Through the Looking-Glass	
		London; New York: Macmillan	John Tenniel
		Macmillan People's Edition. 61st thousand. In olive-green cloth.	

3329	1899	Through the Looking-Glass	

London; New York: Macmillan   John Tenniel

Macmillan People's Edition. 62nd thousand. In olive-green cloth. No copy of the 63rd thousand is known.

3330   1899   Through the Looking-Glass

London; New York: Macmillan   John Tenniel

Macmillan People's Edition. 64th thousand. In olive-green cloth.

3331   1899   Through the Looking-Glass

London; New York: Macmillan   John Tenniel

Macmillan People's Edition. 65th thousand. In olive-green cloth.

3332   1901   Through the Looking-Glass

London; New York: Macmillan   John Tenniel

Macmillan People's Edition. 66th thousand. In olive-green cloth.

3333   1901   Through the Looking-Glass

London; New York: Macmillan   John Tenniel

Macmillan People's Edition. 67th thousand. In olive-green cloth.

3334   1901   Through the Looking-Glass

London; New York: Macmillan   John Tenniel

Macmillan People's Edition. 68th thousand. In olive-green cloth. No copy of the 69th thousand is known.

3335   1901   Through the Looking-Glass

London; New York: Macmillan   John Tenniel

Macmillan People's Edition. 70th thousand. In olive-green cloth.

3336   1902   Through the Looking-Glass

London; New York: Macmillan   John Tenniel

Macmillan People's Edition. 70th thousand. In olive-green cloth.

3337   1902   Through the Looking-Glass

London; New York: Macmillan   John Tenniel

Macmillan People's Edition. 71st thousand. In olive-green cloth.

3338   1902   Through the Looking-Glass

London; New York: Macmillan   John Tenniel

Macmillan People's Edition. 72nd thousand. In olive-green cloth. No copy of the 73rd thousand is known.

3339   1902   Through the Looking-Glass

London; New York: Macmillan   John Tenniel

Macmillan People's Edition. 74th thousand. In olive-green cloth.

3340   1903   Through the Looking-Glass

London; New York: Macmillan   John Tenniel

Macmillan People's Edition. 75th thousand. In olive-green cloth.

3341   1903   Through the Looking-Glass

London; New York: Macmillan   John Tenniel

Macmillan People's Edition. 76th thousand. In olive-green cloth.

3342   1903   Through the Looking-Glass

London; New York: Macmillan   John Tenniel

Macmillan People's Edition. 77th thousand. In olive-green cloth.

3343   1903   Through the Looking-Glass
London; New York: Macmillan   John Tenniel
Macmillan People's Edition. 78th thousand. In olive-green cloth.

3344   1903   Through the Looking-Glass
London; New York: Macmillan   John Tenniel
People's Edition. 79th thousand. In olive-green cloth. No copies of the 80th, 81st, or 82nd thousand are known.

3345   1904   Through the Looking-Glass
London; New York: Macmillan   John Tenniel
People's Edition. 83rd thousand. In olive-green cloth. Known in only 1 copy.

3346   1904   Through the Looking-Glass
London; New York: Macmillan   John Tenniel
People's Edition. 84th thousand. In olive-green cloth.

3347   1905   Through the Looking-Glass
London; New York: Macmillan   John Tenniel
People's Edition. 85th thousand. In olive-green cloth.

3348   1905   Through the Looking-Glass
London; New York: Macmillan   John Tenniel
Macmillan People's Edition. 86th thousand. In olive-green cloth.

3349   1905   Through the Looking-Glass
London; New York: Macmillan   John Tenniel
Macmillan People's Edition. 87th thousand. In olive-green cloth. No copy of the 88th or 89th thousand is known.

3350   1907   Through the Looking-Glass
London; New York: Macmillan   John Tenniel
Macmillan People's Edition. 90th thousand. In olive-green cloth.

3351   1907   Through the Looking-Glass
London; New York: Macmillan   John Tenniel
Macmillan People's Edition. 91st thousand. In olive-green cloth. No copy of the 92nd thousand is known.

3352   1907   Through the Looking-Glass
London; New York: Macmillan   John Tenniel
Macmillan People's Edition. 93rd thousand. In olive-green cloth. No copy of the 94th to 99th thousand is known.

3353   1908   Through the Looking-Glass
London: Macmillan   John Tenniel
Macmillan People's Edition. 100th thousand. In olive-green cloth. No copy of the 101st to 104th thousand is known.

3354   1910   Through the Looking-Glass
London: Macmillan   John Tenniel
Macmillan People's Edition. 105th thousand. In olive-green cloth. No copy of the 106th to 109th thousand is known.

3355   1913   Through the Looking-Glass
London: Macmillan   John Tenniel
Macmillan People's Edition. 110th thousand. No copy of the 111th thousand is known.

3356   1918   Through the Looking-Glass

London: Macmillan   John Tenniel

Macmillan People's Edition. 112th thousand. It is believed that from the 112th to the 130th thousand, copies were printed in batches of 3,000, with all carrying the 1st thousand of the batch. All in olive-green cloth.

3357   1920   Through the Looking-Glass
London: Macmillan   John Tenniel
Macmillan People's Edition. 115th thousand. In olive-green cloth.

3358   1922   Through the Looking-Glass
London: Macmillan   John Tenniel
Macmillan People's Edition. 118th thousand. In olive-green cloth.

3359   1925   Through the Looking-Glass
London: Macmillan   John Tenniel
Macmillan People's Edition. 121st thousand. In olive-green cloth.

3360   1928   Through the Looking-Glass
London: Macmillan   John Tenniel
Macmillan People's Edition. 124th thousand. In olive-green cloth.

3361   1933   Through the Looking-Glass
London: Macmillan   John Tenniel
Macmillan People's Edition. 127th thousand. In olive-green cloth.

3362   1937   Through the Looking-Glass
London: Macmillan   John Tenniel
Macmillan People's Edition. 130th thousand. In olive-green cloth.

3363   1939   Through the Looking-Glass
London: Macmillan   John Tenniel
Macmillan People's Edition. Still listed as the 130th thousand. In olive-green cloth. This may be the last edition with the thousand included.

3364   1948   Through the Looking-Glass
London: Macmillan   John Tenniel
Macmillan People's Edition. No thousand. In olive-green cloth. Dust jacket.

3365   1950   Through the Looking-Glass
London: Macmillan   John Tenniel
Macmillan People's Edition. No thousand. In olive-green cloth. Dust jacket.

3366   1951   Through the Looking-Glass
London: Macmillan   John Tenniel
Macmillan People's Edition. No thousand. In olive-green cloth. Dust jacket.

3367   1952   Through the Looking-Glass
London: Macmillan   John Tenniel
Macmillan People's Edition. No thousand. In olive-green cloth. Dust jacket.

3368   1954   Through the Looking-Glass
London: Macmillan   John Tenniel
Macmillan People's Edition. No thousand. In olive-green cloth. Dust jacket.

3369   1955   Through the Looking-Glass
London: Macmillan   John Tenniel
Macmillan People's Edition. No thousand. In olive-green cloth. Dust jacket.

3370   1962   Through the Looking-Glass
London: Macmillan   John Tenniel
Macmillan People's Edition. No thousand. In olive-green cloth. Dust jacket.

3371   1967   Through the Looking-Glass
London: Macmillan   John Tenniel
Macmillan People's Edition. No thousand. In olive-green cloth. Dust jacket.

3372   1971   Through the Looking-Glass
London: Macmillan   0333066650   John Tenniel
Macmillan People's Edition. No thousand. In olive-green cloth. Dust jacket.

3373   1973   Through the Looking-Glass
London: Macmillan   0333066650   John Tenniel
Macmillan People's Edition. No thousand. In olive-green cloth. Dust jacket.

3374   1976   Through the Looking-Glass
London: Macmillan   0333066650   John Tenniel
Macmillan People's Edition. No thousand. In olive-green cloth. Dust jacket.

3375   1980   Through the Looking-Glass
London: Macmillan   0333066650   John Tenniel
Macmillan People's Edition. No thousand. In olive-green cloth. Dust jacket.

3376   1981   Through the Looking-Glass
London: Macmillan   0333066650   John Tenniel
Macmillan People's Edition. No thousand. In olive-green cloth. Dust jacket.

3377   1983   Through the Looking-Glass
London: Macmillan   0333066650   John Tenniel
Macmillan People's Edition. No thousand. In olive-green cloth. Dust jacket.

3378   1985   Through the Looking-Glass
London: Macmillan   0333066650   John Tenniel
Macmillan People's Edition. No thousand. In olive-green cloth. Dust jacket.

3379   1987   Through the Looking-Glass
London: Macmillan   0333066650   John Tenniel
Macmillan People's Edition. No thousand. In olive-green cloth. Dust jacket.

3380   1988   Through the Looking-Glass
London: Macmillan   0333066650   John Tenniel
Macmillan People's Edition. No thousand. In olive-green cloth. Dust jacket. Believed to be the last People's Edition of
Looking-Glass.

5.3 MACMILLAN *SIXPENNY SERIES*

3381   1898   Through the Looking-Glass
London; New York: Macmillan   John Tenniel
Macmillan Sixpenny Series. 1st edition. Copies were issued in blue cloth boards with a copy in paper wrappers. This series is best identified by paper size of 8½ x 6 inches, which is larger than the Macmillan red cloth 6s or the Macmillan People's Edition. It also has the Illustrators information on the title page in 1 line. It is in 2 lines in the 6s and the People's.

3382   1899   Through the Looking-Glass
London; New York: Macmillan   John Tenniel
Macmillan Sixpenny Series. 1st reprint.

3383   1902   Through the Looking-Glass
London; New York: Macmillan   John Tenniel
Macmillan Sixpenny Series. 2nd reprint.

3384   1904   Through the Looking-Glass
London; New York: Macmillan   John Tenniel
Macmillan Sixpenny Series. 3rd reprint.

3385   1907   Through the Looking-Glass
London: Macmillan   John Tenniel
Macmillan Sixpenny Series. 4th reprint.

3386   1911   Through the Looking-Glass
London: Macmillan   John Tenniel
Macmillan Sixpenny Series. 5th reprint.

3387   1919   Through the Looking-Glass
London: Macmillan   John Tenniel
Macmillan Sixpenny Series. 6th reprint.

3388   1919   Through the Looking-Glass
London: Macmillan   John Tenniel
Macmillan Sixpenny Series. Reprint of the Sixpenny Series, but called the Macmillan's Supplementary Continuous Reader Series.

3389   1923   Through the Looking-Glass
London: Macmillan   John Tenniel
Macmillan Sixpenny Series. 7th reprint.

3390   1926   Through the Looking-Glass
London: Macmillan   John Tenniel
Macmillan Sixpenny Series. 8th reprint.

3391   1930   Through the Looking-Glass
London: Macmillan   John Tenniel
Macmillan Sixpenny Series. 9th reprint.

5.4 MACMILLAN *LITTLE FOLKS'* EDITION

3392   1903   Through the Looking-Glass
London; New York: Macmillan   John Tenniel
Macmillan Little Folks' Edition. 1st edition. With 32 redrawn color illustrations. Abridged for younger readers.

3393   1916   Through the Looking-Glass
London: Macmillan Children's Books (Pan Macmillan)   John Tenniel
Macmillan Little Folks' Edition. With 32 redrawn color illustrations. First published in 1903. Abridged for younger readers.

3394   2016   Through the Looking-Glass
London: Macmillan Children's Books   9781509820498   John Tenniel
Macmillan Little Folks' Edition. With 32 redrawn color illustrations. First published in 1903. Red cloth. A companion to the Little Folks' *Alice* edition. Abridged for younger readers.

5.5 MACMILLAN
ILLUSTRATED POCKET CLASSICS FOR THE YOUNG EDITIONS

3395   1904   Through the Looking-Glass
London; New York: Macmillan   John Tenniel
Macmillan Illustrated Pocket Classics for the Young. 1st edition. The series title is on the verso of the title page of this edition and in all reprints. The binding was usually blue cloth boards (occasionally blue "leatherette") until 1923 when the binding changed to red. Reprinted as a London: Macmillan edition in 1923.

3396   1905   Through the Looking-Glass
London; New York: Macmillan   John Tenniel
Macmillan Illustrated Pocket Classics for the Young. 1st reprint of the Illustrated Pocket Classics for the Young. Blue cloth.

3397   1906   Through the Looking-Glass
London; New York: Macmillan   John Tenniel
Macmillan Illustrated Pocket Classics for the Young. 2nd reprint of the Illustrated Pocket Classics for the Young.

3398   1907   Through the Looking-Glass
London; New York: Macmillan   John Tenniel
Macmillan Illustrated Pocket Classics for the Young. 3rd reprint of the Illustrated Pocket Classics for the Young.

3399   1908   Through the Looking-Glass
London; New York: Macmillan   John Tenniel
Macmillan Illustrated Pocket Classics for the Young. Reprint. The title page has the date of 1908, but the verso of the title page has the 3rd reprint of 1907. In blue écrassé morocco and dust jacket.

3400   1908   Through the Looking-Glass
London; New York: Macmillan   John Tenniel
Macmillan Illustrated Pocket Classics for the Young. Reprint. A copy is known with the title page of 1908 but the verso lists it as the 4th reprint. The copyright page of the 1923 edition fails to mention this reprint.

3401   1912   Through the Looking-Glass
London: Macmillan   John Tenniel
Macmillan Illustrated Pocket Classics for the Young. 5th reprint of the Illustrated Pocket Classics for the Young.

3402   1917   Through the Looking-Glass

London: Macmillan   John Tenniel

Macmillan Illustrated Pocket Classics for the Young. 6th reprint.

3403   1919   Through the Looking-Glass

London: Macmillan   John Tenniel

Illustrated Pocket Classics for the Young. 7th reprint. Published twice in 1919. Appears in both blue and red bindings.

3404   1919   Through the Looking-Glass

London: Macmillan   John Tenniel

Illustrated Pocket Classics for the Young. 8th reprint. Published twice in 1919. Appears in both blue and red bindings.

3405   1923   Through the Looking-Glass

London: Macmillan   John Tenniel

Illustrated Pocket Classics for the Young. 9th reprint. Cover color changed from blue to red. A copy is known with the copyright page listing all reprints except the 2nd of 1908.

3406   1926   Through the Looking-Glass

London: Macmillan   John Tenniel

Illustrated Pocket Classics for the Young. 10th reprint.

3407   1930   Through the Looking-Glass

London: Macmillan   John Tenniel

Illustrated Pocket Classics for the Young. 11th reprint.

3408   1936   Through the Looking-Glass

London: Macmillan   John Tenniel

Illustrated Pocket Classics for the Young. 12th reprint. A copy exists in red cloth with dust jacket. A copy is known with the copyright page listing all reprints except the 2nd of 1908.

5.6 MACMILLAN *MINIATURE EDITION*

3409   1908   Through the Looking-Glass

London: Macmillan   John Tenniel

Macmillan Miniature Edition. 1st edition. Published in October 1908. In red cloth boards until 1920 when various bindings were used. Dust jacket.

3410   1908   Through the Looking-Glass

London: Macmillan   John Tenniel

Macmillan Miniature Edition. 1st reprint in December 1908. Red cloth boards.

3411   1910   Through the Looking-Glass

London: Macmillan   John Tenniel

Macmillan Miniature Edition. 2nd reprint. Red cloth boards.

3412   1911   Through the Looking-Glass

London: Macmillan   John Tenniel

Macmillan Miniature Edition. 3rd reprint. Red cloth boards.

3413   1912   Through the Looking-Glass

London: Macmillan   John Tenniel

Macmillan Miniature Edition. 4th reprint. Red cloth boards.

3414   1914   Through the Looking-Glass

London: Macmillan
Macmillan Miniature Edition. 5th reprint. Red cloth boards.

John Tenniel

3415 1915 Through the Looking-Glass
London: Macmillan
John Tenniel
Macmillan Miniature Edition. 6th reprint. Red cloth boards.

3416 1916 Through the Looking-Glass
London: Macmillan
John Tenniel
Macmillan Miniature Edition. 7th reprint. Red cloth boards.

3417 1918 Through the Looking-Glass
London: Macmillan
John Tenniel
Macmillan Miniature Edition. 8th reprint. Red cloth boards.

3418 1919 Through the Looking-Glass
London: Macmillan
John Tenniel
Macmillan Miniature Edition. 9th reprint. Red cloth boards.

3419 1920 Through the Looking-Glass
London: Macmillan
John Tenniel
Macmillan Miniature Edition. 10th reprint. Starting with this reprint various bindings were used.

3420 1921 Through the Looking-Glass
London: Macmillan
John Tenniel
Macmillan Miniature Edition. 11th reprint. Various bindings. Dust jacket.

3421 1924 Through the Looking-Glass
London: Macmillan
John Tenniel
Macmillan Miniature Edition. 12th reprint. Various bindings Dust jacket.

3422 1927 Through the Looking-Glass
London: Macmillan
John Tenniel
Macmillan Miniature Edition. 13th reprint. Various bindings. Dust jacket.

3423 1929 Through the Looking-Glass
London: Macmillan
John Tenniel
Macmillan Miniature Edition. 14th reprint. Various bindings. Dust jacket.

3424 1931 Through the Looking-Glass
London: Macmillan
John Tenniel
Macmillan Miniature Edition. 15th reprint. Various bindings including some in Ledura and some in transparent "Transmatic." Dust jacket.

3425 1935 Through the Looking-Glass
London: Macmillan
John Tenniel
Macmillan Miniature Edition. 16th reprint. Various bindings including some in Ledura and some in transparent "Transmatic." Dust jacket.

3426 1940 Through the Looking-Glass
London: Macmillan
John Tenniel
Macmillan Miniature Edition. 17th reprint. Various bindings including some in Ledura and some in transparent "Transmatic." Dust jacket.

5.7 MACMILLAN *CHILDREN'S CLASSICS' JUNIOR SERIES*

3427   1913   Through the Looking-Glass
London: Macmillan   John Tenniel
Macmillan Children's Classics' Junior Series. 1st edition. On the verso of the title page of the 1927 *Alice* edition of this book is the following for the *Looking-Glass* edition: 1st edition 1913. Reprinted 1914, 1917, 1919 (twice), 1920, 1922, 1924, 1926, 1927.

3428   1914   Through the Looking-Glass
London: Macmillan   John Tenniel
Macmillan Children's Classics' Junior Series. Not seen. 1st reprint of the Children's Classics' Junior Series edition.

3429   1917   Through the Looking-Glass
London: Macmillan   John Tenniel
Macmillan Children's Classics' Junior Series. Not seen. 2nd reprint.

3430   1919   Through the Looking-Glass
London: Macmillan   John Tenniel
Macmillan Children's Classics' Junior Series. Not seen. 3rd reprint.

3431   1919   Through the Looking-Glass
London: Macmillan   John Tenniel
Macmillan Children's Classics' Junior Series. Not seen. 4th reprint.

3432   1920   Through the Looking-Glass
London: Macmillan   John Tenniel
Macmillan Children's Classics' Junior Series. Not seen. 5th reprint.

3433   1922   Through the Looking-Glass
London: Macmillan   John Tenniel
Macmillan Children's Classics' Junior Series. Not seen. 6th reprint.

3434   1924   Through the Looking-Glass
London: Macmillan   John Tenniel
Macmillan Children's Classics' Junior Series. Not seen. 7th reprint.

3435   1925   Through the Looking-Glass
London: Macmillan   John Tenniel
Macmillan Children's Classics' Junior Series. Paper cover version. Number 24a of the Junior (age 6 to 9) series.

3436   1926   Through the Looking-Glass
London: Macmillan   John Tenniel
Macmillan Children's Classics' Junior Series. Not seen. 8th reprint.

3437   1927   Through the Looking-Glass
London: Macmillan   John Tenniel
Macmillan Children's Classics' Junior Series. The *Alice* edition of this date says this *Looking-Glass* edition is the 9th reprint of the Children's Classics' Junior Series.

3438   ca. 1950s   Through the Looking-Glass
London: Macmillan   John Tenniel
Macmillan Children's Classics' Junior Series. Paper cover version. No. 113.

5.8 MACMILLAN *CHILDREN'S EDITION*

3439   1927   Through the Looking-Glass
London: Macmillan   John Tenniel
Macmillan Children's Edition. 1st edition. The series title Children's Edition is only on the verso of the title page of
this edition and all reprints. Dust jacket.

3440   1928   Through the Looking-Glass
London: Macmillan   John Tenniel
Macmillan Children's Edition. 1st Children's Edition reprint. Dust jacket.

3441   1934   Through the Looking-Glass
London: Macmillan   John Tenniel
Macmillan Children's Edition. 2nd reprint. Dust jacket.

3442   1940   Through the Looking-Glass
London: Macmillan   John Tenniel
Macmillan Children's Edition. 3rd reprint. Dust jacket.

3443   1953   Through the Looking-Glass
London: Macmillan   John Tenniel
Macmillan Children's Edition. 4th reprint. Dust jacket.

3444   1956   Through the Looking-Glass
London: Macmillan   John Tenniel
Macmillan Children's Edition. 5th reprint. Dust jacket.

3445   1956   Through the Looking-Glass
London: Macmillan & Co. New York: St. Martin's Press   John Tenniel
Reprint of Children's Edition, 1st edition of 1927.

3446   1962   Through the Looking-Glass
London: Macmillan   John Tenniel
Macmillan Children's Edition. 6th reprint. Dust jacket.

3447   1965   Through the Looking-Glass
London: Macmillan   John Tenniel
Macmillan Children's Edition. 7th reprint. Dust jacket.

3448   1968   Through the Looking-Glass
London: Macmillan   John Tenniel
Macmillan Children's Edition. 8th reprint. Dust jacket.

3449   1972   Through the Looking-Glass
London: Macmillan   0978041031   John Tenniel
Macmillan Children's Edition. 9th reprint. Dust jacket.

3450   1974   Through the Looking-Glass
London: Macmillan   John Tenniel
Macmillan Children's Edition. 10th reprint. Dust jacket.

3451   1975   Through the Looking-Glass

London: Macmillan   0978041031   John Tenniel

Macmillan Children's Edition. 11th reprint. Dust jacket.

3452   1977   Through the Looking-Glass

London: Macmillan   0978041031   John Tenniel

Macmillan Children's Edition. 12th reprint. Dust jacket.

3453   1977   Through the Looking-Glass

London: Macmillan   0333029461 (*Alice*)   John Tenniel

                                     0333041038 (*L-G*), 0333234175 (boxed set)

Macmillan Children's Edition. 13th reprint. Boxed set. Dark-blue box. Both books with green cloth-covered boards. *Alice* cover with Frog Footman, Alice, and Dodo. *Looking-Glass* with March Hare, Queen Alice between Queens, and Mad Hatter. Illustrated dust jackets. *Alice* has 205 numbered pages, *Looking-Glass* 235. Both *Alice* and *Looking-Glass* with different ISBNs on verso of title pages but same "Boxed Set" ISBN on front flap of dust jacket.

3454   1978   Through the Looking-Glass

London: Macmillan   0978041031   John Tenniel

Macmillan Children's Edition. 13th reprint. Dust jacket.

5.9 MACMILLAN AND ST. MARTIN'S PRESS EDITIONS

3455   1962   Through the Looking-Glass

London: Macmillan & Co. New York: St. Martin's Press   John Tenniel

St. Martin's Press edition. Dated on title page. People's Edition binding but not called People's Edition on the title page or copyright page. Pictorial white dust jacket (Alice and Red Queen, priced 7s 6d) and variant white and red dust jacket (Alice and the Tweedles, priced 8s 6d). 235 pp.

3456   1965   Through the Looking-Glass

London: Macmillan & Co. New York: St. Martin's Press   John Tenniel

Found on COPAC. Might be a reprint of the 1962 edition.

3457   1966   Through the Looking-Glass

London: Macmillan & Co. New York: St. Martin's Press   John Tenniel

Found on COPAC. Might be a reprint of the 1962 edition.

3458   1967   Through the Looking-Glass

London: Macmillan & Co. New York: St. Martin's Press   John Tenniel

Dated on title page. People's Edition binding but not called People's Edition on the title page or copyright page. Might be a reprint of the 1962 edition. No standard book number (SBN).

3459   1971   Through the Looking-Glass

London: Macmillan & Co. New York: St. Martin's Press   0333078225   John Tenniel

Dated on title page. People's Edition binding but not called People's Edition on the title page or copyright page. Might be a reprint of the 1967 or even the 1962 edition.

3460   1973   Through the Looking-Glass

London: Macmillan & Co. New York: St. Martin's Press   0333078225   John Tenniel

No date or city of publication on title page. Not called People's Edition on title page. Copyright page says published by Macmillan London Limited, and Reprinted 1971 and 1973, which provides the date used here. The 1st edition must be earlier than 1971 as that edition is a reprint. People's Edition binding has a Tenniel illustration in color of Alice and Humpty Dumpty shaking hands.

3461   1976   Through the Looking-Glass

London: Macmillan & Co. New York: St. Martin's Press 0333078225   John Tenniel

St. Martin's Press edition. Nelson Classics Series. No date on title page but Library Hub Discover dates it 1976. People's Edition binding but not called People's Edition on the title page or copyright page. With the same SBN as the 1971 and 1973.

5.10 MACMILLAN *NEW CHILDREN'S EDITION*

3462   1980   Through the Looking-Glass

London: Macmillan   0333290372   John Tenniel

Macmillan New Children's Edition. 1st edition. The series title New Children's Edition is found only on the verso of the title page in this edition and all reprints. Includes "The Wasp in a Wig." Green paper binding. Reissued in 1991. Dust jacket.

3463   1981   Through the Looking-Glass

London: Book Club Associates,   0333290372   John Tenniel

by arrangement with Macmillan Children's Books

Macmillan New Children's Edition. 1st reprint. On the title page: "This edition published in 1981 by Book Club Associates by arrangement with Macmillan Children's Books." Same ISBN as the 1980 Macmillan edition. At this time Book Club editions were popular, usually selling at a special price. Dust jacket.

3464   1983   Through the Looking-Glass

London: Macmillan   0333290372   John Tenniel

Macmillan New Children's Edition. 2nd reprint. Dust jacket.

3465   1985   Through the Looking-Glass

London: Macmillan   0333290372   John Tenniel

Macmillan New Children's Edition. 3rd reprint. Dust jacket.

3466   1986   Through the Looking-Glass

London: Macmillan   0333290372   John Tenniel

Macmillan New Children's Edition. 4th reprint. Dust jacket.

3467   1987   Through the Looking-Glass

London: Macmillan   0333290372   John Tenniel

Macmillan New Children's Edition. 5th reprint. Dust jacket. Also published in 1990.

3468   1990   Through the Looking-Glass

London: Macmillan   0333290372   John Tenniel

Macmillan New Children's Edition. Reprint. Also called the 5th reprint. Dust jacket. Also published in 1987.

3469   1991   Through the Looking-Glass

London: Macmillan   0333290378   John Tenniel

Macmillan New Children's Edition. Reissue of the 1980 edition in a publisher's slipcase combined with *Alice*. Dust jacket.

3470   1991   Through the Looking-Glass

London: Macmillan   0333290378   John Tenniel

Macmillan New Children's Edition. 1st reprint of the 1991 reissue. Dust jacket.

3471   1992   Through the Looking-Glass

London: Macmillan   0333290378   John Tenniel

Macmillan New Children's Edition. 2nd reprint of the 1991 reissue. Dust jacket.

3472   1997   Through the Looking-Glass
London: Macmillan   0333290378   John Tenniel
Macmillan New Children's Edition. A later reprint of the 1991 reissue. Dust jacket.

5.11 MACMILLAN PRESS LTD. EDITIONS, *RANGER FICTION 3* SERIES

3473   1982   Through the Looking-Glass
London; Basingstoke, UK: The Macmillan Press Ltd.   0978328354   John Tenniel
Macmillan Ranger Fiction 3 Series. Series edited by Carol Christian. Retold by Deborah Tyler. Includes photographs
courtesy of the National Portrait Gallery. The National Library of Scotland copy was received August 27, 1982, and the
copyright page says first published 1982. There is also an *Alice* of the same Ranger Series and date.

3474   1985   Through the Looking-Glass
London; Basingstoke, UK: The Macmillan Press Ltd.   0978328354   John Tenniel
Macmillan Ranger Fiction 3 Series. 1st reprint of series edited by Carol Christian. Retold by Deborah Tyler. Includes
photographs courtesy of the National Portrait Gallery.

3475   1986   Through the Looking-Glass
London; Basingstoke, UK: The Macmillan Press Ltd.   0978328354   John Tenniel
Macmillan Ranger Fiction 3 Series. 2nd reprint of series edited by Carol Christian. Retold by Deborah Tyler. Includes
photographs courtesy of the National Portrait Gallery.

3476   1986   Through the Looking-Glass
London; Basingstoke, UK: The Macmillan Press Ltd.   0978328354   John Tenniel
Macmillan Ranger Fiction 3 Series. 3rd reprint of series edited by Carol Christian. Retold by Deborah Tyler. Includes
photographs courtesy of the National Portrait Gallery.

3477   1988   Through the Looking-Glass
London; Basingstoke, UK: The Macmillan Press Ltd.   0978328354   John Tenniel
Macmillan Ranger Fiction 3 Series. 4th reprint of series edited by Carol Christian. Retold by Deborah Tyler. Includes
photographs courtesy of the National Portrait Gallery.

3478   1989   Through the Looking-Glass
London; Basingstoke, UK: The Macmillan Press Ltd.   0978328354   John Tenniel
Macmillan Ranger Fiction 3 Series. 5th reprint of series edited by Carol Christian. Retold by Deborah Tyler. Includes
photographs courtesy of the National Portrait Gallery.

3479   1990   Through the Looking-Glass
London; Basingstoke, UK: The Macmillan Press Ltd.   0978328354   John Tenniel
Macmillan Ranger Fiction 3 Series. 6th reprint of series edited by Carol Christian. Retold by Deborah Tyler. Includes
photographs courtesy of the National Portrait Gallery.

3480   1990   Through the Looking-Glass
London; Basingstoke, UK: The Macmillan Press Ltd.   0978328354   John Tenniel
Macmillan Ranger Fiction 3 Series. 7th reprint of series edited by Carol Christian. Retold by Deborah Tyler. Includes
photographs courtesy of the National Portrait Gallery.

3481   1991   Through the Looking-Glass
London; Basingstoke, UK: The Macmillan Press Ltd.   0978328354   John Tenniel
Macmillan Ranger Fiction 3 Series. 8th reprint of series edited by Carol Christian. Retold by Deborah Tyler. Includes
photographs courtesy of the National Portrait Gallery.

3482   [1981]   Through the Looking-Glass
London; Basingstoke, UK: Macmillan Children's Books   John Tenniel
Macmillan Children's Books. Date on verso of title page.

3483   1984   Through the Looking-Glass
London: Macmillan Children's Books   0333370066 cloth;   John Tenniel
           0333370090 slipcase; 0333679393
Macmillan Children's Books. Facsimile edition of the 1872 *Looking-Glass* 1st edition. Issued in red cloth. Also in leather or in a publisher's slipcase with a facsimile of the 1866 London *Alice* edition. Some copies have ISBN 0333679393.

3484   1996   Through the Looking-Glass
London: Macmillan Children's Books   0333651103   John Tenniel;
           Harry Theaker; Diz Wallis
Macmillan Children's Books. 1st edition. New Full Colour Edition. Colored by Harry Theaker and Diz Wallis. Blue paper over boards. Illustrated dust jacket. [7], 240 pp.

3485   1997   Through the Looking-Glass
London: Macmillan Children's Books   0333370066   John Tenniel
Macmillan Children's Books. Reprint of the 1984 facsimile edition of the 1872 *Looking-Glass* 1st edition. Issued in blue paper boards. Paperback.

3486   2006   Through the Looking-Glass
London: Macmillan Children's Books   9781405055680   John Tenniel; Harry Theaker;
           Diz Wallis
Macmillan Children's Books. In paperback. Foreword by Philip Pullman. Colored by Harry Theaker and Diz Wallis.

3487   2011   Through the Looking-Glass
London: Macmillan Children's Books   9780230755413   John Tenniel; Harry Theaker;
           Diz Wallis
Macmillan Children's Books. Foreword by Philip Pullman. Colored by Harry Theaker and Diz Wallis.

3488   2014   Through the Looking-Glass
London: Macmillan Children's Books   9781447273097   John Tenniel;
           John Macfarlane
Macmillan Children's Books. Part of Macmillan Classics Series. With 16 color plates by John Macfarlane. Foreword by Philip Ardagh.

3489   2015   Through the Looking-Glass
London: Macmillan Children's Books   9781447280002   John Tenniel
Macmillan Children's Books. Logo on front cover reads "Macmillan Alice 150 years."

3490   2015   Through the Looking-Glass
London: Macmillan Children's Books   9780230755413   John Tenniel;
           Harry Theaker; Diz Wallis
Macmillan Children's Books. Foreword by Philip Pullman. Colored by Harry Theaker and Diz Wallis.

3491   2018   Through the Looking-Glass
London: Macmillan Children's Books   9781509865734   John Tenniel; Harry Theaker;
           Diz Wallis
Macmillan Children's Books. Paperback.

5.13 MACMILLAN *LITTLE ALICE EDITION*

3492   1988   Through the Looking-Glass
London: Macmillan Children's Books   9780333482247   John Tenniel
Macmillan Little Alice Edition. 1st edition. Also issued in a publisher's box with an edition of *Alice*.

3493   1990   Through the Looking-Glass
London: Macmillan Children's Books   9780333482247   John Tenniel
Macmillan Little Alice Edition. 1st reprint. On the verso of the title page it is called a Little Alice Edition.

3494   1991   Through the Looking-Glass
London: Macmillan Children's Books   9780333482247   John Tenniel
Macmillan Little Alice Edition. 2nd reprint. Also issued in a publisher's box with an edition of *Alice*.

3495   1992   Through the Looking-Glass
London: Macmillan Children's Books   9780333482247   John Tenniel
Macmillan Little Alice Edition. 3rd reprint.

3496   1992   Through the Looking-Glass
London: Macmillan Children's Books   9780333482247   John Tenniel
Macmillan Little Alice Edition. 4th reprint.

3497   1995   Through the Looking-Glass
London: Macmillan Children's Books   9780333482247   John Tenniel
Macmillan Little Alice Edition. 5th reprint. Also issued in a publisher's box with an edition of *Alice*.

3498   2015   Through the Looking-Glass
London: Macmillan Education   9780230469303   John Tenniel
Macmillan English Explorers series. Adapted by Gill Munton.

OTHER PUBLISHER EDITIONS
5.14 OTHER PUBLISHERS OF *THROUGH THE LOOKING-GLASS*

3499   1910   Through the Looking-Glass
London: Harper Press, an imprint of HarperCollins Publishers   John Tenniel
Collins Classics series. Paperback.

3500   1930   Through the Looking-Glass
London; Glasgow, UK: Collins Clear-Type Press   Harry Rountree
This *Looking-Glass* edition is probably a companion volume to an *Alice*. Bound in purple cloth over boards with gold stamped lettering and vignette.

3501   [1932]   Through the Looking-Glass
London; Glasgow, UK: Collins Clear-Type Press   Harry Rountree
Undated. A copy is inscribed "Xmas 1932." Illustrated cover and dust jacket. 4 different Collins editions are known, all illustrated by Harry Rountree ca. 1930s.

3502   [1932]   Through the Looking-Glass
London: Thomas Nelson & Sons Ltd.   Helen Monro
Nelson Classics series. Undated. Date based on the date of a matching edition of *Alice*. Over the years published in a variety of bindings, some with dust jacket.

3503   [ca. 1934]   Through the Looking-Glass
London; Glasgow, UK: Collins Clear-Type Press   Irene Mountfort
With 34 black-and-white drawings and 8 black-and-white full-page plates of photographs from the Paramount film.
Beige cloth stamped in brown.

3504   1936   Through the Looking-Glass
London; Melbourne, VIC: Ward, Lock & Co.   P. B. Hickling
The only illustration is a black-and-white frontispiece. In color dust jacket by the same illustrator. Blue cloth printed
in black.

3505   [1937]   Through the Looking-Glass
London: Thomas Nelson & Sons   Helen Monro
Nelson Classics series. Undated but reprint of the [1932] edition. There are 3 different editions with different
advertisements. Price varies from 1s 6d to 2s 6d. Also, a larger-format edition in the Nelson's Famous Books series is
undated.

3506   1938   Through the Looking-Glass
London; Glasgow, UK: Collins Clear-Type Press   Harry Rountree
Includes Harry Rountree's illustrations, but without attribution on title page. Bound in original red cloth, with a dust
jacket "adapted from a still from the film *Alice in Wonderland*, by courtesy of Paramount Productions, Inc." Back of
jacket contains an advertisement for "Achievement: a book of modern enterprise," which was published in 1937.

3507   1939   Through the Looking-Glass
London; Glasgow, UK: Collins Clear-Type Press   Irene Mountfort
With photographs from the Paramount film.

3508   [ca. 1940]   Through the Looking-Glass
London: Mellifont Press   Anonymous
1st edition. Children's Classic series. Full-color frontispiece and 1 other color illustration. Dust jacket.

3509   [1943]   Through the Looking-Glass
Leeds: E. J. Arnold & Son, Ltd.   Anonymous
L. A. Bright Story Readers. No. 348. The illustrations are from the Clemence Dane and Richard Addinsell stage
productions of *Alice* dated 1943 and 1944.

3510   ca. 1943   Through the Looking-Glass
London: P. R. Gawthorn Ltd.   Rene Cloke
Undated. The ca. 1943 date matches an edition of *Alice* by this publisher of that date.Davis (p. 100) dates this as 1950. 8
color plates and 77 2-color line drawings, 1 of which is color highlighted. These vary from picture to picture—some blue,
red, brown, or green.

3511   1948   Through the Looking-Glass
London: Max Parrish   John Tenniel; Hugh Gee
1st edition. Riverside Series. No. 4. Illustrations in black-and-white by Tenniel plus 8 scenes and figures in photo-
montage color by Hugh Gee. Dust jacket.

3512   1948   Through the Looking-Glass
Harmondsworth, UK: Penguin Books   John Tenniel
1st Penguin Story Book Series, No. 44.

3513   ca. 1949   Through the Looking-Glass
London; Melbourne, VIC: Ward, Lock & Co.   Anonymous
New Prize Library Royal Series. Unsigned color plate frontispiece. A copy is known with the inscription "Xmas 1951".

3514   1950   Through the Looking-Glass
London: Max Parrish   Anonymous
151 pp.

3515   1950   Through the Looking-Glass
Harmondsworth, UK: Penguin Books   John Tenniel
1st Penguin Story Book Series, No. 44. Reprint.

3516   [1950] Alice Through the Looking-Glass Story Book
London: John Shaw   John Tenniel

3517   1951   Through the Looking-Glass
London: Max Parrish   John Tenniel; Hugh Gee
1st edition. Riverside Series, No. 4. Illustrations in black-and-white by Tenniel plus 8 scenes and figures in photo-
montage color by Hugh Gee. Dust jacket.

3518   1951   Through the Looking-Glass
Harmondsworth, UK: Penguin Books   John Tenniel
2nd Penguin Story Book Series. No. 44. Reprint.

3519   [1951] Through the Looking-Glass
London: P. R. Gawthorn Ltd.   Rene Cloke
National Library of Scotland received its copy on August 14, 1951. It may be a reprint of the ca. 1943 edition. 8 color
plates on coated paper and 77 2-color drawings. Red paper-covered boards.

3520   1953   Through the Looking-Glass
London: Thomas Nelson & Sons   Helen Monro
Nelson Classics edition.

3521   [1953] Through the Looking-Glass
London: Thomas Nelson & Sons   Mary A. Brooke
New Prize Royal Series. Date not confirmed. Color dust jacket. Black-and-white frontispiece. No other illustrations.

3522   [1954] Through the Looking-Glass
[London]: Hamlyn Classics and Andrew Dakers Limited   Unillustrated; G. R. Ratcliff.
Undated but the British Library copy was received February 23, 1954. Frontispiece by G. R. Ratcliff

3523   1954   Through the Looking-Glass
Twickenham, UK: Hamlyn Classics   Unknown
Date from WMGC.

3524   1954   Through the Looking-Glass
Harmondsworth, UK: Penguin Books   John Tenniel
3rd Penguin Story Book Series, No. 44. Reprint.

3525   1956   Through the Looking-Glass
Glasgow, UK: Collins Clear-Type Press   Anonymous
Silver Torch Series, No. 81. For a juvenile audience. 96 pp.

3526   1958   Through the Looking-Glass
London: Mellifont Press   Anonymous
Children's Classic Series, No. T18. 3 color plates and front cover. Paper wrappers. Dust jacket.

3527   1959   Alice Through the Looking-Glass
London: W. H. Allen   Libico Maraja
Splendor Books series. 1st edition. Glassine dust jacket. Over 100 illustrations.

3528   ca. 1950s   Through the Looking-Glass
London: Andrew Dakers, Ltd.   Anonymous; G. R. Ratcliff
A Spring House Classics edition. Dust jacket.

3529   ca. 1950s   Through the Looking-Glass
London: Andrew Dakers, Ltd.   Anonymous; G. R. Ratcliff
Hamlyn Classics. Frontispiece by Ratcliff. Red paper boards. Dust jacket.

3530   ca. 1950s   Through the Looking-Glass
London; Glasgow: Collins and Wm. Collins, Sons & Co. Ltd.   Irene Mountfort
Undated. Dated from examination of materials and styles. Light brown cloth over boards.

3531   ca. 1950s   Alice Through the Looking-Glass
London: Hampster Books   Anonymous; Nan Fullarton
Early Reader Series 7. Front and back covers and dust jacket illustrated by Nan Fullerton. The end flap lists 8 books in the series, of which this is No. 4.

3532   ca. 1950s   Alice Through the Looking-Glass
London: Hampster Books   Anonymous; Nan Fullarton
Early Reader Series 7. Front and back covers and dust jacket illustrated by Nan Fullerton. 30 black-and-white images and endpapers by Anonymous. The rear flap lists 19 books in the series, of which this is No. 12.

3533   ca. 1950s   Alice Through the Looking-Glass
London: Spring Books   Unillustrated
Illustrated endpapers in black-and-white. This is a later version of a Hampster Books edition.

3534   ca. 1950s   Through the Looking-Glass
London: Spring House Classics   G. R. Ratcliff
Spring House Classics. 1 color plate frontispiece by Ratcliff, otherwise unillustrated. 14 issues in various bindings exist. Only the color picture varies from issue to issue.

3535   ca. 1950s   Through the Looking-Glass
London; Melbourne: Ward, Lock & Co.   Mary A. Brooke
Color frontispiece by Mary A. Brooke. Dust jacket.

3536   ca. 1950s   Through the Looking-Glass
London; Melbourne, VIC: Ward, Lock & Co.   P. B. Hickling
New Prize Library Series. Color frontispiece by P. B. Hickling. Dust jacket. In various bindings.

3537   ca. 1950s   Through the Looking-Glass
London; Melbourne, VIC: Ward, Lock & Co.   P. B. Hickling
Royal Series. Color frontispiece by P. B. Hickling. Dust jacket.

3538   1962   Through the Looking-Glass
London: Puffin Books   John Tenniel
Reprinted 1997 and perhaps other years.

3539   1962   Through the Looking-Glass
London: The Folio Society   John Tenniel
In publisher's slipcase.

3540   ca. 1962 Alice Through the Looking-Glass
London: Golden Pleasure Books   Leonard
1st edition. Undated but dated to 1962 from the 2nd impression of 1963.

3541   ca. 1962 Through the Looking-Glass
London: Hampster Books   Nan Fullarton
Early Reader Series 7. Retold for younger readers.

3542   1963   Alice Through the Looking-Glass
London: Golden Pleasure Books   Leonard
On the verso of the title page is printed: This edition first published 1962. Second impression 1963.

3543   1964   Alice Through the Looking-Glass
London: Golden Pleasure Books   Leonard
On the verso of the title page is printed: This edition first published 1962. Second impression 1963. Third impression
1964.

3544   1964   Alice Through the Looking-Glass
London: W. H. Allen   Libico Maraja
Splendor Books series. Glassine dust jacket. Over 100 illustrations.

3545   [Pre 1965]   Through the Looking-Glass
London: Nelson   Helen Monro
A copy is known inscribed "Xmas 1964".

3546   1969   Through the Looking-Glass
London: Bancroft Books   Anonymous
1st edition. A Bancroft Classic. 3 unsigned illustrations. Reprinted 1970, 1972, and 1975.

3547   1969   Through the Looking-Glass
London: Mayflower   John Tenniel
1st edition thus. A Mayflower paperback. Companion to the 1969 Mayflower *Alice*.

3548   [1960s] Alice Through the Looking-Glass
London: Spring Books   Nan Fullarton
Retold for younger readers. Cover illustration by Nan Fullarton.

3549   ca. 1960s   Through the Looking-Glass
London: Blackie & Son, Ltd.   Unknown
Blackie's Library of Famous Books, No. 35. Illustrated dust jacket by unknown artist.

3550   [After 1969]   Through the Looking-Glass
London: Mayflower   9780583116435   John Tenniel
Undated reprint of the 1969 London: Mayflower edition. Since it has been assigned an ISBN it is after 1969.

3551   1970   Through the Looking-Glass
London: Bancroft Books   9780430003949   Anonymous
Reprint of the 1969 Bancroft Classics edition.

3552   1972   Through the Looking-Glass
London: Bancroft Books   9780430003949   Anonymous
Reprint of the 1969 Bancroft Classics edition.

3553   1972   Through the Looking-Glass
London: MacGibbon and Kee   9780261633322   Ralph Steadman
Reprint of the 1969 Bancroft Classics edition. Text edited by Selwyn Goodacre. Black cloth stamped in silver.

3554   1975   Through the Looking-Glass
London: Hart-Davis, MacGibbon, Ltd.   9780246109194   Ralph Steadman
2nd impression of the 1970 Bancroft Classics edition. Paperback. Text edited by Selwyn Goodacre.

3555   1975   Through the Looking-Glass
London: Purnell Books   9780430003949   Anonymous
Reprint of the 1970 Bancroft Classics edition.

3556   1976   Through the Looking-Glass
London: J. M. Dent & Sons   9780460027328   John Tenniel
1st edition. Dent Dolphin series.

3557   1977   Alice Through the Looking-Glass
London: Academy Editions   0856702161   John Tenniel
Giant Illustrated Edition. 96 pp.

3558   1977   Through the Looking-Glass
London: Pan Books   9780330252546   Peter Richardson
Piccolo Books edition. Front cover illustrated by Peter Richardson. No other illustrations.

3559   1977   Through the Looking-Glass
Maidenhead, UK: Purnell Books   9780361035521   Anonymous
1st edition thus.

3560   1977   Through the Looking-Glass
London: Purnell Books   0361035527   John Tenniel; McB
1st edition thus. A Purnell Classic. Cover illustration by McB.

3561   1978   Through the Looking-Glass
London: Purnell Books   0361035527   John Tenniel
1st reprint of the 1977 edition. A Purnell Classic.

3562   1979   Through the Looking-Glass
London; Melbourne, VIC; Toronto, ON: J. M. Dent & Sons
New York: E. P. Dutton   9780460010184   John Tenniel; Brian Robins
Reissue of the 1976 edition as An Everyman's Paperback in the Everyman's Library. Color illustration on front cover by Brian Robins.

3563   1981   Through the Looking-Glass
London: Octopus Books Ltd.   9780706415582   John Tenniel
1st edition. Treasury of Children's Classics series. In various bindings.

3564   1984   Through the Looking-Glass
London: Puffin Books   9780140367096   John Tenniel
Pictorial wrappers with series title Puffin Classics. First published 1948 as Penguin Story Book. Reprinted 22 times.

3565   1985   Through the Looking-Glass
London: Penguin Books   9780140367096   John Tenniel
1st reprint of the 1984 Puffin Classics edition. Paperback.

3566   1986   Through the Looking-Glass
London: Victor Gollancz, Ltd.   9780575037564   Justin Todd
1st edition. Dust jacket. 175 pp.

3567   1986   Through the Looking-Glass
London: Victor Gollancz, Ltd.   Justin Todd
21 color plates. Blue cloth.

3568   1987   Through the Looking-Glass
London: Penguin Books   9780140367096   John Tenniel
2nd reprint of the 1984 Puffin Classics edition.

3569   1987   Through the Looking-Glass
London: Treasure Press (Octopus Books Ltd.)   9781850511993   John Tenniel; Unknown
1st reprint of 1981 edition. Cover by unknown artist.

3570   1989   Alice through the Looking-Glass
Limpsfield, Dragon's World   9781850280736   Malcolm Ashman
1st edition. 15 color plates. Dust jacket.

3571   1990   Through the Looking-Glass
London: The Folio Society   John Tenniel
Reissue of the 1962 edition. In publisher's slipcase with a matching volume of *Alice*.

3572   1991   Alice through the Looking-Glass
Limpsfield, Dragon's World   9781850280736   Malcolm Ashman
1st reprint of the 1989 edition. 15 color plates. Dust jacket.

3573   1992   Through the Looking-Glass
London: Andersen Press   9780862643652   Tony Ross
1st edition. Abridged by Tony Ross. There is a 1993 and a 2016 edition.

3574   1992   Through the Looking-Glass
Oxford: Oxford University Press   195852681993   K. Y. Chan
Oxford Progressive English Readers series, Level 2. Cover by K. Y. Chan.

3575   1992   Through the Looking-Glass
London: The Folio Society   John Tenniel
5th printing of the 1962 edition. In publisher's slipcase with a matching volume of *Alice*.

3576   1993   Through the Looking-Glass
London: Andersen Press   9780862643652   Tony Ross
1st reprint of the 1992 edition. Abridged by Tony Ross. There is a 2016 edition.

3577   1994   Through the Looking-Glass
London: Penguin Books   9780140620870   John Tenniel;
                                                                            James Marsh
Reissued as Penguin Popular Classics. Cover illustration by James Marsh.

3578   1994   Through the Looking-Glass
London: Puffin   John Tenniel
Puffin Classics series.

3579   1994   Through the Looking-Glass
London: Red Fox   9780099983408   Tony Ross
Abridged by Tony Ross.

3580   1995   The Penguin Selected Works of Lewis Carroll
London: Claremont Books   John Tenniel
1st edition thus. Includes *Looking-Glass*. Published under license from Penguin Books Ltd. Dust jacket.

3581   1995   Through the Looking-Glass
Oxford: Oxford University Press   9780194227499   John Tenniel
Oxford Bookworms. Stage 3. Green Series. Retold by Jennifer Bassett. Paperback.

3582   1995   Alice Through the Looking-Glass
Bristol, UK: Parragon Book Service Ltd.   9781858137346   Carole Gray
New York: Shooting Press, Inc.
Retold by Stephanie Laslett. Miniature format in the series Mini Classics. Color covers by Carole Gray.

3583   1997   Through the Looking-Glass
London: Puffin Books   9780140383515   John Tenniel
Reprint of 1962 Puffin edition.

3584   1998   Through the Looking-Glass
London: Book People Ltd., Ted Smart   9780333651103   John Tenniel
New edition. In boxed set with *Alice*. Colored by Harry Theaker and Diz Wallis.

3585   2000   Through the Looking-Glass
London: Bloomsbury Books   9780747553731   Mervyn Peake
1st edition. Introduction by Zadie Smith. Dust jacket.

3586   2000   Through the Looking-Glass
[UK]: Creation Books   9781840680210   Trevor Brown
A Creation Classic Portable with introduction by Jeremy Reed. Cover only by Trevor Brown.

3587   2000   Through the Looking-Glass
Oxford: Oxford University Press   9780194230198   John Tenniel
Oxford Bookworms Library. Classics. Stage 3. Retold by Jennifer Bassett. Previous edition 1995. Paperback.

3588   2000   Through the Looking-Glass
Cambridge, UK: Proquest LLC   John Tenniel
Digitized version of an undated earlier edition.

3589   2001   Through the Looking-Glass
London: Bloomsbury Books   9780747553731   Mervyn Peake
Introduction by Will Self and Zadie Smith.

3590   2001   Through the Looking-Glass
Church Hanborough, Whitney near Oxford, UK: Inky Parrot Press   Franciszka Themerson
Foreword about the illustrations by Jasia Reichardt and an afterword by Graham Ovenden. Limited slipcase edition of 48.

3591   2001   Through the Looking-Glass
Church Hanborough, Whitney near Oxford, UK: Inky Parrot Press   Franciszka Themerson
Foreword about the illustrations by Jasia Reichardt and an afterword by Graham Ovenden. Limited edition of 372.

3592   2001   Through the Looking-Glass
        Market Drayton, UK: Tern Press   Nicholas Parry
        Limited edition of 90, with 54 lithographs in orange by Nicholas Parry.

3593   2003   Through the Looking-Glass
        London: Penguin Books   9780140367096   John Tenniel
        Reissue of the 1994 Penguin Popular Classics now titled Puffin Classics – The Essential Collection. Title page author
        name misspelled as "Lewis Carrol."

3594   [2003] Through the Looking-Glass
        London: The Folio Society   John Tenniel
        Reprint of the 1962 edition.

3595   2004   Through the Looking-Glass
        Nottingham, UK: D3 Editions   9780954732400   Peter Blake
        8 color plates. Book size: 22 x 28.5 cm. See also entry 3596.

3596   2004   Through the Looking-Glass
        Nottingham, UK: D3 Editions   0954732405   Peter Blake
        8 color plates. Limited edition of 500 copies signed by Peter Blake, with color plates tipped in. Larger size (24.5 x 31
        cm), with separate ISBN. See also entry 3595.

3597   2005   Through the Looking-Glass
        London: Walker   9781406305777   Helen Oxenbury
        1st edition. Walker Illustrated Classics. Issued in cloth, paper wrappers, and a limited unnumbered edition of 1,000.
        Reprinted in 2009.

3598   2006   Lewis Carroll's Alice Through the Looking-Glass
        London: Merrell   9781858943299   Peter Blake
        8 color plates. Preface by Marco Livingstone.

3599   2007   Through the Looking-Glass
        Oxford: Oxford University Press   9780195462388   K. Y. Chan
        Oxford Progressive English Readers series, Level 2. Paperback. There was a previous edition of 1992.

3600   2008   Through the Looking-Glass
        [London]: Akasha Publishing   9781605123271   Unillustrated
        Issued in cloth and paper wrappers. The dust jacket has an Arthur Rackham picture of Alice, otherwise no
        illustrations.

3601   2008   Through the Looking-Glass
        [London]: Akasha Publishing   9781605124278   Unillustrated
        Paperback. The cover has an Arthur Rackham picture of Alice, otherwise no illustrations.

3602   ca. 2008 Through the Looking-Glass
        Oxford: Oxford University Press   9780194791342   John Tenniel
        Retold by Jennifer Bassett. Oxford Bookworms Library. Stage 3. Classics. Simplified edition. Paperback.

3603   2008   Through the Looking-Glass
        London: Walker   9781406318265   Helen Oxenbury

3604   2009   Alice Through the Looking-Glass
        London: Usborne Publishing Ltd.   9780746096840   Mauro Evangelista
        In Usborne Young Trading: Series 2. Adapted by Leslie Sims. Reading consultant Alison Kelly.

3605	2009	Through the Looking-Glass		
		London: Walker	9781406305777	Helen Oxenbury
		Reprint of the 2005 edition.		

3606	2010	Through the Looking-Glass		
		London: Harper Press	9780007350933	John Tenniel
		Collins Classics Children's Books. Paper wrappers.		

3607	2010	Through the Looking-Glass		
		London: Penguin Books	9780141330075	John Tenniel
		Introduction by Chris Riddell and new endnotes.		

3608	2010	Through the Looking-Glass		
		London: Puffin	9780141946702	John Tenniel

3609   2011   Through the Looking-Glass

Church Hanborough, Oxford, UK: 9780955834318 (std. ed.);   John Vernon Lord
Artists' Choice Editions   9780955834356 (special ed).

Introduction and bibliography by the illustrator. 312 Limited Standard Edition copies, 98 Limited Special Edition copies numbered in Roman numerals and with a set of prints signed by the illustrator in a slipcase, and 10 Limited Exemplary Edition copies. Edited by Selwyn Goodacre. A companion to the 2009 *Alice* edition with the same Standard Edition ISBN.

3610	2013	Alice Through the Looking-Glass		
		London: Harper Collins Children's Books	9780007425082	Emma Chichester Clark
		Best-Loved Classics. Retold and illustrated by Emma Chichester Clark.		

3611	2013	Alice Through the Looking-Glass		
		London: Harper Collins Children's Books	9780007425099	Emma Chichester Clark
		In cloth and paperback. Retold and illustrated by Emma Chichester Clark.		

3612   2015   Through the Looking-Glass

Church Hanborough, Whitney near Oxford, UK: Inky Parrot Press   Angel Dominguez

1st edition. Afterword by the artist. 180 Standard Copies and 52 Special Copies signed by the artist; 32 Exemplary Copies with a portfolio of 4 prints signed by the artist. Includes "The Wasp in a Wig", a suppressed episode from *Looking-Glass* that John Tenniel said he was unable to illustrate.

3613	2015	Alice Through the Looking-Glass		
		London: Palazzo Editions	9780957148390	Robert Ingpen
		Color illustrations.		

3614	2015	Through the Looking-Glass		
		Dorking, UK: Templar Publishing	9781783701841	Robert Ingpen

3615	2016	Alice through the Looking-Glass		
		London: Anderson Press	9781783444120	Tony Ross
		2nd reprint of the 1992 edition. Abridged by Tony Ross. There is a 1993 edition.		

3616	2016	Through the Looking-Glass		
		London: Carlton Kids	9781783121830	Patricia Moffett
		Retold by Kay Woodward.		

3617	2016	Alice through the Looking-Glass		
		[Bedford], UK: Huge Jam Publishing	9781911249016	John Tenniel

3618	2016	Alice through the Looking-Glass		
		Bath, UK: Parragon	9781474851442	Anonymous

Disney edition. Adapted by Kari Sutherland. Based on a screenplay by Linda Woolverton. Paperback.

3619	2016	Through the Looking-Glass		
		London: Transatlantic Press	9781911060239	John Tenniel

3620	2017	Through the Looking-Glass and What Alice Found There		
		[Cookhill, UK]: Pook Press / Read Books	9781528716390	John Tenniel

Various issues in 2017 and 2020 with same ISBN.

3621	2018	Through the Looking-Glass		
		London: Inky Parrott Press	9780995557048	Gennady Kalinovski

Introduction by Ella Parry-Davis. The Kalinovski illustrations are from his 1992 edition.

3622	2018	Through the Looking-Glass		
		London: Scholastic	9781407184494	Unknown

3623	2019	Through the Looking-Glass		
		Berkshire, UK: CCS Books	9781911238645	Anonymous

Classics Illustrated, No. 73. Color illustrations. 48 pp.

3624	2019	Through the Looking-Glass		
		Dundee, Scotland, UK: Evertype	9781782912535	John Tenniel

1st edition. The cover is typical of the Evertype *Looking-Glass* editions but with a gray background.

3625	n.d.	Through the Looking-Glass		
		London: Thomas Nelson & Sons Ltd.		Helen Monro

Nelson's Famous Books series. Undated but reprint of the [1932] edition. In a larger format.

6. *Through the Looking-Glass* Editions Published in the US

6.1 MACMILLAN EDITIONS

3626   1872   Through the Looking-Glass
New York; London: Macmillan   John Tenniel

Macmillan. 1st edition, 3rd issue (according to Hilda Bohem in *Jabberwocky* [Autumn 1984]). Red pebbled cloth, dark green endpapers. A copy known with replaced spine and white endpapers is signed on the half title "Alice P. Hargreaves 1932." Bound in London according to Bohem. *New York Times* ads offered this book for sale on January 6, 1872.

3627   1875   Through the Looking-Glass
New York: Macmillan   John Tenniel

Macmillan. 39th thousand. No copy with a London imprint of the 39th thousand has been found. Macmillan records indicate that the 39th thousand was published only for the American market.

3628   1877   Through the Looking-Glass
London; New York: Macmillan   John Tenniel

Macmillan. 42nd thousand. The 1877 edition also exists in 43rd and 44th thousand, all having the dual London and New York imprint. The 42nd thousand also exists dated 1878 and 1880.

3629   1877   Through the Looking-Glass
London; New York: Macmillan   John Tenniel

Macmillan. 43rd thousand. The 1877 edition also exists in 42nd and 44th thousand, all having the dual London and New York imprint. The 42nd thousand also exists dated 1878 and 1880.

3630   1877   Through the Looking-Glass
London; New York: Macmillan   John Tenniel

Macmillan. 44th thousand. The 1877 edition also exists in 42nd and 43rd thousand, all having the dual London and New York imprint. The 42nd thousand also exists dated 1878 and 1880.

3631   1878   Through the Looking-Glass
London; New York: Macmillan   John Tenniel

Macmillan. 42nd thousand. Copies exist dated 1877 and 1880.

3632   1880   Through the Looking-Glass
London; New York: Macmillan   John Tenniel

Macmillan. 42nd thousand. Red cloth. Lacks the roundel on the back cover. Reset chessboard as in the 45th thousand of 1877, which has the London imprint only. There is also an edition in blue cloth in the style of the 1881 edition; ensuing American editions have the New York imprint only. There may be 4 variants of this edition.

3633   1881   Through the Looking-Glass
London; New York: Macmillan   John Tenniel

Macmillan. 1st edition thus. 50th thousand. Printed at the Norwood Press. Reprints exist of 1883, 1885, 1887, 1888, 1889, 1891, 1895, 1896, 1898, 1899, 1900, and 1901. Macmillan catalog at the rear priced in US dollars. In the typical American green or blue smooth cloth cover with gilt and black floral border at the top of the front cover; at the bottom, a decorative band in black. The cover reads "Through the / Looking-Glass" in a decorative gilt font. Rear cover blank, but both top and bottom borders as on the front cover but in blind. This binding not found in a UK library.

3634   1883   Through the Looking-Glass
London; New York: Macmillan   John Tenniel

Macmillan. First printed in 1881, 50th thousand. Printed at the Norwood Press. Reprints exist of 1883, 1885, 1887, 1888, 1889, 1891, 1895, 1896, 1898, 1899, 1900, and 1901. Macmillan catalog at the rear priced in US dollars. In the typical American green or blue smooth cloth cover with gilt and black floral border at the top of the front cover; at the bottom, a decorative band in black. The cover reads "Through the / *Looking-Glass*" in a decorative gilt font. Rear cover blank, but both top and bottom borders as on the front cover but in blind. This binding not found in a UK library.

3635   1885   Through the Looking-Glass
London; New York: Macmillan   John Tenniel

Macmillan. First printed in 1881, 50th thousand. Printed at the Norwood Press. Reprints exist of 1883, 1885, 1887, 1888, 1889, 1891, 1895, 1896 1898, 1899, 1900, and 1901. Macmillan catalog at the rear priced in US dollars. In the typical American green or blue smooth cloth cover with gilt and black floral border at the top of the front cover; at the bottom, a decorative band in black. The cover reads "Through the / *Looking-Glass*" in a decorative gilt font. Rear cover blank, but both top and bottom borders as on the front cover but in blind. This binding not found in a UK library.

3636   1887   Through the Looking-Glass
London; New York: Macmillan   John Tenniel

Macmillan. First printed in 1881, 50th thousand. Printed at the Norwood Press. Reprints exist of 1883, 1885, 1887, 1888, 1889, 1891, 1895, 1896, 1898, 1899, 1900, and 1901. Macmillan catalog at the rear priced in US dollars. In the typical American green or blue smooth cloth cover with gilt and black floral border at the top of the front cover; at the bottom, a decorative band in black. The cover reads "Through the / *Looking-Glass*" in a decorative gilt font. Rear cover blank, but both top and bottom borders as on the front cover but in blind. This binding not found in a UK library.

3637   1888   Through the Looking-Glass
London; New York: Macmillan   John Tenniel

Macmillan. First printed in 1881, 50th thousand. Printed at the Norwood Press. Reprints exist of 1883, 1885, 1887, 1888, 1889, 1891, 1895, 1896, 1889,1899, 1900, and 1901. Macmillan catalog at the rear priced in US dollars. Issued both in the typical American green or blue smooth cloth cover with gilt and black floral border at the top of the front cover; at the bottom, a decorative band in black. The cover reads "Through the / *Looking-Glass*" in a decorative gilt font. Rear cover blank, but both top and bottom borders as on the front cover but in blind. This binding not found in a UK library.

3638   1889   Through the Looking-Glass
London; New York: Macmillan   John Tenniel

Macmillan. First printed in 1881, 50th thousand. Printed at the Norwood Press. Reprints exist of 1883, 1885, 1887, 1888, 1889, 1891, 1895, 1896, 1898, 1899, 1900, and 1901. Macmillan catalog at the rear priced in US dollars. Issued in both the typical American green or blue smooth cloth cover with gilt and black floral border at the top of the front cover; at the bottom, a decorative band in black. The cover reads "Through the / *Looking-Glass*" in a decorative gilt font. Rear cover blank, but both top and bottom borders as on the front cover but in blind. This binding not found in a UK library.

3639   1891   Through the Looking-Glass
London; New York: Macmillan   John Tenniel

Macmillan. First printed in 1881, 50th thousand. Printed at the Norwood Press. Reprints exist of 1883, 1885, 1887, 1888, 1889, 1891, 1895, 1896, 1898, 1899, 1900, and 1901. Macmillan catalog at the rear priced in US dollars. Issued in both the typical American green or blue smooth cloth cover with gilt and black floral border at the top of the front cover; at the bottom, a decorative band in black. The cover reads "Through the / *Looking-Glass*" in a decorative gilt font. Rear cover blank, but both top and bottom borders as on the front cover but in blind. This binding not found in a UK library.

3640   1895   Through the Looking-Glass
London; New York: Macmillan   John Tenniel

Macmillan. First printed in 1881, 50th thousand. Reprints exist of 1883, 1885, 1887, 1888, 1889, 1891, 1895, 1896, 1898, 1899, 1900, and 1901. Macmillan catalog at the rear priced in US dollars. In the typical American green or blue smooth cloth cover with gilt and black floral border at the top of the front cover; at the bottom, a decorative band in black. The cover reads "Through the / *Looking-Glass*" in a decorative gilt font. Rear cover blank, but both top and bottom borders as on the front cover but in blind. This binding not found in a UK library.

3641   1896   Through the Looking-Glass

London; New York: Macmillan   John Tenniel

Macmillan. First printed in 1881, 50th thousand. Reprints exist of 1883, 1885, 1887, 1888, 1889, 1891, 1895, 1896, 1898, 1899, 1900, and 1901. Macmillan catalog at the rear priced in US dollars. In the typical American green or blue smooth cloth cover with gilt and black floral border at the top of the front cover; at the bottom, a decorative band in black. The cover reads "Through the / *Looking-Glass*" in a decorative gilt font. Rear cover blank, but both top and bottom borders as on the front cover but in blind. This binding not found in a UK library.

3642   1898   Through the Looking-Glass

New York: The Macmillan Company. London: Macmillan & Co., Ltd.   John Tenniel

Macmillan. First printed in 1881, 50th thousand. Reprints exist of 1883, 1885, 1887, 1888, 1889, 1891, 1895, 1896, 1898, 1899, 1900, and 1901. Macmillan catalog at the rear priced in US dollars. In the typical American green or blue smooth cloth cover with gilt and black floral border at the top of the front cover; at the bottom, a decorative band in black. The cover reads "Through the / *Looking-Glass*" in a decorative gilt font. Rear cover blank, but both top and bottom borders as on the front cover but in blind.

3643   1899   Through the Looking-Glass

New York; London: Macmillan   John Tenniel

Macmillan. First printed in 1881, 50th thousand. Reprints exist of 1883, 1885, 1887, 1888, 1889, 1891, 1895, 1896, 1898, 1899, 1900, and 1901. Macmillan catalog at the rear priced in US dollars. In the typical American green or blue smooth cloth cover with gilt and black floral border at the top of the front cover; at the bottom, a decorative band in black. The cover reads "Through the / *Looking-Glass*" in a decorative gilt font. Rear cover blank, but both top and bottom borders as on the front cover but in blind.

3644   1900   Through the Looking-Glass

New York; London: Macmillan   John Tenniel

Macmillan. First printed in 1881, 50th thousand. Reprints exist of 1883, 1885, 1887, 1888, 1889, 1891, 1895, 1896, 1898, 1899, 1900, 1901. Macmillan catalog at the rear priced in US dollars. In the typical American green or blue smooth cloth cover with gilt and black floral border at the top of the front cover; at the bottom, a decorative band in black. The cover reads "Through the / *Looking-Glass*" in a decorative gilt font. Rear cover blank, but both top and bottom borders as on the front cover but in blind.

3645   1901   Through the Looking-Glass

New York: The Macmillan Company. London: Macmillan & Co., Ltd.   John Tenniel

Macmillan. First printed in 1881, 50th thousand. Reprints exist of 1883, 1885, 1887, 1888, 1889, 1891, 1895, 1896, 1898, 1899, 1900, and 1901. Macmillan catalog at the rear priced in US dollars. In the typical American green or blue smooth cloth cover with gilt and black floral border at the top of the front cover; at the bottom, a decorative band in black. The cover reads "Through the / *Looking-Glass*" in a decorative gilt font. Rear cover blank, but both top and bottom borders as on the front cover but in blind.

3646   1906   Through the Looking-Glass

New York; London: Macmillan   John Tenniel

New Edition. The *Harcourt Amory Collection* (p. 34) lists a 1907 edition but fails to mention the Boy's and Girl's Illustrated Series. The catalog entry also says, "first issued in 1906 and issued in red or blue cloth." The 1906 edition is lacking in the Harvard catalog. This imprint was not used in the UK. Lovett 43a says in a 1920 edition that there were "12 additional printings" and lists the 1906, 1908, and 1911.

3647   1907   Through the Looking-Glass

New York; London: Macmillan   John Tenniel

Macmillan Boy's and Girl's Illustrated Series. The *Harcourt Amory Collection* (p. 36) lists the 1907 edition with this imprint but fails to mention the Boy's and Girl's Illustrated Series. The catalog entry also says, "first issued in 1906 and issued in red or blue cloth." This imprint was not used in the UK. Lovett 43a says in a 1920 edition that there were "12 additional printings" and lists the 1906, 1908, and 1911 printings as well as a combined edition of 1917.

3648   1908   Through the Looking-Glass

New York; London: Macmillan   John Tenniel

Macmillan Children's Classics Series. Includes preface to 61st thousand. Verso of the title page reads "Printed March 1898." Lovett 43a says in a 1920 edition that there were "12 additional printings" and lists the 1906, 1908, and 1911 printings.

3649   1911   Through the Looking-Glass

New York; London: Macmillan   John Tenniel

Macmillan Children's Classics Series. Includes preface to 61st thousand. Verso of the title page reads "printed March 1898." Lovett 43a says in a 1920 edition that there were "12 additional printings" and lists the 1906, 1908, and 1911 printings as well as a combined edition of 1917.

3650   1912   Through the Looking-Glass

New York: Macmillan   John Tenniel

Norwood Press on the verso of the title page.

3651   [1920]   Through the Looking-Glass

New York; London: Macmillan   John Tenniel

Originally published in 1906, but Lovett lacked a copy of that date and described this "later printing" of 1920.

6.2 OTHER PUBLISHER EDITIONS

3652   1872   Through the Looking-Glass

Boston: Lee and Shepard. New York: Lee, Shepard, and Dillingham   John Tenniel

1st edition, 1st issue. The Wonderland Library Series. There are at least 5 binding variants: (1) reddish-brown grained cloth, (2) green grained cloth, (3) green pebbled cloth, (4) blue grained cloth, and (5) vivid purplish-blue pebbled cloth. All copies have the Lee and Shepard device at the base of the spine and Macmillan roundels on the front and rear covers. All include the Macmillan device on p. [vi], indicating that they were the printers of the sheets. All copies have "wade" misprint on p. 21. The Lee and Shepard papers held by the American Antiquarian Society include a letter dated December 2, 1871, from Macmillan to Lee and Shepard stating: "We have today sent off for shipment by the Cunard Steamer 'Tripoli' sailing on the 5th inst. 2,000 copies of *Looking-Glass* with your imprint. We hope to send 500 more in a few days, but the remaining 500 of your order will be unavoidably delayed longer." In *Jabberwocky* (Autumn 1984), Hilda Bohem speculated they were shipped unbound and later bound in America. The sheets arrived in Boston on December 19, 1871. An ad in *Boston Daily Evening Transcript* reads "ready at all bookstores" on Saturday, December 23, 1871—4 days after the sheets arrived. A copy exists with the "Lockwood, 812 Broadway, NY" binder's ticket on the lower right of the front paste-down. To support this edition being the 1st edition, 1st issue, consider the letter from Dodgson to Macmillan dated December 17, 1871: ". . . You may think me a lunatic for thus wishing to send away money from the doors, and will tell me that I shall thus lose thousands of would-be purchasers, who will not wait so long but will go and buy other Christmas books. . . ." (from *Letters to Macmillan* by Simon Nowell-Smith, Macmillan/St. Martin's Press, 1967, p. 74). While arguably this could refer to the 2nd printing of 6,000 copies, while the Boston ad noted the books would be ready at all bookstores, the London ad simply noted the book had been published, making no mention of when it might be available on the shelves. Less equivocal is the statement from the Lee and Shepard papers above that " . . . Our desire in this transaction has been to give you every advantage. The shipment now made is considerably in advance of both those we are to send to our house in New York and of the English publication. . . ."

3653   1872   Through the Looking-Glass

Boston: Lee and Shepard; New York: Lee, Shepard, and Dillingham   John Tenniel

1st edition, later issue. The error on p. 21 is corrected from "wade" to the correct "wabe." According to the *Harcourt Amory Collection* (p. 34), Harvard has a copy in green cloth "evidently printed from the 2nd issue of the English plates." This could have been from the final and delayed shipment of 500 sets of sheets after the initial 2,000 sets and a second 500 were sent. The delay could have been to correct the p. 21 error.

3654   ca. 1880–1900   Through the Looking-Glass: Adapted for Very Little Folks from
                        the Original
Buffalo, NY: Berger   John Tenniel
Little Folks' Edition, Alice Series VII. Red paper-covered boards. There is a binding variant with vivid pinkish-orange
paper. Contains both black-and-white and color illustrations.

3655   1885   Through the Looking-Glass
New York: John W. Lovell   Unillustrated
Lovell's Library Series, Vol. 9, No. 48. See Byron W. Sewell, "John W. Lovell's Attempt at Cornering the American
Stereotype Plate Market," *Jabberwocky* (Summer 1982).

3656   [before 1886]   Through the Looking-Glass
New York: R. Worthington   John Tenniel
Green cloth, beveled boards, front with gold-gilt Alice and Borogrove. 50 black-and-white drawings, including
frontispiece. The name "R. Worthington" was used from 1876 to 1885, after which it was changed to "Worthington &
Co."

3657   1886   Through the Looking-Glass
New York: George Munro   John Tenniel
Blue cloth stamped with black and gold.

3658   1886   Through the Looking-Glass
New York: George Munro's Sons   John Tenniel
Seaside Library Pocket Series, No. 789. Blue paper wraps, cover with floral decorations.

3659   1890   Through the Looking-Glass
New York: United States Book Co.   John Tenniel
1st Rugby Series Edition, 1st issue. Emerald-green cloth, green and white head- and tailbands. "Lovell" publisher's
logo at lower spine. Ad in 1890 *PTLA*. Also issued in a 2-volume boxed set with *Alice*. Published by successor to John
W. Lovell.

3660   ca. 1890 Through the Looking-Glass
New York: John W. Lovell   John Tenniel
Lovell's Standard Sets Series. Boxed with *Alice* and sold as a 2-volume set. See Byron W. Sewell, "John W. Lovell's
Attempt at Cornering the American Stereotype Plate Market," *Jabberwocky* (Summer 1982).

3661   ca. 1890 Through the Looking-Glass
New York: United States Book Co.   John Tenniel
Seaside Library Series, No. S.S.789. Paper wraps.

3662   ca. 1890 Through the Looking-Glass
New York: Worthington Co.   John Tenniel
Dark red cloth. Brilliant yellow-orange endpapers.

3663   ca. 1890s   Through the Looking-Glass
New York: Platt and Peck   John Tenniel
1 color illustration.

3664   ca. 1892 Through the Looking-Glass
New York: Hovenden   John Tenniel
Juvenile Books in Sets Series. Issued in 3-volume set with *Alice* and *Rhyme? and Reason?* May be same *Looking-Glass*
as in International Book Company's *Comic Tales for Girls* set and Lovell's 3-volume Standard Set.

3665 ca. 1893 Through the Looking-Glass

New York; Boston: Thomas Y. Crowell

L. J. (Lewis Jesse) Bridgman;
Anonymous (after Tenniel);
Charles Copeland

Children's Favorite Classics Series. 1st edition and 1st printing. Advertised in *PTLA* in 1893. One of 8 titles in series. Boards; cream cloth; olive-green decorative floral borders. Color frontispiece (signed "Copeland"). 51 black-and-white illustrations, including 4 black-and-white plates (1 original by Bridgman and 3 original by Tenniel); the others are after Tenniel. The verso of title page has a copyright of 1893 for all issues in this series. Also published with a different cover design. In various cloth colors. For more information see *MoM*, pp. 143, 144.

3666 ca. 1894 Through the Looking-Glass

New York: International Book Co.

John Tenniel

Comic Tales for Girls Series. Has "Lovell" at base of spine. Sold as part of a 3-volume set. May be same as *Looking-Glass* in Lovell's Standard Sets Series. See Hovenden Company listing and Lovell listing, as well as *Alice* and *Looking-Glass* combined edition listing.

3667 1895 Through the Looking-Glass

Philadelphia: Henry Altemus

After John Tenniel

Series No. 202: Altemus' Young People's Library Series. *Looking-Glass* is No. 3 or 3b in the series. Copies in blue, buff, and gray cloth. This edition is dated on the title page.

3668 [1895] Through the Looking-Glass

Buffalo, NY: New York Publishing Co.

John Tenniel

Advertised in *PTLA* in 1895 only.

3669 [1896] Through the Looking-Glass

New York: A. L. Burt

John Tenniel; Henry Holiday;
Harry Furniss

Little Women Series. 1st printing. Not dated but advertised in *PTLA* in 1896. 14 titles in the series. Includes *Snark* and 3 chapters from *Sylvie and Bruno*. Blue cloth. John Tenniel illustrated *Looking-Glass*; Henry Holiday, *The Hunting of the Snark*; and Harry Furniss, *Sylvie and Bruno*. See *MoM* for more details.

3670 ca. 1896 Through the Looking-Glass

Philadelphia: Henry Altemus

After John Tenniel

Series No. 202: Altemus' Young People's Library Series. One of 18 titles in the series. Blue or cream cloth. Copyright date of 1896 on the verso of title page. Lovett 33a lists this date as ca. 1897. Advertised in *PTLA* in 1896.

3671 ca. 1896 Through the Looking-Glass

Philadelphia: Rodgers

John Tenniel

Popular Classical Series of 16mos, Excelsior Edition, No. 42. No dust jacket. Cloth, silver-gilt and purple lettering on cover (which includes "torch" vignette) and spine. Red, blue, and green binding variants. 43 black-and-white illustrations. Non-integral inserted frontispiece on coated paper. 235 numbered pp.

3672 ca. 1896–1897 Through the Looking-Glass

New York: American Publishers Corporation

John Tenniel

St. Nicholas Series for Boys and Girls, No. 137 of 179 titles. Olive-green cloth covers with panels of green holly and silver-gilt lettering on cover and spine. No frontispiece.

3673 ca. 1897 Through the Looking-Glass

New York; Boston: H. M. Caldwell

John Tenniel

Superb Series. Advertised in *PTLA* in 1897. Issued together with an edition of *Alice* in a 2-volume boxed set.

3674 ca. 1897 Through the Looking-Glass

Philadelphia: Henry Altemus

After John Tenniel

Series No. 202: Altemus' Young People's Library Series. Now 22 titles in the series. Advertised in *PTLA* in 1897. Blue cloth.

3675   ca. 1897 Through the Looking-Glass
Philadelphia: Henry Altemus   Anonymous; John Tenniel
Altemus' Young Peoples Library. 4 color plates by Anonymous and 50 by Tenniel. Off-white cloth printed in blue.
Later reprinted in 1902 and 1911.

3676   ca. 1898 Through the Looking-Glass
New York: A. L. Burt   John Tenniel; Henry Holiday;
                                                              Harry Furniss
Little Women Series. Not dated and not advertised in *PTLA*. Date based on cover description and number of titles
in the series. Ads list 22 titles. Red or blue cloth. Includes *Snark* and 3 chapters from *Sylvie and Bruno*. John Tenniel
illustrated *Looking-Glass*; Henry Holiday, *The Hunting of the Snark*; and Harry Furniss, *Sylvie and Bruno*. See *MoM*
for more details.

3677   ca. 1898 Through the Looking-Glass
New York; Boston: H. M. Caldwell   John Tenniel
Standard De Novo Library Series, No. 188 of 215 titles. 1st edition and 1st printing. Advertised in *PTLA* in 1898. Green
cloth.

3678   ca. 1898 Through the Looking-Glass
Philadelphia: Henry Altemus   After John Tenniel
Series No. 202: Altemus' Young People's Library Series. Advertised in *PTLA* in 1898.

3679   ca. 1898 Through the Looking-Glass
New York: Hurst   John Tenniel
New Argyle Series, No. 221 of 265 titles. 1st printing. Advertised in *PTLA* in 1898. Several issues with binding
variations. Cloth, floral leaf design. For more details see *MoM*. pp. 210–11.

3680   ca. 1898 Through the Looking-Glass
Boston: Lothrop Publishing Company   John Tenniel; Anonymous
Series unknown. Glossy pale tan paper boards. The color frontispiece is non-integral plate on coated paper with 3
other color illustrations. 50 black-and-white illustrations. 208 numbered pp.

3681   ca. 1898 or 1899   Through the Looking-Glass
New York: A. L. Burt   John Tenniel; Henry Holiday;
                                                              Harry Furniss
Wellesley Series. 1st printing. Not dated but advertised in *PTLA* in 1899. The date could be 1898 based on the address
in the ads. One of 30 titles in the series. *MoM* Summary of Editions (p. 117) also gives cover description used in the
dating process. Includes *Snark* and 3 chapters from *Sylvie and Bruno*. John Tenniel illustrated *Looking-Glass*; Henry
Holiday, *The Hunting of the Snark*; and Harry Furniss, *Sylvie and Bruno*. Light blue cloth blocked in brown and black.
See *MoM* for more details.

3682   1899   Through the Looking-Glass
New York: Gilbert H. McKibbin   After John Tenniel
Manhattan Young People's Library Series. Boards; red cloth cover with Alice and fawn. Illustrations after Tenniel;
redrawn and colored by an uncredited artist.

3683   1899   Through the Looking-Glass
New York: M. F. Mansfield and A. Wessels   Blanche McManus
Title page says, "twelve full-page illustrations in color," but there are only 10, including frontispiece. Verso of title
page has copyright 1899 by M. F. Mansfield and A. Wessels. Blanche McManus was married to Milburg Francisco
Mansfield, the co-publisher of this book.

3684   [1899]   Through the Looking-Glass
New York: A. L. Burt   John Tenniel
Burt's Young Folks' Library Series. 1st printing. Not dated but advertised in *PTLA* in 1899. One of 20 titles in the
series. Pictorial cloth. See *MoM* for more details.

3685   [1899]   Through the Looking-Glass
New York; Chicago: Globe School Book Co.   John Tenniel
Pagination, contents, and leaf size identical to the 1899 McKibbin publication.

3686   ca. 1899 Through the Looking-Glass
New York: A. L. Burt   John Tenniel; Henry Holiday;
                                                                         Harry Furniss
Little Women Series. Not dated and not advertised in *PTLA*. Date based on number of titles in the series. The ca.
1899 edition is listed in *MoM* only in the Summary of Editions (p. 117), which gives 25 titles in the edition. Includes
Snark and 3 chapters from *Sylvie and Bruno*. John Tenniel illustrated *Looking-Glass*; Henry Holiday, *The Hunting of
the Snark*; and Harry Furniss, *Sylvie and Bruno*. See *MoM* for more details.

3687   ca. 1899 Through the Looking-Glass
New York: Bay View Publishing   Unknown
Excelsior Library Series, No. 43 of 56 titles.

3688   ca. 1899 Through the Looking-Glass
New York; Boston: H. M. Caldwell   John Tenniel
Young Folks' Library Series, No. 24 of 32 titles. 1st printing. Advertised in *PTLA* in 1899. Cloth. Dust jacket.

3689   ca. 1899 Through the Looking-Glass
Philadelphia: Henry Altemus   After John Tenniel
Series No. 202: Altemus' Young People's Library Series.

3690   ca. 1899 Through the Looking-Glass
Philadelphia: Henry Altemus   After John Tenniel
Series No. 58: Boys and Girls Classics Series. Blue or green cloth.

3691   ca. 1899 Through the Looking-Glass
Philadelphia: Henry Altemus   After John Tenniel
Series No. 130: Marqueterie Series.

3692   ca. 1899 Through the Looking-Glass
Philadelphia: Henry Altemus   After John Tenniel
Series #143: Petit Trianon Series.

3693   ca. 1899 Through the Looking-Glass
Philadelphia: Henry Altemus   After John Tenniel
Series No. 163: Sanspareil Series. At least 4 cloth binding colors.

3694   ca. 1899 Through the Looking-Glass
Philadelphia: Henry Altemus   After John Tenniel
Series No. 180: Vademecum Series. Pink-orange glazed cloth.

3695   ca. 1899 Through the Looking-Glass
New York: Hurst   John Tenniel
New Argyle Series, No. 284 of 335 titles. Advertised in *PTLA* in 1899. For more details see *MoM*. pp. 210–11.

3696 ca. 1899 Through the Looking-Glass

New York: Hurst — John Tenniel

Arlington Series, No. 221 of 250 titles. Advertised in *PTLA* in 1899. Pictorial cloth, medium brown blocked in black. For more details see *MoM.* p. 211.

3697 ca. 1899 Through the Looking-Glass

New York: Hurst — John Tenniel

Laurelhurst Series. 1st printing. Advertised in *PTLA* in 1899. Boxed. Pictorial cloth. Silk ribbon bookmark. 16mo. For more details see *MoM,* p. 212.

3698 1897 Through the Looking-Glass

New York: Mershon — John Tenniel

Standard Series. Dark brown cloth with floral and geometric design, silver-gilt lettering. Also in olive-green cloth. All Mershon issues with New York imprint date to 1897–1901; those with Rahway & New York from 1902–1906.

3699 1897 Through the Looking-Glass

New York: Mershon — John Tenniel

Unknown series. Buff paper boards with repetitive swirling floral pattern in blues and greens, quarter-bound appearance with faux-silk cloth spine and adjacent 3rd of both covers, cloth with ornate gold-gilt on front, plain on rear, [7], 198, [2] pp., tops gold-gilt, no frontispiece, 19 black-and-white drawings of which 4 are integral full-page. Dated 1897 by gift inscription and New York imprint.

3700 1899 Through the Looking-Glass

New York: Mershon — John Tenniel

Standard Series. Buff cloth, red decorations.

3701 1897–1901 Through the Looking-Glass

New York: Mershon — John Tenniel

Sterling Series. Cloth, gold-gilt lettering and blocking.

3702 1897–1901 Through the Looking-Glass

New York: Mershon — John Tenniel

Unknown Series. Yellow-green cloth, front with wide blind-stamped decorative border, central vignette with feathered pen tied with ribbon between 2 small branches, all in silver-gilt, spine lettered in silver-gilt, rear plain, [7], 198 pp., edges plain, no frontispiece, 19 black-and-white drawings of which 4 are integral full-page.

3703 1897–1901 Through the Looking-Glass

New York: Mershon — John Tenniel

Golden Gem Series. Cloth with floral and geometric design, silver-gilt lettering. Frontispiece and title page in color.

3704 1897–1901 Through the Looking-Glass

New York: Mershon — John Tenniel

Unknown Series. Orange cloth, front with green grapes in 3 vertical rectangles, title and author in silver-gilt upper left rectangle and spine, rear plain, [7], 198 pp., no frontispiece, 19 black-and-white drawings of which 4 are integral full-page. Title pages lettered red and black.

3705 1897–1901 Through the Looking-Glass

New York: Mershon — John Tenniel

Miniature Series. Gray-blue cloth, front with title in ornate oval floral frame, both in silver-gilt, spine lettered silver-gilt, rear plain, title page lettered black.

3706 1897–1901 Through the Looking-Glass

New York: Mershon — John Tenniel

Unknown Series. Very dark green cloth, front has blind-stamped wide decorative border, sailing ship in center formed by ornate floral frame, all in silver-gilt, spine with silver-gilt lettering and 5-point star, plain rear, [7], 198, [2] pp., edges plain, no frontispiece, 19 black-and-white drawings of which 4 are integral full-page. Title page lettered red and black.

3707 1897–1901   Through the Looking-Glass
New York: Mershon   John Tenniel

Unknown Series. Gray-green cloth, stem of red and white flowers on both covers and spine, title lettered red on top of front and spine, publisher in red on tail of spine, [7], 198 pp., black-and-white drawings.

3708 ca. 1899 Through the Looking-Glass
New York; Boston: Thomas Y. Crowell   John Tenniel; L. J. (Lewis Jesse)
                                                            Bridgman; Anonymous (after Tenniel); Charles Copeland

Children's Favorite Classics Series. Advertised in *PTLA* in 1899. 16mo. One of 22 titles in the series. Cover design is of girls' heads and interlaced titles. For more details see *MoM*, pp. 143 and 144.

3709 ca. 1899 Through the Looking-Glass
New York; Boston: Thomas Y. Crowell   John Tenniel; L. J. (Lewis Jesse)
                                                            Bridgman; Anonymous (after Tenniel); Charles Copeland

Wonderland Series. Advertised in *PTLA* in 1899. One of 13 titles in the series. Cloth covers with boy and girl holding hoop with title inside.

3710 ca. 1899–1901   Through the Looking-Glass
Philadelphia: Henry Altemus   After John Tenniel

Series No. 48: Beauxarts Series. Boxed. Multi-colored cloth.

3711 [1900]   Through the Looking-Glass
New York: A. L. Burt   John Tenniel; Henry Holiday

Burt's Young Folks' Library Series. Not dated, but date based on inscription and cover illustration. Pictorial green cloth. Includes *Looking-Glass* and *Snark* with only 1 illustration. See *MoM* for more details.

3712 1900   Through the Looking-Glass
New York: A. Wessels   Blanche McManus

Title page says, "twelve full-page illustrations in color," but there are only 10, including frontispiece. Verso of title page has copyright 1900 by A. Wessels Company.

3713 1900   Through the Looking-Glass
Chicago: Donohue Brothers   John Tenniel

Cover with Alice seated before mirror. "Donohue Brothers" was a name used only in 1900. In 1901, it became "M. A. Donohue and Company."

3714 1900   Through the Looking-Glass
Akron, OH: Saalfield   John Tenniel

For details, see Viola A. Smith, "A History of the Saalfield Publishing Company" (master's thesis, Kent State University, 1951).

3715 1900   Through the Looking-Glass
Chicago: W. B. Conkey   After John Tenniel

Amaranth Series. Same as ca. 1900 edition, but illustration is after Tenniel. Pale yellow-brown cloth. Front cover illustrated with Alice in chair playing with Dinah. Color frontispiece same as front cover.

3716 [1900]   Through the Looking-Glass
New York: Wm. L. Allison   John Tenniel

The Snug Corner Series. Publisher recorded as "Allison" on title page but "Donohue Brothers" on spine. See Donohue Brothers listing. Donohue Brothers used that imprint only for the year 1900, hence the dating of this edition.

3717   ca. 1900 Through the Looking-Glass
Chicago: Geo. M. Hill   John Tenniel
Handy Volume Series. One of 150 titles in the series. Yellow-green cloth, front with dark green and red-orange art
nouveau morning glories and gilt lettering. 198 numbered pp., no frontispiece.

3718   ca. 1900 Through the Looking-Glass
Philadelphia: Henry Altemus   After John Tenniel
Series No. 202: Altemus' Young People's Library Series.

3719   ca. 1900 Through the Looking-Glass
Philadelphia: Henry Altemus   After John Tenniel
Series No. 58: Boys and Girls Classics Series.

3720   ca. 1900 Through the Looking-Glass
Philadelphia: Henry Altemus   After John Tenniel
Series No. 87: Favorite Series for Young People. Buff cloth. 50 black-and-white drawings.

3721   ca. 1900 Through the Looking-Glass
New York: Hurst   John Tenniel
Laurelhurst Series. Not advertised in *PTLA*. Now 117 titles in the series. No more information is known.

3722   ca. 1900 Through the Looking-Glass
New York: Hurst   John Tenniel
New Argyle Series, No. 312 of 363 titles. Advertised in *PTLA* in 1900. Pictorial cloth with 8 aquatic-like flowers. For
more details see *MoM*, pp. 210–11.

3723   ca. 1900 Through the Looking-Glass
New York: Hurst   John Tenniel
Cambridge Classics Series, No. 205 of 225 titles. 1st edition, 1st printing. First advertised in *PTLA* in 1900. Several
issues with binding variations. Pictorial cloth.

3724   ca. 1900 Through the Looking-Glass
New York: Hurst   John Tenniel
Universal Library Series, No. 163 of 183 titles. 1st printing. Advertised in *PTLA* in 1900. Light brown paper wraps;
back cover with ads. For more details see *MoM*, p. 211.

3725   ca. 1900 Through the Looking-Glass
New York: Hurst   John Tenniel
Hurst's Gilt Top Library Series, No. 217 of 255 titles. 1st printing. Advertised in *PTLA* in 1900. No. 217 of 255 titles in
the series. Pictorial dark red cloth. For more details see *MoM*, p. 211.

3726   ca. 1900 Through the Looking-Glass
New York: Hurst   John Tenniel
Emerson Series of Popular 16mos, No. 100 of 110 titles. Advertised in *PTLA* in 1900. Decorated floral cloth. For more
details see *MoM*, p. 212.

3727   ca. 1900 Through the Looking-Glass
New York; Boston: Thomas Y. Crowell   John Tenniel; L. J. (Lewis Jesse)
                                                              Bridgman; Anonymous (after Tenniel); Charles Copeland
Children's Favorite Classics Series. Advertised in *PTLA* in 1900. 16mo. One of 24 titles in the series. Illustrated green
cloth. For more details see *MoM*, pp. 143 and 144.

3728   ca. 1900 Through the Looking-Glass

Chicago: W. B. Conkey   John Tenniel

Amaranth Series. Pale yellow cloth with floral pattern or in reddish-brown cloth.

3729   ca. 1900s   Through the Looking-Glass
New York; Boston: H. M. Caldwell   John Tenniel

Editha Series for Little Girls, New Edition, No. 21. Title page printed in red and green.

3730   ca. 1900–1901   Through the Looking-Glass
New York; Boston: H. M. Caldwell   John Tenniel

Young Folks' Library Series. One of 40 titles in the series.

3731   ca. 1900–1913   Through the Looking-Glass
New York; Boston: Thomas Y. Crowell   John Tenniel; L. J. (Lewis Jesse)
                                     Bridgman; Anonymous (after Tenniel); Charles Copeland

Children's Favorite Classics Series. Date based on cover design. Green pictorial boards and green cloth spine. For
more details see *MoM*, p. 144.

3732   ca. 1900–1913   Through the Looking-Glass
New York; Boston: Thomas Y. Crowell   John Tenniel; L. J. (Lewis Jesse)
                                     Bridgman; Anonymous (after Tenniel); Charles Copeland

Children's Favorite Classics Series. Date based on cover design. Smaller leaf size than prior editions. Color and gilt
pictorial boards. For more details see *MoM*, p. 144.

3733   ca. 1900–1913   Through the Looking-Glass
New York; Boston: Thomas Y. Crowell   John Tenniel; L. J. (Lewis Jesse)
                                     Bridgman; Anonymous (after Tenniel); Charles Copeland

Children's Favorite Classics Series. Pictorial green boards with red spine lettered in gilt. Many illustrations that are
within decorative borders. Pictorial green boards and red cloth spine. For more details see *MoM*, p. 144.

3734   ca. 1900–1915   Through the Looking-Glass
Chicago: Homewood   After John Tenniel

Handy Volume Series. Includes *Sleeping Beauty*. Gray-blue cloth cover with Alice and kitten in chair stamped in red,
yellow, green, and black; border and lettering black. Frontispiece same as cover.

3735   1901   Through the Looking-Glass
Chicago; New York: Henneberry   Unknown

Henneberry's Illustrated Boys' and Girls' Library Series. Dust jacket. Cloth-covered boards, cover with girl and boy
reading on tree limb.

3736   1901   Through the Looking-Glass
Chicago; New York: Henneberry   Unknown

Henneberry's Illustrated New Century Library of Standard Books by Popular Authors. Cloth-covered boards above a
vertical floral design. Dust jacket.

3737   1901   Through the Looking-Glass
New York: Hurst   John Tenniel

Hurst's Home Series for Girls, No. 41 of 50 titles Advertised in *PTLA* in 1901. Cloth.

3738   ca. 1901 Through the Looking-Glass
New York: A. L. Burt   John Tenniel, Henry Holiday,
                                              Harry Furniss

Little Women Series. Not dated and not advertised in *PTLA*. Date based on number of titles in the series. The ca. 1901
edition is listed in *MoM* only in the Summary of Editions (p. 117), which gives 32 titles in the edition. Includes *Snark*

and 3 chapters from *Sylvie and Bruno*. John Tenniel illustrated *Looking-Glass*; Henry Holiday, *The Hunting of the Snark*; and Harry Furniss, *Sylvie and Bruno*. See *MoM* for more details.

3739   ca. 1901 Through the Looking-Glass

New York: A. L. Burt

John Tenniel; Henry Holiday;
Harry Furniss

Wellesley Series. The 1901 edition is listed in *MoM* only in the Summary of Editions (p. 117), which gives 42 titles in the edition. Summary also gives cover description used in the dating process. Includes *Snark* and 3 chapters from *Sylvie and Bruno*. John Tenniel illustrated *Looking-Glass*; Henry Holiday, *The Hunting of the Snark*; and Harry Furniss, *Sylvie and Bruno*. See *MoM* for more details.

3740   ca. 1901 Through the Looking-Glass

New York; Boston: H. M. Caldwell

John Tenniel

Chateau Series, No. 150 of 169 titles. Advertised in *PTLA* in 1901. Paper-covered boards backed with cloth spine. Pages with gilt top edges. Ribbon bookmark. Boxed.

3741   ca. 1901 Through the Looking-Glass

New York; Boston: H. M. Caldwell

John Tenniel

Kalon Series, No. 188 of 216 titles. Advertised in *PTLA* in 1901. Cloth with 4 variations of floral surrounding a woman's head. Dust jacket. Tall 16mo.

3742   ca. 1901 Through the Looking-Glass

New York; Boston: H. M. Caldwell

John Tenniel

Chateau Series, No. 150 of 169 titles. Boxed. Paper-covered boards backed with cloth spine. Pages with gilt top edges. Includes bookmark.

3743   ca. 1901 Through the Looking-Glass

Philadelphia: Henry Altemus

After John Tenniel

Series No. 202: Altemus' Young People's Library Series.

3744   ca. 1901 Through the Looking-Glass

Philadelphia: Henry Altemus

After John Tenniel

Series No. 180: Vademecum Series.

3745   ca. 1901 Through the Looking-Glass

Philadelphia: Henry Altemus

After John Tenniel

Series No. 87: Favorite Series for Young People.

3746   ca. 1901 Through the Looking-Glass

Philadelphia: Henry Altemus

After John Tenniel

Series No. 115: La Belle Fleur Series. Multi-colored cloth with art nouveau floral decorative pattern.

3747   ca. 1901 Through the Looking-Glass

Philadelphia: Henry Altemus

After John Tenniel

Series #118: L'Art Nouveau Series. Boxed. Multi-colored covers with art nouveau diamond-shaped decorative pattern.

3748   ca. 1901 Through the Looking-Glass

New York: Hurst

John Tenniel

Emerson Series of Popular 16mos. Advertised in *PTLA* in 1901. Now No. 112 in the series. Decorated floral cloth with 4 carnations. For more details see *MoM*, p. 212.

3749   ca. 1901 Through the Looking-Glass

New York: Hurst

John Tenniel

New Argyle Series, No. 346 of 403 titles. Advertised in *PTLA* in 1901. Pictorial cloth covers with 2 irises beside title. For more details see *MoM*, pp. 210–11.

3750 ca. 1901 Through the Looking-Glass
New York: Hurst   John Tenniel
Hurst's Gilt Top Library Series. Not advertised in *PTLA*. Now 302 titles in the series. No other information known.

3751 ca. 1901 Through the Looking-Glass
New York: Hurst   John Tenniel
Laurelhurst Series, No. 134 of 150 titles. Advertised in *PTLA* in 1901. Pictorial cloth. For more details see *MoM*, p. 212.

3752 ca. 1901 Through the Looking-Glass
New York: Hurst   John Tenniel
Arlington Series. Advertised in *PTLA* in 1901. Medium brown cloth covers with black lettering. For more details see *MoM*, p. 211.

3753 ca. 1901 Through the Looking-Glass
New York: Hurst   John Tenniel
Cambridge Classics Series, No. 249 of 274 titles. Advertised in *PTLA* in 1901. Pictorial cloth, art nouveau poppy design.

3754 [late 1901]   Through the Looking-Glass
Philadelphia: Henry Altemus   After John Tenniel
Series no. 180: Vademecum Series.

3755 1902   Through the Looking-Glass
Boston: DeWolfe, Fiske & Co.   After John Tenniel;
                                                     Anonymous
Favorite Library Series. Binding variants; light yellow/tan cloth-covered boards, cover with Alice climbing into mirror. Black-and-white plates after Tenniel; 4 chromolithograph plates (including frontispiece) by anonymous artist. See 1907 for a later edition.

3756 1902   Through the Looking-Glass
New York; London: Harper and Brothers   Peter Newell
New Holiday Series. Several issues are recorded. [40] leaves of sepia plates. Housed in original publisher's white Japanese vellum box. Heavy green paper dust jacket. Cream Japanese vellum, gilt lettering, and vignette (Alice with cake and candle). Also issued in a later binding variant.

3757 1902   Through the Looking-Glass
Chicago: W. B. Conkey   After John Tenniel
Rosalind Series edition. Includes an abridged version of *Flower Fables* by Louisa May Alcott. There are at least 2 issues of this edition. One is in red cloth with black candelabra-like decoration and single-ruled border on front cover; spine with similar black image and gilt lettering; tan endpapers. Color frontispiece with Alice crawling through mirror.

3758 [1902]   Through the Looking-Glass
New York: A. L. Burt   John Tenniel; Henry Holiday;
                                                     Harry Furniss
Wellesley Series. Not dated but advertised in *PTLA* in 1902. Pictorial cloth. Includes *Snark* and 3 chapters from *Sylvie and Bruno*. John Tenniel illustrated *Looking-Glass*; Henry Holiday, *The Hunting of the Snark*; and Harry Furniss, *Sylvie and Bruno*. See *MoM* for more details.

3759 [1902]   Through the Looking-Glass
New York: A. L. Burt   John Tenniel; Henry Holiday;
                                                     Harry Furniss

Little Women Series. Not dated and not advertised in *PTLA*. Date based on cover description. Blue cloth. Includes *Snark* and 3 chapters from *Sylvie and Bruno*. John Tenniel illustrated *Looking-Glass*; Henry Holiday, *The Hunting of the Snark*; and Harry Furniss, *Sylvie and Bruno*. See *MoM* for more details.

3760   ca. 1902 Through the Looking-Glass
New York; Boston: H. M. Caldwell   John Tenniel
Kalon Series, No. 188 of 217 titles. Advertised in *PTLA* in 1902. Pale orange cloth.

3761   ca. 1902 Through the Looking-Glass
New York; Boston: H. M. Caldwell   John Tenniel
Young Folks' Library Series. One of 41 titles in the series.

3762   ca. 1902 Through the Looking-Glass
New York; London: Harper and Brothers   Peter Newell
New Holiday Series. Same as 1902 edition, but not in box. In various bindings.

3763   ca. 1902 Through the Looking-Glass
Philadelphia: Henry Altemus   After John Tenniel
Series No. 202: Altemus' Young People's Library Series. Beige cloth. 4 color plates and 50 Tenniel illustrations.

3764   ca. 1902 Through the Looking-Glass
Philadelphia: Henry Altemus   After John Tenniel
Series No. 180: Vademecum Series.

3765   ca. 1902 Through the Looking-Glass
Philadelphia: Henry Altemus   After John Tenniel
Series No. 87: Favorite Series for Young People.

3766   ca. 1902 Through the Looking-Glass
Philadelphia: Henry Altemus   After John Tenniel
Series No. 48: Beauxarts Series. Boxed. Multi-colored cloth.

3767   ca. 1902 Through the Looking-Glass
Philadelphia: Henry Altemus   Anonymous; John Tenniel
Altemus' Young Peoples Library. 4 color plates by Anonymous and 50 by Tenniel. Off-white cloth printed in blue. First printed in 1897. Reprinted 1911.

3768   ca. 1902 Through the Looking-Glass
New York: Hurst   John Tenniel
Arlington Series, No. 243 of 274 titles. Cloth. For more details see *MoM*, p. 211.

3769   ca. 1902 Through the Looking-Glass
New York: Hurst   John Tenniel
Laurelhurst Series, No. 161 of 179 titles. Advertised in *PTLA* in 1902. Boxed. Paper-covered boards and decorated cloth spine. Ribbon bookmark. For more details see *MoM*, p. 212.

3770   ca. 1902 Through the Looking-Glass
New York: Hurst   John Tenniel
Hurst's Home Series for Girls. Advertised in *PTLA* in 1902. One of 58 titles in the series. Pictorial cloth covers with a woman walking in winter clothes and holding a book.

3771   [after 1902]   Through the Looking-Glass
New York; London: Harper and Brothers   Peter Newell

New Holiday Series. Same as ca. 1902 edition, but red cloth dust jacket backed with blue paper; maroon diagonal fine-ribbed cloth.

3772 [after 1902]   Through the Looking-Glass
Chicago: W. B. Conkey   After John Tenniel
Rosalind Series edition. No dust jacket. In white cloth with silver-gilt decorations, paper paste-on of man in boat and girl on bank framed in silver-gilt on front cover; white endpapers. Includes 22 pp. of *Flower Fables*.

3773 ca. 1903 Through the Looking-Glass
New York: A. L. Burt   John Tenniel; Henry Holiday;
Harry Furniss
Wellesley Series. Not dated but advertised in *PTLA* in 1903. Pictorial cloth. Includes *Snark* and 3 chapters from *Sylvie and Bruno*. John Tenniel illustrated *Looking-Glass*; Henry Holiday, *The Hunting of the Snark*; and Harry Furniss, *Sylvie and Bruno*. See *MoM* for more details.

3774 ca. 1903 Through the Looking-Glass
Boston; New York; Chicago; San Francisco: Educational Publishing Co.   John Tenniel
Reddish-brown cloth cover with Alice and Humpty Dumpty blocked and framed in black. No frontispiece; black-and-white illustrations. *WMGC*, p. 252 lists a 1912? edition with no details.

3775 ca. 1903 Through the Looking-Glass
New York; Boston: H. M. Caldwell   John Tenniel
Young Folks' Library Series. One of 46 titles in the series.

3776 ca. 1903 Through the Looking-Glass
Philadelphia: Henry Altemus   After John Tenniel
Series No. 180: Vademecum Series.

3777 ca. 1903 Through the Looking-Glass
New York: Hurst   John Tenniel
Cambridge Classics Series, No. 153 of 253 titles. Advertised in *PTLA* in 1903. Light blue or green-gray cloth fading to light gray-yellow-brown cloth.

3778 ca. 1903 Through the Looking-Glass
Philadelphia: Rodgers   John Tenniel
Popular Classical Series of 16mos. Black half leather. Blue marbled boards. Date based on inscription.

3779 ca. 1903 Through a Looking-Glass
New York: Thomas Y. Crowell   John Tenniel; L. J. (Lewis Jesse)
Bridgman; Anonymous (after Tenniel); Charles Copeland
Handy-Volume Classics Series, Pocket Edition. Advertised in *PTLA* in 1903. One of 113 titles in the series. Cloth with decorative design and series title on front cover. Dust jacket. 35 cents.

3780 ca. 1903 Through a Looking-Glass
New York: Thomas Y. Crowell   John Tenniel; L. J. (Lewis Jesse)
Bridgman; Anonymous (after Tenniel); Charles Copeland
Handy-Volume Classics Series, Pocket Edition. Advertised in *PTLA* in 1903. As in the other 1903 edition, but priced at 75 cents. In lambskin. Front cover decorated in gilt. Top edge gilt. Silk bookmark. Boxed.

3781 ca. 1903–1904 Through the Looking-Glass
Chicago: Henneberry   John Tenniel
Henneberry's Illustrated New Century Library of Standard Books by Popular Authors. Magenta cloth cover blind stamped with elaborate floral and geometric design.

3782   1904   Through the Looking-Glass
New York: Frederick A. Stokes   John Tenniel; Maria L. Kirk
Several issues of this edition are recorded. Brown cloth. Alice and Wonderland characters in gold, black, red, and green. 12 color plates by Kirk.

3783   1904   Through the Looking-Glass
Chicago: W. B. Conkey   After John Tenniel
Amaranth Series. Same as above, but textured pale blue cloth cover illustration blocked in dark blue, black, red, and gold. Ad for 25 titles "in uniform style." Date from inscription.

3784   ca. 1904   Through the Looking-Glass
New York: A. L. Burt   John Tenniel; Henry Holiday;
                                                                Harry Furniss
Wellesley Series. Not dated but listed in *MoM* Summary of Editions (p. 117) as having 72 titles in the series. Summary also gives cover description used in the dating process. Includes *Snark* and 3 chapters from *Sylvie and Bruno*. John Tenniel illustrated *Looking-Glass*; Henry Holiday, *The Hunting of the Snark*; and Harry Furniss, *Sylvie and Bruno*. See *MoM* for more details.

3785   ca. 1904   Through the Looking-Glass
New York; Boston: H. M. Caldwell   John Tenniel
Alcazar Classics, No. 170 of 187 titles in the series. Boxed. Binding variants. Cloth.

3786   ca. 1904   Through the Looking-Glass
Philadelphia: Henry Altemus   After John Tenniel
Series No. 180: Vademecum Series.

3787   ca. 1904   Through the Looking-Glass
Philadelphia: Henry Altemus   After John Tenniel
Series No. 87: Favorite Series for Young People.

3788   ca. 1904   Through the Looking-Glass
Philadelphia: Henry Altemus   After John Tenniel
Series No. 87: Favorite Series for Young People. Different ads from the other 1904 edition.

3789   ca. 1904   Through the Looking-Glass
New York: Hurst   John Tenniel
Hurst's Half Leather Classics Series, No. 111 of 120 titles. Advertised in *PTLA* in 1904. Believed to be the 1st, and perhaps only, *Looking-Glass* edition in the series. No. 111 of 120 titles in series. Three-quarter leather with marbled paper-covered boards, gilt lettering on spine. Silk bookmark. Dust jacket.

3790   ca. 1904–1906   Through the Looking-Glass
Philadelphia: Henry Altemus   After John Tenniel
Series No. 180: Vademecum Series.

3791   1905   Through the Looking-Glass
New York: Frederick A. Stokes   John Tenniel; Maria L. Kirk
Gray cloth cover with Alice and Wonderland characters blocked in orange, black, and yellow. 12 color plates by Kirk; 50 black-and-white illustrations by Tenniel. Lovett says there is a later printing but gives no date or information.

3792   1905   Through the Looking-Glass
New York: Frederick A. Stokes   John Tenniel; Maria L. Kirk
Same as 1905 Stokes edition, but with red cloth and cover paste-on of Alice and the Tweedles. 12 color plates by Kirk.

3793   1905   Through the Looking-Glass

Chicago: W. B. Conkey   John Tenniel

Young People's Cloth Library Series. This series includes *Sleeping Beauty* by Charles Perrault. At least 2 issues are known. Light blue-green cloth, Alice in Garden of Live Flowers. Color frontispiece (Alice in chair with Dinah).

3794   ca. 1905 Through the Looking-Glass

Philadelphia: Henry Altemus   After John Tenniel

Series No. 87: Favorite Series for Young People.

3795   ca. 1905 Through the Looking-Glass

Philadelphia: Henry Altemus   After John Tenniel

Series No. 87: Favorite Series for Young People.

3796   ca. 1905 Through the Looking-Glass

Chicago: M. A. Donohue & Co.   John Tenniel

Snug Corner Series. Includes *Dreams* by Olive Schreiner. Dark green cloth, woman on beach with umbrella. No frontispiece. See Wm. L. Allison Company listing for [1900].

3797   ca. 1905 Through a Looking-Glass

New York: Thomas Y. Crowell   John Tenniel; L. J. (Lewis Jesse)

                                       Bridgman; Anonymous (after Tenniel); Charles Copeland

Series uncertain but possibly a Handy-Volume. Not in *PTLA*. Chromolithographed frontispiece. Medium gray-blue cloth spine and corners. Some black-and-white illustrations after Tenniel and others signed "L. J. Bridgman" or "LJB." *MoM* pp. 144.

3798   1906   Through the Looking-Glass

New York: Harper and Brothers   Peter Newell;

                                       Robert Murray Wright

The Popular Edition. 3 issues recorded. Same as New Holiday Series, but smaller format.

3799   1906   Through the Looking-Glass

Rahway, NJ; New York: Mershon   John Tenniel

Miniature Series. Brown cloth, font has title in decorative oval frame, spine with title and publisher, all lettering and decoration in silver-gilt, rear plain, [7], 198 pp., no frontispiece, black-and-white drawings. Title page lettered black. [Date from imprint (Rahway & NY) and from inscription in USC copy.]

3800   ca. 1906 Through the Looking-Glass

New York: A. L. Burt   John Tenniel; Henry Holiday;

                                       Harry Furniss

Wellesley Series. Not dated and not advertised in *PTLA* but listed in *MoM* Summary of Editions (p. 117) as having 87 titles in the series. Summary also gives cover description used in the dating process. Includes *Snark* and 3 chapters from *Sylvie and Bruno*. John Tenniel illustrated *Looking-Glass*; Henry Holiday, *The Hunting of the Snark*; and Harry Furniss, *Sylvie and Bruno*. See *MoM* for more details.

3801   ca. 1906 Through the Looking-Glass

New York; Boston: H. M. Caldwell   John Tenniel

Alcazar Classics. Series now has 188 titles. Boxed. Cloth.

3802   ca. 1906 Through the Looking-Glass

New York; Boston: H. M. Caldwell   John Tenniel

Editha Series for Little Girls, New Edition, No. 21 of 30 titles. Brown calico-textured cloth.

3803   ca. 1906 Through the Looking-Glass
New York; Boston: H. M. Caldwell   John Tenniel
Editha Series for Little Girls, New Edition, No. 21. Cloth cover stamped in gilt; illustrated endpapers. Title page
printed in red and black.

3804   ca. 1906 Through the Looking-Glass
New York; London: Harper and Brothers   Peter Newell
The Popular Edition. Binding variant in blue cloth with gilt Alice holding cake on front cover. Newell frontispiece; 8
black-and-white plates. In various bindings.

3805   ca. 1906 Through the Looking-Glass
New York: Hurst   John Tenniel
Hurst's Home Series for Girls. Advertised in *PTLA* in 1906. One of 104 titles in the series. Medium gray-blue cloth
covers with woman reading on window bench while 2 girls play tennis outside. Lettered in red on front cover and gilt
on spine. For more details see *MoM*, p. 212.

3806   ca. 1906 Through the Looking-Glass
New York: Hurst   John Tenniel
Fleur de Lis Classics Series, No. 52 of 58 titles. Advertised in *PTLA* in 1906. Believed to be the 1st, and perhaps only,
Looking-Glass edition in the series. Boxed. Pictorial cloth with fleur-de-lis pattern. For more details see *MoM* p. 213.

3807   ca. 1906 Through the Looking-Glass
New York: Hurst   John Tenniel
Boys' Own Library Series, No. 57 of 67 titles. Advertised in *PTLA* in 1906. Believed to be the 1st, and perhaps only,
Looking-Glass edition in the series. Cloth with inlaid picture on front cover. Dust jacket.

3808   ca. 1906 Through the Looking-Glass
New York: Hurst   John Tenniel
Ideal Series of Standard Classics, No. 63 of 66 titles. Advertised in *PTLA* in 1906. Believed to be the 1st, and perhaps
only, *Looking-Glass* edition in the series. Boxed. Morocco covers with floral decorations stamped in gilt.

3809   ca. 1906 Through the Looking-Glass
New York: McLoughlin Brothers   John Tenniel
Young Folks Standard Library Series. At least 2 issues. Cloth cover with Alice, White Rabbit, and title blocked in 3
colors. Color frontispiece.

3810   1907   Through the Looking-Glass
Chicago: W. B. Conkey   John Tenniel
Young People's Cloth Library Series. Light blue cloth, Alice in chair with Dinah blocked in pale green, red-orange,
and black. Black-and-white frontispiece (girl reading book). Includes *Sleeping Beauty* by Charles Perrault.

3811   ca. 1907 Through the Looking-Glass
Philadelphia: Henry Altemus   After John Tenniel
Series No. 57: Boys and Girls Classics (new). Linen cloth in 8 different designs.

3812   ca. 1908 Through the Looking-Glass
New York; Boston: H. M. Caldwell   John Tenniel
Editha Series for Little Girls, New Edition, No. 21. Cloth cover stamped in blue. Title page printed in red and black.

3813   ca. 1908 Through the Looking-Glass
Philadelphia: Henry Altemus   After John Tenniel
Series No. 202: Altemus' Young People's Library Series. Calico-textured cloth.

3814   ca. 1908 Through the Looking-Glass
Philadelphia: Henry Altemus   After John Tenniel
Series No. 202: Altemus' Young People's Library Series. With various covers.

3815   ca. 1908 Through the Looking-Glass
Philadelphia: Henry Altemus   After John Tenniel
Series No. 87: Favorite Series for Young People.

3816   ca. 1908 Through the Looking-Glass
Chicago: Reilly and Lee   John Tenniel
No information can be found about this book.

3817   ca. 1908 Through the Looking-Glass in Words of One Syllable
Chicago: Saalfield   John Tenniel
Not paginated. Pictorial boards.

3818   1909   Through the Looking-Glass
New York: A. L. Burt   John Tenniel; Henry Holiday;
                                                               Harry Furniss

Wellesley Series. Not dated and not advertised in *PTLA* but listed in *MoM* Summary of Editions (p. 117) as having 120
titles in the series. Summary also gives cover description used in the dating process. Includes *Snark* and 3 chapters
from *Sylvie and Bruno*. John Tenniel illustrated *Looking-Glass*; Henry Holiday, *The Hunting of the Snark*; and Harry
Furniss, *Sylvie and Bruno*. See *MoM* for more details.

3819   1909   Through the Looking-Glass
New York: Dodge Publishing Company   Bessie Pease Gutmann
1st edition. Blue ribbed cloth with red-and-white Humpty Dumpty on red brick wall; turquoise illustrated endpapers.
10 color plates; 15 line drawings.

3820   ca. 1909 Through the Looking-Glass
New York: Frederick A. Stokes   John Tenniel; Maria L. Kirk
Purplish-gray cloth stamped in gold and printed in orange, yellow, and black. Imprint on verso of title page. Other
details identical to Stokes 1905 edition except "The University Press, Cambridge, USA" on verso of the title page.
Lovett calls this a "later printing."

3821   ca. 1909 Through the Looking-Glass
New York; Boston: H. M. Caldwell   John Tenniel
Alcazar Classics, No. 170 of 190 titles in the series. Paper-covered boards backed with green cloth.

3822   ca. 1909 Through the Looking-Glass
New York; Boston: H. M. Caldwell   John Tenniel
Young Folks' Library Series. One of 49 titles.

3823   ca. 1909 Through the Looking-Glass
New York and Boston: H. M. Caldwell   John Tenniel
Editha Series for Little Girls, New Edition, No. 21 of 36 titles. Light blue, calico-textured dotted-line grain cloth, plain
white endpapers. Front paste-down with publisher's bookplate in red-orange. 50 black-and-white illustrations.

3824   ca. 1909 Through the Looking-Glass
New York: Hurst   John Tenniel
Girls' Own Library Series, No. 50 of 57 titles. Advertised in *PTLA* in 1909. Believed to be the 1st, and perhaps
only, *Looking-Glass* edition in the series. Pictorial cloth covers with 2 girls playing tennis. For more details see *MoM*,
p. 213.

3825   ca. 1909 Through the Looking-Glass
New York: Hurst   John Tenniel
Every Girl's Library Series. Advertised in *PTLA* in 1909. Believed to be the 1st, and perhaps only, *Looking-Glass* edition in the series. Light gray-yellow-brown cloth cover with 3 girls (nurse, tennis player, and one with flowers) within rose. Also published in olive cloth cover with paste-on of boy selling newspapers. For more details see *MoM*, p. 214.

3826   ca. 1909 Through the Looking-Glass
New York: Hurst   John Tenniel
Knickerbocker Classics Series, No. 119 of 130 titles; No. 94 of 101 titles in 1913. Advertised in *PTLA* in 1909. Cloth with paste-on image on right and title on left front cover.

3827   ca. 1909–1910   Through the Looking-Glass
Philadelphia: Henry Altemus   After John Tenniel
Series No. 59: Boys and Girls Own Library.

3828   ca. 1910 Through the Looking-Glass
Buffalo, NY: Hayes Lithographing   After John Tenniel
Wonderland Series. Abridged. No dust jacket. Glossy buff paper-covered boards, cover with multi-colored White Knight and Alice. Includes 6 full-page color illustrations and black-and-white drawings. In 5 of the color illustrations, Alice is unlike Tenniel's, with long blond hair. In the 6th illustration, Alice is much younger and wearing a pink bonnet that covers her hair.

3829   ca. 1910 Through the Looking-Glass
Philadelphia: Henry Altemus   After John Tenniel
Series No. 87: Favorite Series for Young People.

3830   ca. 1910 Through the Looking-Glass
New York: Hurst   John Tenniel
Hurst's Alligator Classics Series. Pale yellow-green cloth. Paste-on of woman in pink Victorian dress and hat holding bouquet of flowers. No frontispiece; 50 black-and-white illustrations. Gift inscription 1910.

3831   ca. 1910 Through the Looking-Glass
New York: McLoughlin Brothers   After John Tenniel;
                                                                   Harry Furniss
Young Folks Standard Library Series, No. 3228. Many issues with different imprints and binding variants. Includes "King Fisher's Wooing and Other Poems." Brown cloth cover with Walrus and Carpenter in black, pink, and green; black lettering on front cover and spine; yellow floral endpapers. Color frontispiece (Knight); black-and-white illustrations. A copy is known inscribed by T. S. Eliot.

3832   ca. 1910s   Through the Looking-Glass
Chicago and New York: Henneberry   John Tenniel
Henneberry's Illustrated New Century Library of Standard Books by Popular Authors. Tan cloth, stamped in white and light blue.

3833   [after 1910]   Through the Looking-Glass
Buffalo, NY: Hayes Lithographing   After John Tenniel
Wonderland Series. Blue-green paper-covered boards, cover with Alice in shower of cards; frontispiece. Includes 6 color illustrations and black-and-white drawings.

3834   [after 1910]   Through the Looking-Glass
New York: McLoughlin Brothers   After John Tenniel;
                                                                   Harry Furniss
Young Folks Standard Library Series, No. 3228. Includes "King Fisher's Wooing and Other Poems." Same as ca. 1910 edition, but green cloth. Several binding variants exist.

3835   1911   Through the Looking-Glass
Philadelphia: David McKay   Frank Godwin;
                                                                             after John Tenniel

McKay's Young People's Classics Series, No. 20 of 26 titles. Several issues in this series. Boards; blue cloth cover with title in top frame and blond Alice in pink pinafore with fawn in lower frame. Black-and-white illustrations after Tenniel and 4 color plates by Godwin; uncredited color frontispiece of Alice crawling through mirror.

3836   ca. 1911 Through the Looking-Glass
New York; Boston: H. M. Caldwell   John Tenniel
Editha Series for Little Girls, New Edition, No. 21 of 46 titles. Brown cloth, cream endpapers.

3837   ca. 1911 Through the Looking-Glass
Philadelphia: Henry Altemus   After John Tenniel
Series No. 202: Altemus' Young People's Library Series. Brown cloth. 1 color plate (frontispiece).

3838   ca. 1911 Through the Looking-Glass
Philadelphia: Henry Altemus   After John Tenniel
Series No. 57: Boys and Girls Classics (new).

3839   ca. 1911 Through the Looking-Glass
Philadelphia: Henry Altemus   Anonymous; John Tenniel
Altemus' Young Peoples Library. 4 color plates by Anonymous and 50 by Tenniel. Off-white cloth printed in blue. First published in 1897 and later in 1902.

3840   1911   Through the Looking-Glass
New York: New York Book Co.   John Tenniel
Our Young Folks Illustrated Books Series. Boards; cream cloth, Frog and Alice on cover.

3841   1911   Through the Looking-Glass
New York: Platt and Peck   John Tenniel
1 leaf of plates. Boards.

3842   [after 1911]   Through the Looking-Glass
Buffalo, NY: Hayes Lithographing   After John Tenniel
Wonderland Series. Same as the "[after 1910]" copy, but with green paper-covered boards, front cover with Trial scene.

3843   [1912]   Through the Looking-Glass
Philadelphia: E. Jacobs   Elenore Abbott
Franklin Classics Series. 2 possible issues; Sewell speculates this may be a 1912 companion issue to the Franklin Classics Series *Alice* from George W. Jacobs.

3844   ca. 1912 Through the Looking-Glass
New York: Chatterton-Peck   Anonymous
Pale green cloth cover with orator and scroll, figures multi-colored and lettering black. Color frontispiece of Alice climbing into mirror; 5 color and 10 black-and-white full-page illustrations, plus other black-and-white illustrations. Includes 8 pp. of *Comrades in New Mexico*.

3845   ca. 1912 Through the Looking-Glass
Boston: Educational Co.   John Tenniel
Found only in *WMGC*, p. 252.

3846   ca. 1912 Through the Looking-Glass
New York; Boston: H. M. Caldwell   John Tenniel
Editha Series for Little Girls, New Edition. Date based on inscription. Blue-green cloth covers with paper paste-on of
girl partially behind curtain holding flowers. Black-and-white frontispiece of Alice and Queen.

3847   ca. 1912 Through the Looking-Glass
Chicago: M. A. Donohue & Co.   After John Tenniel
Our Young Folks Illustrated Book Series. Pink-and-white boards with White Knight blocked in red and black.

3848   ca. 1912 Through the Looking-Glass
Chicago: M. A. Donohue & Co.   John Tenniel
Little Folks' Edition: The Alice Series, No. 2020.

3849   ca. 1912 Through the Looking-Glass
New York: R. F. Fenno   John Tenniel
R. F. Fenno and Company published in New York from 1885 to 1929. No information about this edition could be found.

3850   ca. 1912 Through the Looking-Glass
Cincinnati, OH: Southwestern Publishing   John Tenniel
No copy found. May be a ghost edition.

3851   ca. 1912–1913 Through the Looking-Glass
Philadelphia: Henry Altemus   After John Tenniel
Series No. 200: Young Folks' Quarto Series. Cream cloth.

3852   [after 1912]   Through the Looking-Glass
New York: Chatterton-Peck   Anonymous
Same as [ca. 1912], but front cover colors somewhat different and only 4 full-page color illustrations and 7 black-and-
white full-page illustrations. Includes gilt border added to front cover illustration.

3853   ca. 1913 Through the Looking-Glass
New York; Boston: H. M. Caldwell   John Tenniel
Editha Series for Little Girls, New Edition, No. 17 of 32 titles. Advertised in *PTLA* in 1913. Cloth covers with paper
paste-on. Dust jacket.

3854   ca. 1913 Through the Looking-Glass
New York; Boston: H. M. Caldwell   John Tenniel
Young Folks' Library Series, No. 16 of 18 titles. Advertised in *PTLA* in 1913. Tall 16mo.

3855   ca. 1913 Through the Looking-Glass
Philadelphia: Henry Altemus   After John Tenniel
Series No. 57: Boys and Girls Classics (new).

3856   ca. 1913 Through the Looking-Glass
Philadelphia: Henry Altemus   After John Tenniel
Series No. 202: Altemus' Young People's Library Series.

3857   ca. 1913 Through the Looking-Glass
New York: Hurst   John Tenniel
Hurst's Home Series for Girls. Not advertised in *PTLA*. No other information known.

3858   ca. 1913 Through the Looking-Glass
New York: Hurst   John Tenniel

Knickerbocker Classics Series, No. 94 of 101 titles in 1913. Not advertised in *PTLA*. No other information known.

3859   ca. 1913 Through the Looking-Glass
New York: Hurst   John Tenniel
Ansonia Classics Series, No. 60 of 65 titles. Advertised in *PTLA* in 1913. Believed to be the 1st, and perhaps only, *Looking-Glass* edition in the series. Cloth with color picture pasted to the front cover. For more details see *MoM*, p. 212.

3860   ca. 1913 Through the Looking-Glass
New York: Hurst   John Tenniel
Hurst's Alligator Classics Series, No. 87 of 97 titles. Advertised in *PTLA* in 1913. Believed to be the 1st, and perhaps only, *Looking-Glass* edition in the series. 50 black-and-white illustrations. In various covers, including padded faux alligator stamped in gilt; quarter-bound green cloth over green marbled paper; pale yellow cloth with 3 vertical flowers and title above; and cream paper-covered boards, illustrated with 3 red roses and green leaves at top. Boxed. For more details see *MoM*, p. 214.

3861   ca. 1913 Through the Looking-Glass
New York; Boston: Thomas Y. Crowell   Charles Copeland
Children's Favorite Classics Series. Advertised in *PTLA* in 1913. One of 47 titles in the series. Color frontispiece by Copeland is the only illustration. Dust jacket.

3862   ca. 1913 Through a Looking-Glass
New York: Thomas Y. Crowell   John Tenniel; L. J. (Lewis Jesse)
                                                                Bridgman; Anonymous (after Tenniel); Charles Copeland
Handy-Volume Classics Series, Pocket Edition. Advertised in *PTLA* in 1913. Includes an introduction and critical notes according to *PTLA* but with no other details. See *MoM*, p. 144.

3863   ca. 1913–1920 Through the Looking-Glass
Philadelphia: Henry Altemus   After John Tenniel
Series No. 64: Children's Gift Series.

3864   ca. 1915 Through the Looking-Glass
Chicago: M. A. Donohue & Co.   John Tenniel
Fairy Library Series. Several issues. Light gray-yellow-brown cloth cover with White Knight in red and black. Black-and-white frontispiece of Trial scene on verso of front free endpaper.

3865   ca. 1915–1922 Through the Looking-Glass
Philadelphia: Henry Altemus   After John Tenniel
Series No. 82: Ever New Books for Young People Series. 4 color plates.

3866   [after 1915]   Through the Looking-Glass
Chicago: M. A. Donohue & Co.   John Tenniel
Fairy Library Series. Same as ca. 1915 edition, but black-and-white frontispiece of Alice and Red Queen on verso of front free endpaper.

3867   [after 1915]   Through the Looking-Glass
Chicago: M. A. Donohue & Co.   John Tenniel
Fairy Library Series. Pink dust jacket illustrated: front cover with playing children, back with ads for 25 titles in the Princess Series for Girls (*Alice* and *Looking-Glass* not listed). Olive-green, calico-grain cloth; front cover with red, black, and white fairy in heart-shaped decorative frame with red and white flowers at top; white lettering on cover and spine. Dust jacket and title page says, "*Alice Through the Looking-Glass*," but front cover and spine says, "*Through the Looking-Glass*." Another version exists but with illustrated endpapers.

3868 1916 Through the Looking-Glass

Philadelphia: E. Jacobs   Elenore Abbott

Franklin Classics Series. Sewell cites listing in the *Harcourt Amory Collection* at Harvard for 1916.

3869 1917 Through the Looking-Glass

Chicago; New York; London: Rand, McNally   Fanny Y. Cory

Canterbury Classics Series. Brown cloth stamped in dark brown lettering. Black-and-white photograph of Carroll as frontispiece. 1 black-and-white plate and 21 line drawings. The series bookplate is printed on the front paste-down. Introduction by Florence Milner. Includes a biographical sketch of Carroll, "Notes," "A Reading List," and "Suggestions to Teachers."

3870 ca. 1917–1923 Through the Looking-Glass

Chicago; New York: M. A. Donohue & Co.   After John Tenniel

Looking-Glass plus 6 stories from Arabian Nights' Entertainment. Dust jacket.

3871 ca. 1918 Through the Looking-Glass

Chicago: M. A. Donohue & Co.   John Tenniel

May-Pole Series, Yellow May-Pole Issue. Yellowish-brown cloth cover with title and author in decorative scroll frame, illustrated with 4 girls blocked in black and red dancing around a maypole. Black-and-white frontispiece (Alice and Sheep in boat); black-and-white illustrations. Other bindings known.

3872 [after 1918] Through the Looking-Glass

Chicago; New York: M. A. Donohue & Co.   John Tenniel

May-Pole Series. An abridged edition if the page count is correct. Light green, calico-grain cloth with black lettering and caricature of White Knight falling off horse. Verso of title page lists 6 titles in the Furry Folk Stories Series, *The Jungle Book*, and 3 titles in the Let's Make Believe Stories Series. Front cover says, "*Alice Through the Looking-Glass*," but title page says "*Through the Looking-Glass*."

3873 1919 Through the Looking-Glass

New York: Frederick A. Stokes   John Tenniel; Maria L. Kirk

Same as 1905 Stokes edition, but dust jacket with Alice in yellow dress on stairs. Back lists 9 titles in Fairy Series. One copy signed by Alice Hargreaves.

3874 1919 Through the Looking-Glass

New York: Grosset & Dunlap   John Tenniel

Series unknown. Recorded by Sewell as AT:GRD:5.01 with no description. Cites the *Harcourt Amory Collection*.

3875 1919 Through the Looking-Glass

Akron, OH; New York: Saalfield   John Tenniel

Medium brown cloth, blind-stamped vignette character playing flute in center, gilt lettering on front cover and spine. Colored frontispiece (Alice and Tweedles).

3876 1919 Through the Looking-Glass

Akron, OH; New York: Saalfield   John Tenniel

Unpaginated. No dust jacket. Glazed paper-covered boards, front cover illustrated with Alice in pink dress and Tweedles in blue and tan, landscape in brown and various shades of green. Black-and-white drawings.

3877 ca. 1920 Through the Looking-Glass

Philadelphia: Henry Altemus   After John Tenniel

Series unknown.

3878 ca. 1920s Through the Looking-Glass

New York: Little Leather Library   John Tenniel

Redcroft Edition. Limp green faux leather, rear embossed with "Little Leather Library" logo, below which is embossed "Redcroft Edition." Black-and-white illustrations.

3879   ca. 1920s   Through the Looking-Glass
Akron, OH; New York: Saalfield   John Tenniel
Every Child's Library Series. 1 color plate.

3880   1921   Through the Looking-Glass
New York: Grosset & Dunlap   John Tenniel
Series unknown. Recorded by Sewell as AT:GRD:5.02 with no description. Cites the *Harcourt Amory Collection*.

3881   1921   Through the Looking-Glass
New York; London: Harper and Brothers   Peter Newell
Imaginative Stories for Children Series. Black cloth cover with paper paste-on of Alice and White Queen. Color
frontispiece same as front cover; 39 plates.

3882   1922   Through the Looking-Glass
New York; London: Harper and Brothers   Peter Newell;
Harper's Young People's Series.   Robert Murray Wright
2 issues, both likely the same as the Popular Edition. One priced at 75 cents; the other, 90 cents.

3883   1924   Through the Looking-Glass
Philadelphia: E. Jacobs   Elenore Abbott
Franklin Classics Series.

3884   1924   Through the Looking-Glass
New York; London: Harper and Brothers   Peter Newell
Imaginative Stories for Children Series. Same as 1921 edition, but dust jacket with sheep knitting in boat on front
cover.

3885   1924   Through the Looking-Glass
New York: Harper and Brothers   Peter Newell
Wonderland Series, No. 2 of 10 titles. Series size reduced to 6 in 1934.

3886   ca. 1924–1934 Through the Looking-Glass
New York: Harper and Brothers   Peter Newell
Twilight Series, No. 5 of 10 titles.

3887   ca. 1925 Through the Looking-Glass
Philadelphia: Henry Altemus   After John Tenniel
Series No. 202: Altemus' Young People's Library Series. Pebbled grain green cloth.

3888   ca. 1925–1927 Through the Looking-Glass
Philadelphia: Henry Altemus   After John Tenniel
Series No. 186: Wee Books for Wee Folks. Very pale gray cloth.

3889   ca. 1925 Through the Looking-Glass
Cincinnati, OH: Johnson and Hardin   John Tenniel
Red cloth, gilt lettering. 2 black-and-white illustrations.

3890   ca. 1925 Through the Looking-Glass
Philadelphia: Macrae Smith Company   Elenore Abbott; John Tenniel
Franklin Classics Series. One of 10 titles in the series. At least 2 issues. Boards; blue calico-textured cloth cover with
paste-on of Alice tripping down stairs. 1 color plate and 50 black-and-white illustrations by Tenniel.

3891   [after 1925]   Through the Looking-Glass
Philadelphia: Macrae Smith Company   Elenore Abbott; John Tenniel
Same as ca. 1925, but frontispiece of Alice with White Knight in red armor.

3892   ca. 1926 Through the Looking-Glass
New York: Little Leather Library   John Tenniel
Miniature Edition, "Brown State." Brown limp faux leather.

3893   ca. 1928–1930 Through the Looking-Glass
Philadelphia: Henry Altemus   After John Tenniel
Series No. 186: Wee Books for Wee Folks. Green cloth.

3894   ca. 1928–1945 Through the Looking-Glass
Garden City, NY: Doubleday Classics   John Tenniel
Doubleday Classics Series. Blue dust jacket with Alice and Wonderland characters on the front cover, back cover with ad for 6 unnumbered titles in Doubleday Classics Series (*Looking-Glass* listed last). Boards; pale gray, plastic simulated cloth; Alice in central teal-blue circle surrounded by Wonderland characters and blue dots on cover, all characters reddish-brown. Color frontispiece (Knight); illustrations tinted blue-green.

3895   1929   Through the Looking-Glass
Philadelphia: David McKay   Frank Godwin; John Tenniel
McKay's Young People's Classics Series, No. 14 of 19 titles.

3896   1929   Through the Looking-Glass
Philadelphia; London: J. B. Lippincott   Gertrude A. Kay; John Tenniel
Stories All Children Love Series. Deep red cloth cover with Alice and White Queen; top edges orange. 8 color plates by Kay (including frontispiece) and 50 black-and-white drawings by Tenniel.

3897   ca. 1929 Through the Looking-Glass
Philadelphia: Henry Altemus   After John Tenniel
Adapted for Very Little Folks from the Original Story by Lewis Carroll. Purple pictorial boards backed in red cloth. Lovett 82.

3898   ca. 1929 Through the Looking-Glass
Akron, OH: Saalfield   John Tenniel
Easy-To-Read Series. Abridged; not paginated. Pictorial boards.

3899   1930   Alice Through the Looking-Glass and What Alice Found There
Chicago: Albert Whitman & Co.   After John Tenniel
The Illustrated $1.00 Classics Series. Green cloth, front with paper paste-on of Alice and Humpty Dumpty, lettering and decorations in gold-gilt, orange, and blue. Dust jacket front illustrated same as cover, rear lists 7 series titles, rear flap lists 6, *L-G* not listed in either. 221 numbered pp.; black-and-white drawings. Sewell AT:WHT:2.01; *WMGC*, p. 253.

3900   1930   Through the Looking-Glass
Philadelphia: David McKay   Frank Godwin; John Tenniel
McKay's Young People's Classics Series. Red cloth; front cover paste-on and frontispiece match.

3901   1930   Through the Looking-Glass
Springfield, MA: McLoughlin Brothers   John Tenniel

Young Folks Standard Library Series, No. 3228. Dust jacket illustrated in pink, green, and blue with title in black. Boards; gray-blue cloth. No frontispiece; black-and-white illustrations.

3902   ca. 1930 Through the Looking-Glass
New York: Little Leather Library   John Tenniel
Miniature Edition, "Red State." Limp red faux leather, gilt-stamped with "Miniature Library." 50 black-and-white illustrations. Binding variants known.

3903   ca. 1930s   Through the Looking-Glass
New York: Little Leather Library   John Tenniel
Miniature Edition, "Bronze State." Same as ca. 1930, but bronze wraps, rear embossed with "Little Leather Library" logo.

3904   ca. 1930s   Through the Looking-Glass
Chicago; New York: M. A. Donohue & Co.   John Tenniel
Front cover says, "*Alice Through the Looking-Glass*," but title page says, "*Through the Looking-Glass*."

3905   1931   Through the Looking-Glass
New York: Cheshire House   Franklin Hughes
Limited edition of 1,200 numbered copies. 8 color plates (including frontispiece). Silver-black foil covered slipcase. Glassine dust jacket. White silk covers with silver-gilt Red Queen on right lower corner. Designed and printed by Richard W. Ellis.

3906   1931   Through the Looking-Glass
Philadelphia: David McKay   Frank Godwin; John Tenniel
McKay's Young People's Classics Series. One of 18 titles in the series. Issued in dust jacket.

3907   ca. 1931–1932 Through the Looking-Glass
Philadelphia: Henry Altemus   After John Tenniel
Series No. 186: Wee Books for Wee Folks. Green cloth.

3908   ca. 1931–1940 Through the Looking-Glass
New York: Frederick A. Stokes   John Tenniel; Maria L. Kirk
Probably same as the 1919 Stokes edition.

3909   1935   Through the Looking-Glass
New York: Limited Editions Club   John Tenniel
Limited edition of 1,500 copies. Red cloth slipcase. Dark blue morocco leather boards, gilt lettering and decorations on covers and spine; plain cream endpapers. Hurlbut Special Paper, all edges gilt. Black-and-white drawings. Illustrations re-engraved on metal by Frederic Warde; book and cover fleuron designs by Warde. Introduction by Carl Van Doren. Alice P. Hargreaves (the original Alice) agreed to sign 1,150 copies for $2,250. She signed them on her only trip to the United States. This edition is a companion book to *Alice*, also signed. Signed copies of both *Alice* and *Looking-Glass* are frequently found on the market.

3910   ca. 1940 Through the Looking-Glass
Mount Vernon, NY: Peter Pauper   John Tenniel
Limited edition of 1,650 unnumbered copies. Gray-blue-green slipcase. Ivory paper-covered boards, front cover with floral pattern. Buckeye Text paper. Illustrations in green. One copy has an inscription dated 1940.

3911   ca. 1940 Through the Looking-Glass
Chicago; New York; London: Rand, McNally   Fanny Y. Cory
Canterbury Classics Series. Includes an 1876 Easter Greeting. 20 line drawings. Introduction to the series on pp. 5–6 by editor Katherine Lee Bates. 64 cents. There is confusion whether this is a 2nd 1917 edition or a ca. 1940 edition.

3912   1941   Through the Looking-Glass
New York: Heritage Press   John Tenniel
Light blue slipcase. Yellow cloth cover with bouquet of flowers in green and reddish-brown foil. Introduction by John T. Winterich.

3913   1943   Through the Looking-Glass
New York: Heritage Reprints   John Tenniel
Heritage Reprints Series. Same as 1941, but front cover and spine printed in green and blue.

3914   1944   Through the Looking-Glass
New York: Heritage Reprints   John Tenniel
Heritage Reprints Series. Same as 1941 but boxed with *Alice*.

3915   ca. 1945–1946 Through the Looking-Glass
New York; London: Whittlesey House, McGraw-Hill   John Tenniel
Dust jacket illustrated with Tweedles. Paper-covered boards backed with blue cloth. Shapes of chess pieces floating against a very pale blue background, front cover with title in black oval frame. Title page is light blue with black lettering; vignette of kitten playing with yarn.

3916   1947   Through the Looking-Glass
New York: Maxton   Marjorie Collison
Maxton Books for Little People, Classics Series Edition, No. 14. Abridged by Roselle Ross. Dust jacket. Green paper-covered boards backed with black, front cover with dancing Alice, back with list of 14 Little People Series titles. Color frontispiece (Lion and Unicorn); 22 illustrations.

3917   ca. 1947 Through the Looking-Glass
New York: Maxton   Marjorie Collison
Maxton Books for Little People, Classics Series Edition, No. 14. Abridged by Roselle Ross. Dust jacket. Green paper-covered boards backed with black, front cover with dancing Alice, back with list of 14 Little People Series titles. Color frontispiece (Lion and Unicorn); 22 illustrations.

3918   ca. 1947 Through the Looking-Glass
Mount Vernon, NY: Peter Pauper   John Tenniel
Collector's Edition Series. Plain red cloth-covered slipcase. Decorated paper-covered boards with chess figures in greenish blue and maroon. Type reset.

3919   [after 1947]   Through the Looking-Glass
New York: Maxton   Marjorie Collison
Same as 1947 edition, but [30] pp., 22 illustrations (10 color, 12 black-and-white).

3920   [after 1947]   Through the Looking-Glass
New York: Maxton   Marjorie Collison
Same as 1947, but [32] pp. and blue cloth spine.

3921   [after 1947]   Through the Looking-Glass
New York: Maxton   Marjorie Collison
Maxton Books for Little People, Classics Series. Same as 1947, but 22 illustrations (10 color, 12 black-and-white).

3922   [after 1947]   Through the Looking-Glass
New York: Maxton   Marjorie Collison
Maxton Books for Little People, Classics Series. Same as 1947, but [32] pp. and blue cloth spine.

3923   1949   Through the Looking-Glass
New York; London: Harper and Brothers   Peter Newell
Wonderland Series, No. 2. Pale blue dust jacket with Alice in boat with knitting sheep on front cover flowing onto
spine. Pale blue embossed, calico-grain textured cloth; front cover with Alice and Queens in red and black. Rear
cover lists 10 unnumbered titles in the Twilight Series (including *Alice* and *Looking-Glass*); front flap has brief
summary of the Wonderland Series.

3924   ca. 1950s   Through the Looking-Glass
Philadelphia: David McKay   Anonymous
McKay's Young People's Classics Series.

3925   ca. 1950s   Through the Looking-Glass
Garden City, NY: Junior Deluxe Editions   John Tenniel
Gray decorated paper-covered boards backed in blue cloth. A variant cover is known.

3926   ca. 1950s   Through the Looking-Glass
Garden City, NY: Junior Deluxe Editions   John Tenniel
Gray decorated paper-covered boards backed in blue cloth. A variant cover is known.

3927   ca. 1955 Through the Looking-Glass
Garden City, NY: Doubleday Junior Deluxe Editions   John Tenniel
Doubleday Junior Deluxe Series. Blue dust jacket with *Looking-Glass* characters. Many binding variants. Boards; pale
gray, plastic simulated-cloth cover with title in red decorative frame above with Alice holding cake between Lion
and Unicorn below in black, background of scattered red and black hearts. Color frontispiece (White Knight); other
illustrations tinted red, many full-page.

3928   1956   Through the Looking-Glass
N.P.: L. Melnick   L. Melnick
Boards. Handwritten and illustrated by Melnick; one of a kind.

3929   ca. 1957 Through the Looking-Glass
Garden City, NY: Doubleday   John Tenniel
Junior Deluxe Edition. Same as ca. 1955, but with endpapers with literary characters printed in red and illustrations in blue.

3930   ca. 1950s–1960s   Through the Looking-Glass
Boston: International Pocket Library   John Tenniel
No. 20 of 20 titles in the series. Illustrated paper wraps, IPL logo and lettering within mirror on both wraps and
spine. Verso of title page says, "First printing 10,000 copies."

3931   ca. 1960s   Through the Looking-Glass
White Plains, NY: Peter Pauper   John Tenniel
Same as ca. 1947, but illustrations printed in dark green.

3932   1961   Through the Looking-Glass and The Hunting of the Snark
Garden City, NY: Doubleday   John Tenniel; Henry Holiday
Dolphin Books Series. Includes *The Hunting of the Snark*.

3933   ca. 1963 Alice Through the Looking-Glass
New York; Des Moines, IA: Duell, Sloan, and Pearce   Libico Maraja
Splendor Book Series. The Meredith Press Issue, made and printed in Milan, Italy, by Fratelli Fabbri Editori ©1959.
Glossy illustrated paper-covered boards. 105 illustrations and vignettes. Facing title page is a list of 8 titles, including
Looking-Glass, in the Splendor Book Series. Lovett 353 dates the book to 1963 and calls it "the First American edition."
Lovett says the illustrations were 1st published in London by W. H. Allen in 1959.

3934   1965   Through the Looking-Glass
New York: Random House   John Tenniel
Centennial Edition. Beige paper-covered slipcase with pictorial label, shared with *Alice*. Decorated paper-covered boards backed in red cloth. Front cover with wavy vertical green and purple lines. Black-and-white illustrations.

3935   1966   Through the Looking-Glass
Ann Arbor, MI: Xerox, University Microfilms   John Tenniel
Legacy Library Series. Facsimile of the 1880 Macmillan edition. Boards; beige cloth with gilt "Alice with crown" against blue background on front cover. 25 illustrations tinted in teal blue; 25 in rust. Guiliano states there are "blue and white or brown and white illustrations," implying there may be other issues.

3936   ca. 1966 Through the Looking-Glass
Mount Vernon, NY: Peter Pauper   John Tenniel
Red illustrated slipcase with paper label. Decorated paper-covered boards with vertical bands of card suits and *Looking-Glass* characters in black, blue, and light green; vellum paper with top edges blue, larger leaf. Illustrations tinted blue. Title page has "swelled rule" between lines 2 and 3.

3937   ca. 1966 Through the Looking-Glass
White Plains, NY: Peter Pauper   John Tenniel
The ca. 1966 edition [Lovett 102a] was published in a 2-volume boxed set with *Alice* and in shared red slipcase with decorative label.

3938   ca. 1970s   Through the Looking-Glass
Garden City, NY: Junior Deluxe Editions   John Tenniel
Red and beige paper-covered boards.

3939   ca. 1974–1975   Through the Looking-Glass
New York: Avenel Books   John Tenniel
Glossy brown paper-covered boards, front cover with Alice climbing through mirror. Gold decorations on front cover and spine. Clear plastic dust jacket.

3940   1977   The Wasp in a Wig: The Suppressed Episode of Through the Looking-Glass and What
                Alice Found There
New York: Lewis Carroll Society of North America   Unillustrated
Introduction and notes by Martin Gardner. Carroll Studies No. 2. Pp. xiv + 21 + [14]. Paperback. First publication. Includes a fold-out facsimile of the galley proofs of the episode. See Edward Guiliano's essay in Volume One for complete details.

3941   1977   Through the Looking-Glass
New York: St. Martin's   9780312803742   John Tenniel
Glossy white dust jacket with Alice and a Tweedle. Boards; green cloth cover with black lettering and rules, illustrated at top in red and black with Alice in semi-circle flanked by White Rabbit and Hatter; blue pastel endpapers illustrated with Wonderland characters. [16] color plates, including frontispiece.

3942   [not after 1980]Through the Looking-Glass
Cleveland, OH: World Publishing   John Tenniel
Boards. World Publishing was sold to Collins Publishing in 1980, and they sold off the parts.

3943   ca. 1980s   Through the Looking-Glass
New York: Avenel Books   John Tenniel
6th issue.

3944   ca. 1980s   Through the Looking-Glass
New York: Avenel Books/Barre Publishing   0517118076   John Tenniel
10th issue. Green faux leather. Black-and-white illustrations.

3945   1981   Through the Looking-Glass
New York: Random House   John Tenniel; Fritz Kredel
Reprint of the Special Edition of 1946, but without slipcase. "Jabberwocky" correctly printed mirror image on p. 17.
Dated by inscription. Tenniel illustrations colored by Fritz Kredel.

3946   1982   Through the Looking-Glass
Tarzana, CA: Barbara J. Raheb   John Tenniel
Miniature book. No. 89 of 300 copies. Handbound in red leather. Black-and-white illustrations.

3947   1982   Lewis Carroll's Through the Looking-Glass
West Hatfield, MA: Pennyroyal   Barry Moser
Sesquicentennial Limited Edition of 350 copies. Gray cloth box with red morocco spine, gilt lettering and rulings.
Boards; gray cloth with morocco spine, gilt lettering and lines. Specially made Strathmore paper. 95 wood engravings
and embellishments. Includes blue cloth chemise, which contains a suite of the 91 illustrations from the text, signed
in pencil by Moser. An additional unique original illustration on tracing paper titled and signed by Moser included.
Preface and notes by James R. Kincaid. Selwyn H. Goodacre, editor. Hand-numbered; signed by artist. Printed by
Harold McGrath; bound by Gray Parrot.

3948   1983   Lewis Carroll's Through the Looking-Glass
Berkeley, CA; Los Angeles;   520050396   Barry Moser
London: University of California Press
University of California Press Regular Edition. Dust jacket. 95 wood engravings, some in color. Preface and notes by
James R. Kincaid. Selwyn H. Goodacre, editor. Essay by Barry Moser especially for this edition.

3949   1983   Lewis Carroll's Through the Looking-Glass
Berkeley, CA; Los Angeles; London: University of California Press   Barry Moser
University of California Press. Deluxe Edition. Blue fabric slipcase containing 2 bindings, one of *Looking-Glass*,
and the other a copy of *Snark* in blue paper dust jacket with embossed "Snark" slipped into the binding. 95 wood
engravings, some in color. Preface and notes by James R. Kincaid. Selwyn H. Goodacre, editor. Essay by Barry Moser
especially for this edition. *Snark* has an ISBN of 0520051386, but there is no ISBN in the *Looking-Glass* volume.

3950   1983   Through the Looking-Glass
Berkeley, CA; Los Angeles;   9780520050396   Barry Moser
London: University of California Press
University of California combined edition of *Looking-Glass* and *Snark*. Same as University of California Press
Regular Edition but boxed with *Snark*.

3951   1984   Through the Looking-Glass
New York: Alfred A. Knopf   John Tenniel
A facsimile of the London 1872 1st edition. Red cloth stamped in gold. Included in a slipcase with *Alice* facsimile of
London 1866 edition. With a pamphlet by Michael Hancher titled "On the Writing, Illustration and Publication of
Lewis Carroll's *Alice* Books."

3952   ca. 1985   Through the Looking-Glass
White Plains, NY: Peter Pauper   9780880889919   John Tenniel
Similar to Lovett 102a (ca. 1966) edition, but beige slipcase, illustrated dust jacket, and paper-covered boards.

3953   1986   Through the Looking-Glass
New York: Ariel Books / Alfred A. Knopf   9780394532288   S. Michelle Wiggins
A Borzoi Book published by Alfred A. Knopf, Inc. Dust jacket. Boards; turquoise cloth. 60 color illustrations.

3954   1986   Through the Looking-Glass
New York: Exeter Books   9780671086286   John Tenniel; Julia Christie
Distributed by Bookthrift Marketing, Inc., produced by Octopus Books Ltd. Glossy pink paper-covered boards.
Black-and-white illustrations. Cover by Julia Christie.

3955   [not after 1980] Through the Looking-Glass
Cleveland, OH: World Publishing   John Tenniel
Boards. World Publishing was sold to Collins Publishing in 1980, and they sold off the parts.

3956   1990   Through the Looking-Glass
New York: Children's Classics (Dilithium)   9780517033463   John Tenniel; Bessie Pease
                                                                          Gutmann; Milo Winter; Elenore Abbott
Distributed by Outlet Book Company, Random House Value Publishing. Glossy red paper-covered boards, black
faux-leather cloth spine, Gutmann illustrations on both covers, tailbands, 186 numbered pp., free edges deckle, wide
green decorative border surrounds text, free edges deckle, 8 full-page color illustrations on coated paper (one on each
side of 4 non-integral leaves). Foreword by Ellen S. Shapiro.

3957   1990   Through the Looking-Glass
New York: Putnam Berkley   9780425120224   Kyle Baker
Classics Illustrated, No. 3. Abridged. Glossy paper wraps, cover with multi-colored Alice and Humpty Dumpty. Color
comic panel illustrations.

3958   1991   Through the Looking-Glass
Norwalk, CT: Easton Press   John Tenniel
1st edition. Boards; full black leather, gilt lettering and decorations, vignette on front cover with Alice and Red Queen
in red and gilt; silk page-marker; moire endpapers. Gilt edges.

3959   1991   Through the Looking-Glass
New York: St. Martin's   9780312803742   John Tenniel
Reprint of the 1977 St. Martin's Press edition.

3960   1992   Little Treasury of Alice in Wonderland
New York: Derrydale   9780517067208   Rene Cloke
Retold by Jane Carruth. Miniature 6-volume boxed set.

3961   1993   Through the Looking-Glass
New York: William Morrow   9780688120498   John Tenniel; Paul O. Zelinsky
Books of Wonder Series, No. 5A2. Dust jacket with Alice and Humpty Dumpty on front cover, 5 vignettes of
Wonderland characters on back. Boards; teal blue cloth, silver-gilt triple-rule borders on both covers, silver-gilt
lettering on spine. Illustrations reproduced from original woodblocks. Notes by Peter Glassman.

3962   ca. 1993 Through the Looking-Glass
New York: Avenel Books   John Tenniel

3963   ca. 1993 Through the Looking-Glass
New York: Avenel Books   John Tenniel
Leather binding.

3964   1995   Through the Looking-Glass and What Alice Found There
Norwalk, CT: Easton Press   John Tenniel
Collector's Library of Famous Editions. Limited unnumbered edition. Boards; full black leather, gilt lettering and
decorations on both covers and spine, vignette on front cover with Alice and Red Queen in red and gilt; gold silk
page-marker; rust moire endpapers. Printed in black, page numbers and illustrations with blue borders on cream
white acid-free paper with vellum finish, specially milled, all edges gilt. Black-and-white illustrations printed by
Frederic Warde from originals engraved in metal.

3965   1997   Through the Looking-Glass
Los Angeles: LRS (Library Reproduction Service)   9781581180077   John Tenniel
LRS Large Print Heritage Series. Published by the Thorndike Press. Some copies illustrated by John Tenniel.

3966   1999   Through the Looking-Glass
New York: Adegi Graphics   9780543900562   John Tenniel
Elibron Classics.

3967   1999   Through the Looking-Glass
Mineola, NY: Dover Publications   9780486408781   John Tenniel
Dover Thrift Editions.

3968   2001   Through the Looking-Glass
Franklin, TN: Dalmatian Press   9781577599395   Jason Alexander
1st Dalmatian Press Children's Classic Collection Series Edition, 1st issue. Abridged by Debbie Guthery. Glossy
paper-covered boards, cover with Red Queen prominent in foreground and Wonderland characters in background.

3969   ca. 2001 Through the Looking-Glass
New York; London: Bloomsbury   9781582341750   Mervyn Peake
1st American Edition, 1st issue. Distributed by St. Martin's Press; printed in Italy by Artegrafica S.p.A., Verona, Italy.
Illustrated dust jacket. Boards; white cloth, gilt lettering on spine; silver silk ribbon page-marker, purple-and-white
head- and tailbands, 200 numbered pp. Introduction by Zadie Smith.

3970   2002   Through the Looking-Glass
New York: HarperFestival   9780694015818   John Tenniel
Charming Classics.

3971   2003   Through the Looking-Glass
Franklin, TN: Dalmatian Press   9781577599395   Jason Alexander
Dalmatian Press Children's Classic Collection Series Edition, 3rd issue. Same pagination and binding as 2001 1st
issue. Abridged by Debbie Guthery.

3972   2003   Through the Looking-Glass
Waterville, ME: Thorndike Press   9780786256570 (hardcover); John Tenniel
                                            9780786264544 (paperback)
Hardcover, dust jacket. Large print. Issued 2004 in paper wraps, front with Alice reclining in chair with Dinah.

3973   2004   Through the Looking-Glass
Fairfield, IA: 1st World Publishing   9781595401069   Unknown
1st World Library Literary Society Series Edition, 1st issue. Glossy paper wraps, wide red border with flags, front with
pale-tan central area with title and author, 140 numbered pp., black-and-white illustrations.

3974   2004   Through the Looking-Glass
Whitefish, MT: Kessinger Publishing   9781419190049   John Tenniel
Glossy yellow paper wraps, front with darker hue diagonal feather, title and author lettered black, 100 numbered pp.
Facsimile reprint of 1899 Hurst issue.

3975   2005   Through the Looking-Glass
Fairfield, IA: 1st World Publishing   9781421806563   Unknown
1st World Library Literary Society Series Edition, 2nd issue. Hardbound, same front cover design, dust jacket, 140
pp., black-and-white illustrations.

3976   2005   Alice Through the Looking-Glass
Cambridge, MA: Candlewick Press   9780763628925 (hardback)   Helen Oxenbury
                                            9780763642624 (paperback)
1st American Edition, 1st Issue. Red paper-covered boards, front with Alice and White Queen; dust jacket illustrated
same; 224 numbered pp.; color illustrations, many full-page and some gatefold. Issued in paper wraps 2009.

3977   2006   Through the Looking-Glass
North Hollywood, CA: Aegypan Press   9781598182217   Unknown
Hardcover. Print-on-demand book. 124 numbered pp.

3978   2006   Through the Looking-Glass
Las Vegas, NV: ICON Group International   9780497252946   Unknown
Print-on-demand book. Webster's Thesaurus Edition; 168 numbered pp. An "educational edition" with the bottom of
each page annotated with a mini-thesaurus of uncommon words highlighted in the text.

3979   2007   Through the Looking-Glass
North Hollywood, CA: Aegypan Press   9781598186291   Unknown
Print-on-demand book. 124 numbered pp. Paper wraps.

3980   2007   Through the Looking-Glass
Scituate, MA: DSI (Digital Scanning Incorporated)   9781582187938 (hardcover); John Tenniel
                                                     9781582187921 (paperback)
Print-on-demand book. This is a digital facsimile of an undated McLoughlin Brothers edition. Glossy black paper-
covered boards, Trial on front cover, 132 numbered pp. Black-and-white illustrations. Also issued in paper wraps.

3981   2007   Through the Looking-Glass
Whitefish, MT: Kessinger Publishing   9780548781463   John Tenniel
Later issue of 2004 Whitefish facsimile reprint in paper wraps.

3982   2007   Through the Looking-Glass
Rockville, MD: Wildside Press   9781434492760 (paperback); John Tenniel
                                           9781434492777 (hardcover)
Print-on-demand book. Facsimile reprint of the 1872 edition.

3983   2008   Through the Looking-Glass
Whitefish, MT: Kessinger Publishing   9781436578479   John Tenniel
Facsimile reprint of 1899 Hurst issue, 192 pp. Issued as hardcover, in paper wraps, or as downloadable PDF/Epub.
Print versions with white covers, title and author in black, tops and bottoms with waves of color.

3984   2008   Through the Looking-Glass
New York: Papercutz   9781597071154   Unknown
Classics Illustrated, No. 3. Graphic novel adapted by Kyle Baker.

3985   2009   Through the Looking-Glass
[Charleston, SC]: BiblioLife   978113482280 (paperback); Unknown
                                           9781113482303 (hardcover)
Print-on-demand books. Paper wraps.

3986   2009   Through the Looking-Glass
North Charleston, SC: Chartwell Books   9780785825722   Unknown
In dust jacket.

3987   2009   Through the Looking-Glass
North Charleston, SC: CreateSpace   9781449915995   John Tenniel
Print-on-demand book. 1st issue, September 9, 2009. White paper wraps, front with small drawing of Alice emerging
from mirror, 104 pp., black-and-white drawings.

3988   2009   Through the Looking-Glass
North Charleston, SC: CreateSpace   9781449915995   John Tenniel

Print-on-demand book. 2nd issue, November 24, 2009. White paper wraps, front with small drawing of Alice emerging from mirror, 104 pages; black-and-white drawings.

3989   2009   Through the Looking-Glass
North Charleston, SC: CreateSpace   9781503267206   Unillustrated
Print-on-demand book. 1st issue, September 2009. Paper wraps, front similar to that of Wm. Morrow's Books of Wonder.

3990   2009   Through the Looking-Glass
North Charleston, SC: CreateSpace   9781448654178   Unillustrated
Print-on-demand book. Edited by Tom Thomas. 1st issue, July 2009. Paper wraps.

3991   2009   Through the Looking-Glass
Atlanta, GA: Piggy Toes / Dalmatian Press   9781615242504   Jason Alexander
1st Piggy Toes Great Classics for Children Series Edition, 1st issue. Abridged by Debbie Guthery. Glossy paper-covered boards, maroon faux leather spine with gilt lettering and decorations, both covers illustrated with Alice and cards. Many black-and-white illustrations. Published by a Dalmatian Press subsidiary.

3992   2010   Through the Looking-Glass
Whitefish, MT: Kessinger Publishing   9781164256403   John Tenniel
Print-on-demand book. Legacy Reprint Series. Glossy paper wraps, 189 numbered pp. Facsimile of the 1899 Hurst issue.

3993   2010   Through the Looking-Glass
Charleston, SC: Nabu Press   9781142745264   Unknown
Print-on-demand book. Paper wraps.

3994   2010   Through the Looking-Glass
Atlanta, GA: Piggy Toes / Dalmatian Press   9781615242504   Jason Alexander
Piggy Toes Great Classics for Children Series Edition, 2nd issue. Abridged by Debbie Guthery. Glossy paper-covered boards, maroon faux leather spine with gilt lettering and decorations, both covers illustrated with Alice and cards. Many black-and-white illustrations. Published by a Dalmatian Press subsidiary.

3995   2010   Through the Looking-Glass
Atlanta, GA: Dalmation Press / Piggy Toes   9781615242504   Jason Alexander
2nd issue of the 2009 edition. Great Classics for Children Series. Abridged by Debbie Guthery. Published by a Dalmatian Press subsidiary.

3996   2010   Through the Looking-Glass
Vancleave, MS: Ramble House (Lulu.com)   9781605434339   Gavin L. O'Keefe
Print-on-demand book. Glossy black and orange dust jacket. Blue cloth, gilt lettered spine, white head and tailbands. Black-and-white illustrations. Also issued in glossy black and orange paper wraps. Paper wraps.

3997   2011   Through the Looking-Glass
North Charleston, SC: Dunda Books   9781466322103   Unillustrated
Dunda Books Classic. Carroll misspelled as "Carrol."

3998   2012   Through the Looking-Glass
North Charleston, SC: CreateSpace   9781470156343   Unillustrated
Print-on-demand book. Issued March 2, 2012. The Millenium Fulcrum Edition. Gray-splatter paper wraps. 58 pp.

3999   2012   Through the Looking-Glass
North Charleston, SC: CreateSpace   9781475033953   Unillustrated
Print-on-demand books. Issued March 15, 2012. Birch Tree Publishing Edition. Paper wraps.

4000   2012   Through the Looking-Glass
North Charleston, SC: CreateSpace   9781478219705   Unillustrated
Print-on-demand books. Issued July 10, 2012. Paper wraps. 112 numbered pp. Edited by Tom Thomas. Paper wraps.

4001   2012   Through the Looking-Glass
North Charleston, SC: CreateSpace   9781479227495   Unillustrated
Print-on-demand book. Issued September 1, 2012. Black paper wraps; 116 pp.

4002   2012   Through the Looking-Glass
Franklin, TN: Dalmatian Press   9781453055489   Jason Alexander
1st Junior Classics for Young Readers Edition, 1st issue. Glossy paper wraps, front with Alice in Garden of Flowers. 182 numbered pp. Adapted by Debbie Guthery.

4003   2012   Through the Looking-Glass
North Charleston, SC: Dover Publications   9781306335591   Unknown
E-book version of Dover Thrift Editions.

4004   2012   Through the Looking-Glass
North Charleston, SC: Lulu.com   9781365029271   Unillustrated
Print-on-demand book. Paper wraps.

4005   2012   Through the Looking-Glass
[Memphis, TN]: Rare-booksclub.com   9781151382351   Unknown

4006   2013   Through the Looking-Glass
North Charleston, SC: CreateSpace   9781482629989   Unillustrated
Print-on demand book. Book 2 in *Alice in Wonderland* Series. Edited by Wayne Black. Glossy black paper wraps, front with Jabberwock, 64 pp. Issued February 24, 2013.

4007   2013   Through the Looking-Glass
North Charleston, SC: CreateSpace   9781491054666   Unillustrated
Print-on-demand book. Edited by Elaine Mclean. Glossy purple paper wraps, front illustrated with circular black-and-white Tea Party, 128 numbered pp. Issued August 3, 2013.

4008   2013   Through the Looking-Glass
North Charleston, SC: CreateSpace   9781493626731   Unknown
Print-on-demand book. 1st Large Print Edition. 1st issue, October 30, 2013. Paper wraps, front with Alice reclining in chair with Dinah, 192 numbered pp.

4009   2013   Through the Looking-Glass
North Charleston, SC: CreateSpace   9781494308391   Unillustrated
Print-on-demand book. Issued October 30, 2013. Glossy white paper wraps, front with black-and-white White Knight. 82 numbered pp.

4010   2013   Through the Looking-Glass
North Charleston, SC: CreateSpace   9781494308643   Unillustrated
Print-on-demand book. 2nd issue, November 28, 2013. Glossy white paper wraps, front with black-and-white White Knight, 82 numbered pp.

4011   2013   Through the Looking-Glass
North Charleston, SC: CreateSpace   9781494315160   Unknown
Print-on-demand book. Large print edition. 2nd issue, November 29, 2013. Front cover with an older Alice in bright blue sweater. Paper wraps.

4012   2013   Through the Looking-Glass

North Charleston, SC: CreateSpace ;   9781494810313   Unillustrated
Blacksburg, VA: SaltHeart Publishers LLC
Print-on-demand book. Glossy white paper wraps, front with black-and-white "scrambled" chessboard. 100 numbered pp. Published December 26, 2013.

4013   2013   Alice Through the Looking-Glass

North Charleston, SC: Interactive Media   9781909676367   Unknown
E-book. Edited by Max Bollinger. Available through Hoopla Digital.

4014   2013   Through the Looking-Glass

Charleston, SC: Nabu Press   9781287770435   John Tenniel
Primary Source Edition.

4015   2013   Through the Looking-Glass

New York: Start Publishing   9781627937849   Unknown
E-book. Start Classics Series.

4016   2013   Through the Looking-Glass

Orem, UT: Western Standard Publishing Company   9781631453205   John Tenniel
E-book.

4017   2014   Through the Looking-Glass

Ashland, OH: Bendon   9781453084823   Jason Alexander
Junior Classics for Young Readers Series. Abridged by Debbie Guthery. Dark orange paper wraps, illustrated in red, white, and black.

4018   2014   Through the Looking-Glass

North Charleston, SC: Classic Comic Store   9781681000336   John Tenniel
Issue 147. Electronic graphic novel. Available through Hoopla Digital.

4019   2014   Through the Looking-Glass

North Charleston, SC: CreateSpace   9781499583076   Unknown
Print-on-demand book. There were many more 2014 editions. Issued February 7, May 16, and October 24, 2014.

4020   2014   Through the Looking-Glass

Minneapolis, MN: First Avenue Editions   9781467757546;   Unknown
E-book. First Avenue Classics.

4021   2014   Through the Looking-Glass

North Charleston, SC: Pulpville Press   9780615957906   Unillustrated
Pulpville Press is an imprint of Fiction House Press.

4022   2015   Through the Looking-Glass

North Charleston, SC: CreateSpace   9781507613856   Unillustrated
Print-on-demand book. Paper wraps. Issued January 7, 2015.

4023   2015   Through the Looking-Glass

North Charleston, SC: CreateSpace   9781514200711   Unillustrated
Print-on-demand book. Paper wraps.

4024   2015   Through the Looking-Glass

North Charleston, SC: CreateSpace   9781506090078   John Tenniel
Print-on-demand book. Illustrated. Paper wraps.

4025   2015   Through the Looking-Glass
North Charleston, SC: CreateSpace   9781508486541   John Tenniel
Print-on-demand book. Illustrated. Issued February 15, 2015. Paper wraps.

4026   2015   Through the Looking-Glass
North Charleston, SC: CreateSpace   9781517718312   Unillustrated
Print-on-demand book. Issued October 8, 2015. Paper wraps.

4027   2015   Through the Looking-Glass
[New York]: Diversion Books   9781682301265   S. Michelle Wiggins
E-book. Diversion Classics.

4028   2015   Through the Looking-Glass
New York: Open Road Integrated Media   9781497677166   Unknown
E-book.

4029   2015   Through the Looking-Glass
Seattle, WA: Palala Press   9781340842345   Unknown
Print-on-demand book. Issued September 1, 2015. Paper wraps.

4030   2015   Through the Looking-Glass
Seattle, WA: Palala Press   9781341361296   Unillustrated
Issued September 3, 2015. Paper wraps.

4031   2015   Through the Looking-Glass
Seattle, WA: Palala Press   9781347311479   John Tenniel
Issued December 4, 2015. Paper wraps

4032   2015   Through the Looking-Glass
Sacramento, CA.: Sagwan Press   9781298918468   John Tenniel
Print-on-demand book. Scholar Select Series. Hardback, black covers, 224 pp. First published August 21, 2015.

4033   2015   Through the Looking-Glass
Sacramento, CA: Sagwan Press   9781298952363   Unknown
Print-on-demand book. Scholar Select Series. 2nd printing issued August 22, 2015. Hardback, black covers, 326 pp.

4034   2015   Through the Looking-Glass
Sacramento, CA: Sagwan Press   9781340081881   Unknown
Print-on-demand book. Scholar Select Series. 3rd printing issued August 23, 2015. Hardback, black covers, 258 pp.

4035   2015   Through the Looking-Glass
North Charleston, SC: St. Paul Press / CreateSpace   9781519573001   Unknown
Print-on-demand book.

4036   2016   Through the Looking-Glass
San Diego: Classroom Complete Press   9781771676229   Unknown
Literature Kit for Grades 5–6. Adapted by Chad Ibbotson. Features reading comprehension and vocabulary questions.

4037   2016   Through the Looking-Glass
North Charleston, SC: CreateSpace   9781535247870   John Tenniel
Print-on-demand books. Issued January 7, 2016. Many 2016 issues, each with a different ISBN even when published only a few days apart. Some are listed here.

4038   2016   Through the Looking-Glass
North Charleston, SC: CreateSpace   9781523440931   Unknown
Print-on-demand book. Issued January 17, 2016.

4039   2016   Through the Looking-Glass
North Charleston, SC: CreateSpace   9781530256785   Unknown
Print-on-demand book. Issued February 26, 2016.

4040   2016   Through the Looking-Glass
North Charleston, SC: CreateSpace   9781530589036   Unknown
Print-on-demand book. Issued March 17, 2016.

4041   2016   Through the Looking-Glass
North Charleston, SC: CreateSpace   9781533206558   Peter Newell
Print-on-demand book. Issued May 14, 2016.

4042   2016   Through the Looking-Glass
North Charleston, SC: CreateSpace   9781533304551   Unknown
Print-on-demand book. Issued May 17, 2016.

4043   2016   Through the Looking-Glass
North Charleston, SC: CreateSpace   9781530256785   Peter Newell
Providence Books Edition. Print-on-demand book. Issued May 18, 2016.

4044   2016   Through the Looking-Glass
North Charleston, SC: CreateSpace   9781534875203   Unknown
Print-on-demand book. Issued June 24, 2016. Edited by Angel Sanchez.

4045   2016   Through the Looking-Glass
North Charleston, SC: CreateSpace   9781535075879   Unknown
Print-on-demand book. Issued July 3, 2016.

4046   2016   Through the Looking-Glass
North Charleston, SC: CreateSpace   9781536817553   Peter Newell
Print-on-demand book. Issued July 30, 2016.

4047   2016   Through the Looking-Glass
San Bernardino, CA: CreateSpace   9781533557124   John Tenniel
Print-on-demand book. Issued September 1, 2016.

4048   2016   Through the Looking-Glass
North Charleston, SC: CreateSpace   9781539974512   Unknown
Print-on-demand book. Issued November 10, 2016. Includes audiobook.

4049   2016   Through the Looking-Glass
North Charleston, SC: CreateSpace   9781540414830   Unknown
Print-on-demand book. Issued November 15, 2016. Edited by Paula Benitez.

4050   2016   Through the Looking-Glass
North Charleston, SC: CreateSpace   9781540547453   Unknown
Print-on-demand book. Issued November 21, 2016.

4051   2016   Alice Through the Looking-Glass

Glendale, CA: Disney Press   9781484729595   Walt Disney Company

Retold by Kari Sutherland. Red cloth boards, black cloth spine, front with paper paste-on of (very) mature Alice; no dust jacket; 299 numbered pp., free edges deckle; color illustrations. Adaptation based on the Linda Woolverton screenplay for the 2013 Disney motion picture directed by Johnny Depp.

4052   2016   **Through the Looking-Glass**

Glendale, CA: Disney Press   9781484729601   Walt Disney Company

Retold by Carla Jablonski. Color illustrations.

4053   2016   **Through the Looking-Glass**

Glendale, CA: Disney Press   9781484729595   Walt Disney Company

Retold by Linda Woolverton.

4054   2016   **Alice Through the Looking-Glass**

North Charleston, SC: Lulu.com   9781365029196   Unknown

Print-on-demand book.

4055   2016   **Through the Looking-Glass**

Seattle, WA: Palala Press   9781355299660   Unknown

Issued May 3, 2016. Adapted/edited by Florence Milner.

4056   2016   **Through the Looking-Glass**

North Charleston, SC: Providence Books / CreateSpace 9781533321213   Unknown

Print-on-demand book. Issued May 18, 2016.

4057   2016   **Through the Looking-Glass**

San Bernardino, CA: CreateSpace   9781533557124   John Tenniel

Print-on-demand book. Paper wraps, 146 pp. Issued June 1, 2016.

4058   2016   **Looking-Glass House: The Lost Manuscript of Through the Looking-Glass**

[Los Angeles]: Roverzone Press   9780692704721   Daniel Rover Singer

Imagines the rough draft of Carroll's 1871 sequel to *Alice's Adventures in Wonderland* in Carroll's meticulous handwriting, with more than 30 pen-and-ink illustrations that replicate Carroll's artistic and handwriting style. Text is an abridgement of the original. Illustrations by Daniel Rover Singer, book adapted by Jonathan David Dixon, book design by Andrew Ogus, and editorial oversight by Mark Burstein.

4059   2016   **Through the Looking-Glass**

New York: Scholastic Inc.   9780545933551   John Tenniel; Jill Howarth

1st paper wraps edition of Scholastic's First Avenue Classics series. Glossy green paper wraps, front with Alice and Red Queen; 197 numbered pp.; black-and-white illustrations. Jill Howarth credited for cover illustration but Alice's face quite like that repeatedly drawn by Mary Blair for Disney.

4060   2017   **Through the Looking-Glass**

North Charleston, SC: CreateSpace   9781546659198   John Tenniel

Print-on-demand book. 1st Page Classics Series. Paper wraps, unabridged.

4061   2017   **Through the Looking-Glass**

North Charleston, SC: CreateSpace   9781542329736   Unknown

Print-on-demand book. Classical Book Series. January 5, 2017. Paper wraps.

4062   2017   **Through the Looking-Glass**

North Charleston, SC: CreateSpace   9781544984797   Unillustrated

Print-on-demand book. Issued March 28, 2017. Vintage Edition. Bestsellers: Classic Books Series. 80 pp. Paper wraps.

4063	2017	Through the Looking-Glass		
	North Charleston, SC: CreateSpace	9781545406687	Unknown	
	Print-on-demand book. Issued April 16, 2017. 110 pp. Paper wraps.			

4064	2017	Through the Looking-Glass		
	North Charleston, SC: CreateSpace	9781545500132	Unknown	
	Print-on-demand book. Issued April 20, 2017. RGV Classic Series. 110 pp. Paper wraps.			

4065	2017	Through the Looking-Glass		
	North Charleston, SC: CreateSpace	9781548683382	Unillustrated	
	Print-on-demand book. Issued July 7, 2017. 88 pp. Paper wraps.			

4066	2017	Through the Looking-Glass		
	North Charleston, SC: CreateSpace	9781973728474	Unillustrated	
	Print-on-demand book. Issued July 20, 2017. Paper wraps.			

4067	2017	Through the Looking-Glass		
	North Charleston, SC: CreateSpace	9781974502653	Unknown	
	Print-on-demand book. Issued August 14, 2017. Paper wraps.			

4068	2017	Through the Looking-Glass		
	North Charleston, SC: CreateSpace	9781976234767	Unknown	
	Print-on-demand book. Issued September 10, 2017. 86 pp. Paper wraps.			

4069	2017	Through the Looking-Glass		
	North Charleston, SC: CreateSpace	9781979762540	Unknown	
	Print-on-demand book. Issued November 20, 2017. Albrite Classics Edition. Down the Rabbit Hole Series. 268 pp. Paper wraps.			

4070	2017	Through the Looking-Glass		
	North Charleston, SC: CreateSpace	9781979943734	Unillustrated	
	Print-on-demand book. Millennium Fulcrum Edition 1.7. Issued November 21, 2017. Adapted/edited by David Widger. 164 pp. Paper wraps.			

4071	2017	Through the Looking-Glass		
	Mineola, NY: Dover Publications	9780486819242	John Tenniel	
	Dover Evergreen Classics. Paperback. Reprinted in 2018.			

4072	2017	Through the Looking-Glass		
	Los Angeles, CA: Enhanced Media Publishing	9781365996641	Unknown	
	83 pp.			

4073	2017	European Classics: The Lighter Side		
	Solon, OH: Findaway World, LLC	9781509456352	Various	
	Electronic text of numerous novels, including *Through the Looking-Glass*.			

4074	2017	Through the Looking-Glass		
	North Charleston, SC: Lulu.com	9781365997341	Unknown	
	Print-on-demand book.			

4075	2017	Lewis Carroll's Through the Looking-Glass		
	Gainesville, FL: Moth House Press	9780999532508	Maggie Taylor	
	Deluxe Signed Limited Edition of 100. The standard edition was published in 2018. This edition is housed in a brown cloth Solander box and comes with original archival print hand numbered and signed by the artist.			

4076   2017   Through the Looking-Glass
North Charleston, SC: The Whale Books (CreateSpace) 9781542389358   Unillustrated
Print-on-demand book. Whale Book Series. Issued January 5, 2017. 94 pp. Paper wraps.

4077   2018   Through the Looking-Glass
Mineola, NY: Dover Publications   9780486819242   John Tenniel
Dover Evergreen Classics. Paperback. Reprint of 2017 edition.

4078   2018   Through the Looking-Glass
North Charleston, SC: CreateSpace   9781983724800   Unillustrated
Print-on-demand book. Issued January 9, 2018. 118 pp. Paper wraps.

4079   2018   Through the Looking-Glass
North Charleston, SC: CreateSpace   9781718751910   Unknown
Print-on-demand book. Issued May 6, 2018. 36 pp. Paper wraps.

4080   2018   Through the Looking-Glass
North Charleston, SC: CreateSpace   9781724344892   Unknown
Print-on-demand book. Issued July 26, 2018. 82 pp. Paper wraps.

4081   2018   Through the Looking-Glass
North Charleston, SC: CreateSpace   9781720652694   Unknown
Print-on-demand book. Issued June 3, 2018. 78 pp. Paper wraps.

4082   2018   Through the Looking-Glass
Mineola, NY: Dover Publications   9780486819242   John Tenniel
Dover Evergreen Classics. Paperback. Reprint of 2017 edition.

4083   2018   Through the Looking-Glass
[Massachusetts?]: Hypothesis Press   9781948785020   John Tenniel
Haverhill Classics Volume 3.

4084   2018   Lewis Carroll's Through the Looking-Glass
Gainesville, FL: Moth House Press   9780999532508   Maggie Taylor
Gray-green cloth boards, silver-gilt lettering, dust jacket has Alice on front, Queen on rear, 196 coated pp., 64 integral
full-color photo-montages and other color illustrations. Includes essays by Carol McCusker and Thomas W. Southall.
In 2017, a Deluxe Signed Limited Edition of 100 was issued.

4085   2018   Through the Looking-Glass
Seattle, WA: Palala Press   9781378179130   John Tenniel

4086   2018   Through the Looking-Glass
North Charleston, SC: SeaWolf Press   9781949460506   John Tenniel
1st issue, October 19, 2018. Illustrated Classics Collection Series. 126 pp. Paper wraps.

4087   2018   Through the Looking-Glass
North Charleston, SC: SF Classic   9781772265231   John Tenniel
Limited edition of 100 unnumbered copies. Brown cloth with gold-gilt lettering and decorations. 112 pp. Illustrated
dust jacket.

4088   2019   Through the Looking-Glass
New York: Scholastic   9781338585278   John Tenniel

4089   2019   Through the Looking-Glass
North Charleston, SC: SDE Classics   9781951570026   John Tenniel
137 pp. Paper wraps.

4090   2019   Through the Looking-Glass
North Charleston, SC: SeaWolf Press   9781949460896   John Tenniel
2nd issue of the 2018 edition. Illustrated Classics Collection Series. 126 pp. Paper wraps.

4091   n.d.   Through the Looking-Glass
Garden City, NY: Doubleday Classics   John Tenniel
Gray decorated paper-covered boards backed in blue cloth.

7. *Alice's Adventures under Ground* Editions Published Worldwide

4092   1862–1864   Alice's Adventures under Ground
Manuscript   Lewis Carroll

First told in 1862 by Lewis Carroll to Alice Liddell and her two sisters on a boat trip on the river Isis. Later expanded to the present MS and given to Alice for Christmas, 1864. See Selwyn Goodacre and Denis Crutch, *Jabberwocky*, (Autumn 1978); 89–90 for details on this manuscript, which is now at the British Library.

4093   1886   Alice's Adventures under Ground
London; New York: Macmillan   Lewis Carroll

Proof sheets for the London and New York facsimile printed edition of 1886 printed by Macmillan. The sheets are printed one side only and measure 9¾ inches x 5⅝ inches, whereas the printed leaves measure 7 ³/₁₆ x 4 ⅞ inches. Lacking 9 pp. Defective printing on some pp. The only set known in private hands. Pages contain 2 staple marks on the left side. In a red cloth box.

4094   1886   Alice's Adventures under Ground
London; New York: Macmillan   Lewis Carroll

A facsimile of the original MS, which was afterwards developed into *Alice's Adventures in Wonderland*. With 37 illustrations. viii, 95, [2 ads]. Red cloth on boards with gilt lettering. Black endpapers. The price was 4s until 1919 when the price became 6s. Published in an edition of 5,000 sets of sheets bound up over a period of time. Presentation bindings in various colors. One copy known in black pebble grain cloth inscribed to Alice's mother: "To Her, whose children's smiles fed the narrator's fancy and were his rich reward: / from the Author. / Xmas.1886". A copy exists at Christ Church, Oxford, with a similar inscription to Alice. A copy exists in red cloth inscribed: "John Tenniel from the Author Jan 1887." A copy is known that came from the Harold Hartley collection. Hartley attended the Carroll sale of 1898, so that copy was likely in the Carroll library.

4095   [1931]   Alice's Adventures under Ground
London and New York: Macmillan   Lewis Carroll

Remainder edition. Red cloth blocked in gilt. White endpapers. The remainder price is printed on the dust jacket at the base of the spine "5/-" along with the Macmillan logo, which is also on the front cover. The dust jacket is beige with black lettering. The price of the 1866 edition when published was 4s until 1919 when it went to 6s. *WMGC*, p. 144, says the remainder editions were bound in [1931].

4096   1932   Alice's Adventures under Ground
New York: Macmillan   Lewis Carroll

Centenary issue. First American edition. Red cloth. 104 pp. Pale green dust jacket with the printed title and Macmillan logo on the front cover. Both the front jacket flap and verso of the title page give the date of 1st publication as 1876 rather than the correct 1886.

4097   [1936]   Alice's Adventures under Ground
[Vienna, Austria]: [Privately Printed by Max Jaffe for Eldridge Johnson]   Lewis Carroll

A facsimile of the original manuscript. Privately printed for Eldridge Johnson by Max Jaffe in Vienna, Austria, in commemoration of Johnson's purchase of the original. 90 pp. Dark green morocco stamped in gilt. Issued in a green slipcase. 500 sets of sheets printed, 50 bound for presentation by Johnson. The remaining sheets were thought to have been destroyed in Vienna during World War II, but in fact after the war they were located and sent to A.S.W. Rosenbach in Philadelphia, with some 200 bound copies sent to Mrs. Johnson and the remainder retained for sale by Rosenbach. The Rosenbach Museum and Library has three copies, one in the common green and gilt binding and two slightly different in size, one larger and one smaller, including having red and gilt headbands. The Johnson papers are at the Victor Talking Machine Museum in Dover, Delaware, where, among other objects, they have a model of Johnson's yacht *Alice*.

4098   [1953]   Alice's Adventures under Ground
New York: Panda Prints   Lewis Carroll

Boxed and not dated. A newspaper suggests 1953. Likely a reprint of the [1936] privately printed edition. 96 pp. Tan paper-covered pictorial boards.

4099   1960   Alice's Adventures in Wonderland
London: Hutchinson Educational   Lewis Carroll; Douglas Hall
Junior Classics Series. Title is a misnomer because content is actually *Alice's Adventures under Ground*. Dust jacket.

4100   1961   Alice's Adventures under Ground
London: The Folio Society   Lewis Carroll
Quarter cloth with printed paper sides. Pale blue boards with red Tenniel illustrations.

4101   1964   Alice's Adventures under Ground
Ann Arbor, MI: Xerox, University Microfilms, Inc.   Lewis Carroll
Introduction by Luther H. Evans, former Librarian of Congress. Blue cloth. In a slipcase. According to a publicity handout, it was published in September 1965 (but dated 1964) in an edition of 60,000 copies. A separate portfolio of prints was available. In white cloth. A variant exists with slight change to the imprint.

4102   1965   Alice's Adventures under Ground
Toronto, ON: General Publishing   Lewis Carroll
Martin Gardner is listed as an author.

4103   [1965]   Alice's Adventures under Ground
New York: Dover Publications. Toronto, ON: General Publishing   Lewis Carroll
A facsimile of the 1886 edition. A new introduction by Martin Gardner. In stiff glazed wrappers. Price $1.00. Distributed in Britain by Constable at 8 shillings. An undated later printing exists with ISBN 0486214826.

4104   [1965]   Alice's Adventures under Ground
New York: McGraw-Hill   Lewis Carroll
Reprint of Dover edition in green cloth boards with dust jacket. With a new introduction by Martin Gardner.

4105   [1965]   Alice's Adventures under Ground
Gloucester, MA: Peter Smith Publishing   Lewis Carroll
Reprint of Dover edition in hard covers. With a new introduction by Martin Gardner.

4106   1966   Alice's Adventures under Ground
New York; Toronto, ON; London: McGraw-Hill   Lewis Carroll
Reprint of Dover edition in hardback. Green cloth with dust jacket. New introduction by Martin Gardner.

4107   1966   Alice's Adventures under Ground
New York: McGraw-Hill Book Co.   1851454713   Lewis Carroll
Chrysalis Children's Books series.

4108   1966   Alice's Adventures under Ground
Ann Arbor, MI: Xerox, University Microfilms   Lewis Carroll
Introduction by Luther H. Evans, former Librarian of Congress. In a slipcase.

4109   1969   Alice's Adventures in Wonderland: A Critical Handbook
Belmont, CA: Wadsworth Publishing Company   Lewis Carroll
Edited by Donald Rackin, Temple University. Includes *Alice's Adventures under Ground*. Pictorial wrappers.

4110   1970   Alice's Adventures under Ground
New York: Dover Publications   9780486214825   Lewis Carroll
Bright red cloth. Introduction by Martin Gardner.

4111   [1971]   Alice in Wonderland
New York: W. W. Norton & Company   0393043436 (hardback);   Lewis Carroll
                                           0393099776 (paperback)

Norton critical edition. Edited by Donald J. Gray. Includes a 9-page excerpt (22 pages in the 1886 edition) of *Alice's Adventures under Ground*. 1.5 pp. (7 in the 1886 edition) of Chapter II, "The Mouse's Tale," and 5.5 pp. (15 in the 1886 edition) of Chapter IV, "The Croquet Game, and the Lobster Quadrille," starting on p. 76 in the 1886 edition, to "The End" on p. 90.

4112   [ca. 1972] Alice's Adventures under Ground
Ann Arbor, MI: University Microfilms   Lewis Carroll
Photocopy with no ISBN. Undated. In wrappers.

4113   1973   Alice's Adventures under Ground
Johannesburg, SA: DALRO   9780869641507   Lewis Carroll
An adaptation by Nigel Vermaas. 50 leaves. Edition of 250 copies.

4114   1979   Alice's Adventures under Ground
Brookvale, NSW: Australia & New Zealand Book   9780904351118   Lewis Carroll
A copy of the Genesis edition.

4115   1979   Alice's Adventures under Ground
Guildford, UK: Genesis Publications   9780904351118   Lewis Carroll
Foreword by Philip Dodgson Jaques, great-nephew of Charles Dodgson. Introduction by Morton Cohen. Boxed. Limited edition of 500 copies.

4116   1980   Alice's Adventures under Ground
Tokyo, Japan: Eihosha   Lewis Carroll
Facsimile of the 1886 1st edition. Annotated by Yasuichirō Ōhashi.

4117   1980   Alice's Adventures under Ground
New York: Mayflower Books   9780831702403   Lewis Carroll
1st Mayflower edition. A Windward edition, With Easter Greeting (1876) and Christmas Greeting (1867); with Illustrated dust jacket.

4118   1980   Alice's Adventures under Ground
Leicester, UK: Windward   9780711201019   Lewis Carroll
This appears to be the same as the Mayflower edition of 1980.

4119   1980   Alice's Adventures under Ground
Lakeville, MN: Windward Publishing   9780711201019   Lewis Carroll
A Windward Reprint. 112 pp. Red cloth.

4120   1982   England in Literature
Glenview, IL: Scott, Foresman and Company   John Tenniel; Jean-Michel Folon
Full text of *Alice's Adventures under Ground* but without Carroll's illustrations. Pp. 386–408.

4121   1982   Alice's Adventures under Ground
Ann Arbor, MI; London: University Microfilms   Lewis Carroll
Print-on-demand edition.

4122   1985   Alice's Adventures under Ground
Tokyo, Japan: Eihosha   Lewis Carroll
2nd printing of the 1980 edition. Facsimile of the 1886 1st edition. Annotated by Yasuichirō Ōhashi.

4123   1985   Alice's Adventures under Ground
London: HarperCollins Distribution Services   Lewis Carroll

4124   1985   Alice's Adventures under Ground
New York: Holt, Rinehart and Winston   9780030061134   Lewis Carroll
American reprint of the 1985 Pavilion edition.

4125   1985   Alice's Adventures under Ground
London: Pavilion/Michael Joseph   9780907516941   Lewis Carroll
Published October 1985. First published in Great Britain. Foreword by Mary Jean St. Clair, Alice Liddell's granddaughter. Decorated paper-covered boards backed in green cloth. This edition includes a reproduction of Carroll's drawing of Alice Liddell under her photograph on the final page of the *Alice's Adventures under Ground* manuscript. This was first described by Morton Cohen in the *New York Times Book Review* of October 9, 1977. See Lovett 1526 for details.

4126   1985   Alice's Adventures under Ground
Ann Arbor, MI: University Microfilms, Inc.   Lewis Carroll
Reprint of 1964 edition. In burgundy cover with copper lettering and silver border. On verso of title page: copyright 1964, reprinted 1985. Copies of this 1985 reprint were distributed as a gift at the 2nd European Conference on Archives, May 9, 1989, with a laid-in sheet that read "University Microfilms International reproduced the book by photo offset in 1965 in celebration of its 100th anniversary. This special edition has been printed specially to commemorate your visit." .

4127   1986   Alice's Adventures under Ground
New York: Henry Holt & Co.   9780030061134   Lewis Carroll
A reprint of the 1985 edition of Holt, Rinehart and Winston as it has the same ISBN. Published March 1986.

4128   1986   Alice's Adventures under Ground
London: Macmillan   Lewis Carroll
Not in COPAC.

4129   1987   Alice's Adventures under Ground
Tokyo, Japan: Shoseki Jōhōsha   9784915999109   Lewis Carroll; John Tenniel
Introduction by Russell Ash. Consisting of 2 books: Republication of Pavilion Books and the British Library. English edition illustrated by Lewis Carroll and Japanese edition illustrated by John Tenniel. Japanese edition translated by the editorial staff of Shoseki Jōhōsha.

4130   1988   Alice's Adventures under Ground
Tokyo, Japan: Eihosha   9784269010109   Lewis Carroll
3rd printing of the 1980 edition. Facsimile of the 1886 1st edition. Annotated by Yasuichirō Ōhashi.

4131   1989   Alice's Adventures under Ground
London: Pavilion Books   9781851454716   Lewis Carroll

4132   1990   Alice's Adventures under Ground
[New York]: Viking Press   9781851455416   Lewis Carroll

4133   1992   Alice's Adventures under Ground: The Story That Became Alice in Wonderland
London: Pavilion Books Ltd.   9781851454716   Lewis Carroll
Hard cover. Published March 1992.

4134   1995   Alice's Adventures under Ground
London; Boston: Faber and Faber   9780571176014   Lewis Carroll
Adapted from the writings of Lewis Carroll by Christopher Hampton in collaboration with Martha Clarke.

4135   1995   Alice's Adventures under Ground
London: Pavilion Books   9781851454716   Lewis Carroll

4136   [1996]   Alice's Adventures under Ground
New York: Dover Publications   9780486214825   Lewis Carroll
Reprint of 1965 edition.

4137   1998   Alice's Adventures under Ground
London: Pavilion Books   9781851454716   Lewis Carroll

4138   1998   Alice's Adventures in Wonderland and Through the Looking-Glass
London: Penguin Books   9780140433173   Lewis Carroll; John Tenniel
Centenary edition. Edited with introduction and notes by Hugh Haughton. Includes *Alice's Adventures under Ground*.

4139   2000   Alice's Adventures in Wonderland
Peterboro, ON; Orchard Park, NY: Broadview Press   9781551112237   Lewis Carroll; after John
                                                                             Tenniel; E. Gertrude Thomson
Edited by Richard Kelly. Includes *Alice's Adventures under Ground* (pp. 157–208), *Alice's Adventures in Wonderland*, and *The Nursery "Alice,"* as well as selected reviews, parodies, remembrances of Carroll, and extracts from Carroll's diaries and letters.

4140   2000   Alice's Adventures under Ground
San Francisco: Cottage Classics   1892847000   Kim Deitch
250 copies numbered and signed. Foreword by Mark Burstein.

4141   2000   Alice's Adventures under Ground
San Francisco: Cottage Classics   1892847019   Kim Deitch
1,600 unnumbered copies. Foreword by Mark Burstein.

4142   2000   Alice's Adventures under Ground
London: Pavilion Books   9781851454716   Lewis Carroll
5th impression of the 1998 edition.

4143   2001   Alice's Adventures under Ground
New Delhi, India: Bloombury   9781847490957   Lewis Carroll

4144   2002   Alice's Adventures under Ground
Tokyo, Japan: Shoseki Jōhōsha   9784915999109   Lewis Carroll; John Tenniel
Introduction by Russell Ash. Consisting of 2 books: Republication of Pavilion Books and the British Library. English edition illustrated by Lewis Carroll and Japanese edition illustrated by John Tenniel. Japanese edition translated by Hiroshi Takahashi.

4145   2003   Alice's Adventures under Ground
London: Chrysalis Children's Books   9781851454716   Lewis Carroll

4146   2004   Alice's Adventures under Ground
Whitefish, MT: Kessinger Publishing Co.   Lewis Carroll
Print-on-demand book.

4147   2005   Alice's Adventures under Ground
London: The British Library   9780712305259   Lewis Carroll
Print book and CD. Preface by Miriam Margolyes.

4148   2006   Alice's Adventures under Ground
Montreuil, France; Brussels, Belgium: FRMK   9782350650166   Lewis Carroll
A facsimile of the 1886 edition. With a French translation in the margins by "Professeur A." and a postface on pp. 93–95.

4149   2006   Alice's Adventures under Ground
US: Project Gutenberg   Lewis Carroll
E-book. Project Gutenberg is an American project to digitize books and other printed work.

4150   2008   Alice's Adventures under Ground
Montreuil, France; Brussels, Belgium: FRMK   9782350650333   Lewis Carroll
2nd edition.

4151   2008   Alice's Adventures under Ground
London: The British Library   9780712309707   Lewis Carroll
Preface by Sally Brown. In the series Treasures in Focus.

4152   2008   Alice's Adventures under Ground
London: The British Library   9780712350426   Lewis Carroll
For a juvenile audience.

4153   2008   Alice's Adventures under Ground
London: The British Library / The Folio Society   9780712309707   Lewis Carroll
Boxed with *The Original Alice* by Sally Brown; limited to 3,750 copies.

4154   2009   Alice's Adventures under Ground
Richmond, UK: Alma Classics   9781847490957   Lewis Carroll
Reprinted in 2010, 2011, and 2013.

4155   2009   Alice's Adventures under Ground
Westport, Ireland: Evertype   9781904808398   Lewis Carroll
Not a facsimile edition but typeset in the style of other Evertype editions. Orange front cover with Alice and the Caterpillar. The back cover has Alice and the Ostrich. In printings until July 2012 Alice had a blue dress and thereafter she wears a yellow dress. Foreword by Michael Everson.

4156   2009   Alice's Adventures under Ground
US: International Business Publications, USA   9781433092084   Lewis Carroll

4157   2009   Alice's Adventures under Ground
Richmond, UK: Oneworld Classics   9781847490957   Lewis Carroll
Reprinted 2010.

4158   2009   Alice's Adventures in Wonderland and Through the Looking-Glass
London: Penguin Books   9780141192468   Lewis Carroll; John Tenniel
Includes *Alice's Adventures under Ground*.

4159   2010   Michael Foreman's Alice's Adventures in Wonderland
Scoresby, VIC: Five Mile Press   9781742481487   Michael Foreman
Includes *Alice's Adventures under Ground*.

| 4160 | 2010 | Alice's Adventures under Ground | | |
| | | Los Angeles: Indo-European Publishing | 9781604442670 | Lewis Carroll |

4161	2010	Alice's Adventures under Ground		
		Whitefish, MT: Kessinger Publishing Co.		Lewis Carroll
		Print-on-demand.		

4162	2010	Alice's Adventures under Ground		
		Richmond, UK: Oneworld Classics	9781847490957	Lewis Carroll
		Reprint of the 2009 edition. Formerly Alma Classics.		

| 4163 | 2010 | The umpteenth translation of Alice's Adventures under Ground | | |
| | | Tokyo, Japan: Switch Publishing | 9784884183080 | Lewis Carroll |

In English and Japanese. Included in the May 2010 issue of *Switch* magazine (vol. 28, no. 5), pp. 52–59. Japanese version translated by Miu Sakamoto.

4164	2010	The Complete Alice in Wonderland.		
		Fitchburg, WI: Wonderland Imprints		Lewis Carroll; John Tenniel
		Kindle e-book. Includes *Alice's Adventures under Ground*.		

| 4165 | 2011 | Alice's Adventures in Wonderland | | |
| | | Peterborough, ON: Broadview Press | 9781554810390 | Lewis Carroll; John Tenniel; E. Gertrude Thomson |

2nd edition of the 2000 edition. Edited by Richard Kelly. Includes *Alice's Adventures under Ground*, *Alice's Adventures in Wonderland*, and *The Nursery "Alice."* Also selected reviews, parodies, remembrances of Carroll, and extracts from Carroll's diaries and letters.

4166	2011	Alice's Adventures under Ground		
		Montreuil (Seine Saint-Denis), France: Frémok	9782930204611	Lewis Carroll
		3rd edition.		

4167	2011	Alice's Adventures under Ground		
		Richmond, UK: Oneworld Classics	9781847490957	Lewis Carroll
		Reprint of the 2009 edition. Formerly Alma Classics.		

| 4168 | 2012 | Alice's Adventures under Ground | | |
| | | New York: Cosimo | 9781616407131 | Lewis Carroll |

4169	2012	Alice's Adventures under Ground		
		[Dayboro, QLD]: Emereo Publishing	9781486417643	Lewis Carroll
		E-book.		

| 4170 | 2012 | Alice's Adventures under Ground | | |
| | | Chelmsford, MA: Lee Ann Borgia Miniature Books | | Lewis Carroll |

150th Anniversary Keepsake Edition of the Lewis Carroll Society of North America. 2012 marked the 150th anniversary of the telling of the *Alice's Adventures under Ground* story. About 1 in. tall. Produced by Alan and Alison Tannenbaum. All numbered "Number 42 of 50." Signed by the printer. Reproduces the photo and drawing of Alice Liddell.

4171	2012	Alice's Adventures in Wonderland; Through the Looking-Glass; and Alice's Adventures under Ground		
		New York: Penguin Classics	9780147509079	Lewis Carroll; John Tenniel
		With an introduction and notes by Hugh Haughton.		

4172   2013   Alice's Adventures under Ground
Oxford, UK; London: Artists' Choice Editions   Lewis Carroll; Ian Beck
22 "Specials" in publisher's box, with 3 lithographs "from the hand coloured original," each signed by Ian Beck.

4173   2013   Alice's Adventures under Ground
Richmond, UK: Oneworld Classics   9781847490957   Lewis Carroll
Reprint of the 2009 edition. Formerly Alma Classics.

4174   2014   Alice in Wonderland: The Complete Collection
London: Classic Good Books   9780692228722   Unillustrated
Includes *Alice's Adventures under Ground* and *The Hunting of the Snark*. Also has quiz questions and numerous notes
on adaptations, etc.

4175   2014   Alice in Wonderland: The Complete Collection
London: Classic Good Books   9780692228722   Anonymous
As the unillustrated 2014 edition but with illustrations. Includes *Alice's Adventures under Ground* and *The Hunting of
the Snark*. Also has quiz questions and numerous notes on adaptations, etc.

4176   2014   The Complete Novels of Lewis Carroll With All the Original Illustrations
[Cork, Ireland]: E-artnow Editions   9788026805106   Lewis Carroll; John Tenniel
E-book. Includes: *Alice's Adventures under Ground*; *Alice's Adventures in Wonderland*; *Through the Looking-Glass*;
Sylvie and Bruno; *Sylvie and Bruno Concluded*; *The Life and Letters of Lewis Carroll*. Page counts may vary depending
on e-reader. Amazon Kindle copy has 1,382 pp.; others may have as many as 1,670 pp. *Under Ground* contains Carroll's
illustrations, and *Looking-Glass* contains Tenniel illustrations. Other illustrated books contain the original illustrations.

4177   2014   Alice's Adventures under Ground
Olympia, WA: Last Word Press   Unillustrated?
Imprint from publisher's website. G. Edward Cassady Collection, University of Southern California.

4178   2014   Alice's Adventures under Ground
London: British Library   9780712356008;   Lewis Carroll; Maggi Smith
                                         0712356002
Preface by Sally Brown; reprint of the 2008 edition, with a new dust jacket designed by Maggi Smith.

4179   2015   Alice's Adventures in Wonderland and Through the Looking-Glass
Richmond, UK: Alma Classics   9781847494078   John Tenniel; Lewis Carroll
Includes *Alice's Adventures under Ground*.

4180   2015   Alice's Adventures under Ground
Kennebunkport, ME: Cider Mill Press   9781604335729   Charles Santore
Introduction by Michael Patrick Hearn. In the back matter is Santore's "Conversation."

4181   2015   Alice's Adventures under Ground
[Marsden, QLD]: Cobblestone Productions 9780994333711   Lewis Carroll
150th Anniversary edition. "Limited Edition" (of 500). In publisher's box with white glove and an accompanying
booklet containing 5 essays. $499.95.

4182   2015   Alice's Adventures under Ground
[Marsden, QLD]: Cobblestone Productions 9780994333704   Lewis Carroll
150th Anniversary edition. "Premium Edition" (of 2,000). In publisher's box with white glove and an accompanying
booklet containing 5 essays. $59.95.

4183   2015   Alice's Adventures under Ground: being a facsimile of the original Ms. book
                  afterwards developed into "Alice's Adventures in Wonderland"
London: Forgotten Books   9780259949879   Lewis Carroll
Classic Reprint Series.

4184   [2015]   Alice's Adventures under Ground
Peterborough, ON: Broadview Press   9781554812417   Lewis Carroll; John Tenniel;
                                                                            after John Tenniel; E. Gertrude Thomson

3rd edition of the 2000 edition. Edited by Richard Kelly. Includes *Alice's Adventures under Ground*, *Alice's Adventures in Wonderland*, *Through the Looking-Glass*, and *The Nursery "Alice,"* as well as selected reviews, parodies, remembrances of Carroll, and extracts from Carroll's diaries and letters.

4185   2016   Alice in Wonderland (Deluxe Complete Collection)
[Lexington, KY]: [Christian Books Today]   9781499336924   Anonymous
Includes *Alice*, *Looking-Glass*, *under Ground*, and *The Hunting of the Snark*.

4186   2016   Alice in Wonderland Collection
Los Angeles: Enhanced Media   9781530917563   Unknown
Includes *Alice*, *Looking-Glass*, *under Ground*, and *The Hunting of the Snark*.

4187   2017   Alice's Adventures under Ground: being a facsimile of the original manuscript book
                  afterwards developed into "Alice's Adventures in Wonderland"
Surrey, UK: Alma Classics   9781847497772   Lewis Carroll

4188   2017   Alice's Adventures under Ground
New Delhi, India: Kalpaz Publications   9789351289838   Lewis Carroll

4189   2017   The Complete Novels of Lewis Carroll (Illustrated Edition)
Frankfurt am Main, Germany: Musaicum Books   9788027218509   Lewis Carroll; John Tenniel;
                                                                            Others

E-book. 1,670 pp. Includes: *Alice's Adventures under Ground*, *Alice's Adventures in Wonderland*, *Through the Looking-Glass*, *Sylvie and Bruno*, *Sylvie and Bruno Concluded*, and *The Life and Letters of Lewis Carroll*.

4190   2017   Alice in Wonderland: The Complete Collection
Frankfurt am Main, Germany: Musaicum Books   9782377939190;   Lewis Carroll;
                                                 9791097338756   John Tenniel; Others

E-book. The Greatest Fictional Characters of All Time Book Center. 483 pp. Includes *Alice's Adventures under Ground*, *Alice's Adventures in Wonderland*, *Through the Looking Glass*, *The Hunting of the Snark*, The Nursery *"Alice"*, and the lost chapter, "The Wasp in the Wig," from *Through the Looking-Glass*.

4191   2019   Alice's Adventures under Ground
Amsterdam, The Netherlands: Magic Touch Books   9789493087064   Anonymous

"Based on the original manuscript." On cover: "Alice comes to your screen in Augmented Reality." Publisher description: "a unique, updated edition with fully modernized text and amazing 3D illustrations which will guide readers through its many twists and turns.... This book is also available as an animated movie-book with amazing videos, captivating narration, and enchanting music. With Alice in Augmented Reality downloadable for free, Alice can even step out of the book, right in front of the children, creating an unforgettable reading experience!"

4192   2019   Alice's Adventures under Ground: The Original Manuscript
London: British Library   9780712352437   Lewis Carroll
Accompanying commentary by former British Library curator Sally Brown.

4193   2019   Alice's Adventures under Ground

[Amsterdam, The Netherlands]: Zoomikon Press   9789493087125   Anonymous

Same as the 2019 Magic Touch Books edition, but with a different ISBN. Imprint on the page facing the title page, with this note: "also available as a movie book, ISBN 9789493087057 (e-book)." A search on this ISBN retrieved no related entries. A QR code on the last page enables one to "Play with Alice. Take photos and videos with Alice in Augmented Reality." Barcode on back cover refers to magictouchbooks.net.

4194   n.d.   Alice's Adventures under Ground & Alice's Adventures in Wonderland

Garden City, NY: Dolphin Books / Doubleday & Company   Lewis Carroll; Sydney Butchkes; John Tenniel

In the series A Doubleday Dolphin Master. The cover includes a Tenniel illustration adapted by Sydney Butchkes. Pictorial wrappers. 95 cents.

4195   n.d.   Alice's Adventures under Ground

Tokyo, Japan: Shoseki Jōhōsha   Unillustrated

With cassette tapes.

8. *The Nursery "Alice"* Editions Published Worldwide

4196   1889   The Nursery "Alice"
London: Macmillan

John Tenniel;
E. Gertrude Thomson

WMGC 215. Printed in a run of 10,000 sets of sheets but rejected by Dodgson as "far too bright and gaudy." In a letter to Macmillan of June 23, 1889 he asked that they be reprinted. The *WMGC* 215d copies of the 1889 sheets are found with "Three Shillings" overprinted with "One Shilling." So, there must be sheets saying "Three Shillings" alone but none have been found. It seems likely that the decision to reject these sheets was made before any copies were bound.

4197   1889   The Nursery "Alice"
London: Macmillan

John Tenniel;
E. Gertrude Thomson

1st edition. *WMGC* 215a. No price on title page or in advertisements. Intended as samples for the American market. Received by Dodgson on October 29, 1889. Orange illustrated front and rear covers. Orange front and rear endpapers. Half title, x, 56 pp, [6], [2 pp ads]. Copies are known with blank cream-colored covers, a number of which have survived. They were probably intended for America. However, their title pages, inadvertently, had not been replaced by the 1890 American title page (*WMGC* 215b). Some of these may have been given by Dodgson to members of his family, as inscribed copies from family members exist. 2 pages of ads at the rear list "Works by Lewis Carroll." At the end is Carroll's "Caution to Readers." about a story in the August 1, 1881, issue of *Aunt Judy's Magazine* (no. 184), falsely attributed to him.

4198   [1889]   The Nursery "Alice"
Color proof sheets

John Tenniel;
E. Gertrude Thomson

6 color proof sheets exist, probably for the 1889 edition. These may have been part of a larger group of proofs from Dodgson's library. See Stern, p. 63.

4199   1890   The Nursery "Alice"
New York: Macmillan

John Tenniel;
E. Gertrude Thomson

2nd issue. With the imprint New York: Macmillan. *WMGC* 215b. 4,000 sets of sheets of the 10,000 sets rejected by Dodgson were sent to America. Title page dated 1890. It is unpriced. Only a few copies can be located.

4200   1889 [1891]   The Nursery "Alice"
London: Macmillan

John Tenniel;
E. Gertrude Thomson

3rd issue. The title page reads 1889 but it was published in 1891. *WMGC* 215c. "Macmillan People's Edition. Price Two Shillings" at the top of the title page. Ads at rear give price of 3s. The remaining 6,000 sets from the original 10,000 rejected by Dodgson after 4,000 sets were sent to America. 2 pages of ads at the rear list "Works by Lewis Carroll." In 1896 these were withdrawn from sale and given to hospitals. Copies exist with the cover reading *The Nursery Alice* (no quotes around "Alice") Cover faded to brown; the cover illustration is Tenniel's "Alice and the shower of cards." Rear cover is blank. This is a remainder binding.

4201   1889 [1897]   The Nursery "Alice"
London: Macmillan

John Tenniel;
E. Gertrude Thomson

4th (cheap) issue published from 1889 sheets in 1897. *WMGC* 215d. Original price of "Three Shillings" overprinted "One Shilling" on the title page and 3s in the ads. White endpapers and white covers faded to brown. Copies exist in the remainder binding.

4202   1890   The Nursery "Alice"
London: Macmillan

John Tenniel;
E. Gertrude Thomson

2nd edition. *WMGC* 216. White illustrated covers. Title page and ads give price of "Four Shillings." Ads say "(First published in 1889.)" One inscribed copy by Carroll reads on the half title "For Else, / from L.C. / flourish / Oct. 10. 1890." Copies exist with a tipped-in addendum dated March, 1890, advertising *Sylvie and Bruno*. Copies exist in the remainder binding.

4203   1890 [1896]   The Nursery "Alice"
London: Macmillan   John Tenniel;
                                                                    E. Gertrude Thomson

WMGC 216a. 2nd (cheap) issue of [1896]. Sales of 215c and 216 were slow so Dodgson decided to reissue 215c and on the title page overprinted the original price of "Four Shillings" with "One Shilling." The rear ads still show 4s. White covers and endpapers. A copy of this issue was reproduced in facsimile in 1966 by Dover.

4204   [1938]   The Nursery "Alice"
[London]: Hodder & Stoughton   Gwynedd M. Hudson
Retold for the nursery by Irene Pearl.

4205   [ca. 1960s]   Alice in Wonderland
London: Murray's Sales and Service Co.   Vittorio Accornero

The title page states *Alice in Wonderland* but the text is *The Nursery "Alice."* Glazed pictorial boards. This edition is organized in 12 chapters versus the original 15 chapters. The publication date is shown as 1968 in Davis.

4206   1966   The Nursery "Alice"
New York: Dover Publications   John Tenniel;
                                                                    E. Gertrude Thomson

Introduction by Martin Gardner. Reproduced from *WMGC* 216a, the 1s reduced price version [1896] of the 1890 1st edition. A copy exists in red cloth boards with "Peter Smith" at the base of the spine but not on the title page.

4207   1966   The Nursery "Alice"
London: Dover Publications   John Tenniel;
                                                                    E. Gertrude Thomson

Introduction by Martin Gardner. Reproduced from *WMGC* 216a, the 1s reduced price version [1896] of the 1890 1st edition.

4208   1966   The Nursery "Alice"
New York; London; Toronto, ON: McGraw-Hill   John Tenniel;
                                                                    E. Gertrude Thomson

Introduction by Martin Gardner. Bright green pictorial cloth. 56 pp. Reproduced from *WMGC* 216a, the 1s reduced price version [1896] of the 1890 1st edition. Color illustration by E. Gertrude Thomson for the back cover. Pictorial dust jacket with blurb.

4209   [1966]   The Nursery "Alice"
New York: McGraw-Hill   John Tenniel;
                                                                    E. Gertrude Thomson

Introduction by Martin Gardner. Reproduced from *WMGC* 216a, the 1s reduced price version [1896] of the 1890 1st edition.

4210   1967   Alice for the Very Young
New York: The Grolier Society   John Tenniel;
                                                                    E. Gertrude Thomson

A reprint of *The Nursery "Alice."* A slightly reduced format of the 1890 edition *WMGC* 216. In wrappers. 1st edition thus.

4211   ca. 1969 The Nursery "Alice"
New York: McGraw-Hill   John Tenniel; Anonymous

Introduction by Martin Gardner. Green cloth with Alice and Duchess outlined in black on the cover by an anonymous illustrator.

4212	1979	The Nursery "Alice"		
		London: Macmillan / Godfrey Cave	9780333273869	John Tenniel;
				E. Gertrude Thomson

Facsimile of the 1890 "Four Shilling" 2nd edition, *WMGC* 216. Reprinted in 1980, 1986, and 1990 with the same ISBN.

4213	1979	The Nursery "Alice"		
		New York: Mayflower Books	9780831764784	John Tenniel;
				E. Gertrude Thomson

Uses the *WMGC* 215b 1890 edition text from the New York: Macmillan issue.

4214	1979	The Nursery "Alice"	
		Tokyo: Holp Shuppan	John Tenniel;
			E. Gertrude Thomson

Facsimile edition reproduced from a copy of the 1889 Macmillan People's Edition at the Osborne Collection in Toronto. *WMGC* 215c. No reprint of this edition had an ISBN. Reprinted in 1980, 1981 (three reprints), 1982 (two reprints), 1983, 1984, 1985, 1987, 1988, 1989, 1991, and 1993.

4215	1979	The Nursery "Alice"	
		Tokyo: Tsurumi Shoten	John Tenniel;
			E. Gertrude Thomson

Annotated by Yozo Muroya.

4216	1980	The Nursery "Alice"	
		Tokyo: Holp Shuppan	John Tenniel;
			E. Gertrude Thomson

2nd printing of the 1979 edition.

4217	1980	The Nursery "Alice"		
		London: Macmillan / Godfrey Cave	9780333273869	John Tenniel;
				E. Gertrude Thomson

Reprint of the 1979 facsimile edition of the 1890 "Four Shilling" 2nd edition *WMGC* 216. Also reprinted in 1986 and 1990. All with the same ISBN.

4218	1981	The Nursery "Alice"	
		Tokyo: Holp Shuppan	John Tenniel;
			E. Gertrude Thomson

3rd, 4th, and 5th printings of the 1979 edition.

4219	1981	The Nursery "Alice"	
		Tokyo; London: Holp Shuppan, distributed by Bodley Head	John Tenniel;
			E. Gertrude Thomson

First published by Holp Shuppan, Tokyo, 1979. This and later editions published in Tokyo and London were not sold in Japan. No Japanese university library or the National Diet Library has a copy. A copy exists in a slipcase and is a facsimile reproduced from the Osborne copy at Toronto Public Library.

4220	1982	The Nursery "Alice"	
		London: Bodley Head. Tokyo: Holp Shuppan	John Tenniel;
			E. Gertrude Thomson

A facsimile reproduced from the Osborne copy at Toronto Public Library by Holp Shuppan Publishers, Tokyo and printed in Japan. This and later editions published in Tokyo and London were not sold in Japan. No Japanese university library or the National Diet Library has a copy.

4221   1982   The Nursery "Alice"
Tokyo: Holp Shuppan   John Tenniel;
                                                                        E. Gertrude Thomson

5th printing of the 1979 edition.

4222   1982   The Nursery "Alice"
Tokyo: Holp Shuppan   John Tenniel;
                                                                        E. Gertrude Thomson

6th printing of the 1979 edition.

4223   1983   The Nursery "Alice"
Tokyo: Holp Shuppan   John Tenniel;
                                                                        E. Gertrude Thomson

7th printing of the 1979 edition.

4224   1984   The Nursery "Alice"
Tokyo: Holp Shuppan   John Tenniel;
                                                                        E. Gertrude Thomson

8th printing of the 1979 edition.

4225   1985   The Nursery "Alice"
Sydney, NSW: Child, Henry & Page   978086777066X   John Tenniel;
                                                                        E. Gertrude Thomson

A facsimile edition of the 1890 "Four Shilling" edition but lacking the original title page. Dated from the preface which reads "Easter-tide, 1890." The ads in the back include the price of "4s."

4226   1985   The Nursery "Alice"
Tokyo: Holp Shuppan   John Tenniel;
                                                                        E. Gertrude Thomson

9th printing of the 1979 edition.

4227   1985   The Nursery "Alice"
Ware, Hertfordshire, UK: Omega Books   9781850070511   John Tenniel;
                                                                        E. Gertrude Thomson

Dust jacket.

4228   1986   The Nursery "Alice"
London: Macmillan / Godfrey Cave   9780333273869   John Tenniel;
                                                                        E. Gertrude Thomson

Reprint of the 1979 facsimile edition of the 1890 "Four Shilling" 2nd edition *WMGC* 216. Also reprinted in 1980 and 1990. All with the same ISBN.

4229   1987   The Nursery "Alice"
Tokyo: Holp Shuppan   John Tenniel;
                                                                        E. Gertrude Thomson

10th printing of the 1979 edition.

4230   1988   The Nursery "Alice"
Tokyo: Holp Shuppan   John Tenniel;
                                                                        E. Gertrude Thomson

11th printing of the 1979 edition.

4231	1989	The Nursery "Alice"		John Tenniel; E. Gertrude Thomson

Tokyo: Holp Shuppan

12th printing of the 1979 edition. Dated on the colophon.

4232	1990	The Nursery "Alice"	9780333273869	John Tenniel; E. Gertrude Thomson

London: Macmillan / Godfrey Cave

Reprint of the 1979 facsimile edition of the 1890 "Four Shilling" 2nd edition *WMGC* 216. Also reprinted in 1980 and 1986. All with the same ISBN.

4233	1991	The Nursery "Alice"		John Tenniel; E. Gertrude Thomson

Tokyo: Holp Shuppan

13th printing of the 1979 edition.

4234	1993	The Nursery "Alice"		John Tenniel; E. Gertrude Thomson

Tokyo: Holp Shuppan

14th and final printing of the 1979 edition.

4235	2000	Alice's Adventures in Wonderland	9781551112237; 015511223X	John Tenniel; E. Gertrude Thomson; Lewis Carroll

Peterborough, ON; Orchard Park, NY: Broadview Press

Combined edition. In "Broadview Literary Texts" edited by Richard Kelly. Includes *The Nursery "Alice," Alice's Adventures in Wonderland*, and *Alice's Adventures under Ground* along with selected reviews, parodies, remembrances of Carroll, and extracts from Carroll's diaries and letters.

4236	2009	The Nursery "Alice"	9789738882683	John Tenniel; E. Gertrude Thomson

Bucharest, Romania: Mediamorphosis

Reprint of the 1980 London: Macmillan / Godfrey Cave edition.

4237	2010	The Nursery "Alice"	9781904808428	John Tenniel; E. Gertrude Thomson

Westport, Ireland: Evertype

Edited with a foreword by Michael Everson. This edition omitted in error the "Alice and Jury box" illustration. The frontispiece is Thomson's cover illustration from the 1890 edition. That edition's March Hare faces page 1.

4238	2010	The Nursery "Alice"	9780230747708	John Tenniel; E. Gertrude Thomson

London: Macmillan Children's Books

Dust jacket.

4239	2011	Alice's Adventures in Wonderland	9781554810390	John Tenniel; E. Gertrude Thomson; Lewis Carroll; Others

Peterborough, ON: Broadview Press

2nd edition. Combined edition. In "Broadview Literary Texts" edited by Richard Kelly. Includes *The Nursery "Alice," Alice's Adventures in Wonderland*, and *Alice's Adventures under Ground*. With a new appendix, George MacDonald writing on the fantastic, contemporary reviews, a section on film and TV adaptations of *Alice*, new illustrations and bibliographical references.

4239a	[2015]	Alice's Adventures under Ground	9781554812417	Lewis Carroll; John Tenniel; after John Tenniel; E. Gertrude Thomson

Peterborough, ON: Broadview Press

3rd edition of the 2000 edition. Edited by Richard Kelly. Includes *Alice's Adventures under Ground*, *Alice's Adventures in Wonderland*, *Through the Looking-Glass*, and *The Nursery "Alice,"* as well as selected reviews, parodies, remembrances of Carroll, and extracts from Carroll's diaries and letters.

4240	2015	The Nursery "Alice"		
		London: Pan Macmillan	9781447287117	John Tenniel; E. Gertrude Thomson

4241	2015	The Nursery "Alice"		
		Portlaoise, Ireland: Evertype	9781782011170	John Tenniel; E. Gertrude Thomson

4242	2017	The Nursery "Alice" (from naught to five)		
		[Great Britain?]: Robin Books	9781910880470	John Tenniel; Arthur Hughes; Arthur Claude Strachan

Book designed by Marie-Michelle Joy. Includes cover illustration and page border paintings by Arthur Hughes and Arthur Claude Strachan.

4243	n.d.	The Nursery Alice in Wonderland		
		London: Hodder and Stoughton		Gwynedd Hudson

Glazed paper boards. Retold for the Nursery by Irene Pearl. A small 48-page adaptation with 6 color plates and 8 black-and-white pictures.

9. *The Annotated Alice* Editions Published Worldwide

4244   1960   The Annotated Alice: Alice's Adventures in Wonderland and Through the Looking-Glass
New York: Clarkson N. Potter   John Tenniel
1st edition. Annotated by Martin Gardner. Tan cloth.

4245   1960   The Annotated Alice
London: Anthony Blond   John Tenniel
1st UK edition. Paper boards. Includes *Looking-Glass*. All editions with annotations by Martin Gardner. Probably uses sheets from the American edition. Dust jacket.

4246   1960   The Annotated Alice: Alice's Adventures in Wonderland and Through the Looking-Glass
New York: Clarkson N. Potter   John Tenniel
Book Club issue. Annotated by Martin Gardner. Otherwise, identical to the 1st edition.

4247   1962   The Annotated Alice: Alice's Adventures in Wonderland and Through the Looking-Glass
New York: Bramhall House   John Tenniel
Published by a division of Clarkson N. Potter. Annotated by Martin Gardner.

4248   1963   The Annotated Alice: Alice's Adventures in Wonderland and Through the Looking-Glass
New York: Meridian   John Tenniel
New American Library of World Literature. Annotated by Martin Gardner. Paperback.

4249   1963   The Annotated Alice: Alice's Adventures in Wonderland and Through the Looking-Glass
Cleveland, OH: World Publishing   John Tenniel
Annotated by Martin Gardner.

4250   1965   The Annotated Alice
London: Thomas Nelson and Sons   John Tenniel
Claims to be the first UK printed edition. Internally as the 1960 edition. Includes *Looking-Glass*. With annotations by Martin Gardner. Dust jacket.

4251   1965   The Annotated Alice
Harmondsworth, UK: Penguin Books   John Tenniel
First Penguin edition. Paperback. Includes *Looking-Glass*. With annotations by Martin Gardner.

4252   1966   The Annotated Alice
Harmondsworth, UK: Penguin Books   John Tenniel
1st reprint of the 1965 Penguin paperback edition. Includes *Looking-Glass*. With annotations by Martin Gardner.

4253   1968   The Annotated Alice: Alice's Adventures in Wonderland and Through the Looking-Glass
Cleveland, OH: World Publishing Co.   John Tenniel
Annotated by Martin Gardner.

4254   1970   The Annotated Alice
Harmondsworth, UK: Penguin Books   0140013873   John Tenniel
Revised edition. Includes *Looking-Glass*. With annotations by Martin Gardner. Numerous dated reprints to 1987. Many later reprints are all dated 1970. Goodacre copy is inscribed "To Selwyn Goodacre / from / Martin Gardner - / May 1987" with a note from Gardner to Goodacre laid in.

4255   1970   The Annotated Alice
Harmondsworth, UK: Penguin   97801400138   John Tenniel
Includes *Looking-Glass*. Introduction and notes by Martin Gardner.

4256   1971   The Annotated Alice: Alice's Adventures in Wonderland and Through the Looking-Glass
Cleveland, OH: World Publishing Co.   9780529020529   John Tenniel
Annotated by Martin Gardner.

4257   1972   The Annotated Alice
Harmondsworth, UK: Penguin Books   0140013873   John Tenniel
2nd reprint of the Revised edition of 1970. Includes *Looking-Glass*. With annotations by Martin Gardner.

4258   1974   The Annotated Alice
Harmondsworth, UK: Penguin Books   0140013873   John Tenniel
3rd reprint of the Revised edition of 1970. Includes *Looking-Glass*. With annotations by Martin Gardner.

4259   1975   The Annotated Alice
Harmondsworth, UK: Penguin Books   0140013873   John Tenniel
4th reprint of the Revised edition of 1970. Includes *Looking-Glass*. With annotations by Martin Gardner.

4260   1975   The Annotated Alice
London: Thomas Nelson and Sons, Ltd.   0171460537   John Tenniel
1st edition thus. Dust jacket. Includes *Looking-Glass*.

4261   1976   The Annotated Alice
Harmondsworth, UK: Penguin Books   0140013873   John Tenniel
5th reprint of the Revised edition of 1970. Includes *Looking-Glass*. With annotations by Martin Gardner.

4262   1978   The Annotated Alice
Harmondsworth, UK: Penguin Books   0140013873   John Tenniel
7th reprint of the Revised edition of 1970. Includes *Looking-Glass*. With annotations by Martin Gardner.

4263   1979   The Annotated Alice
Harmondsworth, UK: Penguin Books   0140013873   John Tenniel
8th reprint of the Revised edition of 1970. Includes *Looking-Glass*. With annotations by Martin Gardner.

4264   1982   The Annotated Alice
Harmondsworth, UK: Penguin Books   0140013873   John Tenniel
10th reprint of the Revised edition of 1970. Includes *Looking-Glass*. With annotations by Martin Gardner.

4265   1984   The Annotated Alice
Harmondsworth, UK: Penguin Books   0140013873   John Tenniel
11th reprint of the Revised edition of 1970. Includes *Looking-Glass*. With annotations by Martin Gardner.

4266   1985   The Annotated Alice
Harmondsworth, UK: Penguin Books   0140013873   John Tenniel
12th reprint of the Revised edition of 1970. Includes *Looking-Glass*. With annotations by Martin Gardner.

4267   1986   The Annotated Alice
Harmondsworth, UK: Penguin Books   0140013873   John Tenniel
13th reprint of the Revised edition of 1970. Includes *Looking-Glass*. With annotations by Martin Gardner.

4268   1987   The Annotated Alice
Harmondsworth, UK: Penguin Books   0140013873   John Tenniel
14th reprint of the Revised edition of 1970. Includes *Looking-Glass*. Reprints after 1987 are all dated 1970. With annotations by Martin Gardner.

4269	1990	More Annotated Alice: Alice's Adventures in Wonderland and Through the Looking-Glass

New York: Random House   0394585712   Peter Newell

Includes "The Wasp In a Wig."

4270	1998	The Annotated Alice

New York: Wings   9780517189207   John Tenniel

Annotated by Martin Gardner.

4271	2000	The Annotated Alice: The Definitive Edition

London: Allen Lane, The Penguin Press   9713994177   John Tenniel

The "Definitive Edition." 1st edition thus. Includes *Looking-Glass*. With annotations by Martin Gardner. Dust jacket.

4272	ca. 2000	The Annotated Alice: Alice's Adventures in Wonderland and Through the Looking-Glass

New York: Norton   9780393048476   John Tenniel

The definitive edition.

4273	2001	The Annotated Alice: The Definitive Edition

London: The Penguin Press   9780140289299   John Tenniel

1st paperback Definitive Edition. Includes *Looking-Glass*. With annotations by Martin Gardner. There have been later reprints indicated by reducing number coding, all with same date.

4274	2014	The Annotated Alice in Wonderland & Through the Looking-Glass by Lewis Carroll

Norderstedt, Germany: Books on Demand   9783735790408; 9783735764423   Unknown

E-book. 1st edition. Adapted by Davies Guttmann. 320 pp. Starts with background information. Then both stories follow.

4275	2015	150th Anniversary Deluxe Edition of The Annotated Alice

New York; London: W. W. Norton & Company Ltd.   9780393245431   Elenore Abbott; Pat Andrea; Uriel Birnbaum; Peter Blake; Lewis Carroll; Charles Copeland; F. Y. Cory; Salvador Dalí; Charles Folkard; Harry Furniss; Iassen Ghiuselev; Leonor Solans Gracia; Tatiana Ianovskaia; Alfred Edward Jackson; Gertrude A. Kay; Walt Kelly; Maria Louise Kirk; John Vernon Lord; Ian McCaig; Blanche McManus; L. Melnick; Barry Moser; John R. Neill; Peter Newell; Andrew Ogus; Charles Pears; Bessie Pease Gutmann; Adriana Pelliano; Willy Pogany; Beatrix Potter; Arthur Rackham; Charles Robinson; Harry Rountree; Byron W. Sewell; Mary Sibree; Mahendra Singh; George Soper; Millicent Sowerby; Ralph Steadman; Margaret W. Tarrant; John Tenniel; Franciszka Themerson; Michel ("Mixt") Villars; W. H. Walker; Leonard Weisgard; Milo Winter

150th Anniversary Deluxe Edition. Includes *Looking-Glass*. Edited by Martin Gardner. Expanded and updated by Mark Burstein. Includes at the end a Preface, an Introduction, the suppressed episode "The Wasp in a Wig" illustrated by Ralph Steadman, a note about Lewis Carroll Societies, Selected References, a section titled "Alice on the Screen" with a checklist by David Schaefer of *Alice*-related films, a section on the many illustrators contained within this edition, and Acknowledgments.

10. Pop-up and Movable Editions Published Worldwide

4276 ca. 1900 Alice in Wonderland Panorama with Movable Pictures

London: Raphael Tuck & Sons   Anonymous

Very abbreviated text by "G. C. F." accompanied by black-and-white illustrations. Also, 2 full-color background spreads and many cut-out figures to be inserted into them.

4277 [1932] Alice in Wonderland

London: Raphael Tuck & Sons   A. L. Bowley

The Storyland Treasury series. Pictorial paper boards, with Come to Life Panorama in central pages. An Easy pop-up. 1 pop-up in color. A later issue, date unknown, exists with minor changes.

4278 1934   Stand-ups #954: Adventures of Alice in Wonderland

Akron, OH: The Saalfield Publishing Co.   Sidney Sage

Die-cut figures to be popped out. Very abbreviated text.

4279 ca. 1940s Alice's Adventures in Wonderland

London: Raphael Tuck & Sons, Ltd.   A. L. Bowley

Decorated boards with red back strip. 2 color plates. 2-page, 3-level pop-up style Come to Life Panorama and 16 black-and-white full-page plates.

4280 ca. 1940s Alice's Adventures in Wonderland

London, Paris, and New York: Raphael Tuck & Sons, Ltd.   A. L. Bowley

Illustrations by Bowley but not credited to her. 16 panel panoramas.

4281 1942   Tony Sarg's Treasure Book: Rip van Winkle, Alice in Wonderland, and Treasure Island

New York: B. F. Jay & Company   Tony Sarg

[22] pp. Color illustrations; 29.2 x 24.2 x 7.6 cm. Imprint from spine; copyright 1942. Shortened, adaptation of 3 famous children's stories. Movable illustrations.

4282 ca. 1943 Alice in Wonderland

Springfield, MA: McLoughlin   Emma McKean

Magic Fairy Tales, No. 2943. Color illustrated boards, plastic comb binding with color and movable illustrations.

4283 [1945] The Animated Picture Book of Alice in Wonderland

New York: Grosset & Dunlap   Julian Wehr

Including 8 movable pictures and 4 pull-outs. Spiral bound. Little is known of this book. See Lovett 306 for more information. WorldCat gives [1947] as the date of publication.

4284 ca. 1960 Alice's Adventures in Wonderland

Baltimore, MD: Bancroft Press   V. Kubasta

With 2 elaborate pop-ups. Illustrated in color. Unpaginated.

4285 ca. 1960s Alice in Wonderland

London: Bancroft & Co.   Voitech Kubasta

Pictorial paper boards. A pop-up edition probably published first in Europe as it is an Artia Production of Prague.

4286 1968   Alice in Wonderland

New York: Graphics International   Dave Chambers; Gwen Gordon;
                                                                             John Spencer

A pop-up book. Adapted by Albert G. Miller, designed by Paul Taylor. Also exists in a smaller format.

4287 1969   Walt Disney's Alice and the Mad Hatter's Tea Party

London: Purnell Books   3610013868   Anonymous
3 double-page scenes.

4288   ca. 1970s   Alice in Wonderland
New York: Playmore   Anonymous
Giant 3-D Fairy Tale Books. Plastic 3-D onlay. Abridged.

4289   1973   Alice's Adventures in Wonderland
Prague, Czechoslovakia: Artia   071960253X   J. Pavlin; G. Seda
Pop-up book with 6 color pop-up scenes. Retold and severely edited by Lornie Leete-Hodge. Might be the 1st edition.

4290   1973   Alice's Adventures in Wonderland
London: Brown Watson   0709702175   J. Pavlin; G. Seda
Retold by Lornie Leete-Hodge. Pop-up edition. An English version of a Czech edition. There was a later edition published in 1980.

4291   1973   Alice's Adventures in Wonderland
London: Murray's Sales and Service   0071960253   J. Pavlin; G. Seda
Reprint of the Prague edition.

4292   1974   Alice in Wonderland: A Giant Pop-Up Book
New York: Modern Promotions,   3009929540   Anonymous
a division of Unisystems, Inc.
Printed in Cali, Colombia, South America. Copyright 1974, 1979, 1983. Multiple editions known, including 2 with "Honey Bear Books" on the cover, and some that say "edited by Ron Stover." Also see an edition dated "n.d."

4293   1975   Alice's Adventures in Wonderland
London: Octopus Books   0706412648   J. Pavlin; G. Seda
Retold by Lornie Leete-Hodge. In an accordion folding of a single sheet of heavy paper. 6 color pop-up scenes. There was a later edition published in 1980.

4294   1976   Alice's Adventures in Wonderland
London: Academy Editions. New York: St. Martin's Press   John Tenniel
Giant Illustrated Edition.

4295   1979   Alice in Wonderland: A Giant Pop-Up Book
New York: Modern Promotions,   3009929540   Anonymous
a division of Unisystems, Inc.
Printed in Cali, Colombia, South America. Copyright 1974, 1979, 1983. Multiple editions known, including 2 with "Honey Bear Books" on the cover, and some that say "edited by Ron Stover." Also see an edition dated "n.d."

4296   1980   Alice's Adventures in Wonderland
London: Brown Watson   0709702175   J. Pavlin; G. Seda
Retold by Lornie Leete-Hodge. Pop-up edition. An English version of a Czech edition. There were later editions published by Brown Watson, and by Octopus Books in 1980.

4297   1980   Alice's Adventures in Wonderland
New York: Delacorte Press   0440003539   Jenny Thorne
                                             (after John Tenniel)
Reprint of Pan Macmillan Children's Books edition.

4298   1980   Alice's Adventures in Wonderland
London: Macmillan Children's Books   9780333293522   Jenny Thorne
                                             (after John Tenniel)

1st edition. Also reprinted multiple times (as listed below). 6 pop-ups and 5 moving scenes. Paper engineer James Roger Diaz. Designed by John Strejan. Glazed pictorial paper boards.

4299   1980   Alice's Adventures in Wonderland
London: Octopus Books   0706412648   J. Pavlin; G. Seda
Retold by Lornie Leete-Hodge. Pop-up edition. An English version of a Czech edition. A later issue.

4300   1980   Alice's Adventures in Wonderland
London: Pan Macmillan Children's Books   9780333293522   Jenny Thorne
                                                                   (after John Tenniel)
1st reprint of the 1980 1st edition. 6 pop-ups and 5 moving scenes. Paper engineer James Roger Diaz. Designed by John Strejan. Glazed pictorial paper boards.

4301   1981   Alice in Wonderland
Barcelona: Brown Watson   9780709701149   Anonymous
Minipanorama Pop-Up series, no. 3. 6 pp. Book is composed of a single piece of stiff paper folded and pasted to create an outer wrapper and 3-color pop-up scenes and 6 pp. of (severely edited) text, printed vertically bottom to top. In wrapper.

4302   1981   Alice's Adventures in Wonderland
London: Pan Macmillan Children's Books   9780333293522   Jenny Thorne
                                                                   (after John Tenniel)
2nd reprint of the 1980 1st edition. Pop-ups and movables on every page. Paper engineer James Roger Diaz. Designed by John Strejan.

4303   1981   Alice's Flip Book
[Amherst, Mass.]: [Swamp Press]   Edward Rayher
Miniature edition (5.5 x 7.5 cm). White wrappers, printed in black and orange. Stapled.

4304   1981   Alice's Flip Book of the Cheshire Cat
Oneonta, NY: [Swamp Press]   Edward Rayher
Miniature edition (5.2 x 7.4 cm). Press name and copyright date on spine. Letterpress printed on one side, printed paper wrappers. "This third edition was made possible by Victor the Golding letterpress." —Colophon

4305   ca. 1981 Alice in Wonderland
London: Brown Watson   0709701144   Magda
Minipanorama Pop-up Series. A UK version of a Spanish original.

4306   1982   Alice's Flip Book
New York: B. Shackman   Edward Rayher
Miniature book (5 x 7.5 cm).

4307   1982   Alice's Flip Book
New York: Merrimack Publishing   Edward Rayher
Miniature book (5 x 7.5 cm).

4308   1983   Alice's Adventures in Wonderland
Melbourne, VIC: Budget Books   0868011002   Anonymous
Giant 3-D Fairy Tale Books. Adaptation. 8 pp. Distributed in Australia and New Zealand.

4309   1983   Alice in Wonderland: A Giant Pop-Up Book
New York: Modern Promotions,   3009929540   Anonymous
a division of Unisystems, Inc.

Printed in Cali, Colombia, South America. Copyright 1974, 1979, 1983. Multiple editions known, including 2 with "Honey Bear Books" on the cover, and some that say "edited by Ron Stover." Also see an edition dated "n.d."

4310   1984   Alice in Wonderland: A Favorite Pop-Up Book
New York: Derrydale Book   0517462311   Anonymous
Copyright by Ottenheimer Publishers. Also see other copies.

4311   1984   Alice in Wonderland
Guipuzcoa, Spain: Ediciones A. Saldaña   9780709405757   Anonymous
Pop-up book. Wonder Pop-Up series. Color illustrations.

4312   1986   Alice's Adventures in Wonderland
London: Macmillan   9780333293522   Jenny Thorne
                                                                           (after John Tenniel)
3rd reprint of the 1980 edition. Pop-ups and movables on every page. Paper engineer James Roger Diaz.

4313   1987   Alice's Adventure in Wonderland: The Classic Story Retold in Rhyme
                for Young Children
Kansas City, MO: Hallmark Cards   Pat Paris
Adapted by Karen Ravn. 1 pop-up and several movables.

4314   1988   Alice's Adventures in Wonderland
London: Macmillan   9780333293522   Jenny Thorne
                                                                           (after John Tenniel)
4th reprint of the 1980 edition. Pop-ups and movables on every page. Paper engineer James Roger Diaz.

4315   ca. 1980s Alice in Wonderland
Manchester, UK: Children's Leisure Products Ltd.   0709404948   Anonymous
In the Petite Series. 8-page adaptation. Red card wrappers. Another copy known in darker red wrappers. 3 bright color pop-ups.

4316   1990   Alice's Adventures in Wonderland
London: Macmillan   9780333293522   Jenny Thorne
                                                                           (after John Tenniel)
5th reprint of the 1980 edition. Pop-ups and movables on every page. Paper engineer James Roger Diaz.

4317   1991   Alice's Adventures in Wonderland
New York: Dell   0440405408   Jenny Thorne
                                                                           (after John Tenniel)
Reprint of the 1991 Macmillan edition. A Yearling Book. Paper engineer James Roger Diaz.

4318   1991   Alice in Wonderland Pop-up Storybook
London: Grandreams Ltd.   0862278910; 9780862278915 Anonymous
A pop-up book probably first published in Europe. 6 double-page scenes. Printed in Czechoslovakia.

4319   1991   Alice's Adventures in Wonderland
London: Macmillan   9780333293522   Jenny Thorne
                                                                           (after John Tenniel)
6th reprint of the 1980 edition. New front cover design. Pop-ups and movables on every page. Paper engineer James Roger Diaz.

4320   1992   Alice in Wonderland
London: Binky Books   1856271722   Samantha Smith

4 pop-up books in illustrated card case, retold by Elsa Knight Bruno. The books are titled: *Down the Rabbit Hole* (ISBN 1856271773); *Curiouser and Curiouser* (185627182X); *The Mad Hatter's Tea-Party* (1856271927); and *The Queen of Hearts* (1856271870).

4321   1992   Alice in Wonderland: Pop-up Picture Story

London: Brown Watson   070970805X;   Pamela Storey
                                        9780709708056

Glazed pictorial paper boards.

4322   1992   Walt Disney's Alice's Tea Party

New York: Disney Press   1562821458   Jesse Clay
Text adapted by Lyn Calder. Dust jacket

4323   1992   Down the Rabbit Hole

Chicago: Lexicon Publications, Inc.   Samantha Smith

Volume 1 of 4 pop-ups. Created and manufactured by Ottenheimer Publishers, Inc. for Lexicon Publications, Inc. Copyright Ottenheimer Publishers, Inc. Retold by Elsa Knight Bruno. Paper engineered by Bruce Foster. Printed and bound in Colombia by Carvajal S.A.

4324   1992   Curiouser and Curiouser

Chicago: Lexicon Publications, Inc.   Samantha Smith

Volume 2 of 4 pop-ups. Created and manufactured by Ottenheimer Publishers, Inc. for Lexicon Publications, Inc. Copyright Ottenheimer Publishers, Inc. Retold by Elsa Knight Bruno. Paper engineered by Bruce Foster. Printed and bound in Colombia by Carvajal S.A.

4325   1992   The Mad Hatter's Tea Party

Chicago: Lexicon Publications, Inc.   Samantha Smith

Volume 3 of 4 pop-ups. Created and manufactured by Ottenheimer Publishers, Inc. for Lexicon Publications, Inc. Copyright Ottenheimer Publishers, Inc. Retold by Elsa Knight Bruno. Paper engineered by Bruce Foster. Printed and bound in Colombia by Carvajal S.A.

4326   1992   The Queen of Hearts

Chicago: Lexicon Publications, Inc.   Samantha Smith

Volume 4 of 4 pop-ups. Created and manufactured by Ottenheimer Publishers, Inc. for Lexicon Publications, Inc. Copyright Ottenheimer Publishers, Inc. Retold by Elsa Knight Bruno. Paper engineered by Bruce Foster. Printed and bound in Colombia by Carvajal S.A.

4327   1992   Alice's Adventures in Wonderland

London: Macmillan   9780333293522   Jenny Thorne
                                                                 (after John Tenniel)

7th reprint of the 1980 edition. Pop-ups and movables on every page. Paper engineer James Roger Diaz.

4328   1993   Alice in Wonderland: A Pop-Up Storybook

Montreal, QC: Brimar   9782894330388   Anonymous
A Pop-Up book.

4329   1993   Alice in Wonderland Pop-up Storybook

London: Grandreams Ltd.   0862278910   Anonymous
A pop-up book probably first published in Europe. 6 double-page scenes.

4330   1994   Walt Disney's Alice in Wonderland: Down the rabbit hole

New York: Disney Press   9780786830008   Robbin Cuddy
"A Lift-the-Flap Rebus Book." Adapted by Lisa Rojany; designed by Suzanne Ferguson; paper engineering by José R. Seminario.

4331	1994	Alice in Wonderland Pop-up Storybook		
	London: Grandreams Ltd.		1858302137	Anonymous
	A pop-up book probably first published in Europe.			

4332	1994	Walt Disney's Alice in Wonderland: Down the Rabbit Hole		
	Santa Monica, CA: Intervisual Books		078683000x	Robbin Cuddy
	"A Lift-the-Flap Rebus Book." Adapted by Lisa Rojany; designed by Suzanne Ferguson; paper engineering by José R. Seminario.			

4333	1994	Alice's Adventures in Wonderland		
	London: Macmillan		0333293525	Jenny Thorne
				(after John Tenniel)
	8th reprint of the 1980 edition. Pop-ups and movables on every page. Paper engineer James Roger Diaz.			

4334	1997	Alice's Adventures in Wonderland		
	London: Grandreams Ltd.		1858302137	Anonymous
	A musical pop-up book. 4 double-page scenes.			

4335	1998	Alice's Adventures in Wonderland		
	London: Macmillan Children's Books		9780333293522	Anonymous
	Reprint of a 1980 edition. 6 pop-ups and 5 moving scenes. Paper engineer James R. Diaz.			

4336	1999	Alice in Wonderland "Running Late"		
	New York: B. Shackman		9669183780	Alyse M. Newman
				(after John Tenniel)
	Miniature edition (4.8 x 7.5 cm). Illustrates White Rabbit checking his watch, and then running and jumping into a rabbit-hole.			

4337	2000	Alice's Adventures in Wonderland		
	London: Grandreams Ltd.		1858302137	Anonymous
	A musical pop-up book. 4 double-page scenes. Reprint of the 1997 edition.			

4338	2000	Alice's Pop-Up Wonderland		
	London: Macmillan Children's Books		0333901134	Alex Vining
	Adapted by Nick Denchfield. 6 pop-up scenes and a fold-down board game with over 30 press-out pieces.			

4339	2002	Alice's Pop-Up Theatre Book		
	London: Macmillan Children's Books		0333901134	Alex Vining; Angela Edwards;
				Peter Vining
	Adapted by Nick Denchfield. 6 pop-up scenes and a stage with over 30 press-out pieces. 20-page. book of theater scenes. Alternate ISBN: 0333961374.			

4340	2003	Alice's Adventures in Wonderland		
	New York: Little Brown		9780689847431	Robert Sabuda
	Classic Collectible Series. A pop-up adaptation. [12] pp. Same as the London: Simon & Schuster edition.			

4341	2003	Alice's Adventures in Wonderland		
	New York: Little Brown			Robert Sabuda
	Large foldout of shower of cards, and small booklet within with 3 smaller pop-up previews.			

4342	2003	Alice in (Pop-Up) Wonderland		
	New York: Orchard Books		043941184X;	J. Otto Seibold
			9780439411844	

Pop-up book. Published by Orchard Books, an imprint of Scholastic, Inc. Orchard Books and design are registered trademarks of Watts Publishing Group Ltd. 1st edition September 2003. Paper engineering by James R. Diaz. Also issued in a limited boxed edition.

4343   2003   Alice's Adventures in Wonderland
London: Simon & Schuster   9780689837593   Robert Sabuda
Classic Collectible Series. A pop-up adaptation. [12] pp. Also issued as a limited edition of 10, lettered A to J and retained by the illustrator; and in a numbered edition of 50. Some copies signed but not numbered. As a promotional item there was also a large foldout of shower of cards, and a small booklet with 3 smaller pop-up previews.

4344   2003   Alice's Adventures in Wonderland
London: Simon & Schuster   0689847432   Robert Sabuda
Little Simon edition.

4345   2003   Alice's Adventures in Wonderland
London: Simon & Schuster   Robert Sabuda
Large foldout of shower of cards, and small booklet within with 3 smaller pop-up previews.

4346   2010   Lewis Carroll's Alice's Adventures in Wonderland
London: Carlton Books Ltd.   9781847324368   Zdenko Basic
1st edition. Retold by Harriet Castor. Pop-up and movable book. Various later issues all with the same date.

4347   2010   Lewis Carroll's Alice's Adventures in Wonderland
Prahran, VIC: Hardie Grant Egmont   9781921564215   Zdenko Basic
Retold by Harriet Castor. With pop-up and pull-out pages.

4348   2010   Alice in Wonderland: A Classic Story Pop-up Book with Sounds
Dorking, UK: Templar Publishing   9781848770010   Richard Johnson
1st edition. Retold by Libby Hamilton. A Classic Story Pop-up Book with Sounds. Various later issues all with the same date.

4349   2013   Alice in Wonderland
Tokyo: Lyric   Yui
Pop-up book.

4350   2014   Alice in Wonderland Creativity Book
[London]: Carlton Kids   9781783120451   Zdenko Basic;
                                                                  Manuel Sumberac
Includes games, cut-outs, art paper, stickers, and stencils. Printed in Shenzhen, China.

4351   2014   Alice in Wonderland
London: Tango Books Ltd.   9781857078145   Maria Taylor
Adapted by Sheri Safran. With 3-dimensional pop-up scenes. Paper engineering by Manth.

4352   2015   Alice's Adventures in Wonderland
London: Walker Books   9781406361728   Graham Baker-Smith
A panorama pop-up book in 3 dimensions showing 10 scenes.

4353   2016   Alice Through the Looking Glass
London: Carlton Books   9781783121830   Patricia Moffett
Retold by Patricia Moffett. Lift-up flaps.

4354   2016   Alice in Wonderland: Down the Rabbit Hole
London: Macmillan Children's Books   9781509820511   John Tenniel
Macmillan Children's Books. The book opens out to a carousel shape showing *Alice's Adventures in Wonderland* in 6 3-dimensional scenes.

4355   2019   Alice's Adventures in Wonderland and Through the Looking-Glass
New York: Harper Design   9780062936615   MinaLima
"Lavishly illustrated with interactive elements."

4356   n.d.   Alice's Adventures in Wonderland
London: Brown Watson   0709702175   J. Pavlin; G. Seda
Pop-up edition. Retold by Lornie Leete-Hodge. An English version of a Czech edition.

4357   n.d.   Alice in Wonderland: My Favorite Pop-Up Book
New York: Modern Promotions, a division of Unisystems, Inc.   Unknown
Printed in Colombia, South America

PUBLICATION HISTORY, AND
PUBLISHER AND ILLUSTRATOR INDEXES

APPENDIX 1: Publication History of the Four *Alice* Books

Arnold Hirshon

ASSUMPTIONS AND DECISIONS

USING INFORMATION from the checklists, the data table presented here documents the publication history of the four *Alice* books (including "Combined Editions") from the date of the first publication through April 2021. For this analysis, I had to make some assumptions when assigning the date of publication. Given the size of the total data set, it is unlikely that the application of a different set of assumptions would have significantly altered the trendlines for any of the four books. For the record, here are the assumptions underlying the data table and analysis.

- Excluded from the data table are books where no date could be ascertained ("n.d.").

- Qualified dates (i.e., those appearing in brackets in the checklist) are treated as if they were unqualified. Therefore, single-year dates enclosed in brackets were counted as if the dates were certain; e.g., [1924] was included as a 1924 imprint. In addition, approximated dates in the checklist were treated as confirmed dates; e.g., "ca. 1908" was counted as if the date was 1908

- When multiple dates appear in the checklist, the earliest date was used. Therefore, a date range of "[1930–1933]" was treated as if the date of issue was 1930. Dates in approximated ranges, such as "1930s," were similarly treated as if the date was 1930. For Macmillan combined editions with double dates, such as "1899 and 1900," the former being the date for *Looking-Glass* and 1900 for *Alice*. the earlier of the two dates was used.

- Although *The Annotated Alice* editions appear in a separate list in the checklists, in the data table they are included with the data set for the Combined Editions of *Alice* and *Looking-Glass*. In addition, the combined editions in the checklists of the "Other English-Language" and the "Rest of the World" editions were added to the Combined Editions list for the data compilation.

- Since nearly all the titles of the pop-up and movable editions refer only to *Alice*, they are included entirely with the *Alice* editions, recognizing that some will likely have included text, characters, or scenes from *Looking-Glass*.

- To make the data table more readable and to smooth insignificant year-by-year changes, the publications are grouped by decade rather than shown separately for each year over the nearly 160 years of the history of the works.

	Alice	Looking-Glass	Combined Editions	under Ground	The Nursery "Alice"	TOTAL
1865–1869	28	0	0	1	0	29
1870–1879	54	40	0	0	0	94
1880–1889	49	32	5	3	5	94
1890–1899	157	99	41	0	3	300
1900–1909	221	158	54	0	0	433
1910–1919	188	79	27	0	0	294
1920–1929	188	48	41	0	0	277
1930–1939	137	32	63	3	1	236
1940–1949	135	26	60	0	0	221
1950–1959	124	44	65	2	0	235
1960–1969	118	29	103	11	7	268
1970–1979	128	28	107	6	4	273
1980–1989	178	44	94	16	15	347
1990–1999	174	51	71	7	3	306
2000–2009	190	53	57	20	2	322
2010–2020	272	146	77	35	6	536
TOTAL	2,341	909	865	104	46	4,265
PERCENT OF TOTAL	54.9%	21.3%	20.3%	2.4%	1.1%	

DATA ANALYSIS

UNDER GROUND AND THE NURSERY "ALICE" EDITIONS. Although the *Alice's Adventures under Ground* manuscript preceded *Alice's Adventures in Wonderland,* the former did not appear in a published facsimile edition until 1886. Similarly, *The Nursery "Alice"* was not published until 1890—a quarter-century after the original *Alice,* and four years after the facsimile of *under Ground.* Together, *under Ground* and *The Nursery "Alice"* represent only 3.5% of all the English-language published editions of the four books. The trendline for each one (separately and together) is much lower than for the two main books, *Alice* and *Looking-Glass* (published separately and in combination).

Of the two lower-ranked titles, *under Ground* represents nearly 70% of the total activity. Given the small population size of each, it is difficult to intuit any statistically significant trends for either. Throughout most of their histories, these two books have similar trendlines. For half of the decades, their publishing activity was either identical (including four decades when neither was published) or nearly identical (including two where there was only a one-book publishing differential, and two decades with only a two-book difference). So, what can we intuit when 33% of all editions of *The "Nursery" Alice* were published in the decade from 1980 to 1989? Similarly, what are we to intuit when, beginning with the 1990 decade, publishing activity for *The Nursery "Alice"* began to drop significantly compared to new editions of *under Ground,* but the total difference in publishing activity over the thirty-year period was only fifty-one books?

ALICE EDITIONS. Since *Alice* was the first and most published of the titles (55% of the total of all editions), its sustained success and activity growth are assured. However, the trendline shows that *Alice* experienced some significant hills and valleys over the decades. For example, *Alice* hit its first peak in the 1900–1909 decade, and this peak was not exceeded until 110 years later. Beginning in 1910, there was a long and nearly continuous period of general decline in *Alice* publishing activity. We can make some reasonable conjectures as to possible causes of this slump, one that did not fully reverse itself until the twenty-first century. A major factor driving the issuance of new editions was the creation of new illustrated works, and so following the expiration of the UK copyright in 1908 there was a significant flurry of new editions for the next few years. This likely saturated the market and satiated the public appetite for some time. Another possible explanation for the slump may be that for this period *Alice* was no longer in vogue, as more contemporary books captured the imaginations of children.

New *Alice* editions continued to decline significantly beginning in the 1930s. Surely the occurrence of World Wars I and II (along with a troubled economic history in the intervening years) shifted public appetites. Disruptions in the publishing business might also have been a factor, including the general economic conditions caused by the Great Depression of the 1930s, and the later war mobilization and paper rationing required during and after the World War II years.

New illustrated editions generally increased the publishing activity, but with only a few notable exceptions the period from 1930 through at least the 1950s was not a particularly fertile time for newly illustrated works. Three other important factors might have been expected to cause a significant increase in the rate of publication but failed to do so: the 100th anniversary of Carroll's birth in 1932 (which was recognized by Alice Hargreaves's trip to New York), the 1933 release by Paramount Pictures of its version of *Alice in Wonderland*, and the 1951 release of Disney's *Alice in Wonderland* film.

Regarding the 100th anniversary, the Tenniel illustrations were still much in the public consciousness in 1932. Rightly or wrongly, in the public mind, especially in the UK and US, Hargreaves as the "real" Alice was inextricably associated with the "real" illustrations by Tenniel. Publishers probably saw no need to issue brand-new illustrated editions given the existence of myriad cheap editions containing the Tenniel illustrations.

The Paramount film generated a few associated new book editions that employed black-and-white still photographs from the film. However, those books created barely a tiny ripple in the market, not a wave. It did not help that the film was a box office failure, and that the set and costume designs were largely inspired by Tenniel. Although Disney released collateral books to its film (and continues to mine that trove today), new publications by Disney alone were insufficient to move the overall trendline. Therefore, it is no surprise that the film did not cause publishers to issue large numbers of newly illustrated editions.

The decline of newly published *Alice* editions did not abate during the economic recovery of the postwar 1950s. In the UK, paper shortages continued through the early years of the decade, which delayed the availability of newer editions from respected illustrators such as Mervyn Peake.

It was only in the 1960s, the decade in which the publication of *Alice* celebrated its 100th anniversary, that a significant number of new editions began to be issued. This growth accelerated somewhat in the 1970s, but the most significant increase in the number of new *Alice* editions did not begin to emerge until the 1990s, a trend that continued over the next three decades. Indeed, it was only in the most recent decade (2010–2020) that the previously highest peak of publishing activity (which ended in 1909) was finally exceeded. It is reasonable to assume that the 150th anniversary of publication in 2015 was the cause for this most recent sharp increase.

LOOKING-GLASS EDITIONS. This sequel usually is not regarded as being as popular as *Alice*. Most illustrators of *Alice* did not illustrate a *Looking-Glass*, so fewer new editions of *Looking-Glass* tended to appear. Although the publication trendlines for *Looking-Glass* as a stand-alone publication generally align closely to those of *Alice*, the volume of new editions of *Looking-Glass* is much lower. *Looking-Glass* editions peaked in the same decade as *Alice* (1900–1909), but there were about 30% fewer editions of *Looking-Glass* published during that period than of *Alice*. Subsequently, and unlike *Alice*, the published editions of *Looking-Glass* never exceeded their 1900–1909 peak, though they did come within about 10% of that mark in the most recent decade.

Looking-Glass went out of copyright in 1948, but unlike the flourishing of new editions following the copyright expiration of *Alice*, the expiration of *Looking-Glass* did not spawn much new publishing activity. There are likely at least four reasons. First, while there was always an interest in *Looking-Glass*, its success was never the same as that of *Alice* in the public imagination, and so publishers were likely less inclined to test the market. Second, the potential lack of an audience likely caused publishers to be hesitant to authorize new editions, a risk-avoidance choice intensified by limited paper resources in the early post-WWII years in the UK. Third, some publishers may have felt burned by the reception given to many of the new 1907 *Alice* editions. (As mentioned in my essay in Volume One, we know that Arthur Rackham, and perhaps others, shied away from illustrating *Looking-Glass* because of the critical reactions beginning in 1907.) Fourth, it is rare to find an illustrator who illustrated only *Looking-Glass*, but not *Alice*.[1] Perhaps many illustrators did not see the same joys or challenges in illustrating *Looking-Glass*, or they simply moved on to other projects. Even artists who did illustrate both books usually worked on *Alice* first, and then many years sometimes elapsed before they illustrated *Looking-Glass*. (For example, fifteen years passed between F. Y. Cory's editions of the two books.)

COMBINED EDITIONS. In the United States, the first combined editions were issued in 1881, and in the United Kingdom the first ones were issued by Macmillan in 1911. Other publishers did not begin to do so in the UK until 1920.

Although the number of *Alice* editions issued alone was greater than the number of combined editions over the entire 150 years of publishing activity, the visual trendlines of the two generally mirrored each other until the 1970s. The trendline for *Alice* as a stand-alone volume decreased

---

1. Among the very few illustrators who had a hand in illustrating *Looking-Glass* (including a full edition, a frontispiece, or a cover), but whose work is not represented with an *Alice* in the English-language checklists, are Kyle Baker, Mary A. Brooke, Trevor Brown, K. Y. Chan, Frank Godwin, P. B. Hickling, Franklin Hughes, Incco, Ken Leeder, Patricia Moffett, Gwyneth Richardson, Daniel Rover Singer, and Franciszka Themerson.

from 1930 through 1979, but over the same period the trendline for new combined editions rose. Nonetheless, in terms of sheer numbers, in every decade the number of *Alice* stand-alone editions significantly exceeded those of combined editions—on average by 38% over the entire period, and by more than 70% during the 1900–1909 decade.

Beginning in the 1920–1929 decade, the number of combined editions began significantly to exceed that of *Looking-Glass* editions. It is possible that sales interest in combined editions either absorbed or cannibalized sales of *Looking-Glass* alone—perhaps because publishers may have considered that *Looking-Glass* lacked the sales potential of the more popular *Alice* and thus chose to intensify the impact of *Looking-Glass* by issuing the two books in combination. Publishers also did not commission new illustrated editions with the same gusto as they had for *Alice*; had they done so, perhaps the sales volume for *Looking-Glass* as a separate volume may have increased.

Beginning in the 1970–1979 decade, the trendlines of the two began to diverge substantially. Over the next three decades, the number of new *Alice* stand-alone editions increased while the number of combined editions decreased.

The two trendlines intersected the 2000–2009 decade. It is too soon to determine whether this is an anomaly or a new trendline, but in the 2010–2020 decade *Looking-Glass* editions significantly outpaced combined editions by over 100%. Although the rate of rise was far less than that of *Alice* editions, the delta between the number of editions still spiked at 54%.

THE FUTURE. History may not be an accurate guide to conjecture what may occur in the future publication history of the *Alice* books, or what unanticipated factors may cause future shifts. For example, whereas anniversaries of *Alice* tend to be associated with the issuance of new editions, the 50th anniversary of *Looking-Glass* did not stave off its general publication downward trendline, nor did its 100th anniversary. The early signs are that, unlike the 150th anniversary of *Alice* in 2015, the 150th anniversary of *Looking-Glass* in 2022 may not spark a significant increase in the number of new editions.

APPENDIX 2: Publisher Index

Arnold Hirshon

INTRODUCTION

THIS INDEX LISTS publishers and imprints under 1,046 different entities.

Since the first publication of *Alice* more than 150 years ago, the publishers of the four related books have had many different corporate relationships, as reflected in the different forms of their names on title pages. Not only was the form of the name of the same publisher sometimes inconsistently represented on title pages, but different checklist compilers followed different conventions for recording those names. Due to these variations in forms of publisher names, below is a brief explanation of some of the most common differences, and the conventions applied within this index.

- Some checklist compilers recorded the full form of the name as found on the title page, while others may have shortened the entry by (1) removing names and abbreviations such as "Co.," "Ltd.," etc., (2) using an ampersand rather than spelling out the word "and," or (3) adding the word "Sons" to the name. In this index, such variations usually are normalized and combined, but in some cases a checklist entry may include the full name as a variant if the difference is likely to be important to identify different editions.

- The index does not attempt to trace or record the corporate history of each publisher; such a task is well beyond our scope. The objective is to enable readers to find books identified with an imprint as found in a book-in-hand, and so a pragmatic approach was adopted. For example, in the United States, Doubleday published editions under many imprints, including Bantam Books, Bantam Doubleday Dell Publishing Group, Blue Ribbon Books, the Book League of America, Doubleday Doran, Doubleday Editions, Doubleday Page & Company, Garden City Publishing, Junior Deluxe, and Nelson Doubleday. Both the checklist entries and this index record the form of the name as found in the book. For differences that are likely significant, the entries may appear in the index under separate names; e.g., "Collier-Macmillan" appears as a separate entry from "Collier" or "Macmillan" alone, and "Donohue Brothers" is separate from "Donohue, Henneberry & Co." or "Henneberry." In addition, where one organization served as a distributor for another publisher, or when one publisher had different corporate offices and names in two different countries (e.g., in both the UK and the US), this index includes entries under both organizations. Therefore, the same book may appear two or more times within the index under two or more publisher names.

- This index omits the title of an edition from the publisher's name when the title is included in the name; e.g., the edition name ("People's Edition") was omitted when the checklist entry lists the publisher as the "Macmillan 'People's Edition.'" In these cases, only the publisher's imprint as found on the title page appears in the index, but the full entry may include more complete information.

- Regarding the presence of the initial article "the" as part of a publisher's name (e.g., "The Continental Book Company" or "The Folio Society" or "The British Library"), different checklist compilers observed different conventions. We recognize that in some cases the publisher itself considers the article to be an essential part of its name and identity. (This is especially a common practice among publishers in the UK.) For each publisher, this index usually consolidated these entries under the predominant form (i.e., with or without the initial article) as found in most of the checklist entries for that publisher's name. To aid the reader, cross-references to alternate forms of names have been included throughout the index.

For additional information about the listing of publishers within the checklist, see the "Introduction to the Checklists."

Publisher Index of the Checklist Entries

PUBLISHER NAME	CHECKLIST ENTRY NUMBERS
1st World Publishing	3973, 3975
A. & C. Black Ltd.	645, 705, 729, 742, 764, 787, 827
A. Colish	2262
A. Flanagan	2027
A. Francke	3192
A. L. Burt	1870, 1871, 1894, 1908, 1909, 1910, 1961, 1964, 1965, 1977, 1989, 1990, 1991, 2000, 2028, 2029, 2059, 2060, 2061, 2068, 2093, 2117, 2130, 2131, 2132, 2369, 2370, 2388, 2390, 2391, 2395, 2397, 2398, 2399, 2414, 2415, 2416, 2424, 2430, 2431, 2432, 2439, 2440, 2451, 2465, 2506, 3669, 3676, 3681, 3684, 3686, 3711, 3738, 3739, 3758, 3759, 3773, 3784, 3800, 3818
A. Wessels	1925, 2407, 2428, 3712. *See also* M. F. Mansfield and A. Wessels
Abbey Classics	942, 945, 1451, 1458
Abrams	2277
Academic	3140
Academy	2244, 2611
Academy Editions	985, 1475, 1497, 3557
AD Classics	2819
Adegi Graphics	3966
Adelaide Observer	2732
Adprint Ltd.	778, 788, 820, 834, 845
Aegypan Press	3977, 3979
Agents Digest	3105
Aionas	2995, 2996
Airmont	2218, 2592
Akasha Publishing	3600, 3601
Alan Wingate	1382
Albert Whitman	2483, 2493, 3899
Aldine Co.	483
Alfred A. Knopf	2265, 2269, 2278, 2287, 2288, 2646, 3951, 3953
Alka Publications	3002
Allen and Richard Lane	794
Allen Lane	4271
Alligator Books	1195
Alma Classics	1671, 1682, 4154, 4179, 4187
Almqvist & Wiksell	2927
Amazon	1256
American Book Company	2090
American News Company	1829
American Publishers Corporation	1872, 2396, 2400, 3672

Cider Mill Press	2366, 4180
Claremont Books	1604, 3580
Claremont Classics	2772
Clarkson N. Potter	2236, 2238, 4244, 4246
Classic Comic Store	4018
Classic Communications Co.	3200
Classic Good Books	1668, 1669, 4174, 4175
Classic Press	2227
Classic Publishing	2604, 2605
Classroom Complete Press	4036
Cobblestone Productions	4181, 4182
Collector's Library	1660, 1631
Collier	443, 1413, 1818, 1827, 2581, 2585, 2595, 2613
Collier Macmillan	443, 444, 445, 446, 447, 1412, 1413, 1818, 1819, 1820, 1821, 1822, 1827, 2581, 2595, 2613
Collins	709, 727, 823, 824, 825, 2756
Collins and Wm. Collins, Sons & Co. Ltd.	3530
Collins Clear-Type Press	499, 509, 512, 519, 520, 531, 544, 552, 594, 612, 664, 670, 671, 672, 701, 722, 732, 759, 821, 828, 829, 835, 839, 847, 850, 854, 857, 858, 862, 880, 1279, 1280, 1281, 1282, 1283, 1284, 1285, 1286, 1287, 1312, 1316, 1317, 1318, 1319, 1325, 1326, 1327, 1328, 1336, 1337, 1346, 1347, 1353, 1374, 1375, 1380, 1383, 1384, 1385, 1389, 1392, 1393, 1397, 1403, 1414, 1422, 1433, 1464, 1465, 1482, 1518, 3500, 3501, 3503, 3506, 3507, 3525
Collins Design	2345
Collins World	2614
Colorgravure Press	2747
Colourgravure Publications	2739
Commercial Press	2870, 2871, 2872, 2873, 2876, 2879, 2880, 2889
Compass Publishing	3148
Consolidated Press	2740, 2741, 2743, 2745
Contemporary Books, Inc.	2652
Continental Book Company	See The Continental Book Company; see also Zephyr Books
Cornelsen	2965, 2966
Cornelsen Hirschgraben	2964
Cornerstones Education	1215
Cornhill Co.	2139
Cosimo	4168
Cosmos Culture	3216, 3218, 3219, 3220
Cottage Classics	4140, 4141
Courage Books	1167, 2289, 2329
CreateSpace	2340, 2349, 2351, 2353, 2357, 2688, 3987, 3988, 3989, 3990, 3998, 3999, 4000, 4001, 4006, 4007, 4008, 4009, 4010, 4011, 4012,

Dodd, Mead & Co.	2105
Dodge Publishing Company	2007, 3819
Dolphin Books	2712, 4194
Donohue	*See* Donohue Brothers; Donohue, Henneberry & Co; M. A. Donohue
Donohue Brothers	1926, 2408, 3713
Donohue, Henneberry & Co.	1859, 1863, 1864, 1888, 2405
Dorling Kindersley	1150, 1261, 2316
Doubleday	2204, 2712, 2831, 3929, 3932, 4194
Doubleday Classics	2376, 3894, 4091
Doubleday Junior Deluxe Editions	3927
Doubleday, Doran	2009, 2078, 2086, 2092, 2106, 2114, 2122, 2124, 2137, 2143, 2165, 2449
Doubleday, Page & Co.	480, 481, 533, 562, 566, 576, 602, 611, 641, 654, 669, 2013, 2014, 2107
Dover Publications	2308, 2321, 3967, 4003, 4071, 4077, 4082, 4110, 4136, 4206, 4207
Dragon's World	1091, 3570, 3572
Dreamland Publications	3005, 3010, 3013
DSI [Digital Scanning Incorporated]	2335, 3980
Duell, Sloan and Pearce	2212, 3933
Duffield & Co.	2017
Dufour	2577
Dunda Books	3997
Dutton	*See* E. P. Dutton
Dutton Children's Books	2309
Dynamite	2680, 2702
E. A. Weeks & Co.	1865
E. Arnold	521
E. J. Arnold & Son, Ltd.	556, 3509
E. Jacobs	3843, 3868, 3883
E. P. Dutton	882, 905, 907, 908, 955, 956, 968, 969, 970, 986, 987, 988, 1025, 1321, 1322, 1323, 1324, 1334, 1338, 1341, 1348, 1386, 1396, 1411, 1423, 1425, 1434, 1454, 1466, 1483, 1504, 1519, 2010, 2034, 2079, 2104, 2126, 2127, 2479, 2484, 2504, 2541, 2561, 2563, 2578, 2596, 2609, 2615, 2621, 2623, 2626, 2634, 3562
E. W. Cole, Book Arcade	2733
E-artnow Editions	1689, 2838, 4176
East China Normal University Press	2898
East China University of Science and Technology Press	2917
Easton Press	2249, 2274, 3958, 3964
EDC Publishing	2352
Ediciones A. Saldaña	4311
Ediciones Dos Amigos	2861

Firefly Books	1067, 2325, 2812
Firmin-Didot	2941
First Avenue Editions	4020
Five Mile Press	*See* The Five Mile Press Pty Ltd.
Flame Tree Publishing	1687
Fleetway Books	1046, 1047, 1055
Fleurus Editions	2945, 2946
Floating Press	2857, 2858, 2859, 2860
Folio Society	*See* The Folio Society
Foreign Language Press	2877, 2883
Foreign Language Teaching and Research Press	2920
Forgotten Books	4183
Foulsham & Co.	706, 798
Foxton Books	1265
Frances Lincoln's Children's Books	1244
Franklin Library	2258, 2264
Franklin Mint	2243
Franklin Watts	2219
Frederick A. Stokes	1982, 2062, 3782, 3791, 3792, 3820, 3873, 3908
Frederick Warne & Co.	613, 673
Frederick Watts	2588, 2597
Frémok	4166
FRMK	4148, 4150
Funk and Wagnalls	2069
Funtastic	2778, 2779
G. Bell & Sons Ltd.	540, 546, 565, 568, 572, 579, 609, 627, 665, 693, 723
G. G. Harrap	711
G. K. Hall	2260
G. Malipiero	3028, 3030
G. P. Putnam	2043, 2149, 2443, 2498, 2508, 2533
Gakusei-sha	3068
Galley Press	1522
Galley Press, W. H. Smith	1563
Gama	3141
Garden City Publishing	2072, 2095, 2111, 2138, 2140
Geddes & Grosset	1632, 1643
General Publishing	4102, 4103
Genesis Publications	4115
Geo. M. Hill	3717
Geographica Ltd.	603
George Allen & Unwin	530, 608, 779

International Book Company	1861, 1862, 3666
International Business Publications, USA	4156
International Learning Systems Corporation	1429, 1430, 1431
International Pocket Library	2153, 2206, 3930
International Readers League	2172, 2535
Intertaal Dist.	3126
Intervisual Books	4332
J. Alfred Sharp	*See* The Epworth Press, J. Alfred Sharp
J. B. Lippincott	2110, 2525, 3896
J. Brodie	633
J. Coker & Co., Ltd.	618, 649, 650, 682, 683, 694, 707, 724, 781, 790, 802, 1289, 1331, 1332
J. G. Ferguson & Associates	2379, 2716
J. H. Sears & Co.	2468, 2478, 2481
J. M. Dent [including J. M. Dent & Sons]	667, 882, 886, 892, 905, 907, 908, 949, 956, 968, 969, 970, 987, 988, 1025, 1290, 1321, 1322, 1323, 1324, 1334, 1338, 1341, 1343, 1348, 1357, 1377, 1386, 1395, 1396, 1411, 1423, 1425, 1434, 1454, 1466, 1471, 1483, 1498, 1499, 1504, 1519, 1585, 1601, 1605, 1608, 2104, 2479, 2484, 2504, 2541, 2561, 2563, 2578, 2596, 2609, 2615, 2621, 2623, 2626, 2634, 3556, 3562
James Brodie, Ltd.	635, 812, 1291
Jan Förlag	3185, 3186, 3188, 3189
Jazzybee Verlag	2974
Jesse Haney	1830, 1831
John C. Winston Co.	2064, 2195, 2203, 2467, 2471, 2476, 2526, 2562, 2570, 2717, 2718
John F. Shaw Ltd.	536, 537, 553, 557, 583, 595, 702, 1292, 1293
John Lane	479, 515, 599, 607, 637, 713, 2011
John Long & Co. Ltd.	501
John Milne	495
John Shaw	3516
John W. Lovell	1842, 1845, 1868, 3655, 3660
Johnson and Hardin	3889
Jonathan Cape	1549, 1550
Jordan, Marsh & Co.	2097
Julia Macrae Books	1065
Julian Messner	2641
Junior Deluxe Editions	2147, 2181, 3925, 3926, 3938
Jupiter Books	1505, 1506, 1690, 2627
Juvenile Productions	703, 725, 730, 763, 769, 803, 841, 869
K.K. Publications	2197
Kadokawa	3103
Kaibunsha	3066

Little Brown	4340, 4341
Little Leather Library	2073, 2121, 2141, 2380, 2719, 3878, 3892, 3902, 3903
Little Sun	3114
Liveright Publishers	2501
Longman	542, 989, 1057
Longman Green and Co., Ltd.	651
Longman Group	990, 991, 1004, 1012, 2327
Longmans	2058
Longmeadow Press	2638, 2648
Los Libros más Pequeños del Mundo E.I.R.L.	3129
Lothrop Publishing Company	2404, 3680
Lothrop, Lee and Shepard	1889, 1987, 2403, 2442
Lovell, Coryell & Co.	2386
LRS [Library Reproduction Service]	3965
Lulu.com	3996, 4004, 4054, 4074
Lynx	1063, 4349
M. A. Donohue	1940, 1941, 1953, 1954, 1955, 1956, 1957, 1958, 1959, 1981, 1992, 2012, 2036, 2037, 2052, 2098, 2100, 2109, 2113, 2119, 2123, 2128, 2129, 2135, 2136, 2144, 2150, 2162, 2413, 2461, 2464, 2520, 3796, 3847, 3848, 3864, 3866, 3867, 3870, 3871, 3872, 3904
M. F. Mansfield and A. Wessels	3683
M. Kellerer	2955
Ma Ling Publishing Co.	3193
Macenas Press	*See* Random House
MacGibbon and Kee	3553
Macmillan	227, 228, 229, 230, 231, 232, 233, 237, 238, 239, 240, 241, 242, 243, 244, 245, 246, 247, 248, 249, 250, 251, 252, 253, 254, 255, 256, 257, 258, 259, 260, 261, 262, 263, 264, 265, 266, 267, 268, 269, 270, 271, 272, 273, 274, 275, 276, 277, 278, 279, 280, 281, 282, 283, 284, 285, 286, 287, 288, 289, 290, 291, 292, 293, 294, 295, 296, 297, 298, 299, 300, 301, 302, 303, 304, 305, 306, 307, 308, 309, 310, 311, 312, 313, 314, 315, 316, 317, 318, 319, 320, 321, 322, 323, 324, 325, 326, 327, 328, 329, 330, 331, 332, 333, 334, 345, 346, 347, 355, 374, 375, 376, 377, 378, 379, 380, 381, 382, 383, 384, 385, 386, 387, 388, 389, 390, 391, 392, 393, 394, 395, 396, 397, 398, 399, 400, 401, 402, 403, 404, 405, 406, 407, 408, 409, 410, 411, 412, 413, 414, 415, 416, 417, 418, 419, 420, 421, 422, 423, 424, 425, 426, 427, 428, 429, 432, 433, 434, 435, 436, 437, 439, 440, 441, 442, 445, 446, 448, 449, 450, 451, 452, 453, 454, 455, 456, 457, 458, 459, 460, 461, 464, 1698, 1699, 1700, 1701, 1702, 1704, 1705, 1706, 1707, 1708, 1709, 1710, 1711, 1712, 1713, 1714, 1715, 1716, 1717, 1718, 1719, 1720, 1721, 1722, 1723, 1724, 1725, 1726, 1727, 1728, 1729, 1730, 1731, 1732, 1733, 1734, 1735, 1736, 1737, 1738, 1739, 1740, 1741, 1742, 1743, 1744, 1745, 1746, 1747, 1748, 1749, 1750, 1751, 1753, 1754, 1755, 1756, 1757, 1758, 1759, 1760, 1761, 1762, 1763, 1765, 1766, 1767, 1768, 1769, 1770, 1773, 1774, 1775, 1776, 1777, 1778,

1779, 1781, 1782, 1783, 1784, 1785, 1786, 1787, 1788, 1790, 1791, 1792, 1793, 1795, 1796, 1798, 1799, 1815, 1817, 1819, 1820, 1821, 1822, 1823, 1824, 1825, 1826, 1988, 1994, 2016, 2032, 2102, 2755, 3232, 3233, 3234, 3235, 3236, 3237, 3238, 3239, 3240, 3241, 3242, 3243, 3244, 3245, 3246, 3247, 3248, 3249, 3250, 3251, 3252, 3253, 3254, 3255, 3256, 3257, 3258, 3259, 3260, 3261, 3262, 3263, 3264, 3265, 3266, 3267, 3268, 3269, 3270, 3271, 3272, 3273, 3274, 3275, 3276, 3277, 3278, 3279, 3280, 3281, 3282, 3283, 3284, 3285, 3286, 3287, 3288, 3289, 3290, 3291, 3292, 3293, 3294, 3295, 3296, 3297, 3298, 3299, 3300, 3301, 3302, 3303, 3304, 3305, 3306, 3307, 3308, 3309, 3310, 3311, 3312, 3313, 3314, 3315, 3316, 3317, 3318, 3319, 3320, 3321, 3322, 3323, 3324, 3325, 3326, 3327, 3328, 3329, 3330, 3331, 3332, 3333, 3334, 3335, 3336, 3337, 3338, 3339, 3340, 3341, 3342, 3343, 3344, 3345, 3346, 3347, 3348, 3349, 3350, 3351, 3352, 3353, 3354, 3355, 3356, 3357, 3358, 3359, 3360, 3361, 3362, 3363, 3364, 3365, 3366, 3367, 3368, 3369, 3370, 3371, 3372, 3373, 3374, 3375, 3376, 3377, 3378, 3379, 3380, 3381, 3382, 3383, 3384, 3385, 3386, 3387, 3388, 3389, 3390, 3391, 3392, 3393, 3394, 3395, 3396, 3397, 3398, 3399, 3400, 3401, 3402, 3403, 3404, 3405, 3406, 3407, 3408, 3409, 3410, 3411, 3412, 3413, 3414, 3415, 3416, 3417, 3418, 3419, 3420, 3421, 3422, 3423, 3424, 3425, 3426, 3427, 3428, 3429, 3430, 3431, 3432, 3433, 3434, 3435, 3436, 3437, 3438, 3439, 3440, 3441, 3442, 3443, 3444, 3446, 3447, 3448, 3449, 3450, 3451, 3452, 3453, 3454, 3462, 3464, 3465, 3466, 3467, 3468, 3469, 3470, 3471, 3472, 3626, 3627, 3628, 3629, 3630, 3631, 3632, 3633, 3634, 3635, 3636, 3637, 3638, 3639, 3640, 3641, 3643, 3644, 3646, 3647, 3648, 3649, 3650, 3651, 4093, 4094, 4095, 4096, 4128, 4196, 4197, 4199, 4200, 4201, 4202, 4203, 4212, 4217, 4228, 4232, 4312, 4314, 4316, 4319, 4327, 4333

Macmillan and Co.

1, 2, 3, 4, 5, 6, 7, 8, 9, 10, 11, 12, 13, 14, 15, 16, 17, 18, 19, 20, 21, 22, 23, 24, 25, 26, 27, 28, 29, 30, 31, 32, 33, 34, 35, 36, 37, 38, 39, 40, 41, 42, 43, 44, 45, 46, 47, 48, 49, 50, 51, 52, 53, 54, 55, 56, 57, 58, 59, 60, 61, 62, 63, 64, 65, 66, 67, 68, 69, 70, 71, 72, 73, 74, 75, 76, 77, 78, 79, 80, 81, 82, 83, 84, 85, 86, 87, 88, 89, 90, 91, 92, 93, 94, 95, 96, 97, 98, 99, 100, 101, 102, 103, 104, 105, 106, 107, 108, 109, 110, 111, 112, 113, 114, 115, 116, 117, 118, 119, 120, 121, 122, 123, 124, 125, 126, 127, 128, 129, 130, 131, 132, 133, 134, 135, 136, 137, 138, 139, 140, 141, 142, 143, 144, 145, 146, 147, 148, 149, 150, 151, 152, 153, 154, 155, 156, 157, 158, 159, 160, 161, 162, 163, 164, 165, 166, 167, 168, 169, 170, 171, 172, 173, 174, 175, 176, 177, 178, 179, 180, 181, 182, 183, 184, 185, 186, 187, 188, 189, 190, 191, 192, 193, 194, 195, 196, 197, 198, 199, 200, 201, 202, 203, 204, 205, 206, 207, 208, 209, 210, 211, 212, 213, 214, 215, 216, 217, 218, 219, 220, 221, 222, 223, 224, 225, 226, 348, 349, 350, 351, 352, 353, 354, 356, 357, 359, 360, 361, 362, 363, 364, 365, 366, 367, 368, 369, 370, 372, 373, 1703, 1771, 1772, 1780, 3445, 3455, 3456, 3457, 3458, 3459, 3460, 3461, 3642, 3645

Macmillan Children's Books

234, 235, 236, 335, 336, 337, 338, 339, 340, 341, 342, 343, 344, 358, 462, 463, 465, 466, 467, 468, 470, 471, 472, 473, 1674, 1828, 3463, 3482, 3483, 3484, 3485, 3486, 3487, 3488, 3489, 3490, 3491, 3492, 3493, 3494, 3495, 3496, 3497, 4238, 4298, 4335, 4338, 4339, 4354

National Sunday School Union   *See* The National Sunday School Union
Nelson   3545
Nelson Doubleday   2208
Nelson Regency   2295
New American Editions   *See* The New American Editions
New American Library of World Literature 2571, 2572, 2582, 2583, 2589
New English Library   *See* The New English Library
New Era Publishing Company   *See* The New Era Publishing Company
New Orchard Editions   1542, 1691
New York Book Co.   2050, 3840
New York Post   2381, 2866
New York Publishing Co.   1850, 3668
Newman Wolsey   753
Nichieisha   3077
Nihon Eigo Kyoiku Kyokai   3075, 3078
Nihon Yosho Hanbai, Tokyo   3093, 3094
Nimbus   1644
Nonesuch Press   1339, 1340, 1342, 1344, 1345, 1349, 1351, 1358, 1378, 1418, 1419, 1435,
                                      1436, 1472, 1500, 1636, 1693, 2548

Norderstedt Books on Demand   2984, 2985, 2986, 2987, 2990, 2991
Nórdica   3173
North Books   2663, 2664
Northern Paper Mills   2382
North-South Books   1148, 2313
Norton   2607, 2686, 4111, 4272, 4275
Oberon   1198, 1624
Obunsha   3076, 3079, 3086
Octopus Books   1013, 1015, 1023, 1156, 1169, 1508, 1543, 1567, 3563, 3569, 4293, 4299
Odhams Press   893, 909, 1314, 1329, 1404
Olivetti   971, 3029
Om Books International   3009, 3012, 3020, 3023
Omega Books   4227
Omniprose   2807
Oneworld Classics   4157, 4162, 4167, 4173
Open Road Integrated Media   4028
Orchard Books   4342
Oregan Publishing   2993
Ottenheimer   2180, 2232, 2266, 2281, 2285, 3030
Otto Hattrem   1979
Oudepote Press   2270
Oxford University Press   581, 606, 617, 622, 623, 629, 630, 636, 648, 686, 695, 712, 717, 718,
                                      1016, 1119, 1294, 1460, 1461, 1462, 1484, 1485, 1486, 1494, 1495,
                                      1523, 1524, 1541, 1551, 1572, 1578, 1613, 1645, 1647, 1656, 1670, 2742,

Rylee Ltd.	873, 941, 1372, 1438, 1439, 1440, 1456
S. W. Partridge & Co., Ltd.	496, 497, 503, 504, 505
S. WN. Co.	2056
Saalfield	2018, 2441, 3714, 3817, 3875, 3876, 3879, 3898, 4278
Sagwan Press	4032, 4033, 4034
Salt Heart Publishers	4012
Sam'l Gabriel & Sons	2077, 2142, 2384
Sampson Low	620
Sampson Low, Marston & Co., Ltd.	586
Sandle Brothers Ltd.	983, 1408, 1441
Sandle's	874
Sands Print Group	2769
Santillana	3127
Santillana-Richmond	3128
Schinozaki Shorin	3067
Schocken Books	2625
Scholastic	2790, 3622, 4088
Scholastic Australia	2794
Scholastic Book Services	2221, 2234, 2239
Scholastic Inc.	4059
Scholastic Ltd.	1268
Scholastic Publications Ltd.	1069
Science Research Associates	2247
Scott, Foresman and Company	4120
SDE Classics	4089
SeaWolf Press	4086, 4090
SE-Education, Plc.	3224
Sesame Publishing Company	615
Seven Seas Entertainment	2690
Seymour Lawrence	2248
SF Classic	4087
Shanghai Foreign Language Education Press	2888, 2895, 2896, 2899, 2915
Shanghai Scientific and Technological Literature Press	2910
Shanghai Translation Publishing House	2904
Sharon	2636
Shaw's Children's Books	815, 855
Shdn Books	3061
Shepherd Moon	2797
Shooting Press, Inc	3582
Shoseki Jōhōsha	4129, 4144, 4195
Shrewsbury Publishing Co.	2099

Sydney Sunday Herald	2749, 2750
T. Nelson	575
Tait, Sons and Co.	1858, 2389
Tango Books Ltd.	4351
Tania Press	2814, 2816, 2823
Tarry at the Taft	2492
Tate, Sons	1208
Ted Smart	1137, 1153, 1170, 1612, 3584
Templar Publishing	1158, 1182, 1188, 1192, 3614, 4348
Tempo Books	2233
Tern Press	1143, 3592
Thames Publishing Co.	*See* The Thames Publishing Co.
The Blue Book Company	773
The Bodley Head	479, 515, 599, 607, 637, 713, 1476, 1479, 1481, 1491, 1528, 2011, 4219
The Book Company	2765, 2768
The British Library	4147, 4151, 4152, 4153, 4178, 4192
The Brockhampton Press	676
The Caxton Publishing Company	*See* Caxton Publishing Company
The Cheshire Cat Press	*See* Cheshire Cat Press
The Children's Golden Library	1162
The Children's Press	677, 733, 734, 806, 817, 833, 859, 861, 883, 894, 901, 919, 923, 934, 950, 975, 976, 977, 1007, 1299, 1300, 1301, 1302, 1303, 2603
The Commercial Press	*See* Commercial Press
The Continental Book Company	1350, 3187
The Epworth Press, J. Alfred Sharp	660, 1304
The Five Mile Press Pty Ltd.	1177, 1214, 2777, 2783, 2784, 2789, 2791, 4159
The Folio Society	884, 889, 910, 1084, 1101, 1138, 1264, 1571, 3539, 3571, 3575, 3594, 4100, 4153
The Golden Press	*See* Golden Press
The Grolier Society	4210
The Heirloom Library	1359, 1360, 1376, 1381, 1387, 1390, 1398, 1399
The Little Blue Book Co.	*See* Little Blue Book Co.
The Macmillan Company	*See* Macmillan and Co.
The Modern Library	*See* Modern Library
The National Sunday School Union	513, 600
The New American Editions	1409
The New Education Fellowship	610
The New English Library	994, 1409, 1428
The New Era Publishing Company	610
The Nonesuch Press	*See* Nonesuch Press
The Porcupine's Quill	*See* Porcupine's Quill
The Readers Library Publishing Company	625, 638, 643, 678, 688, 697
The Shepherd Moon	*See* Shepherd Moon

APPENDIX 3: Illustrator Index

Arnold Hirshon

STATISTICAL OVERVIEW

T HE CHECKLISTS CONTAIN 4,358 unique editions in which 792 different illustrators played a part. Most volumes had only a single illustrator, some had two or three who contributed, and some had as many as 150 illustrators who each had one or two illustrations represented in a single collaborative volume. In a few cases the illustrator provided only the cover design or page borders, or colorized the images to supplement the work of another illustrator. The tables below include all illustrators—regardless of their role or the number of illustrations they provided—who bore some responsibility for illustrating an aspect of each edition represented in the checklists.

Here are the top twenty-five named illustrators (i.e., excluding "anonymous," "unknown," "various," and "other"). They account for 65% of all editions.

RANK	ILLUSTRATOR	EDITIONS
1	Tenniel, John	2,151
2	Carroll, Lewis	149
3	Rountree, Harry	68
4	Disney Studio	54
5	Rackham, Arthur	49
6	Thomson, E. Gertrude	47
7	Jackson, A. E.	36
8	Holiday, Henry	32
9	Copeland, Charles	30
10	Gutmann, Bessie Pease	30
11	Newell, Peter	30
12	Tarrant, Margaret W.	29
13	Bridgman, L. J. (Lewis Jesse)	28
14	McManus, Blanche	26
15	Pears, Charles	24
16	Stanley, Diana	23
17	Peake, Mervyn	22
18	Macfarlane, John	21
19	Theaker, Harry	21
20	Cloke, Rene	20
21	Furniss, Harry	20
22	Hudson, Gwynedd M.	20
23	Robinson, Charles	19
24	Thorne, Jenny	19
25	Thompson, E. Heber	18
	TOTAL	2,986

The following is a summary of the number of illustrators, and the percentage of the total number of editions they represent.

ILLUSTRATORS REPRESENTED BY	NUMBER OF ILLUSTRATORS	% OF ALL ILLUSTRATORS
1 edition	519	65.0%
2 editions	95	11.9%
3 editions	39	4.9%
4 editions	31	3.9%
5 editions	23	2.9%
6 editions	13	1.6%
7 editions	10	1.3%
8 editions	7	0.9%
9 editions	8	1.0%
10 editions	4	0.5%
11–15 editions	15	1.9%
16–30 editions	21	2.6%
31–100 editions	9	1.1%
101+ editions	2	0.3%

NAMING CONVENTIONS USED IN THE ILLUSTRATOR INDEX

THIS INDEX PROVIDES entries for all named illustrators recorded in the checklists, regardless of whether the illustrator was the primary illustrator or served in a secondary role (e.g., colorizing Tenniel illustrations, providing only the cover art, illustrating only the page borders, or contributing only the frontispiece).

This index normalizes names for consistency, and so the form of a particular name in the index may differ from the form as found in some of the checklist entries or in indexes of other bibliographies or indexes to other books. In general, the form of the name by which the illustrator was most identified in published works is what is used in this index.

Imposing consistency is important in an index to ensure that all work by the same person appears under a single form of an illustrator's name, even when a person's name may appear under different forms on the title pages of different editions. Inconsistencies in the form of the name may occur for a variety of reasons.

- The illustrator may have changed names later in life or mid-career, such as adopting a married name, but is better known or cited by the maiden name (such as Christian Yandell Waller, whose *Alice* editions were published under Christian Yandell), or by the married name (such as Bessie Pease, whose original publications were issued under that name, but the later ones under Bessie Pease Gutmann).

- The person may have most often used only an initial for a forename or middle name on published editions rather than being identified with the name spelled out in full. Sometimes the full name of the person is known, but the illustrator published only under her or his initials, such as Fanny Young Cory publishing under F. Y. Cory, and Alfred Edward Jackson publishing under A. E. Jackson.

- The illustrator also may have used a pseudonym, such as Irene Mabel Neighbor publishing under the name Rene Cloke, or used a single name rather than the full form, such as Costanza Magda publishing under the name Magda, or Manuel Gutiérrez Garulo publishing under the name Gutmaga.

- The name may also have been transliterated inconsistently from a non-Roman alphabet to a Roman one, such as the forename Iassen versus Jassen, or the surname Kalinovski versus Kalinovskii or Kalinovsky.

Taking such variations into account, and to aid the user, when there are two or more forms of an illustrator's name that a reader may know, a "*see*" reference appears from the variant to the indexed form. In addition, if a fuller form of a name is known, that may be added to the index entry in parentheses, such as: Bridgman, L. J. (Lewis Jesse).

In particular, the form of the name used in Appendix 2 of the *Translations* edition of *Alice in a World of Wonderlands* may not be the same form used in this index. However, where the two forms differ, there is a "*see*" reference from the form used there to confirm when two identities are for the same person.

In addition, there are some situations where the role and attribution of an illustrator's work may require clarification or may not always be consistently represented in the checklists.

- When an edition has multiple illustrators, the name of each illustrator is indexed separately. For example, the secondary illustrator may have only provided the cover illustration, a frontispiece, or a border design. The specific role of the illustrator is not stated in the index, but often can be found in the notes of the checklist entry. When the checklist entry lists two or more illustrators and there is no note as to their roles, these illustrators shared relatively equal responsibility, e.g., Anne Grahame and Janet Johnstone.

- Sometimes, a compiler of one checklist may have positively identified the illustrations in a book as being the work of a named illustrator, but another compiler may have attributed the same illustrations to "Anonymous." For example, there are checklist entries in which Harry Rountree is listed as the primary illustrator and a second illustrator is listed as either "E. Heber Thompson" or "Anonymous." No attempt has been made in this index to try to resolve any such differences.

- As discussed both in my essay on "Beyond Tenniel" in Volume One, and in the introduction to Volume Two, the attribution of "after Tenniel" often is in the eye of the beholder. For this index, the description found in each checklist entry is the one used to create the index entry.

Illustrator Index of the Checklist Entries

ILLUSTRATOR NAME	CHECKLIST ENTRY NUMBERS
A.in.Z	2343
Abbott, Elenore	2444, 2447, 2448, 2470, 2477, 3843, 3868, 3883, 3890, 3891, 3956, 4275
Abbott, Elenore Plaisted	*See* Abbott, Elenore
Abbott, Rowan	2913
Abe, Mayumi	3083
Accornero, Vittorio	4205
Ackroyd, Winifred M.	664, 732
Adams, Frank	534, 1218, 1599, 2299
Adreani, Manuela	3054, 3056, 3063
After Tenniel	1385, 1890, 1940, 2065, 3184, 3667, 3670, 3674, 3678, 3682, 3689, 3690, 3691, 3692, 3693, 3694, 3710, 3715, 3718, 3719, 3720, 3734, 3743, 3744, 3745, 3746, 3747, 3754, 3755, 3757, 3763, 3764, 3765, 3766, 3772, 3776, 3783, 3786, 3787, 3788, 3790, 3794, 3795, 3811, 3813, 3814, 3815, 3827, 3828, 3829, 3831, 3833, 3834, 3835, 3837, 3838, 3842, 3847, 3851, 3855, 3856, 3863, 3865, 3870, 3877, 3887, 3888, 3893, 3897, 3899, 3907, 4139. *See also* individual illustrator names with "(after Tenniel)"
Aitch	2913
Akita, Julien	2949, 2951
Alexander, Jason	2320, 2674, 3968, 3971, 3991, 3994, 3995, 4002, 4017
Alexandersen, Peter Bay	2927
Alfeyevsky, Valerie	1258
Alí, Facundo	2861
Allen, Olive	521
Alvear, Belén Eizaguirre	3154, 3161, 3164, 3165, 3175
Anderson, Walter	2268
Andrea, Pat	4275
Andronic, Madalina	2343
Angeles, Ricardo De los	2913
Anonymous	483, 501, 586, 623, 661, 686, 703, 714, 717, 733, 734, 737, 759, 767, 769, 773, 774, 799, 801, 803, 828, 844, 858, 861, 868, 871, 872, 874, 875, 887, 890, 891, 896, 898, 903, 904, 912, 916, 919, 921, 923, 926, 929, 934, 940, 942, 945, 946, 947, 951, 952, 953, 954, 959, 960, 965, 966, 993, 999, 1007, 1020, 1024, 1026, 1033, 1043, 1053, 1076, 1082, 1088, 1093, 1095, 1097, 1103, 1110, 1127, 1130, 1131, 1140, 1171, 1173, 1179, 1195, 1269, 1275, 1276, 1277, 1278, 1290, 1297, 1310, 1311, 1355, 1362, 1365, 1366, 1368, 1369, 1370, 1371, 1373, 1391, 1394, 1406, 1410, 1438, 1443, 1452, 1480, 1501, 1573, 1580, 1587, 1599, 1602, 1618, 1635, 1688, 1692, 1853, 1889, 1902, 1912, 1932, 1938, 1966, 1971, 1979, 1987, 2027, 2049, 2054, 2087, 2098, 2129, 2141, 2145, 2168, 2180, 2442, 2452, 2460, 2481, 2491, 2492, 2494, 2497, 2512, 2520, 2550,

Backhouse, G. W.	821, 835, 839, 847, 850, 854, 857, 862, 880, 1279, 1280
Baines, Muriel	673
Baker, Kyle	3957
Baker-Smith, Graham	4352
Balantenysheva, Anastasia	1258
Ball, Alexandra	1252
Ball, Allison	2343
Banks, Eulalie	1303
Bartlett, Aaron	2343
Bašić, Zdenko	1196, 1204, 1243, 4346, 4347, 4350
Batakov, Nikolay	1258
Baynes, Pauline	842, 865, 866, 867, 872, 915, 942, 945, 1077, 1364, 1401, 1402, 1405, 1451, 1458
Bazanova, Elena	1258
Beck, Ian	1246, 4172
Becker, Greg	2316
Bejenaru, Alexandra Stefanel	2913
Bello, Marina	2913
Bennion, Robin	1636
Bergevin, Dan	2343
Berkova, Dagmar	1258, 1581
Berkum, Petra van	2913
Berman, Julia Steffy	2913
Bianchi, Fausto	1184
Birch, Stéphanie	1072
Bird, Eric	2913
Birmingham, Christian	1273
Birnbaum, Uriel	4275
Blackman, Charles	2753, 2754, 2856
Blair, Landis	2913
Blair, Mary	2336
Blake, Peter	3595, 3596, 3598, 4275
Blampied	1306
Blasco	1006
Blasco, Jesus	*See* Blasco
Blithe, Arabella	786, 1355
Bloomfield, Frances	1645, 1647
Blum, Alex A. (Anthony)	816, 877, 2175, 2220, 2228
Bolima, Isaiah	2913
Bolle, Frank	1001
Bond, Anna	2355, 2359
Bone, Hildegard	867
Bowley, A. L.	*See* Bowley, Ada L. (Louise)

Caruana, Deno	1077, 1081, 1469
Castro, Estefanía de	2913
Ceder, Gilly	2913
Cekauskas, Justas	2343
Cernuschi, Claudio	1118, 3031
Chambers, Dave	4286
Chambers, David	*See* Chambers, Dave
Chan, K. Y.	1119, 2892, 2893, 3574, 3599
Chance, Tony James	1569, 1575
Chaves, Maisa	2913
Chehardy, Kelly	2343
Chen, Yucci	2343
Chizhykov, V.	*See* Chizhykov, Victor
Chizhykov, Victor	1258
Christie, Julia	1543, 1544, 1545, 1556, 1557, 1558, 2648, 3954
Christotinoy, Eugenia	1258
Chronis, Theo	2913
Chryssanthopoulou, Antigoni	2343
Chuklev, Petr	1258
Clair, Nathan	1596
Clark, E.	2117, 2130
Clark, Emma Chichester	1191, 1197, 3610, 3611
Clavijo-Telepnev, Vladimir	1258
Claxton, Adelaide	1115, 1582, 1583, 1591, 1625, 1626
Clay, Jesse	4322
Clements, M. L.	710, 1335
Cloke, Rene (Irene Mabel Neighbor[1])	746, 749, 750, 751, 755, 756, 761, 782, 930, 1079, 1089, 1096, 1107, 1116, 1163, 1295, 2290, 3510, 3519, 3960
Colles, Dorothy (after Tenniel)	1383, 1414, 1422, 1433, 1465, 1482, 1492, 2567, 2720
Collison, Marjorie	2173, 3916, 3917, 3919, 3920, 3921, 3922
Comes, Tania	2786
Cooke, Donald E.	2466, 2569, 2579, 2580, 3118
Cooper, Jessica	2913
Cooper, John	1417, 2639
Copeland, Charles[2]	1856, 1867, 1923, 1924, 1980, 1986, 2006, 2044, 2067, 2107, 2385, 2388, 2391, 2395, 2399, 2415, 2430, 3665, 3708, 3709, 3727, 3731, 3732, 3733, 3779, 3780, 3797, 3861, 3862, 4275. *See also* Bridgman, L. J. (Lewis Jesse)

---

1. Rene Cloke was a pseudonym for Irene Mabel Neighbor according to WorldCat Identities (https://www.worldcat.org/identities/lccn-n79065549/). "Rene" likely came from a shortening of "Irene," but the origin of "Cloke" as the surname is unknown. Another source notes that the "information on René [*sic*] Cloke is oddly various. One source claims she was a woman born in Plymouth, England on October 4th, 1904. The British Library says René Cloke was a man, though they agree about the birth in Plymouth, but offer no birthdate. Another source has her born on the 5th, 1904." https://laughingelephant.com/authors-and-illustrators-born-in-octoberren-cloke-october-4th/.

2. As noted in the checklist entries, Charles Copeland provided only the frontispiece for the Bridgman editions.

Corrêa, Pedro	2343
Cortés, Ester	1217
Cory, F. Y. (Fanny Young)	1968, 1993, 3869, 3911, 4275
Corydon	2534
Cosanti, Francesca	3064
Cosareanu, Luminita	2913
Coster, Thomas de	*See* de Coster, Thomas
Cotiw-an, Kizel	2913
Couri, Kathryn A.	2259
Criado, Pilar	2913
Crockett, Rebecca	2913
Cuddy, Robbin	4330, 4332
D'Agostini	983
D'Aquino, Andrea	2360
Dabrowska, Olga	2913
Dahlgren, Björn	2913
Daily, John	2913
Dalí, Salvador	2230, 2358, 2962, 4275
Danaila, Adriana	2913
Danielsen, Peter	2343
Daude, Cecilia	2913
Davis, J. Watson	1990, 1991, 2068, 2440, 2506
de Coster, Thomas	2331
De Filippo, Maria	1118, 3031
de la Fuente, Esteban Quintana	*See* Fuente, Esteban Quintana de la
Deitch, Kim	4140, 4141
Delamare, David	2365
Dempster, Al	2177, 2773
Derevyanko, Nataliya	1258
DeWitt, Patricia	2297
DeWitt, Robin	2297
Deyn, Elenka	1258
Diddit, Glenn	2340, 2357
Dijk, Reuben Van	2343
Disney Co.	*See* Disney Studio
Disney Productions	*See* Disney Studio
Disney Studio	822, 823, 824, 825, 829, 963, 973, 984, 994, 1005, 1031, 1042, 1046, 1047, 1053, 1055, 1056, 1092, 1112, 1132, 1160, 1166, 1174, 1199, 1202, 1209, 1212, 1261, 1262, 1271, 1296, 2182, 2183, 2184, 2187, 2188, 2189, 2190, 2197, 2217, 2233, 2253, 2254, 2255, 2257, 2364, 2758, 2779, 2806, 2818, 2917, 4051, 4052, 4053
Dmitry, Kosub	1258
Dodon, Alexander	1258
Doherty, D. A.	*See* Doherty, Dorothy A.

Doherty, Dorothy A.	1372, 1407, 1408, 1439, 1440, 1441
Dominguez, Angel	2304, 3612
d'Onofrio, Mollie	2913
Doré, Guy	943
Dørge, Mille	2343
Dragomir, Anda	2913
Dryha, Zhanna	2913
Duff, Lindsay	1589
Duff, Lyndsay	*See* Duff, Lindsay
Dunn, Robert	1207, 1241
Dunthorne, David John	2913
Dyer, Gil	706, 739, 798, 818
Dzhiganskaya, Alexandra	2913
E. C.	2039
Earnshaw, Peggy	1302
Edwards, Angela	4339
Egiguren, Beñiat Olaberria	2913
Ekman, Marlene	2653
Elder, Jenay M	2913
Elias, Monica	2659
Eliseeva, Kseniya	2913
Entwhistle, H.	1388
Entwisle, M.	1363
Erko, Vladislav	1258
Escuadra, Mark Torres	3129
Evangelista, Mauro	1178, 1193, 1232, 1253, 1637, 1649, 3604
Evernden, Graham	2296
Everson, Michael	2835, 2839
Ewing, Carolyn	2307
Faissal, João	2913
Fajardo, Guillermo	2343
Federer, C. A	2140, 2143
Federis, John Frederick	2913
Fidalgo, Patricia	2913
Figueira, Raquel	2343
Figueroa, Brenda	2913
Filippo, Maria de	*See* De Filippo, Maria
Fimbres, Maria Fernanda Fierro	2913
Fiorese, Juliana	2913
Fiorini, Constantina	3033, 3035
Fisher, Jeff	1126
Fisher, Jeffrey Brian	*See* Fisher, Jeff
Flis, Małgorzata	3132, 3135

Goodall, J. S.	900
Gorban, Anna	2913
Gorde, M.	*See* Gorde, Monique
Gorde, Monique	918, 1075, 2305, 2310, 2945, 2946
Gordon, Gwen	4286
Gorokhovski, E.	*See* Gorokhovski, E. S.
Gorokhovski, E. S.	1258
Gough, Philip	1359, 1360, 1376, 1381, 1387, 1390, 1398, 1399, 2566
Goulding, June	1161, 1175, 1628, 1629
Gourrat, Carole	2948
Grabiański, Janusz	2211
Gracia, Leonor Solans	4275
Gram, Anja	2913
Grant, Campbell	2751
Gray, Carole	1120, 1135, 3582
Greene, Julia	658, 2084, 2085, 2094, 2120
Grey, Mini	1246
Grinchuka, Anna	2913
Grisolfa, Carmen Virginia	2343
Guide, Gill	*See* Guile, Gill
Guile, Gill	1139, 1144
Guimarães, Igor Tadeu Paiva	2913
Gukova, Julia	1258
Gulina, Francesco	2343
Gulliver, Amanda	1211
Gutiérrez, Manuel Garulo	*See* Gutmaga (Manuel Garulo Gutiérrez)
Gutmaga (Manuel Gutiérrez Garulo)	3149
Gutmann, Bessie Pease	495, 580, 616, 618, 646, 647, 649, 650, 655, 682, 683, 694, 707, 724, 781, 790, 802, 1289, 1313, 1315, 1320, 1331, 1332, 2007, 2280, 2299, 2801, 3819, 3956, 4275
H. K.	2077
Hagialas, Nikolas	2913
Hague, Michael	1040, 2274, 2275
Hahner, Chris	1567
Hall, D.	902, 939
Hall, David	1049, 2276
Hall, Douglas	879, 4099
Hallmark Entertainment	2666
Hamiche, Samir	2343
Hammarlund, Regina	2913
Hanna, H.	3100
Hannah, Jonny	1246
Hannen, Holly	2300

Harchy, Atelier Philippe | 2771, 2778
Hardy, E. S. | *See* Hardy, E. Stuart
Hardy, E. Stuart | 536, 537, 553, 557, 583, 595, 1292, 1293
Hargreaves, Georgina | 967, 1102
Hawes, Walter | 507, 620, 659, 1220, 1297
Haywood, Helen | 815, 855
Henderson, Gary | 1083
Henderson, Hume | 625, 638, 688, 697
Henriquez, Pablo Lara | 2343
Herbert, Jack | 2913
Herford, Oliver | 2082
Hernández, Eduardo Alejandro Ramírez | 2913
Hewetson, Nicholas | *See* Hewetson, Nick
Hewetson, Nick | 1128
Hickling, P. B. | 3504, 3536, 3537
Hicks-Jenkins, Clive | 1246
Hidalgo | 941
Hildebrandt, Greg | 1167, 2284, 2329
Hirata, Shōgō | 2303
Hirshon, Dan | 2362, 2363
Hofsten, Hugo von | 2019, 2046, 2047, 2080
Högfeldt, Robert | 3185, 3189
Holiday, Henry | 667, 892, 1104, 1418, 1419, 1436, 1447, 1476, 1479, 1481, 1491, 1528, 1812, 2559, 2586, 2593, 2594, 2608, 3669, 3676, 3681, 3686, 3711, 3738, 3739, 3758, 3759, 3773, 3784, 3800, 3818, 3932
Holland, Janice | 2194
Honeybourne, Rosemary | 933
Hovhannisyan, Nune | 2913
Howarth, Jill | 4059
Hudson, Gwynedd M. | 597, 598, 628, 676, 684, 728, 1021, 1022, 1036, 1100, 1125, 1146, 1237, 1263, 1288, 2105, 2154, 2299, 4204, 4243
Huehnergarth, John | 2064, 2195, 2203
Huella ilustración | 3172
Huertas, Alice | 897, 911, 912, 925
Hughes, Arthur | 4242
Hughes, Franklin | 3905
Hutchings | 979, 981
Hutchings, S. | *See* Hutchings
Hutchings Studio | *See* Hutchings
Ianovskaia, Tatiana | 1258, 2814, 2816, 2823, 4275
Iborro | 1017
Iglesias, M. C. | 2353
Iida, Masami | 3090

Alice in a World of Wonderlands

Leonard, Andre	2343
Leone, S.	*See* Leone, Sergio
Leone, Sergio	906, 2214
Letica, Tena	2343
Lewicki, James	2249
Lewis, T.	2652
Lipchenko, Oleg	1258, 2815, 2817, 2832
Lira, Giuseppe	2913
Livraghi	893
Loginov, Sergey	2913
Loiseaux, M.	1064, 1113, 1114
Lord, John Vernon	1190, 1659, 3609, 4275
Lornie, June	2837
Louceiro, Maria do Carmo	2343
Louw, Johan	2913
Lozano, Santiago	2913
Luna, Leandro	2913
Macfarlane, John	294, 295, 296, 297, 298, 299, 300, 301, 302, 303, 304, 305, 306, 307, 308, 309, 432, 433, 439, 472, 3488
Macias Sampredo, José Luis	937, 1008, 1009, 1010
MacKnight, Ninon	1555, 2518
Magda	4305
Magda (Costanza)	*See* Magda
Máhr, Peter	2913
Maiorana, Andrea	2913
Makiela, Daria	2913
Makienko, Elvira	2913
Manna, Giovanni	2981, 3053
Manson, Beverly	1623
Maraja	*See* Maraja, Libico
Maraja, Libico	856, 860, 878, 924, 2212, 2752, 3527, 3544, 3933
Marciante, Enzo	2867, 2868, 3151, 3152, 3153, 3155
Marinov-Oummaia, Rosen	2913
Maristane, Victor (after Jan Švankmajer)	1246
Marsh, James	1121, 1142, 1611, 3577
Martynov, A.	*See* Martynov, Andrei
Martynov, Andrei	1258
Martynov, M.	1258
Masaru, Schichinhoe	1246
Massari, Alida	3044, 3168, 3171, 3174
Mateu, Franc	2286, 2300
Matic-Kuriljov, Vladimir	2913
Matlack, Elizabeth	2343

---

3. There are two checklist entries in which Charles Pears is listed as the only illustrator, but in at least one of these cases T. H. Robinson is an unattributed contributor. All of the T. H. Robinson editions also contain the Pears illustrations.

Sburelin, Glenda	1258
Scavino, Alicia	2861
Schermele, Willy	841
Schindler, H. L.	489
Schneider, Rex	2330
Schoett, Marianna	3134
Schroeder, Ted	2606
Šeda, G. (Gustav)	4289, 4290, 4291, 4293, 4296, 4299, 4356
Seery, Valerie	2833
Seibold, J. Otto	4342
Sergienko, I.	1258
Sewell, Byron W.	4275
Sexton, D. R.	702, 703, 725, 730, 763
Shalvashvili, Inga	2913
Shatunov, V.	*See* Shatunov, Victor
Shatunov, Victor	1258
Shau, Natalie	2343
Sherborn	1362
Shi, Xingwen	2913
Shields, Sue	1035, 2757
Shiko	2913
Shōgō, Hirata	*See* Hirata, Shōgō
Shukayev, V.	1258
Shulgina, Lidia	1258
Sibree, Mary	4275
Silivonchik, Anna	1258
Silva-Freimane, Jehanne	2913
Šimon, Ana	2343
Simon, Ute	2347
Simpson, Kate	1080
Sinclair, J. R.	506, 513, 600
Singer, Daniel Rover	4058
Singh, Mahendra	4275
Singh, Manish	3009
Singh, Niharika	2913
Sison, Kriss	2690
Sissolak, Dagmar	1246
Smajic, Susanne	2969, 2976, 2977
Smith, Graham	*See* Baker-Smith, Graham
Smith, Luke Stephen	2343
Smith, Maggi	4178
Smith, Mary	790
Smith, Samantha	4320, 4323, 4324, 4325, 4326

Tenniel, John   1, 2, 3, 4, 5, 6, 7, 8, 9, 10, 11, 12, 13, 14, 15, 16, 17, 18, 19, 20, 21, 22, 23, 24, 25, 26, 27, 28, 29, 30, 31, 32, 33, 34, 35, 36, 37, 38, 39, 40, 41, 42, 43, 44, 45, 46, 47, 48, 49, 50, 51, 52, 53, 54, 55, 56, 57, 58, 59, 60, 61, 62, 63, 64, 65, 66, 67, 68, 69, 70, 71, 72, 73, 74, 75, 76, 77, 78, 79, 80, 81, 82, 83, 84, 85, 86, 87, 88, 89, 90, 91, 92, 93, 94, 95, 96, 97, 98, 99, 100, 101, 102, 103, 104, 105, 106, 107, 108, 109, 110, 111, 112, 113, 114, 115, 116, 117, 118, 119, 120, 121, 122, 123, 124, 125, 126, 127, 128, 129, 130, 131, 132, 133, 134, 135, 136, 137, 138, 139, 140, 141, 142, 143, 144, 145, 146, 147, 148, 149, 150, 151, 152, 153, 154, 155, 156, 157, 158, 159, 160, 161, 162, 163, 164, 165, 166, 167, 168, 169, 170, 171, 172, 173, 174, 175, 176, 177, 178, 179, 180, 181, 182, 183, 184, 185, 186, 187, 188, 189, 190, 191, 192, 193, 194, 195, 196, 197, 198, 199, 200, 201, 202, 203, 204, 205, 206, 207, 208, 209, 210, 211, 212, 213, 214, 215, 216, 217, 218, 219, 220, 221, 222, 223, 224, 225, 226, 227, 228, 229, 230, 231, 232, 233, 234, 235, 236, 237, 238, 239, 240, 241, 242, 243, 244, 245, 246, 247, 248, 249, 250, 251, 252, 253, 254, 255, 256, 257, 258, 259, 260, 261, 262, 263, 264, 265, 266, 267, 268, 269, 270, 271, 272, 273, 274, 275, 276, 277, 278, 279, 280, 281, 282, 283, 284, 285, 286, 287, 288, 289, 290, 291, 292, 293, 294, 295, 296, 297, 298, 299, 300, 301, 302, 303, 304, 305, 306, 307, 308, 309, 310, 311, 312, 313, 314, 315, 316, 317, 318, 319, 320, 321, 322, 323, 324, 325, 326, 327, 328, 329, 330, 331, 332, 333, 334, 335, 338, 339, 340, 341, 342, 343, 344, 345, 346, 347, 348, 349, 350, 351, 352, 353, 354, 355, 356, 357, 358, 359, 360, 361, 362, 363, 364, 365, 366, 367, 368, 370, 371, 372, 373, 374, 375, 376, 377, 378, 379, 380, 381, 382, 383, 384, 385, 386, 387, 388, 389, 390, 391, 392, 393, 394, 395, 396, 397, 398, 399, 400, 401, 402, 403, 404, 405, 406, 407, 408, 409, 410, 411, 412, 413, 414, 415, 416, 417, 418, 419, 420, 421, 422, 423, 424, 425, 426, 427, 428, 429, 430, 431, 432, 433, 434, 435, 436, 437, 438, 439, 440, 441, 442, 443, 444, 445, 446, 447, 448, 449, 450, 451, 452, 453, 454, 455, 456, 457, 458, 459, 460, 461, 462, 463, 464, 465, 466, 467, 468, 469, 470, 471, 472, 473, 474, 547, 548, 667, 770, 771, 772, 778, 788, 791, 793, 794, 813, 815, 820, 831, 834, 848, 855, 884, 888, 889, 892, 910, 914, 922, 928, 931, 932, 935, 962, 972, 985, 995, 1002, 1013, 1014, 1015, 1016, 1023, 1028, 1029, 1030, 1034, 1041, 1044, 1051, 1052, 1057, 1058, 1068, 1069, 1078, 1084, 1101, 1104, 1106, 1108, 1110, 1121, 1122, 1123, 1124, 1138, 1141, 1142, 1149, 1151, 1176, 1181, 1186, 1187, 1189, 1216, 1223, 1231, 1242, 1246, 1254, 1257, 1263, 1267, 1270, 1308, 1339, 1340, 1342, 1344, 1345, 1349, 1351, 1352, 1354, 1358, 1378, 1379, 1386, 1396, 1409, 1411, 1412, 1413, 1415, 1416, 1418, 1419, 1420, 1423, 1424, 1426, 1427, 1428, 1429, 1430, 1431, 1432, 1434, 1435, 1436, 1437, 1442, 1444, 1445, 1446, 1447, 1448, 1449, 1450, 1453, 1454, 1455, 1459, 1460, 1461, 1462, 1463, 1464, 1466, 1468, 1470, 1471, 1472, 1473, 1474, 1475, 1477, 1478, 1479, 1481, 1483, 1484, 1485, 1486, 1487, 1488, 1491, 1493, 1494, 1495, 1496, 1497, 1498, 1499, 1500, 1502, 1505, 1506, 1508, 1509, 1510, 1514, 1517, 1518, 1519, 1520, 1521, 1522, 1523, 1524, 1525, 1526, 1528, 1529, 1531, 1535, 1536, 1537, 1539, 1541, 1542, 1546, 1548, 1551, 1552, 1555, 1559, 1562, 1563, 1565, 1566, 1567, 1568, 1570, 1571, 1572, 1573, 1574, 1576, 1577, 1578, 1582, 1584, 1585, 1586, 1588, 1590, 1591, 1592, 1593, 1594, 1595, 1596, 1597, 1598,

Tenniel, John (continued)

1600, 1601, 1603, 1604, 1605, 1607, 1608, 1609, 1610, 1611, 1612,
1613, 1614, 1615, 1616, 1617, 1619, 1625, 1626, 1630, 1631, 1632, 1633,
1636, 1641, 1642, 1643, 1645, 1646, 1647, 1648, 1652, 1655, 1657,
1660, 1661, 1663, 1664, 1665, 1666, 1669, 1671, 1673, 1674, 1676,
1677, 1678, 1679, 1680, 1681, 1682, 1685, 1686, 1690, 1693, 1694,
1695, 1696, 1697, 1698, 1699, 1700, 1701, 1702, 1703, 1704, 1705,
1706, 1707, 1708, 1709, 1710, 1711, 1712, 1713, 1714, 1715, 1716, 1717,
1718, 1719, 1720, 1721, 1722, 1723, 1724, 1725, 1726, 1727, 1728, 1729,
1730, 1731, 1732, 1733, 1734, 1735, 1736, 1737, 1738, 1739, 1740, 1741,
1742, 1743, 1744, 1745, 1746, 1747, 1748, 1749, 1750, 1751, 1752, 1753,
1754, 1755, 1756, 1757, 1758, 1759, 1760, 1761, 1762, 1763, 1764, 1765,
1766, 1767, 1771, 1772, 1773, 1774, 1775, 1776, 1777, 1778, 1779, 1780,
1781, 1782, 1783, 1784, 1785, 1786, 1787, 1788, 1789, 1790, 1791, 1792,
1793, 1794, 1795, 1796, 1797, 1798, 1799, 1800, 1801, 1802, 1803,
1804, 1805, 1806, 1807, 1808, 1809, 1810, 1811, 1812, 1813, 1814, 1815,
1816, 1817, 1818, 1819, 1820, 1821, 1822, 1823, 1824, 1825, 1826, 1827,
1828, 1829, 1830, 1831, 1832, 1833, 1834, 1835, 1836, 1837, 1838, 1839,
1840, 1841, 1842, 1843, 1844, 1845, 1846, 1847, 1848, 1849, 1850,
1851, 1852, 1853, 1854, 1855, 1857, 1858, 1859, 1860, 1863, 1864, 1865,
1866, 1868, 1870, 1871, 1872, 1873, 1874, 1875, 1876, 1877, 1878,
1879, 1880, 1881, 1882, 1883, 1884, 1885, 1886, 1887, 1888, 1889,
1894, 1895, 1896, 1897, 1898, 1899, 1902, 1904, 1905, 1906, 1908,
1909, 1910, 1911, 1912, 1913, 1914, 1915, 1916, 1917, 1918, 1919, 1920,
1921, 1922, 1926, 1927, 1928, 1929, 1930, 1931, 1933, 1934, 1935, 1936,
1938, 1941, 1942, 1943, 1944, 1945, 1946, 1947, 1948, 1949, 1950,
1951, 1953, 1954, 1955, 1957, 1959, 1961, 1962, 1963, 1964, 1965, 1967,
1969, 1970, 1977, 1981, 1982, 1984, 1985, 1987, 1988, 1989, 1990,
1991, 1992, 1994, 1995, 1996, 1997, 2000, 2001, 2002, 2004, 2005,
2012, 2015, 2016, 2023, 2024, 2025, 2026, 2028, 2029, 2030, 2032,
2033, 2035, 2036, 2037, 2038, 2039, 2040, 2042, 2043, 2052, 2053,
2057, 2058, 2059, 2060, 2061, 2062, 2063, 2068, 2074, 2081, 2083,
2087, 2088, 2090, 2091, 2093, 2097, 2098, 2099, 2100, 2102, 2103,
2109, 2110, 2113, 2117, 2118, 2119, 2123, 2125, 2128, 2130, 2131, 2132,
2133, 2134, 2135, 2136, 2139, 2144, 2149, 2150, 2151, 2153, 2156, 2157,
2161, 2162, 2163, 2164, 2165, 2167, 2169, 2170, 2172, 2174, 2176,
2178, 2181, 2185, 2205, 2206, 2207, 2208, 2209, 2210, 2215, 2216,
2218, 2221, 2222, 2224, 2226, 2229, 2233, 2234, 2235, 2237, 2239,
2240, 2243, 2244, 2247, 2249, 2250, 2258, 2262, 2269, 2271, 2280,
2287, 2293, 2294, 2295, 2298, 2309, 2317, 2318, 2321, 2324, 2326,
2335, 2338, 2354, 2369, 2370, 2371, 2372, 2373, 2374, 2375, 2376,
2377, 2379, 2386, 2387, 2389, 2390, 2391, 2392, 2393, 2394, 2395,
2396, 2397, 2398, 2399, 2400, 2401, 2402, 2405, 2406, 2408, 2411,
2412, 2414, 2415, 2416, 2417, 2418, 2419, 2420, 2421, 2422, 2424,
2425, 2426, 2427, 2429, 2430, 2431, 2432, 2433, 2435, 2436, 2438,
2439, 2440, 2441, 2442, 2443, 2444, 2447, 2448, 2450, 2451, 2452,
2454, 2456, 2457, 2458, 2460, 2461, 2462, 2463, 2464, 2465, 2466,
2467, 2469, 2470, 2471, 2472, 2473, 2474, 2475, 2476, 2477, 2482,
2485, 2486, 2487, 2488, 2489, 2490, 2491, 2494, 2496, 2497, 2500,
2501, 2505, 2506, 2507, 2514, 2516, 2517, 2519, 2520, 2521, 2522,
2523, 2524, 2525, 2526, 2528, 2529, 2531, 2532, 2533, 2535, 2538,

Tenniel, John (continued)

2539, 2540, 2542, 2543, 2545, 2546, 2548, 2549, 2551, 2553, 2554,
2555, 2556, 2557, 2558, 2559, 2562, 2563, 2568, 2569, 2570, 2571,
2572, 2573, 2574, 2575, 2576, 2577, 2578, 2579, 2580, 2581, 2582,
2583, 2584, 2585, 2586, 2587, 2588, 2589, 2590, 2591, 2592, 2593,
2594, 2595, 2596, 2597, 2598, 2600, 2601, 2608, 2609, 2610, 2611,
2613, 2614, 2615, 2616, 2617, 2618, 2619, 2620, 2621, 2622, 2624,
2625, 2627, 2628, 2629, 2630, 2633, 2634, 2635, 2636, 2637, 2638,
2640, 2642, 2643, 2644, 2645, 2646, 2647, 2648, 2649, 2650, 2654,
2656, 2658, 2659, 2660, 2661, 2662, 2664, 2665, 2667, 2669, 2670,
2672, 2673, 2676, 2677, 2678, 2679, 2681, 2682, 2684, 2685, 2687,
2689, 2692, 2693, 2694, 2697, 2698, 2700, 2703, 2704, 2706, 2708,
2709, 2710, 2711, 2712, 2713, 2714, 2716, 2717, 2718, 2722, 2723,
2724, 2725, 2728, 2755, 2782, 2785, 2811, 2819, 2820, 2821, 2822,
2826, 2828, 2829, 2833, 2834, 2835, 2836, 2838, 2839, 2840, 2841,
2867, 2868, 2885, 2889, 2894, 2936, 2937, 2938, 2939, 2955, 2959,
2961, 2968, 2969, 2972, 2975, 2976, 2977, 2979, 2984, 2985, 2986,
2989, 2990, 2992, 2993, 2995, 2996, 2998, 2999, 3000, 3065, 3070,
3071, 3072, 3073, 3077, 3082, 3083, 3085, 3087, 3089, 3091, 3093,
3094, 3095, 3096, 3098, 3099, 3101, 3102, 3118, 3121, 3122, 3124,
3136, 3148, 3151, 3152, 3153, 3155, 3178, 3180, 3181, 3182, 3183, 3193,
3199, 3221, 3222, 3223, 3232, 3233, 3234, 3235, 3236, 3237, 3238, 3239,
3240, 3241, 3242, 3243, 3244, 3245, 3246, 3247, 3248, 3249, 3250,
3251, 3252, 3253, 3254, 3255, 3256, 3257, 3258, 3259, 3260, 3261, 3262,
3263, 3264, 3265, 3266, 3267, 3268, 3269, 3270, 3271, 3272, 3273,
3274, 3275, 3276, 3277, 3278, 3279, 3280, 3281, 3282, 3283, 3284,
3285, 3286, 3287, 3288, 3289, 3290, 3291, 3292, 3293, 3294, 3295,
3296, 3297, 3298, 3299, 3300, 3301, 3302, 3303, 3304, 3305, 3306,
3307, 3308, 3309, 3310, 3311, 3312, 3313, 3314, 3315, 3316, 3317, 3318,
3319, 3320, 3321, 3322, 3323, 3324, 3325, 3326, 3327, 3328, 3329, 3330,
3331, 3332, 3333, 3334, 3335, 3336, 3337, 3338, 3339, 3340, 3341, 3342,
3343, 3344, 3345, 3346, 3347, 3348, 3349, 3350, 3351, 3352, 3353,
3354, 3355, 3356, 3357, 3358, 3359, 3360, 3361, 3362, 3363, 3364, 3365,
3366, 3367, 3368, 3369, 3370, 3371, 3372, 3373, 3374, 3375, 3376,
3377, 3378, 3379, 3380, 3381, 3382, 3383, 3384, 3385, 3386, 3387,
3388, 3389, 3390, 3391, 3392, 3393, 3394, 3395, 3396, 3397, 3398,
3399, 3400, 3401, 3402, 3403, 3404, 3405, 3406, 3407, 3408, 3409,
3410, 3411, 3412, 3413, 3414, 3415, 3416, 3417, 3418, 3419, 3420,
3421, 3422, 3423, 3424, 3425, 3426, 3427, 3428, 3429, 3430, 3431,
3432, 3433, 3434, 3435, 3436, 3437, 3438, 3439, 3440, 3441, 3442,
3443, 3444, 3445, 3446, 3447, 3448, 3449, 3450, 3451, 3452, 3453,
3454, 3455, 3456, 3457, 3458, 3459, 3460, 3461, 3462, 3463, 3464,
3465, 3466, 3467, 3468, 3469, 3470, 3471, 3472, 3473, 3474, 3475,
3476, 3477, 3478, 3479, 3480, 3481, 3482, 3483, 3484, 3485, 3486,
3487, 3488, 3489, 3490, 3491, 3492, 3493, 3494, 3495, 3496, 3497,
3498, 3499, 3511, 3512, 3515, 3516, 3517, 3518, 3524, 3538, 3539, 3547,
3550, 3556, 3557, 3560, 3561, 3562, 3563, 3564, 3565, 3568, 3569,
3571, 3575, 3577, 3578, 3580, 3581, 3583, 3584, 3587, 3588, 3593, 3594,
3602, 3606, 3607, 3608, 3617, 3619, 3620, 3624, 3626, 3627, 3628,
3629, 3630, 3631, 3632, 3633, 3634, 3635, 3636, 3637, 3638, 3639,
3640, 3641, 3642, 3643, 3644, 3645, 3646, 3647, 3648, 3649,

Tenniel, John (continued)	3650, 3651, 3652, 3653, 3654, 3656, 3657, 3658, 3659, 3660, 3661, 3662, 3663, 3664, 3666, 3668, 3669, 3671, 3672, 3673, 3675, 3676, 3677, 3679, 3680, 3681, 3684, 3685, 3686, 3688, 3695, 3696, 3697, 3698, 3699, 3700, 3701, 3702, 3703, 3704, 3705, 3706, 3707, 3708, 3709, 3711, 3713, 3714, 3716, 3717, 3721, 3722, 3723, 3724, 3725, 3726, 3727, 3728, 3729, 3730, 3731, 3732, 3733, 3737, 3738, 3739, 3740, 3741, 3742, 3748, 3749, 3750, 3751, 3752, 3753, 3758, 3759, 3760, 3761, 3767, 3768, 3769, 3770, 3773, 3774, 3775, 3777, 3778, 3779, 3780, 3781, 3782, 3784, 3785, 3789, 3791, 3792, 3793, 3796, 3797, 3799, 3800, 3801, 3802, 3803, 3805, 3806, 3807, 3808, 3809, 3810, 3812, 3816, 3817, 3818, 3820, 3821, 3822, 3823, 3824, 3825, 3826, 3830, 3832, 3836, 3839, 3840, 3841, 3845, 3846, 3848, 3849, 3850, 3853, 3854, 3857, 3858, 3859, 3860, 3862, 3864, 3866, 3867, 3871, 3872, 3873, 3874, 3875, 3876, 3878, 3879, 3880, 3889, 3890, 3891, 3892, 3894, 3895, 3896, 3898, 3900, 3901, 3902, 3903, 3904, 3906, 3908, 3909, 3910, 3912, 3913, 3914, 3915, 3918, 3925, 3926, 3927, 3929, 3930, 3931, 3932, 3934, 3935, 3936, 3937, 3938, 3939, 3941, 3942, 3943, 3944, 3945, 3946, 3951, 3952, 3954, 3955, 3956, 3958, 3959, 3961, 3962, 3963, 3964, 3965, 3966, 3967, 3970, 3972, 3974, 3980, 3981, 3982, 3983, 3987, 3988, 3992, 4014, 4016, 4018, 4024, 4025, 4031, 4032, 4037, 4047, 4057, 4059, 4060, 4071, 4077, 4082, 4083, 4085, 4086, 4087, 4088, 4089, 4090, 4091, 4120, 4129, 4138, 4144, 4158, 4164, 4165, 4171, 4176, 4179, 4184, 4189, 4190, 4194, 4196, 4197, 4198, 4199, 4200, 4201, 4202, 4203, 4206, 4207, 4208, 4209, 4210, 4211, 4212, 4213, 4214, 4215, 4216, 4217, 4218, 4219, 4220, 4221, 4222, 4223, 4224, 4225, 4226, 4227, 4228, 4229, 4230, 4231, 4232, 4233, 4234, 4235, 4236, 4237, 4238, 4239, 4240, 4241, 4242, 4244, 4245, 4246, 4247, 4248, 4249, 4250, 4251, 4252, 4253, 4254, 4255, 4256, 4257, 4258, 4259, 4260, 4261, 4262, 4263, 4264, 4265, 4266, 4267, 4268, 4270, 4271, 4272, 4273, 4275, 4294, 4354
Theaker, Harry	338, 339, 340, 341, 342, 343, 344, 370, 373, 428, 429, 465, 468, 471, 473, 1828, 3484, 3486, 3487, 3490, 3491
Themerson, Franciszka	3590, 3591, 4275
Thompson, E. Heber	619, 632, 639, 652, 668, 689, 698, 708, 726, 738, 744, 747, 748, 762, 776, 795, 814, 885
Thomson, E. Gertrude (Emily)	1884, 4139, 4165, 4184, 4196, 4197, 4198, 4199, 4200, 4201, 4202, 4203, 4206, 4207, 4208, 4209, 4210, 4212, 4213, 4214, 4215, 4216, 4217, 4218, 4219, 4220, 4221, 4222, 4223, 4224, 4225, 4226, 4227, 4228, 4229, 4230, 4231, 4232, 4233, 4234, 4235, 4236, 4237, 4238, 4239, 4240, 4241
Thorne, Jenny	1489, 1490, 1503, 1511, 1532, 1553, 1554, 1579, 4297, 4298, 4300, 4302, 4312, 4314, 4316, 4317, 4319, 4327, 4333
Thurstan, Edgar B.	1314, 1329, 1404
Todd, Justin	1018, 1032, 1063, 2272, 3566, 3567
Toniţa, Nicolae	3141
Topor, Roland	1246
Torrey, Marjorie	843, 845, 849, 899, 2171, 2198, 2199, 2200, 2201, 2383
Toshima, Tetsuya	2913

Tovey, R. M.	727
Toyoda, Wendy Cogan	2324, 2662
Trapo, Thiago	2913
Triebsee, Kim	2343
Trimby, Elisa	792, 831, 848, 1029, 1041, 1051, 1052
Trimby, John	792
Turner, Helen Monro	*See* Munro, Helen
Turner, Lindsey	1198
Tutus, Milos	2913
Unillustrated	369, 524, 589, 604, 642, 651, 810, 1011, 1081, 1133, 1162, 1168, 1248, 1256, 1394, 1400, 1421, 1457, 1515, 1516, 1624, 1644, 1656, 1662, 1668, 2073, 2158, 2159, 2160, 2202, 2213, 2380, 2468, 2492, 2508, 2511, 2632, 2719, 2760, 2799, 2800, 2857, 2858, 2859, 2918, 2924, 3066, 3068, 3069, 3080, 3084, 3104, 3130, 3131, 3156, 3157, 3158, 3159, 3522, 3533, 3600, 3601, 3655, 3940, 3989, 3990, 3997, 3998, 3999, 4000, 4001, 4004, 4006, 4007, 4009, 4010, 4012, 4021, 4022, 4023, 4026, 4030, 4062, 4065, 4066, 4070, 4076, 4078, 4174, 4177, 4195
Unknown	542, 575, 584, 593, 674, 692, 743, 745, 760, 846, 870, 1136, 1152, 1183, 1185, 1215, 1251, 1260, 1265, 1268, 1272, 1405, 1451, 1453, 1456, 1458, 1467, 1547, 1653, 1768, 1769, 1770, 1861, 1862, 1892, 1893, 1975, 1976, 1983, 1998, 1999, 2056, 2121, 2196, 2277, 2292, 2302, 2314, 2319, 2327, 2334, 2349, 2351, 2381, 2527, 2560, 2651, 2657, 2663, 2671, 2688, 2691, 2699, 2721, 2732, 2734, 2737, 2748, 2759, 2762, 2766, 2767, 2770, 2774, 2775, 2776, 2780, 2787, 2788, 2790, 2793, 2795, 2797, 2803, 2804, 2805, 2807, 2827, 2860, 2862, 2863, 2866, 2870, 2871, 2872, 2873, 2875, 2876, 2877, 2878, 2879, 2880, 2883, 2895, 2896, 2897, 2898, 2899, 2900, 2901, 2902, 2903, 2905, 2906, 2907, 2908, 2909, 2910, 2912, 2914, 2915, 2919, 2920, 2950, 2952, 2953, 2954, 2958, 2960, 2967, 2978, 2982, 2983, 2987, 2988, 2991, 2994, 2997, 3001, 3002, 3004, 3006, 3007, 3008, 3011, 3014, 3015, 3017, 3018, 3019, 3020, 3021, 3024, 3032, 3034, 3036, 3037, 3039, 3041, 3042, 3045, 3046, 3048, 3051, 3052, 3055, 3057, 3058, 3059, 3060, 3062, 3067, 3074, 3125, 3126, 3133, 3137, 3138, 3147, 3179, 3191, 3192, 3196, 3197, 3198, 3200, 3215, 3217, 3231, 3523, 3549, 3569, 3622, 3687, 3735, 3736, 3973, 3975, 3977, 3978, 3979, 3984, 3985, 3986, 3993, 4003, 4005, 4008, 4011, 4013, 4015, 4019, 4020, 4028, 4029, 4033, 4034, 4035, 4036, 4038, 4039, 4040, 4042, 4044, 4045, 4048, 4049, 4050, 4054, 4055, 4056, 4061, 4063, 4064, 4067, 4068, 4069, 4072, 4074, 4079, 4080, 4081, 4186, 4274, 4357
Upton, Oliver	2668
Urbańczyk, Karolina	2913
Utashiro, Arina	3103
Valenza, Valeria	1210
Valero, Maria Gómez-Pintado	*See* Gómez-Pintado Valero, Maria
Van Gool, A.	1064, 1113, 1114
Van Gool-Lefevre-Loiseaux	*See* Lefèvre, André M.; Loiseaux, M.; Van Gool, A.

Set in Adobe Minion Pro types.
Design & typography by Jerry Kelly.

www.ingramcontent.com/pod-product-compliance
Lightning Source LLC
Chambersburg PA
CBHW040258100426
42811CB00011B/1310